T S ELIOT

Lyndall Gordon was born in Cape Town, South Africa and received her doctorate from Columbia University. Before becoming a full-time writer in 1995 she taught at St Hilda's College, Oxford. Her prize-winning two-part biography of T S Eliot is now revised and published in this one volume edition. *Eliot's Early Years* won the British Academy's Rose Mary Crawshay Prize and *Eliot's New Life* won the Southern Arts Prize.

Her other books include *Virginia Woolf: A Writer's Life* (winner of the James Tait Black Prize for Biography), *Shared Lives* (chosen by the *New York Times* as one of the notable books of 1992), *Charlotte Brontë: A Passionate Life* (winner of the 1994 Cheltenham Prize) and most recently *A Private Life of Henry James, Two Women & His Art*. Lyndall Gordon lives in Oxford.

ALSO BY LYNDALL GORDON

Eliot's Early Years
Virginia Woolf: A Writer's Life
Eliot's New Life
Shared Lives
Charlotte Brontë: A Passionate Life
A Private Life of Henry James, Two Women & His Art

Lyndall Gordon

T S ELIOT
An Imperfect Life

VINTAGE

Published by Vintage 1998

2 4 6 8 10 9 7 5 3 1

Eliot's Early Years was first published
in Great Britain in 1977 by Oxford University Press
Eliot's New Life was first published in
Great Britain in 1988 by Oxford University Press

The author has made every effort to
trace holders of copyright and much regrets
if any inadvertent omissions have been made.

Vintage
Random House, 20 Vauxhall Bridge Road,
London SW1V 2SA

Random House Australia (Pty) Limited
20 Alfred Street, Milsons Point, Sydney
New South Wales 2061, Australia

Random House New Zealand Limited
18 Poland Road, Glenfield,
Auckland 10, New Zealand

Random House South Africa (Pty) Limited
Endulini, 5A Jubilee Road, Parktown 2193, South Africa

Random House UK Limited Reg. No. 954009

A CIP catalogue record for this book
is available from the British Library

ISBN 0 09 974221 7

Papers used by Random House UK Ltd are natural,
recyclable products made from wood grown in
sustainable forests. The manufacturing processes
conform to the environmental regulations of
the country of origin

Typeset by Deltatype Ltd, Birkenhead, Merseyside
Printed and bound in Great Britain by
Mackays of Chatham PLC

CONTENTS

FOREWORD

ELIOT ONCE SPOKE of a lifetime burning in every moment. He had the mind to conceive a perfect life, and he also had the honesty to admit that he could not meet it. This biography explores the divide between saint and sinner in the greatest poet of the twentieth century. Its core is still my two-volume work, *Eliot's Early Years* and *Eliot's New Life*, but these have been extensively rewritten with new material and changes that go beyond revision. I was driven to this, in part, because I believe that we are now ready to view Eliot from the vantage point of the next century, more detached from the spiritless disillusion of his own time and less beguiled than his contemporaries by his normative masks, with a keener sense of his strangeness, his prejudice, and extremism. The aim, though, is not to reduce Eliot to the level of others in an extremist century, but to follow the trials of a searcher whose flaws and doubts speak to all of us whose lives are imperfect.

Research for this book began at the Berg Collection in New York in 1970, and I have continued ever since to collect material. From the outset I resolved to focus on primary sources: manuscript poems which, when dated, lit up the trajectory of Eliot's course; the visionary early stages of *The Waste Land*, overlaid by the city scenes that made it appear so dazzlingly modern; the vast treasure of still-buried essays; and quantities of letters scattered in libraries across England and America. So, my first book, *Eliot's Early Years* (1977), brought together his life and work. It was a portrait of a confessional poet, reversing the view of an older generation who, hanging on Eliot's lips, had stressed his impersonality. It also challenged the dismissive view of Eliot's wife, Vivienne, and redrew the map of Eliot's career starting from a shadowy 'upheaval' with sexual and religious conflicts from 1910 to 1914. The American Eliot was another side to be stressed as a counter to the English façade. His move from America to England has continued to intrigue me as an expatriate: however much an expatriate takes on the colouring of another country, native origins remain of course ineradicable. I was struck by the persistence of American traditions in Eliot, especially his renewal of the dominant genres of sermon and spiritual autobiography. And these approaches then encouraged me to attempt a sequel on the years of Eliot's maturity and great fame, *Eliot's New Life*, which was published at the time of his centenary in 1988.

This second volume, based again on unpublished papers, followed his ties with two women. Emily Hale and Mary Trevelyan, and also the way he left his first wife. In 1976 Vivienne's brother, Maurice Haigh-Wood, gave me permission to quote from her diaries and writings. Since it has emerged (in the course of time) that no others were allowed to quote, at this point I added further material from Vivienne's diaries and writings so that what she called her '*huge*' voice might be heard (as she wished when she bequeathed her papers to the Bodleian Library). *Eliot's New Life* turned out to be a biographical experiment in drawing forward the unseen collaborative element in a writer's life. With Eliot, as with Henry James, women who were vital to the creative life were kept under wraps. Eliot had four quite different relationships with women who were all remarkable and, in various ways, entered his work. The more I come to know of Eliot's life, the surer I am that these four women – together with his high-minded mother, Charlotte Stearns – provide essential clues to a guarded, even elusive character who at times and especially with women, would be simple – a combination so tantalising that throughout his life, and well into old age, women fell in love with him.

One incentive to revise the earlier biographies was the publication of the first volume of Eliot's correspondence in

1988, not only for the quantity of new and accurate information, including letters from Vivienne and a young Frenchman Jean-Jules Verdenal, but because it changed my impression that the letter was Eliot's least distinctive mode. I had thought him adept at the distant letter: the kindly letdown to would-be poets, the business letter, the droning or jokey letter, above all the letter of excuse with such a profusion of elaborate detail that it carried politeness, sometimes, to the verge of insult. Eliot's letters to good friends – Pound, Virginia Woolf, John Hayward, Polly Tandy – were performances: clowning, not intimate. But to his mother, to his brother, and to his cousin Eleanor Hinkley, he wrote with discreet yet absorbing truth.

Another incentive was that the ban on quotation from Eliot's poems in manuscript was lifted in 1997 by the publication of *Inventions of the March Hare*. I can now confirm paraphrases of manuscript poems which suggested the novel view of Eliot's development, as well as the chronology I worked out in the early seventies. Biography always has a detective appeal, but I have never experienced it so intensely as in that tomb-like room, as still and unchanging as a single plastic rose in one back corner, at the top of the New York Public Library. It was there that I became obsessed with dating Eliot's undated poems and the early fragments of *The Waste Land* manuscript, as dates began to show how unexpectedly early Eliot was formulating a search for salvation. And more, his drafts seemed to prefigure the events of his life with uncanny exactness. There is now much to add, but my premise about the clairvoyant directedness of Eliot's life remains unchanged.

Inventions of the March Hare reveals his obscene poems. Long ago, when I came across lines here and there, I assumed these were puerile aberrations, but seeing how the full poems incite the common impulse to sexual violence, and finding recently from an unpublished letter that Eliot continued to circulate these loathsome things as late as his forties, I have to recognise that this was part of a larger problem: disgust with the flesh in conflict with repressed desire. So, I now look more closely at what *Eliot's Early Years* called 'vitriolic' jibes, expanding my initial focus on Eliot's misogyny to his anti-

Semitism – a prejudice common, almost automatic, in his time, but having in Eliot a special character determined by a lofty 'hatred of life' that he called 'a mystical experience'.

Some of the best new material has come to me privately over the years in response to publication: Dorothy Elsmith's letter from Woods Hole, Massachusetts in the late seventies about Eliot and Emily Hale; and a letter in 1993 from Basil Saunders in London whose mother was involved in Vivienne's attempt to escape imprisonment in a 'home'. Lorraine Havens brought me a confidential letter from Emily Hale about Eliot's decision not to marry her when Vivienne died in 1947. Professor Willard Thorp, the widower of another of Emily Hale's friends, preserved her comments on the thousand letters Eliot wrote to her – letters sealed by his wish until 2019. Mary Trevelyan, Eliot's companion between his two marriages, has left an eloquent memoir, still unpublished, of her friendship with the poet. In the early nineties, Lesley Roberts of the BBC discovered that her neighbour, a pig farmer, was about to throw out piles of Eliot letters. She salvaged them and brought them in shopping bags to Oxford, and together we sifted through them on my kitchen table. Best of all, Judy Harvey Sahak, a curator of Emily Hale papers in California, alerted me to her recent acquisition of the unusually expressive Eliot-McPherrin letters which show his concern for the stresses of Emily Hale's life and for her breakdown at the height of their contact in the mid-thirties.

In the past, many have seen Eliot as a disillusioned sophisticate who suddenly turned religious poet; admirers would choose their preferred half of a divided career, but this act of choice was misleading, for Eliot himself urged us to see a poet in terms of the complete sequence of works. Approached as a whole, Eliot's story has an extraordinary coherence. In fusing the two books, I have tried, above all, to bring out the continuity of a single-minded career, as though life and work were reciprocal parts of one design.

Oxford. June 1998.

ILLUSTRATIONS

I

EARLY MODELS

THOMAS STEARNS ELIOT was born on 26 September 1888 in St Louis, Missouri, the son of a New England schoolteacher and a St Louis merchant. Thirty-eight years later he was baptised as an Anglican in an English village. Such facts tell little of a man for whom there was usually a gap between his outward and his private life, the constructed, highly articulate surface and the inward ferment. Wyndham Lewis painted Eliot's face as if it were a mask, so that he might distinguish Eliot's formal surface from his hooded introspective eyes, and the severe dark lines of his suit from the flesh of his shoulders beneath. Virginia Woolf wrote that his hazel eyes seemed oddly lively and youthful in a pale, sculptured, even heavy face.

Eliot's admirers played up his mask, while detractors stripped it only to find the flaws: both overlooked a man of extremes whose deep flaws and high virtues were interfused. Obsessed by 'this self inside us' and determined to guard it, he was barely famous in 1925 when he decided there should be no biography. He urged those close to him to keep silence, and sealed many letters until the next century. Meanwhile, he devised his own biography, enlarging in poem after poem on the character of a man who conceives of his life as a spiritual quest despite the anti-religious mood of his age and the distracting claims of women, friends, and alternative careers. He once spoke of the man who tries to explain to himself 'the sequence that culminates in faith', and in a letter, written in 1930, mentioned his long-held intention to explore a mode of

1

writing neglected in the twentieth century, the spiritual autobiography.

Eliot aimed to be a 'poet who, out of intense and personal experience, is able to express a general truth'. In some sense his own works do retain 'all the particularity' of personal experience, though to work back from the work to the life can only be done through imaginative transformations that intervene, the discarded fragments of *The Waste Land* or the ten layers of Eliot's most confessional play, *The Family Reunion*. The challenge is to discern the bonds between life and work in a way that brings out the greatness of major works which are, after all, the most important facts in the poet's life. To do this we must imagine a man with immortal longings, and reconstruct the strategy by which he attained immortality. The strategy was extraordinary, so willed in its acts of surrender, so directed in its doubts, so sure in its single-mindedness, that we see all the way the pure line of that trajectory – leaving broken lives in its wake.

Eliot was recognised in his lifetime as the moral spokesman of the twentieth century, but as that century now recedes from view the question is rising whether the huge power of his voice to engage our souls can sustain sympathy for a man who was stranger and more intolerant than his disarming masks would have us believe, a man who grew progressively harder to know during the inscrutable years of fame. Eliot's guardians, most now dead, no longer block the crucial issue whether his intolerance for the masses, for women and Jews in particular, infects his greatness. The anti-Semitism is integral to the poetry, said a lawyer, Anthony Julius, who built up a formidable case against Eliot in 1996, thirty years after the poet's death. Biography, though, can't reduce a man to the adversarial categories – guilty or not guilty – of the courtroom. Courts construct set dramas that rarely elicit the complexity of motives in actual lives. Undoubtedly, an infection is there in Eliot – hate – and we can't explain it away; and yet biographers, of all people, know it is naïve to expect the great to be good. Dickens was monstrous to his wife and children, while his works laud the social ideal of the

2

family; Tolstoy was a self-willed autocrat who parades an image of humble holy man; Carlyle was another domestic tyrant, while Hardy estranged his wife and then wrote touching elegies after her death. Eliot's superiority invites scrutiny. In his case, we must walk a difficult path through a thicket of 'things ill done and done to others' harm'. Shall we find that Eliot's great poems answer ill-doing? Is it conceivable that they are all the greater, in fact, for their admission of failure to match the perfect life to which Eliot aspired from the start?

Eliot's Notebook and other manuscript poems (published thirty years after his death) show that he began to measure his life by the divine goal as far back as his student days, in 1910 and 1911, and that the turning-point came not when he was baptised in 1927 but in 1914 when he first interested himself in the motives, the ordeals, and the achievements of saints. In later years Eliot seemed to beg off personally in favour of a routine life of prayer and observance, but the early manuscripts suggest that for a time in his youth he dreamed of the saint's ambitious task, of living by his own vision beyond the imaginative frontiers of his civilisation.

At the heart of the hidden life was a hunt for signs. One came to him in an English garden seven years after his conversion, a renewal of a sign he had as a student moving through the streets of Boston in June 1910. It had cut through the urban clamour, cut through sense perception, cut through time itself with an intuition of timeless 'reality'. Emily Dickinson called it

> Eternity's disclosure
> To favorites – a few –
> Of the Colossal substance
> Of Immortality.

Eliot would not call it anything, unwilling to wrench it to fit words that fall short of the Word. But there is no question that he recognised whatever it was as momentous. He said simply there was nothing else to live for – 'there is nothing else beside'. This absolute conviction explains his view of ordinary life as waste. In *The Waste Land*, the waste is a place, a city filled with hopeless inhabitants. Later, in *Four Quartets*, the waste is time, the 'waste sad time' between signs.

Whether the waste was place or time, it meant the failure of the human mind to grasp the sign. There followed, a bit automatically, Eliot's disgust with the debasement of the human condition. This was confirmed by a wretched marriage and early struggles to make a living in what seemed, to a newcomer, a squalid and soulless London. His London, like the equally squalid Boston of his 'Preludes', is not really an objective scene but a correlate for the collapse of a private vision. If this is true, Eliot's famous disgust is no common élitism. It is a stranger, soul-sick state of his own.

Eliot is most outspoken in his poetry, guarded by his celebrated theory of impersonality which, he once admitted, was a bluff. As more is known of Eliot's life, the clearer it becomes that the 'impersonal' façade of his poetry – the multiple faces and voices – masks an often quite literal reworking of personal experience. Eliot wrote that there is a 'transfusion of the personality or, in a deeper sense, the life of the author into the character'. This book will follow the confessional element in Eliot's poetry by measuring the poetry against the life. It may be called a biography, but in Eliot's sense of the genre. Whenever he wrote about lives Eliot was not so much concerned with formal history and circumstance as with what he called 'unattended' moments. 'The awful daring of a moment's surrender,' he wrote in *The Waste Land*. 'By this, and this only, we have existed.' The external facts of Eliot's life are here, but only to prop what was for him the definitive inward experience that shaped the work. By limiting biographic trivia, it is possible to trace the continuity of Eliot's career and see poetry and life as complementary parts of one design, a consuming search for salvation. Throughout his life and throughout his work, Eliot was testing the sublime plot of spiritual biography, the plot laid down in Exodus: an exit from civilisation followed by a long trial in a waste place, followed by entry into the

4

promised land. To obscure this plot with too much detail would be to miss the point, and that is why, with Eliot, the form of full-scale biography is simply unsuited to an understanding of his life.

A poet, Yeats said, 'is never the bundle of accident and incoherence that sits down to breakfast; he has been reborn as an idea, something intended, complete.' It is hard to say exactly how or when the commanding idea is born but, in Eliot's case, an obvious source suggests itself in the figures that surrounded his American youth. The shadowy exemplary figure that haunts Eliot's poetry may be traced to his grandfather, whom Emerson called 'the Saint of the West', to his mother's heroes of truth and virtue, to the hardy fishermen of Cape Ann, Massachusetts, who all shaped Eliot's imagination. Towards the end of his life he came to see his poetry as more American than English: '. . . in its sources, in its emotional springs, it comes from America.'

*

Eliot said he was brought up to believe that there were 'Eliots, non-Eliots and foreigners', and that amongst Eliots the pinnacle was his grandfather, the Revd William Greenleaf Eliot (1811–87): '. . . the most one could possibly achieve was to be a Credit to the Family, though of course one's Grandfather was the Great Man, so there was no hope of reaching that eminence.' His grandson was never 'whacked', in fact as the last of seven children he was 'spoilt', but he had no sense of importance in his own right.

Eliot's parents were both forty-five when he was born, and seemed to him remote, like 'ancestors'; he felt closer to his only brother, Henry Ware Eliot, Jr, and to his sister Marian, nine and eleven years older. His father, Henry Ware Eliot, Sr, was a man of refined bearing with a taste for art and music, and an acute sense of smell. He had a habit of smelling his food before he ate it and could identify which of his daughters owned a stray handkerchief. He started with wholesale groceries, then went bankrupt making acetic acid.

Although he eventually found success as a manufacturer of bricks, he lived under the shadow of his own father, William Greenleaf Eliot, a financial genius of whom it was said that, had he not been called to the ministry, he might have owned nearly everything west of the Mississippi. There is little sign of imagination in Henry's autobiography; he presents himself as rather a plodder, proud of his industry and filial piety. He could be, in a studied way, playful and liked to draw faces on his children's boiled eggs. He commended Tom as a modest and affectionate son, not as a promising one, and this left the boy rather 'mournful', since his grades, mostly C's, gave no indication of latent gifts.

His mother, on the other hand, may have thought more of him than he granted, for she spoke to him as an equal. He, in turn, was devoted to her. Later, when he was cut off from her by a comfortless marriage, struggling through war years in a gloomy England, he recalled lying in bed at home in St Louis, his mother by his side, telling the tale of the 'little Tailor' as the firelight played on the ceiling. His strongest recorded expression of emotion is on the flyleaf of a copy of *Union Portraits* which he sent to her 'with infinite love'. High-minded and plain-living, Charlotte Champe Stearns taught her children to perfect themselves each day, 'to make the best of every faculty and control every tendency to evil'.

T. S. Eliot spent his first sixteen years in a city distinguished at the turn of the century for the corruption of its business-men, its inadequate sewers, and sulphurous fumes. Yet he could still say: 'I am very well satisfied with having been born in St. Louis.' Whenever he recalled St Louis in later life he did not think first of the city's blemishes but of the childhood memories that overrode them: the moods and rhythms of the great Mississippi ('the river is within us . . .'); the steamboats blowing in the New Year; the river in flood in 1892, 1897, and 1903 'with its cargo of dead Negroes, cows and chicken coops'; his Irish nurse, Annie Dunne, who discussed with him, at the age of six, the existence of God, and took him with her to a local Catholic church on the corner of Locust Street and Jefferson Avenue. '. . . I liked it very much,' he recalled, 'the lights, the coloured statues and paper flowers, the lived-in atmosphere, and the fact that the pews had little gates that I could swing on.' There is a photograph of Eliot, aged seven, with his dimpled nurse, his beret perched jauntily on his head and his face mischievous; Annie's lips are pursed, one hand on her hip. Years later, Eliot wrote a rhyme about some naughty Jim Jum Bears who got up to tricks to exasperate their Nurse ('Was ever a Nurse so put about?'). It recalls the secure intimacy of early days with Annie, to whom he said he was 'greatly attached'.

Annie took him to Mrs Lockwood's school, what was called in those days a dame school. When he was ten, in 1898, he moved on to Smith Academy, a school founded by his grandfather; his mother sent him in a sailor-suit, and the boys laughed. There was one other 'terrible' humiliation as he described it: 'I sat between two little girls at a party. I was very hot. And one of the little girls leaned across . . . to the other and whispered loudly: "Look at his ears!" So one night I tied some rope round them when I went to bed, but my mother came and took it off and told me they would fold themselves back so I needn't worry.' He avoided another children's party: 'I walked round and round the streets until it was time to go home.'

The Eliots lived in Locust Street, an unfashionable part of St Louis, not far from the saloons and brothels of Chestnut and Market Streets, at a time when pianists in back rooms were joining 'rags' together as jolting tunes. At the turn of the century St Louis became the world's ragtime capital, where Scott Joplin produced his ragtime opera in 1903. An impresario called Turpin set up a National Ragtime Contest for the 1904 St Louis World's Fair. This music was the first popular hit of the twentieth century, and there are Americans who claim that Eliot's improvisation in *The Waste Land* (1922) is a kind of rag, joining snatches of tunes and voices in a single composition. Certainly, a rag of 1902 'Under the Bamboo Tree' by Johnson, Cole, and Johnson, was to enter Eliot's Jazz Age play, *Sweeney Agonistes* (1926).

Since most of the Eliots' friends moved to quieter suburbs

further west, and since Tom's sisters and brother were a good bit older, he had few playmates and spent most of his time reading. One favourite was Poe. From the age of ten he had to go to a dentist twice a week for two years: he found the collected works of Poe in the waiting-room, and managed to read them through. From 28 January to 19 February 1899 he brought out fourteen numbers of a magazine called *The Fireside*, boasting 'Fiction, Gossip, Theatre, Jokes and all interesting'. At the same age he could identify some seventy kinds of birds on Cape Ann, Massachusetts, where the family spent the summer. He had a congenital double hernia and his mother, afraid it would rupture, forbade football and strenuous sports. When 'the Skipper' gave him sailing lessons, Charlotte would go along, fortified by a guard of grown-up sisters, to ensure that he did not get too wet or too hot or too tired. He accepted his mother's domination in good humour.

There was in Eliot's mother a moral passion and a gift of eloquence. She had the intellectual ardour of able nineteenth-century women – like Dorothea Brooke in *Middlemarch* – a natural scholar whose sex and circumstance debarred her from higher education. She set out to be a poet, and when her youngest child showed talent, hoped that he might redeem her sense of failure. She wrote in a letter to Eliot at Harvard:

> I hope in your literary work you will receive early the recognition I strove for and failed. I should so have loved a college course, but was obliged to teach before I was nineteen. I graduated with high rank, 'a young lady of unusual brilliancy as a scholar' my old yellow testimonial says, but when I was set to teaching young children, my Trigonometry and Astronomy counted for nought, and I made a dead failure.

In 1862, after her graduation from the State Normal School of Framingham, Massachusetts, she had moved from one teaching post to another – Pennsylvania, Milwaukee, Antioch College in Ohio, and then back to Framingham. It was when she moved yet again to teach at the St Louis Normal School that she met a handsome clerk who shipped goods on the Mississippi. This was Henry Ware Eliot, and they married in

1868. She then devoted her energies to her growing family and local reforms, particularly a separate house of detention for juveniles. When her husband went bankrupt in the 1870s, she supported the family for a year, teaching at an adjoining girls' school, the Mary Institute. Her room displayed no sign of conventional femininity except for a pincushion on the dresser. There was a comfortable armchair next to a sunny window even though it blocked a chest of drawers. The bed faced a mantelpiece draped with a velvet cloth on which rested a painting of the Madonna and child. On her wall there hung an engraving of Theodosius and St Ambrose, illustrating the triumph of holy over temporal power.

After her death, when Henry Ware Eliot, Jr, placed Charlotte's poems in Harvard's Eliot Collection, he wrote to the librarian: 'Perhaps a hundred years from now the connection with T. S. Eliot will not seem so remote. Of all the family, my brother most resembled my mother in features and ... if there is anything in heredity, it must have been from that side that T. S. Eliot got his tastes.' Apart from Charlotte herself, there were no writers on the Stearns side, but there was that moral fervour. The statue called 'The Puritan' in Springfield, Massachusetts, shows a Stearns ancestor striding forward with a huge Bible grasped under one arm and, in the other, a pilgrim's staff.* A reserved uncle, the Revd Oliver Stearns, used to startle his students at Harvard Divinity School with sudden floods of eloquence. Whatever he saw to be true or right, that would he say and do, 'though the heavens fell'.

It is telling to read Charlotte Eliot's poetry in the context of her son's work. She writes of 'the vision of the seer' and 'the prophet's warning cry'. Her poems recount turning-points in the lives of the chosen: the Apostles and 'The Unnamed Saints', St Barnabas and St Theodosius. Her heroes are 'truth-inebriated', 'God-intoxicated' individualists modelled on nine-teenth-century New Englanders Emerson and Channing; her

* Saint-Gaudens's statue of Samuel Chapin was done in 1887. Thomas Stearns (1710–84) married Abigail Reed, great-granddaughter of Chapin.

Savonarola, her Giordano Bruno, her St Francis trust the private vision. Her image of the thinker who, from unfathomed depths, seizes on the sublime truth is almost identical with the dominant figure in her son's vigil poems of 1911 and 1912.

Charlotte Eliot's strength is essentially that of a preacher. All the force of her poetry lies in passionate argument and dramatic illustration. She speaks particularly to those who 'by gift of genius' are set apart; her message is to endure with faith periods of religious despair:

> Ye who despair
> Of man's redemption, know, the light is there,
> Though hidden and obscured, again to shine . . .
>
> ('Saved!')

Her gift is didactic; she lacks the inventiveness and imaginative freshness of the great poet. Her son, using the same traditional images, rescued them from triteness – the beatific light, the fires of lust and purgation, the pilgrimage across the 'desert waste', and the seasonal metaphor for spiritual drought that pervades his mother's poetry. In the extremity of 'the dying year' the boughs in her garden go stiff and dry, no flower blooms, while a new power awaits its birth. 'April is the cruellest month,' her son was to write, 'breeding lilacs out of the dead land'. Mother and son used the same traditional images to signal grace. In 'The Master's Welcome' she hears children's voices. Bells signal recovery of faith after a period of doubt. Water – the 'celestial fountain' and 'the healing flood' – promises relief after long ordeals.

Charlotte Eliot mapped out states of being between loss and recovery of grace, a map her son redrew in his poetry in twentieth-century terms. The main difference was his mother's optimism. She felt an assurance of grace her son could not share. His faint-hearted character, J. Alfred Prufrock, feels obliged to frame an 'overwhelming' question but shirks it. In the context of his lack of nerve, it is curious to note the many questions Charlotte Eliot posed in her poetry: How does one face 'blank annihilation'? Is life worth living since we know we must die? 'And is this all [,] this life so incomplete?' 'What shall I do to be saved?' Eliot had a model of the perfect life before he left his mother's side; the long-term issue was whether he could make it his own.

He was later to lead a double life: publicly at the centre of a sycophantic buzz; privately there was the incommunicable life of a solitary that was all the stranger because it was conducted in the stir of the city, in the glare of fame. There was an inward silence and, at the same time, a speaker on platforms across Europe and America. Eliot's face acquired a sort of exposed reticence˙ from the habit of looking down from a lectern into rows upon rows of eyes. His skin had a look of being drawn tightly across his face. His features, though sharp, were delicate, especially the softly indented mouth. It was his nature to have scruple within scruple and to regulate his conduct on principles ignored by men of the world, like Lot in Sodom or Daniel in Babylon who, Eliot said, kept silence because they could do no good.

He often spoke of the 'unspoken'. In a solitude guarded by public masks he lived a hidden life. It would be unreachable if he had not been a poet with a need to explore and define that life. His poetry distils a predetermined drama from the dross so that what emerges is the coherent form of spiritual autobiography, direct, honest, and more penetrating than any outsider could dare to determine – a life so closely allied to creative works as to be a reciprocal invention. This biography follows his own formulation, testing it against the facts of his actual existence.

*

In a talk, 'The Influence of Landscape upon the Poet', Eliot called himself a New England poet because he had been so deeply affected when he came east as a child. He was always happy near the sea and would remember with joy his boyhood summers at Gloucester, Cape Ann.

Until he was eight, the family stayed at the Hawthorne Inn; then, in 1896, his father built a large, solid house at Eastern

Point, beyond the town, on land bought in 1890, an uncultivated rough coast, surrounded by wild bush and slabs of rock going down to the sea's edge. The upper windows looked out on the granite shore, the white sails on the sea and, looking the other way, the harbour. Eliot remembered Gloucester harbour as one of the most beautiful on the New England coast. A photograph by his brother, Henry, shows it at the turn of the century, the tall masts of what was then an all-sail fishing fleet dominating the village in the background with its clapboard houses and sloping roofs. From the beginning, fishing was the main occupation in Gloucester. When a divine came among the first settlers in the seventeenth century and said: 'Remember, brethren, that you journeyed here to save your souls,' one of the brethren added, 'And to ketch fish.' In Eliot's day fishermen lounging at the corner of Main Street and Duncan Street told yarns of storms and shipwrecks on the half-hidden rocks offshore from Cape Ann. Working in hard winter gales, the deep-sea fisherman put out from the schooner in a tiny dory which often capsized or went astray in fog or snow. And when a man lived through such an experience, he told the kind of yarn Eliot listened to as a boy, of risk and tenacity beyond belief.

Glory in the fisherman's casual acts of heroism and hardy self-reliance is reflected in Eliot's schoolboy compositions and sustained through his writings. In 'A Tale of a Whale', published in the *Smith Academy Record* in April 1905, and in 'The Man Who Was King', published the following June, Eliot made proud use of sailing jargon. Later, in *Marina* (1930), the dross of civilisation is blown away by the sea wind, and an awakening to redemptive love, its mystery and promise, is aligned with the perilous crossing of the Atlantic and slow approach to the New World, the dim New England shore with its woods and grey rocks. Eliot imagined forebears in the mould of the Cape Ann sea captains he admired. In an article called 'Gentlemen and Seamen' (1909) he extols as 'plebeian aristocrats' men like the old Eliots – small-town patriarchs, seamen, small printers, and tradesmen, who established themselves in villages along the New England coast. His great-grandfather William Greenleaf Eliot, Sr, had been a New Bedford ship-owner, and acquired a dinner service of Chinese 'willow-ware' porcelain which survives in the family. Eliot calls up old sombre faces, old compressed lips, old Eliot natures difficult and unyielding as a consequence of religious principle and endless struggle with the narrow resources of New England.

As a child Eliot explored the Cape Ann beaches for what the sea tossed up – starfish, a whale bone, a broken oar, a horseshoe crab.* The pools offered, for his curiosity, 'the more delicate algae and the sea anemone'. He collected, dried, and classified algae. When he was ten, peering through water in a rockpool, he saw the sea anemone for the first time, an experience, he remembered, 'not so simple, for an exceptional child, as it looks'.

Eliot was to return again and again to the Cape Ann shore and sea for scenes of crisis and revelation in his poetry. To the Cape Ann summers of his youth he owed his model, drawn from the Gloucester fisherman, of a sailor 'faring forward' on the thin edge of mortality. His imagination fastened, too, on the still pool and the light-filled water that recurred in his poetry as a tantalising memory of unspeakable bliss.

*

When Eliot was sixteen his mother published a biography of her father-in-law, William Greenleaf Eliot, and dedicated it to her children 'Lest They Forget'. 'I was brought up to be very much aware of him,' Eliot said. 'The standard of conduct was that which my grandfather had set: our moral judgements, our decisions between duty and self-indulgence, were taken as if, like Moses, he had brought down the tables of the Law, any deviation from which would be sinful . . .'

William had a narrow frail body and large, calm, benign eyes. His son, Henry, recalled those magnificent eyes in his

---

* *The Dry Salvages*, *CP*, p. 191. Eliot explained, in a letter to the *NEW* (25 Jan. 1941) that he had used the term 'hermit crab' in error for 'horseshoe crab'.

autobiography, and said that they seemed to read one's innermost thoughts. William's expression was sensitive and serene, the face of a man who looks on suffering from a citadel of moral assurance. He was not stern, but it would have been unthinkable, said his son, to argue with him or to attempt undue familiarity. 'How can one be familiar with the Day of Judgement?' said James Freeman Clark, a classmate at Divinity School. 'One feels rebuked in his presence. . . . Yet he is playful, fond of fun, and there is a sweet smile appearing on the corner of his mouth. But there is no *abandon*.'

Charlotte revered her father-in-law and brought up her children to observe two of his laws in particular, those of self-denial and public service. T. S. Eliot acknowledged that his early training in self-denial left him with an inability to enjoy even harmless pleasures. He learnt, for instance, that it was self-indulgent to buy candy, and it was not until he was forced to stop smoking in his sixties that he could bring himself to eat it as a substitute. This kind of upbringing was, of course, not peculiar to the Eliot home. Henry Adams, also constrained by the virtue of New England ancestors, recalled that he would eat only the less perfect peaches in his grandfather's garden.

Eliot's grandfather had died in 1887, the year before his birth, but a vice-regent in the shape of his grandmother lived on next door all through his youth. Abigail Adams Eliot (1817–1908), who had spent her childhood in Washington, could recall her great-uncle, the second President, for whose wife she was named, and she knew his son, John Quincy Adams, the sixth President, grandfather of the writer Henry Adams (1838–1918) with whom Eliot felt much in common.

As Eliot grew up he had to face the most important of his grandfather's laws, the subordination of selfish interests to the good of Community and Church. William Greenleaf Eliot exemplified the family ideal of manhood, combining piety and public enterprise. In 1834 he moved from Harvard Divinity School to found the Unitarian Church on what was then the American frontier. A brilliant fund-raiser, he helped found both the Academy of Science in St. Louis and

Washington University, where he served as unpaid professor of metaphysics. He was an early advocate of women's suffrage and of prohibition. During the terrible typhoid epidemic of the 1840s he visited sickbeds indefatigably, and during the Civil War organised the Western Sanitary Commission in Missouri which looked after the medical services of the Northern army and its fleet on the Mississippi. For three decades, he opposed slavery in his border state, appalled by whippings, mob violence, and the 'vile traffic' of chained gangs led through the streets to the steamboats going South; he was known as St Louis' 'only open abolitionist'. A portrait of Lincoln hung in the front hall when Eliot was a child – his grandfather had known him slightly. In 1852, when Emerson visited St Louis, he reported that the Unitarian minister had 'a sumptuous church and crowds to hear his really good sermons'.

William Greenleaf Eliot fulfilled Emerson's ideal of an individual with the power to remake his world. 'All history resolves itself very easily into the biography of a few stout and earnest persons,' Emerson said. 'The man must be so much that he must make all circumstances indifferent. Every true man is a cause, a country, and an age.' The gambling and drinking habits of the French Catholics and American pioneers from Kentucky and Virginia (who settled St Louis) had called, said Eliot, for his grandfather's strong missionary hand. Brought up to applaud William's reforming zeal, it is not surprising that his grandson should confront, a century later, the moral wilderness of post-war London. Even as a boy, said one cousin, 'Tom had a great sense of mission.'

Generations of Eliots before him had responded to the call to family and communal duties. Those Eliots who lived in Somerset, Wiltshire, and Gloucestershire in early Tudor times made wills which did not forget the poor, and sent their sons to institutions of higher learning, and tended to marry rich widows of the landed gentry.

Little is known of the Andrew Eliott (1627–1703) who emigrated from Somerset to Salem, Massachusetts, except that he was a man of property and education, that he was

15

accompanied by his second wife, Mary Vivion, and four children, and that he became a member of the First Church of Beverly in 1670 and in 1690 Beverly's first Town Clerk. He was drawn into the frenzy of the Salem witch trials, where he condemned innocents to death, along with the notorious 'hanging' Judge Blood, a forebear on the Stearns side (Eliot's grandmother Charlotte Blood was a descendant). In 1692 Andrew Eliott confessed that he had acted on insufficient evidence. He and eleven others signed a declaration that they had been 'sadly deluded and mistaken', unable 'to withstand the mysterious delusions of the powers of darkness', which now left them 'much disquieted and distressed in our minds'. Andrew Eliott asked forgiveness of God and of the sufferers. For he and others, he owned, 'fear we have been instrumental . . . to bring upon ourselves and this people of the Lord the guilt of innocent blood – '.

In the tight network of cousinage in New England, reaching down from the colonial period, the Eliots were interrelated with all the leading New England families: William Greenleaf Eliot was distantly related to John Green-leaf Whittier, Noah Webster (the lexicographer), and Herman Melville, and there were also links on both sides of the family to Louisa May Alcott. There was a political tie between William's brother, Thomas Dawes Eliot, and Edward Dickinson (father of Emily Dickinson) who shared rooms in Washington as representatives to Congress in the 1850s, where they set up meetings that led to the formation of the anti-slavery Republican Party. The Eliot network included, besides the eminent Adamses, the Lowells, and, most closely, Nathaniel Hawthorne, another direct descendant of the first Andrew Eliott, whose ancestor (on the Hathorn side – Colonel John Hathorn) was another of the jurors at the witchcraft trials – not one of the repenters. By the next century the Eliots were flourishing as city people, conspicuous in the affairs of Boston. The first to distinguish himself was the Revd Andrew Eliot (1718–78). Chubby-faced, with neat features and a double chin, he seldom gave controversial sermons from his pulpit in the New North

Church. His Calvinism was moderate in temper but he practised it most earnestly. When Boston was blockaded during the Revolution, he was the only Congregational minister, apart from Samuel Mather, to open his church every Lord's Day. When he was proposed as successor to President Holyoke at Harvard, and again after the resignation of Locke, he declined because of religious duties. One acquaintance used to call him 'Andrew Sly' because of his political prudence and circumspection. When he felt his temper rising he used to retire until he had controlled it.

The Eliots were a prudent lot but the best of them had moral courage. T. S. Eliot was proud of Sir Thomas Elyot, who risked reproving Henry VIII to his face on account of Anne Boleyn, and in *The Boke Named the Governour* (1531) attacked kings for their luxury and frivolity, urging them to rule for the common good. Two centuries later, in 1765, the Revd Andrew Eliot preached a censorious election-day sermon before the colonial governor of Massachusetts. Both Eliots escaped charges of treason because their tones were sober. They felt strongly about morals, conduct, and the public good, but they did not resort to flaming rhetoric.

There was much in the model Eliot man to admire. Throughout his life, T. S. Eliot was to feel the disjunction between his poetic impulse and his compulsion to conform to the Eliot ideal. 'The primary channel of culture is the family,' he wrote: 'no man wholly escapes from the kind, or wholly surpasses the degree, of culture which he acquired from his early environment.' At a prestigious New England boarding-school, Milton Academy, which Eliot attended in 1905–6, and as a student at Harvard, Eliot prepared for the professional career his family would applaud, but came to feel that the claims of his poetic gift had priority over the claims of his family: 'The Arts insist that a man shall dispose of all he has, even of his family tree, and follow art alone. For they demand that a man be not a member of a family or a caste or of a party or of a coterie, but simply and solely himself.' Eliot puzzled and alarmed his parents by staying in London in 1915 instead of finishing his doctorate at Harvard, and by

17

spending years writing poetry that was published only sporadically and in little-known magazines. His father died in 1919 under the impression that his youngest child had made a mess of his life. Yet although Eliot resisted the family pattern he also followed it, first as a poor clerk like his father in the early Mississippi days, and later, when he became a publisher, as a successful man of business. To the end of his life he faithfully performed the kind of responsible daily labour that had been, for generations, the self-affirming activity of the Eliot family.

*

Bred in a family which belongs at the very heart of Boston Unitarianism, Eliot's fervent nature found no nourishment there, and by the time he enrolled at Harvard he had become indifferent to the Church. The religion taught by William Greenleaf Eliot was strict rather than spiritual. He was not concerned with perfection, or doctrine, or theology, but with a code that would better the human lot. With Unitarian scorn for evangelical enthusiasm, he said that educated, practical people reject 'sudden miraculous conversion, wrought by divine power, independently of the human will . . . by which the sinner of yesterday is the saint of today.' True salvation comes from human effort. 'It is at once arrogant and dangerous to claim direct and extraordinary guidance. It is virtually to claim inspiration, and that which begins in humility ends in pride.' He passed on to his children and grandchildren a religion which retained Puritan uprightness, social conscience, and self-restraint, but which had been transformed by the Enlightenment. T. S. Eliot was taught to be dutiful, benevolent, and cheerful. He was always acutely sensitive to the power of evil, but was taught a practical common-sense code of conduct. He once mentioned that his parents did not talk of good and evil but of what was 'done' and 'not done'. In abandoning Unitarianism, Eliot rebelled against those tepid, unemotional distinctions. 'So far as we are human,' he wrote, 'what we do must be either evil or good.' Like Jonathan Edwards, who had rebelled in the first half of the eighteenth century against religion tamed as a respectable code and re-evoked the fervent religion of the previous century, so Eliot in the first half of the twentieth century sought an older, stricter discipline, unsoftened by nineteenth-century liberalism. Edwards and Eliot each seemed, to his own time, an isolated reactionary.

Unitarianism arose in America in the mid-eighteenth century, during the Great Awakening, in opposition to the Puritan conviction of man's innate sinfulness. The Unitarians were confident of man's innate nobility (Eliot's grandfather was a protégé of the leading Unitarian of the early nineteenth century, William Ellery Channing, who spoke of man's 'likeness to God'). They rejected the Puritans' doctrine of damnation, their tests of orthodoxy and heresy, and undemocratic distinctions between church members. Their God was benevolent not wrathful. The year before Eliot was born, his mother praised a benign, rational universe in her poem, 'Force and God':

> While worlds harmonious move in breathless awe
> We whisper 'God is here, and God is Law.'

In view of the sincere piety of Eliot's mother and grandfather and his father's lifelong support of the Unitarian Church, it may seem odd that he should have come to think of himself as one brought up 'outside the Christian Fold'. He had in mind the Unitarians' denial of the Trinity as against his own definition of Christianity as a belief in the Incarnation. In 1931 Eliot wrote to the critic Middleton Murry that the perfection of a Lord who was merely human did not seem to him perfection at all. His antagonism to England's greatest religious poet may be traced to his grandfather's view of Milton as a Unitarian. Similarly, Eliot's wish to exclude free thinking Jews has to do with the easy association of such Jews and Unitarians in his youth. 'The Jewish religion is unfortunately not a very portable one,' Eliot said in 1940, 'and shorn of its traditional practices, observances and Messianism, it tends to become a mild and colourless form of Unitarianism.'

19

So, Eliot disliked 'the intellectual and puritanical rationalism' of his early environment. In his revival of ideas of depravity and damnation, and in his craving for orthodoxy, he opposed his Unitarian background. Probably the most important difference was his sense of man's unlikeness, his distance from an unknowable deity.

Eliot said that to understand a modern writer it is necessary to classify him according to the type of decayed Protestantism which surrounded his childhood. Already in the 1830s Emerson resigned his pulpit in protest against 'corpse-cold Unitarianism'. The Transcendentalists of the 1840s liberated themselves from formal Christianity and trusted, like Emerson, in the private light, but the next generation found themselves, as one historian puts it, 'in a chilling void . . . The heir of Emerson was Henry Adams who turned away from the barren chaos of American life to the certitudes of Dante and St Thomas; and after Henry Adams came Eliot who not only admired the lost traditions of Catholicism from a distance, but made a heroic attempt to recapture them.'

For sensitive Unitarian children growing up in America in the nineteenth century, the bland surface presented by their religion must have seemed to resist too much of life. Eliot himself made only passing critical comments, but Henry Adams's analysis of the insufficiencies of Unitarianism suggests what Eliot reacted against:

> Nothing quieted doubt so completely as the mental calm of the Unitarian clergy . . . They proclaimed as their merit that they insisted on no doctrine, but taught . . . the means of leading a virtuous, useful, unselfish life, which they held to be sufficient for salvation. For them, difficulties might be ignored; doubts were a waste of thought . . . Boston had solved the universe . . . The religious instinct had vanished, and could not be revived, although one made in later life many efforts to recover it . . . That the most intelligent society, led by the most intelligent clergy, in the most moral conditions he ever knew, should have . . . quite ceased making itself anxious about past and future . . . seemed to him the most curious social phenomenon he had to account for in a long life.

The Unitarian code, with its optimistic notion of progress ('onward and upward forever', Eliot said as a student), glossed over unpleasant changes in American life, particularly after the Civil War. Walt Whitman, commenting on a widespread 'hollowness at heart', wrote: 'The great cities reek with respectable as much as non-respectable robbery and scoundrelism . . . A sort of dry and flat Sahara appears, these cities, crowded with petty grotesques, malformations, phantoms . . .' with manners 'probably the meanest to be seen in the world'. The authority of the class to which Adams and Eliot belonged, genteel responsible descendants of the Puritans, was superseded by the business power of the Gilded Age. In St Louis the moral law of William Greenleaf Eliot was ousted by the motive of profit, and in 1902 the city's corruption was scandalously exposed. Eliot was sensitive to the monotony that resulted from immense industrial expansion at the end of the nineteenth century and to the loss of native (New England) culture to a new America in which, as he put it, Theodore Roosevelt* was a patron of the arts. The muscular Virginian was the popular hero during Eliot's adolescence, not Lambert Strether.† Eliot belonged to an older America, before 1828 he said, when the country seemed like 'a family extension'. What that date meant to Eliot must be a guess. It was soon after that Eliot's grandfather left Boston for the frontier. It was also then that the civilised élite of the eastern seaboard lost their power in the bitter election of 1828, when John Quincy Adams fell before the rude, uncultivated Andrew Jackson.‡ Was Eliot still resisting the impact of Jacksonian democracy – more Western, more individualistic – a hundred years on? Or was it some more subtle change: the fading of the last traces of Calvinist piety before the cheery optimism of a new age of self-reliance? For

* President of the United States from 1901 to 1909.
† Sensitive and thoughtful hero of *The Ambassadors* (1903) by Henry James.
‡ Eliot referred jokingly to Uncle John (John Adams, the second President and father of John Quincy Adams) when he praised the American Cantos in a letter to Pound (1 Jan. 1931).

Emerson, the very advocate of self-reliance, that old demanding piety remained a lingering force through his memory of his Calvinist aunt, Mary Moody Emerson: 'What a debt is ours to that old religion which, in the childhood of most of us, still dwelt like a Sabbath morning in the country of New England, teaching privation, self-denial and sorrow'.

During Eliot's youth his mother guarded him from the jarring aspects of the new America. It is necessary to look rather to the more trying years that followed in Boston to explain why Eliot came to feel oppressed by the American scene and had to escape it.

2

A NEW ENGLAND STUDENT

AT THE TIME Eliot graduated from Harvard College, while walking one day in Boston, he plunged into a strange silence like a parting of the sea. In June 1910 he wrote a poem he never published called 'Silence', his first and perhaps most lucid description of the timeless moment:

> Along the city streets
> It is still high tide,
> Yet the garrulous waves of life
> Shrink and divide
> With a thousand incidents
> Vexed and debated: –
> This is the hour for which we waited –
>
> This is the ultimate hour
> When life is justified.
> The seas of experience
> That were so broad and deep
> So immediate and steep,
> Are suddenly still.
> You may say what you will,
> At such peace I am terrified.
> There is nothing else beside.

At the age of twenty-one Eliot had an experience which, he said, many have once or twice in their lives and are unable to put into words. 'You may call it communion with the Divine or you may call it temporary crystallization of the mind,' he said on another occasion. Eliot's peace in the noisy street is similar to Emerson's on Boston Common when he felt 'glad to the brink of fear'. For some, such a moment is part of an orthodox religious life, for others – like Emerson – it is terminal, sufficient in itself, and gratefully received. For Eliot, though, the memory was to remain through the years that followed as a tantalising reminder of an experience beyond his grasp.

Silence came to a prepared mind – a moment for which, already, he had 'waited' – and Eliot's Notebook traces the course of this preparation during the undergraduate years in Cambridge, Massachusetts. Through his mother, in particular, Eliot was steeped in Emerson, who granted authority to the private light. During the formative years in New England this was reinforced by Eliot's solitary habits, by his discovery of the alienated voice of nineteenth-century French poets, and by his growing distrust of family norms, Harvard clichés, and Boston manners. The Boston of Eliot's youth was no longer the 'old Boston' governed by Puritan conscience, but a society in decline. Eliot deplored turn-of-the-century Boston – as he would probably have deplored any city that he happened to be in at the time – but he was not unaffected by its gentility, its high-mindedness, its avidity for culture, experience, and Europe.

Eliot was one of those rare people who have a sense of their own age when its image is yet incomplete and secret. He salvaged from Boston's society and slums a certain sense of his time and place which he projected in his juvenilia, in 'Prufrock', in the 'Preludes', and even in *The Waste Land*. Eliot reacted against an emotional inertia, a moral blight, and in *The Waste Land* located it in England after the First World War, but its inception belonged to his youth in America at the beginning of the century.

John Jay Chapman, a contemporary critic, located the blight in the pervasiveness of the commercial mind in America, which was, he said, indifferent to truth, to love, and to religion – all things, in fact, Eliot tried to recover. 'I regret', wrote Chapman, 'the loss of the old cultivation; and yet I know that none of our older cultivation was ever quite right. The American has never lived from quite the right place in his bosom.' This was not a new idea. It had certainly perturbed Hawthorne, Twain, and James. Eliot first knew it as a mood that engulfed Eastern society after the Civil War: a loss of assertiveness. His class lost its moral leadership to men whose energies were the greater, the less they wasted on thought. *The Bostonians* (1886) demonstrates the demoralisation of cultivated men: 'a nervous, hysterical, chattering, canting age, an age of hollow phrases and false delicacy and exaggerated solicitudes and coddled sensibilities which, if we don't look out, will usher in the reign of mediocrity, of the feeblest and flattest and most pretentious that has ever been.' Eliot knew this flatness first-hand, and suffered himself from the inertia of his class.

The energetic vulgarity of St Louis had not posed to his particular temperament a serious threat or temptation. Boston, on the other hand, proved disturbing, and all the more for his affinity. 'I loathe mankind,' said Henry Adams, and he blamed Boston. 'Indeed Boston cankers our hearts. I feel it in me . . . I recognize the strange disease.' Eliot lived during his most formative years in a city whose heart and life had become defective. The political and moral power of its oldest and most distinguished citizens, the descendants of the Puritans, had been displaced by commercial corporations. The Brahmins' culture had been challenged by an invasion of immigrants. To Santayana the source of their deadness lay in tenacious gentility: 'Serious poetry, profound religion (Calvinism, for instance), are the joys of an unhappiness that confesses itself; but when a genteel tradition forbids people to confess that they are unhappy, serious poetry and profound religion are closed to them by that.' Their evil was vulgarity. In Back Bay innumerable windows watched one another hopelessly for revelations and indiscretions which never disturbed the peace. The smug righteousness and propriety of Beacon Street, of the Eliots, Millses, Bullards, Coolidges, and Parkmans, was the triumph of a bourgeoisie without the shadow of an aristocracy to worry it. 'I yearn', said Henry Adams in 1906, 'for St. Simeon Stylites or sin.'

Eliot was put in touch with Boston society through his uncle, Christopher Rhodes Eliot, a prominent Unitarian minister, and the branch of the Eliot family which had remained in the city and flourished in its affairs. He was related to Charles William Eliot, a stately chemist who was then President of Harvard and whose father had been Mayor of Boston and a congressmen. The latter, Samuel Atkins Eliot, was connected by marriage with the inner circle of Boston society, for one of his sisters married a leading figure, Andrews Norton, and another married George Ticknor, publisher and professor at Harvard from 1817–35. It was a society steeped in the values of Unitarianism, which made conduct a prime concern. This Boston was Eliot's birthright, and yet he came to it with the detachment of an alien. Later, Eliot caricatured Bostonians in a few poems which stressed their 'consanguinity' – almost everyone in his circle was related. There is 'Cousin Nancy', who rebels rather awkwardly against her genteel aunts. It is not a passionate Puritan rebellion but a thinner kind, involving arid acts of will, smoking, drinking, riding the New England hills until she 'broke them'. On the library shelves favourite nineteenth-century authors, Emerson and Arnold, sanction the gentility of the aunts and the self-expression of the girl. There is, too, wealthy 'Miss Helen Slingsby', who lives in a fashionable area of the city and contrives to shut life out by observing the secret codes of her milieu. The important things are her four servants, her small house (mansions are vulgar), her pets, her Dresden clock. Eliot, who had been brought up to his grandfather's ideals of unselfish service to the community, was struck by the absurdity of such oblivious, self-serving habits. Finally, there is 'Cousin Harriet', to whom a young man delivers the *Boston Evening Transcript*, her substitute for life. The youth, parting mentally from La Rochefoucauld, is rather worn, as though traversing the Boston street were like wading through time.

A society 'quite uncivilized', Eliot called it, 'but refined beyond the point of civilization'. To some extent he mastered Boston by understanding it; he felt aversion for it, but aversion did not mean he was immune. He took upon himself, perhaps involuntarily, the character of late nineteenth-century Boston, its rigid manners, its loss of vigour, its estrangement from so many areas of life, its painful self-consciousness. Adams said of his generation, whose influence presided over Boston when Eliot arrived there, that there existed only one mind and nature and that the only differences lay in 'degrees of egotism'. 'We looked through each other like microscopes. There was absolutely nothing in us that we did not understand merely by looking in the eye. There was hardly a difference in depth for Harvard College and Unitarianism kept us all shallow. We knew nothing – no! but really nothing! of the world . . . God knows that we knew our want of knowledge! the self-distrust became introspection – nervous self-consciousness – irritable dislike of America, and antipathy to Boston. . . . Improvised Europeans, we were, and – Lord God! – how thin!'

Failing to find life amongst his own class, Eliot prowled the slums. He later said that 'the contemplation of the horrid or sordid or disgusting by an artist, is the necessary and negative aspect of the impulse toward the pursuit of beauty. The negative is the more importunate.' To Roxbury, then, and North Cambridge,* Eliot went in search of squalor, but found it as life-destroying as the well-to-do Boston squares. He was repelled by smells and depressed by slums. In so far as this derived from Baudelaire, it was, in part, a literary posture. Baudelaire taught him the poetic possibilities 'of the more sordid aspects of the modern metropolis, of the possibility of fusion between the sordidly realistic and the phantasmagoric, the possibility of juxtaposition of the matter-of-fact and the fantastic'. In St Louis, before he read Baudelaire, the bleaker aspects of the city had passed him by; in Boston, for the first time, he conceived a horror of the

* Eliot's first three 'Preludes' were originally called 'Preludes in Roxbury'. North Cambridge was the scene of two of his Notebook 'Caprices'.

commercial city, its clutter and the sordid patience of its dwellers. In his 'Caprices in North Cambridge', a series preliminary to his 'Preludes', he described bottles, broken glass, dirty window panes, trampled mud mixed with grass, broken barrows, and tatty sparrows scratching in the gutter. His mind came to rest, with grim satisfaction, on vacant lots filled with the city's debris of ashes, tins, bricks, and tiles. He was horrified and, in a way, engaged. It seemed a far cry from his studies, the neat definitions and laws he was piling up at college, but it touched him as Harvard did not. It was his first image of a wasteland, a scene he was to make his own.

*

Although the transition from St Louis to Boston changed Eliot, Harvard itself barely touched him. From December 1906 to February 1907 he was put on probation 'for working at a lower rate than most Freshmen' despite 'an excellent record of attendance'; he 'loafed' for the rest of his first two years. His poor grades seemed to confirm those of the schoolboy, but two teachers did touch a responsive growth: Irving Babbitt, who helped him to become cultivated, and Dean Briggs, who used to read, with persuasiveness and charm, the poems of Donne to freshmen.

Eliot did not comment on social life at Harvard, but others who knew it during the presidency of Charles William Eliot (1869–1909) converge on a sense of coldness. 'Cold as an icicle', one of his students recalled. To John Jay Chapman, President Eliot was the father of a 'glacial era' at Harvard. Henry Adams, explaining his reasons for resigning his professorship, said that Cambridge was a social desert that would have starved a polar bear. Even before the advent of President Eliot, the young Henry James had remarked to his brother William in November 1867: 'Life here in Cambridge . . . is about as lively as the inner sepulchre.' There was no society, 'only the ghastly simulacrum of it'. Cambridge lacked the social idea. Professors were encouraged to make observations but not to converse, Adams observed. 'The liveliest and most agreeable men – James Russell Lowell, Louis Agassiz, John Fiske, William James, who would have made the joy of London or Paris – tried their best to break out and be like other men ... but society called them professors and professors they had to be ... Society was a faculty meeting without business.'

When Bertrand Russell came to Harvard as a visiting professor (while Eliot was a graduate student) he found his colleagues impossibly pompous and laborious. Eliot satirised them and their relation to Russell in his poem 'Mr Apollinax'. The scene is a house where he and Russell were guests of a snob called Fuller whom Russell despised because he and his mother aped the English manner. Eliot gleefully described Russell's assault on the gentility of the professor's tea party with his passionate talk, his grinning foetus face, and easy laughter. The dowager 'Mrs Phlaccus' and the Professor and Mrs 'Channing-Cheetah', bewildered but at all costs correct, concentrate on lemon slices and bitten macaroons. Eliot, who had first met Russell at a tea in the mansion of the art collector Mrs Jack Gardner, immediately allied himself with the alien. In his imagination the shy man among the birch trees and the amorous gentleman were united in a frivolous eighteenth-century pastoral by Fragonard. Russell quickly recognised the allegiance. 'My pupil Eliot was there', he wrote home afterwards, ' – the only one who is civilized.'

In Eliot's time students at Harvard did not live in Houses, but got together through clubs. Eliot conformed; he lived in the approved affluent area of Cambridge called the 'Gold Coast' and joined numerous clubs, but experienced little in the way of enlightened companionship. He roomed with a plump schoolmate from Milton Academy, Howard Morris, who loved to eat and drink, and had few artistic interests. 'Triflers' abounded who were satisfied with the 'gentleman's C' and took four-day weekends in New York. Eliot joined the staff of the *Harvard Advocate*, which provided, at best, 'hilarity', while the Southern Club seemed a 'drinking and poker hell'. But he thought he had to discipline himself so as not to miss experiences he did not naturally take to. He dutifully joined the Digamma, a social club, and went to a few initiations and punch nights. Occasionally, tall, sybilline, and attractive, but rather shy, he appeared at Buckingham and Brattle Hall dances. More often he visited the Signet, a writers' club, attended editorial meetings with rum tea in the *Advocate*'s sanctum at the top of the Union, and read in their small library to the perpetual sound of Debussy on the piano. Uneasy about his physique, he exercised his chest according to 'the Sandow system' at August's gymnasium in the basement of Apley Hall, hoping he might expand to forty-six inches. To most students, Eliot was a bit of a recluse who kept to his room in Russell Hall, Holyoke House, or 42 Apley Court. And he always immured himself behind a 'somewhat Lamian smile'.

It pleased Eliot to have been, as he saw it, an isolated cultural phenomenon:

> What the help and encouragement of men of an older generation may be like, what it feels like, what useful stimulus or perhaps misdirection it may give, I do not know. At a time which may be symbolized by the figures 1910, there was literally no-one to whom one would have dreamt of applying. One learnt something, no doubt, from Henry James, and might have learnt more . . . As for other writers then rising to celebrity . . . they lived in another world altogether.*

Later, he recalled that he had read Yeats, 'but it was the early Yeats. It was too much Celtic Twilight for me. There was really nothing except the people of the 90's who had all died of drink or suicide or one thing or another.' W. G. Tinckom-Fernandez, a fellow-editor of the *Advocate*, showed Eliot some verse by Ezra Pound, *Exultations* and *Personae*.

'This is up your street,' he said, 'you ought to like this.'

Eliot was not impressed. It seemed to him 'rather fancy old-fashioned romantic stuff, cloak and dagger kind of stuff'.

Apart from two or three teachers and some brilliant instruction in reading Dante in Italian, Harvard was not

---

* TSE's 'Views and Reviews' column in the *NEW* (12 Sept. 1935), 351–2. The writers he referred to were Shaw, Wells and Chesterton.

particularly stimulating. The educational bias was encouraging to scientists (Eliot took no science courses), while the humanities suffered from President Eliot's notion that cultivation was for women. 'Art is left to languish and die,' wrote Eliot's brother Henry Ware Eliot, Jr, in 1902.* 'The study of classics is practically dead at Harvard,' wrote his cousin Fred Eliot in 1910 – dead because they never helped build better bridges, or manipulate a market, or win battles. To the average undergraduate it was simply 'not a man's work'. All that was necessary for cultivation, decreed President Eliot, could be found on a five-foot shelf.

In the English department Copeland, whose composition course Eliot took in 1908–9, taught histrionic effects and an entertaining, journalistic style. Eliot was one of a minority – which included Conrad Aiken, John Dos Passos, Van Wyck Brooks, and George Santayana – out of sympathy with his tastes. 'I never really hit it off with him,' Eliot recalled. The feeling was mutual. Copeland regarded his pupil's classical fastidiousness with irritable incomprehension. 'Youthful rashness', Copeland told him, 'is not likely to be one of your attributes till you are middle-aged.'

In the philosophy department Eliot remained impervious to William James's optimism, his faith in men's agency, his version of truth as plural rather than absolute. His *Pragmatism* (1907) was one celebrated book published while Eliot was at Harvard, but Eliot remained unimpressed. He said that the error of pragmatism was making man the measure of all things. His courses with Palmer and Santayana were somewhat more useful. George Herbert Palmer, a teacher of ethics who had trained as a Congregational minister, behaved to students like a father confessor 'never shocked by sin, never despairing at sinners'. He taught Eliot pre-Socratic philosophy, and introduced him to Heraclitus. Eliot noted that the highest good was a combination of the greatest

* The line is from a parody of Charles Eliot Norton, Professor of Fine Arts, now in the Eliot Collection, Harvard. Norton points feebly to Ruskin and Rossetti but a herd of collegiates rushes past him, entranced with 'brutal sports'.

intellectual activity and the greatest receptivity to the divine around us.

He said repeatedly in later life that he had not liked George Santayana, a Spanish-born philosopher who stood out at Harvard for his supercivilised bearing and his classes so small and select that President Eliot enquired into them. Eliot felt that 'his philosophy was a dressing up of himself rather than an interest in things', an attitude Eliot called 'feminine'. All the same, he did read Santayana's *Three Philosophical Poets*, which included Dante as a poet who expressed a philosophical system. Eliot would draw on this book in his first essay on Dante in 1920, where he said that Dante's poetry contains 'the most comprehensive, and the most *ordered* presentation of emotions that has ever been made'. Dante's narrative of his journey to paradise through hell and purgatory was to provide the model for Eliot's own journey. Santayana himself had rejected the dogma of the Catholic Church, but he may have passed on to his student his admiration for rituals and forms he thought very beautiful.

At the same time as Eliot took a course in the philosophy of history with Santayana in the fall of 1909, he took a course in the history of allegory, and another in French literary criticism with Irving Babbitt, who would say, 'before we can have any literature worthy of the name, we must have a sound foundation of criticism.' Babbitt made his class read widely in the classics of the past and alerted them to the dangers of the modern secular world. Eliot later slighted Babbitt for not being a believer and deplored the inadequacy of his humanism, yet Eliot admitted that he had been an auxiliary to religion, for he had suggested to his students that the Catholic Church might perhaps be the only institution left in the West that might be counted on to preserve the treasures of the past. If one followed him to the end, said Eliot, one came to 'a Catholicism of despair'.

In November 1909 Eliot produced a new batch of poems. They were the result of private reading and emotions, but perhaps the lonely cultivation and intellectual intransigence of these two teachers fortified him. For a long time he remembered Babbitt as a man who had been 'very often right quite alone'.

*

During his summer vacation in East Gloucester in 1910 Eliot decided to collect his unpublished poems. He bought a marbled notebook from the Old Corner Bookstore, inscribed his title – INVENTIONS OF THE MARCH HARE – and copied in the more experimental poems he had been writing since November 1909.* (He did not include earlier poems, those published in the *Advocate*.) He continued to use the Notebook during the following year in Paris, on his return to Harvard and, finally, on arrival in London in 1914. He also maintained a loose collection of rough drafts and of typescripts of poems composed after he acquired his own typewriter in about 1913–14. With extraordinary patience and self-restraint Eliot hoarded many poems – some very fine – without attempting publication. In 1914, the slightly older Pound was amazed to come across a young American who had trained and modernised himself entirely on his own. Even in the first batch of poems, Eliot's sense of the central issues of his life is already clear. Two great poems that followed in 1910–11, 'Portrait of a Lady', and 'The Love Song of J. Alfred Prufrock', give these issues a more sophisticated formulation.

From the first, Eliot took up the task of recording the private habits of mind, the fears and solitary impulses that led him to a religious position. That position took hold in about 1914, but many of the earlier poems, particularly those he never published, record an underground phase of religious searching, a slow incubation and maturing of motives. 'Towards any profound conviction', said Eliot, 'one is borne gradually, perhaps insensibly over a long period of time, by

* The first poems in the Notebook were copied at the same time, i.e. in the same hand and blue ink. The latest is dated August 1910. The poems were later revised in pencil and dates added.

what Newman called "powerful and concurrent reasons".' At the end of his student years, in 'The Love Song of Saint Sebastian' (1914) and in 'The Death of Saint Narcissus' (early 1915), Eliot imagined the role of martyr, emphasising the martyr's abandonment of the ways of other men. As a person his martyr or 'saint' is absurd, but his ordeal is serious. Eliot was gradually formulating a choice all through his juvenilia: an Absolute or Pure Idea or Soul set against women, time, and society, who were the Absolute's enemies (although he scrupulously acknowledged the pomposity of the project and always guarded it with mocking humour). In 'Conversation Galante' (November 1909) he indicts woman as 'the eternal enemy of the Absolute'. In 'Spleen' (January 1910) a fastidious man turns his back on the tedious habits of Sunday church-going and waits impatiently 'on the doorstep of the Absolute'. In a Notebook poem of the same month, 'The First Debate between the Body and Soul', he calls on the Absolute to rescue the soul from the 'mud of physical sense'. He was rewarded, not immediately, but six months later, by the Silence in the Boston street.

The debate shows Eliot's state of mind more clearly than any other poem of the undergraduate period. He feels the sanctuary of the soul is violated by insistent material facts about him – 'twenty leering houses' in a shabby Boston square, the wheezing street piano, a blind old man who coughs and spits – and by the distractions of physicality – defecations, masturbations, 'The withered leaves / Of our sensations'. His mother's high-minded appeals in her poems to 'loose the spirit from its mesh, / From the poor vesture of the flesh' provided Eliot with the unacknowledged standard against which, in poem after poem, he would list his quarrels with the world of sense. The soul struggles unaided by an inert brain unable to distil meaning from these 'dull precipitates of fact'. He would like to dispose of a multiplicity of mundane observations with the 'pure Idea'. Driven by an as yet vague and inherited notion of perfection, Eliot made body and soul enemies and set up the uncompromising dichotomy that ordered his early years.

34

Perfection was only dimly perceived, while its enemies were quickly identified and reviled. For Eliot, time was the first enemy: at sixteen he wrote, 'For time is time, and runs away.' He started his poetic career with the smell of decay in his nostrils. Almost before he felt desire he watched its bloom fade. In all three of the first poems he published in the *Advocate*, blooming and withering flowers are images of love, and the fragrance of decay interweaves with the fragrance of bloom. Even before love's dawn, a young man notices that the leaves in a woman's wreath are already brown. Lines he wrote many years later in 'Salutation', about the rose of love with its worm-eaten petals, suggest that to satisfy love was to spoil it forever.* He deploys Poe's fragile world poised on the brink of dissolution and a grim nostalgia like Laforgue's, a youth writing as if youth were already reminiscent of itself, so conscious is he that time is passing. At the end of a Notebook poem, 'Opera', written in November 1909, the poet feels 'like the ghost of youth / At the undertakers' ball.'

It is easy to dismiss Eliot's juvenile melancholy as no more than a *fin de siècle* routine. But his horror of time and decay was real: it blew up later, in a discarded section of 'Prufrock', into a prophetic vision of the world dissolving:

> – I have seen the darkness creep along the wall
> I have heard my Madness chatter before day
> I have seen the world roll up into a ball
> Then suddenly dissolve and fall away.

Later yet, it was the impulse behind 'Whispers of Immortality', and behind the falling towers of London, Jerusalem, Alexandria, Athens, and Vienna in *The Waste Land*. It was logical that he should come to feel, eventually, that the temporal world had to be transcended.

The next opponent of perfection was less abstract, more immediately formidable: women. In each of the poems written in 1908 and 1909 a woman manages to humble a

---

* *Criterion*, vii (Jan. 1928), 31–2. This poem, revised, became part of *Ash-Wednesday*.

man in a different way. First there is Circe, who cultivates deadly flowers, very different from the delicate flowers he had previously imagined. Her flowers are fanged and red. Her fountain flows with the sound of men in pain. A snake lies sluggish along the garden stairs. The sinister and emasculating witch who presides over this garden of experience gathers strength from Madeline Usher and Rappaccini's daughter, who radiate an energy that Poe and Hawthorne regard as dangerous, perverse, or abnormal. Male American writers (with the notable exception of James) do not readily conceive women with the depth and humanity they accord to their great heroes – Fiedler, in his study of the American novel, suggests that the perfunctory and forced cataloguing of females according to type was 'prompted by a secret hate!' In Eliot's earliest poems, he followed a tradition in which women exist as predetermined types of manipulative energy or sickly pallor. His Circe appeared in November 1908. By January 1909 he had already created the traditional counterpoise: a pale white woman, thin as a sea-mist, fragile as a moonflower, elusive as a snowy owl. Her escort, like Dimmesdale, the sinful minister in *The Scarlet Letter*, has momentary regrets for the Circe spirit. 'Have you no brighter tropic flowers', he groans, 'with scarlet life for me?'

Turning irritably from one extreme possibility to another, Eliot looked on women from a literary distance. The distance was supported partly by his own inhibition, partly by a society in which the sexes were artificially separated. In the Long Island house of Theodore Roosevelt, rooms full of horns, tusks, and other hunter's trophies alternated with rooms full of fragile teacups and fussy upholstery. There was no overlap, no meeting-ground. Eliot had come across girls only as creatures on the other side of a wall that separated his parents' house from the Mary Institute. He used to sneak into the school-yard to play when they were gone. On one occasion he arrived too early and when he saw some girls staring at him through a window, fled at once. He remained 'extremely shy' with girls. Yet there were many spirited, humane, and active women around Eliot in his youth, not least his own mother who undertook social work through the Humanity Club of St Louis; his clever eldest sister, Ada (who Eliot often said was the Mycroft to his Sherlock Holmes); his sister Charlotte, who studied art, mainly sculpture; and his sensible Boston cousins Martha and Abigail Eliot, who were to distinguish themselves as professional women. It is puzzling that women kin to Eliot in no way shaped his judgement of their sex, as though that judgement excluded every attribute women share with men beyond sexual instinct. Though this distortion of women is, of course, a commonplace in Eliot's time, it is inexplicable in a man of questioning intelligence. In his early sonnet 'On a Portrait' (it was Manet's *La Femme au perroquet* which hung in a friend's drawing-room) Eliot chose to write about woman as a baffling and alien creature, frozen in an image, with exotic secrets but no ideas. 'Beyond the circle of our thought she stands,' he states in January 1909.

Again and again in his student poems – in 'Conversation Galante', in 'Circe's Palace', in 'Portrait of a Lady', and in 'Prufrock' – Eliot caricatured his embarrassing friendship with an emotional older woman, Adeleine Moffatt, who used to serve tea to Harvard men in a home crowded with bric-à-brac, behind Boston's State House. Conrad Aiken, who sometimes accompanied Eliot to these teas, recalled the 'oh so precious the oh so exquisite, Madeleine, the Jamesian lady of ladies, the enchantress of the Beacon Hill drawingroom – who, like another Circe, had made strange shapes of Wild Michael and the Tsetse (T. S. Eliot)'. Adeleine is so elusive in Eliot's poems because he does not strive to elicit her character, in the manner of James, but fits her to a variety of female types – the gushy romantic, the dangerous enchantress, the languid socialite. The interest of these poems lies not in the woman but in her effect on a potential lover. He is uneasily aware that the woman points up his pallid appetite for what others might readily desire but is, at the same time, defensively scornful of her taste, conversation, and brains. Prufrock has fleeting erotic sensations – the perfume from the woman's dress, or her arms moving to wrap her shawl or throw it off, can whip his attention from his foggy self-absorption – but she is not capable of a real exchange and is therefore unworthy of his confession. In 'Portrait of a Lady' a youth finds himself set to act in a darkened room with candles. Ill at ease and bored, blocking out a woman's voice with a savage 'tom-tom' in his head, he resists her absurd romantic ploys. When Eliot saw *Tristan* in 1909 he felt irritated by the lovers' passionate extravagance: 'And love torturing itself / To emotion for all there is in it, / Writhing in and out / Contorted in paroxysms . . .'. It seemed to him so futile, that in the end life itself departs with a feeble smile:

> We have the tragic? oh no!
> Life departs with a feeble smile
> Into the indifferent.

The characteristic irritability of Eliot's pieces on women was the rankling of inhibition compounded by a fear of having dared too little. In 'Portrait of a Lady' the young man struggles to preserve his self-possession against the tide of an emotion that makes him queasy. Fastidiousness was not a sign of diminished sexuality, but the result of inhibitions caused, in the first place, by distrust of women. Subtle and Jamesian in his analyses of gentlemen's consciousness, Eliot lacked insight when it came to women. Many of his youthful poems reinvigorate prejudice. 'Conversation Galante' (November 1909), 'Nocturne' (November 1909), and the Notebook poem 'Convictions' (January 1910) aim to demonstrate the shoddiness of women's minds and the poverty of their conversation. Eliot places women in sentimental situations, beneath a moon, surrounded by tissue-paper roses, exchanging the usual compliments, guesses, and promises – only the moon is bored and the conversation monotonous. He imagines in these poems a twittering, self-absorbed woman yearning to engulf a man in emotional claims, and assures us that female readers drip tears of gratification at such scenes.

One likely reason for Eliot's prejudice and associated inhibition was his father's view of sex as 'nastiness'. Henry

Eliot, Sr, considered public instruction tantamount to giving children a letter of introduction to the Devil. Syphilis was God's punishment and he hoped a cure would never be found. Otherwise, he said, it might be necessary 'to emasculate our children to keep them clean'. How far such an attitude affected his son is impossible to know, but later in life Eliot called the sex act evil – though he tempered this by saying that sex as evil was less boring than the cheery automatism of his contemporaries.

*

One day, in December 1908, Eliot went into the library of the Harvard Union and picked up the newly published second edition of *The Symbolist Movement in Literature* by Arthur Symons'. He was immediately struck by its call for a spiritual vision to eclipse the realistic tradition. Art which becomes religion, wrote Symons, may be an escape from time and mortality. He advised poets to wait on every symbol by which 'the soul of things can be made visible'. The sacred task of the poet is to shed the 'old bondage of exteriority' and become a prophet of the unknown, even if to shed externals is to come close to madness. The generation of Freud, Durkheim, Bergson, Croce, William James, and Weber gave prestige to half-glimpsed, half-articulated meaning, whose only logic lay in the emotions. Of that generation, Sir James Frazer, in particular, was to interest Eliot as an elucidator of the 'obscurities of the soul'. But this mood – the growing interest in consciousness – first came to Eliot through Symons, who presented the artist in the role of privileged seer.

His quotations from late nineteenth-century French poets had the effect of a mirror that flashed back to Eliot an image clearer, larger, and more dramatic than anything he had imagined. He saw at once not only the form that Modern poetry might take but a reflection of what he himself might be, particularly in the account of Jules Laforgue. A poet, Symons revealed, could be 'eternally grown-up'; he did not have to be a Byronic *enfant terrible* to be a hero. There were others, Eliot discovered, who spoke with mature irony, others whose dreams dissolved in the grim business of the grown-up world. The main difference between the poems Eliot wrote before and after he encountered Laforgue is that the latter contain at their centre a wilfully defeatist figure.

Laforgue's short life was full of dramatic change. Born in 1860 in Montevideo, he was brought to France at the age of six. (The seventy-five-day voyage supplied the first intimations of the famous *ennui*.) He had a talent for attracting loyal friends; he also attracted women. These ties were ephemeral but provided him with a subject for his women-ridden poetry. His poems play off the voice of a wry, defeated lover against the banal yap of some woman. The problem, Laforgue states repeatedly, is how to reconcile instinctive adoration of an angel with the mundane facts: the angel wears knickers, covets necklaces, and is generally ignorant of the fact that life is hurtling towards the graveyard. Sorrowfully, the clowns of *L'Imitation de Notre-Dame la Lune* (1885) come to see through female vacuity. Her eyes are divine, but there is nothing behind them.

Laforgue himself is invisible behind the façade of vulnerable clown, but it is not impossible to discern the ordinary cold-hearted flirt. Simone de Beauvoir was not convincing when she praised him as a man who pities women for their submission to masculine myths. Laforgue's rancour and mocking *ennui* are all the more brutal for those flickers of understanding that women found so seductive. Eliot shared Laforgue's irritability at women as well as an ascetic temper which regards sensuality as degrading. Laforgue ended a letter of 1885 with the drawing of a man walking away from a 'Lighthouse of Bitterness' to which his leg is attached by a ball-and-chain labelled 'Desire', while from his mouth issues the word 'Spleen'. Underneath, Laforgue wrote: 'This allegory will explain everything.' Eliot copied the self-pitying voice of the disillusioned idealist, and hunted out those women of the drawing-room or slum who were easy to cut down as mental lightweights and prostitutes. Women became more incidental in Eliot's poetry, allegoric figures of tinsel artifice, false emotion, and pathetic nonentity, to be bypassed on the way to the City of God. The bitten-off words of Laforguian repartee hint of suffering depths which, in both poets, mask their sealed-off detachment. This changed for Laforgue when he began to take English lessons with Leah Lee. For a long time he had admired Englishwomen in theory, and in 1886, when he was twenty-seven, he married this 'Petit Personnage' from Teignmouth in Devon. During 1886 there was a burst of creativity, and the interesting women in Laforgue's new poems, *Des fleurs de bonne volonté*, and his stories, *Moralités légendaires*, are perhaps his finest achievement. Leah became the model for his tender portrait of the red-headed Andromède, an impatient girl who declines to be rescued from a vulnerable dragon by a smug hero. 'As you know, there are three sexes,' Laforgue wrote to a friend, 'men, women and English girls.' Soon after, he died of tuberculosis, followed a year later by the death of his young wife of the same disease. He felt, it seems prophetically, in his poems, the waste, the futility, the grotesqueness of effort when lives are abruptly cut short.

Laforgue offered Eliot a new kind of poetry. In 1882, he had the idea of 'a kind of poetry which would be psychology in the form of dream . . . with flowers and scents and wind . . . complex symphonies with certain phrases (motifs) returning from time to time'. It was from Laforgue that Eliot would learn to control the drift of interior monologue through an ironic dialogue between rival aspects of the self. In the summer of 1885 Laforgue developed *vers libre*, which Eliot would later perfect in 'Prufrock' and 'Portrait of a Lady'. 'I forget to rhyme,' Laforgue wrote, 'I forget the number of syllables, I forget to set it in stanzas – the lines themselves begin in the margin like prose. The old regular stanza only turns up when a popular quatrain is needed.' Eliot would also make Laforgue's tricks with words a norm of Modernist method: the undercutting contrast of sublime and banal phrases.

The modish Modernism of verbal dazzlement and disillusioned airs goes back to Laforgue, but the great Moderns

were only secondarily showmen. Primarily, they were search-
ers for a way out of cultural despair. They were ideologues,
with messages of salvation of one sort or another, and
Laforgue, by contrast, has nothing to suggest beyond a
preoccupation with the self and with the difficulties of being
true to it. 'Night falls on the town: we shave our mask, don a
funereal coat, dine artistically, and then among sickly virgins,
take an idiotic stance' – Aldous Huxley would see, in that
stanza, all modern life. But this is only the posture of the
Modern, something with which Eliot would simply begin.

At once, on discovering Symons, Eliot ordered three
volumes of Laforgue from France. The Œuvres complètes
must have arrived in the spring of 1909, certainly in time for
Eliot to read them over the summer, and late in the autumn
he began to pour out new poems. 'I puzzled it out as best I
could, not finding half the words in my dictionary,' he said.
No other writer 'meant so much to me as he did at that
particular moment, or that particular year'. Many times in his
life he would return to this initiation, and try to explain what
happened: 'it was a personal enlightenment such as I can
hardly communicate,' he said on one occasion, and on
another spoke of 'a feeling of profound kinship, or rather of a
peculiar personal intimacy, with another, probably a dead
author. It may overcome us suddenly. . . ; it is certainly a
crisis; and when a young writer is seized with his first passion
of this sort he may be changed, metamorphosed almost,
within a few weeks even, from a bundle of second-hand
sentiments into a person.' Laforgue, he noted, was 'always
himself' in the sense that 'every mental occupation had its
own precise emotional state, which Laforgue was quick to
discover and curious to analyse' – this was 'always personal
in the right sense'. The shock of recognition roused for the
first time in Eliot 'an unshakeable confidence'. It had the
impact of a secret intimacy that would pass yet remain
'ineffaceable', much like 'personal intimacies in life'.

Laforgue, Eliot said, 'was the first to teach me how to
speak, to teach me the poetic possibilities of my own idiom of
speech'. It is not usually an exalted master who does this;

rather, someone more approachable. Laforgue wrote relatively little – his voice was original without being overwhelming. Eliot learnt to confess through the defeatist character; to broadcast secrets, and, at the same time, to shield himself with a mélange of voices: the wry voice of the failure, the scathing or flippant voice of a commentator, the banal voice of a woman who blocks truth. The last was at once evident in 'Conversation Galante' (modelled on 'Autre complainte de Lord Pierrot', which Symons had quoted in full). He learnt, too, another confessional strategy useful to a cautious and shy sensibility: to dramatise his most serious ideas as irrational, even ridiculous.

Laforgue's pierrot inspired Eliot's marionette and clown poems. They were exercises and not very good ones, but helped Eliot to develop his image of a performer fixed in his silly role, unable to take command of his real self which is socially unacceptable, outcast, or elusive. Eliot discovered in Laforgue an alienation in accord with his own feelings:

Nous nous aimions comme deux fous,
On s'est quitté sans en parler
Un spleen me tenait exilé,
Et ce spleen me tenait de tout. Bon.
('Solo de lune')

He read of an earth whirling inexplicably and lightly with its rotten cargo of war, suffering, and death, and about a solitary loser who invites experience only to spurn it. He spurns especially the unclean couplings of brutes and at the same time suffers through all his nerves ('Souffrir par tous mes nerfs, minutieusement'). He yearns for a perfection which he knows is not to be found in the world in which he lives.

Yet while Eliot learnt from Laforgue, he also transformed that state of mind into something cooler, more relentless, that came from himself. He shared with Laforgue and Baudelaire a powerful sense of evil and a passionate antagonism towards society, but he did not share their tenderness. The pleasure of hating, said Henry Adams sourly, one's self if no better victim offered, was not the New Englander's rarest amusement.

43

Laforgue's appearance also intrigued Eliot. He proceeded to cultivate the *dandysme* of his hero, the polished image described in Symons' book: 'fort correctes, de haut gibus, des cravates sobres, des vestons anglais, des pardessus clergyman, et de par les nécessités, un parapluie immuablement placé sous le bras.' Eliot elaborated his polish in imitation of Laforgue but, as one critic noted, he probably did not have to alter himself that much: 'There was an element of Laforgue already in him: it was easy to progress to the pose from the urbane dandyism, the perfection of dress, manners, and accomplishments, which was the Harvard style of his time and in which he excelled.' 'Manners', wrote Conrad Aiken, 'is an obsolete word nowadays, but he had them. He did things with an enviable grace.'

This public image became, in various guises, Eliot's most useful persona. In a Notebook poem, 'Suite Clownesque', he invents the 'First born child of the absolute', turned out neatly in 'the quintessential flannel suit'. With 'Spleen', published in January 1910, he pursues the image of a middle-aged gentleman whose absurd proprieties impede his advance on some final knowledge:

> And Life, a little bald and gray,
> Languid, fastidious, and bland,
> Waits, hat and gloves in hand,
> Punctilious of tie and suit
> (Somewhat impatient of delay)
> On the doorstep of the Absolute.

The character was finally perfected in the course of 1910–11 when Eliot created J. Alfred Prufrock. In 'Prufrock' the Laforguian split into mocking commentator and droll sufferer is reworked as split into prophet and groomed conformist. Eliot's prophet-commentator evaluates experience from a withdrawn position, exhorts, mocks, and offers salvation; the conformist suffers the experience, doubts, despairs, and resigns himself to his absurd ties with society.

Although Eliot got his initial clue from Laforgue, he shaped this character with materials close at hand. His speech was not the bitter, passionate speech of Laforgue but the understated, sour speech of New England. His *ennui*, associated with fear of action, was the neurosis of late nineteenth-century Boston. Eliot's impulse towards caricature was probably reinforced by a native tradition of burlesque. His comic repertoire – Prufrock wriggling and pinned to the salon wall, broadbottomed Sweeney whose hands dangle like an ape's, the hippo whose voice at mating time is hoarse and odd, the elephant who never forgets* – these versions of the actor-fool are reminiscent of American popular humour. As a student Eliot enjoyed the fad for comic strips, and used to frequent the vaudeville with his friend Conrad Aiken. It would have been at a Boston vaudeville house that Eliot heard 'That Shakespearian Rag', lyric by Gene Buck and Herman Ruby, music by Dave Stamper, for the 1912 Ziegfeld Follies, which would find its way into *The Waste Land*. 'There was something of the actor in Tom,' said Aiken, 'and some of the clown too. For all his liturgical appearance . . . he was capable of real buffoonery.'

*

Eliot's first batch of poems, written in November 1909, were modelled directly on French poems. Then, in 1910, he dropped his newly acquired façades for the confessional 'I'. Except for 'Spleen', the 1910 poems were all unpublishable because they fumbled with very strong feelings whose direction was not quite clear to the author. The year 1910, in fact, marked the beginning of a religious ferment and a rebellion against the world's dull conspiracy to tie him to its lifeless customs. These two tendencies persisted side by side but, at the time, the former was only dimly perceived in brief poems, while the latter was definite enough in his mind to induce the first act to separate him from his family and what they stood for: his decision to live in Paris.

* Eliot used the elephant on his bookplates. It was also his identity in a privately printed collection of his and his friends' light verse, *Noctes Binanianae* (see ch. 7 below).

During his Junior and Senior years, he became aware that there was 'not one older poet writing in America whose writing a younger man could take seriously'. At that stage Poe and Whitman had to be seen through French eyes: Laforgue's free verse derived from Whitman, but Eliot read Whitman only later. It was inevitable to want to leave 'a country in which the status of poetry had fallen still lower than in England'. Undergraduates at Harvard were reading the English poets of the nineties who were dead: 'that was as near as we could get to any living tradition', Eliot remembered. At the same time he needed to get away from the set scenes of youth, dalliance with women, his family's insistent questions about his future career, his siblings and cousins – all those dutiful grandchildren of William Greenleaf Eliot who were settling into practical, public-spirited careers. His eldest sister, Ada, had trained in social work and been a probation officer from 1901 to 1904 in New York City's prison, where she was known as 'the angel of the Tombs'. Another sister, Marian, had studied at Miss Folsom's school for social service in Boston. Of his Boston cousins, Martha was to be a physician – she later specialised in child care and public health – and her sister Abigail was going into education – her school in Roxbury was to be the precursor of all programmes for special needs. Their brother, Frederick, was destined for Harvard Divinity School. Another cousin, William Greenleaf Eliot II, was to be, like his father, a minister in Portland's Unitarian church.

In the context of these careers, Tom's decision to go to Paris appeared bizarre to his family. To him Paris might have meant a place where, as a poet, he might feel less at odds with society, and he probably dreamed, like any provincial, of belonging in a great centre of artistic and intellectual innovation. To the average American, however, Paris was for tourists and for female dilettantes to potter at art. American men simply did not go there seriously to live. 'Our people have forgotten', wrote Henry Adams, 'that any world exists outside America and their heads are excessively swelled . . . One might as well talk about Babylon or Nineveh as about

England or France.' Predictably then, Eliot's mother wrote, on 3 April 1910, to her 'dear Boy' expressing her surprise that he had not settled for New York if he wished to write. To her France was incredibly remote and corrupt:

> I suppose you will know better in June what you want to do next year ... I can not bear to think of your being alone in Paris, the very words give me a chill. English speaking countries seem so different from foreign. I do not admire the French nation, and have less confidence in individuals of that race than in English.

Eliot held out against this opposition, but in May went down with scarlet fever, and his mother rushed to Boston. He was put in Stillman Hospital. It was not serious, but prevented him from taking his final examinations that spring. Nevertheless, on 24 June, he graduated from Harvard, attended the huge garden party in the Yard, sat in Sanders theatre amid the waving fans, and heard the Orator speak of the debt a Harvard man owed to the community. Ever since the Civil War Harvard had cultivated a strenuous ideal which President Eliot had defined as steady nerve to endure fatigue and moral stress. Harvard men were expected to rein their bodies as so many forces to be controlled, to fight and subdue their emotions. At Commencement in 1908 the urgent message was: 'the farther away we get from Harvard, the more is expected of the Harvard man in spreading the faith.' So effective was this indoctrination that Harvard men became wary of anyone who undermined their assumptions about what it was to be a man. So it was that men who were conscious of their leadership in society damaged their lives trying to be 'manly'. Tom Eliot came at the end of this era – talk of manliness died out at Harvard after about 1910 – but at Commencement that year he did still hear that he should strive to be a man of affairs like the two presidents of his time, Charles William Eliot and A. L. Lowell, and of efficiency as the quality to be desired above all others.

Possibly it was during the next two months of idle summer at Cape Ann that he wrote a series of 'Goldfish' poems about the rituals of family life and friends about him. He was impatient with white flannels, with teacups and sounding 'the depths with a silver spoon', the summer afternoons on the veranda, the waltzes turning on hot August evenings, *The Chocolate Soldier* and *The Merry Widow*, the sunlight on the sea, the salty days, and boys and girls together. These pleasures seemed to him trivial, the 'Essence of summer magazines', and in another Notebook sequence, 'Mandarins' (dated August 1910), he turns to the similar outlines of a civilised Chinese scene: tea in thin, translucent porcelain, two tranquil ladies at a window, a distant prospect of the sea, and the oldest mandarin so enviably at ease in his obese repose. He had the world in his fist, and could close in on himself. He was not haunted by perfection.

The last of the 'Goldfish' poems describes a cleaning-up session in October. Jumbled amongst the debris of the past academic year, the old letters, bills, photos, programmes, and tennis shoes in a bureau drawer, the poet comes upon a poem, 'Barcarolle', which brings back 'problems of the soul', walking the waves like gospels from a 'fourth dimension', as he paces the shore.

Eliot's 1910 poems are mostly rejections of family and Boston life, but he also recorded two experiences that struck a different note. In 'Easter: Sensations of April' (April 1910), the smell of some geraniums on a third-floor sill calls up a long-forgotten scene, perhaps in Missouri, a little black girl across the alley with a red geranium in her hands that she had brought from church. He imagines her obedient prayers and thinks wistfully – 'She is very sure of God.' Eliot's Easter poem is insignificant as poetry, but it marks his growing distance from his family's religious certainties – and his nostalgia for them. His mother wrote numerous Easter/Spring poems promising the waking of the spirit to 'the new life in its blessedness'. For her son the spring only mocked his failures of faith.

Then in June there came the indescribable Silence in the midst of the clatter of graduation, the exhortations of practical men, the questions of parents, the frivolity of millinery and strawberries in the Yard. Suddenly able to shed the world, he experienced a fugitive sensation of peace that he would try all his life to recapture. Eliot once said that his mind was naturally inclined to the metaphysical, and any mystical experience which put him in touch with another kind of existence would be treasured and made much of. 'Silence' was the forerunner of later beatific moments in Eliot's work, and in each case it seems to him he has received some kind of message that disperses and obliterates ordinary reality, a message he badly needs to interpret. At first, Eliot did not conceive of the religious implications, simply that the Silence was antithetical to the world (perhaps reinforced by Laforgue's invective against the pitiful world and its wretched history: 'And thou, Silence, pardon the Earth; the little madcap hardly knows what she is doing'). The revelation in the spring of 1910, at the age of twenty-one, had no immediate repercussions but remained the defining experience of his life. His immediate response may have been like that of Hawthorne, who distrusted it as a transient sensation, surrounded by the inescapable facts of the material world which could not be shed.*

Still, there was in the spring and summer of 1910 some vital intersection of problems: Eliot's isolation, his uneasiness in Boston, his resentment against women, his fear of time and decay, the encounter with the French poets and Arthur Symons, and the secret wish to know the Absolute. At this intersection we might locate the beginning of Eliot's religious journey. For a long time his caution and self-distrust kept him at a stage of religious intimation rather than of surrender and

---

* In *The Blithedale Romance*, ch. 8, the hero suddenly sees through nature's mask and enjoys the novelty. 'But that was all,' Hawthorne says. (For Emerson, of course, it would have been everything.) Melville, too, wrote in a letter to Hawthorne (1 June 1851): 'This "all" feeling . . . You must often have felt it, lying in the grass on a warm summer's day. Your legs seem to send out shoots into the earth . . . But what plays mischief with the truth is that men will insist upon the universal application of a temporary feeling or opinion.'

conviction. The latent interest remained balanced against the distractions of his immediate surroundings. During the next year in Paris the recurrence of the Silence provided only a brief escape from insistent inspections of Parisian decadence. Yet though Eliot failed to find the truth he sought, his sense of special destiny gradually hardened and reached a point of articulation in the 'saint' poems at the end of his student years.

3

BEYOND PHILOSOPHY

ELIOT CROSSED THE Atlantic to an imaginary Paris filled with the spiritual malaise and morbidness of the late-nineteenth-century poets he admired. ('La France représentait surtout, à mes yeux, la poésie,' he declared many years later.) He planned to 'scrape along' in Paris, and gradually give up English and write in French.

In October 1910 Eliot settled at 151 bis rue Saint Jacques, a pension on the Left Bank. He visited Jacques Rivière, editor of the *Nouvelle revue française*, and studied French language and literature with Rivière's brother-in-law, Alain-Fournier (1886–1914), who would publish a nostalgic novel, *Le Grand Meaulnes*, in 1913 just before his death in the Great War. Eliot recalled his 'exquisite refinement, quiet humour and his great personal charm'. He introduced his pupil to French translations of *Crime and Punishment, The Brothers Karamazov*, and *The Idiot*, and late in 1910 Eliot saw the first dramatisation of *The Brothers Karamazov*, by Jacques Copeau, at the Théâtre du Vieux-Colombier. Eliot recognised that one of Dostoevsky's best themes was humiliation, one of the major experiences in life, Eliot remarked, and under-exploited in writing. Humiliation began to blend in his poetry with his brand of Boston refinement which was close to that of Henry James. At this time, November 1910, Eliot was subverting the Jamesian title of 'Portrait of a Lady' with the portrait of a young man who fears humiliation at the hands of a demanding 'lady', a fear which provokes the savagery of a 'dull tom-tom' in the brain. In return for Dostoevsky, Eliot introduced Alain-Fournier to new English writing, in particular Conrad's allegory *Typhoon*, where an unseen hero, Captain MacWhirr, holds firm between the outward onslaught of a storm at sea, on the one hand, and, on the other, interior anarchy, the uproar of men fighting for money in the ship's hold.

Eliot had also befriended a fellow-lodger at his pension. Jean-Jules Verdenal had a round-faced inoffensiveness, with a neat moustache and a dimple in his chin, and that doomed look of men of his generation who were soft and ripe for sacrifice. He was born in 1890 at Pau in the French Pyrenees, the son of a doctor and now a medical student. The two students sat politely at table each evening while Mme Casaubon, the owner, tucked a napkin between chin and chest as she mixed the salad with wrinkled hands. In contrast with Eliot's punctiliousness, Verdenal would come downstairs collarless, comfy in slippers and an old jacket, and chat in Eliot's room where the bed was in a recess and the wallpaper, according to Verdenal, got on one's nerves. After Eliot left, Verdenal moved to his room, and contemplated sending Eliot a snip of that wallpaper; then realised this gesture came from Laforgue – Verdenal too read Laforgue, and he too cultivated a philosophic *ennui*. He admired Eliot's 'gracieuse nonchalance', and reflects it in his letters.

'. . . Je ne sais guère agir; et si j'agis', Verdenal wrote, 'je suis assez malin pour qu'un sincère regard vienne bientôt analyser la joie d'agir et la détruire. . . . Toutes mes ardeurs, aujourd'hui vaines comme un feu d'artifice raté, pourront-elles un jour pleinement s'épanouir?' ('I have little gift for action; and if I act . . . I am bright enough to take a sincere look at the joy of action and destroy it by analysis. . . . Will my enthusiasms, now as inoperative as damp squibs, ever be able to flower fully?')

Many attitudes, familiar to readers of Eliot, can now be traced to letters Verdenal wrote to him between July 1911 and December 1912. Verdenal believed that while materialism spread downwards through society, an aspiration towards the Idea was growing amongst the élite – in evidence in modern poetry and music – which frequently took the form of a return to Christianity. Common to each case was '*en quelle mesure il peut influencer notre vie intérieure vers la connaissance du bien suprême*' ('*how far it can influence our inner life towards knowledge of the supreme good*').

These letters reflect Eliot's capacity for friendship without the bravado he went in for with buddies like Aiken: his new friend was devoid of the ostentatious masculinity American men felt compelled to construct; his unaffected seriousness was charming. Eliot was struck by the French determination to catch the most elusive feelings in the net of language. Long after, he remembered Verdenal coming towards him across the Luxembourg Gardens, waving a spray of lilac – the rare sentiment in this memory has raised the question whether the feeling between them was 'queer'. Eliot denied this absolutely, and spoke of 'nervous sexual attacks' which he 'suffered' in Paris: 'One walks about the street with one's desires, and one's refinement rises up like a wall whenever opportunity approaches.' He made it plain that these desires were for women. Who can now determine the exact ways people of the past bent their inclinations in order to construct gender according to absurd models of masculinity and femininity? Verdenal was easy with Eliot who, stiff himself, had a stiffening effect on others when he did not deliberately unbend. The Frenchman's most important legacy for Eliot was to offer a blend of sensibility and intellect missing in the English intellectual tradition since the seventeenth century.

Eliot never acknowledged this influence, and made light of French ties. His temperament was, of course, solitary, but it was also part of his mystique to project an image of solitary genius. He declared that the best way to know Paris as a place and a tradition was to cut oneself off from it. 'When I was living there years ago,' he added, 'I had only the genuine stimulus of the place, and not the artificial stimulus of the people, as I knew no-one whatever, in the literary and artistic world, as a companion – knew them rather as spectacles, listened to, at rare occasions, but never spoken to.' Eliot adopted this pose and cultivated a spectatorial distance in his poems, in the manner of the young Emerson, who wrote in his *Journal*, 'I am solitary in the vast society of beings; I consort with no species; I indulge no sympathies. I see the world, human, brute and inanimate nature; I am in the midst of them but not *of* them . . .' Though Eliot was nourished in Paris by the kind of intellectual ferment he had missed in America, the poetry he wrote during 1910 and 1911 affects more alienation than ever.

He brought with him to Paris some promising fragments. 'No! I am not Prince Hamlet, nor was meant to be', modelled on Laforgue, was a preliminary bit of 'J. Alfred Prufrock', Eliot's first famous poem, in which an indeterminate character confronts himself with negations and questions, and still finds it 'is impossible to say just what I mean!' Though he has 'wept and prayed', Prufrock admits he has had no call. His disclaimers reveal heroic pretensions absurdly at odds with inhibition in a man who can hardly venture across the threshold of a Boston party.

The pressure of Eliot's own inhibition burst its barriers in a riot of obscene verse – exactly what his mother had feared in the immoral influence of Paris. Later, Eliot excised from his Notebook this start of an 'epic' about the sexual exploits of Christopher Columbus, King Bolo, and his Big Black Kween: 'The Triumph of Bullshit' (Eliot's is the first usage recorded in the *Oxford English Dictionary*) is the obverse of his polite refinement. It addresses 'Ladies' who find the attentions of the speaker (like 'Prufrock among the Women'*) 'ineptly meticulous', but he gets back at them with a rude retort at the close of each stanza: 'For Christ's sake stick it up your ass.'

Otherwise, Paris did not change Eliot very much. Henry James was intrigued by the fate of solitary Americans who worked out, like Columbus, a conception of the other side of the globe, the world 'imagined always in what one had read and dreamed'. Eliot imposed upon his observations of the city a point of view already manifest at Harvard, a mixture of

* The original subtitle of 'The Love Song of J. Alfred Prufrock' was 'Prufrock among the Women', *IMH*, p. 39.

horror at the monotonous drabness of the poor and boredom with the smug formulae of academics. A thinker in a gloomy garret gazes at the constellations and they do not enlighten him: the universe reverberates with empty abstractions, 'the Pure Idea' and 'a Place in Life', 'the relation of life to matter', and 'the scheme of Vital Force'.* From early January to 17 February 1911 Eliot attended seven weekly lectures by the philosopher Henri Bergson. Bergson was at this time 'the most noticed figure in Paris', and Eliot was impressed that 'the mondaines who attended lectures at the College de France were in a sense using their minds'. Bergson's *Creative Evolution* (1907) gave agency to the human spirit, rescuing evolution from a mindless, crass materialism. Change was the core of experience, for 'an ego which does not change does not endure'.

This was the only time that Eliot was ever converted by the influence of any individual. As it turned out, his conversion was temporary; he found some of the philosophy suspect – the use Bergson made of biology and psychology, for instance; also his 'somewhat meretricious' promise of immortality – but Eliot was to draw on Bergson's challenge to the technological artifice of clock-time which enforces the present and ignores the cumulative incursions of the past. Duration, the lived experience of Time, is subjective and continuous, not measured out in ticks and tocks. (To experience the even monotony of measured time – the 'petty pace' of Macbeth's tomorrows – is the unspeakable torment of vacated souls.) Bergson had an immediate impact on poems in which Eliot cultivates indirect habits of mind. Discard solid intellectual supports, Bergson urged, admit only the fluid consciousness and intuitions in the making.

By February 1911 Eliot was already disillusioned with

* 'Inside the gloom . . .', untitled draft of a holograph series of couplets. *IMH*, pp. 72–3. Eliot's handwriting changed during the year he was in Paris. From about November 1910 his neat small hand became large and spiky, with few loops, tall capitals, and long tails. After November 1911 he reverted to a smaller, rounder hand. These changes make it possible to align the undated with the dated holographs.

Paris. Bored with the proper gatherings he had known in Boston, the young traveller had looked forward to his initiation into a sophisticated society. He exhorted himself to have his fling but, as in Boston, the life he sought eluded him. In 'The smoke that gathers blue and sinks . . .' he describes a dinner in a Parisian nightclub inducing only torpor. A woman of indeterminate age, all breasts and rings, singing 'Throw your arms around me – Aren't you glad you found me', does not enliven him. Why is he so hard to please? the poet asks himself. The French sauces, the smoke of rich cigars, the after-dinner liqueurs seem to blanket his perceptions.

When he paced the streets of Paris he saw a grey city, rows of blackened trees, and rain dripping from slated roofs into a mess of mud. In 'Fourth Caprice in Montparnasse' he is faintly amazed that the indifferent plastered houses should have such a resilient life of their own, should so insolently go on without fear of dissolution.

Whether it was Boston or Paris, people were the same: too apathetic and undisciplined to escape their banal fates. The exaggerated hopelessness of Eliot's poems is partly a Laforguian gesture, but there is a genuine craving for experience and a fear that experience might easily pass one by. Lovefancies had risen like waves as he had paced the Cape Ann shore the previous summer; now, in Paris, he thinks of the passion of Bacchus for Ariadne whose 'lives curl upward like a wave'. At the same time he craves a sign to 'annul' such agitations. Silence came to Eliot a second time in March 1911. In a '2nd Debate between the Body and Soul'* he writes: 'a ring of silence closes round me'. It seals him off, in a state of beatific security, from the 'floods of life' that threaten to break like a wave against his skull. There, momentarily, he hangs in his chrysalis. The soul lies still in its cell, sensing its wings, longing to unfurl its purity, and fearful it will miss its moment of birth through excessive caution:

* I have used the second title, which stresses the continuity of Eliot's thought. The first is 'Bacchus and Ariadne'.

Yet to burst out at last, ingenuous and pure
Surprised but knowing – it is a triumph not
   endurable to miss!
Not to set free the purity that clings
To the cautious midnight of its chrysalis
Lies in its cell and meditates its wings
Nourished in earth and stimulated by manure.
– I am sure it is like this
I am sure it is this
I am sure.

Throughout his career, Eliot tried to interpret this release from a time-bound world. In 1911 he calls it 'the wind that breathed across', a wind from 'beyond the world'. It sweeps by leaving no trace, and Time begins again its relentless attrition. It's a jolt to come back from 'beyond the world', similar perhaps to what people who have crossed into death experience when brought back to life: 'The world of contact sprang up like a blow.' Subsequent poems picture a young man who walks the Paris streets and beats his brains in fevered efforts to understand the implications for his life.

At this point and for a long while to come, Eliot resisted a conventional religious answer. Given his sensitivity to urban degradation, he could not easily accept the benign, enlightened deity of his family. In his first blasphemous poem ('He said: this universe is very clever . . .' dated March 1911) the Absolute is likened to a sexual monster. Here, he contrasts the rational universe of scientific laws, with the comic horror of an Absolute waiting in the middle of a geometric net 'like a syphilitic spider'. Her victims end their lives inside her.

It was less the sophisticated or innovative of Paris who interested Eliot, rather the prostitutes and *maquereaux* of the Boulevard Sébastopol, the grave façades of the buildings which seemed to darken the sidewalks, and the men who nosed after pleasure, especially men who had never known it. Slumming, for Eliot, was no pastime: he took it too seriously. He allowed lust and drunkenness to circle round him, so that he might contemplate with horror a life bereft of morale or dignity.

He clung to decadence, like Laforgue before him. Laforgue had liked to alternate between the domestic gentility of the Prussian court (where he held a post as French Reader to the Empress) and the low dives of Berlin. His diary for 5 June 1883 records a sexual marathon: 'A Jewess with black armpits – a blonde made of wood – the red-faced English girl, unbelievable.' As a foreigner in Paris, Eliot duly tried out the studied kind of slumming he describes in 'Rhapsody on a Windy Night' (dated March 1911). The difference is that Laforgue was a participant, Eliot an inspector of vice, which gave Eliot as a poet the decided advantage of a more incisive spectatorial distance. While Laforgue tended to reproach women for his sense of banality, Eliot understands the banality of vice itself.

He began to explore the streets during those hours of the night when they were deserted except for the occasional prostitute or scavenging cat. He, too, was a kind of scavenger, turning over his observations to find some clue to the meaning of life – a rusty spring in a factory yard, the unfathomable eye of a soliciting prostitute, his own eyes peering through the lighted shutters of other people's houses. In 'Rhapsody on a Windy Night' Eliot tried out Bergson's approach to truth not by analysis but by casting oneself on a current of immediate perception as it flowed through time. Bergson said:

> I perceive at first, as a crust solidified on the surface, all the perceptions which come to it from the material world. These perceptions are clear, distinct, juxtaposed ... Next, I notice memories which more or less adhere to these perceptions and which serve to interpret them. These memories have been detached, as it were, from the depth of my personality, drawn to the surface by the perceptions which resemble them; they rest on the surface of my mind without being absolutely myself. Lastly, I feel the stir of tendencies and motor habits – a crowd of virtual actions, more or less firmly bound to these perceptions and memories. All these clearly defined elements appear more distinct from me, the more distinct they are from each other.

Accordingly, in 'Rhapsody', a wanderer drifts from one hour to the next, while the moonlit street dissolves 'the floors of memory'. The twisted corner of a prostitute's eye reminds him of a twisted branch on a New England beach; the automatic lick of a cat's tongue recalls an old crab gripping the stick held out to him. Finally, the stir of habit takes the wanderer back to his room at four in the morning – to his toothbrush on the wall and his shoes neatly at the door. Eliot thought the most important passage in Bergson's work had to do with the difference between 'the heterogeneous qualities which succeed each other in our concrete perception', perceptions which are discontinuous, and an underlying harmony which we should be able to deduce. In an essay on Bergson's philosophy Eliot asks whether reality is to be found in the observer's consciousness or in the material object. And where, he asks, is the one reality to subsume both of these, and can one know it?*

'Rhapsody' marvellously evokes a mood and a state of mind, an almost painful sensitivity to his impressions of the deserted, vaguely sinister streets of Paris after midnight. But, from a philosophical point of view, this experiment failed: the impressions do not converge; there is no intuition to be seized. I think, behind the poem, there lies an Emersonian premise that we might cultivate an angle of vision whereby diverse objects are penetrated and illumined as part of one design. 'What would we really know the meaning of?' Emerson asked. 'The meal in the firkin; the milk in the pan; the ballad in the street; the news of the boat; the glance of the eye; the form and the gait of the body; – show me the ultimate reason of these matters, show me the sublime presence of the highest spiritual cause lurking, as always it does lurk, in these suburbs and extremities of nature . . . and

* Holograph paper, perhaps a lecture, on Bergson (Eliot Collection, Houghton Library). It is not in Eliot's Paris hand, and must have been written some time after Eliot's return to Harvard. My guess is 1913 or 1914 since he mentions F. H. Bradley, whom he was reading at that time, and uses the same paper as that of an address to Harvard's Philosophical Society in 1913 or 1914.

the world lies no longer a dull miscellany and lumber-room, but has form and order; there is no trifle, there is no puzzle, but one design unites and animates the farthest pinnacle and the lowest trench.' Eliot did eventually confirm this hidden attunement of the universe in *Burnt Norton* in 1935, but in 1911 the sublime design refused to compose itself and the objects fell apart. He wished to find meaning, but could not say, with Emerson's blithe assurance, 'it always does lurk'.

Apart from the poet, there is only one other distinct character in the Paris poems. In 'The Little Passion: From "An Agony in a Garret" ' the poet meets a lost soul in a bar, a man of religious gifts, but damned for his inability to use them.* The drunk is aware his soul has been dead a long time, yet continues to waste his energies in futile diving into dark retreats. The alternative, if he could reach it, is martyrdom:

> Upon those stifling August nights
>   I know he used to walk the streets
> Now following the lines of lights
>   Or diving into dark retreats
>
> Or following the lines of lights
>   And knowing well to what they lead:
> To one inevitable cross
>   On which our souls are pinned and bleed.

This is a later, distilled version. In the first, more decadent draft, instead of following the lights, the drunk lets them spin round him like a wheel. The first draft of 'The Little Passion', really only fragmentary jottings, is, all the same, a reservoir of themes for some of Eliot's greatest poems. The dead soul in a Parisian bar is the predecessor of those wanderers of the city, those heroes of the wasted passions, J. Alfred Prufrock and

---

* The first draft is undated, but is written in the spiky Paris hand. A later, more compact version (quoted below) was written in about 1914 and is the last poem copied into Eliot's Notebook (*IMH*, pp. 57–8). It might appear that the Notebook draft in ink came first, and a longer, laid-in draft in pencil came second – I would judge the reverse.

Gerontion. The fragment also points to Eliot's martyr poems of 1914 and to the wastefulness of the turning world in the fourth 'Prelude'. It is curious that the path, which in other poems of this period is so tortuous, should lead, in this one case, directly to a Christian terminus.

The '2nd Debate between the Body and Soul' and 'The Little Passion' show Eliot's mind edging beyond 'Silence' and 'The First Debate' towards a religious, even Christian, point of view. In one fragment, 'He said: "this crucifixion was dramatic . . ."', Eliot imagines for a moment an *imitatio Christi* and then falls back on his own paltry alternatives, on the one hand the Parisian garret, the seedy life of the would-be artist up six dingy flights of stairs, or on the other the office chair, an equally unenticing inheritance from his businessman father. Eliot posed God briefly as an alternative to an unwanted relationship in 'Entretien dans un parc'. He imagines the interior monologue of a youth strolling hand-in-hand with a woman up a blind alley, filled with nervous embarrassment and 'exasperation' in the face of her composure: 'Simmering upon the fire, piping hot / Upon the fire of ridicule.' It would be relief, he tells himself, to turn at length to faith:

> Some day, if God –
> But then, what opening out of dusty souls!

In April Eliot made a brief stay in London, together with a school friend. Bon's Surrey Hotel in Duke Street had a coffee room, butler, and maids in starched aprons bringing hot water in great brass cans. The two young men bought ties for ninepence ha'penny in the Burlington Arcade, and suits, the most expensive they could find, for seven guineas. Eliot's 'Interlude in London' observes a people hibernating behind their bricks, shut in by sudden rains, and tied to their routines – '. . . marmalade and tea at six'. Eliot did the last thing expected of a tourist: he made a 'pilgrimage' to unvisited suburbia: Cricklewood, then part of the outlying hamlet of Hendon.

'Where *is* Cricklewood?' enquired an austere Englishman at the hotel.

Eliot produced a map and pointed silently, as evidence that Cricklewood existed.

'But why go to Cricklewood?' The Englishman was puzzled.

'There is no reason.' Eliot was triumphant. 'Cricklewood is mine,' he thought. 'No one will go there again.' It seemed to him like a town in a fairytale, which existed for an hour and only one man saw it. Part of his 'triumph' was *not* to have seen the Tower or Madame Tussaud's or even Westminster Abbey. But he did visit City churches: St Helen's Bishopsgate, St Stephen Walbrook, St Bartholomew the Great, West Smithfield (where an inscription records that one John Eliot gave £30 to the poor), and St Sepulchre Old Bailey. He also visited the medieval Catholic church, St Etheldreda, in Ely Place, Holborn. His Baedeker (inscribed 'Thomas S. Eliot October the 14th. 1910') marks Lower Thames Street (where Chaucer was said to have lived from 1379 to 1385) and its church: already, in 1911, Eliot's eye is trained on one of the *non*-wasteland sites in *The Waste Land* (1922), sites of potential change into something rich and strange: 'Inexplicable splendour of Ionian white and gold'. This is St Magnus the Martyr, built by Christopher Wren in 1676, the very high Anglo-Catholic church in Lower Thames Street, where Miles Coverdale, translator of the Bible (1535), had preached from 1563 to 1566.

Eliot's poems of 1911 fall into two groups. In the first half of the year, chiefly February and March, they touch on local scenes: a glossy Parisian restaurant, the nocturnal life of the street, the sedate wintriness of London. In the second half of the year and into 1912 the poems retreat into a private world of the mind, drawn there by some secret hovering on the edge of consciousness. The hero of the great poem of this period, J. Alfred Prufrock, is driven by a secret just beyond his grasp which he terms 'the overwhelming question'.

Eliot said several years later that a poet should state a vision which includes a coherent formulation of life outside the poem. Eliot did not wish to create a rag-bag of moods, insights, and sensations: he wanted his poetry to terminate in a formulated philosophy and extend, further, into a way of life. He decided a poet should realise emotionally and dramatically 'that which constitutes the truth of his time, whatever that may be'. In Paris, in 1911, Eliot witnessed *la ferveur bergsonniene*, and took in the anti-democratic anti-romantic notions of the Action Française, but these did not provide the larger philosophic view he needed. The latter would come to him eventually from men outside his own time, Dante and St John of the Cross.

In the summer of 1911 Eliot told his college friend Conrad Aiken, over *sirop de fraises* at an outdoor café, that he had to return to Harvard to study philosophy. He had lived for nine months in the most sophisticated centre of Western civilisation but had not found 'the truth of his time'. Eliot came to Paris to be a poet; he left a philosophy student.

*

About the time Eliot made his decision to study philosophy, he began to write poems in which the nocturnal wanderer of the city is replaced by a new dominant figure, an almost demented philosopher, keeping all-night vigils in his room.* 'Thought ought to govern spiritual reality', Eliot underlined in his copy of Hegel's *Philosophy of History*. In his new poems a philosopher makes his way along various mental paths, asking questions, but they seem to lead nowhere. It is a torture reserved for the intellectual that nothing speaks to him but his own questionable logic. At dawn, the solitary

---

* Most of these poems Eliot left undated, but the change in handwriting makes it possible to group them. The third 'Prelude' and most of 'Prufrock', dated July and August 1911, were copied into the Notebook in the spiky Paris hand. All the other poems in this batch, including a later, discarded section of 'Prufrock', were copied in the smaller, rounder hand Eliot developed after his return to Harvard. The rounder hand is very similar to the pre-Paris hand, but distinguishable by the capital 'I' – which gains a lower loop – and by a different flourish beneath the poems.

meditations are curtailed by the damp breeze and rattling shutters, by menacing shadows, stretching their tentacles, or by a 'vision of the street / As the street hardly understands.' He thinks of broken lives in Roxbury, Massachusetts, or on the Left Bank. While the gas-jets flicker in the morning draught, the sound of a drunk singing in the gutter reminds him of children whimpering in corners, women spilling out of their corsets in doorways, men in shirt-sleeves leaning out of windows, and smoking boys drifting together in the fan of light from a corner drugstore. The outside world then seems so hateful that it dissolves, fades away.

Eliot once said that a narrow, unique, and horrible vision of life might come, as the result of a few or slender experiences, to a highly sensitive youth. His own hatred of humanity was in no way commensurate with what he actually saw – to see a drunk in the gutter or dirty, broken fingernails tapping on the counter in a bar filled Eliot with extreme loathing, some horror of his own. After he became a Christian, Eliot said that the religious life, for a certain temperament, began with a sense of 'the disorder, the futility, the meaninglessness, the mystery of life and suffering'. Particularly after his return to Harvard for the fall semester of 1911, he was greatly troubled to explain such feeling: in a manuscript poem, 'Do I know how I feel? Do I know what I think?',* a prospective suicide – a 'gentleman' who does not forget to take his hat and gloves – fears 'what a flash of madness might reveal' and wishes that just one person, say the porter on his stair, could share his horror at the common plots of fate: beauty wasted in convenient marriages, or worn away in commuter trains, or stifled in darkened rooms. Will the doctor with a pointed beard and black bag, chemicals and a knife, who arrives to perform the post-mortem, 'touch the secret which I cannot find?' Vestiges of consciousness which might remain will be blacked out by ether. He will not have

* This rough draft was not completed, or possibly the poem was designed to break off, like the suicide's existence. There is no date, but it is in the post-Paris hand.

to care what happens after. A dead soul will not, like Hamlet, question the afterlife.

This period of intellectual stress (a 'brain twisted in a tangled skein', fixated on 'something which should be firm but slips, just at my finger tips') came from a latent prophetic power Eliot could not quite grasp or express. He felt an overwhelming need to question a drably abhorrent world based on attrition, but did not know in what direction to carry his questions or what exactly to do.

Eliot's mother gave him a blueprint he could only partially follow. She relied on private revelation, but insisted it be given a firm rational basis 'that superstition with inconstant light / May not allure my steps from Reason's way'. One of Charlotte Eliot's most eloquent models, Giordano Bruno, spends sleepless nights in search of truth. His imagination is racked with a brood of loathsome shapes, yet he is able to say at last: 'The truth dawns on my vision . . .' He realises God is to be found 'upon the paths of knowledge everywhere / He dwelt in truth.' Eliot duly explored 'the paths of knowledge' – he speaks of them in 'Prufrock' and other poems – but they led him into dark corners, wound him in question marks, finally abandoned him in an intellectual maze.

The first vigil poems, the third 'Prelude' (dated July 1911) and 'Prufrock' (completed during a visit to Munich in July–August 1911) were more dramatic and less obviously autobiographical than the others, which were written after Eliot's return to Boston. In the third 'Prelude', Eliot describes the rather improbable thoughts of a grimy woman in curl papers. She lies on her back in a poor suburb of Boston, staring at the ceiling, where she projects 'a thousand sordid images' from her miserable mind – images, Eliot insists, the common man would not understand. Eliot is vague about the sordid images, but there are more explicit details in 'Prufrock's Pervigilium', a section of 'Prufrock' which Eliot added in 1912 and then cut on the advice of Conrad Aiken.*

---

* 'Prufrock's Pervigilium' is undated, but it was probably copied into

I have aligned 'The Love Song of J. Alfred Prufrock' with the vigil poems firstly because the discarded section is about an all-night vigil; secondly because Prufrock's visit to the fashionable lady is merely a possibility turning over in the mind of a nervous Bostonian* who never, in fact, leaves his room. (Eliot wrote the poem just before his return to Boston, his thoughts turning to the social ordeals of the Beacon Hill drawing-room and solitary walks past Boston's sawdust restaurants with oyster shells.)

Eliot said J. Alfred Prufrock was in part a man of about forty and in part himself. The demarcation between fiction and autobiography fits neatly along the lines of Prufrock's divided self.[†] Prufrock the timid, middle-aged lover is a caricature of a character from the fiction of Henry James. In 'Crapy Cornelia' (1909), a middle-aged bachelor, White-Mason, goes to propose to a worldly woman, but at the point of doing so, decides against it – in James, this is far from pathetic; it is a recuperation of his unworldly soul. Eliot believed that initially he developed in the manner of James,

Eliot's Notebook in 1912. The rest of 'Prufrock' (i.e. the poem as it was eventually published) was copied into the Notebook, in his spiky hand, in Munich, July–August 1911. But Eliot deliberately left four pages in the middle of the poem blank, which suggests he had a rough draft of the 'Pervigilium' which awaited completion. In a letter to the *TLS* (3 June 1960) Aiken writes: 'Mr. Eliot maintains to this day that on my suggestion a certain passage – now presumably lost – had been dropped from the poem. I can only say that I have no recollection of this, but if so, what a pity!' Eliot wrote to the *TLS* (8 July 1960) that in 1912 he did make some additions to the poem and Aiken perceived their inferior quality. What survived in print, he said, was the version written in 1910–11. The date 1912 also derives from TSE's recollection in a letter to William Force Stead (12 Nov. 1931), that this was the time Aiken took the poem to London. (Osborn Collection, Beinecke Library, Yale.) In a later letter (to John C. Pope on 8 Mar. 1946), Eliot gives the date of Aiken's promotion of 'Prufrock' as spring 1914. It is rare for Eliot to be confused as to dates, unless it happened that Aiken tried twice to place 'Prufrock'.

* Prufrock's wonderfully prudish, boxed-in name was probably derived from a furniture company in St Louis: Prufrock-Littau.

† Eliot used the notion of the split personality, first studied and widely popularised in his youth.

and when he compared the influence of James with that of Dostoevsky he conceded that the spirit of James, 'so much less violent with so much more reasonableness and so much more resignation than that of the Russian', was more useful to him. Eliot – with beauty, wit, and grace – had little in common with the graceless lover with his bald spot and conspicuous lack of muscle who wishes to establish rapport with a rather overpowering lady at a late-afternoon tea party.

Elements of Eliot are transfused into the lover – his shyness, his propriety of dress – but Eliot is more obviously aligned with Prufrock's other self, a solitary thinker who wishes to ask an 'overwhelming question' and assault the genteel surfaces of Boston society with an apocalyptic truth. 'Do I dare / Disturb the universe?' he wonders, and gropes in vain among New Testament models – Lazarus and John the Baptist – for the appropriate manner.* Prufrock's philosophic daring is continually checked by genteel scruples. At the same time, his imaginary social drama is continually eroded by the emotions of a prophet who may have 'a hundred visions' and a need to disturb the universe. Yet Prufrock doubts his calling ('I am no prophet'), for truth is dispersed in fog that curls in questions. Prufrock's natural arena, like Eliot's, is not the social gathering, but the lonely winding streets that express his sentience, streets that follow like his tedious arguments to their unnerving end in dark retreats.

To what exactly did Prufrock's question point? In the Notebook a confession follows Prufrock's distraught query, 'How should I begin?' He imagines he might reveal his vision of the end of the world to mannered women who 'come and go' talking of Michelangelo. In the published poem he fades into silence – a blank on the page – but in 1912 Eliot tried to translate the vision into words: a night-long vigil when midnight 'turned and writhed in fever' and darkness crawled 'among the papers on the table'. At dawn Prufrock opens his

---

* Charlotte Eliot was devoted to these two figures. Her poem 'The Raising of Lazarus' dramatises Lazarus's emergence from his tomb.

window 'to hear my Madness singing, sitting on the kerb-stone . . . / And as he sang the world began to fall apart . . .'. The 'Pervigilium' is poised on the edge between vision and madness: if what Prufrock has seen is valid then he is potentially a prophet, albeit a shy one; if it's a projection of himself, he must be mad.

Prufrock's overwhelming need is to ask not a lover's question but a metaphysical one, suggested by Bergson, about the point of man's accumulated experience. 'To live', says Bergson, 'is to grow old.' ('I grow old . . . I grow old . . .' Prufrock murmurs.) Life is a succession of psychological states, memories, and roles, 'a continual rolling up, like that of a thread on a ball, for our past follows us, it swells incessantly with the present that it picks up on its way . . .'. Prufrock (in his Pervigilium) has 'seen the world roll up into a ball' and 'fall away' – and he hears the chatter of his own imminent 'Madness'. He longs to confide in someone, an admired woman, but fears women only want lovers' talk 'of you and me'.

Eliot learned from Dostoevsky how a writer can exploit his own weakness in writing. He saw how Dostoevsky's epilepsy and hysteria 'cease to be defects of an individual and become – as fundamental weakness can, given the ability to face it and study it – the entrance to a genuine and personal universe'. Eliot exploited his own inhibition in Prufrock-the-prophet's stifling fears: his head brought in, like John the Baptist's, upon a platter. He imagines persecution. He sees his greatness flicker, and is afraid.

When, in spring 1914, Conrad Aiken took 'Prufrock' to a 'poetry squash' in London and showed it to Harold Monro, the editor of *Poetry and Drama*, Monro flung it back saying it was 'absolutely insane'. Those first readers of 'Prufrock' who thought it the morbid ravings of a madman were shamefully discredited, but they may, in fact, have been closer to the poem's message than Pound, who applauded its contemporary satire. Despite the poem's mannered surface, Eliot is looking beyond the Jamesian scene and the obligation to enter into others' lives – towards a characteristic theme of his own, a prophet's obligation to articulate what he alone knows.

At the end of the poem the sound of voices disturbs Prufrock from his solitary ruminations, and images of lover and prophet die away. Neither are stable identities. Prufrock cannot be a lover, a mindless body, seduced by mermaids he does not respect; but neither can his mind pursue overwhelming issues without distraction from his senses. The debate between would-be lover and would-be prophet is a more dramatic and complicated version of Eliot's earlier debates between body and soul. Eliot could forgo human attachments, but the alternative – the Absolute in the first debate, the ring of silence in the second, the prophetic figures in 'Prufrock' – could not, at any point, compose a durable vision.

Eliot revived Prufrock's debate between two selves in a typescript poem he wrote some time after his return to Harvard, 'Oh little voices . . .'.* The shadowed abject self (sitting all night in an armchair muffled in a shawl) complains that he has searched all the byways, the dark retreats and twisty streets, but has ended in an intellectual 'maze'. The philosophic self replies that what he has seen are appearances not realities, and exhorts him not to delay taking possession of some truth. Yet to the abject self the babbling men and women of this world *are* real, for they seem so confident on their 'wrinkled ways of wrong', while he, striking out for the frontier of heaven and hell, driven by his impulse to 'blow against the wind and spit against the rain', contemplates his future audience with confused unease. The philosopher urges him to face up to the 'unreal', and to break through the façades of appearance with this 'truth': 'No other time but now, no other place than here, he said.'

In both 'Oh little voices' and the fourth 'Prelude', also written after Eliot's return to Boston, a speaker is oppressed

* 'Oh little voices . . .' is undated but is typed on the same paper as Eliot used for his 1914 poems. Thematically, it is an outgrowth of the vigil cluster, but the issues of appearance and reality associate it with the period when Eliot was reading F. H. Bradley, beginning in the summer of 1913.

by multitudes of insistent, undirected feet of small-minded men. (The same theme reappears in an early *Waste Land* fragment, 'So through the evening . . .', where a wanderer, bruised by ordinary jostling men, drifts away from the town.) In the fourth 'Prelude', Eliot tests the prophetic role with momentary confidence.* He speaks of the lone conscience of a blackened street, the only one who sees beyond the common knowledge of the evening rush-hour crowd who guards its oblivion with newspapers and stuffed pipes. The soul stretches, impatient to 'assume the world', yet still gropes for an idea. Curled round the insistent feet and mind-killing routines lurks a 'notion', not an idea but something less – and more: 'The notion of some infinitely gentle / Infinitely suffering thing'. Thing. This is not a casual word for an articulate poet. Whatever it is transcends the limitations of language in the same manner as 'Silence', emphasised by blanks on the page: a space precedes 'thing' and a space follows it, before we fall back into the 'vacant lots', the waste grounds of cities. Here, Eliot begins to formulate the falling movements of *The Waste Land*, the collapse of an intangible intuition into the vacant routines of the city. The commuters and collectors of fuel don't suffer this collapse, only a mind capable of conceiving a 'thing' beyond the waste. The poem ends with an attempt to laugh off a vision that can't hold, and the speaker resigns himself to watching the world go round.

Years later Eliot told Leonard and Virginia Woolf that he had experienced an upheaval after writing 'Prufrock' that had altered his rather Jamesian inclinations. Eliot's poems of 1911 and 1912 document this upheaval, a period of nightly vigils, visions, and panic – 'the nightly panic / Of dreaming dissolution'. Eliot's night-long watches as an air-raid warden during the Second World War revived memories of 'the dark night in the solitary bedroom', essential to his future:

* *CP*, pp. 14–15. Since the fourth 'Prelude' is in the post-Paris hand it must be dated some time after September 1911.

Remember rather the essential moments
That were your times of death and birth and change
The agony and the solitary vigil . . .*

*

Eliot returned to Harvard at a time when its prestigious philosophy department had just lost its leading figures – Santayana, George Herbert Palmer, and William James. While Eliot had been an undergraduate, the department had an idealist bias dominated by Hegel, but in 1912 Ralph Barton Perry and five others inaugurated a doctrinal change with a book on the New Realism. Eliot admitted that the Realists might be refreshing, but he was put off by their subservience to mathematics and the exact sciences. He could not accept that a course on symbolic logic, given in 1914, by the English philosopher and mathematician, Bertrand Russell (1872–1970) had 'anything to do with reality'. Instead of joining the Realists, he turned first to Indian philosophy and, after two years, devoted himself to the work of an Oxford idealist, F. H. Bradley. With Bradley's help, Eliot was able to chart a way through the intellectual maze in which he found himself in 1912.

In June 1913 Eliot bought Bradley's *Appearance and Reality* (1893) and probably read it over the summer vacation. He found an immediate acknowledgement of the disturbing gap that separates hints of Absolute truth from everyday experience. Bradley granted that common knowledge does not go far enough, in other words the necessity of a religious point of view. To Eliot, Bradley seemed to radiate 'the sweetness and light of the medieval schoolmen'. His prose borrowed none of the persuasiveness of science or literature; it was 'pure' philosophy, yet throbbed, said Eliot, like the prose of Henry James 'with the agony of spiritual life'.

Bradley followed the same paths Eliot explores in 'Oh little

---

* The line 'The agony and the solitary vigil' replaced 'The dark night in the solitary bedroom' in a draft of *Little Gidding*. (CFQ, pp. 183, 228.)

voices', but he admitted bafflement without Eliot's sense of defeat. Bradley's attraction for Eliot was not speculative bravery, but the graceful intellectual poise with which he accepted human failure to know final truth: 'We justify the natural wonder which delights to stray beyond our daylight world, and to follow paths that lead to half-known half-unknowable regions. Our conclusion . . . has confirmed the irresistible impression that all is beyond us.' The sanity and range of Bradley's enquiries saved Eliot from a terrifying sense of intellectual isolation.

Bradley asked the same question as Eliot (in 'Rhapsody on a Windy Night'): 'whether the universe is concealed behind appearances'. But where Eliot despairs of finding meaning in commonly observed objects – he complains, as early as February 1911, that these either pass right through or else clog the brain – Bradley was more hopeful that through common objects 'we can discover the main nature of reality'. In 'Oh little voices' Eliot posed irreconcilable worlds of appearance and reality; Bradley insisted the two were linked; also that there was 'no province of the world so low but the Absolute inhabits it. Nowhere is there even a single fact so fragmentary and so poor that to the universe it does not matter.' Eliot, who had seen appearances dissolve, was perhaps comforted by Bradley's firm statement: 'We may keep a fast hold upon this, that appearances exist.'

As in Eliot's debates between body and soul, Bradley felt the 'infection' of the material world and that perfection lay beyond it, with the Absolute. He was discouraging about the quality of possible contact, for his Absolute was remote and impervious and its nature inexplicable: 'As an object of contemplation it seems simply to *be*.'

Bradley described a soul within a closed circle of consciousness. Eliot echoes this in his dissertation – 'My mind . . . is a point of view from which I cannot possibly escape' – and later repeats it, quoting Bradley, in one of his more serious notes to *The Waste Land*. A private centre of consciousness is opaque to others surrounding it, Bradley thought, but he still asserted its 'palpable community with the universe'. Bradley warned against solipsistic interpretations of immediate experience: 'It would not follow . . . that all the world is merely a state of myself.'

One issue, crucial to Eliot, Bradley bypassed. In his harmonious universe evil and ugliness were 'subordinate aspects' in the Absolute's kingdom. For Eliot, evil and ugliness were his most commanding experience to which, for years to come, even Silence was subordinated.

Eliot wrote his doctoral dissertation, 'Experience and the Objects of Knowledge in the Philosophy of F. H. Bradley', between 1913 and 1916. Based on *Appearance and Reality*, it strayed beyond Bradley's bounds of enquiry. Eliot was less committed to a community of understanding, more willing to indulge in solipsistic speculation. He emphatically contradicts Bradley's dictum 'my experience is not the whole world', and asserts the primacy of subjective knowledge: 'What is subjective is the whole world.' 'All significant truths are private truths.' When he tried to be objective, to adjust his private truths to accepted intellectual formulae, the connection seemed 'obscure'. His perceptions were 'shrunk' or 'impoverished' when he shut off personal feeling.

Eliot's tortuous style obscures the content so that the dissertation is almost unreadable, but it becomes a significant document in the context of Eliot's manuscript poems of 1911 and 1912. The dissertation's concern with a maddeningly brief visionary moment and its contradictory interpretations may be seen as a continuation of Eliot's introspective vigils in his Parisian room, where he would mull over the elusive message contained in the ring of silence and fail to make sense of it. And the dissertation's denial of the substantiality of the material world confirms poetic fantasies of a dissolving world. Neither the vigil poems nor the dissertation could formulate a coherent vision. All hinted at an extraordinary experience, an intuition of sublime truth, that was wretchedly curtailed. In *Knowledge and Experience* (the published dissertation) Eliot's trains of thought trailed, stopped, started in differing directions, like the streets Prufrock had followed. Eliot wrote like a restless sleeper, turning over and over, as he was tapped on the shoulder by new considerations. His long exercise in philosophy only taught him that approach was futile. Whereas Bradley was willing to accept incomplete truth gained by the calculations of 'mere intellect', Eliot strained towards a final truth contained in heightened moments of 'lived' experience – experience indeed so 'mad and strange' as to elude common understanding.

By 'lived' experience Eliot meant something wholly mental. He found that if he cast his mind into the flux between different viewpoints, and held them momentarily together, he could sometimes discern a 'half-object', a composite of the viewpoints which yet transcended them. When he made the necessary intuitive 'leap' he discovered his power to see 'the real future of an imaginary present'. The language, though vague and abstract, suggests a quasi-religious experience: there is a 'pilgrimage' into the space between two worlds; prophetic power is the reward of an 'act of faith'. In Harvard classes Eliot kept suggesting that 'illusion', 'hallucination', or 'superstition' might deserve more serious philosophical attention than social or material objects. In February 1914 he complained of the failure to find an explanation for illusion that would not *diminish* the illusion. In March he asked, 'Can we do without superstitions as to casuality?' In May, in a paper on the classification of different types of objects, he asserted the primacy of mental events like hallucinations, like God.

In his thesis Eliot insisted that the half-object appears only to a mind floating free, almost unconscious, from which all accidents of socially conditioned personality are removed. In view of Eliot's future rejection of personality, it's interesting that his thesis distinguished between subjectivity, which he endorses, and personality, which he rejects only in the special context of visionary experience. He said that the vision is timeless ('Any object which is wholly real is independent of time')* and unlocalised and independent also of social

* 'Immediate experience is a timeless unity,' Eliot writes (p. 164). It is curious to see, here, an early source for an idea that came to fruition several decades later in *Four Quartets*.

consequences: 'We are led to the conception of an all-inclusive experience outside of which nothing shall fall.' It is only when the visionary power fails, said Eliot, that people resort to social custom and common knowledge. Eliot was unsure of his truth – his subjective self half-recognised it, his rational self half-resisted – but he was confident that it could be said to 'diverge' from common knowledge.

Eliot looked upon the world as a precarious, artificial construction. Divergent images were rather arbitrarily drawn into a frame of common knowledge which was eroded at every moment by fresh subjective experience. Eliot's world was dangerously fragile – poised, like Poe's city in the sea, on the edge of dissolution.* It had no permanent substance: it was 'essentially vague, unprecise, swarming with insoluble contradictions'. Yet it tugged. It insisted on acknowledgement. It made itself felt as a background to the heightened moments. And then, when he approached, it fell apart. Like Prufrock, owning to madness at the end of his vigil, Eliot watched the great world dissolve and fade.

Knowledge and Experience was written by a haunted young man, torn between the truth of his visions and his rational distrust of them. 'I have lived with shadows for my company,' Eliot quotes. The shadows point towards a higher reality which should suggest the meaning of the material world and confirm its lesser status. But he cannot be sure. The half-objects might be only 'figments of imagination' or, worse, plausible hallucinations. The dissertation resounds with confessions of suffering: the 'agony' when the vision refuses to be realised and the observer falls back into artificial life; the fatal persecution of an obsessional idea 'for one crazed by fear or passion'; the wrenching beginning and end of the vision – 'annihilation and utter night'.

The problem Eliot posed in his dissertation was his own. To live like a visionary in the dangerous space between two worlds was to court madness. But to fall back into the net of the material world, and to live enmeshed in its artificial

---

* Eliot owned a volume of Poe's poems (1906) at Harvard.

customs and beliefs, was to risk his gift for sublime knowledge.

Bradley, with his saving wisdom, his scepticism and air of sophisticated disillusion, helped Eliot towards a sane formulation – not a solution – of the questions posed in the vigil poems. But with Bradley, Eliot came to the end of the philosophic path. Bradley asked all Eliot's overwhelming questions but was careful to abstain from pretensions beyond verifiable knowledge. Together with him Eliot gazed on the vast territories that stretched beyond philosophy on all sides while Bradley planted flags marking intellectual frontiers that should not be crossed. 'His philosophy seems to give you everything that you ask,' said Eliot in despair, 'and yet to render it not worth wanting.'

*

Eliot returned to America with a polished European air. He affected a malacca cane and hung a copy of Gauguin's *Yellow Christ*, brought from Paris, on his wall. Aiken recalled a travelled, sophisticated young man rather at odds with a New England college town still, in the early years of the twentieth century, a kind of village with white picket fences and horse-drawn watering carts to lay the summer dust. But Eliot was now less of a lone figure than during his undergraduate and Paris years, particularly in 1913 and 1914 when he went so far as to enrol for dancing and skating lessons. Photographs show him laughing with his sisters at Eastern Point or sprawled on the floor of the porch against the whitewashed wall.

He continued to write ribald verses for the entertainment of Harvard friends like Aiken, including 'Ballad for Big Louise', about King Bolo's hairy Kween who 'pulled her stockings off / With a frightful cry of "Hauptbahnhof!!" ' Grown-ups will find this Eliot puerile and unexpectedly tedious in his obsession with 'big hairy balls', a black 'knotty penis', 'assholes', and quantities of 'shit'. His women are all 'whores', including one who takes on a jolly tinker with a 'babyfetcher' hanging to his knee:

> O mother dear mother I thought that I was able
> But he ripped up my belly from my cunt to my navel.

'Bolo' also has sneers for blacks ('An interview from Booker T. / Entitled, "Up from Possum Stew!" / Or "How I set the nigger free!" ') and chaff about 'a bastard jew named Benny', a Spanish doctor, who 'filled Columbo's prick / With Muratic Acid'. Humane this is not, nor was it meant to be. There's a sick fury here, an obsessional hatred of women and sex, punitive in its virulence. The Bolo poems were written exclusively for men – women weren't asked to enjoy them because, in them, women exist only as prey or predators. Obscene spew is not entirely disconnected from Eliot's serious verse: the 'crooked' eye of the Parisian prostitute and the 'syphilitic spider' are figments of the same hatred. As an adult, Eliot did not discard these lines; he did want them published and, failing that, pressed them on appreciative buddies like Ezra Pound. Eliot regretted that Wyndham Lewis, editor of the avant-garde magazine *Blast*, declined to publish words 'Ending in -Uck, -Unt, and -Ugger'.

Meanwhile, the other Eliot – the refined, well-mannered graduate – was attending concerts of Ravel, Dvořák, Wagner, Sibelius, and Chopin. He heard violin recitals by Mischa Elman and Fritz Kreisler at Symphony Hall, and saw Puccini operas and *Tristan*, once more, at the Boston Opera House. Eliot was well thought of by his teachers. For two years he taught undergraduate courses in philosophy in Emerson Hall, and in his last year was elected president of Harvard's Philosophical Society.

In an address to the Philosophical Society in 1913–14 Eliot complained that no radical is so radical as to be a conservative. He scorned those optimists who offered glib solutions, economic or socialist, to human misery. Even more pernicious was a contemporary fear of dogma, which resulted in a light devotion to change as an end in itself. Instead of upholding absolute moral standards of good and evil, Eliot

---

saw his contemporaries becoming subject to two fallacies, the idea of Progress (which he associated with Bergson) and the idea of Relativity (which he ascribed to *Pragmatism*). Eliot saw what neither Bergson nor William James acknowledged, that their absorption in a private psychological world of need and change was, in effect, a withdrawal from the great world and resulted from despair of a perfect political order. He was exasperated that neither philosopher followed his theory through to its pessimistic end. His hero of pessimism was the Greek philosopher Heraclitus, an uncompromising aristocrat (Eliot notes),* contemptuous of the democracy which has deprived his class of power. Heraclitus scorns the inability of the ordinary man to pierce the appearance of stability, and seeks a knowledge beyond logic, to do with a soul changeable as fire. These jottings are highly suggestive of Eliot's future work. His note that Heraclitus disowned the city and withdrew into the hills forecasts similar renegades in early *Waste Land* fragments.†

On 17 February 1913 Eliot took part in a 'Stunt Show', beginning at 8 p.m. at 1 Berkeley Place, the Cambridge house of his mother's sister, Mrs Holmes Hinkley. Scenes from *Bleak House* by Dickens ('An Evening at the Bayham Badgers'), *Emma* by Jane Austen ('An Afternoon with Mr Woodhouse'), and Maria Edgeworth were played by the parlour fireplace. The audience were relatives, friends, and neighbours, and Eliot's humorous cousin Eleanor Hinkley, three years younger, devised the scenes. Eliot played M. Marcel in a sketch entitled 'M. Marcel and his latest Marvel', and then played the hypochondriacal Mr Woodhouse, pressing on visitors the healthy abstemiousness of thin gruel, in the scene from *Emma*. Eleanor's friend Emily Hale played the ill-bred snob Mrs Elton ('as elegant as pearls and lace could

---

* TSE heard a lecture on Heraclitus on 20 Oct. 1912 as part of a class on Greek philosophy, given at Harvard in 1912–13. He made further notes on 23 Oct. 1912. (Houghton.)
† 'So through the evening' and 'The Death of Saint Narcissus'. See below, ch. 5.

make her', with a habit of bringing the conversation round to her sister's barouche-landau), and sang songs called 'Ecstasy', 'May Morning', 'Serenata' by Tosti, and 'Julia's Garden' – six in all, introducing each half of the programme. Eliot fell in love with her.

She was born on 27 October 1891, into the same Boston Brahmin milieu as Eliot's family. Her birthplace was East Orange, New Jersey, but her parents returned to Boston and she spent her childhood on Chestnut Hill. Her uncle, Philip Hale, was well known as music critic for the Boston *Herald*. Her father, Edward Hale, was an architect turned Unitarian minister. He taught for many years at Harvard Divinity School, and became first assistant to Edward Everett Hale at the Southern Congregational Church in Boston. Emily later said that her father had been like another son to Edward Everett Hale though they were not blood relations.

Early in the girl's life came tragedy. An infant brother died, and her mother, Emily Milliken, took ill. She remained a permanent mental invalid, unable to care for her remaining child who was sent to live with her mother's sister. The Revd and Mrs John Carroll Perkins were old friends of the Eliot family and stood, like them, at the very heart of Boston Unitarianism. (Eliot once joked that his family's relation to Boston Unitarianism was like that of the Borgias to the papacy.)

Aunt Edith Perkins and Uncle John gave her the kind of advantages that were then considered appropriate for well-bred young women. Her preparatory schools were Miss Ingalls' and the Berkeley Schools in Cambridge, and Miss May's School in Boston. For seven years she had singing lessons with Boston teachers. When she was older, she was sent to Miss Porter's exclusive boarding-school at Farmington, Connecticut. There she made a lifelong friend, Margaret Ferrand, who was to become a teacher at Smith College. For the rest of their lives they wrote to each other every fortnight, each on alternate weeks. These letters were strictly confidential – after Margaret's marriage to Willard Thorp in 1931, she never showed them to her husband and took care to destroy them before her death.

The major omission in Emily's education, in view of her future, was not going to college. Later, when she applied for posts, she said it had happened 'because at the time I was not considered strong enough'. This has the sound of a polite excuse. She wanted to go on the stage; her family objected; and for a space she was overruled. Instead, she had a 'presentation' in Boston society. A portrait painted of her at this time shows a poised young woman, in a pink lace dress, seated with a posy of flowers on her lap. Her dark brown hair is drawn simply and softly up and her back is straight and long. Her presence was even more arresting than her beauty.

A shared passion for the theatre brought Emily together with her exact contemporary Eleanor Hinkley, who hoped to be a playwright. Eleanor enrolled in the '47 Workshop' under Professor George Pierce Baker at Radcliffe College. (There were forty-seven in the class and their plays were published.) She always hoped that her plays would reach New York; only one did (*Dear Jane*[Austen], a comedy in three acts, produced by Eva Le Gallienne at the Civic Repertory Theater in 1932). Since her aunt and uncle would not allow Emily to go on the stage professionally, she had to content herself with private performances, amongst them the amateur theatricals put on by her friend Eleanor. Emily had a natural stage presence and a resonant voice that were to prove effective in commanding comic roles. Many years later, she created a sensation as Edith Wharton, one Valentine's day, when guests were invited to come to Laura Scales House at Smith College dressed as books. Emily Hale chose Wharton's *A Backward Glance*. She put on an Edwardian gown of pale green silk that had belonged to her mother or aunt. Her hair was dressed, her neck bejewelled. Carrying an old silver mirror, held at arm's length, and peering imperiously into it, she made a dramatic 'entrance'.

Eliot first met Emily as a family friend at the Hinkley house where he was a frequent visitor. After his return from

Europe a shared interest in drama brought them together, certainly by 1912.*

Emily Hale became the source for a series of garden encounters in Eliot's poetry, moments of romantic attraction to a woman. He wrote 'La Figlia che Piange' in 1912 and 'Hidden under the heron's wing . . .' in the same period after his return to Harvard. In the latter the bird and the lotus (revived in the garden setting of *Burnt Norton* seventeen years later) reveal a woman walking lightly across the grass in the evening. A lover cherishes a dream of 'fragile arms dividing the evening mist', but instead of seeking the answer to his question, 'Oh my beloved what do you bring – ' – an answer which might centre the woman as a responsive being – the lover centres himself with an abrupt and brutal self-pity as a suicide who lies on the floor 'a bottle's broken glass / To be swept away by the housemaid's crimson fist.' The poem offers no chance that they might come together. Nor has love a chance in 'La Figlia che Piange', where a lover and a girl holding flowers, her hair irradiated by sunlight, part with artistic grace:

> Stand on the highest pavement of the stair –
> Lean on a garden urn –
> Weave, weave the sunlight in your hair –
> Clasp your flowers to you with a pained surprise –
> Fling them to the ground and turn
> With a fugitive resentment in your eyes:
> But weave, weave the sunlight in your hair.

The poet does wonder 'how they should have been together', but prefers his fantasy of the beautifully controlled, unmessy parting – 'a gesture and a pose' – which he may enshrine forever in his memory and his art. The lover loses flesh and blood; the poet yet possesses her. There is more than a hint of triumph amidst his regret, like Henry James lamenting Minny

* Emily Hale told Marianne Moore that she and Eliot met when he was a graduate (letter, 24 Sept. 1959, copy at Smith College). Valerie Eliot gives the date of the meeting as 1912 – presumably this date derived from her husband, who had an excellent memory.

Temple's death. (Minny would be 'a pure and eloquent vision' locked, incorruptibly, 'within the crystal walls of the past'.) Ten years later Eliot worked this scene, or one very like it, into *The Waste Land* and, from that distance in mood and time, a regretful voice recalls when 'we came back late, from the hyacinth garden, / Your arms full, and your hair wet . . .'. Later in the poem the unlovable wife asks the disaffected husband, 'Do you remember / Nothing?' and, in an earlier draft, he gives his silent inexorable answer: 'I remember / The hyacinth garden.' He shuts off his wife with that recollection of fertile love and its power to transform him: 'Those pearls that were his eyes, yes!'

Eliot froze Emily Hale into art so that he could possess her in memory as one might possess a statue of poignant beauty. There was a curious precedent in Laforgue's early relations with a poet called Sanda Mahali. At a distance in Berlin, he turned her into a figment of his imagination as the embodiment of the sensual, sophisticated Paris for which he longed. But during his vacations in Paris, he dodged calling on Mahali, with the feeblest excuses. She was understandably bewildered by her would-be lover's evasions. In a private paper written in his sixties, Eliot claimed that before he left for Europe in 1914 he told Emily Hale that he was in love with her. He said that he had no reason to believe, from the way in which his declaration was received, that his feelings were returned 'in any degree whatever'. In other words, Eliot presents himself in a sympathetic role as rejected lover. There is no way, at this point, that we can know the whole truth: Eliot's second wife, Valerie Eliot, who reports his words, doesn't say that Eliot proposed to Emily. We don't know if there was an explicit refusal, and we don't know whether certain words that might have been said were *not* said, given the modesty expected of well-bred girls. The ladylike construct of passivity and silence begs the question of what a girl at such a time was permitted to say. Eliot's poems invariably lock her into silent poses, though the facts of Emily's history tell us that here was a girl who was lively, humorous, and capable of extravagant devotion.

Eliot's tortuous views of women suggest that whatever took place between him and Emily in the spring or early summer of 1914 was likely to have had its nuances and complications. It's possible to declare love and, at the same time, avert commitment. To be formally engaged would have been inconvenient, as Eliot took off for a year in Europe. Emily's subsequent attachment to him – he was undoubtedly the love of her life – suggests the possibility of stronger feeling than he perhaps perceived. His poem evokes a tie that is Jamesian in its ambiguities: a young man orchestrating an untrammelled departure from a young woman in such a way that her 'pained surprise' and the 'fugitive resentment' in her eyes are muted. We can't equate Eliot with a poetic character, but what we can say with certainty is that two years before his departure, when he composed his poem about the abandoned girl, Eliot could imagine the reverse of the story which an elderly Eliot tells posterity: as a young man, he could concoct a sexual power-game in which a lovely, weeping girl is cast as victim of an ambitious youth resolved to use her for art alone. Though this purports to be a poem, not life, it was prophetic of Eliot's long future with Emily Hale.

The sexual instinct and associated sense of sin, flickering rather half-heartedly in Eliot's undergraduate years, came suddenly to life in 'The Love Song of Saint Sebastian' which, evidence suggests, Eliot drafted before he left for Europe and completed just after. This is the time of his unsuccessful declaration to Emily. A desperate and insecure lover fans his passions with fantasies of violent action which enforce the beloved's attention. In the first fantasy the lover, wearing 'a shirt of hair', flogs himself at the foot of the lady's stair until his blood flies:

> I would flog myself until I bled
> And after hour on hour of prayer
> And torture and delight
> Until my blood should ring the lamp . . .

Eliot adds in the margin: 'I mean stand all about in a pool on the floor'. Only after this spectacular martyrdom can the speaker follow the woman to her bed. In pity, she takes him in – she can do so without shame because he is dead. Purged of sin, he spends the night, his head between her breasts. So, a man lashes himself with an eye to a lady and then, bespattered in the blood of penitence, is permitted a love-death of extraordinary intimacy. An ominous move to 'put out the light' en route to her bed, recalling Othello's murder of Desdemona, leads into a second fantasy where the lover's relation to the woman is reversed. This time, he will be a sexual menace, exerting brute power over the white-clad body he loves. He comes at her with a towel and bends her head below, then between, his knees, fingering the curve of her ears which, he tells her fondly, 'curl back in a certain way / Like no one's else in all the world.' For a moment he holds back to stroke the curve of her ear and her head locked there between his knees. And then when he strangles her, she loves him for his 'infamy'. This man believes in the woman's assent – it's a horrific poem, especially for women, because though the speaker is mad, he's actually making the common plea of the rapist that his victim wants it. As in Browning's 'Porphyria's Lover',* the strangler's love is liberated by the act of mutilation which is also a triumphant act of self-assertion and possession. For a dead woman will no longer be desirable to anyone else.

Whether she is drawn from Emily Hale or anyone else does not matter, since she has no real existence except as a projection of male fantasy – a traditional one in the literature and theology of the West, alternating woman as sinner or saint, a strategy for denying her equal humanity. In the *Waste Land* manuscript Eliot would write off women with 'unreal emotions and real appetite'; in *Ash-Wednesday* (1930) he invented idealised figures he might revere, the Rose of memory, the Mother, and above all a veiled Lady who develops from the spotless object of Sebastian's distempered

---

* The poem is in a slim selection of Browning which Eliot owned at Harvard.

passions: 'The Lady is withdrawn / In a white gown, to contemplation, in a white gown . . .'.

It is possible to connect the idealised Figlia, on the highest pavement, with the pure and remote lady on a stair in the love-starved song of St Sebastian and with the divine Lady in *Ash-Wednesday*. If so, La Figlia was to become a pervasive figure in Eliot's work.

*

Eliot's main objection to his department was its divorce of philosophy from religion. He craved philosophy in an ampler sense – wisdom, insight, revelation. Upon his return to Harvard he began to study Eastern philosophy: Sanskrit and the Pantañjali's metaphysics under James Woods, and Indic Philology under Charles Lanman who, on 6 May 1912, gave his pupil a copy of *Upanishads, the Twenty-Eight* by Vasudev Laxman Shastri Phansikar, published by Tukaram Javaji in Bombay (1906). Eliot said he was glad to uncover in the *Bhagavad-Gita** philosophical and religious beliefs different from those of his family. He acquired a catalogue of books on Vedanta and, in August and October 1913, bought two books by Paul Deussen, *Upanishads des Veda* and *Die Sûtras des Vedânta*. From 1911 he carried in his pocket an Italian edition of Dante, and memorised long passages while lying in bed or on a railway journey. He marked lines that were to appear in his own poetry: 'I never should have thought death had undone so many' in the *Inferno*, and the punishment of Arnaut Daniel for lust in the *Purgatorio*: 'Then he hid him in the fire that refines them.' Dante was to become the most profound and persistent influence in his life because, said Eliot, he helped him see the connection between the medieval Christian inferno and modern life. More important for him than any canto was the complete schema. For Eliot, as for

* Eliot acquired a copy of a translation by Lionel D.Barnett (J. M. Dent pocket ed., 1905) inscribed 'Cambridge 1912'. He pasted in a slip showing the line-up of the battles of the *Mahabharata* relevant to his poem, *The Dry Salvages* (1941). Houghton.

Dante, there was to be no shortcut to paradise: he had to plumb the depths of hell and bear the ordeals of purgatory. The inscription over Dante's hell inspired Eliot to write a prayer promising to come to terms with accepted beliefs:

> O lord, have patience
> Pardon these derelictions –
> I shall convince these romantic imitations
> By my classical convictions.*

There was one teacher at Harvard who might have helped Eliot effect a transition between philosophy and religion. Josiah Royce, pudgy, gnarled, who looked like a janitor with a battered hat tilted on a bulging forehead and red eyes (from strain), was Harvard's leading idealist philosopher. One of his books, *The Problem of Christianity*, was published in 1913, just before Eliot entered his advanced seminar in Comparative Methodology. Here Royce argued that Christian doctrine expresses 'universal human needs' and, in the twentieth century in particular, a need for community based on shared traditions. As Eliot was to do later in *The Idea of a Christian Society*, Royce put private needs to one side, and stressed the social order, its dependence on religion for survival.

Eliot took up the notion of human need in a report on primitive religions, which he read in Royce's class on 9 December 1913. He criticised the anthropologists – Frazer, Jane Harrison, Durkheim, and Lévy-Bruhl – for giving no explanation of religious rituals 'in terms of need'. He criticised their 'wanton interpretation' based on uninvestigated assumptions, and suggested there was no adequate truth in the study of religion short of an absolute truth. And that would be found, not through methodological enquiry, only through intuitive sympathy. Again, on 16 December, Eliot tried to bypass anthropologists' records of behaviour with the question: What is he [the believer] sincere about?'

---

* Written on Boston paper (Carter Rice & Co.), therefore before Eliot left America. (*IMH*, p. 83 which reads 'imitations' as 'irritations'.)

Behaviour is mere mechanism, Eliot added, unless it has some sort of meaning. 'The question is, what is that meaning?' Finally, on 24 February 1914, Eliot criticised all theories of knowledge for their inability to 'treat illusion as real'.

The turning-point in Eliot's life came not at the time of his baptism in 1927, but in 1914 when he was circling, in moments of agitation, on the edge of conversion. This supposition is based on a group of intense religious poems Eliot never published. He wrote four of these poems before he left Harvard, 'After the turning . . .', 'I am the Resurrection . . .', 'So through the evening . . .',* and 'The Burnt Dancer' (dated June 1914). 'The Love Song of Saint Sebastian' was revised in Germany in July 1914, and 'The Death of Saint Narcissus' was composed at the end of 1914 or beginning of 1915, after Eliot's move to England. In the new cluster, a bold convert, martyr, or saint displaces the frustrated philosopher of 1911–12. There is a confusing night visitation and the poet's fear of divine commerce. There is a monastic impulse to isolate himself from the crowd, to take off for mountain or desert in search of initiation and purification. There is, most persistently, a fantasy of a martyr's passion. Eliot's imaginary commitment to faith is both wild and tentative, cloudy with flitting possibilities and overburdened with resolution.

Eliot's comments both in Royce's class and in his Bradley dissertation showed his disillusion with logic. 'After the turning', 'I am the Resurrection', and 'So through the evening', the earliest visionary fragments of the *Waste Land* manuscript, signal Eliot's liberation from the studied paths of philosophy, his new willingness to give rein to strange intuitions and images:

One tortured meditation dragged me on
Concatenated words from which the sense was gone –

---

* These *Waste Land* fragments are described in detail in ch. 5. The evidence of the paper and Eliot's hand suggest they were written before he left America.

87

. . . .
The This-do-ye-for-my-sake . . .
The one essential word that frees
The inspiration that delivers and expresses
A chain of reasoning whereof the thread was gone
Gathered strange images through which I walked alone

'I am the Resurrection' acknowledges the unknowability of the divine force which decides our destiny but which cannot be judged in human terms. The implicit question, throughout this group, is how to behave in relation to the unknown. Eliot's answer in 'The Burnt Dancer' and the two 'saint' poems seems to be to attract attention by an extraordinary display of self-inflicted pain.

In 'The Burnt Dancer' an insomniac, listening all night to children whimpering behind walls, observes a black moth dancing round a yellow ring of flame. The moth compels the watcher hovering on the edge of a ring of illumination; its dance invites him to some portentous fate beyond our understanding. He watches curiously while the moth singes its wings on the flame, as though witnessing the expiation of a martyr. The extraordinary deliberation of the moth's passion exhilarates him, its pain 'nearest to delight' as the 'singèd reveller of the fire'. But the end is forbidding. For the moth, now broken, loses its passion and desires only the fatal end of its ordeal.

The poem has its sequel in the martyrdom of St Narcissus. The moth dances about a yellow flame; the saint dances to God on the hot sand while arrows pierce his flesh. In both cases there is a savage joy in pain.

Throughout his career Eliot was fascinated by the motives, the behaviour, the achievement of saints. Only saints can know 'a lifetime's death in love, / Ardour and selflessness and self-surrender', wrote Eliot in 1941, and begged off in favour of a humbler life of prayer and observance. But the 1914 poems suggest that, for a time in his youth, Eliot's imagination toyed with the saint's ambitious task.

This preoccupation can be traced to his mother – her

numerous poems about 'Priests and prophets, saints and sages, / Martyred in successive ages'. During Eliot's last years at Harvard he made a study of the lives of saints and mystics, St Teresa, Dame Julian of Norwich, Mme Guyon, Walter Hilton, St John of the Cross, Jacob Böhme, and St Bernard. He noted their visions: Dame Julian's steady gazing on the Crucifix, Böhme's at a dazzling light reflected from a tin vessel, and St Teresa's assertion that she never saw visions with the eye of the body. Eliot made copious notes from Evelyn Underhill's *Mysticism* (1911), and copied in detail one passage which explains vision as a work of art derived from actual experience: 'If we would cease, once for all, to regard visions and voices as objective, and be content to see in them forms of symbolic expression, ways in which the subconscious activity of the spiritual self reach the surface-mind, many of the disharmonies noticeable in visionary experience which have teased the devout, and delighted the agnostic, would fade away. Visionary experience . . . is a picture which the mind constructs . . . from raw materials already at its disposal.'

Eliot's later resolve in 1928 'to construct something / Upon which to rejoice' goes back to his note in 1912 that the Dark Night of the Soul is a period of construction, not of negativity; and his repeated cry in the same conversion poem, 'Lord, I am not worthy / Lord, I am not worthy' (1929), goes back to another note in 1912: purgation is a sense of unworthiness. There were two aspects to purgation, *Mysticism* taught Eliot: detachment and mortification.

Eliot noted the dangers and the maladies of the religious life and also its disciplines and cures to be found in *Spiritual Exercises* by St Ignatius Loyola and in *Dark Night of the Soul* by St John of the Cross. At this time Eliot first came upon the disease of doubt, *aboulie*, by which term he was to describe his depression while writing *The Waste Land* in 1921. Reading of Mme Guyon, he noted that when the divine command is withheld it becomes impossible to act. *The Story of My Heart* (1891) by Richard Jeffries warned of another danger of the religious life, delusional insanity, which Eliot described as mysticism turned upside down, become diabolical. He was more concerned, though, with what one of his sources termed 'la vie religieuse normale', the traditional pattern of progress towards sainthood through phases of awakening, unworthiness, mortification of the senses, and illumination. As Underhill points out, the potential saint will naturally look to the historic life of Christ as 'an epitome . . . of the essentials of all spiritual life' with its pattern of birth and rebirth. Her three classic identities – pilgrim, lover, ascetic – appear immediately in Eliot's poems and fragments of 1914.

'The Love Song of Saint Sebastian' represents Eliot's debates between body and soul carried beyond possibility of resolution. A respectable context for the poem's bizarre sexual violence came from three fifteenth-century paintings which struck Eliot's fancy as he passed through the galleries of Italy in the summer of 1911 and of Belgium in the summer of 1914: the first is by Mantegna (1437–1506) in the Palazzo della Cà d'Oro in Venice, and has in one corner an extinguished candle, the smoke winding in a curve on which are written words which Eliot noted: 'nil nisi divinum stabile est; caetera fumus' ('nothing endures except the divine; the rest is smoke');* the second is attributed to Antonello da Messina (1430–79) at Bergamo; the third is by Hans Memling (1430?–94) in the Brussels Museum. They show innocent, firm-fleshed youths exposed to penetrant arrows. In a letter to Aiken on 25 July 1914, in which he enclosed a final draft of the poem, Eliot noted the eroticism, and emphasised that, for him, 'there's nothing homosexual about this – rather an important difference perhaps – but no one ever painted a female Sebastian, did they?'

The sado-masochism is fired only superficially by a sense of sin, more by an avidity for sensation. Eliot's pervert-

---

* TSE used this as part of the epigraph to 'Burbank with a Baedeker, Bleistein with a Cigar' (1919). In October 1932 he pointed out this source to Professor Theodore Spencer at Harvard, who copied it into his volume of Eliot's *Poems 1909–1925* (now in the Matthiessen Room, Eliot House, Harvard).

Sebastian has only tenuous links with the real saint, a Roman martyr in the time of Diocletian who, the fable goes, was sentenced to be shot by archers. Although the arrows pierced his flesh, he did not die but was rescued by a woman and nursed in her lodgings. In the case of Eliot's 'saint', the martyrdom is not only self-inflicted, but is an exhibitionistic attempt to gain a woman's attention. The counterpart to this bloody revel is sexual murder – both scenes bring to mind a constrained man who can't express sexual needs in a natural way.* From the instinctual side of Sebastian, wielding his towel, came Eliot's later characters, Sweeney, playful with his razor in a brothel, and Harry, Lord Monchensey, with his murderous heart.

On the surface Eliot seems the antithesis of a St Sebastian or a Sweeney. He appeared particularly lacking in 'crude insistent passion', as Russell put it in a letter of May 1914, an exquisitely well-conducted student amidst a horde of 'vigorous intelligent barbarians'. Yet his poems' antithesis between extremes of body and soul expressed a genuine dilemma. Many years later he wrote of his sense of the void in the middle of all human happiness and all human relations: 'I am one whom this sense of the void tends to drive towards asceticism or sensuality.' Constrained in love, defeated in his search for religious identity, Eliot projects these elements into the single-minded actions of allegorical characters.

The last of the visionary poems, 'The Death of Saint Narcissus', was based on T. E. Hulme's 'Conversion', which Eliot must have read, at Pound's direction, soon after arriving in England. Hulme's 'conversion' takes place in a wooded valley, covered with hyacinths, when he is stunned by a

* There are two typescripts of the poem, one in the McKeldin Library, University of Maryland, and one in the Berg Collection. Both are undated, but Eliot mentions in a letter to Aiken (Marburg, Germany, 19 July 1914) that he had recently written about fifty belaboured lines of a poem (the length and laboriousness fits 'Oh little voices') and, in the next letter (25 July) enclosed 'St. Sebastian' together with 'Oh little voices'. Although the two poems now coalesced in Eliot's mind, he intimates that Aiken will have seen one part, presumably 'Saint Sebastian', some time before.

revelation of beauty. St Narcissus is similarly rapt before his own beauty. Neither is enlarged by his sensations. Both in the end overreach themselves and suffer a psychic blow, some kind of ignominious death of the spirit. In Hulme's metaphor, the convert sinks silently in the 'final river' in a sack; Narcissus is burnt dry in the desert.

A large section of the poem is characteristically Eliot's and in no way derives from Hulme: the scene where the would-be saint chooses a solitary life of deprivation and worship. Narcissus sets out to win immediate experience of divinity by retiring from the world, like the Desert Fathers of the fouth century. It is a logical, if extreme, answer to the Prufrockian world of ridiculous conformity. Eliot would demonstrate an ascetic's motives more plausibly in *The Family Reunion*, where Harry seeks to subdue his murderous heart in 'the heat of the sun and the icy vigil'. Harry has willed his wife's death, and his atonement is real. Narcissus, on the other hand, has nothing particular for which to atone; his solitariness is self-serving. He tries to win the glow of fervour through abuse of his body, but whatever glow he achieves quickly subsides, leaving him exhausted and without grace.

Like St Sebastian, St Narcissus represents an idea. He is not a realistic character and, of course, Eliot cannot be identified with him. But take away the caricature of twisted motives and excessive egotism, and the poem reveals the consuming issues of Eliot's life – his longing for metamorphosis, his vision and loss of vision, and the avidity of his religious emotions.

Why did Eliot not make a serious religious commitment in 1914? Among his student notes there is a warning from Evelyn Underhill that vision through the senses is imperfect, capricious, often a delusion. One must await purely spiritual communication. Eliot refused to make more of feverish excitations and abasements than a kind of stunt. The wry, derisive note, entirely absent in 'The Burnt Dancer', under-cuts the posturing of St Narcissus six months later. Eliot's heroes of the spirit experience the attractions of asceticism; they have glimpses of Silence, but these possess no decisive life-transforming power. There is awe in Eliot's 1914 cluster, but no enduring vocation; there is penance, but no real sense of sin.

His feverish fantasies of a martyr's passion and monastic dreams of taking off for a mountain-top or desert in search of purification, show, once again, a temperamental correspondence with Laforgue, whose letters and diaries show that for five months in the winter of 1879–80 he, too, played at asceticism as a kind of stunt: 'I acted the little Buddha on two eggs and a glass of water per day. . . . At nineteen I dreamed of going out into the world barefoot and preaching the word.' After a breakdown, he planned a novel about 'the macabre adventure of humanity', with an epilogue about the last days of humanity 'when Illusion is dead, the cities deserted and Man, his head shaved and covered with ashes, awaits Nothingness'. There is an obvious affinity with the mind that conceived the earliest fragments of *The Waste Land* during a period of religious extravagance. What Laforgue lacked was Eliot's moral acumen and his will to find a way out of urban despair.

Eliot owned to Aiken that these martyr poems were 'strained and intellectual'. His models were traditional and literary, his scenes oddly unlocalised as though the mind that conceived them were floating free in space and time. What we miss most is the individual, contemporary note of 'Prufrock'. Eliot failed to imagine saints in an appropriate contemporary guise as, in the fourteenth century, William Langland conceived of a Christlike ploughman, an appropriate curative figure in a time of disastrous famine, or as Malory's prosaic and quarrelsome knight, a fifteenth-century gentleman thug, can be converted without too much strain into a *miles Christi*. It is difficult to pinpoint the sensibility that moves through Eliot's poems. Perhaps, if Eliot's prowlers and flawed saints were merged, one might come up with one of Nathaniel Hawthorne's shadowed souls – say Arthur Dimmesdale, the saintly New England minister, who keeps vigils night after night but cannot purify his mind, who has secret sympathies with the vilest of sinners, whose self-loathing drives him to punish himself with a scourge, and to whom the whole universe appears so false and impalpable that it shrinks to nothing. The vein Eliot admired in the New England writers Hawthorne and Henry James is their 'exceptional awareness of spiritual reality', their 'profound sensitiveness to good and evil', and their 'extraordinary power to convey horror'.

In 1914 Eliot moved too fast, riding on intuitions and truncated visions without experience beyond his self-absorbed fantasies. His poems did not satisfy him: 'I know the kind of verse I want, and I know this isn't it, and I know why,' he wrote to Aiken. 'I shan't do anything that will satisfy me (as some of my old stuff *does* satisfy me . . .) for years.' A long period of poetic sterility followed, but by immersing himself in the metropolis of a foreign country and by marrying a wild, haunted woman he found, during this very period, the genuine trials against which he might refine his soul.

4

ELIOT'S ORDEALS

ALL THROUGH HIS last semester Eliot was planning another journey abroad. In February 1914, or earlier, he decided to complete his training in Europe as many leading American teachers of philosophy had done. In 1914 Professor Palmer declared that an academic career represented an ideal 'type toward which all organised society moves'; he spoke of the teaching profession as 'a consecrated brotherhood'. The Harvard authorities, who looked on Eliot as a possible brother, awarded him a Sheldon travelling fellowship. Officially, he was to spend a year at Merton College, Oxford, studying Aristotle under Harold Joachim, a disciple of Bradley who was almost inaccessible in his rooms overlooking Christ Church meadow. Eliot also had a stint in Germany in mind. He planned to participate in Marburg University's summer programme for foreign students in July and August 1914.

Eliot's first response to Europe was some distaste for the 'past-putridity' of old towns in Italy and Belgium, but Marburg, built on the side of a steep hill, had beautiful, unkempt gardens and he had the impression of great waves of roses. Each day he walked in the woods, but not too far lest he be late for the five excellent meals served by Frau Pfarrer. Lulled by a sudden tranquillity, Eliot planned his first long work, which, like the master-works of later years, was to piece together poems written at different times. A tentative title, he told Aiken, was the 'Descent from the Cross'. The poem was to include first 'Oh little voices' and 'Saint

Sebastian'; to be followed by an insane section; a love song of a happier sort with a refrain in the manner of 'Portrait of a Lady'; a mystical section and, to conclude, a Fool-House section in the manner of 'Prufrock' in which the speaker attends not a tea party but a masquerade. He goes in his underwear as St John the Divine. 'Descent from the Cross' was never completed. Eliot had barely settled down in Marburg when war broke out. On 3 August he moved, via Rotterdam, to London, and thence, in October, to a new retreat, Oxford, where he remained till June 1915.

In London he was merely a tourist, politely curious about local habits. He saw determined matrons in tailor-made suits and ugly hats advance on Assyrian art in the British Museum and then fade beyond the Roman statuary. He saw a shopgirl in a department store, and her false teeth and the pencil stuck in her hair spoke to him of heated nights in second-storey dance halls. From his room at 28 Bedford Place he saw an old woman sing 'The Rosary' for pennies. London itself seemed like a scene from *Bleak House*: all brown waves of fog and trampled edges and muddy skirts.

While London at least seemed to offer some promise of life behind the iron railings and curtained windows, Oxford seemed quite dead. He deplored the dons' smug domesticity, their pregnant wives, and the lack of female society. His senses felt numbed. To cheer himself he wrote comically to his cousin Eleanor Hinkley, and to Emily Hale. When he heard she was in a Cambridge Dramatics production of *Mrs. Bumstead-Leigh* in December 1914, he sent Aiken $4 with instructions to send Emily a bouquet of pink or red Killarney roses for the Saturday performance. There were few men up in 1914–15, and these Eliot appraised, as one fellow-student remembered, 'with feelings that were singularly disengaged'. Men in the leading literary society, the Heretics, seemed 'narrow and plebian', while the one or two brilliant men recalled 'the clever Jew undergraduate mind at Harvard; wide but disorderly reading, intense but confused thinking, and utter absence of background and balance and proportion'. A fellow-student named Karl Culpin, with whom Eliot took a holiday in Swanage, Dorset, at the end of his first term, joined the army and was killed on his first day in the trenches. The membership of a class on Plotinus, initially six, dropped to two. The other remaining student, E. R. Dodds (later, Professor of Greek at Oxford), found Eliot reserved but 'seriously interested in mystical experience'. Dodds invited him to a group called The Coterie where men read their poems (women like Dorothy Sayers and Naomi Mitchison – then, Haldane – were excluded). A few days after he joined, Eliot read 'Prufrock', which puzzled the young Englishmen, who were sufficiently aware of the dead-end of sweet Georgian verse to hold back from tearing the poem to pieces. This fell short of encouragement. 'O Conversation, the staff of life, shall I get any at Oxford?' Eliot wrote dejectedly to Conrad Aiken.

Yet beneath his quiet life, Eliot was slowly moving, in 1914 and 1915, from a position of avoidance or retreat to make a resolute advance on experience. For Eliot this would be the most difficult of tasks, to stab himself awake. And when he failed to awaken to religious emotions, he abruptly tried an alternative, to awaken himself through marriage. It was probably this effort to bestir himself that lay at the root of *The Waste Land*, the origins of which date back to this time.

Two compelling individuals made claims on Eliot during this crucial year. The one was a young American poet, Ezra Pound (1885–1972), stalwart, with exuberant reddish-blond hair and pince-nez, wide cheekbones, and a narrow chin accentuated by a pointed beard, who flung himself into chairs and gave out strange cries. He was interested in Eliot as a poet. The other was the vivacious Vivienne (often Vivien)* Haigh-Wood, who was to become his wife. Neither's claim

---

* Though she often used 'Vivien', the correct spelling was 'Vivienne', as on her marriage certificate, and it's the spelling Eliot uses when he writes of her officially (in the fiftieth anniversary report of the Harvard class of 1910 and in the private paper written in his sixties). This is the spelling used in the records of *The Family of William Greenleaf Eliot and Abby Adams Eliot* (1952).

was unreasonable, but each distracted Eliot from his saint's dream.

In the summer of 1913 Pound had heard from Aiken that, as he put it, 'there was a guy at Harvard doing funny stuff'. Eliot then invited Pound's attention by calling on him at 5 Holland Place Chambers, Kensington, on 22 September 1914. He showed Pound 'Prufrock', and Pound was immediately captivated by Eliot's natural language and grasp of 'an extant milieu, and an extant state of comprehension'. Pound dashed off an excited letter to Harriet Monroe, the Chicago editor of *Poetry*, raving about his new find. 'Prufrock' was the best poem he had yet seen from an American. To H. L. Mencken he wrote: 'I enclose a poem by the last intelligent man I've found – a young American, T. S. Eliot. . . . I think him worth watching.' Eliot was excited in turn by Pound's enthusiasm, and by the idea that he should stay on in London, write more (under Pound's guidance), and bring out a volume of poems after the war that would have the substance to establish him as a leading poet. Pound argued that a poet had readier access to American magazines from England, whereas English publication was practically impossible for any man outside England unless he was as established as Kipling. London, he urged, was the only possible place for a poet, for only in London was there 'a disciplinary body of fine taste', of powerful writers who insisted that publishers act in accord with dictates other than those of sheer commercialism. London accepted no other standard but its own, and if it took to Eliot it would impose that acceptance on all the English-speaking world. Pound was well aware that new writing came mostly from Americans, but planned to keep this quiet, as English publishers and reviewers would not like to be reminded of this fact.

Pound energised Eliot at a time when he was more or less resigned to an academic career in philosophy, and turned him firmly in the direction of a poet. They were drawn together as two young lapsed professors in exile from America. Eliot looked up to his older and better known contemporary as a teacher and campaigner, and was grateful for his truly generous attention and concern. 'He would cajole, and almost coerce, other men into writing well,' Eliot remarked, 'so that he often presents the appearance of a man trying to convey to a very deaf person the fact that the house is on fire.' Pound gave Eliot entrée to his first artistic milieu in London, the group which included Miss Weaver, a woman of integrity and private means who became editor of the *Egoist* magazine and backed James Joyce;* Wyndham Lewis, artist and editor of *Blast*; an American writer, Hilda Doolittle, known as HD, an old college friend of Pound; and her English husband, who fought in the war and became a minor critic, Richard Aldington. From mid-1915 Eliot attended their Thursday night gatherings in Soho and Regent Street restaurants where – tall, lean, and hollow-cheeked – he would listen to gossip of Amy Lowell's amazing descent on London, and Ford Madox Ford booming anecdotes of the great Victorians, and Arthur Waley on Chinese poetry, while overhead the air-raid sirens whined.

Pound was in many ways a marvellous sponsor and teacher, wholeheartedly devoted to his disciples, but his sponsorship had it drawbacks. Eliot recalled that Pound was so passionately concerned about works of art that he sometimes tended to regard his protégés 'almost impersonally, as art or literature machines' to be oiled for the sake of their potential output. Pound said explicitly that he was interested in Eliot's personal feelings only in so far as they affected his poetic productivity. One observer said he treated Eliot as a kind of collector's piece. With his prize beneath his eye, he would recline in an American posture of aggressive ease, and squint sideways up at the visitor, over the rims of his pince-nez, to see how impressed he was with Eliot's apt answers. Eliot allowed Pound to groom him as a sophisticated poet in some ways as Gurnemanz groomed Parzival as a knight. Parzival obediently polished his manners, Eliot his diction and versification.

* Eliot later dedicated his *Selected Essays 1917–1932* 'To *Harriet Shaw Weaver* IN GRATITUDE, AND IN RECOGNITION OF HER SERVICES TO ENGLISH LETTERS'.

Pound announced that artists were the dictators of the future, and scorned the 'mass of dolts': 'the greasy vulgus will be directed by us'. The modern artist, conceived by Pound, had 'no intention of trying to rule by general franchise. He at least is born to the purple. Modern civilisation has bred a race with brains like those of rabbits and . . . we artists who have been so long the despised are about to take over control.' Without the great artist, the 'rabble' was aimless and drifting. Eliot's letters to Pound in 1914–15 show the infection of Pound's diktats. Or perhaps it's truer to say that Pound's pugnacious backing brought into the open the pride of Eliot's inheritance – pride that was all the fiercer for its formal control. Where Pound verged on the comic in his extravagance, Eliot grew deadly, and directed his venom against the monopolisation of literature by women and the Evil Influence of Virginity on American Civilisation. Too many women lowered the tone of artistic gatherings. When he approached an influential woman, the Boston art collector Isabella Stewart Gardner, he switched his contempt to Germans for being hospitable: inferior races are hospitable, he said, forgetting that a few months before, when war broke out, he had welcomed the hospitality of German hosts who invited stranded foreigners to stay free of charge. He had been relieved, then, to be treated with kindness.

These letters reverberate with pre-echoes of an Eliot with unexpected sides to him, a man of scrupulous correctness who in youth spews foul words, in middle age slaps on make-up, and in old age shocks people close to him with sudden bolts of annihilation. Less shocking to Eliot's contemporaries, but more so to us, is the prejudice emerging so nakedly in letters to Pound – it struts out with the glint of a giggling knifer.

For all Pound's importance to Eliot as backer, Eliot was not in these early years an admirer of Pound's poetry. 'His verse is touchingly incompetent,' Eliot wrote to Aiken.*

---

* 60th Birthday Collection, 23. Pound complained of Eliot's 1919 review of *Quis Pauper Amavi* that it was all 'granite wreaths' and 'leaden laurels, no sign of exhilaration'.

While Pound was impressed with Eliot's note of modernity, Eliot thought Pound old-fashioned. In *After Strange Gods* he would charge Pound with being attracted to the Middle Ages by everything except that which gives them their significance. 'I confess I am seldom interested in what Pound . . . is saying,' Eliot wrote in the *Dial* in 1928, 'but only in the way he says it.' He listened to Pound's pleas for exact objective presentation, hard reality, chiselled statement, and allowed himself to be turned from the exalted hazy impressions of his visionary poems. Composing reviews on the typewriter helped him slough off long sentences, an improvement in lucidity, he thought, at the expense of subtlety. An eight-line poem, 'Suppressed Complex', sent to Pound on 2 February 1915, has a lover dancing about a girl's bedroom and flying out through the window like the thrilling Russian dancer, Vaslav Nijinsky, in *Spectre de la rose*, but where in the ballet the spectre is a figment of the girl's awakened feeling after a ball, Eliot's spectre, 'a shadow upright in the corner', is more of a conventional sexual threat. He is self-regarding, and lacks both the tenderness of the ballet and the delicate voluptuousness of the way Nijinsky grants a girl's response. Eliot's lover has no sense of the sleeping girl, who is merely a prop to arousal, and the result is an immature bore boasting an imaginary escapade. The title pretends to the Imagism that Pound was promoting: 'an intellectual and emotional complex in an instant of time' – 'complex' being used in the technical sense of the new psychologists to mean obsessions arising from repressed drives. But the poem is neither sophisticated in its psychology nor advanced as art. It is of a piece with Eliot's first two letters to Pound, where he postures as a sexual athlete, and talks airily of a debauch and two more candidates for 'Portrait of a Lady'.

Pound concerned himself with the material details of Eliot's life – his jobs, his poverty, his need for contacts and publication. It was as though Eliot were a precious plant to be watered and tended with care. 'Pray God', Pound wrote, ' "Prufrock" be not a single and unique success.' Without Eliot's knowledge, Pound later borrowed money to pay for printing his first volume. Eliot recalled that one might sometimes chafe against Pound's beneficence, though one never resented it. Once, when Eliot struck up an acquaintance with the Bloomsbury artist Roger Fry and his Cambridge friend Goldsworthy Lowes Dickinson at the seaside in 1916, Pound behaved rather jealously and got Eliot to agree Fry was 'an ass'. Eliot had to keep up an attitude of discipleship, but he felt that Pound deserved it.

Pound reinforced Eliot's impulse at this time to cast off what they believed to be the thinness of American civilisation. Pound saw a 'blood poison' in America, and Eliot, he said, had the disease. '. . . Perhaps worse than I have – poor devil,' he wrote; '. . . the thin milk of . . . New England from the pap.' Disinherited together, they would float through other civilisations and ransack them for souvenirs. Henry James once spoke of the American appetite, 'morbid and monstrous, for colour and form, for the picturesque and romantic'. Half a century before Pound and Eliot started to write, he had predicted American writers who would discover their freedom to pick and choose and synthesise the various tendencies of foreign civilisations with an unprecedented lightness and vigour 'and in short (aesthetically &c) claim our property wherever we find it'.

In 1919 Eliot caricatured himself as a 'Burbank with a Baedeker', a New Englander more at ease with literature than life in a foreigner's Venice pinpointed by an epigraph from *The Aspern Papers* by Henry James, who had found himself unable to surrender to Venice (as he told his brother William, 'I might have been born in Boston'). Eliot was not apologetic to be a foreigner, and wrote in 'Henry James: In Memory' (1918): 'It is the final perfection, the consummation of an American to become not an Englishman, but a European, something which no born European, no person of any European nationality can become.' Soon after James had settled in England (in 1876), he had come to the identical conclusion. The New England genius, Eliot claims, was not only 'discriminable' but 'improved and given its chance, not worked off, by transplantation'. He aligns himself with the

'Hawthorne aspect' of Henry James: their deeper psychology and sense of the past, a sense he calls 'peculiarly American'.

It is curious – unprecedented – how often Eliot's letters refer to this essay on James devised for a James issue of the *Little Review*, planned and written almost wholly by himself two and a half years after the Master's death in 1916. As he wrote it he took up the mantle of the Master, as James had taken up the mantle of Hawthorne. It was at this moment that Eliot found a peculiar kinship with the Europeanised James of *The Europeans* (1878), *Hawthorne* (1879), and *The Aspern Papers* (1887), which gave him, for the first time, 'a real, an unshakable confidence'. In the *Egoist* he elaborated on this kind of intimacy: 'That you possess this secret knowledge, this intimacy, with the dead man, that . . . you should have appeared with this indubitable claim to distinction; who can penetrate at once the thick and dusty circumlocutions about his reputation, can call yourself alone his friend: it is something more than *encouragement* to you. It is a cause of development, like personal relations in life . . . Our friendship gives us an introduction to the society in which our friend moved; we learn its origins and endings; we are broadened. We do not imitate, we are changed, our work is the work of a changed man; we have not borrowed, we have been quickened, and we become bearers of a tradition.' In the absence of a poetic tradition they could follow, Pound was shoulder to shoulder with Eliot in their allegiance to the great prose fiction of the nineteenth century, mainly Flaubert and James.

It's impossible to know if Pound was aware of Eliot's religious bent. Eliot himself retreated from the initial impulse, but he may have been further discouraged by Pound's disapproval of Western religions. 'Christianity has become a sort of Prussianism, and will have to go,' Pound thought. 'It has its uses and is disarming, but it is too dangerous. Religion is the root of all evil, or damn near all.' On another occasion he attacked monotheism: 'I consider the *Metamorphoses* [by Ovid] a sacred book, and the Hebrew scriptures the record of a barbarian tribe, full of evil.' In a 1917 issue of the *Little*

Review (in which Eliot also appeared) Pound said: 'Organized religions have always constituted a danger.' In 1918 he said Christianity should be taken lightly and sceptically, until it drifted back into a realm of fairy-lore and picturesque superstition. Pound disapproved when Eliot eventually settled for Christianity as the cure for cultural despair. 'His diagnosis is wrong,' he commented flatly. 'His remedy is an irrelevance.'

Eliot was writing quasi-religious poems when he met Pound. Pound convinced him to return to the social satire of 'Prufrock' and, by 1918, proudly announced 'new and diverting verses'. They *were* diverting, but also bitter for, when Eliot focused on society, he saw only stupid men and fearful women – Sweeney copulating and Mrs Porter's whores and Grishkin the female jaguar and pimply youths at Sunday Service. He fell into the habit of writing jibes at creatures so patently futile as hardly to warrant the energy of his attack.

Eliot once owned to a 'suspicious' and 'cowardly' disposition driven by a hidden force. In suspicious and worried times, it relieved him to hit out at common targets. It is often suggested that his anti-Semitism is too much a commonplace of the time to warrant particular notice, but, as Anthony Julius points out, it was not inevitable in his milieu: Joyce, E. M. Forster, Middleton Murry, and Aldous Huxley all countered it in different ways. It is also suggested that Eliot is at his most brilliant when he incites prejudice. On the contrary, I find Eliot banal in his caricature of the profiteering Jew as 'Money in furs' (conveniently forgetting that his own Blood forebears had dealt in beaver hats); banal in his snigger at upstart names of his own invention 'Lady Kleinwurm', 'Lady Katzegg'; and banal yet again when he plants the Jew beneath the rats of a decayed Venice. Eliot saw himself above his age, looking beyond it as a prophet. In the hatred he incites for a Chicago 'Semite' from Vienna, forcing on us the 'protozoic slime' of Bleistein's 'lustreless protrusive eye', Eliot himself falls into the savagery of the age he affects to abhor.

Yet what those who attack Eliot for anti-Semitism tend to overlook is what often goes with it: misogyny.

A prostitute is reduced to a set of slits – 'Slitted below and gashed with eyes' – and a mouth like an 'oval 0 cropped out with teeth', a human zero. The 'sickle motion from the thighs' – all there is to sex – turns into the alarming jerk of an epileptic fit. The neat quatrains with their pat rhymes suggest the studied rationality of the madman. The poet's hatred of women's sexuality is in line with the murderous fit in 'The Love Song of Saint Sebastian' and the sex act that rips up the woman in the Bolo cycle, both of which precede Eliot's marriage. Vivienne was not the cause. This hatred, clothed as comedy, is too common to strike us as it ought – the matter of magazines, movies, and fashion shows that debase women and do dirt on life. The dirt is literal: not only the 'shit', 'kuk', and 'a-pissin' of the Bolo cycle but the 'liquid siftings' that seem to fall on Agamemnon's shroud in a poem Eliot regarded as especially serious, 'Sweeney Among the Nightingales' (1918). (Pound provided 'siftings' in place of Eliot's first choice, 'droppings'.)* Modernist disillusion bags the tragedy at Argos as a woman's low intrigue: nowadays, it's a Jew, 'Rachel *née* Rabinovitch' – stripped of the cover of her married name† – who tears at grapes 'with murderous paws'.

Women in Eliot's quatrains of 1917–19 are animals in ways that reduce animals to 'murderous paws' and 'rank' smell – a jaguar does not emit 'so rank a feline smell' as

---

* 'I had "droppings" at first,' Eliot said, 'but Pound gave me "siftings" – his own word. He hadn't then used it in Mauberley [Pound's poem *Hugh Selwyn Mauberley*] – it was typical of his generosity.' He was talking in 1933 to Professor Theodore Spencer at Harvard, who copied the words into *Poems 1909–1925* by Eliot (now in the Matthiessen Room, Eliot House, Harvard).

† Christopher Ricks points out that it is not English to use *née* without the married name. The line does not tell us if she is now 'Rachel Winthrop or Rachel Lowell or Rachel Eliot. . . . She might be Rachel Bleistein, *née* Rabinovitch.' Since we can't know, the line incites suspicions in the reader – suspicions, Ricks notes, which are related to anti-Semitism (*T. S. Eliot and Prejudice*, pp. 30–1).

Grishkin in a drawing-room. The social-climbing Jew, 'Sir Ferdinand Klein', courts the wolfish and tubercular 'Princess Volupine'. There are faint links between the last and Eliot's attack on the leading short-story writer Katherine Mansfield, the source for his portrait of 'Scheherazade' from Honolulu in 'Eeldrop and Appleplex' (1917), the only prose fiction Eliot ever published and a rare dead-end in his career. For the story fails to bring off a slice-of-life in the vein of Mansfield. Like Eliot, Mansfield (a New Zealander) was an expatriate who was establishing herself at the heart of London's intelligentsia: her long story, *Prelude*, was chosen by Leonard and Virginia Woolf as publication number 2 for the Hogarth Press, following the Woolfs' own *Two Stories*. Eliot was to be their choice for publication number 3, but he hadn't met the Woolfs as yet and could not endure to see a woman a step ahead of himself. In 1920 he called Mansfield 'a dangerous WOMAN' for no evident reason beyond the fact that she was influential; she thought well of Eliot, and offered him hospitality and no harm; in truth, she was poor, wasted, and dying slowly of tuberculosis without much help from her handsome, self-centred husband, John Middleton Murry, who busied himself in the literary marketplace while Mansfield had long, lonely spells in the South of France, trying in vain to heal her lungs. Eliot's portrait of 'Scheherazade' is spiteful without being clever. He hates what reflects himself: her detachment, 'what is called her impenetrable mask', her failure to live 'at all upon instinct', her tendency to present herself 'too well', and her command of herself as the material of her art. 'I cannot use her; she uses herself too fully.' He wants to say that she is not as good as she and others think ('I think of her as an artist without the slightest artistic power').

In 1922, Lady Rothermere, the financial backer for Eliot's journal, the *Criterion*, said that Katherine Mansfield was the most intelligent woman she had met, and wished Eliot to publish one of her stories.

Eliot exploded in fury. 'K. Mansfield is not by any means the most intelligent woman Lady R. has ever met,' he raged to Pound. 'She is simply one of the most persistent and thickskinned toadies and one of the vulgarest women Lady R. has ever met and is also a sentimental crank.'

Envy did not melt with Mansfield's early death two months later: Eliot told his assistant, Richard Aldington, of a wish to 'deal' with her 'inflated reputation'. Her death bilked him of Eeldrop's wishful scenario: Scheherazade was to have lived on, forgotten, a fat frump who would go 'motoring with a Jewish stockbroker', rolling in motorcars, 'rolling towards a diabetic end in a seaside watering place'.

Eliot does not have the excuse of ignorance or failure or reluctance to question the commonplaces of his time. In his chosen capacity as moral authority, he can't be absolved from inciting prejudice; he did not hold back from the mass-prejudice that played a part in the largest atrocity of the century. In 1936, Eliot published a review of *The Yellow Spot: The Extermination of the Jews in Germany*. Eliot's reviewer Montgomery Belgion claimed that the book's amply documented reports of persecution were exaggerated. In 1943, when the gas-ovens were working at full steam, Lionel Trilling objected to Eliot's inclusion of an anti-Semitic poem in his choice of Kipling's verse. Eliot replied: 'I am not aware that [Kipling] cherished any particularly anti-Semitic feelings.' Trilling commented dryly: 'As anti-Semitism goes these days, I suppose Kipling is not – to use Mr Eliot's phrase – particularly anti-Semitic.' Following this exchange, Christopher Ricks concludes that 'Eliot should never have descended to these shifts on behalf of such a poem.'

After the Holocaust, after the exposures of the Nuremburg Trials, Eliot still kept the 'jew' he had aligned with rats and the 'jew' who was 'spawned' in Antwerp in the lower case until 1963.* Nor did he question the provocation in his disgust for women's bodies, which appears now increasingly ugly as women reveal the extent of sexual violence. Does hatred come from sexual failures, or suppressed affinities, or resentful envy? Another woman writer is called 'Shitwell' – a

---

* See Eliot's selection of his poems for Penguin (1948, repr. 1951), pp. 29, 33.

reward for the affability which the eccentric aristocrats Edith Sitwell and her brothers offered Eliot when, a newcomer in London, he used to sit with them in dank tearooms that seemed to be papered with their tea leaves. In the end, there is no adequate explanation for a man of Eliot's sensibilities – it is as though women are not regarded as fellow-humans unless, like La Figlia or Pipit,* they are stripped of sexuality, adulthood, or agency.

In a man-to-man account of himself as an editor of the *Egoist*, a little magazine owned by a woman called Dora Marsden, Eliot wrote to his father in 1917: 'I struggle to keep the writing as much as possible in Male hands, as I distrust the Feminine in literature . . .'. He was put out by 'women in

* Pipit is an old-fashioned innocent from the speaker's childhood past in 'A Cooking Egg' (1919), *CP*, pp. 36–7, but readers tend to agree that the poem remains impenetrable without knowing more about Pipit as its emotional centre (the literary source Eliot once gave seems an elaborate dodge). There is a close-guarded tenderness for Pipit, rare in these quatrain poems, that does make readers want to place her. This is a mere guess, but since Eliot based a quatrain poem on his Boston cousin Fred Eliot, I have wondered if the source of Pipit in another quatrain poem might be Fred's younger sister Abigail Eliot, who was due to study at Oxford in 1919–20 (Pipit has a book on the Oxford colleges in her room). Abigail Eliot was born in 1892, four years after her cousin Tom, and a photograph of them as children shows them sharing a hammock with Fred and another sister, Martha. Abigail took her first degree at Radcliffe College in 1914, and engaged in social work until she came to England in 1919. Eliot did not see her until 1920. After the year in Oxford she was a student at the Rachel McMillan Nursery School and Training Centre in London in 1921. From 1922 she began her distinguished career as Director of the Nursery Training School of Boston (until 1952). She would be the first close family member the homesick Eliot would see since 1914, and the prospect could have evoked his nostalgia for childhood innocence over against a catalogue of disgust with the dubious sophistications and post-war gloom of a debased Europe (including the menace of a Lucretia Borgia bride). In a final stanza to a first draft of 'Whispers of Immortality' (1918), the speaker says:

> As long as Pipit is alive
> One can be mischievous and brave;
> But where there is no more misbehaviour
> I would like my bones flung into her grave.

Pound, puzzled ('why'), cut this stanza. (*IMH*, pp. 365–7.)

business' while husbands fought: 'not being wholly dependent on their salary they are rather *in*dependent, and sometimes irritating to men who *are* dependent on their salary.'

Readers are now tempted to blast Eliot with political
correctness. In later years he established a protective barrier
about himself, sustained by his wish since his death. Criticism
of Eliot has therefore been difficult. He set himself up as a
moral authority and throughout the twentieth century his
reputation was idolised; the result is now a reaction that is all
the fiercer when the idol is revealed to be made in part from
certain waste products of his century.

Idol-smashing has its base as well as its brave side. We
must take care not to make Eliot an easy target in the same
way he made easy targets of pimply youths and women and,
of course, Jews. I propose to look flaws in the face without
seeing flaws alone. The difficulty, if we are to see a complete
picture, is to admit that flaws in lesser works can coexist with
moral urgency and poetic greatness in other works. Eliot's
greatness, I believe, shows itself not in glib jibes but in a
struggle with certain flaws in his nature, a long struggle that
gave birth to the spiritual journeys of his maturity.

While Eliot was honing the jibes, and smoking brutal black
French cigarettes in pubs about London with Pound's coterie,
he continued to brood about Christianity, its dogma and
institutions. Christian dogma, he realised, was not subject to
logic, but could not be skipped over. 'Philosophy may show,
if it can, the meaning of the statement that Jesus was the son
of God. But Christianity – orthodox Christianity – must base
itself upon a unique fact: that Jesus was born of a virgin: a
proposition which is either true or false, its terms having a
fixed meaning,' he wrote in 1917. In 1916 and 1917 he
reviewed a number of books about the relation of philosophy
to religion, criticising writers who tried to reformulate
Christianity so as to make it more palatable to the enlightened bourgeoisie. He criticised specifically their removal of
asceticism and radicalism from Christianity – it made it too
tepid, too liberal, too much like the enlightened Unitarianism
of his family. 'All that is anarchic, or unsafe or disconcerting

in what Jesus said and did is either denied or boiled away,' he complained. He scorned one writer's suggestion that following Christ could be made easier. 'Certain saints', wrote Eliot crushingly, 'found the following of Christ very hard, but modern methods have facilitated everything.'

His reviews also showed a concern for the religious emotions and for mystical experience. He read, with interest, the anthropologist Lévy-Bruhl's *Les Fonctions mentales dans les sociétés inférieures*, and found there a recognition of the mystical side to the primitive mind which, he felt, Sir James Frazer neglected in his study of primitive ritual, *The Golden Bough*. It struck him how much more mystical experience engrossed the daily life of the savage than that of civilised man.

Eliot also worried about the Church as an institution. His resentment against the empty proprieties of Sunday church-going dated back to Boston days and must have been associated with the Unitarian churches attended by his family. In particular, he resented Sunday morning services conducted by his cousin Frederick May Eliot, who graduated from Harvard a year behind him, in 1911, went on to Harvard Divinity School, and was ordained as a Unitarian minister. Between 1915 and 1917 Fred Eliot took up a post as Associate Minister of the First Parish in Cambridge, Massachusetts – in other words, where Tom had made a mess of his life in the view of the Eliot family, Fred was the boy who made good – to the annoyance of his superior but as yet unsuccessful cousin. He remarked once, '. . . some Eliots are wiser than others, and my cousin Frederick . . . is an ass'. In 'Mr. Eliot's Sunday Morning Service', Eliot denounced empty idolatry of forms with the reforming zeal of his forebears. In the eighteenth century the Revd Andrew Eliot had written: 'The greatest prodigies of wickedness have been those who have put on the guise of religion.' In *Savonarola*, Charlotte Eliot had said:

> The church of old
> Had chalices of wood, while all of gold

Her prelates were. Now arc her prelates wood,
Her chalices of gold, and it is good
For this to rob the poor.

T. S. Eliot's own comparison of modern congregants clutching 'piaculative pence' with the fervent asceticism of early Christians, stemmed from his desire for a revival. Ten years later, Eliot was campaigning to save churches from destruction, parading at the head of a protest march through City streets, and chanting 'Onward Christian Soldiers'. During his first years in London he wrote blasphemous poems, notably the rather juvenile 'Hippopotamus', but explained later that genuine blasphemy stemmed from the 'partial belief' of a mind in a peculiar and unusual state of spiritual sickness. Blasphemy might even be 'a way of affirming belief'.

Eliot's belief had its foundation, in 1914, in his sense of man's flawed nature and the necessity for drastic measures of purification. He cultivated a state of mind that was the very antithesis of the eclectic, tolerant, democratic mind that had surrounded his mid-Western childhood. In one of Eliot's Oxford University Extension lectures in 1916, 'The Reaction against Romanticism', he alluded to T. E. Hulme's theory: 'The classicist point of view has been defined as essentially a belief in Original Sin – the necessity for austere discipline.'

As Eliot had sought depravity in Montparnasse in 1911, he sought it again in disreputable suburbs in South London. He found 'neighbourhoods of silence' which, hc said, were more evil than neighbourhoods of noise. In 'Eeldrop and Appleplex' he wrote about the secret life of a bank clerk called Eeldrop (Eliot called himself 'Eeldrop' in a letter to Pound, was a bank clerk at the time, and described by Pound as serpentine), who would indulge his taste for witch-hunts and smell out evil with the implacable curiosity of a master detective.* He and his friend Appleplex 'aim at experience

* Donald Gallup suggested that Eeldrop and Appleplex seem to have been Eliot and Pound. See *T. S. Eliot and Ezra Pound: Collaboration in Letters* (New Haven: Henry W. Wenning, 1970). We recall that the first Andrew Eliott was one of the jurors in the Salem witch trials and Eliot's

in the particular centres in which alone it is evil'. His passion is to surprise truth behind the masks and façades, and he prides himself on his moments of pure observation and insight that transcend the usual pigeon-holes. (Scheherazade defeats this because her self-consciousness pre-empts investigation.) The larger aim is to grasp the uniqueness of each event, a sense of which, the clerk feels, had vanished with the decline of the religious view. He is particularly fascinated by the medieval mind's identification of evil through the punishment – the eternal punishment – that followed. He himself is a sceptic 'with a taste for mysticism'.

Eliot's preoccupation with questions of Christianity, theology, and evil was undercover because he remained in doubt. 'For people of intellect I think that doubt is inevitable,' Eliot once told an interviewer. 'The doubter is a man who takes the problem of his faith seriously.' In July 1917 he acknowledged that life was poor without religion, but as yet he was unconvinced it was the greatest of all satisfactions and so worth the effort. It was for Eliot a time of exile, when his own visions and signs dried up, a time of 'silence from the sacred wood'.

*

When Eliot failed to awaken his religious emotions in 1914, or to make much of Oxford's Buddhist Society, he had a sudden impulse 'to be a moment merry . . .'. He was ready for women to fall in love with him – several, preferably, would be less testing on the 'practical side', he confided to Aiken. 'And I should be very sorry for them, too.'

In London, during the Christmas vacation in 1914, desires seemed to rise up as he walked the streets. 'How much more self-conscious one is in a big city!' he wrote to Aiken. It was another of his 'nervous sexual attacks. . . . This is the worst since Paris. I never have them in the country. . . . I am very dependent upon women (I mean female society); and feel the

Stearns grandmother, Charlotte Blood, was a descendant of Judge Blood.

112

deprivation at Oxford – one reason why I should not care to remain longer – but there . . . the deprivation takes the form of numbness only; while in the city it is more lively and acute.' Refinement blocked any possible relief. 'I should be better off, I sometimes think, if I had disposed of my virginity and shyness several years ago: and indeed I still think sometimes that it would be well to do so before marriage.'

During the Trinity term of 1915 Eliot went punting with another American, Scofield Thayer, whom he had known at Milton Academy. The party included Thayer's sister, Lucy, and an English girlfriend by the name of Vivienne Haigh Haigh-Wood.* They met again at a lunch party in Thayer's rooms at Magdalen. Vivienne's excitable, eager nature, her quick fire, stirred in Eliot a hope that she might supply the defining experience he needed. Marriage was Eliot's one memorable act of self-surrender and perhaps served as a compensation for the self-surrender he had failed to achieve during his religious crisis. A little more than a year after his marriage Eliot wrote of the attractions of passion after a practical, sensible, and emotionally undernourished upbringing: 'For the boy whose childhood has been empty of beauty, who has never known the *detached* curiosity for beauty, who's been brought up to see goodness as practical and to take the line of self-interest in a code of rewards and punishments, then the sexual instinct when it is aroused may mean the only possible escape from a prosaic world.' He goes on to say that both sexual and religious passion offer possibilities of 'escape' into feeling, but already he recognises – he was twenty-eight when he wrote these words – that religion promised a more durable satisfaction: 'We must learn to love always, to exercise those disinterested passions of the spirit which are inexhaustible and permanently satisfying.'

* Pound surmised that Vivienne was Thayer's best girl or that he was, at least, an admirer. (Letter to Quinn (24 Mar. 1920). Quinn Coll.) Valerie Eliot says (*L*, i, 112) that neither TSE nor Vivienne was aware of the attraction. When Thayer declared himself 'nettled' after Eliot married her, Eliot replied that in his view it was 'vanity' not passion that had suffered – he afterwards apologised to Thayer for this unkindness.

Vivienne Haigh Haigh-Wood was four months older than Eliot. When they met, both were twenty-six. She was, at the time, a governess with a Cambridge family, and was keen on the arts. Her father, whom she loved, was a painter; she herself painted and did ballet; later, she tried film-acting; then wrote poetry and prose sketches; and finally, she took up music. Her fancy name was deceptive; her origins were plain. She was born in Bury in Lancashire, the granddaughter of Charles Wood, who had a flourishing trade there as a carver and gilder. In 1850, he had married Mary Haigh, and their son, Charles, born in 1854, became an artist. In 1870 Charles went off to study at Manchester Art School, and at an early age made a successful approach to the Royal Academy in London. He held his first exhibition in 1874, and later had several works accepted for the RA Summer Exhibition. Charles Haigh-Wood married Rose Esther Robinson in 1885, and their first child, Vivienne Haigh, was born on 28 May 1888; a son, Maurice, followed in 1896. He fought all through the war, and survived – a dark, strapping, well-conducted young man who was fond of his sister.

To Russell, who took her up at Eliot's request – the idea was to help him cope with her, which Russell did with a dubious blend of concern and gleeful alacrity – she seemed like an actress. She liked original, dramatic clothes and bold colours – she owned a scarfdress in the post-war years and, in the thirties, got herself up in a cape and waistcoat and flourished a cigarette-holder. She was attractive to men, but not the kind of woman a gentleman would introduce to his mother.* Though her parents lived comfortably in Hampstead, Eliot's background was very much grander. Silent and shy, he was eased by her lavish temperament, and her downright opinions, frank to the point of what was then thought vulgar – but still charming. She was quite devoid of cultural snobbery, and would never say she liked Bach or Cézanne if she did not. Eliot was fascinated by a flamboyant

---

* In his *Journals 1982–1986*, Anthony Powell imagines what his mother might have said on meeting Vivienne (p. 230).

woman who could dispense so perfunctorily with masks and façades. He admired her daring, her lightness, her acute sensitivity, and her gift for speech. Later, the very qualities that attracted him – her emphatic rhetoric (she spoke with what she called a 'strong Welsh shriek'), her unashamed behaviour, her frank eyes – accused him of his insufficiencies when their marriage failed.

Both had recently been in love with someone else, and were in need of consolation. Eliot had kept in contact with Emily Hale while he was in Oxford. When he did not return to Boston, Emily's connections concluded that Eliot had turned away because her mother's mental illness might prove hereditary. This seems unlikely. Even less likely was Emily's high-flown notion that, with the outbreak of war, Eliot, not strong enough to fight himself, took a job in order to release a fighting man. In fact, the prime cause was Pound, who had turned Eliot against his prospects at Harvard, and a lifetime in Boston. Eliot's change of direction during 1915 is evident in new poems which mock Harvard academics and other Bostonians. The contempt was a measure of the wrench, bombarded as he was by images of his patrician family with their stern sense of public duty – authoritarian men like Charles William Eliot, ex-President of Harvard, who urged Eliot not to stay abroad and ruin his art like Henry James.

Vivienne's recent love affair with a schoolmaster, Charles Buckle, had ended six months before she met Eliot. Her diary of that time is an ominous record of fluctuating moods. For nine months 'B' endured Vivienne's emotional scenes, screams and reproaches, 'heavenly' (but brief) reconciliations, frantic telegrams and phone calls until in August 1914, with a relief evident even to Vivienne, he enlisted at the War Office, and so escaped. The diary does not do Vivienne credit: it exhibits a shallow and self-centred prima donna, preoccupied with her romance.

On 24 April 1915, Eliot reported to Eleanor that during the spring vacation, at a dance held in a London hotel, he had met English girls with 'amusing' names – one was Vivienne.

She was a pliant dancer, the kind of woman who seems to offer a shy scholar a holiday from the seriousness of his superior world. Eliot started to 'dip' in his one-step in a style unknown in England where, he reported, 'dancing is very stiff and old fashioned'. He was up on new dances called the foxtrot and the grizzly bear, and could hum the latest ragtime, 'That Shakespearian Rag' (published in New York in 1912). Its chorus, which haunts a failing marriage in *The Waste Land* ten years later, went: 'That Shakes-pea-ri-an rag, – Most in-tel-li-gent, ve-ry, el-e-gant, . . . Des-de-mon-a was the col-ored pet, Ro-me-o – loved his Ju-li-et – And they were some lov-ers, you can bet, – and yet, I know – if they were here to-day, They'd Grizz-ly Bear in a different way, And you'd hear old Ham-let say, "To be or not to be," That – Shakespea-ri-an Rag.'

Vivienne caught on quickly. She seemed more 'adaptable' than the run of English girls; most of them, especially in Oxford, were completely managed by mothers. As 'emancipated Londoners', Vivienne and a friend were free to go out to tea and dinner several times. Eliot found them 'quite different from anything I have known at home or here. . . . They are charmingly sophisticated (even "disillusioned") without being hardened; and I confess to taking great pleasure in seeing women smoke . . .'.

Dancing, dining, and punting in the company of others told him little about Vivienne. He was a foreigner who until then had had no contact with Englishwomen. At Oxford, he stiffened in surprise at the sight of women students at lectures for men. For a long time to come, gentlemen at Oxford regarded the women students as earnest oddities – one didn't associate with them socially. Vivienne appeared the opposite, wild, mercurial, a world apart from his serious mother, his professional women cousins, and the perfect propriety of Emily Hale. As an Englishwoman, she was a mystery to Eliot, who may not have known what to make of her staring eyes and open mouth – beyond their challenge. Her impulsiveness, her smoking and dancing, and her eloquent intelligence teased his cautious nature. Not least of Vivienne's attractions was her faith in Eliot as a coming poet. In this, Pound saw a prospective ally. He and Vivienne got on rather well – both madcaps, with darting insights but little interest in what others felt.

Eliot went down from Oxford when Trinity term ended on about 20 June. This was the end of his travelling fellowship: was he now to return home? In the fourth week of June, he faced the decision of his life. Pound's persuasions, at this moment, carried enormous force.

Pound's strongest ploy was to play on Eliot's fear of provincialism. Robert Frost had published *North of Boston* in 1914. Pound dismissed it as too local, too remote from poetry 'which accepts the tone and difficulties of modern civilization'.

'No one in London cares a hang what is written in America,' Pound pressed his point. 'After getting an American audience a man has to begin all over again here if he plans for an international hearing. He even begins at a disadvantage. London likes discovering her own gods.' He urged Eliot to go 'the whole hog', and cited the celebrated precedent: 'Henry James stayed in Paris and read Turgenev and Flaubert; Mr Howells returned to America and read Henry James.'

The issue that faced Eliot at this point was whether, on the strength of 'Prufrock', four years earlier, he was justified in abandoning an academic career. There was no proof, beyond the publication of 'Prufrock' in June 1915, that Eliot had it in him to make poetry his life. The challenge is neatly expounded in retrospective lines written in the early 1940s when Eliot was completing his masterpiece:

It seems just possible that a poem might happen
To a very young man: but a poem is not poetry –
That is a life.

Pound, who would stop at nothing for the sake of art, put it into Vivienne's head to save Eliot for poetry – a notion designed to captivate her bent for fantasy. Eliot, whom she hardly knew, was at the centre of a drama which seemed to offer this thin little governess, hungry for a big scene, a dashing part. Her free manner invited Eliot to make love to her at a moment when he longed to lose his virginity, and it would be in character, given his rectitude, that he felt obliged to marry her. The marriage took place suddenly on 26 June 1915 at the Hampstead Registry Office, near Vivienne's home at 3 Compayne Gardens. The witnesses were Lucy Thayer and Lillia C. Symes, Vivienne's aunt. It was done without the knowledge of either set of parents. Two days later, Pound – closely involved, it would appear, in this turn of events – sent off an apologia to Eliot's father, with a deluge of reasons for staying in London to be a poet. It's a cogent apologia from a poet's point of view, but unlikely to impress a manufacturer of bricks who had no expectation of having to support his son any further. With airy ease, Pound suggested to Henry Ware Eliot, Sr, that $500 would do for the first year, and $250 for the second to get his son started on a new life in another country.

There are several explanations of Eliot's unplanned marriage, all non-explanations, as he was ready to admit. 'I can't tell you,' he said in middle age to Mary Trevelyan. 'Not because I don't want to, but because I cannot find the words to express it.' The printed extract from the private paper written in his sixties offers no new insight. It links the marriage to his decision to remain in England, and underlines the rashness of a shy young man who wanted to have a little fling, no more, but was too inexperienced to know how to do so without commitment. Again, as in his departure from Emily Hale, Eliot puts himself in a pathetic light. The tone is measured, official. Vivienne's claims and merits are not acknowledged – or not in the extract relayed to readers. A less calculated explanation lies buried in an obscure letter to one Mrs Tandy, whose husband left her in 1946. Her plight stirred Eliot's memory, and on this occasion his words were heated: he confided to Mrs Tandy that during the four years he had tried to be a philosopher and future professor of philosophy, a rebellion had seethed inside him. As a graduate he had discovered how much he baulked at the deadliness of academe – Oxford proved to him that one university town was much like another – and his choice of the wrong career had been a constant worry undermining his capacity to write the kind of poetry he was turning out before he began this course. The result had been a maddened feeling of failure and inferiority. To escape this, he had to deal an all-out blow to an unwanted life. Vivienne happened to be at hand. It was as casual as that. And here is the strangeness of Eliot: a lesser man might have spared a thought for the woman. Officially, Eliot conceded there was a mutual trauma, but his unguarded version to Mrs Tandy suggests that he saw the marriage as *his* drama. He was not disposed to see the wrong he did a woman with whom he was not in love. A year after the marriage, he found himself still in love with Emily Hale.

In all this, there remains something unstated if we look at the marriage in the trajectory of this life – so extraordinary in its directedness. Eliot's private paper tells posterity that out of the marriage to Vivienne came the state of mind that 'led to *The Waste Land*'. He's saying that Vivienne led him into hell; but wasn't hell – genuine suffering – just what his masochist-martyrs lacked in the mediocre poems of 1914 and early 1915? In this sense, his marriage to Vivienne in mid-1915 was not an inexplicable aberration in a prudent life; it was precisely what that life required at precisely the point at which poetry became 'a life'.

Six days after marriage, Eliot told his brother on 2 July that he was less 'suppressed'. It seems that, for a brief spell, Vivienne Haigh Haigh-Wood freed Eliot in some way, but whatever daring she induced was soon replaced by a grim sense of responsibility. The momentum that carried them both to reckless consummation made Eliot think of Dante's Paolo and Francesca. He quoted the line 'ma solo un punto fu quel che ci vinse' ('but one moment alone it was that overcame us'), and Francesca's assertion that her lover shall never be divided from her. He recalled how their torment in hell was not to lose all recollected delight – that would have been a relief – but to continue to experience desires they could no longer gratify.

Eliot married on the crest of a moment of rapport, so abruptly that there was no time to inform his family. It was almost necessary for him to act impulsively – to forestall habitual scruples – if he were to act at all. He once said that it was better to do wrong than to do nothing. 'At least we exist.' He was impatient with the remote, stuffy atmosphere of universities, and Vivienne tempted him to fling himself inescapably into a 'real' world – where people made love and took care of each other and worried about money. That the adventure into the 'real' world did not turn out well, that Eliot was disillusioned with the relationship before it had fairly begun, should not dispel the important fact: Eliot, at this point, took a plunge that would change his life. 'There are always some choices', he said eighteen years later, 'which are irrevocable and, whether you make the right one or the wrong one, there is no going back on it. "Whatever you do," I wish someone had said to me then, "don't whimper, but take the consequences." ' One of Eeldrop's favourite observations is the rash marriage of a young man who awakens to his ruin three months later. He is classed with the unhappily married. But what that man feels 'when he wakes up in the morning, which is the great important fact' no one but Eeldrop conceives. 'The awful importance of the ruin of a life is overlooked.' Eliot's marriage was to be the grim underside of his life, the secret inferno to be traversed before he might be worthy of the genuine awakening only faith could supply.

I think Eliot's disillusion with his marriage was associated with sexual failures, and preceded his discovery of his wife's chronic illness. At dinner, on Friday 9 July 1915, two weeks after their marriage, Vivienne Eliot told Bertrand Russell that she had married her husband to stimulate him, but found she could not do it. Russell's sympathies were, at this point, with the wife, whom he saw as a spirited English girl tied to an over-refined New Englander. He thought she would soon tire of him. Eliot brought into the marriage an intellectual recoil from the flesh ('the mind deserts the body it has used') that fought its baser attractions. His acute awareness of mortality made contact with flesh ephemeral. The result was a curious alignment of women with the evanescence and triviality of Time. This view is present long before he met Vivienne, as well as a more common resentment, born of fear, that imposes on women the blame for a male's transformation into sexual beast. Eliot did not contradict his wife's complaint to Russell, but reclined listlessly on the other side of the table.

Russell's mistress, Lady Ottoline Morrell, was showing signs of indifference at this time, and his eye fell on Vivienne, unloved and smarting from sexual failure. She was twenty-seven; Russell forty-three. Given the silence enjoined on wives, Vivienne was unusually honest, and it was her clarity of statement, I think, as well as the generous but self-defeating impulse behind her union with Eliot, that drew Russell. Her generosity sparked his wish to help her, but his motives were not, as they appeared to Eliot, disinterested. In his 1996 biography of Russell, Ray Monk shows how Russell's letters admit repeatedly that he 'used' Vivienne. Though Russell normally kept *everything*, he destroyed letters Vivienne is known to have written to him, obviously because he felt guilty. His *Autobiography* which appears disarmingly candid – he is content to divulge the bad breath which marred his affair with Lady Ottoline Morrell, and endless affairs with other women – obscures a long affair with Vivienne that lasted, his biographer speculates, from the summer of 1915 to January 1918.

What made this affair different from others, and why did Russell wish to obliterate it? There is no knowing the whole truth, but we may deduce from Russell's correspondence with two mistresses of the time, Lady Ottoline and Lady Constance Malleson (the actress, Colette O'Neill), that Russell was toying with a sickly woman who lacked the independence of the titled or professional women to whom Russell was habitually attracted. He told Lady Ottoline that it was, indeed, odd that he should like Vivienne, yet he did. Putting together what facts do survive, we might conclude that he 'used' Vivienne's keen responses as a stimulus at two particular times when his self-esteem dwindled: in the summer of 1915 when Lady Ottoline neglected him for the writers and artists she invited to Garsington Manor, near Oxford; and again, in 1917, when his affair with Constance Malleson broke up. Russell explained in one letter to Lady Ottoline (with whom he remained an intimate friend) that sexual success energised his work – and the primacy of his work can't be overestimated. Vivienne turned out to be more than a stimulus; she could type from dictation, and Russell employed her on two anti-war publications, *Justice in War Time*, published in November 1915, and a reply to Professor Gilbert Murray's defence of British foreign policy leading to war, *The Policy of the Entente 1904–1914*, published in December. In return for Vivienne's help, Russell undertook to 'help' her, and through her, Eliot. With diabolical sophistry he argued that if he invited Vivienne to fall in love with him, he would divert Vivienne's darts of cruelty from her withdrawn bridegroom whom she blamed 'for having tricked her imagination'.

Lady Ottoline warned Russell that to make the bride fall in love with him was not the way to help an uneasy couple at the start of their marriage: 'I feel *very* strongly that in getting her confidence you are rather separating her from Eliot.' But Russell ignored this advice. While Eliot sailed to America to placate and beg help from his parents, Russell (who, as yet, had not gone out of his way for Eliot) now drew close to Vivienne. By the time Eliot returned in early September, it was agreed that the couple would move into Russell's flat at 34 Russell Mansions, Bury Street, London. The subsequent disaster of their 'pseudo-honeymoon' in Eastbourne (as Russell called it, very much in the know) may not have been unconnected with his attentions to Vivienne, playing the engaging compatriot against his image of Eliot as listless alien. Eliot later confirmed to Lady Ottoline that Russell had damaged Vivienne. The most satanic conduct is when an exploiter appears to himself as well as to others the kindest of benefactors. For Russell was also generous: he gave the couple the equivalent of £3,000 in engineering debentures, no mean sum in 1915, as well as dancing lessons and (according to Ottoline) silk underwear for Vivienne. The ambiguities of Russell's involvement are hopelessly intricate – he said he was 'fond' of his ex-pupil, and may well have been – but, on balance, Russell brought evil on the marriage, and I think in his sealed-off soul, he knew this.

The Eliots' room in Russell's flat was not much bigger than a closet, with the result that Eliot often slept in the hall or sitting-room, when he wasn't lodging in High Wycombe where he began a lack-lustre career as a schoolmaster. This means that, for three months, Russell and Vivienne were sometimes alone in the flat, whenever Russell was able to leave a deadly, war-time Cambridge. He took the precaution of asking Eliot's permission, and Eliot declared his trust in the following reply:

> 8 Hartington Mansions,
> Eastbourne, Sussex
> 11 September [1915]

Dear Mr Russell,

Your letter coming on top of all your other kindnesses, has quite overwhelmed me. Such generosity and encouragement means a great deal to me at present, above all coming from you . . .

As to your coming to stay the night at the flat when I am not there, it would never have occurred to me to accept it under any other conditions. Such a concession to conventions never entered my head; it seems to me not only totally unnecessary, but also would destroy for me all the pleasure we take in the informality of the arrangement . . .

> Sincerely yours
> Thomas Stearns Eliot

For a long time Eliot continued to trust Russell and his wife. He felt bound to Vivienne by gratitude for taking him on. 'She has been ready to sacrifice everything for me,' he wrote to his father on 23 July. 'She has everything to give that I want, and she gives it. I owe her everything. I have married her on nothing, and she knew it and was willing for my sake. She had nothing to gain by marrying me.' For her part, she, too, felt bound by more than a legal bond. Her diary recalls her husband's clean-cut mouth, fine head, and keen, deep, hawk-like eyes. 'He was a very attractive fellow then,' one acquaintance wrote, 'a sort of looks unusual this side of the Atlantic.' At times he seemed like a Harvardian Rupert Brooke – with a Gioconda smile, dimples, and a graceful neck – and at times like a sleek cat, with an exactly articulated drawl that made a sleepy droning like 'some heavy hymenopter, emitting a honeyed buzz'. His charm, part of which was his reserve, and her faith in his artistic promise spurred Vivienne to save him from his cagey constraint. Both willed this awakening, but it failed.

There is no denying that many of Eliot's early poems suggest sexual problems – not lack of desire, but inhibition, distrust of women, and a certain physical queasiness. Vivienne, with continuous ill health, would have been surrounded by smelly medicines, and disordered hormones led to heavy, unpredictable periods which stained the sheets. Eliot wrote of a bridegroom offended by blood on the marriage-bed, and of French perfume that disguised 'the good old hearty female stench'. Vivienne's slightly vulgar manner perhaps liberated him momentarily from his genteel constraint, but he was soon put off by it, and it was clear to friends who observed them early on that he felt ashamed of her. Years later, she wrote a sketch about a loud-mouthed wife trying to energise her husband on the dance floor. 'Now *dance*, for a change,' she says, exasperated. 'You never do dance, you know, you simply march about. . . . You've got no energy.' The wife exhorts; the husband smiles feebly. (Someone remembered how Eliot and his wife used to foxtrot, very solemnly, in the twenties.) Vivienne never quite accepted their incompatibility, while Eliot accepted it too quickly. After a year, he said he had been through 'the most awful nightmare of anxiety that the mind of man could conceive', but at least it had not been dull.

In Eliot's 'Ode' to disastrous sex, an inexperienced bridegroom, sailing expectantly towards a 'golden apocalypse', is frustrated by what appears to be a premature ejaculation. He is left, a good way below the stars, 'indignant / at the cheap extinction of his taking-off'. 'Ode' alludes to Whitman's lines about sexual exasperation:

O Hymen! O Hymenee! why do you tantalize me thus?
O why sting me for a swift moment only?

But while the bridegroom contrives to recompose his neat façade, he feels (probably exaggerated) guilt towards his partner, who appears to him a 'succuba eviscerate', a sexual creature deprived of her force.* It is impossible to know how far 'Ode' recalls Eliot's own experience, but there actually was that postponed 'pseudo-honeymoon' at Eastbourne in September 1915, with Vivienne 'not far removed from suicide'.

On their return, the couple moved into Russell's flat in the same month. When Vivienne was suicidal again a few months later, Eliot seemed grateful to Russell for taking her to Torquay (at Russell's expense) from 7 to 16 January. 'Vivien says you have been an angel to her,' Eliot wrote to Russell. 'I am sure you have done everything possible and handled her in the very best way – better than I. I often wonder how things would have turned out but for you – I believe we shall owe her life to you, even.'

Eliot's male characters suffer either from a sense of inadequacy, like Prufrock or Burbank, or automatic lust like Sweeney, or emotional barrenness in the case of a house agent's clerk. With the first the woman is unapproachable, with the second she has a fit, with the third she remains indifferent. I am not suggesting that Eliot should be identified with these lovers, for they are caricatures, but simply that all his scenes of sexuality in his early years, except 'Suppressed Complex', show it to be joyless, forced, sporadic, and sordid. While Eliot completed his doctoral thesis during the early months of 1916, Vivienne and Russell used to meet twice a week for lunch or dinner. Russell gave Lady Ottoline to

* The Latin *succuba* (strumpet) came to mean, in the folklore, a female demon thought to have sexual intercourse with sleeping men.

understand that he wished to avoid 'any permanent entanglement' as well as any risk to his reputation, but to do so without giving Vivienne 'the feeling that I have played her false'. Vivienne cost him time, money, and worry; his 'affection' for her was 'not constant'; and yet the tie continued. On 4 September 1916, Russell brooded over it in a long letter to Lady Ottoline: 'It is odd how one finds out what one really wants, & how very selfish it always is. What I want permanently – not consciously, but deep down – is stimulus, the sort of thing that keeps my brain active & exuberant. I suppose that is what makes me a vampire. I get a stimulus most from the instinctive feeling of success . . . I had a sense of success with Mrs E. because I achieved what I meant to achieve (which was not so very difficult) . . .'

Russell told his next mistress, Colette, about Vivienne: 'If you met her you would be utterly unable to understand what I see in her – you would think her a common little thing, quite insignificant.' Before he went off with Colette, Russell went to see Vivienne who felt he was 'deserting' her. He recognised 'some truth' in this.

In late October 1917 Russell and Vivienne were alone at Senhurst Farm on Abinger Common, Surrey, where Vivienne was lodging. According to Russell it was Vivienne who wanted something more than friendship. He wrote to Colette on 30 October:

> I thought I could manage it – I led her to expect more if we got a cottage – at last I spent a night with her. *It was utter hell.* There was a quality of loathsomeness about it which I can't describe. I concealed from her all I was feeling – had a very happy letter from her afterwards. I tried to conceal it from myself – but it has come out since in horrible nightmares which wake me up in the night & leave me stripped bare of self-deception. So far I have not said a word to her – when I do, she will be unhappy. I should like the cottage if we were merely friends, but not on any other footing – indeed I cannot bring myself to face anything closer. . . . A sort of odour of corruption pervades everything, till I am maddened by nausea.

I have to break Mrs. Eliot's heart & I don't know how to face it. It mustn't be done all of a sudden.

This has been taken on trust as a moral upheaval. But Russell is writing to another woman whom he now wants back – and his letter succeeds in its purpose. After the smears on Vivienne, he can tell Colette: 'I want you to understand that the one & only thing that made the night loathsome was that it was not with you. There was nothing else to make me hate it.' Isn't this the self-serving histrionics of a practised seducer? Vivienne is being used as foil in yet another round of Russell's sex games. So can we believe his version? One thing is clear: Russell was treacherous to Eliot, who had been grateful for his help, and treacherous also to Vivienne in maligning her so vilely. He had expected her to fall in love with him from the first – so he confided to his preceding mistress, Lady Ottoline Morrell, and ignored her warning that if he really wished to help Vivienne this was not the way. When Russell met Vivienne on 6 November he was relieved to get 'out of the troublesome part of the entanglement by her initiative – she behaved very generously . . .'. But for Eliot it was a double betrayal, a spectacle of evil which, he told Lady Ottoline later, had a part in his conversion. It reinforced his student need to stimulate higher faculties in recoil from female flesh. Vivienne's adultery and Russell's unscrupulous lust may have fuelled the bitter rhymes Eliot was writing between 1917 and 1919. A line in 'Gerontion' (1919) puns on 'adultery' in a suggestive way:

I have lost my passion: why should I need to keep it
When what is kept must be adulterated?

Eliot never really forgave Russell, and afterwards attacked him in writing – most subtly, as we shall see, in his play *Murder in the Cathedral*.

The women in Eliot's new poems were all predatory, barren, or parasitic: the sick Princess Volupine stretching a wasted hand, and Grishkin who plays jaguar to the male's scampering marmoset. She was based on the Russian dancer Serefima Astafieva (1876–1934), whom Pound introduced to

Eliot, hoping a poem would result.* Later, there is the frantic wife in *The Waste Land* and, in the same poem, the fashionable, pampered Fresca. In this section (which Eliot cut on Pound's advice) he makes his fullest anti-feminist statement:

Fresca! in other time or place had been
A meek and lowly weeping Magdalene;
More sinned against than sinning, bruised and marred,
The lazy laughing Jenny of the bard
(The same eternal and consuming itch
Can make a martyr or plain simple bitch);
Or prudent sly domestic puss puss cat,
Or autumn's favourite in a furnished flat,
Or strolling slattern in a tawdry gown,
A doorstep dunged by every dog in town.
For varying forms, one definition's right:
Unreal emotions, and real appetite.

Eliot seems to have regarded a seductive woman as a man's ordeal, a view that had more to do with traditional prejudice than with the reality of his marriage, however unsuitable. Vivienne's 1919 diary shows the mundane interests that engaged most of her energies – a woman buying a hat or vegetables, making blackberry jam, enjoying a 'roaring time' amongst her own friends. With Sydney and Violet Schiff, she shone as an actress in the private theatricals the Eliots enjoyed with them in 1919–20. Whenever Vivienne demonstrated some flair as actress, dancer, or writer, Eliot liked to show her off. Katherine Mansfield noted rather enviously the way he kept a wing over Vivienne when they came to dinner in the summer of 1920, 'admiring, listening, making the most of her'. There were, in fact, a number of affinities between

* Related by Pound's biographer Humphrey Carpenter, in *A Serious Character: The Life of Ezra Pound* (Boston: Houghton Mifflin; London: Faber, 1988), pp. 332–3. Pound told Charles Olson of a dance of Astafieva called 'spermatopyros' about the making of the seed of life, the 'female equivalent of sperm' which turns to fire. Astafieva opened her own ballet school in London.

Eliot and Vivienne: her hatred of the 'fug and slop' of sentiment, her alienation from most people, her susceptibility to horror, and her taste for night prowls with the likes of Eeldrop. She recalls in her diary how she and Eliot once, in the dark of night, spat into a letterbox at the *Adelphi*.* Yet, strangely, in her own sketches, Vivienne's self-image merges with the fictional type of the alluring female whose energy and intelligence become, for the sensitive male, monstrous. The hyacinth blooms 'mis-shapen'.

Vivienne's crises in the first year of the marriage remained the pattern of the rest of her life: a pattern of illness, convalescence, and relapse. In April 1919, when Virginia Woolf met her, she saw a prematurely old and washed-out little woman. Eliot said Vivienne made a heroic struggle against ill health, but one major or minor illness followed another, starting with tuberculosis of the bones in infancy. She told Eliot she had had so many operations before she was seven that she was able to recall nothing before that age. In 1914 she mentions a liver complaint, neuralgia, fainting. Eliot's letters in 1916 mention her stomach upsets, exhaustion, and again a tendency to faint when not lying down. In 1919 she speaks of migraines and a swollen face. In 1922 Eliot told Pound that her symptoms seemed to point to pituitary trouble, a cramped *sella turcica*. He said that Vivienne had all along behaved very finely and even offered to live on her own so that her illnesses should not interfere with his work. In 1923 there followed an attack of colitis when she very nearly died. In the spring of 1924 she nearly died again, and in frightful pain, of what was tentatively (but obviously unsatisfactorily) diagnosed as rheumatism. There was pleurisy in 1929, and her diary of 1936 complains of a permanent injury to the spine.

Worse than these physical ordeals was her perennial nervous self-consciousness, amounting at times to panic and, in crowds, near-delirium. There were frequent 'nervous'

---

* It belonged to Monty Shearman. Vivienne recalls this in her diary (18 Mar. 1935).

collapses, associated with severe headaches and heavy, dazed sleep all day and night for weeks, sometimes months. In one of Vivienne's sketches the voices of guests drive an invalid mad as she lies in the dark. Could her panics have been the side-effect of drugs or sedatives which she had started to take, quite innocently, under doctor's orders, when she was sixteen? Russell considered that the difficulty between Vivienne and Eliot in the first year of their marriage had a lot to do with her taking drugs and the consequent hallucinations. (She used ether, which was, after opium, a common sedative in the ninteenth century.) The Haigh-Woods, Vivienne's parents, seem to have contributed little or nothing to the expense of taking a shaky daughter off their hands – Eliot had to resort to begging his own parents for subsidies when money ran out. There is no sign of similar pleas to the Haigh-Woods, who (Eliot informed his parents at the outset) were in 'very straitened circumstances owing to the war'. We must conclude that it was left almost entirely to Eliot to care for his wife, which he did responsibly as she deteriorated year after year. 'I think that in some ways I have improved (somewhat less selfish and more considerate),' he wrote to Eleanor, 'also hardened a bit.'

Once, when the Haigh-Woods went away on holiday, the Eliots were allowed to stay in the smooth-running house in Hampstead. Mr Haigh-Wood allowed them £1 a week for the servants' food. Vivienne complains, not to her parents, but to Eliot's family in America that this did not suffice for their expenses in living in Haigh-Wood style. She was unaware of false notes in her letters which can't have endeared her to the Eliot family: there's unmistakable triumph in her voice when she informs them that a doctor had declared the cause of her migraines to be 'starvation', and that he has ordered her not to 'economise' – as though she had been a selfless heroine starving herself to pale fever for the sake of her husband – forgetting that another letter had revealed a lapse in the strictest economy. When the Eliots had moved into a flat at 18 Crawford Mansions on the border of Paddington and Marylebone in March 1916, Vivienne had 'chosen' a striking orange wallpaper for the dining-room and striped wallpaper for the hallway – luxuries, surely, for a starving woman, especially with rising prices in wartime. Vivienne wished Eliot's mother to know that she was wearing herself out darning her husband's worn-out underwear for untold hours. There's no getting to the bottom of Vivienne – at this distance in time, truth and untruth lie so close that it is almost impossible to sort them. I'm not inclined to believe in Vivienne's darning, nor in Bertrand Russell when he reassures the Eliot parents and the professors at Harvard that Vivienne was a good thing – Henry Ware Eliot, Sr, was sufficiently shrewd to take a cool view of Russell – but I do believe Eliot's report to his mother that Vivienne was a good cook. He doesn't say, of course, how *much* she cooked. She presents a familiar form of self-defeat: loads of flair, initiative, eloquence diverted into private dramas – someone who competes successfully for attention but for some reason can't grow up.

Vivienne presented a wifely image in letters to the Eliot family, and kept up a pretence that she couldn't wait to go to America – just as soon as the war would be over. She may well have pretended to herself, for she was one of those manoeuvrers who shift ground, not vaguely but boldly, persuading themselves as they go of a rock-fast rationale. The art of lying took precedence amongst her gifts – Vivienne gave bravura performances – fired by the will to score in private battles. A battle for Eliot was constantly underway in the years following his marriage when, from his family's point of view, he failed to bring his wife home: call it England versus America, poet versus academic philosopher, present versus past, Vivienne versus the Eliots for the prime claim on Tom's conscience. During these early years Vivienne seemed to win all the way, firstly because she sided with the prospective poet (in this, supremely useful to Eliot in so far as she kept him away from Harvard), secondly because she had an effective weapon in her ill health, and finally because she had no scruples. She boldly admits to Eliot's brother that she has opened his letter to her husband: '. . . I opened and read it

... I read the postscript which you did not intend me to see.'
Her argument is the legalised 'we' of marriage: 'we always do
this with *family* letters'; her action is therefore legitimate. She
then defends her husband's right to pursue a future as a poet.
'... Tom knows perfectly well that I share his feeling over the
poetry – in fact, he knows that of the two of us perhaps I
worry most. ... I look upon Tom's poetry as real genius – I
do think he is made to be a great writer – *a* poet. His prose is
very good – but I think it will never be *so* good as his poetry.'

She is more than a wife who stands by her husband. 'I
provide the motive power,' she exults, 'I *shove.*'

Her shove at a time when Eliot's genius stood on one poem
alone, when parents opposed a poetic career and urged a
professorship, suggests that this marriage may not have been
entirely wrong for him at this point. The force his wife
provides, as well as a justification for his physical distance
from family pressure, may well have been vital to his promise.
Vivienne exerts her force not solely on Eliot's behalf – she
enjoys the fight and exults as she wins: from now on, neither
Henry nor any other Eliots need think they can make a move
that will escape her eye.

An alternative and less certain weapon was pathos. She
discovered ordeals in ordinary actions: her hand cannot write
in ink on any but the smoothest paper, she claims almost
proudly. Many of her letters link pathos to poverty in order
to play on the Eliots. In the bold letter to her brother-in-law,
written on a train north to her birthplace in Lancashire, she
laments the fact that they have only £22 left in the bank – and
then, suddenly, she blunders into a defensive position,
possibly a replay of a recent difference with her husband:
she'd had to have new clothes for this visit to old friends who
were very, *very* rich. 'Unfortunately it has meant writing to
your Father for help again.' (Imagine the pressed lips of plain-
living Eliots reading this in their rockers in the sparely
furnished living-room at Eastern Point – generations of New
England thrift behind them: 'Buy it new, wear it out, make it
do – *do without.*')

Vivienne blundered on blithely, forgetting that her father-in-law manufactured bricks: she would have the Eliots know that she had left *provincial* manufacturing people behind her, and now moved in a superior 'set' – she was going to 'hate' this return to old friends, and meant to drop them as soon as she 'decently' could. This has a Veneering not a classy sound. And we hear the on-and-on of Vivienne's voice: she couldn't possibly be expected to cancel a visit arranged long before (though she was prepared to cross others' plans when her interests required it: in 1915 her husband had been compelled to cut short a fraught visit to his family and cross the Atlantic without delay because she was 'very ill').

Both Eliot and his wife used the image of a couple in a cage. Vivienne, in one of her sketches, pictured the cage as a deadly isolation, where the confined woman beats herself against the bars. To Eliot the cage meant the opposite, the perennial lack of privacy: 'It is terrible', he wrote, 'to be alone with another person.'

One of Eliot's friends said that posterity would probably judge Vivienne Eliot harshly. She could turn on her husband with barbed accusations. She must have been, in her thwarted, insomniac moods, grim company. Eliot had no notion how to cope with her moods – during the first year of marriage and again, ten years later, he turned helplessly to Russell and others for advice.

It seems that, from Vivienne Eliot's angle too, the marriage must have been a miserable trial. She mentions that her husband, too, was often sick at night. She reports to Charlotte Eliot how 'very very trying' it was to have him entirely at home – his 'black silent moods, and the irritability' – at the start of 1917 when he had given up his teaching post at Highgate school and had not yet found another job. In 1919 she writes to a friend: 'Tom is IMpossible – full of nerves, really not well, very bad cough, very morbid and grumpy. I wish you had him!' Vivienne's diary for 1919 (the only year she kept a diary during her married life) shows a physically energetic woman, an enthusiastic bather and ballroom dancer, who is self-sufficient and high-spirited, but only when her husband is not there. Signs of neurotic complaining reappear on summer weekends when, after a week or a fortnight's separation, she and Eliot are reunited. When he leaves her in the country and returns to town she becomes exhilarated by her natural surroundings. On 10 July 1919 she has a 'wonderful impression of Bosham [near Chichester, on the south coast] in the evening, last thing. Full moon, and only half dark at 10, and a mist. The water like glass.' On 19 September 1919 (at Wittering, nearby, with a favourite companion, Mary Hutchinson): 'Cold stormy day. Sat in the shed with the wind roaring & the shed creaking like a ship.' By contrast her references to her husband are laconic: Tom had a cold, and was cross. Tom went to France. Alone, in August, she enjoys 'the feeling of London in the still heat'. Her husband returned 'very nice at first, depressed in evening'. The diary suggests that, quite possibly, she was not a parasite all the time (mainly when ill), that she tried hard with her husband and encouraged an unusual degree of freedom.

Vivienne's writings show an eager, emotional manner, with vague romantic yearnings, and a daring and nerve that could be easily daunted. Although she hadn't the health or confidence to pursue any one of her talents, she is not to be dismissed lightly. In the last month of the war, in October 1918, she expounds a state of waiting in which a public mood blends with her own: 'life is so feverish and yet so dreary at the same time, and one is always waiting, waiting for something. Generally waiting for some particular strain to be over. One thinks, when this is over I will write. And then there is something else. For *months* now I have waited for T. to be settled [over joining the army]. . . . I am also waiting to be well.'

In this way she receded into the background of her husband's life and remained there, a phantom of pain and reproach. 'Vivien's assistance' which 'preserved' the poet in Eliot (as he owned after four years), was in time obscured: in later years, he did not acknowledge it, unlike his gratitude to Pound. His friends remembered a chic and literate woman who became, through illness, too 'hysterical' to be endured.

We feel invited to dismiss her as a burden Eliot painstakingly upheld, beyond the call of duty, for many long years. She left no one to speak for her, and no evidence in her diaries that the marriage was disastrous from her point of view, but we know that her initial impulse towards Eliot was generous and that she continued to back him as a poet. After a talk with Mary Hutchinson about giving oneself up to others, she wrote on her husband's thirty-first birthday in 1919: 'I had never seen before we spoke how much I have done that with Tom.' She offered her sea-hoard of curious oddments and trophies, gossip, and spars of knowledge, like the woman in Pound's 'Portrait d'une Femme'. She wished to make herself part of the poet's mind. Eliot would not grant her fantasy – he would not allow her the inspirational role – but remained flat and sometimes ashamed of her. And so she, in turn, retreated – into attention-getting illness. She ended tragically as the emblem of the material world against which Eliot's religious impulse tugged, to free itself.

Two Viviennes – one pathetic, one terrible – appear in photographs. There is a small timid woman, a visitor hesitating in the doorway at Garsington, pretty and delicate in skirts drooping about her slender ankles, or dwarfed by the confident stature of Philip Morrell in the garden. She did not much care for literary gatherings. In her 1919 diary she comments that Edith Sitwell's party was dull, a Hutchinson dinner – with Nancy Cunard, Osbert Sitwell, and Duncan Grant – was 'very drunken and rowdy but not fun'. Then there is the other, later image, in their next home at 9 Clarence Gate Gardens in 1922. Her face is harder and her nose bolder beneath a modish bob. She stands in her own domain – next to a tea-kettle on a gas-ring – her hands on her hips, her feet slightly apart.

After Eleanor Hinkley, Emily Hale, and the controlled moral world of Jane Austen, Eliot found himself, unprepared, in the bottomless pit of a Dostoevsky novel. 'If I have not seen the battlefields, I have seen other strange things . . . and it all seems like a dream,' he tried to explain to Eleanor. His wife's reckless touch of madness rode in tandem with a mania of his own – sexual and racial furies harnessed by icy rigour in tight rhymes. 'We were off our heads all the summer,' Vivienne announced at the end of 1918. Together, they fronted a world of extremes. Vivienne 'is a person who lives on a knife edge and will end a criminal or a saint,' Russell said. 'She has a perfect capacity for both.'

*

When Eliot was living in Russell's flat during the second year of the war, Russell confided strange observations which later found their way into *The Waste Land*. After watching the troop trains – full of patriots – depart from Waterloo, he would see London's bridges collapse and sink, and the whole great city vanish like a morning mist. 'Its inhabitants began to seem like hallucinations,' he said. He would wonder whether the world in which he thought he lived was not merely a product of his own nightmares.

In the autumn of 1915 Eliot came to settle in a city at war and saw it from the estranged angle of a non-participant. He saw a London from which almost all its young men were withdrawn, and only the sick and unfit, the elderly, the women, the workers, and a few pacifist intellectuals – outcasts – remained. He knew the gloom, the privation, and the deadness of London in those war years. 'In the winter of 1915–16,' wrote D. H. Lawrence, 'the spirit of the old London collapsed. The city, in some way, perished, perished from being the heart of the world, and became a vortex of broken passions, lusts, hopes, fears, and horrors. The integrity of London collapsed, and the genuine debasement began . . .' Virginia Woolf recalled silent people huddled in buses, looking cadaverous in the blue light (for the lights were all shrouded in blue paint) and the consenting mass of civilians whom one did not wish to join – 'the strutting; the tiptoeing; the pasty; the ferret-eyed; the bowler-hatted, servile innumerable army of workers'. Eliot shared in the horror of the English intellectual at the dehumanisation of his countrymen, but I imagine that he felt less shocked, more resigned. The war bore out his dim view of human nature.

Verdenal had joined up at the outbreak of war, and early in 1915 was sent to the Dardanelles. There, he was cited for bravery when, after an attack of pleurisy, he did not hesitate to spend most of a night in water up to his waist in order to evacuate the wounded. Shortly after, on 2 May 1915, he was killed while tending a wounded soldier on the battlefield. Eliot dedicated his first volume to 'Jean Verdenal *mort aux Dardanelles*'. The wording does not acknowledge Eliot's indebtedness to Verdenal; it is a gesture towards the war and its sacrifice – with which Eliot personally had little to do.

Although he said he was not sure what he thought of the war, he was sure he was not a pacifist. After the United States entered the war in 1917, he made belated but feverish efforts to enlist in August and September 1918. There were conventional incentives – a sense of duty, the wish to belong, and (he hoped) more freedom for writing. He wished to please his mother, who for years had been writing urgent newspaper appeals to Americans to fight and even wrote a war song for the Boston *Herald*. Pound, it is almost needless to say, opposed Eliot's enlistment, and he went so far as to go to the Embassy in person to point out that if this were a war for civilisation, not merely for democracy, it was folly to shoot one of the six or seven Americans capable of understanding the word. Eliot was disqualified (as expected) for active service in the US navy on account of tachycardia and his old hernia, nor, to his frustration and chagrin, did he get a commission in the Quartermasters or Interpreters Corps or in Army Intelligence despite excellent letters of recommendation from sixteen worthies including the Dean of Merton, Harold Joachim, Osbert Sitwell, Arnold Bennett, Charles William Eliot, and George Herbert Palmer. This seems to have been more the result of red tape than rejection. The year after the war ended he re-created in one of his poems the emotions of a man who had not fought in rain or knee-deep in mud –

someone who had never ventured from city retreats into heroic scenes.

Not only did Eliot miss the battles of his generation, he was also at a distance from civilians at home. His first encounters with Londoners – apart from his wife, Russell, and Pound's circle – were brief and unsatisfactory. Vivienne describes wonderfully their sense of themselves as two people from sheltered, middle-class homes who found themselves adrift 'in a little noisy corner, with slums and low streets, and poor shops close around us – . . . it is like being in a wilderness, we are just 2 waifs who live perched up in our little flat – no-one around us knows us, or sees us, or bothers to care how we live or what we do, or whether we live or not.'

Eliot's first post was as a schoolmaster at High Wycombe for one term at an annual salary of £140; then he moved to his next school in Highgate at the slightly increased salary of £160. For a little over a year, from September 1915 to the end of 1916, his days were spent with schoolboys to whom he was a foreigner, 'the American master'. He felt no interest in them, and looked upon teaching not as a means of expression but as a barrier to it. 'After all,' he said, 'all I wanted to do was write poetry, and teaching seemed to take up less time than anything else, but that was a delusion.' Teaching drained his energy so that he had no desire to write, even during vacations. 'To hold the class's attention you must project your personality on them, and some people enjoy doing that; I couldn't, it took too much out of me.'

Eliot loathed schoolmastering but stuck to it, partly because he needed money for his wife's medical bills, partly for self-respect. Honest toil – regular employment, set hours, a full-scale commitment – had been for generations the self-affirming activity of the Eliot family. It would have been unlikely for Eliot to make a precarious living, as did many English writers, by freelance or part-time work. He had to prove himself to his father, who had decided, when Eliot made his rash marriage and deferred his prospects at Harvard, that he had wrecked his life. He had to recover the approval of his mother, who had always scorned 'the man without a hoe'. Rather bend beneath the strain of work, she urges in one of her poems, than lose your pride in action. She pitied him – 'it is like putting Pegasus into harness' – but she felt that he had, in the past, been overprotected and should now make his own future.

In the summer of 1916 Russell asked the art critic Clive Bell to befriend Eliot and, through Bell, Eliot came in contact with Roger Fry, Lytton Strachey, and other members of the Bloomsbury Group. At the same time, again through Russell, he was gathered into the social orbit of Lady Ottoline Morrell, who entertained leaders of the English intellectual scene like Aldous Huxley and Middleton Murry. He was treated kindly, invited to dinner at 46 Gordon Square, the home of Clive Bell, and to Garsington Manor, but he remained an outsider. They did not feel at ease with him. His correct dress and prim manners were not particularly endearing. His ostentatious learning (partly effrontery, he later admitted) did not impress. When Huxley met him, in December 1916, he wrote him off as 'just a Europeanized American, overwhelmingly cultured, talking about French literature in the most uninspired fashion imaginable'. Eliot, for his part, was 'bewildered' by Aldous, his biologist brother Julian Huxley, Eddy Sackville-West, and David Cecil, all clever young Oxford men of the time. His studied reserve constrained Cambridge disciples of the philosopher G. E. Moore who observed candour and truth as the highest good. Lytton Strachey found him nice at times, at other times 'rather ill and rather American; altogether not quite gay enough'. He added, though: 'But by no means to be sniffed at.'

Vivienne offended Lady Ottoline by walking Russell away, arm-in-arm, when they met in London – a show of possession or a bid for attention that others call bad manners. Lady Ottoline dismissed Vivienne as kittenish and refused to have her at Garsington. So long as Vivienne retained her hold on Russell, Eliot went to Garsington alone. His gravity appeared so monotonous, that Lady Ottoline named him 'the Undertaker'.

He was more appreciated by his wife's friend Mary

Hutchinson, a daughter of Winifred Strachey, petite, feminine, with a sleek head and a mask-like face. She was a long-time mistress of Clive Bell. Her tastes were avant-garde, and Eliot began to write to her about his reading and poetry with unusual openness. In June 1917, he attended one of the parties she gave with her husband, St John (known as Jack, a barrister and legal adviser to the Ministry of Reconstruction), at River House on the Thames at Hammersmith. Katherine Mansfield, who found it 'infernally boring', recorded Jack's performance as the butcher of America: 'Jack tied a white apron round himself and cut up, trimmed and smacked into shape the whole of America and the Americans. So nice for poor Eliot who grew paler and paler and more and more silent . . .'.

Lady Ottoline grew sympathetic after Russell discarded Vivienne. Between about 1919 and 1921, Vivienne was so winsome and affectionate that Ottoline could understand why some women fell in love with their own sex. According to Vivienne, Ottoline knew how Eliot was hurt and by whom. Vivienne mentions 'how often Ottoline used to say to me – and *how sadly* – "isn't Tom beautiful, Vivienne, such a *fine mind*, such a grand impression. Such a good *walk*." '

Even with her, one was expected, as everywhere Eliot went in English society, 'to be as brilliant as possible in the evenings – which does not necessarily imply *intellectual*'. It was foreign to the 'barbarous life in America', and 'damned hard work to live with a foreign nation and cope with them – one is always coming up against differences of feeling that make one feel humiliated and lonely. One remains always a foreigner.' His inherited caution as a New Englander made him fear to be frank – he might reveal 'a savage'. So he disguised himself, painstakingly, with protective resemblances to local society. 'It is like being always on dress parade – one can never relax. It is a great strain. And society is in a way much *harder*, *not* gentler. People are more aware of you, more critical, and they have no pity for one's mistakes or stupidities. . . . They are always intriguing and caballing; one must be very alert. They are sensitive, and easily become enemies.'

That Eliot was not really accepted was not wholly his fault. He had not been in any way fashioned by English life – neither by a public school, nor by a great university, nor by childhood or family associations – and had only his manner to recommend him. He was unaffected and charming with Sydney Schiff, who published under the name Stephen Hudson, and his wife, Violet, a musician who had studied with Tosti and accompanied Caruso. Like Vivienne she was given to unexplained temperatures, and perhaps this is one reason why the Schiffs warmed to the Eliots. Schiff liked Vivienne for her 'natural sincerity'. Violet was the warm-hearted and socially adept sister of Ada Leverson, whom Wilde had called 'the Sphinx'. She had married Schiff in 1911. He ran an influential magazine called *Arts and Letters* to which Eliot contributed, and he translated the final volumes of Proust into English. The Schiffs were friends of Proust and entertained a cosmopolitan circle. At their home Eliot met Arthur Symons, who had led him to Laforgue in 1909; the composer Frederick Delius; Middleton Murry and Katherine Mansfield; Wyndham Lewis; Charles Scott-Moncrieff, the future translator of Proust; and most important for Eliot's future, the first Viscountess Rothermere, who founded the *Criterion*, the ruling journal Eliot was to edit for nearly twenty years between the wars. After Pound left London for Paris at the end of the war, Schiff took his place as Eliot's backer – but by this stage Eliot was beginning to show a steely assurance of his own. By now he had the measure of the literary marketplace, what Virginia Woolf called 'the Underworld', and it remained only to conquer Virginia Woolf herself.

From the first, she rather liked him – his formidable air entertained her – but he remained peripheral to her life and, for a while in the early twenties, his self-pity became a bit tiresome. She did not look forward to his visits and used to sigh over him in her diary: O dear, Eliot on the phone again. It took her till 1935 – seventeen years of teas and talks and weekends – to decide that he was one of 'us'. In spite of God, she said, averting her eyes from what appeared to her (as the unbaptised daughter of a Victorian agnostic) incomprehensible piety. In truth, she had a sense of the soul and its 'moments of being' that meshed with the 'unattended moments' (the infinite 'thing') that provided unobtrusive high points in Eliot's poems. They were at one in their attention to life on an ordinary day, in their switch from visible action to invisible trains of consciousness, and not least in their Jamesian taste for the shadows of hidden lives. After his death, Virginia Woolf observed that James had shaped his art in 'the shadow in which the detail of so many things can be discerned which the glare of day flattens out'. A similar shadow haunts the crepuscular habitats of Eliot, as it haunts Woolf herself who, at the time of her comment, was setting up the antinomy of *Night and Day* (1919). She wanted to crack through the paving stone of public life and be enveloped in a mist. For both writers, the shadow in James made him a precursor of Modernism, reinforced by the Modernist shadow in Joseph Conrad: it falls upon the Thames, reflecting on the centre of civilisation an obscurity at the heart of *Heart of Darkness* (1902). Eliot's *Waste Land* (1922) was to expand that novel's 'sepulchral city', the deadly routines of London which an alien sees with a visionary 'horror' inaccessible to blinkered natives.

The main difference was that Eliot was by nature a solitary. He disguised this, of course, when it suited him, but Bloomsbury sensed something profoundly alien to their humanist faith in 'personal relations' – expressed most famously by 'only connect', the refrain of E. M. Forster's *Howard's End*. A yet deeper difference was Eliot's sternness and political conservatism, which jarred the skipping irreverence of the Bloomsbury Group. The Woolfs and the Bells coped with Eliot's punctiliousness by treating him as a family joke. They found him deliciously comic. 'Come to lunch,' Virginia would write to her brother-in-law. 'Eliot will be there in a four-piece suit.'

After Pound left, Eliot was aware of the pre-eminence of

the Bloomsbury Group, and continued to attach himself to its members and friends, in particular to Virginia Woolf and Mary Hutchinson. Pound wrote scornfully from Paris that they were an 'arse blasted lot' and urged Wyndham Lewis to 'get Eliot out of England somehow'. But Eliot remained, and welcomed Virginia Woolf's invitations. She, on her side, tried to ignore Eliot's allegiance to Pound, and challenged his façades that she might know him better. One night at a dinner party she dared to laugh in Eliot's white marble face and, to her surprise, was rewarded by an answering twinkle. In March 1921, after a visit to the theatre, she challenged him to confess his faults while they were cruising in a taxi through the damp market gardens of Hammersmith. He said that the worst thing in life for him was humiliation. From that time he began to relax his formality and, by the end of 1921, their friendship was firm. During the next twenty years of her life he cherished her good opinion, and once said that whoever else gave him approval, he only hoped 'that Mrs. Woolf'll'.

The turning-point in Eliot's relations with English writers came when the Egoist Press published his first volume of poems in 1917. When Eliot settled in London he had been an embryo professor; in 1917 he was born a poet. The critical time was probably March 1916 when he put off returning to America to defend his dissertation. In April, Eliot noted that he had fifteen to twenty publishable poems, and began to plan his first volume, *Prufrock and Other Observations.** Clive Bell took ten or twelve badly printed copies bound in cheap yellow jackets to an Easter party at Garsington. They were distributed; Katherine Mansfield read 'Prufrock' aloud, and Murry, Aldous Huxley, the Morrells, and Lytton Strachey applauded Eliot's talent.

By December 1917 Eliot was reading his poems under the auspices of the Red Cross to fashionable society in the Mayfair drawing-room of Lady Colefax. Also giving readings were troops of nervous Sitwells, Robert Graves, Siegfried

---

* 'Observations' was a title which the editor of *Poetry*, Harriet Monroe, gave to a few of these poems published earlier in her magazine, and which Eliot had approved.

Sassoon, Aldous Huxley, a writer called Bob Nichols, who hooted and moaned war poetry, and Viola Tree, who declaimed in a voice cloyed with syrup. The elder statesman of English letters, Sir Edmund Gosse, who introduced the poets as 'bards', was shocked by Eliot's blasphemous 'Hippopotamus'. Eliot was also noticed for his polite manners. When Gosse rudely reproved him for being late, he listened quietly and did not protest, although he had come straight from his new post at Lloyds Bank. It occurred to Osbert Sitwell that he looked like an Aztec carving with his wide bone structure and 'yellow' eyes.

His failure to obtain a position with US Intelligence in August–September 1918 left a residue of resentment towards his country, and encouraged a shift in allegiance towards England. Americans were immature, he decided. They had certainly neglected to appreciate what he had to offer, unlike Lloyds Bank (who paid less than US Intelligence, but advanced him steadily, and with kind words, as an expert on foreign loans, work that verged on what he came to see as the interesting field of economics). More important to him was the respect of his growing circle of influential English contacts. 'No other nationality perhaps provides so dense an environment as the English,' he wrote in September. 'The *intelligent* Englishman is more aware of loneliness, has more reserves, than the man of intelligence of any other nation.' He recognised in the English flair for humour 'the instinctive attempt of a sensitive mind to protect beauty against ugliness; and to protect itself against stupidity'. Up to this point, he had kept open a channel with Harvard that would allow for a return, should his venture abroad fail; when his supporter at Harvard, Professor Woods, came to London in the summer of 1919, Eliot closed this off.

Towards the end of the war, he had begun to put in order his more recent poems written under Pound's eye. Leonard Woolf had approached him with a proposal:

Hogarth House
Paradise Road, Richmond, S.W.
19 Oct. 1918

Dear Mr Eliot,
  My wife and I have started a small private Printing Press,
and we print and publish privately short works which would
not otherwise find a publisher easily. We have been told by
Roger Fry that you have some poems which you wish to find a
publisher for. We both very much liked your book, *Prufrock*;
and I wonder whether you would care to let us look at the
poems with a view to publishing them.

Yours very truly
Leonard Woolf

I should add that we are amateurs at printing but we could, if
you liked, let you see our last production [Katherine Mans-
fields' *Prelude*].

On 15 November 1918, Eliot took three or four poems to
show the Woolfs at their workplace-home, Hogarth House,
in Richmond. Seven poems, including 'Mr. Eliot's Sunday
Morning Service', 'Whispers of Immortality', and 'Sweeney
Among the Nightingales', were printed by the Hogarth Press
in 1919 and bound in one of Fry's designs. Leonard and
Virginia Woolf made 190 copies, to be sold at half a crown
each.* It was a gesture of faith which helped strengthen
Eliot's position. 'There is a small and select public which
regards me as the best living critic, as well as the best living
poet, in England,' he informed his mother at this time, on 29
March 1919. 'I really think that I have far more *influence* on
English letters than any other American has ever had, unless
it be Henry James. I know a great many people, but there are
many more who would like to know me, and I can remain
isolated and detached.'

When Aiken returned to London after the war he found
Eliot 'so rootedly established, both socially and in the
"politics" (as it were) of literature . . . as to have achieved
what Emily Dickinson had called "overtakelessness": he had

---

* The edition sold out in a year with a net profit of £12-8-6. Eliot's
share was £3-2-6.

built the splendid ramparts round that rare new domain of his, and behind them he had become all but invisible, all but intangible'.

During this time of transformation Eliot was writing brief autobiographical fragments and poems which he kept separate from the quatrain poems he was writing for immediate publication. Between 1914 and 1919 the hoard consisted of three distinct batches, corresponding to Eliot's private trials: first the problems of religious awakening, then the problems of adaptation to a foreign city and to a demanding new wife. By 1919 Eliot had material for one long poem or series of poems. This was to emerge, three years later, as *The Waste Land*, the poem that fired the imagination of the 'lost' generation and made Eliot famous.

5

'THE HORROR! THE HORROR!'

MARY HUTCHINSON, WHO read *The Waste Land* soon after its completion, said it was 'Tom's autobiography'. Aiken called it 'his Inferno', parallel to a stage of 'his own emotional development'. Eliot himself said that it was only 'the relief of a personal . . . grouse against life'. *The Waste Land* is clearly more than this – it may be read as a satire on post-war London – but I shall trace the confessional element which, though covert or deliberately muted in the poem itself, is more obvious in the manuscript which goes back to 1914, a time when Eliot remarked to Aiken: 'It's interesting to cut yourself to pieces once in a while, and wait to see if the fragments will sprout.' Over the next seven and a half years, Eliot was accumulating a hoard of fragments, the earliest of which show a different bias from what emerged in 1922 as the poem of the century.

He justified the necessity for autobiography as opposed to formal biography. The definitive experiences in the life are so private – 'the awful daring of a moment's surrender' – no one else could know them. To know the man, we must follow the poem which alone will 'give the pattern . . . of the personal emotion, the personal drama and struggle, which no biography, however full and intimate, could give us'. We must venture, then, beyond biography, into the morass of the manuscript to determine the chronology of the accretions, and then, on the basis of that chronology, we may perceive the shaping pattern of the private life. There is no other hope of recovering this after death, Eliot is saying at the end of *The*

147

Waste Land, neither in wills or obituaries, nor in the memoirs of well-meaning friends and critics.

In the earliest fragments of the manuscript Eliot starts with what he called 'some rude unknown psychic material'. He speaks of impulses so inward that they are obscure even to himself. Such 'dark' experience must take its own unique form but, says Eliot, there is a 'shadowy' traditional form against which it shapes itself. From the beginning Eliot had in mind the traditional form of the spiritual journey through deathly ordeals. 'So through the evening . . .', written in 1914 and the source of part V (according to Eliot the most important part) of *The Waste Land,* is a quest for a sign.*

Faceless, nameless, the composite narrator of *The Waste Land* turns out to be a world-weary intellectual who has given up life for books, and can't find his way out of the stale plots of existence, stale words, stale ways of thinking and feeling. He is trapped to the point of horror, and escapes only momentarily into the soundless beat before the frenzied rhythms of the Jazz Age. Those silences are sites where residual emotion breaks through the clamour of horoscopes, dirty weekends, brothels, and other meaningless diversions. Contained within a workaday London from nine in the morning to nightfall, the poem achieves its extraordinary impact from an abrupt fusion of dramatic vignettes of urban degradation with an unspoken confession beating with violence against sealed lips. It signals, and shuts us out, waving us ironically towards the coupling of a bored typist and crass clerk – one of the repellent scenes of sexual history.

It was fashionable for long stretches of the twentieth century to read the poem as an intellectual game for scholars who could identify allusions. Lesser readers were to have access to it only through their guidebooks.† Many erudite

---

* This is a more sophisticated version of one of his mother's traditional poems, 'Ring Easter Bells', in which the soul tends nearer to God along an upward path, and bells herald 'the faith that clearer vision brings'.

† 'Ignore any book calling itself a guide to Eliot', the great Eliot scholar, Helen Gardner, advised students at Oxford at the start of her last Eliot lectures before her retirement in 1975.

readers of Eliot's century actually had no idea what the poem was about, while readers with any sort of religious background knew at once: they saw through the crust of erudition to the residue of timeless forms – sermon, soul history, confession – almost drowned out by the motor-horns, pub talk, and the beguiling patter of a bogus medium, all that noise of wasted lives.

Soul history and sermon are the dominant forms of American writing from the time of the Puritan settlement in the seventeenth century; to retrieve them is to be that quintessential New Englander which Eliot claimed transplantation brought out. For he shared with Emerson, Thoreau, and Dickinson, and Whitman too, a guarded mode of confession. Unlike St Augustine or Rousseau, who draw us into intimacy, these Americans throw the onus of introspection back into the lap of the reader. Their confessions, like *The Waste Land*, are fragmentary and, left so deliberately incomplete, demand a reciprocal effort. The point lies not in their content so much as in the reader's act of self-discovery and judgement. The purpose is not to expose the speaker but to create the reader.

This requires from atrophied souls an act of recognition and renewal, closed to those imprisoned in the waste. To reach through *The Waste Land* to the sermon that haunts it, transforms the reader – any reader. Literacy is not necessary, for it's a poem best heard. The rhythms of the Bible beat behind it, speaking to us subliminally with prophetic power: the lamentation of Jeremiah, 'For my people . . . have forsaken me the fountain of living waters, and hewed them out cisterns, broken cisterns, that can hold no water'; and Ezekiel's warning cry, 'And your altars shall be desolate, and your images shall be broken. . . . In all your dwelling places the cities shall be laid waste . . .'.

At a distance from Eliot's age, we look back to a poem that seemed to speak for and to its time, and read it anew as a poem that speaks beyond its time about the ordeals of a life in the process of becoming exemplary.

Eliot was haunted by the exemplary lives of the chosen,

Dante and St Augustine. For several years, between writing the first fragments in 1914 and the finale of the poem in 1921, Eliot was cut off from a 'sign', so that the soul's advance and the 'grouse' could not cohere. It was not until he heard 'What the Thunder Said', during a breakdown in December 1921, that he was able to conceive, once more, a special destiny, and so complete his long-unfinished poem.

*

At the age of twenty-eight, when Eliot was still a graduate student living in an attic at 16 Ash Street in Cambridge, Massachusetts, and toying with fantasies of religious extravagance, he wrote three fragments from which he later took lines, setting, and ideas for the finale of *The Waste Land*. All three fragments are concerned with revelation and its aftermath: the attractions and problems of 'turning' or conversion.

In 'After the turning . . .' a seeker is turning from the daily world. By night he faces another world – inaccessible as yet, hovering behind bristling spears and flickering lights. If he repudiated the futile shows of our world, would it of itself fall away? After prayers and much painful soul-searching, it does, at least momentarily, disappear. As the stars go out, he finds himself on the brink of a river filled with tears and blackened by suffering. On the further bank, a pagan garrison threatens oncoming sinners, suggesting an inferno yet to be traversed. There seems to be for Eliot, as for Dante, no other way.

Another fragment tries to put into words the substance of a vision. There is a strange infusion of power:

> I am the Resurrection and the Life
> I am the things that stay and those that flow.
> I am the husband and the wife
> And the victim and the sacrificial knife
> I am the fire, and the butter also.

This divine voice speaks, like Emerson's Brahma, of an all-

encompassing energy through which we transcend the vicissitudes of fortune.* Neither Emerson nor Eliot found truth in
what William James called the 'professional philosophy
shop'. As a philosopher, William James acknowledged that
for certain minds truth would seem to exist for the express
confusion of the machinery of philosophy and to reveal itself
in whispers to the meek lovers of the good in their solitude.

The third fragment is 'So through the evening . . .' As the
poet-pilgrim climbs the pathway of the mind, two companions appear, dreamlike other selves. One is a crazed adventurer. He dares to turn himself upside down to see a new
world of reversed images; he hears unexpected, miraculous
voices:

A man distorted by some mental blight
Yet of abnormal powers
I saw him creep head downward down a wall
And upside down in air were towers
Toiling reminiscent bells
And there were chanting voices out of cisterns and of wells.

The poet sees a conversion scene and is drawn to
participate ('My feverish impulses gathered head'). Then,
suddenly, this dream is replaced by another in which a diver
sinks through layers of water, discarding all ordinary faculties
of perception and communication. He surrenders to

*.Obviously, the first line comes from Christian liturgy. Valerie Eliot
noted (*facs. WL*, p. 130) the source of both poems in the *Bhagavad-Gita*, ix.
16:

> I am the rite, the sacrifice
> The offering for the dead, the healing herb:
> I am the sacred formula, the sacred butter am I,
> I am the fire, and I the oblation [offered in the fire].

Michael Wood noticed another likely source in Baudelaire's 'L'Héauton-
timo-rouménos':

> Je suis la plaie et le couteau!
> Je suis le soufflet et la joue!
> Je suis les membres et la roue,
> Et la victime et le bourreau!

an irrational impulse, swimming down rather than up, to the calm still deep where seaweed, purple and brown, crowns him. It is a reckless quest, an act of faith.

A final apparition presents a different type: a man lies on his back, passive and inert. He feels estranged from people he knows, even though, like Prufrock, he chooses to remain among them. 'It seems to me I have been a long time dead,' he confesses. 'Do not report me to the established world.' Two seers are reckless explorers, transgressing the boundaries of normal experience; the last is a jaded and time-worn malingerer on the rim of the old world. What they have in common is that all despise the known world; all have, in their different ways, to 'die' that a new order may come into being.

If Eliot had lived in the time of Dante or, more plausibly, in colonial New England, the sanity of seers would not have been the issue it was for a man coming to adulthood in the second decade of the twentieth century. Eliot argued that once there existed 'a psychological habit, the trick of which we have forgotten, but as good as any of our own. We have nothing but dreams, and we have forgotten that seeing visions – a practice now relegated to the aberrant and uneducated – was once a more significant, interesting, and disciplined kind of dreaming. We take it for granted that our dreams spring from below: possibly the quality of our dreams suffers in consequence.'

It is not possible to understand Eliot's dreams and the associated confessional impulse outside the context of a native tradition. It is true that Eliot's bonds were not with the American of his own day, but he shared with earlier Americans a barely acknowledged bond: with those who opposed spiritual deadness through revivals like the Great Awakening and Transcendentalism, and with those New England saints who were subject at all times to incursions from the unknown. In the seventeenth century New Englanders kept private records of their soul's health, their setbacks or progress towards grace. Spiritual autobiographies flourished in England after 1640 and then declined towards the end of the century, but in America they never flagged and, in fact, the habit of self-examination never really died out. In the journals of Emerson a Yankee is still taking his pulse, as in the poems of Dickinson and Eliot, and in *The Education of Henry Adams*, a book Eliot recommended to his mother, calling Adams our 'cousin'. In the early, more obviously personal fragments of the *Waste Land* manuscript, Eliot climbed the twisting path of his mind; he dived into his own deep waters; he kept an account of signs and balanced them against the soul's diseases.

It is easy to dismiss these earliest fragments as unpromising scraps, but together they announce a persistent mood. *Ash-Wednesday* revives the 'turning' towards the religious life. Other dreamlike poems of the twenties – 'Doris's Dream Songs', 'The Hollow Men' – move so naturally out of the fragments of 1914 that, in retrospect, the satires Eliot wrote between 1917 and 1919 seem like something of a digression from his poetic career. During his first years in England, Eliot played half-heartedly at coming alive through emigration, marriage, and a new milieu. His experiment was reinforced by Pound's urgent poetic ambitions and Vivienne's equally urgent emotional claims. In 1914 Eliot, still free, imagined 'turning' from the material world – but Pound and Vivienne turned him back to face it.

Early in the history of the manuscript, in February 1915,* there appears a would-be saint who vanished from the more impersonal *Waste Land*. Eliot named the character after Narcissus, Bishop of Jerusalem, who, towards the end of the second century, hid himself in the desert for many years. 'The Death of Saint Narcissus' is a martyr's tale, the last of the martyr cluster at the close of Eliot's student years. 'Come,' he says in the opening lines, 'I will show you . . . his bloody cloth and limbs.' Of the 'saint's' actual career Eliot

---

* The paper of the first draft of 'The Death of St Narcissus' (*facs. WL*, p. [90]) is British, 'Excelsior Fine British Make', the same paper Eliot used for 'Mr. Apollinax'. On 2 February 1915 Eliot alluded to the two poems in a letter to Pound ('I understand that Priapism, Narcissism, etc. are not approved of').

says virtually nothing; he concentrates on the inner life of a solitary who feels most intensely alive when God's arrows pierce and mar his flesh. St Narcissus wishes to become 'a dancer to God' and cuts himself off from his kind, but sees no divine light, only his own flaws – his self-enthralment, his indifference to others, his delight in the burning arrows. So, Narcissus fails to receive a sign. And in that failure lies the necessity for a more demanding venture. We might see *The Waste Land*, in fact all of Eliot's subsequent work, in the context of this failed saint.

If St Narcissus fails the desert ordeal and succumbs to disappointment, such setbacks are common, in fact essential, to the plot of spiritual biography. Bunyan set the pattern for a life that persists in an atmosphere of risk and frightful doubt. God's abandonment of Bunyan did not disqualify him from the pursuit of grace. On the contrary, it excited in him, as in Eliot, more rigorous self-analysis and self-condemnation. Behind both stands Augustine's exhibition of his life as a pathological development, from the evil effects of which he is saved by a dramatic call.

The *Confessions*, the first of their kind, were written in 397–8 when Aurelius Augustinus was forty-four. To confess – the Latin *confiteor* – means to reveal, to acknowledge, to proclaim, to praise God, and he intends all these, and more: to reveal more than he knows: 'I will confess therefore, what I know, yea, and what I know not.' His emphasis is less on the past than on being and becoming: 'not discovering what I have been but what I now am, and what I am yet'. Augustine does not intend to confess in the ordinary way: the ultimate aim is divine revelation, but somehow self-revelation steals the show: what he calls the 'disease of the flesh' and its 'deadly pleasures' in conflict with his higher will. 'My two wills, one carnal one spiritual were in conflict and in the conflict wasted my soul.' God is *medice meus*: 'Behold I hide not my wounds; thou art the physician and I the patient.' His life is a celebration of divine power which heals a man of an extreme temper, a fornicator who wished to be an ascetic. After his conversion to Christianity, he became Bishop of

Hippo in North Africa, and in 413–26, following the sack of Rome, wrote *The City of God* (*De Civitate Dei*). A saint in the making, he exposed himself as a lustful man who for too long failed to find a cure. 'Da mihi castitatem et continentiam, sed noli modo,' he begged God, 'give me chastity and continence, but do not give it yet.'

Eliot's fascination for 'Saint Narcissus' lies in diagnosing his failure. The well-known dangers of gazing into the mirror of election are pride and despair. Those, Eliot would face later; his concern here is with the sensuality of self-regard. It gratifies his senses to think of himself as a tree tangling its roots together, or as a slippery fish, or as a smooth girl raped by an old man. He dares to court God with the same appetite for self-gratifying sensation. Narcissus has no moral impulse, only a masochistic one ('His flesh was in love with the burning arrows'). He wants to reform himself, to be more than himself, but instead of self-enhancement there is, at the end, the shock of self-loss. After the encounter he finds himself burnt out, abandoned on the hot sand, dry and stained, his beauty gone, his clothes bloody, and the taste of death in his mouth.

Although Eliot derides the passion of Narcissus, the portrait is in some ways more penetrating than earlier caricatures, Prufrock or St Sebastian. This is a case study of peculiar narrowness and moral intimacy. Eliot ignores the kind of physical and social detail which enlivened the portrait of Prufrock, and narrows in on the 'saint's' secret pretensions and obsession with pain. Narcissus went, we are told, to the death *he* wanted. His death is not, as it purports to be, a religious drama, but a self-indulgence: the redness of his wounds 'satisfied him'. In an essay on Dante, Eliot distinguished between the pain which issues from the damned themselves, from 'their own perpetually perverted nature', and the pain of purgatory, which is 'deliberately and consciously accepted by the penitent'. Eliot's saint is too grotesque to be fully human, but his emotional vices are real. His attitudinising is deplorable, but his sense of abandonment is genuine:

Now he is green, dry and stained
With the shadow in his mouth.

This final picture of the failed saint, sealed in Eliot's matter-of-fact condemnation, generates unexpected sympathy.

The condition of dryness came to dominate *The Waste Land*. Associated with this condition is the desert setting which here and in *The Waste Land* offers a proper place for a religious drama. The mood of the solitary under his rock was the vantage-point from which Eliot chose to reflect on urban despair in the twentieth century. In 'Saint Narcissus', *The Waste Land*, and later 'The Hollow Men', he cultivated the state of mind of those early Christians who looked forward to the imminent ruin of a decadent civilisation. Precedents in the Bible and among the desert saints of the early Middle Ages were revived in the imagination of American Puritans who transported themselves 'into a *desert land* in America ... in the way of *seeking first the Kingdom of God*'. 'So through the evening' ends with a decision to leave town. Narcissus leaves because 'men's ways' interfere with self-expression:

He could not live men's ways, but became a dancer to God.
If he walked in city streets, in the streets of Carthage
He seemed to tread on faces, on convulsive thighs and
knees.
So he came out to live under the rock.   (first draft)

The city evokes images of hell and sin, Dante walking over bodies beaten down on the ground and Augustine's cauldron of unholy loves during his youth in Carthage. Narcissus sets up an antithesis that persists in *The Waste Land* between damned city and the desert. Here is the hot sand and rock, glimpsed in part I, 'The Burial of the Dead', and measured at length in part V, 'What the Thunder Said'.

Eliot's imaginary desert has a parallel in the Grail romances where a knight will traverse a waste in his quest for grace. Eliot's desert has a parallel too in the way the Puritans conceived of New England – as a howling desert – because they associated their Migration with the Israelite exodus.

Their errand in the wilderness was to create a new ideal for mankind. In 'The Man Without the Hoe' Charlotte Eliot hails America as the place where pilgrims came, not out of greed, but to try themselves morally in a wilderness, to face 'the rocky shore' and 'a churlish climate'. This notion of pilgrimage from imperfection to perfection was deeply rooted in Eliot's family and their Puritan past. For him to experience the world as a waste was a prerequisite to experiencing it in faith.

The first three pieces of the *Waste Land* manuscript were obviously fragments, but 'The Death of Saint Narcissus' was a complete poem. Pound submitted Eliot's second draft to *Poetry* in August 1915, while Eliot was briefly in America. Evidently, this was against Eliot's wishes – he might have considered the poem too confessional – for when he returned to London he withdrew it from publication. There is another possible explanation. As the conditions of Eliot's own life in London, bound up as he was in 1915 with Pound and Vivienne, undermined the prospect of solitary commitment, he began to play down the issue in his poetry. By the time Eliot produced the final draft of *The Waste Land* the dream of sainthood had almost wholly disappeared.

*

For a year and a half after Eliot's marriage he felt as if he had dried up. He often feared that Prufrock was 'a swan-song'. Yet almost immediately, he perceived his marriage as future material. In January 1916, he confided to Aiken that although he was not actually writing he had '*lived* through material for a score of long poems in the last six months'. It was during this period with a suicidal wife he could not console, pressured further by financial hardship in a country at war which, Eliot told his father, belittled private suffering, that he accumulated in their first sharpness the impressions of London that formed the basis of the first three, urban sections of *The Waste Land*. In new fragments written between 1916 and 1919* Eliot turned from his earlier preoccupation with model lives to see what could be learnt from ordinary lives around him – a wife, a merchant, and fishermen lounging on the banks of the Thames. The two ventures are complementary, and remained so throughout *The Waste Land*: one way of proclaiming sainthood is by abandoning civilisation for a solitary watch; the other is by discerning in one's civilisation the moral contours of a wasteland – lust and avarice, mindless workers bound upon the wheel of fortune, and undone women.

Eliot's most confessional fragments have to do with a mismatched couple. In 'The Death of the Duchess' (rewritten in 1921 for part II of *The Waste Land*) the wife is playing a scene in a love-drama while the husband is absorbed in a quite different, more sinister plot of life and death.† The

---

* My supposition is that 'The Death of the Duchess' and a collection of fragments written on small 'Hieratica Bond' sheets from a notepad – 'Elegy', 'Dirge', 'O City City', 'London', and 'The river sweats . . .' – were written between 1916 and 1919. This cannot yet be conclusively proved and I have doubts about the date of 'The river sweats . . .'. The fact that fragments were written on the same paper is no guarantee that they were written at the same time. Valerie Eliot tells me there is a letter to Eliot, written in 1919, in which the correspondent refers to 'The Death of the Duchess' and Mr Bleistein (in 'Dirge'). The theme of death by water and the name Bleistein appear in poems written in 1918 and 1919. The idea for 'Dirge' and its first line came from the Proteus episode of *Ulysses*, published by the *Little Review* in May 1918 and republished by Eliot in the *Egoist* in March–April 1919. The form of 'Elegy', on the verso of 'Dirge', suggests it was written during Eliot's quatrain period (1917–19). The two City fragments would have been written after the spring of 1917 when Eliot began his career as a bank clerk in the City. Taking in all the evidence, 1918 seems a reasonable date for the Hieratica fragments.

† *facs.* WL, pp. [104–6]. It might be possible to be more specific about the date by matching the paper with that of non-*Waste Land* manuscripts but, in the absence of other clues, the paper evidence is inconclusive. The paper matches that of an unpublished review (1916) of HD's translation of choruses from *Iphigenia in Aulis* (Berg Collection). It also matches a draft of 'Gerontion', which Eliot sent to John Rodker in the summer of 1919 (David Schwab Collection, Alderman Library, Univ. of Virginia at Charlottesville). In a letter to Rodker (9 July 1919) Eliot mentioned the prospect of another poem, about the same length as 'Gerontion'; this might be 'The Death of the

husband is a solitary who finds the continual physical proximity of his wife unendurable. His only hope of life is to escape from the marriage, but to do so would mean death – psychological death – for his mate. The title suggests a sequel to 'The Death of Saint Narcissus': as God denies the saint his chosen role, so the husband shuns the wife. 'The Death of the Duchess' shows a couple trapped in a hotel bedroom and unable to communicate their separate needs. (Eliot called the 1921 version 'In the Cage'.) Silently, the wife urges her claims as she brushes her hair in the firelight, her bare arms poised above her head. Silently, the husband longs to escape through the door. There is no respite from their differences, not even sleep, only barren diversions, a game of chess, an afternoon drive. (In one of his January 1916 health-bulletins to Russell, while Vivienne recuperated from a suicidal state at the Torbay Hotel, Torquay, Eliot mentioned an afternoon drive in a hired car after one of her bad nights: 'Vivien is not very well today. . . . As it was a lovely afternoon, however, we took a taxi drive along the shore. . . . You could not have chosen a better place for Vivien: it's a sign how badly she needed it, when even under the absolutely *perfect* conditions you have provided for her she is still so weak and fatigued. . . . She is alright when she is lying down, but immediately she gets up is very faint.' Two days later came the next bulletin: 'Vivien is wretched today – another bad night.')

Duchess'. I think it likely Eliot wrote the fragments before 1918. There is a joking reference among Pound's comments on 'Whispers of Immortality' to a Duchess who is outraged by Grishkin's animality (*IMH*, p. 371). Pound may have been alluding to 'The Death of the Duchess' in his *Egoist* review of Eliot's poetry, June 1917, when he says that a great deal of the poetry is personal and in no way derives from Webster and others.

The poem is the first of the *Waste Land* fragments in typescript: Eliot used his own typewriter which he had brought with him from Harvard. According to Eliot there were never any handwritten drafts of the sections in typescript, only scattered lines (letter to Quinn, 21 Sept. 1922). Eliot composed some *Waste Land* fragments on his Harvard typewriter, others on an alternative typewriter, probably the one his brother left for his use in August 1921.

Eliot's Duchess would seem to point to Webster's Duchess of Malfi, a proud, self-assertive woman whose reckless marriage to her steward leads to her ruin. But this allusion, like most of Eliot's is so coloured by personal circumstance that to pursue it is pointless.* Eliot shapes his marital scene ostensibly in terms of drama, but there is no dialogue and the husband shuns his role, craves solitude and anonymity.† Within the privacy of his mind he dwells on memories and dreams of metamorphosis, but he cannot act or speak in relation to his mate. Eliot's later comments about the dead wife in *The Family Reunion* are suggestive of the Duchess: 'She has sometimes talked of suicide,' Eliot wrote. 'She is trying to play one of her comedies with him [the husband] – to arouse *any* emotion in him is better than to feel that he is

---

* The same applies to 'In the Cage', which, like 'Portrait of a Lady', is a title derived from Henry James, but like so many of Eliot's allusions has little bearing on the poem. It is almost always best to respond to the literal import of Eliot's words. At first, many of Eliot's reviewers were all too conscious that, as they offered their readings, the poet himself might mutter deprecatingly, 'That is not what I meant at all. / That is not it, at all.' Critics began to evade the emotional demands of the verse by fastening on the erudition that studs its surface. By the 1950s pedants seemed to have settled for the routine business of identifying allusions. The Bloomsbury critic Desmond MacCarthy shrewdly analysed the appeal of Eliot to academic vanity: 'when a reader seizes an obscure reference he is flattered; it gives him a little thrill. But though this thrill may seal him one of the poet's admirers, it is not an aesthetic thrill.' Eliot confirmed this in an address to the Author's Club (6 May 1955), reported in the *TLS* as 'Author Against Critics': source-hunting, he said, is necessary to Joyce, but 'when applied to most poetry, more likely to lead the reader farther *away* from the true meaning of the poem (the meaning of which is communicated first emotionally, by the rhythms and the imagery) instead of leading him to it'. Anyway, as Eliot is always repeating himself in one way or another, it matters less to miss an allusion than to miss the moments of emotion that break through the crust of erudition.

† The silences and obscure menace of the dramatic poetry Eliot wrote outside of the theatre seem to lead into the plays Harold Pinter would write in the 1960s. Vivien Merchant taking five deathly silent minutes (it seemed) to cross her knees in *The Homecoming* in a New York production in about 1968 reminds me of Eliot's Duchess in this scene and also of the secret Furies in Eliot's 'homecoming' play of 1939, *The Family Reunion*.

not noticing her.' In 1917 Eliot was generalising crassly from private misfortune: his letters to Pound repeatedly dismiss women as unworthy of attention, lower beings. In one of the drafts of 'Whispers of Immortality', in May–June 1918, he deplores the social framework that demeans a Son of God to tending his wife. Hopefully, she'd die:

> Our sighs pursue the vanishd shade
> And breathe a sanctified amen,
> And yet the Sons of God descend
> To entertain the wives of men.

> And then the Female Soul departs
> The Sons of Men turn up their eyes.
> The Sons of God embrace the Grave –
> The Sons of God are very wise.

'Elegy' is another manuscript poem about a mismatched couple. Although it was not retained in any form in *The Waste Land*, it is interesting for the husband's psychological terror and the same clash of two irreconcilable plots. The wife belongs in a tale of Poe, and her determination to possess her mate beyond death conflicts with Eliot's old plot of sainthood. The 'Poe-bride' haunts her husband's mind with an energy that becomes more perverse, overwrought, and malevolent in proportion to his evasiveness. Again the wife is a complex of victim and demon (like the 'succuba eviscerate' in the honeymoon 'Ode'), and again the husband would be rid of her. Her revenge for having been emotionally dismissed is to refuse to go away. She will not allow the man to retire, but follows him tenaciously with her reproaches and emotional claims. She appears no longer lovely, but filled with avenging poison.* Scorpions hiss about her head.

In the last stanza, a holy plot is superimposed on Poe: the wife is followed by God. Both make fearful claims, both are avengers, both are associated with a man's sense of failure – yet they act not in conjunction but in competition. And the

---

* Another suggestive parallel is 'Lucretia Borgia shall be my bride' in 'A Cooking Egg'.

wife loses. Her presence intrudes upon the husband's welcome of God, and interferes with his receptivity. In the end she is forced to recede before a more compelling claim. Pursued by God, obsessed, his mind has no place for her. The poem ends:

> God in a rolling ball of fire
> Pursues by day my errant feet.
> His flames of anger and desire
> Approach me with consuming heat.

From the man's angle 'Elegy' is about an awakening sense of sin in which a woman plays a crucial part. He regrets having wronged her, but wishes he might dispose of her and, after sanctimonious mourning, get on with his own destiny. In his scenario remorse is followed by expiation and then, hopefully, bliss.

Like 'Elegy', 'The river sweats . . .' (the earliest section of what would become part III of *The Waste Land*) associates religious emotions with remorse for sexual wrong. In each, guilt for violation or abandonment of women precedes purgatorial pain. Eliot believed we might hold to the visionary power promised in 'I am the Resurrection' only if the flesh were purged. The raining arrows of 'The Death of Saint Narcissus' are one attempt to punish the flesh. They are followed by the consuming flames of 'Elegy' and by the burning agony which follows scenes of promiscuity on the River Thames, at Moorgate, and on Margate sands:

> To Carthage then I came
>
> Burning burning burning burning
> O Lord thou pluckest me out
> O Lord thou pluckest
>
> burning

Again, sexual guilt precedes religious fervour. The voice of Augustine confesses to promiscuity in Carthage, and penitence propels him into the burning routine. Over the course of his career Eliot repeatedly alluded to the refining fire, the

cure for lust, on the highest terrace of Dante's *Purgatorio*.*
A parallel voice comes from the Fire Sermon in which the
Buddha directs his followers to the holy life through the
cultivation of aversion for all the impressions of the senses.
But Eliot's own impulse towards asceticism can possibly be
traced back, past his wrongs with Vivienne, past the Buddhist
Society at Oxford, and the spiritual biographies of Augustine
and Dante, to his mother, who wrote:

> Purge from thy heart all sensual desire,
> Let low ambitions perish in the fire
> Of higher aims. Then, as the transient dies,
> The eternal shall unfold before thine eyes
> The fleeting hours will grant thee thy request:
> Take thou immortal gifts and leave the rest.

The pattern of spiritual biography is to move from a dead
world to a new life. Eliot associated the dead world with the
City of London, where he went to work as a bank clerk in
1917, and two new manuscript fragments are associated with
that move. 'O City City' (inserted later into part III of *The
Waste Land*) suggests ways of transcending the sordid city:
the fishermen lounging near Billingsgate fish market and the
splendour of churches nearby. Since his Gloucester childhood
Eliot idolised fishermen, whom he saw as unworldly gallant

---

* *Purgatorio*, XXVI:

> '. . . consiros vei la passada folor;
> e vei jausen lo joi qu'esper, denan.
> Ara vos prec, per aquella valor
> que vos guida al som de l'escalina,
> sovenha vos a temps da ma dolor!'
> Poi s'ascose nel foco che li affina.

('I see with grief past follies and see, rejoicing, the day I hope for before me.
Now I beg you, by the goodness which guides you to the summit of the
stairway, to take thought in due time for my pain.' Then he hid himself in
the fire that refines them.) The last line was the original epigraph to
'Prufrock' and was one of the fragments to be 'shored' for future use in *WL*:
V. 'Ara vos prec' was the title of Eliot's second collection of poems. 'Som de
l'escalina' was the title of one section of *AW*. Lines 1 and 5 were quoted in
'Exequy', a *Waste Land* fragment Pound persuaded Eliot to cut.

adventurers. During his lunch hours at Lloyds Bank he used to wander along Lower Thames Street to a fishermen's wharf, perhaps the oldest on the Thames, in use from Saxon times. Seeing fishermen at rest in the middle of the day, he imagined they 'spat time out', freed of the timebound routines that locked him in place. From there he moved on to view the 'inviolable splendour' of Magnus Martyr.

In the summer of 1918, when he and Vivienne had a house at 31 West Street, Marlow, Eliot took the train each morning, indistinguishable in a dark suit and bowler hat from the crowd of suburban commuters, and then, still in the crowd, he walked from the railway station across London Bridge amidst horse-drawn carts, open-topped buses, canvas-topped lorries, and street vendors. As he moved, he saw in the distance St Magnus the Martyr rising out of the dingy mass of London buildings, its white tower and fine Wren steeple surmounting the brown tatty buildings near a quayside edged with rusty machinery. A circle of windows stood out beneath the dome and spire.* In Eliot's London, Wren's lovely empty churches soared above the city as a splendid counterpoise to banks and commercial houses, somehow enduring against all those 'flying feet'. In the evening, after work, he observed the tower of St Michael, Paternoster Royal, its red windows lit up in the dark sky, a marvellous antidote to the 'ghastly hill of Cannon Street'. At other times, on winter mornings, as he emerged from Bank Station, buried in the mass of hurrying workers, he would look up and see the church of St Mary Woolnoth (built by one of Wren's pupils) and hear it strike nine from its oblong tower with square turrets. In the lunch hour a tower down a grimy lane would strike his eye and empty naves would receive him, a solitary visitor, from the dust and tumult of Lombard Street.

The second fragment, 'London', was eventually cut, but contains the germ of the Unreal City scenes in The Waste

* Eliot owned an album of London Views containing a photograph of this scene, c. 1924. There is a photograph of a similar scene preserved in the Eliot Collection, Houghton Library, together with one of men hurrying outside Bank Station with St Mary Woolnoth on the right.

Land. Briefly, Eliot contrasts the city of men, swarming and dead, with the City of God. Ghostly gnomes burrow in brick and steel, huddled between concrete and sky, with bodies mechanical as toys. But around them curls an 'ideal meaning' which a 'penumbral consciousness' may yet decipher. As yet it appears 'indistinctly', 'vaguely', 'doubtfully', a non-wasteland phenomenon obscured by the obtrusive visibility of tarnished creatures, blindly gratifying immediate needs and unconscious of a 'formal destiny'.

Eliot was invisible as a man of destiny: superman in the guise of a clerk. Pound and others thought it pitiful to spend his days in a bank, but it left imagination free, and he relished the completeness of his disguise, for he excelled as a clerk. His salary rose steadily from the meagre £120 a year when he started in March 1917, to £200 from 1 January 1918, to £500 at the end of 1922, to £600 by 1925 – not a lot, but a secure income. He preferred this to a precarious post with an arty journal, despite Vivienne's urgings: she had a keen sense of getting ahead in the literary world; as she put it, 'What's the use of being famous after you're dead?' Though Eliot worked at the right contacts and wrote quatrains with an eye to an audience who cultivated snide brilliance, he was determined to publish nothing that was second-rate. Journalism, he believed, had nothing to do with literature. He wished to choose what to write, not churn out ephemeral copy. Then, too, he liked the bank, and this was not only because he was good at business but because it was a stratagem of sorts. He wrote to Lytton Strachey: 'I am sojourning among the termites.' The violent fragments written during the early years in London – dramatic deaths and purifications of the flesh by fire and water – foretell a growing purpose, realised at the end of *The Waste Land*, to denounce civilisation and declare it 'Unreal'.

*

By 1919 Eliot had amassed a collection of visions and ordeals. 'Gerontion', written in May–June 1919, marks the imaginative turning-point between assorted fragments and a single poem. Six months after Eliot finished 'Gerontion' he confided to his mother and to a New York patron, a lawyer called John Quinn, that he was about to write a long poem he had had in mind for some time.

The case study of Gerontion takes us back to the question of failure. Reviewing his life, Gerontion deplores its lack of action or commitment and the unenlightened death he faces. The self-absorption of Prufrock and Gerontion and their anxiety for experience recall the unlived life in late tales of Henry James: middle-aged gentlemen who crave and dodge an overwhelming experience, like the leap of a beast in the jungle. 'Came Christ the tiger', Gerontion muses.* His theological position recalls that of the American Puritan who sees himself without spiritual agency, abject, wholly at the mercy of divine omnipotence.

At the same time as Eliot wrote 'Gerontion' he analysed the New England temperament in a review of *The Education of Henry Adams*. 'A Sceptical Patrician' is clearly a bit of self-analysis and suggests links between Eliot, Gerontion, and Adams. This refined type of American, Eliot said, had a strong Puritan conscience which laid upon him 'the heavy burden of self-improvement' and an obligation to experience more than liberal Unitarianism, an imperfect education at Harvard, and a narrow Boston horizon might have provided. His native curiosity was balanced by a scepticism which Eliot called 'the Boston doubt'. The Boston variety was not a solid scepticism but quirky, dissolvent rather than destructive, a kind of vulnerability 'to all suggestions which dampen enthusiasm or dispel conviction'. Eliot contemplated the respectfully attentive New England congregation who would have heard Emerson announce that he would not administer the Communion because it did not interest him. Wherever the well-bred American steps, said Eliot, the moral ground does not simply give way, it fragments. Gerontion's ground, too,

---

* Eliot reversed a line from Whitman: 'Christ is no tiger'. He mentioned this to Mary Trevelyan (July 1956). PRS.

flies into 'fractured atoms'. Gerontion's last thought is of a traveller blown about by winds like the white feathers of birds in a snowstorm.

Later in 1919 Eliot wrote of his sense of the artist as an Eye curiously, patiently watching himself as a man. Gerontion's distinction derives in part from Eliot's circumstances: he was sojourning in an alien place, he had failed to fight the battles of his generation, he had not subscribed to its outdated values – romantic heroism, physical courage, and sentimental nostalgia.

Gerontion tries to give his depleted spirit a clearer intellectual basis by defining it against the backdrop of history. He thinks of history as a mistress, and secular leaders as her dupes. She panders to men's vanities and deludes them with bogus favours, sometimes granting them more than they expect, but in the end leaving them graceless and baffled. Throughout the ages she toys with and betrays the human race. Most immediately, through the Great War she betrays Western pride in progress, knowledge, and civilisation. History induces men to forsake the salvation plot for her own tortuous plots. In this passage Gerontion denounces secular history as a reasonable alternative to faith.

During 1919 Eliot read the sermons of John Donne, Hugh Latimer, and Lancelot Andrewes, and became interested in the sermon as 'a form of literary art'. It is a form that merges readily with Eliot's confessional-instructive mode. Gerontion's statement uses preachers' terms of 'forgiveness', 'vanities', 'unnatural vices', 'virtues', 'our impudent crimes', and 'the backward devils'. While the post-war generation rebelled against Victorian cant and religious hypocrisy, Eliot held to an older faith – devouring, passionate, and mystical. From his earliest juvenilia Eliot consistently deplored contemporary life and secular history, not with the helpless voice of his generation, but with the authoritative voice of Old Testament prophet or New England divine.

Gerontion and, later, a pilgrim in *The Waste Land*, are poised at the extremity of a dry season, waiting for rain, the traditional sign of spiritual fertility. 'We would see a sign!'

Gerontion says in the words of Lancelot Andrewes, and his wish is answered by the thunder's message and promise of rain at the end of *The Waste Land*. Gerontion knows he may yet be saved from withering if only he can recover some passion. His cry, 'I have lost my passion . . . I have lost my sight, smell, hearing, taste and touch', recalls a sermon on Divine Calls by the greatest nineteenth-century convert, Cardinal Newman: 'Let us beg and pray Him day by day to reveal Himself to our souls more fully, to quicken our senses, to give us sight and hearing, taste and touch of the world to come.' But, for Gerontion, these senses have atrophied, and all that is left to him are fearful premonitions of savage experience, analogous to fighting in the warm rain or heaving a cutlass in a salt marsh or drowning, like a seagull, off some distant shore. The warm rain, the marsh, the Gulf Stream are the mirages of a man dying for want of water.

*

It is not easy to follow the sequence of *The Waste Land*'s composition during 1921, but some facts are clear. After resolving to write the poem at the end of 1919 Eliot did nothing about it during 1920. That year he busied himself with a volume of criticism, *The Sacred Wood*. The reviews were disappointing and he went about looking pale and ill. Then, in the autumn of 1920, Vivienne's father became dangerously ill and she and Eliot sat up night after night nursing him. The anxiety was too much for Vivienne, who broke down. Though in March and April 1921 she was in bed and complaining of pain that made her scream continuously for several days, Eliot began to see there would be no end to domestic crises, and that he must keep a part of his mind intact if he wished to get on with his long-delayed poem.

There were two periods of composition in 1921. New evidence reveals activity at the beginning of the year, for in an unpublished letter of 6 February, Wyndham Lewis reports to Mrs Schiff that Eliot, whom he had seen at a production of

Volpone, 'seems to be engaged in some obscure & intricate task of late'. Lewis must have pressed him further, for the very next day Lewis writes again to tell Schiff that Eliot had shown him 'a new long poem (in 4 parts) which I think will be not only very good, but a new departure for him'. Between then and May, there are repeated indications that Eliot was pulling it together: in April he was revising, and hoped to have it in a final form by June. May, while Vivienne was away at the seaside, was an opportunity to get more on paper.

It is not possible to know for sure what he had in hand at this point, but it was not the poem as we know it. He continued to envisage a poem in four parts, and it is likely that, by now, he had written the first version of parts I and II, drawing heavily on scenes from his own life. These he rehearsed years later when he drove about London with Mary Trevelyan. He told her that in 1921 he went to dine in Hampstead or Primrose Hill with a woman he had met at the poetry circle of the Lyceum Club, who had showed him her tarot pack, the only time he had seen one. Eliot transformed this into the fortune-teller who introduces the characters of *The Waste Land* through her tarot cards. In 1942, as Eliot and Mary Trevelyan passed the dingy flats of Crawford Mansions on the border of Paddington, he said: 'We lived there – I was very unhappy. There was a pub – I used to watch people coming out at Closing Time. That's the origin of "HURRY UP PLEASE IT'S TIME".' In Trafalgar Square, he said, pointing: 'It was from there that Vivienne threw her nightdress out of the window into the street in the middle of the night.' Her power to shame his sense of propriety was transformed into the frenzied wife in part II who threatens, 'I shall rush out as I am, and walk the street / With my hair down, so.' Vivienne remarked at the time of publication that *The Waste Land* became 'a part of me (or I of it)'.

The second period of composition came in the autumn, from October to December, a more concentrated stretch of writing. For, finally, Eliot himself broke down, and during his recuperation at Margate and Lausanne at the end of 1921 he had, at last, the continuous time he needed to complete his poem.

The event that immediately preceded his breakdown was a long-awaited visit from his mother, accompanied by his sister Marian and brother Henry. He had not seen his mother for six years. He feared that Charlotte, now seventy-seven, would be old and weak, but when they arrived he was taken aback by his mother's formidable energy. Most of the strain was keeping marital problems under wraps and Vivienne at a distance in the country. When she did appear she strove to preserve the even manners an Eliot would take for granted, but Charlotte could tell that her son was afraid of his wife, and at the very last moment Vivienne exploded. She wrote regretfully, and rather touchingly, to Henry Eliot:

Wigmore Street
Tuesday 23 [August 1921]

Dear Henry,

. . . Now I want you to tell me something truly. You are not to lie. Did your mother and sister show, think, say or intimate that I behaved like 'no lady', and just like a wild animal when [we] saw you off? I was perfectly stunned on that occasion. I had no idea what I was doing. I have been more or less stunned for many months now and when I come to, I suppose it seems deadful, to an American. I have worried all the time since. Tom said it was perfectly allright, etc, but I am sure he has lived here so long he hardly realises how *very* much less English people mind showing their emotions than Americans – or perhaps he does realise it so perfectly. But I was extremely anxious to show no emotion before your family at any time, and then I ended in a fit!

I found the emotionless condition a great strain, all the time. I used to think I should burst out and scream and dance. That's why I used to think you were so terribly failing me. But I won't talk about that now, except to ask you if ever two people made *such* a fearful mess of their obvious possibilities. I don't understand, and I never shall. . . . Both flats are equally unbearable to us [they had moved to Lucy Thayer's flat, so as to leave Clarence Gate Gardens to their visitors], so we stay here morosely. . . .

Good-bye Henry. And *be personal*, you must be personal,
or else it's no good. Nothing's any good.

Vivien

Henry took a cool view. 'I have a feeling that sub-
consciously (or unconsciously) she likes the role of invalid,'
he remarked to his mother, 'and that, liking it as she does to
be petted, "made a fuss over", condoled and consoled, she
. . . encourages her breakdowns, instead of throwing them off
by a sort of nervous resistance. It is hard to tell how much is
physical and how much mental and controllable by will
power; but I think that if she had more of "the Will to Be
Well" she would have less suffering. . . . She needs something
to take her mind off herself; something to absorb her entire
attention.'

After his mother left, Eliot collapsed. 'I really feel very
shaky', he wrote to Aldington, 'and seem to have gone down
rapidly since my family left.' He felt as though he might lose
self-control, but it was 'impossible to describe these feelings
even if one wants to'. When overstrained, he said, he used to
suffer from a vague but acute sense of horror and apprehension. Clarence Gate Gardens without his family seemed no
home, and his brother's departure seemed 'as unreal as
death'. Vivienne's lamentations over missing his mother
seemed to vie with his own. In late September he went to see a
nerve specialist. Though it was Vivienne who proposed the
specialist, she was taken aback by the serious view he took of
Eliot's case. '. . . Look at *my* position,' she urged Scofield
Thayer. 'I have not nearly finished my own nervous breakdown yet.'

When Henry Eliot heard of his brother's condition, he was
inclined to blame Vivienne. He put it to their mother: 'I am
afraid he finds it impossible to do creative work (other than
critical) at home. Vivien demands a good deal of attention,
and I imagine is easily offended if she does not get it well
buttered with graciousness and sympathy.'

Henry took the view that his brother suffered also from his
disguise. 'The strain of going out among people who after all
are foreigners to him, and, I believe, always must be to an

171

American – even Henry James never became a complete Englishman – has, I think, been pretty heavy. I remember a year or more ago, in a letter to me, he spoke of always having to be ... alert to the importance of appearances, always wearing a mask among people. To me he seemed like a man playing a part.'

On 12 October, Eliot was given three months' sick-leave from the bank. It now became clear to him that he was suffering neither from 'nerves' or insanity, but from 'psychological troubles' which, he complained, English doctors at that time simply did not acknowledge. He decided to seek help abroad, and the biologist Julian Huxley and Ottoline Morrell recommended Dr Vittoz in Lausanne. Both had been his patients. Roger Vittoz was an austere Catholic, to some a living saint, who trained his patients in meditation, similar to yoga and Buddhism. His book, *Treatment of Neurasthenia by Means of Brain Control* (1913) appeared in English in 1921. He did not advocate lengthy psychoanalysis, rather mastery, through reason and will, of what he termed *clichés*, the painful thoughts in which a diseased mind had become imprisoned. The method was not to suppress memories and desires, but through a return to moral equilibrium, to free a patient of his pain.

In the meantime, on 22 October, Eliot moved to the Albemarle Hotel, Cliftonville, Margate. Vivienne bought him a mandolin and accompanied him, at his request; after two weeks, she left him to follow the rest-cure his doctor prescribed. He was to be alone, and in the open air, and not think of the future. It is likely that it was during the last of his three weeks there, after Vivienne left, that he did 'a rough draft of part of part III',* calling it 'The Fire Sermon'. 'I do not know whether it will do, & must wait for Vivien's opinion as to whether it is printable,' he informed Schiff. 'I have done this while sitting in a shelter on the front – as I am out all day except when taking rest.'

* The reference to 'part III' confirms the supposition that parts I and II were already by then in existence.

172

Eliot attached his hotel bill to the manuscript: the work he did at Margate cost him about £16 in all. The first week he indulged himself in the 'white room' and took all his meals. The next two weeks were spent rather more frugally in a modest room *en pension*. Vivienne, reporting to Russell, said that he seemed to like Margate. He was in a precarious state, but the purposeful letters he wrote at this time suggest that he was convalescing rather than declining. Pound, briefly in England in early October, found him enlivened by the prospect of leisure. There was evidently no discussion of Eliot's poem, and I doubt that Eliot showed it to him before he went to Margate.

During the final stages of *The Waste Land*'s composition Eliot put himself under Pound's direction. On 18 November, on his way to Switzerland, Eliot passed through Paris and left his wife with the Pounds, who were then living there. It seems likely that Eliot now showed Pound what he had done in Margate. Pound called Eliot's Swiss draft 'the 19 page version', which implies that he had previously seen another. He marked certain sheets on two occasions: once in pencil, probably on 18 November; once in ink, on Eliot's return from Lausanne early in January.* Pound undoubtedly improved particular passages: his excisions of another anti-Semitic portrait of Bleistein and a misogynist portrait of a woman writer called Fresca† curbed Eliot's excessive

---

* 'Exequy' and 'The Fire Sermon' are typed with Eliot's brother's typewriter on yellowish sheets with a 'Verona' watermark. The carbon of 'The Fire Sermon', with Pound's marginalia in pencil, was clearly shown first. Eliot then revised the top copy in accordance with Pound's suggestions before submitting it for further consideration on his return from Lausanne.

† In an appendix to a biography of Nancy Cunard, Anne Chisholm suggests that she could have been a source for Eliot's Fresca: his 'bitterness may be explained by the contrast between the struggles of Eliot and his wife against illness and poverty, and the affluent, leisured existence of Nancy'; also by 'the ease with which the well-connected amateur, Nancy, found publishers and respectful reviewers for her poems'. TSE had met Nancy several times by 1921, and Vivienne's 1919 diary mentions her presence at an evening the Eliots spent with the Hutchinsons, when Osbert Sitwell and Duncan Grant were also guests.

animus, and his feel for the right word improved odd lines throughout.* Pound was proud of his hand in *The Waste Land* and wrote:

> If you must needs enquire
> Know diligent Reader
> That on each Occasion
> Ezra performed the caesarian Operation.

Pound's influence went deeper than this comment during the winter of 1921–2, going back rather to 1918, 1919, and 1920 when he and Eliot were engaged in a common effort to modernise their poetry. Pound's *Hugh Selwyn Mauberley* (1920) is a covert dialogue with Eliot, a composite biography of two great unappreciated poets whose flaws are frankly aired. Pound criticises a Prufrock-like poet too given to hesitation, 'maudlin confession', and the precipitation of 'insubstantial manna' from heaven. As though in answer, Eliot put aside his more confessional fragments, 'Saint Narcissus' and 'Elegy', and in 1921 overlaid them with contemporary characters – the pampered Fresca (like Pound's Lady Valentine), Venus Anadyomene (another *Mauberley* character), Cockneys, a typist in a bedsit, and a 'low' clerk. The Pound colouring in these sketches did not suit Eliot. Where Pound is exuberant in his disgust, Eliot becomes callow or vitriolic – and Pound himself recognised this in his comment on typist and clerk who couple like 'crawling bugs': 'Too easy', he scribbled in the margin. Eliot's characters are not as realistic as Pound's. They are projections of Eliot's consciousness – they could be termed humours.† Unlike the satirist, Eliot does not criticise an actual world but creates

---

* Pound changed 'When Lil's husband was coming out of the Transport Corps' to 'When Lil's husband was demobbed', and suggested that Mr Eugenides should not issue his invitation to lunch in 'abominable' but in 'demotic French'.
† See Eliot on the comedy of humours, *SW*, pp. 112, 116. In the essay on Ben Jonson, Eliot writes of characters that conform to the logic of their creator's emotions. Each character is 'a simplified and somewhat distorted individual with a typical mania'.

a 'phantasmal' world of lust, filth, boredom, and malice on which he gazes in fascinated horror. *The Waste Land* is about a psychological hell in which someone is quite alone, 'the other figures in it / Merely projections'.

In 1921 Eliot deliberately played down the loner's voice, and transferred the weight of his poem to the Voices of Society. He had Dickens in mind, the panoramic range of *Our Mutual Friend*, where disconnected fragments of lives on the river and all over London gradually cohere in the horror of the reader.* In *The Waste Land* there is no longer a central figure, like Narcissus or Gerontion, hovering between the remote role of religious candidate and a more immediate despair. Yet the medley of voices is put on, even mocking, for the lone voice is never wholly submerged. Stripped of divine love in 'The Death of Saint Narcissus', stripped of marital love in 'The Death of the Duchess', stripped of misplaced fame in 'Exequy', it is the voice of a dissembling ghost, without stable shape. In the guise of St Augustine he repents sexual excess. And in the form of a poet who has misused his gift and buried himself in suburbia, he pleads pity for his pain: 'SOVENHA VOS A TEMPS DE MA DOLOR.'

One difficulty of attempting to speak from the centre of a society was its variety. Eliot had a more ordering mind than Pound; the collage of representative characters to be found in *Hugh Selwyn Mauberley* would not have satisfied him. In 'Rhapsody on a Windy Night' and in his doctoral thesis on Experience, Eliot had despaired of a philosophic principle that would master disparate perceptions. But in 1921, while *The Waste Land* gestated in his mind, Eliot found an answer in the Russian Ballet.

It was a time when Diaghilev's ballets represented a collaboration of Stravinsky, Picasso, Nijinsky, de Falla, and Massine, the greatest innovators in music, art, and choreography, and London's intelligentsia went night after night to

---

* Eliot used a snatch of *Our Mutual Friend*, 'He do the Police in Different Voices', as his title on typescripts of parts I and II. He refers to the orphan Sloppy, who read the newspaper statements of London policemen 'in different voices'.

Covent Garden. Eliot was struck by the strange effect of 'a simplification of current life' in *La Boutique fantasque* and *The Three-Cornered Hat*. The phenomenon was particularly striking in the strange, harsh music of Stravinsky's *Le Sacre du Printemps*. Eliot was so infuriated with the audience for laughing that he poked his neighbours with the point of his umbrella. The music seemed to 'transform the rhythm of the steppes into the scream of the motor-horn, the rattle of machinery, the grind of wheels, the beating of iron and steel, the roar of the underground railway, and the other barbaric noises of modern life'. Stravinsky, like *Ulysses* and *The Golden Bough*, provided a revelation of a vanished mind of which the modern mind was a continuation. Primitive man on the dolorous steppes, modern man in the city with its noises: there is an unchanging predicament, said Eliot. He saw that one might strip brute experience of its contexts and explanations, leaving the abrupt fact exposed, and simplify it further by showing the repetition of the same experience along the continuum of history. (As far back as 1914, in Josiah Royce's seminar, Eliot had insisted that 'there is no importance *at one time* historically'.) Eliot used real men and women and real historical events but reduced them to emblems of vice, lust, weakness, mediocrity. The typist awaiting the clerk, Elizabeth flirting with Leicester, Cleopatra in her barge, and the frenzied wife: 'all the women are one woman', said Eliot (not quite convincingly) in his notes.

Throughout his career he framed a choice between body and soul, between the sordid city and the transcendental silence, between shuttling to no purpose on London's commuter trains and communing with God on holy ground. On the one hand, the speaker of 'Song'* is tantalised by an

---

* *facs. WL*, p. [98]. Eliot published 'Song' in Wyndham Lewis's *Tyro* (April 1921) under the pseudonym Gus Krutzsch, which appears in the original opening scene of *WL*: I. The name suggests someone deformed or maimed. It also sounds a bit like Kurtz, the hero of *Heart of Darkness* by Conrad. Eliot referred to Kurtz again in the original epigraph to *The Waste Land* ('The horror! the horror!') and in the epigraph to 'The Hollow Men' ('Mr. Kurtz – he dead').

intangible golden foot in the shadow of his bed, on the other alarmed by his proximity to his wife, whose face 'sweats with tears'.* The husband, swinging 'between two lives', rehearses yet again a debate that was a favourite with Eliot's mother. 'Ring out the world's temptation and illusion!' cried Charlotte in one of her sermon-poems. 'Ring in immortal hopes that shall endure!' For her son hope was less easy, but there was no more question of choice. The abandonment of the city, civilisation, and history – the world as we know it – near the end of *The Waste Land* is as inevitable as it has been for St Narcissus. The only difference is that Narcissus acts instinctively whereas the *Waste Land* pilgrim acts rationally – before his exit from history, he accumulates evidence against it and makes his categoric judgement: 'Unreal'.

*

If civilisation is 'unreal' and God sends no 'sign', where do we find a reliable authority? The Moderns looked first to the authenticity of the writer's life. Eliot took his original epigraph from Conrad's *Heart of Darkness*:

> Did he live his life again in every detail of desire, temptation, and surrender during the supreme moment of complete knowledge? He cried in a whisper at some image, at some vision, – he cried out twice, a cry that was no more than a breath –
>
> 'The horror! the horror!'†

Here is the heart of Eliot's *aboulie* in the autumn of 1921: a horrified glimpse of innate depravity and the related fear that few have the stature to transcend it. Pound should not have dismissed this epigraph for, as Eliot modestly protested, it is 'somewhat elucidative'. It certifies the authority of the shocked, knowing heart stripped of cultural superstructures.

* Eliot told Pound in late January 1922 that 'sweats with tears' would fit the 'nerves monologue' of the wife in *WL*: II (*L*, i, 504).
† The epigraph is typed under the title 'The Waste Land' on the same 'Verona' paper that Eliot used for 'The Fire Sermon' and 'Exequy'.

'To live his life again', to master the facts of his autobiography, could not alone cure Eliot. His sense of 'horror' was not a symptom of derangement but a fair judgement, and his only hope of patching up his 'ruin' was by following the pattern of certain authoritative lives. In the lives Eliot invokes – Dante, Christ, Augustine, the Grail knight, Ezekiel – there is always a dark period of trial, whether in a desert, a slough of despond, or hell, followed by initiation, conversion, or the divine light itself. The external biographic events that form part of this plot do not have to cover the lifespan from birth to death, for time has nothing to do with redemption. Augustine's *Confessions* end at the age of thirty-two. *The Waste Land* ends with three thunderous calls.

The traditional schema of the exemplary life usually opens with the kind of confession of youthful vanities with which Eliot originally opened *The Waste Land*. The young Bostonian, humming tunes of the early 1900s, seeks out the clichés of wine, women, and song, but soon finds his appetite jaded. The painful awakening to sin is the substance of 'The Fire Sermon', which ends with a recognition of the necessity for punishment. There follows a stage of committed action and purification in 'Death by Water' and then, at last, enlightenment in 'What the Thunder Said'. While Eliot could safely expose the heart of darkness to a modern audience, the blueprint for salvation had to be subdued. To intellectuals of Eliot's generation it would have seemed an anachronism.

The first two parts put forward autobiographical material of a different order from the introspective outposts of the manuscript. Here are visible actions (recognisably Eliot's life to his mother and Mary Hutchinson): a worldly young man in Boston having a drink at the Opera Exchange; an inspiring moment of love for a 'hyacinth girl'; a tormenting marriage; the sage advice of Mme Sosostris, a bogus clairvoyante (Eliot's friends would have recognised Bertrand Russell);* the routines of a commuter to the City. Eliot transforms these

---

* Mr Scogan, who impersonates Sesostris the Sorceress in Aldous Huxley's *Crome Yellow*, is modelled on Bertrand Russell.

actions as a set of instructive ordeals. In part I, 'The Burial of the Dead', the demeaning routines of suburban corpses are aligned with Dante's abject neutrals on the outskirts of hell. Part II, 'A Game of Chess', is hell itself, the diabolical routines of marital powerplay.

Pound wrote 'photography' on the draft of the first marital scene in 'A Game of Chess'. This is the scene which originated in 'The Death of the Duchess' where a woman plays a scene from a love-drama while her mate devises a more sinister plot of life and death. He longs to escape her room, though this would end her. Entrapped 'In the Cage', he shuns the physical proximity of his wife, refusing to notice her barrage of anxious questions:

'Why do you never speak. . . . What are you thinking of? What thinking? What? . . . What is that noise now? What is the wind doing? . . . You know nothing? Do you see nothing? Do you remember / Nothing? . . . Are you alive, or not? Is there nothing in your head?' The gaps are filled with silent denial of her frantic plea for communication. He will remember only his own dream of metamorphosis: 'Those are pearls that were his eyes.' This secret commitment is a drama which he must enact alone, as voyager or pilgrim. What did Vivienne make of that silent retort? At any rate, she applauded the frenzy of the woman: 'wonderful, wonderful'.

The prestige of normality since the Enlightenment that isolates frenzy as a form of deviance must not deceive us, said Foucault, to its 'original exuberance'. Eliot gave Vivienne's voice a measure of expression in so far as it complements his own breakdown at the time of *The Waste Land*. Before the wife speaks, she brushes her hair before the fire, and it stands out around her head in fierce burning points, like the burning words that alternate with the savage stillness of non-communication. It is an uncompromising exhibition of temperamental violence: partners so evenly matched that their powerplay must end in deadlock. The husband's cruelty is disguised as gentlemanly forbearance. Mockingly, he drowns out her voice in the syncopated rhythms of ragtime. The silent vehemence of his refusal to hear is matched by the outspoken threat of the wife to expose their torment in public.

Eliot's tie with his wife meant more to him than legal responsibility: she gripped his imagination because her lashing, uncontrolled emotions reflected some part of his own nature. He was, Virginia Woolf saw, 'thrown like an assegai into the hide of the world'. His violence, controlled by the perfection of his manners, manifested in the early poetry as disgust with sexual licence, intellectual pretension, rotting cities, and Jews fallen from moral grandeur into avarice. This fallen world Eliot transmutes into *The Waste Land*'s vision of hell of which Vivienne, with her anarchic abandon, was arch embodiment.

Though the Eliots were physically incompatible from the start, they shared something else that, at a deeper level, bound them: a mutual susceptibility to horror. 'As to Tom's *mind*, I am his mind,' Vivienne wrote to Jack Hutchinson. She bore him beyond the normal: her nerves, like her hair, stretched out tight, she was ready to throw off decorum. In 'Hysteria', 'Ode', and *The Waste Land*, the woman's companion stares appalled – and fascinated. Already, in 'Hysteria', written in Oxford in 1915, just before Eliot's marriage, an embarrassed man in a tea garden tries to stop the shaking of a woman's breasts while he feels drawn into the exposed, pulsating tunnel of her throat. In 'Ode' a bridegroom finds the 'succuba eviscerate' in his bed. Again, a man makes a vain effort at a semblance of decorum: the bridegroom, smoothing down his hair, is trying to detach himself from the creature who has claimed him for her own. The creature is not without her own outrage: she is cut open, her entrails exposed. The couple, like the Eliots, discover a mutual nightmare with their first damaging contact. For Eliot, horror mounted swiftly to a vision of hell: he spoke of 'horror of life' as 'a mystical experience'. For Vivienne, horror came from hidden motives. Women rattling prams behind her in the street might be 'dying to propagate their own loathesomeness'. Their menace complements Eliot's red-eyed scavengers creeping in from the suburbs.

In Vivienne's nightmares a glaring figure would appear in chains or on crutches with strange looks, shrieks and imprecations, a frightful other self which, she told Sydney Schiff, she must learn to accept. For Eliot, Vivienne may have been the one character in *The Waste Land* who is *not* projected from the poet's inner world of nightmare. The fact that she did exist validated the poem's mood of horror, for she enacted that swift conversion of fact into nightmare that was an essential strategy of Eliot's art.

Sanity or detachment is maintained by the exercise of wit. But with the growing sense of horror in part III, 'The Fire Sermon', wit is no longer possible. The manuscript shows Pound levelling off Eliot's revulsion for the 'carbuncular' clerk, 'spotted about the face' whose hair is thick with scurf and thick with grease, and who spits and urinates in corners. 'Probaly [*sic*] over the mark', Pound scrawls in the margin, levelling the build-up of contamination. The only hope is to escape. It is obvious why Eliot had to leave London to recuperate, and the poem follows the course of his sickness and recovery. From the close of 'The Fire Sermon' the sordid city is blotted out by exemplary characters who escape contamination either by the practice of asceticism – like the Buddha or St Augustine – or by dreams of a voyage, a journey, a pilgrimage, the usual metaphors of spiritual biography. Eliot gives over urban realism for the far and strange: a bold sailor, washed clean and refashioned by the ocean, and the hooded figure of the resurrected Christ on the road to Emmaus.

'Death by Water', part IV, which Eliot completed at Lausanne, was initially a narrative of a fishing expedition from Cape Ann to the Grand Banks, off Nova Scotia.* In the London of 'The Fire Sermon' someone fishes futilely in the polluted canal; here, in the North Atlantic, the New

* *facs.* WL, pp. [54–60]. Eliot did his handwritten drafts at Lausanne on quadruled paper. These were 'What the Thunder Said', fair copies of 'Death by Water' and 'Dirge', and a rough draft of 'Venus Anadyomene' (which was soon discarded along with the Fresca episode for which it was designed). Eliot used the same black ink for the two fair copies.

England fishermen lead purposeful, honest lives, far from the contamination of cities. They are constantly in danger of death off some remote shore, but to Eliot this is preferable to death-in-life, like Gerontion's, in a soiled corner of familiar trade-routes.

The transition from the London of 'The Fire Sermon' to the New England of 'Death by Water' revives an ancestral sense of release from the sinfulness of the Old World. Eliot's North Atlantic is unexplored territory, a testing-ground. He thinks of the New Englander as pure will confronting the sea, 'something inhuman, clean and dignified'. As the vessel flies north, far off course, the voyage turns into an allegorical dream. As the stars become invisible, the voyager sees three crosses and, in front of them, three women with foaming hair, singing a siren's song. Prufrock longed for mermaids to sing to him; Londoners were charmed by the Thames daughters' 'la la' to their senses; but the voyager rejects women. For him, their song blends with the 'illimitable scream' of the whole natural world. At the height of the storm, it occurs to him that the shrill world with its provocative women is simply an illusion:

> . . . while I was
> Frightened beyond fear, horrified past horror, calm
> (Nothing was real) for, I thought, now when
> I like, I can wake up and end the dream.

No sooner does he reject this world as a dream than he knocks up against it. Literally, the vessel drives against an iceberg. One moment he looks into infinity, a meeting of sea and sky; the next, a long white line breaks into it like 'a wall, a barrier'. The drowning at the end of 'Death by Water' is not seen to be a disaster but a stage of purification and metamorphosis.

Eliot found no answer to his *aboulie* in psychiatry with its romantic ethos of self-expression. He favoured the sterner medieval view that one should 'look to *death* for what life cannot give'. In this view the death of the flawed natural self is preliminary to a new life. In 'The Death of Saint Narcissus',

'The Death of the Duchess', 'Elegy', and 'Dirge', and finally, at the end of 1921, in 'Death by Water', Eliot conducts violent annihilations of flawed characters.

At the same time as Eliot made his fair copy of the New England voyage, he found the pilgrim's journey of 1914 reviving in his imagination – the sunbaked road winding among the mountains, the bells and chanting voices, the reversed point of view of the saint. Eliot said that part V was the only part of *The Waste Land* 'that justifies the whole at all'. Here, in 'What the Thunder Said', the heroes of the spirit in the earliest manuscript fragments are depersonalised. In place of a man with extraordinary powers there is now a 'form' and, in a later revision, merely a bat. And instead of a voice saying plainly 'I am the Resurrection', the thunder now rumbles obscure Sanskrit words.

In the sanatorium in Lausanne, Dr Vittoz saw Eliot for half-an-hour each day when he would place his hand on a patient's forehead to determine the agitation of what he believed were physical brain waves. The cure was to concentrate on a simple word with a view to 'calm' and 'control'. Vittoz abjured learned words in favour of 'quelques paroles, nette et lumineuses', which he hoped would heal by their clarity – for Vittoz, simplicity was based on religious belief. The final part of *The Waste Land*, written at one sitting at the Hotel Ste Luce, carries out this meditative exercise, choosing to focus on 'water' to the point when agitation is dissolved in 'calm', 'beating obedient / To controlling hands'.

The speaker, with two companions, journeys away from the cities, across a sandy desert, where the rock will not yield miraculous water, as it did for the Israelites in Sinai. It is a wasted, barren land dotted with empty, exhausted wells. This quest for water in a desert recalls St Narcissus' passion; his thirst fever recalls Gerontion's parched body and his plea for rain. Both Narcissus and Gerontion lived in a state of feverish anticipation, awaiting an experience that would shape and define them; both were left unrewarded. But drawn into intense intimacy with the mind of the nameless seeker we can, for a space, concentrate on the spiritual refreshment of water in a way that leaves fragmented thoughts behind. This is the first passage of sustained concentration in the poem.*

Behind us, the city explodes – the fate of all great cities in the course of time, Jerusalem, Athens, Alexandria, Vienna. We move out of 'unreal' history into a bracing atmosphere of stirring grass and gusts of wind. Caught up in the grandeur of the triple thunderbolt that follows, the distant fall of London may be as insignificant as the fall of the Roman Empire for St Augustine. For the real plot is an inward journey.

The seeker makes it to a deserted chapel in the mountain, like the best of knights in search of the Holy Grail. ('Than sir Galahad com to a mountayne where he founde a chapell passynge old, and found therein nobody, for all was desolate. And there he . . . harde a voyce . . .'.) The thunder's first law is 'Datta', to give. We are to understand it as 'the awful daring of a moment's surrender'.

The thunder's next law is to sympathise: 'Dayadhvam'. We are imprisoned, like Narcissus, in self-absorption. But now we are offered a release through nocturnal intimations. 'Aetherial rumours' are breaking through. By 'sympathy' the thunder means receptivity to intimations and signs. 'I carry the keys of my castle in my hand,' wrote Emerson, 'ready to throw them at the feet of my lord, whenever and in what disguise soever he shall appear.' And then, quite suddenly, the 'angel-whispering' comes to him.

Thunder is, in fact, spelling out an old formula for conversion:† self-surrender; hope – of aetherial rumours; and then, finally, 'Damyata' or control. Spiritual biography traditionally ends with this gesture of obedience towards a

---

* This is the inception of the poetic language of Eliot's later years. Helen Gardner suggested that Eliot's new style began in *The Waste Land*: V, in an interview for a BBC 'Bookmark' programme on Eliot in September 1984. Unfortunately, the producer cut this insight.

† Daniel Shea, *Spiritual Autobiography in Early America* (Princeton Univ. Press, 1968; London: OUP, 1969), pp. 90, 100–1, shows that the settlers of New England had 'an early reputation as English Protestantism's most sophisticated students of the process, the signs and stages of conversion'.

superior power which has directed a life to this moment. It is that sense of 'beating obedient / To controlling hands'.

Eliot wrote this 'in a trance', and explained his extraordinary facility in terms of the 'illness' from which he was, at this time, recuperating. 'It is a commonplace that some forms of illness are extremely favourable, not only to religious illumination, but to artistic and literary composition. A piece of writing mediated without progress for months or years, may suddenly take shape and word, and in this state long passages may be produced which require little or no touch.'

The thunder prompts the speaker to put a psychological waste behind him. He might shore up his 'ruin' through attention to instructive moments in others' lives: Arnaut Daniel suffering for lust in the flames of purgatory, and Nerval's disinherited prince who experienced hell and returned to life, and conceived his *mélancolie* to be the sign of a saint. A vengeful rage could drive one into madness – that possibility remains. An alternative is a prayer for mental peace: 'Shantih'. Eliot again uses Sanskrit to convey an untranslatable truth 'which passeth understanding'.*

*

On 2 January 1922, Eliot stopped again in Paris and stayed about two weeks en route for home. At this late stage, Pound's emphatic criticisms cut the poem by half (in Lausanne, Eliot spoke of 800–1,000 lines, double its final length).

Pound thought badly of the narrative in 'Death by Water'. He drew a thick line through the focal 'London' fragment of 'The Fire Sermon' and cancelled the churches, St Mary Woolnoth and Michael Paternoster. What excited Pound was

---

* Eliot's original note to the line, 'The Peace which passeth understanding', is a feeble translation of 'Shantih'. Cleo McNelly Kearns, in *T. S. Eliot and Indic Tradition*, 228–9, explains 'the full context of *shantih* in Hindu tradition, where it is . . . simultaneously a mantra, a closing prayer for many ritual occasions, and one of the most prestigious terms in the Sanskrit language for the goal of meditative truth'.

not private hallucinations and spiritual hopes but helpless submission ('deploring action') to the stings of fortune, to London's odour of putrefaction and dull routines. He congratulated Eliot on the outline he had found for their 'deformative secretions'.

Pound could be ruthless about lines or passages that suggest an imaginative control of the waste. He refused Eliot the authority of St John the Divine when he bears witness to his generation's muddled efforts to communicate with spirits: 'I John saw these things, and heard them'. Pound also scratched a prophecy of metamorphosis: '(Those are pearls that were his eyes. Look!)' He persuaded Eliot to omit his most penitential fragment, 'Exequy', in which a poet confesses having abused his gifts in order to court immediate fame and resolves to carry through the Dantean schema. Silly devotees admire what is fake and celebrate the poet with fireworks; but he is warmed by a 'constant fire' within, a purgatorial fire. Pound, who for years had helped Eliot to fame, could not see the reason for Eliot's cry of 'DOLOR'. 'Song', also rejected by Pound, is a nocturnal vigil for the divine 'touch'.

On 20 January 1922, when Eliot offered *The Waste Land* to his friend Scofield Thayer, editor of the New York *Dial*, he said it had been three times through the sieve by Pound and himself and should soon be in its final form. Eliot probably left the manuscript, or part of it, in Paris so that Pound might consider it a third time. With the last sieving of the manuscript Eliot cut the whole of the fisherman's voyage in response to Pound's numerous cancellations on the typescript copy, though doubts lingered as to the effect of this on the poem as a whole. This was a sustained counter to urban stagnation, but Pound was hostile to narrative, and had his way. He thought Conrad was not 'weighty enough', and Eliot dropped the telling epigraph. But the main force of Pound's attack in his late-January letters was directed against the three closing lyrics of the Lausanne draft: 'Song', 'Dirge', and 'Exequy'. On 24 January Pound advised Eliot repeatedly 'to abolish 'em altogether'. Eliot replied that he accepted criticism 'so far as understood'. They were not impressive pieces, aesthetically, but essential facets of Eliot's emotional ensemble. What Pound called 'superfluities' were cut.

When Quinn saw the original manuscript he wrote to Eliot that he would not have cut as Pound advised. In the Lausanne draft the urban documentary in the first half of the poem had been more or less evenly balanced by allegoric trials in the second half. The effect of Pound's last suggestions is to curtail the second half so that urban documentary comes to dominate the poem. So, Pound blocked, at several points, Eliot's impulse to exhibit the strength as well as the sickness of a suffering soul. When Eliot left Lausanne he was master of his autobiography, but from the time Pound revised the manuscript in Paris, Eliot's gloom returned. In Paris, he added his last, most emotional fragment, a lament for an improper marriage.

In 'The river's tent is broken . . .' a man weeps for his bondage. Like many scenes in the poem, it had its source in the private circumstances of Eliot's life during his first years with Vivienne. In June 1918, when they had a house at Marlow, on the Thames, Eliot wrote to his mother of his intention to 'go out on the river' during a week's vacation – it would have been there and then that he had the opportunity to observe the detritus of summer nights when the heirs of city directors enjoyed girls whom they would not expect to marry. Eliot himself had been too proper to use Vivienne in this way, but the combination of sex and rectitude had proved disastrous for both of them. Eliot took responsibility for his wife's 'catastrophic' state of health: he told Pound in November 1922 that his 'mistakes' had been 'largely the cause'. Nor could he forget that Vivienne had saved him by changing his life. He was convinced that had he returned to America and become a professor, he would probably never have written another line of poetry.

The Waste Land is filled with broken women betrayed by sex or marriage: Philomela, whose tongue gets ripped out by Tereus so that she can't report his rape; a frenzied wife unable to get through to her husband, who hums ragtime, 'O – O –

O – O that Shakespeherian Rag', to block her out; a woman in a pub prematurely aged by too many pregnancies whose husband, back from the war, 'wants a good time'; the typist who feels no desire for the clerk but consents to couple with him as automatically as, afterwards, she puts a record on the gramophone; the London woman who raised her knees, out on the river. 'I made no comment,' says a streetwalker of her undoing. She had it coming to her: 'What should I resent?' Here, Eliot has replaced hatred of women with their pathos as the city's victims – all loveless and without hope. With extraordinary attentiveness, he hears – as poetry – their silenced voices.

Back in London, Eliot complained to Pound that he was sick, miserable, and 'excessively depressed'. He wrote to America: 'I have been led to contemplate, for many moments, the nature of the particular torpor or deadness which strikes a denizen of London on his return.' He saw everywhere a cowardly fear of independent thinking. That winter he used to meet Conrad Aiken regularly for lunch, and would confess to him – over rump steak at a pub in Cannon Street – how he would come home from work, sharpen his pencil, and then be unable to write. Yet it seemed to him there was material there, waiting. He told his mother he planned another poem. She understood that it was to be a sequel to *The Waste Land*, a more optimistic poem about the coming of the Grail. More than anything he wanted to give the spirit's ordeal back to his generation, and the dimensions of a moral universe in which such an ordeal belonged. At the time he was finishing *The Waste Land* he carried Dante everywhere with him in his pocket – Dante who had surveyed that universe and then written his autobiography in colossal cipher.

In October and November 1922 Eliot published *The Waste Land* in his own new journal, the *Criterion*, in London and in the *Dial* in New York, but remained uneasy. He said *The Waste Land* seemed like something he had written as far back as 'Prufrock', and could no longer speak for him. In November 1922 he repeated to Aldington that, for him, *The Waste Land* was a thing of the past. 'My present ideas are very different,' he told Gilbert Seldes, a *Dial* editor, in the same month. In 1930, still chafing at the outcome of the poem, he told McKnight Kauffer, an American illustrator, that he did not want anything he wrote to have *The Waste Land* stamped on it. His uneasiness was confirmed when he came to be hailed as spokesman for a disillusioned post-war generation.* They fastened on his despair and erudition and ignored the fact that these were subsidiary to a search for belief. In 1933 Eliot remarked to Virginia Woolf that he was no longer sure there was a science of criticism. He felt that critics had mistakenly fastened on the erudition of his poetry, and got things very wrong. When the critic I. A. Richards stated that the poem was devoid of belief, Eliot published a personal statement: 'As for the poem of my own in question, I cannot for the life of me see the "complete separation" from all belief – or it is something no more complete than the separation of Christina Rossetti from Dante. A "sense of desolation", etc. (if it is there) is not a separation from belief; it is nothing so pleasant. In fact, doubt, uncertainty, futility, etc., would seem to me to prove anything except this agreeable partition; for doubt and uncertainty are merely a variety of belief.'

The manuscript of *The Waste Land* shows that at first Eliot made the divine 'touch' an unmistakable priority, but played this down in the winter of 1921–2. The poem originated in the record of a man who saw himself as a potential candidate for the religious life but was constrained by his own nature and distracted by domestic claims. Eliot began writing spiritual autobiography in an age not cordial to the genre. He decided he could reach his audience only by indirection. Like many autobiographers, he compelled attention by presenting himself as a child of the times, but the gambit proved so

---

* See 'Thoughts After Lambeth', *SE*, p. 324: 'I dislike the word "generation", which has been a talisman for the last ten years; when I wrote a poem called *The Waste Land* some of the more approving critics said I had expressed the "disillusionment of a generation", which is nonsense. I may have expressed for them their own illusion of being disillusioned, but that did not form part of my intention.'

catchy that readers ignored the would-be saint. Eliot's strategy – pushed by Pound – failed by its success, for the strategy took over the poem. The cacophony of horns and motors, ragtime and gramophone, the Jazz Age and the post-war clamour seem to drown out the silence between the lines, which invites the reader to reciprocal effort. This silence circles repeated hints of what is *not* waste. We hear it in the space that follows the 'DA' of thunder; and in the space which in the early printings of the poem preceded the sublime peace of 'Shantih shantih shantih'; and in the weight of prophetic voices and lyric moments: above all in a memory of 'looking into the heart of light, the silence' in the presence of the 'hyacinth girl' with her arms full of flowers in a garden of fertile love.* The fishermen exposed to the sea are also beyond the waste; so too the 'inexplicable splendour' of St Magnus the Martyr, the children chanting in the chapel ('*Et O ces voix d'enfants, chantant dans la coupole!*'), and the tolling bells of the finale. Their presence suggests that this is a poem not solely about collapse, but also about a possibility of regeneration.

The Waste Land is defined in part by a visionary alternative we can't quite grasp before it fades and eludes us. To lose what is *not* a wasteland is the very condition of being in a wasteland. The mass of the inhabitants of the Unreal City – the clerks hurrying over London Bridge, the typist, the habitués of the pub – are too oblivious of their condition to suffer the experience the poem grants us. For it terminates in us, its readers.

The last lines divide our feeling between antithetical states. On the one hand are three holy words and a damp gust bringing rain to the arid land; on the other, London Bridge is falling down and madness returns. *The Waste Land* stops short of salvation, and leaves us between collapse and recovery, between 'The horror! the horror!' of the Unreal

---

* Hyacinths are purple or dark red flowers. In mythology, Hyacinthus, the god of love, was loved by Apollo, who accidentally killed him. Emerson wrote of 'The hyacinth boy, for whom / Morn well might break / and April bloom.'

City and some unspoken 'reality' – we are haunted by hints of 'reality' but unable to possess them. The last lines jolt us faster between these extremes. There are intimations of sublime peace, but are they fading or approaching? In either case, there is no finality, no full stop. Completion remains for the reader.

6

CONVERSION

WHEN ELIOT VISITED Rome in 1926 he fell on his knees before Michelangelo's *Pietà*, to the surprise of his brother and sister-in-law who were with him. His entry into the Church of England the following year astonished many friends and readers, but for Eliot there was no dramatic change, only 'an expansion or development of interests'.

Churchmen who knew Eliot in later life denied that he was in any way distinguishable from an Englishman born into the Anglican Church. In the early 1970s when I spoke to men like Canon Demant of Christ Church, Oxford, who was part of Eliot's church circle, they seemed – all of them – a little put out to be reminded of his American origin, as though they had forgotten it. He was one of 'us'. His last confessor, Father Hillier, stressed his humility and called him 'a thoroughly converted man'. The completeness of Eliot's adaptation to the Anglican community was in itself extraordinary, given the man as he appeared in the intellectual milieu of the early 1920s. His inward development was largely invisible, for the saint's dream had been edited out of *The Waste Land* and the visionary element almost obliterated in the cacophony of the day. Eliot was hailed as the sceptic of the hour, the spokesman for the 'lost' generation, venting the bitterness of its disillusion with the elders who had led them into a needless war; he was also, in his mid-thirties, a man taking control of opinion through his international journal, the *Criterion*.

Vivienne was central to this enterprise. A letter from Eliot to his assistant, Richard Aldington, reveals that she did a lot of *Criterion* work, and that she had an original mind – not at all a feminine one, Eliot considered. Because she was diffident about her untrained mind, she began to write for the *Criterion* under assumed names. Eliot did not hesitate to publish her extensively, completing some of her stories if she was too ill to do so, or touching them up. She cultivated an ironic detachment like Eliot's own, and took on an array of pseudonyms: Fanny Marlow, Feiron Morris, Felise Morrison, FM, and Irene Fassett. Vivienne saw Fanny Marlow as the money-maker, spinning on forever like a spider. 'There is no *end* to Fanny! But Feiron will never make money. And he does not spin. He is a nasty fellow.'

Vivienne's infiltration into the *Criterion* was part of a secret policy, confided to Pound at the outset in November 1922: to back the 'jailbirds' – himself, Pound, Wyndham Lewis, Dostoevsky (an outline for 'The Life of a Great Sinner' which came through a Russian émigré, Samuel Solomono-vitch Koteliansky), as well as 'nasty' Feiron. Eliot once confided to his mother that 'getting recognised in English letters is like breaking open a safe – for an American.' To gain access and crack the combinations to the safe could only be done as an inside job. In this Eliot was helped by his confidence as an Eliot, which made him feel the equal of anyone. Henry James, after all, had been 'comparatively parvenu'. Eliot's plot was to slide the 'jailbirds' between impeccable contributors like Professor Saintsbury and under sober grey covers.

The *Criterion* was 'so heavily camouflaged as Westminster Abbey,' Pound protested, 'that the living visitor is not very visible'.

Eliot reassured him that certain passengers, required to steer a respectable vessel out to sea, would soon 'walk the plank'.

He told a favoured contributor, the poet and art critic Herbert Read, that too visible an association might suggest to the public a Gunpowder Plot. Under cover, he was forming a phalanx. The plot was nothing less than to take over the literary establishment. A Gunpowder Plot fits the Guy Fawkes* mood of 'The Hollow Men' (1925). We should not be fooled by a straw man who's about to burn: politically, he is something of a stalking horse. A plot is yet in the making. An audible whimper is not defeat; it is a reasonable fear that the bang won't go off. The plotter naturally hesitates to explode 'the world'. Beyond the incidental fact that we, in the world, will be wiped out, it is a venture that has little to do with us and everything to do with ambition on a scale most of us could not imagine: literary and moral dictatorship.

It is worth remembering that, at this point in his career, Eliot was considered by many to be unacceptable, or at the very least questionable – just as the primitive rhythms of Stravinsky, or Nijinsky masturbating at the climax of his performance at the 1912 première of *L'Après-midi d'un faune*, or the Post-Impressionist paintings exhibited in London in 1910 and 1912, had shocked or infuriated the wider public. The avant-garde had welcomed *The Waste Land*, the *Dial* had awarded the poem a prize and found it impossible to fill a thousand new orders for its November number, and yet many accomplished readers found the poetry incomprehensible. It was 'like something in cipher', Henry Eliot, no fool, remarked to their mother. It was marginal to the non-avant garde as represented by the 'Squirearchy', the coterie of Sir John Squire (1884–1958) who was literary editor of the *New Statesman* from 1913, chief reviewer for the *Observer*, and editor of a new magazine, the *London Mercury* from 1919. The Squirearchy championed traditional literature against a Modern incursion which seemed anarchic and obscure. In 1923, Squire himself complained that *The Waste Land* was 'a faithful transcript, after Mr. Joyce's obscurer manner, of the poet's wandering thoughts when in a state of erudite depression.' Quite. But what follows is blank dis-

---

* Guy Fawkes was a seventeenth-century Englishman who joined a plot to blow up Parliament with gunpowder. He was hanged, drawn and quartered. In England and its colonies, this event was (and sometimes still is) celebrated with fireworks and bonfires of straw men every 5 November.

missal: 'A grunt would serve equally well'. In the mid-twenties All Souls College, Oxford, did not elect Eliot to a fellowship when he was proposed, and a faction of Cambridge dons opposed his appointment as distinguished lecturer. The most intransigent proved to be Eliot's own college. 'He is not a poet at all', was the ruling opinion at Merton as late as the 1950s.

So, the old guard looked upon Eliot with suspicion, and the young were defying these elders when an undergraduate at Oxford blasted *The Waste Land* through a megaphone over Christ Church meadow. Upholders of public opinion like Sir Edmund Gosse did not take to Eliot. And Eliot was not impervious to public opinion: he intended to rule it. 'Would you care to cut up —?' he might say to a prospective reviewer. 'I think what reputation he has should be exploded.' I. P. Fassett cuts up *The Tents of Israel* by G. B. Stern: 'no Jew', this reviewer says, 'can ever be a great artist' – the best Jews can do by the dint of cleverness and hard work is 'a marvellous imitation of art'.

In a poem 'Necesse est Perstare?' Vivienne Eliot (as 'F.M.') describes a moment after a literary luncheon when the guests have departed. The wife is thankful for an end to gossip about Clive Bell, Elizabeth Bibesco, and Aldous Huxley. She longs to win her husband from his resolve to master the cultural scene. But he stretches his arms above his head with the weary air of a very old monkey, impervious to her silent plea. One of Vivienne's sketches accounts for Eliot's block during 1923 and 1924 by his distracting urge to possess all the kingdoms of this world:

> 'Isn't he wonderful?' whispered Felice. 'He is the most marvellous poet in the *whole world*.'
> 'He might be if he wrote anything,' said Sybilla dryly.
> 'Yes, why *doesn't* he write more?'
> 'Because he wants to be everything at once, I expect. Perhaps the devil took him up into a high mountain and showed him all the kingdoms of the world – unfortunately for him!'
> 'And so, I suppose,' asked Felice naggingly, 'that he doesn't know which kingdom to choose?'

'He's still up on the mountain so far as I know . . .'

Vivienne pounced on the omnivorousness but she didn't understand it – that American hunger for experience, knowledge, people, Europe that Henry James presented sympathetically in a similar image of Milly Theale, poised on a mountain in Europe 'in a state of uplifted and unlimited possession . . . She was looking down on the kingdoms of the earth . . . Was she choosing among them, or did she want them all? . . . It would be a question of taking full in the face the whole assault of life, to the general muster of which indeed her face might have directly presented as she sat there on her rock.' Eliot differed from Milly in his suspicion of the world as a snare, and in his vulnerability to the devil's temptations. Pound's wife, Dorothy, said that Eliot was 'always wrestling with a devil or an angel', which made life uncomfortable.

Vivienne channelled her frustration into a diatribe against America in her 'Diary of the Rive Gauche' (under the name of Fanny Marlow). The narrator reminds herself (mimicking the repetitive manner of Vivienne's own talk) 'that I never did understand Americans. I simply do not understand Americans. When I see an American coming I ought to say immediately, "Please do not speak to me, because if you do I shall not understand you. I shall never understand you, so will you please pass on." For instance, why do Americans insist that all European women are *au courant* with every form of vice (to them all pleasure or amusement really means vice, so far as I can see) – whereas they insinuate that the female of their own species is supremely innocent and unsullied . . . Why? Because they cannot cope with European women. Ha! they can't cope with us!'

Between 1923 and 1925, the mutual misfortune of the Eliot marriage came to a crisis. Eliot's complaints of poverty – of long hours at the bank that left him exhausted, or huge doctors' bills during Vivienne's bouts of illness – had some foundation, but chiefly they provided a front for other problems, moral and domestic, which disturbed him more profoundly. Not the grandest stipend, not the pleasantest part-time post could have assuaged Eliot's misery during these years. Pound and Ottoline Morrell set up separate funds to rescue Eliot for poetry;* Leonard Woolf told a friend on 22 February 1923 that Eliot 'continually consults us as to his future'; the Woolfs schemed to appoint him literary editor for the *Nation*; then all were baffled when he turned their offers down.

The problem, briefly, was Eliot's obligation to secure the future for a wife who would never manage to shift for herself or endure any privation. And at the very time that Vivienne's needs mounted, Eliot first tasted fame and began to feel more strongly than ever the claims of his poetic career. At the age of thirty-four, he had worked in the bank for five years, and now, he owned, 'the prospect of staying there for the rest of my life is abominable to me'. Eliot's friends urged him to leave the bank, but he had to think of Vivienne. He had $2,000 from the *Dial* prize, and could rely on Quinn for substantial gifts – Quinn had been willing to pledge £300 a year to Pound's scheme. In 1923 Pound sent Eliot such funds as Bel Esprit had accumulated (about £120), which he received gratefully in two instalments. His mother had given him 200 shares from his father's Hydraulic Brick Company, worth about $10,000, yielding £635 a year. Eliot also had a substantial inheritance from his father, but Henry Ware Eliot, Sr, had disapproved of his son's marriage and had not left the money outright, as to his other children. On Eliot's death the money was to revert to the Eliot family. Until 1923 (when Charlotte Eliot provided for Vivienne in her will) Vivienne's main security appeared to be Lloyds Bank, which meant an annual income of £500 and provision for employees' widows, and she insisted that her husband should not leave his job. 'Indeed, if he did take such steps I should bear him a considerable grudge,' she wrote to Mary Hutchinson on 4 March 1923, detailing her ills. She was having 'Plomblière'

* Pound set up the 'Bel Esprit' scheme. Ottoline Morrell set up the 'Eliot Fellowship Fund'. Eliot told Pound that he would need at least £600 a year, a flat in London, and six months abroad.

treatment for 'catarrh of the intestines with occasional enteritis'. Although she had been one of the first to believe in Eliot as a poet, she refused the romantic demand that a wife sacrifice herself in the cause of genius. She took the defensible view that it is *not* picturesque to die in a humble cot.

In fact, Vivienne was less vulnerable than she appeared: her parents lived in comfort without a salary, which meant that she and her brother could expect to live in equal comfort when her parents died. She also had some property coming to her from an aunt. If Eliot died before her, she would inherit his Hydraulic stock. Altogether, as Henry Eliot discerned, Vivienne was not penniless 'as we once supposed'.

Early in April the crisis broke when Eliot considered leaving the bank without an alternative position and, at the same time, tried to settle Vivienne alone in a cottage near Chichester. Vivienne's colitis took a dangerous turn. Within three weeks she wasted away to a skeleton. She was at the point of death seven or eight times. Eliot, shaken, gave up his plan to leave the bank and fretted over the expense of two specialists from London, the local doctor twice a day, not to mention the year's rent on a cottage that had proved rather disagreeable. In a despairing cable and letter to Quinn on 25 and 26 April Eliot said that his affairs were in complete chaos. In May, he reported to Pound 'a hell of a time' with Vivienne, who had threatened suicide.

As she had once sought consolation in the faithless Russell, so in the twenties she flirted with Prince Dimitry Mirsky, according to Ottoline Morrell 'a dreadful man . . . a fraud . . . a brute'. Yet another ill-judged man added to the sum of Vivienne's distress.

She was a deviser of tortured situations and also their victim. All this she saw like a clever bad child. Eliot told Bertrand Russell that she had an uncanny astuteness, and in Vivienne's copy of *Poems 1909–1925* he wrote that only she would understand them. 'He is a Prophet,' she declared, understanding the exact character of his vehemence. He made her feel, with him, 'a sort of super-being'. His poetry displays her in overweening roles, playing Duchess, Cleopatra, or the lady of situations, conspicuously vocal compared with an ideal Lady of silences. Vivienne was not disposed to be her husband's inferior. Eloquent, febrile, perpetually sick, she had needs of her own. These Eliot met with conscientious patience and an inward detachment that only made her more demanding. Vivienne's health, Eliot told Russell in 1925, was now a thousand times worse than when he had married her. For a whole year, she had lain in an 'abyss', as she put it, 'a helpless and unspeakable wreck of drugs, fear and semi-paralysis'. In intermittent dramas between 1923 and 1925 the tension rose: Vivienne's explicit; Eliot's repressed.

In April 1925 he burst out to Virginia Woolf that he had spent three months mewed up in Vivienne's room. Vivienne's doctor had released her childhood fears of loneliness, and she would not let her husband out of her sight. If he did go out, he would come back to find her staging a faint. It is as though the scenario which he had set out years before in 'The Death of a Duchess' were coming to life: the wife's fear of abandonment; the husband's wish to escape from the room. The open terror of the woman may actually be a response to that unspoken but vehement wish.

'To-morrow will be wretched,' Eliot said. He had to go out from eight to eleven.

Virginia Woolf laid an arm on his shoulder. Over the next few years she watched him 'drown, wrapped in swathes of dirty seaweed'. So the mermaid sang to Eliot, a vengeful muse who dragged him down to her dark seabed. It became a struggle for survival, projected into the menace of *Sweeney Agonistes*, which Eliot began in about September 1923:

> I knew a man once did a girl in
> Any man might do a girl in
> Any man has to, needs to, wants to
> Once in a lifetime, do a girl in.

As this took shape in Eliot's mind between 1923 and 1926, Vivienne worsened. A collapse of morale in 1925 seems to mark the start of irreversible decline.

'Am ill (*still* ill) not ill again (always ill),' she told Pound, with insistent, rhythmic cries, like the wild wife in *The Waste Land*.

Current opinion held that a woman who showed signs of strain should be stopped from writing. The case was similar to Virginia Woolf's, and Eliot approached Leonard Woolf for advice. They exchanged more than thirty letters at this time and lunched together weekly. Vivienne, Eliot explained, was naturally immoderate and had never been trained in regular habits of work. When she got an idea, she wanted to work it out at once. When she was not allowed to write, she would think and think the whole time. Should her writing be curtailed, he wanted to know, or should she have a free hand?

Vivienne stated her protest in a draft of a letter which she pasted into her writing book. She might be speaking here for all who are struggling to find a voice. It was 'torture' to follow standard ways of writing at appointed times. She argued that her material could not be regulated because it came not from books but from some 'very overgrown and hidden inner spirit':

> When this begins to spurt, it is intolerable to choke it up, & will lead to my going mad. It is agony either way, of course, but I think at first, until one has got the spout of this long disused fountain clear, it is better to let the water burst out when it will & so *force* away the accumulation of decayed vegetation, moss, slime & dead fish which are thick upon & around it.

Eliot defined Vivienne's case as a nervous rather than mental breakdown. He made this distinction, granting reasons for her collapse: her loneliness in their marriage and her fear that he would leave her. Eliot implied that it was he, if anyone, who was in need of mental treatment and asked Leonard Woolf to recommend a doctor with psychoanalytic knowledge. Leonard sent him to Sir Henry Head, a peculiar choice since Virginia Woolf had attempted suicide immediately after a consultation with this man in 1913. (Henry James, who consulted Head in 1912, found him worse than useless: his cures sent you down 'into hell'.) Eliot merely found him not modern enough. Leonard conceded, 'Head can be rather brusk in manner.'

Vivienne herself had no illusions about doctors, whose tampering usually did her more harm than good. One doctor, obsessed with glands, started her on 'a very violent treatment' in 1922 which, she confided to Pound, 'I do not think will be of any use. He gave me some glands to take called Ovarian Opocaps and told me that this was a "shot in the dark". I think that English doctors are more fond of "shots in the dark" than any treatment based on scientific knowledge. It appeals to the "sporting" side of the English character.' Another time she was 'crying with rage' against a Dr West, who was convinced that all her ills lay in a rock-hard liver. She hammered poor Pound with sarcastic questions:

Is West alrite?
Do you *know*?
Do you believe in Vichy [for cures of the liver]?
Do you believe in Liver?

There is an element in this of hilarious enjoyment, even pride in her drama. At this time she 'took to' trances. 'Spouse all of a dither,' she boasted. 'Am very *hypnotic, always* was. Could be 1st class MEDIUM'.

Eliot, worn out, went away to Rapallo at the end of 1925. He left Vivienne at a Health Institute in Watford, Hertford-shire. From there she sent an SOS via Pound: 'All I can utter are abstract yells.' Ezra must make Tom 'rescue' her at once. When Eliot rushed back to England, he found her fairly normal. She was affectionate, but he could not respond. He wrote to Pound that her behaviour left much to be desired, and returned forthwith to Italy, warning Vivienne that he might turn vampire if not allowed some respite. Vivienne took on the role of a doomed Little Nell, and declared herself 'anxious to die'.

Such dire exchanges are close to the threatening world of *Sweeney Agonistes*, which Eliot published in two fragments in October 1926 and January 1927. The epigraph to the early typescript quotes Brutus, the high-minded assassin, the same words Eliot was to use again in 1933 about ending his marriage:

> Between the acting of a dreadful thing
> And the first motion, all the interim is
> Like a phantasma, or a hideous dream.

The play is about a dream of murder that has rooted itself in Sweeney's mind and which he is compelled to relive. In the final version Sweeney speaks of the murderer as some other man, but in the early typescript Sweeney himself appears to shoot Mrs Porter (the madam of the brothel which Sweeney frequents in *The Waste Land*). Mrs Porter is carried out for dead, but is resurrected. Her voice coming from the next room taunts Sweeney with a bawdy ballad about the sexual prowess of a hero of the red-light district. Murderer and victim accept the roles assigned by fate, and the victim returns to Sweeney's side, so that a murder scene can repeat itself eternally. Man and woman are locked by their natures in a savage, inescapable ritual, propelled by unceasing drum taps.

Sweeney is a familiar type of brute innocence who stumbles on the scene of a crime. In 'Sweeney Among the Nightingales', it is a conspiracy in a low dive; in *Sweeney Agonistes* it is a fatal tie to a woman, no longer Mrs Porter but Doris, the epileptic prostitute of 'Sweeney Erect'. Doris has a moment of horror in the first scene, an intimation of her death which is matched, in the second scene, by Sweeney's horror at what murder – or the intent to murder – does to a man. The main difference between Eliot's early and final draft is that, in the latter, sin itself is not dramatised: what interests him is the aftermath of sin in the lives of sinners. As Eliot put it in a contemporary essay, a not bad but undeveloped nature awakens to moral consequences. Sweeney finds himself trapped in the toils of remorse, pursued by 'hoo-ha's', as he waits for Judgement. The fragments end with a chorus of Hoo's followed by nine loud knocks.

Sweeney is haunted, like Sykes after his murder of Nancy (in *Oliver Twist*), where the real nightmare is not the pursuit by the police but the resurrection of his victim. Her eyes are upon him wherever he flees. Eliot, too, was haunted by eyes in the 'Dream Songs' of this time. There is a drowning face that 'sweats with tears'. There are the remembered tears of the rejected Figlia che Piange: the speaker is afflicted by a lifelong division from these eyes, which have since dried and become eyes of judgement. As the brute becomes a hollow man – a lost soul – he comes to fear the eyes of his victim and dare not meet them in his dreams. Yet, at the same time, he holds to a distant, fading image of other eyes that could restore his soul and revive poetic sight. These eyes, which he must not approach, are sublime, a 'perpetual star'. This is the futile dream of empty men: the 'multifoliate rose' of paradise.

The dreaming that connects *Sweeney Agonistes*, 'Doris's Dream Songs', and 'The Hollow Men' seems to veer between supernatural terror and grace that have their source in Eliot's contrasting relations to his wife and Emily Hale. It has come to light that Emily Hale was in London in 1923, presumably in the summer, between the marital 'hell' of April–May and the start of *Sweeney* in September.

In May 1915, as Eliot had shifted towards Vivienne, Emily Hale had been playing the title role in *Eliza Comes To Stay* with a company called The Amateurs. In 1917 she directed the same play for the Cambridge Social Dramatic Club. The year before she had begun to coach students who joined the drama club at Simmons College in Boston. If family debarred her from the professional stage – and she was scrupulously observant of her duty to them – she could at least teach. Because she had no formal training and no college degree, she had to find her way into colleges as an administrator. In 1918 she took up a post as Assistant Matron of the dormitories at Simmons College. Unofficially, she continued as drama coach. As matron, she distinguished herself in the flu epidemic that followed the war. At the same time she continued to act with amateur companies like the Footlight Club. In April 1919 she played the Comtesse in J. M. Barrie's farce, *What Every Woman Knows*. Eleanor Hinkley must have written about her to Eliot, because on 17 June 1919 he replies to his cousin: 'I have written to Emily – I hope it was a nice letter. I should, I think, like her to know what a keen interest I take in everything that happens to her.' The college authorities noted that she was a 'superior type', and from 1919 to 1921 she became Director of Dormitories. All the while she pursued her alternative career in numerous plays, including *Bluebeard* (May 1920), *Overtones* (1921, staged with Eleanor Hinkley's play *A Flitch of Bacon*), and as the female lead in *Cyrano de Bergerac* at the Copley Theatre. As an actress and director her training took place on the stage. Formal study was no more than the odd summer course: one at the Leland Powers Summer School of the Spoken Word in Boston in 1920; another at the Cornish School of the Theatre, Seattle, in 1921.

In 1921, when she was thirty, she moved to a combined post as administrator and drama teacher at Milwaukee-Downer College, a private women's school now part of the University of Wisconsin. There had been predictable opposition over her lack of qualifications, but she was persuasive, and the college agreed to pay her $1,000 a year. During her first year there, in March 1922, she played Dorimène, a marchioness, in a production of *Le Bourgeois Gentilhomme*, to celebrate Molière's tercentenary. A collection of photographs shows her as a highly painted young woman wielding a fan. That year she also took the lead in a Pulitzer Prize-winning play *Miss Lulu Bett* in Milwaukee's main theatre, infusing a down-trodden role with dry wit. At the same time she took up teaching with the panache of Miss Jean Brodie, a born teacher who always attracted a set of special girls. A college bulletin outlines her admirable aims: 'to find each student's need or gift and to guide it to better and fuller means of expression', grounded in 'honest, direct interpretation of life – off the stage.' She demanded an erect carriage and flexible, open mouths. Tongues that were lazy were exercised; accents and colloquialisms were toned down in favour of 'standards of phonetic excellence'.

Little is known, as yet, of her contact with Eliot from the time of his marriage until the revival of their tie in the thirties.

It may have been in 1923 that she enrolled in a course she took at some undetermined point at the Speech Institute in London – according to a curriculum vitae, one of five visits to England by 1930. There is no proof, so far, that she and Eliot met, and yet it is unlikely that Emily would have stayed in London and not let him know. It may even be that their common interest in theatre encouraged Eliot to begin his first play in September 1923.

That month, Eliot sent Emily Hale a copy of his 1920 collection of poems, *Ara Vos Prec*. There was something he wanted to say to Emily, and he found a way to say it through a particular title. 'Ara vos prec' are the words of Arnaut Daniel, the lustful sinner who, in Dante's *Purgatorio*, owns his fault and accepts his punishment in purgatory, but cries out for pity: 'I beseech you ... take pity on my pain'. 'For Emily Hale with the author's humble compliments, T. S. Eliot', he wrote conventionally, then the date '5. ix. 23', and then another Dantean inscription which resonates with unstated import:

'sieti raccommandato il mio Tesoro
nel qual io vivo ancora, e più non cheggio.'
Poi si rivolse.

A man of learning speaks from hell, asking that his book be remembered: ' "Keep my *Treasure*, where I yet live on, and I ask no more." Then he turned round.' Both Dantean passages were special to Eliot – he repeated them in his works, and there is no other instance where he addressed these words to a living person. From the pit, as it were, he offered Emily, the minister's daughter, a glimpse of his soul.

In Eliot's dream-poetry, the antithesis to the hollow men are stars, like heavenly eyes, recalling a lost purity of feeling. A golden foot 'I may not kiss or touch' glows in the shadow of the bed, and the eyes appear in a 'golden vision'. The dreamer swings 'between two lives' as he strains towards the angelic touch or breath and then wakes alone, trembling with tenderness, with lips that would kiss or frame prayers to the broken image of a girl once loved.

The dream-poetry draws us into some very delicate and unspeakable emotion, while *Sweeney* distracts us with the restless activity of visionless characters, prostitutes and noisy transatlantic visitors to London, ex-soldiers on a spree, nudging one another into bravado and propping their meagre personalities with stale phrases. 'We did our bit', they say loudly, 'got the Hun on the run'.

Into this routine patter explodes Sweeney's tale of murder. The killer keeps the woman's body in a bath of lysol while he maintains a façade of respectability. He pays the rent and takes in the milk. Inwardly, though, he is dead, more truly dead than his victim since he is damned for all eternity. The play, originally called 'The Marriage of Life and Death', had at its core this buried state of death-in-life which will bind killer to victim more completely and permanently than in life. And this tie will cut him off from all humanity. Sweeney's story had its origin in Eliot's prose piece of 1917 where Eeldrop, the bank clerk, analyses a man in Gopsum Street who has murdered his mistress: 'The important fact is that for the man the act is eternal, and for the brief space he has to live, he is already dead. He is already in a different world from ours. He has crossed the frontier. The important fact is that something is done which cannot be undone.' Ordinary minds concern themselves with the body and the weapon, but 'the medieval world, insisting on the eternity of punishment, expressed something nearer the truth'.

Fantasies of escape from a sexual tie persist in Eliot's works – in 'Elegy', in 'The Death of the Duchess', in *Sweeney Agonistes* ('Any man might do a girl in'), and, eventually, in *The Family Reunion* (1939). Eliot's marital and religious crises were inextricably mixed: through his impulsive commitment to Vivienne, Eliot made 'that frightful discovery of morality' when 'the not naturally bad but irresponsible and undeveloped nature [is] caught in the consequences of its own action' and 'becomes moral only by becoming damned'. The sense of damnation, the remorse and guilt that Vivienne evoked, were essential to Eliot's long purgatorial journey. He might escape her, morally, only by embracing the ascetic Way of the Catholic mystics.

Eliot drew on the words of St John of the Cross for one epigraph to *Sweeney Agonistes*: 'Hence the soul cannot be possessed by the divine union, until it has divested itself of the love of created beings.' Some of Eliot's friends were taken aback. 'I don't think that ordinary human affections are capable of leading us to the love of God,' Eliot explained, 'but rather that the love of God is capable of informing, intensifying, and elevating our human affections, which otherwise have little to distinguish them from the "natural" affections of animals.' This position is the opposite of the humanist view of his mother and grandfather that it is through love of one's kind that one approaches love of God. Eliot's disgust with the body and misfortunes with 'natural' love confirmed his monastic idea of divine love as utterly different in kind.

*

People who met Eliot casually were charmed by his manners and modest silence, but those on whose friendship he relied saw a man constantly on the verge of a breakdown, peevish and 'desperate', weakened by weariness, and preoccupied with fears of poverty. Eliot wrote to John Quinn: 'I have not even time to go to a dentist or to have my hair cut. . . . I am worn out. I cannot go on.' These days, he turned to the whisky bottle. Lady Ottoline often found it hard to be near him. His other comfort was Alida Monro (wife of Harold Monro, founder of the *Poetry Review*) the only woman, according to Vivienne, to understand her husband. Virginia Woolf was baffled by Eliot's sudden withdrawals from friendship, by his refusal to respond when his shell was prodded, and by the laboured perplexities of his rhetoric in which he would enshroud his feelings. One day she, her sister, and husband found him in a state of collapse in his flat. His eyes were blurred, his face ashen, and he could barely stand up to see them out.

Virginia Woolf could at times divine others with darting acumen. Suddenly, four years before Eliot's conversion, she caught sight of what would emerge:

> That strange figure Eliot dined here last night. I feel that he has taken the veil, or whatever monks do. . . . Mrs Eliot has almost died at times in the last month. Tom, though infinitely considerate, is also perfectly detached. His cell, is I'm sure a very lofty one . . .

Virginia Woolf saw the 'cell' with amazing clairvoyance. Conversion meant not only joining a church, but declaring himself ready to begin to close the gap between human frailty and superhuman perfection.

This dream, so fragile, so daring, so inadmissible, needed the protection of an array of masks. A 'crowskin' must mask the approach to God's Kingdom: 'Let me also wear / Such deliberate disguises . . .'. The interest of Eliot's life, as well as his work, has seemed to many readers to lie in a game of masks and unmaskings, yet it is not enough to see only an Eliot who changes inexplicably from one disguise to another, according to his company. Hawthorne presents a New Englander, Holgrave, who shifts all the time yet 'never violated the innermost man' but 'carried his conscience with him'. So, with Eliot, there is an inward certainty that invites confidence, yet it remains elusive behind the many façades: 'I was still the same, knowing myself yet being someone other.'

As Eliot advanced into middle age he shed his American youth and cultivated the anonymous front of an English gentleman. At Lloyds Bank he wore City trousers, slate-blue with black stripes, and a black business coat with a bowler and grey spats. He surrounded himself with the props of respectability: the modest manner, the deferential attentiveness, the voice so measured as to sound almost deadpan. The most long-lived mask was an ageing man, tired out at twenty-one: 'I grow old . . . I grow old . . .'. By playing Possum, as Pound called him, he could evade unwanted demands. He liked, playfully, to adopt an alias. In 1923 he had a hideaway at 38 Burleigh Mansions, St Martin's Lane, almost over the publishing house of Chatto & Windus. There, he answered to the name of 'Captain Eliot' – you were instructed to knock at his door three times. Another hideaway in the mid-twenties was a small top-floor flat in the Charing Cross Road: here, again, you were to enquire at the porter's lodge for 'The Captain'. Osbert Sitwell said the feeling was nautical not military, but, either way, Eliot was playing his favourite Sherlock Holmes role, a mysterious character whose incognitos and purposes were unguessable by people of ordinary brain. To artistic Bloomsbury of the twenties Eliot presented a face tinted green with powder to look cadaverous.

Eliot's visible life offers only the shell of a character who was almost antithetical to what appeared. To all appearance Eliot was conventional, mild, decorous, yet the hidden character was daring and savage. The outward appearance proclaimed normality; the hidden self refused all norms as it struck out for the frontiers of experience. To understand Eliot's life it is necessary to see the continuity of this venture through the poetry so that, with him, it's futile to dab at individual poems.

Eliot's masks disguise an extraordinary singleness of mind. To follow the course of his development it is necessary to walk a narrow path: not to be dazzled by Eliot's performances – the smokescreen of absence, and the deadpan intoning. It is necessary, also, to resist the opposite: to be tempted to crude exposé, for there was, of course, the disturbing side to Eliot: the irrational contempt – 'no women worth printing', he declared to Pound at the very time, privately, he was praising Virginia Woolf for her experimental novel *Jacob's Room*, accepting Vivienne's name for the *Criterion* (in place of his own idea, 'The London Review' which she thought dismal), and publishing May Sinclair alongside *The Waste Land* in the first number – and, disturbing too, his questionable treatment, as we shall see, of three women who gave their love to him during his creative years. Yet these are partial truths and must be seen in the perspective of a man who, while he performed the routines of work, commuting, and dining out in mid-century London, existed all the time, in his imagination, beyond the pale of civilisation and within sight of eternity. No one in the rush-hour would have suspected that the immaculate gentleman, with his carefully rolled umbrella, his bowler hat, and a white handkerchief in the breast pocket of his sober suit, was trying out – 'For thine is . . . For thine is the . . .'. Attempts at prayer seal his remoteness from the urban setting in which he placed himself almost, it might seem, as cover. Masked by apparent conformity, he had passed by in the midst of the workaday swarm, an anonymous Judgement ('The horror! the horror!') in the urban waste. Now, still masked by anonymity, an awakening soul infiltrates the crowd.

*

Self-transformation begins from what precedes it: a person who feels weak, helpless, and locked in fears: on the one hand, fear of action; on the other, fear of inaction. Behind these lurks a greater fear of the unknown.

'I am afraid of the life after death,' Eliot said to Pound in 1923 in Verona.

'This beats me,' Pound replied, 'beats me.'

Pound was drunk on the beauty and culture of Italy, which was life enough. They were sitting with Bride Scratton at the Caffè Dante towards sundown by the arena. Eliot, in some theatrical get-up with a little (not very clean) lace falling over his knuckles, was in the role of *il decaduto* (the decadent) but also, Pound recognised, Arnaut Daniel burning for his sins in Dante's *Purgatorio*.

The last work on which Eliot consulted Pound was 'The Hollow Men'. So brilliantly does it fuse the gleeful gunpowder plot with the purgatorial plot (the purposeful 'burning burning') that it is easy to confuse what are, in fact, different (though parallel) ventures. The religious plot has come to a crossing, 'a tumid river', in which a man of straw would disintegrate. Is he a man of straw? He draws back from the plunge. The alternative is equally daunting: an ordeal by fire. The old guy filled with straw, like effigies of Guy Fawkes, must burn. Either way, the old life must be washed or burnt away if a new is to come into being, whimpering like a newborn, as secular existence comes to an end.

In the last part of 'The Hollow Men' we are allowed to overhear an act of conversion as it begins in the utmost privacy of the mind. A potential convert, still hollow of belief, tries to make the Lord's Prayer ('*For Thine is the Kingdom*') his own prayer. On the right of the page are the eloquent responses of the given prayer; on the left, the potential convert struggles to utter the words, in vain:

For Thine is

The shadow of doubt and fear draws him back. He ventures once more, edging slightly further, only to fall, again, short of completion:

For Thine is the

Eliot's entry into the Church was not brought about by a ferment that mounted naturally to a point of action. He said that the thought of the intelligent believer 'proceeds by rejection and elimination' until he finds a satisfactory explanation both for the disordered world without and the moral world within. Eliot stressed rational progress rather than emotional states. He accepted the morality of damnation, and could not save himself without help. It seems that at this time he felt no fervour, and was driven to the Church almost as a last resort.

Eliot had first visited an Anglican chapel at Merton College, Oxford, in 1914. (He kept a picture postcard of its interior.) He began to frequent Anglican churches in the City of London, between 1917 and 1921, in search of a quiet spot to think during lunch hour. At first, he enjoyed St Magnus the Martyr aesthetically, for its 'splendour'; later he appreciated its 'utility' when he came there as a sinner. He was struck, once, by the sight of a number of people on their knees, a posture he had never seen before. Eliot's family was not accustomed to kneel. Mrs Charles William Eliot wrote censoriously to a friend who had joined the Episcopalian

Church: 'Do you kneel down in church and call yourself a miserable sinner? Neither I nor my family will ever do that!' But Eliot admired this gesture of abasement and worship.

The first serious impetus towards the Church of England coincided with Eliot's lowest point in 1923. It was then that the printer of the *Criterion*, Richard Cobden-Sanderson, introduced Eliot to a fellow-American, William Force Stead, who also had a disturbed wife and was ordained in the Church of England. This priest became Eliot's confidant in the years before and after his conversion, encouraging his attention to the writings of seventeenth-century Anglicans, in particular those of the Bishop of Winchester, Lancelot Andrewes. Eliot read the sermons on the Incarnation (a notion his Unitarian family would not have stressed). He saturated himself in Andrewes' prose ('but sure there is no joy in the world to the joy of a man saved') and found his examination of the words 'terminating in the ecstasy of assent'. When Eliot had first read sermons in 1919 he had been attracted by Donne's spellbinding personality. He now came to prefer the 'pure', 'medieval' temper of Andrewes, who did not stir the emotions so much as stress a settled and resolute will to holiness. This stage of patient waiting demands that one shed personality so as to concentrate on a mystery beyond the self. In the sermons of Lancelot Andrewes, Eliot said, one 'is finally "alone with the Alone" '.

His essay 'Lancelot Andrewes' explored a distinction between poets with self-riveted emotions (Donne is his prime exemplar) and the austere spirit of Andrewes: 'Donne belonged to that class of persons, of which there are always one or two examples in the modern world, who seek refuge in religion from the tumults of a strong emotional temperament which can find no complete satisfaction elsewhere.' Donne had something in common with the Jesuits or Calvinists in their understanding of sin, but Andrewes had the purer concentration. So Eliot reminded himself that there were still higher places 'in the spiritual hierarchy'.

His first success at sustained contemplation had come in the last (and, to him, most important) section of *The Waste*

Land. There, for the first time, attention does not flit distractedly, but concentrates on the absence of water (spiritual fertility). The concentration is so intense that water is, at times, imagined and, though it proves a mirage, the speaker does go some way towards a new poetic language of longing and prayer, using the biblical images of thirst and journey for a Modern pilgrimage away from the sterile site of urban despair.

Eliot craved a stronger, more dogmatic theological structure than was to be found in his own ethical background. Associating his parents' injunctions about 'what is done and not done' with Puritanism, he scribbled on the back of an envelope in about 1923 or 1924: 'There are only 2 things – Puritanism and Catholicism. You are one or the other. You either believe in the reality of *sin* or you don't – *that* is the important moral distinction – not whether you are good or bad. Puritanism does not believe in sin: it merely believes that certain things must not be done.' Eliot's 'Puritan' mother nevertheless prepared the way for his interest in Catholic forms by her own tolerant interest. One of her poems beckons the stranger to the stately Cathedral with its art treasures, its sweet music, and fragrant incense. 'Must not the Lord be near?' she asks. 'Wilt thou not pause to kneel?'

Eliot regretted the cultural impoverishment which, he felt, resulted from the Reformation. 'Milton's celestial and infernal regions are large but insufficiently furnished apartments filled by heavy conversation,' he said, 'and one remarks about Puritan mythology an historical thinness.' Of all the reformed churches the Church of England retained the closest connection, in formal creed and ritual, with the ancient Roman Church. Eliot, with his interest in a revival of the Catholic tradition, found it freshest in the prayers and sacraments of the Anglo-Catholic inheritors of the Oxford Movement, which, a hundred years before, had attempted to revive within the Church of England the best aspects of the Roman Church. For Anglo-Catholics the pulpit was less significant than the sacraments; faith centred on the altar and the confessional, which had the advantage of being constant, free from the local limitations of individual pulpits, exempt from competition with the media, and unimpaired by the fallibility of individual clergymen which had so troubled the learned congregant in 'Mr. Eliot's Sunday Morning Service'. The Anglo-Catholics were a dominant party within the Church at that time, prescribing a regulated life of high sanctity and service.

Why should someone who was not born an Anglican not go directly to Rome? He may have considered it, for amongst his books is a *Liturgical prayer book: mass, vespers, ritual, and principal Catholic devotions*, compiled by the Right Reverend Dom F. Cabrol, OSB. Eliot's main consideration was his growing attachment to England. He was drawn to the Anglican Church through his historical imagination, associating its creation with the reign of Elizabeth rather than with that of Henry VIII. He used to recall with pleasure its flourishing under Elizabeth, and the scholar-clerics who had dignified it in the seventeenth century.

By 1925 it was clear to Eliot that he must make some deliberate change. That year many anxieties came to a head – another near-fatal illness for Vivienne in the winter of 1924–5, the *Criterion* in danger, and his new collected edition of poems which seemed to him merely an ejection of things he wanted to get out of the way. Eliot quoted Orestes saying that Furies were hunting him down and he must move on.

His first thought was to leave his wife. By 1925 Eliot was finally convinced that his marriage was doomed. In ten years nothing had really changed – her condition and their relations had only deteriorated. One of Vivienne's unpublished sketches provides a sympathetically detached portrait of a fraught husband. 'Anthony' comes home very quietly and hangs about in the hall for a minute, dreading his wife. 'There were many things he dreaded. That Ellison might have a headache, that she might be irritable and hate him, that she might be in despair or have with her her greatest friend who would have been quarrelling with her.' He moves almost stealthily to his study, hoping it will be empty, to find his wife lying in wait on the sofa. Vivienne's moods and nervous states must have given her husband ample cause for self-pity, but I think their marriage was also blighted by something else, something in Eliot, that he half-recognised as the underlying cause of their troubles. What exactly it was, one can only conjecture from other fragmentary remarks in his poems and in Vivienne's sketches. He seemed to suffer from an inability to empathise with suffering outside his own experience. In a strange guilty poem he published in 1924 he said he could see eyes in a golden vision, but not eyes in actual life, in tears. The latter he saw only through a blank, almost sealed-off division. 'This is my affliction,' he repeated. 'This is my affliction.'

There is another picture of Eliot's detachment in a sketch by Vivienne called 'Fête Galante'. At a bohemian party, a lively girl called Sybilla encounters an American financier-poet. She describes him leaning with exaggerated grace against the fireplace, refusing to speak. Her portrait is rather like the one painted by Wyndham Lewis of Eliot a few years later – a heavy, slumbering, white face; long hooded eyes, unseeing and leaden-heavy; a large sleek head. She is fascinated, but recognises that there is something strange about him. 'I like him, I like him,' she muses, ' – if only he would – What? What is wrong, what missing?'

If there is any truth in this sketch it is not surprising that Vivienne should have had a hopeless sense of exclusion. 'Sybilla' is Eliot's Sybil in the epigraph to *The Waste Land*. She who had directed Aeneas to the Underworld now withers eternally in a cage. A scrap in Vivienne's writing scrapbook muses over Stravinsky's *Firebird*: 'at the end of the first act, after the bird is captured, it tries to fly, over and over again, wings beating. The music suggests it _/ _/ _/'. Another obvious parallel is an ambitious story called 'The Paralysed Woman' by Feiron Morris. Sybilla, a writer, is in pain as she types but realises she is envied by a youngish woman across the way who is paralysed. Standing in her chemise at the window, Sybilla watches this woman, her other self. The woman resplendent in white, including hat and gloves, and wheeled in and out by a chauffeur and uniformed maid, lives a life of immaculate order, eating exquisite meals on a sunny, glassed veranda with a grey-haired man and a boy, presumably a son. Sybilla's husband, André, won't look at her because he can't do anything. To Sybilla this is not the point. In cold fury, André turns on Sybilla's friend, Felice, to ask if the milk is pasteurised. Sybilla is staying with Felice (based perhaps on Mary Hutchinson) in a seaside flat where André comes at weekends, wearing a bowler hat and an anxious expression, and carrying two suitcases, one full of books and periodicals, the other full of medicine bottles. He gets up in the morning liverish and ill-tempered; makes copious notes; and packs and unpacks his suitcases. The seaside flat is high up; the people in it are in a cage – fretful, squabbling over small expenses like grapenuts for breakfast or seven pence for the laundry. Another inmate, Mike, is needled for reading Proust; Sybilla for her attachment to *Holy Dying*. There is a brief flutter when the two women kick up their heels at a tea-dance – Sybilla imagines herself as an exhibition dancer, blissfully mindless, and her sudden enthusiasm draws André into a frenzy of assent. Then, all Sunday, Sybilla lies inert in bed, longing to be independent. And always there in her mind is that paralysed woman like a doll.

Vivienne became more obviously disturbed following a curt rejection of this story by the *Dial*. There were wild accusations of the editor's sister, her old friend Lucy Thayer, who had encouraged its submission, and she called on Eliot to 'curse out' the American poet Marianne Moore and the *Dial*. Vivienne became increasingly prey to lightning switches of mood in which she would pounce at random on a scapegoat for self-despair. Vivienne's sketches show extraordinary self-insight. In her pencil notes for 'Au Revoir' Sybilla gets caught up in a fit of rage and passion. Throwing all her parcels down the stairs, she hits André in the face with her umbrella, and having done it, she does it again. Then she sits on the stairs in a silent convulsion while André collects the parcels. He then takes her arm tightly, gets her out into the street, where she walks mechanically beside him, steeped in utter blackness. Now and then a gust of violent rage returns.

All very well in writing, but socially, of course, unacceptable. Vivienne was aware that if she dared to express a minute portion of what she felt to be the truth about herself, she was liable to let loose 'an *avalanche*, and in the end turn ... one's confidant into an implacable enemy'. There is a pathetic description of a convalescent Vivienne – heavily powdered, shaky, overdressed – driven into the country to enjoy Sunday afternoon tea with the Woolfs, where her husband pressed her to take medicine and Virginia lightly snubbed her small effort at conversation. In this character she is like the sickly, curled-up dormouse in A. A. Milne who has treats forced upon him, outings by car, when all he wants is his bright old life amongst delphiniums blue and geraniums red. Eliot wrote to Virginia Woolf that Vivienne's disease of 1924–5 was diagnosed as rheumatism, although the doctor admitted she had never seen anything like it. The drugs Vivienne took, and their side-effects, probably obscured whatever ailed her. What with pain and near-delirium she hardly slept, and it seemed to Eliot, at times, that she would die from exhaustion. From February 1924 to July 1925 she had been publishing a lot in the *Criterion*. In her husband's opinion she wrote 'EXTREMELY well'. Her sketches of a dingy Parisian hotel and its inhabitants, a *thé dansant* in London, or a boring bohemian party where ballet dancers are shepherded in by a 'macaw', are all emotionally alive and observant, with plangent minutiae, reminiscent of Katherine Mansfield.

'By the way, the F.M. who wrote the Letters you liked is the author of "Thé Dansant",' she wrote to Conrad Aiken. 'I think it has a distinct quality, though apparently very slight.' She planned an interlinked series which could appear separately but which could make up a book; by 1924 she had done a little over half. To write, she 'removed' herself to the hideaway at 38 Burleigh Mansions. She still preferred 'life' to writing: 'No one will ever persuade me that writing is a substitute for living.' She enjoyed her success, but feared (she confided to Schiff in 1924) that it 'is a sort of flash in the pan – that it won't *go on*'. She spoke of writing as 'this temporary aberration of mine'.

In 1925 Eliot told Russell that the obvious alternative to their present life was that they should part – if only Vivienne could manage to live on her own. He did not complain of her illnesses; he blamed himself – 'living with me has done her so much damage' – and her immaturity. 'I find her still perpetually baffling and deceptive,' he wrote. 'She seems to me like a child of 6 with an immensely clever and precocious mind. . . . And I can never escape from the spell of her persuasive (even coercive) gift of argument.' At Garsington, in March 1926, Lady Ottoline spoke out. In front of Henry Eliot and his new wife, Theresa, she urged Vivienne to curb her frenzies over health which forced her husband to cancel engagements at the last minute – Vivienne was jealous of the attention he got, Ottoline believed. Eliot told his brother that his wife was 'perfectly well now though subject to querulous moods occasionally'.

But it was never as simple as that. For all her eloquence, there was something unspoken in Vivienne's shifts from wildness to pathos and back again, as though she despaired of expression, and found a language in collapse – a protest Eliot might have divined but was not prepared to hear. Was she protesting that he had not come to love her – that he reserved his emotion for a drama in which she had no part? Excluded, her clamour grew the wilder, more arresting. She muttered, raged, plucked at her clothes. A year later, no longer quite normal in her husband's opinion, she would take herself to a centre for nervous disorders at Divonne-les-Bains, near Geneva. A fellow-patient remembered his first sight of Vivienne 'as she walked almost as though in a trance along the wooded path. Her black hair was dank, her white face blotched – owing, no doubt, to the excess of bromide she had been taking. Her dark dress hung loosely over her frail form; her expression was both vague and acutely sad.'

In the end Eliot did not leave her as yet, but made other attempts to change his life. In 1925 they moved to a pleasanter neighbourhood, 57 Chester Terrace in SW1, in a charming row of houses with iron railings in front and pretty doors. It was comfortable, with a neat, bright kitchen, a cosy dining-room, and a small garden paved with flagstones. He also went to beg help from Geoffrey Faber, who agreed to take him into his new publishing firm, Faber & Gwyer, in September 1925. Eliot's *Poems 1909–1925* were published by Faber* in November, followed by Charlotte Eliot's *Savonarola* – Eliot had a copy ready to show his brother, Henry, early in 1926. There is a photograph of Eliot in Bloomsbury in 1926 in his new role of elegant publisher: his bowler hat very straight, he leans casually on his tightly rolled umbrella.

As a publisher who was also a businessman, Eliot set himself to make poetry pay, and the phrase 'Faber poetry' a byword. By the time he stated this aim, in 1955, Faber was publishing the foremost English and American poets of the age, including Auden, Spender, Day Lewis, Pound, Muir, Robert Lowell, Marianne Moore, Ted Hughes and, later, Sylvia Plath. In the late twenties and thirties, Faber was a new firm, and Eliot's publishing ambitions still in the making. The tedious aspect comes out in letters to Pound. Eliot tried in vain to curb the cryptic allusions in the *Cantos*. How could Pound expect Britons to be excited about a president like Martin Van Buren when they were unaware of Jefferson and John Quincy Adams? As Eliot toiled over Pound's disorderly manuscripts, struggling (with help from Geoffrey Faber) to correct quotations from obscure Greek texts, he reflected how little publishers had to show for their efforts to act as psychiatrists, labour exchange, school of authorship, and soup kitchen. He was attentive to authors' needs. Stead once witnessed his anxiety to discover the address of an author who had faded into obscurity and poverty. 'I spend a great deal of time talking to authors whose work I do not want to print,' he noted in a 1935 report for the Harvard class of

---

* The Woolfs, who had published Eliot since 1919, were hurt by what they saw as his defection to a rival publisher.

1910. 'And I have read a great many manuscripts, most of which are uninteresting. . . . I forgot to say that I am obliged to spend a great deal of time answering letters from Ezra Pound, but my firm pays for the stamps.'

Eliot was quick and decisive in his rejections of manuscripts – 'all out', he would often say at Wednesday afternoon meetings – though his letters of rejection were kindly and hopeful. Years later he said that the bulk of his literary criticism was buried in letters and marginal comments on manuscripts. He set before young poets a standard of civilisation against barbarism, as Kathleen Raine put it. It was part of his job to help with general submissions, many of which were, of course, unsolicited. Everyone in the firm took part: 'blood and thunder' went to the office boy; 'novelettish' novels to the secretaries; and those few manuscripts that might actually be publishable to the directors, Faber himself, Richard de la Mare, Eliot, and another American settled in England, Frank Morley.

The main attempt to change his life was his conversion. There is always a public and a private side to conversion, and the private side remained in shadow until the publication, in 1993, of a set of lectures which Eliot delivered in 1926. These lectures open up a private turning.

He was offered the Clark lectures at Trinity College, Cambridge, in the face of opposition. Only two Americans had ever preceded him, Professor Barrett Wendell of Harvard in 1902 and William Everett, a Trinity College graduate and Harvard Latin professor, in 1907. The election of a thirty-six-year-old bank clerk who was a controversial poet with no college affiliation had been, by Cambridge standards, extraordinary. By October 1925, Eliot had made little progress: Vivienne was suffering from neuralgia, rheumatism, and shingles, while he had infected gums and had to have an operation on his jaw. Vivienne was dispatched to the Health Institute until Christmas, while he went to the South of France and Ravenna to recuperate. At the Savoy Hotel, La Turbie, in the Alpes-Maritimes, he prepared the lectures hastily, playing too hard to academe and losing himself in mazes of subtlety. But it so happened in the course of preparation that he read a book by Remy de Gourmont, *Dante, Béatrice et la poésie amoureuse*. At this low point, the scenario for a future drama came into view.

'For love, one had to be married and love outside marriage,' Eliot quoted from this book in a lecture on the *trecento* at Trinity College between January and March 1926. The Provençal lady was not angelic, but the new Florentine school, including Dante, modified this profoundly: 'the poets' love becomes pure, almost impersonal; its object is no longer a woman but beauty, femininity personified in an ideal creature. No idea of marriage or of possession haunts them. . . . It is a date in the history of the evolution of human feelings . . .'.

Other extracts from Dante's *Vita Nuova* link past and future in an unbroken continuity through the memory of Emily Hale as Eliot transformed her in his imagination. His epigraph to his series of lectures salutes the lady 'wherein alone I found that beatitude which is the goal of desire'. When Dante is asked where his beatitude 'abideth', he answers: 'In those words that do praise my lady.' Here is the transforming hope, latent in *The Waste Land*, which propels Eliot's new life and the 'new verse' it will shape. Eight or nine months before he resolved on conversion, Eliot came upon an idea that could retrieve 'the heart of light, the silence': a love which cannot be had *in*, but which may be had *through*, human relations. This could be an alternative to marriage, a partner to conversion. The twentieth century was preoccupied with the sensations of physical union; it was at the farthest remove from the way Dante loved Beatrice in the thirteenth century. Turning from the debased sexuality of his time, in the winter of 1925–6, Eliot took up a medieval dream of a lady who might pity him, forgive him, guard his soul, and redeem the mess he had made of his life.

*

Playing a curious part in the run-up to conversion was a

contest between Eliot and Middleton Murry for supremacy in the literary establishment. Ostensibly, it was a power-struggle between the *Criterion* and the *Adelphi*, edited by Murry, but the contest carried within it larger issues that bore on what was shaping in the chrysalis of 1926. Back in 1919, Murry, as editor of the *Athenaeum*, had been top dog in the literary establishment, with Eliot cultivating his friendship and grateful to be offered reviewing. Soon after, they had begun to diverge as they took up increasingly polemical positions as romantic and classicist – Murry rash, Eliot ruthless – in their respective journals. At the same time, each was searching for a religious answer to post-war despair, Murry through the kind of sublimated humanism against which Eliot set his face. In effect, this was an intellectual battleground which terminated in a reversal of fortune, with the once-central Murry ousted and Eliot entrenched as foremost critic. At the end of 1926, Eliot informed Pound that his main source of income was his journal – a statement of success. No one now remembers Middleton Murry except as the unsatisfactory husband of Katherine Mansfield.

Eliot's hostility to 'Mr. Muddleton Moral' may be a sign of how close Murry had come to Eliot's still-secret position. Eliot was about to explode the public's view of himself as devoid of belief with a revelation of his route to spiritual authority – a higher authority than the ephemeral glamour of disillusion. And here was Murry along the same route, claiming mystical experience, writing a life of Jesus, and divining what Eliot had in mind. A draft of his attack on Eliot in 1926 was annotated by Eliot himself. Underlining a section of the typescript in which Murry predicted Eliot's conversion ('it might conceivably be done, by an act of violence, by joining the Catholic Church'), Eliot added the cagy comment, 'to be proved'.

Murry followed Modern theologians who developed a Bergsonian view of a God invested with the creative potentiality of an individualist; Eliot was drawn rather to the Catholic view of a static prime mover whose immobility is not inertia but the immobility of pure and supreme activity which can become nothing because it already has in itself all that can be had. This position denies the validity of individual revelation and supports the medieval assumption of man's innate depravity. Eliot felt at home with Catholic doctrine in the way he felt at home with the strict New England of his forebears. Like them, he welcomed the rigour with which the warped individual must submit to the *via disciplina*. So, in May 1926, he fell on his knees when he entered St Peter's in Rome.

*

In 1927 Eliot joined the Church of England and, in November, exchanged American for British nationality (sponsored by Leonard Woolf). In 1914 he might have become a Christian in a mood of passionate assent; by 1927 he had hesitated too long for such a mood to be possible. He no longer hoped to recover 'the one veritable transitory power' of his youth, nor waited like Gerontion for a sign, but began to see religion as a long-term regimen. Starting in 1926 he began to attend early-morning Communion. He learnt the morality of patience ('teach us to sit still'), and that 'humility is the beginning of anything spiritually or even culturally worthwhile'.

On 13 November 1926 Eliot had asked Stead if he might be confirmed in the Church of England. He had wished for absolute secrecy; he hated, he said, spectacular conversions. As a Unitarian, Eliot had the idea he had not been baptised in the name of the Trinity, so Stead arranged for his baptism in his own village of Finstock, in the Cotswolds. Eliot's sponsors, whom he barely knew, were to be B. H. Streeter, a theologian of Queen's College, Oxford, who did much to recommend the Church to educated agnostics, and Vere Somerset, a historian, a fellow of Worcester (the college with which Stead was associated). On Wednesday 29 June 1927 the doors of Finstock Church were locked against idle spectators, and Stead poured the waters of regeneration over Eliot's head. Eliot later told Mary Trevelyan it had been rather hole in the corner – but the secrecy was orchestrated according to his wish. Stead felt a little embarrassed. If Eliot had been baptised already, this wasn't really necessary. After supper, they took a walk in Wychwood, and got lost. Stead recalled Eliot 'pacing under the mighty oaks and pushing his way through hazel thickets attired in a smart suit, a bowler hat, and gray spats'.

Next morning Eliot was taken to be confirmed by the Bishop of Oxford, Thomas Banks Strong, at Cuddesdon. The Bishop talked to him for twenty minutes, rather hurriedly as though determined Eliot should 'pass'. No one had 'prepared' him, but there was a general idea he had read some learned things. Then, in his private chapel, the Bishop laid his hands on Eliot's head and said: 'Defend, O Lord, this thy Servant with thy heavenly grace, that he may continue thine forever.'

The third, and for Eliot probably the most important, ceremony came nine months later when he made his first confession, in March 1928, after finding a spiritual director in Father Underhill. Eliot wrote to Stead of his extraordinary sense of surrender and gain, as if he had finally crossed a very wide and deep river, never to return. This was the crossing feared at the end of 'The Hollow Men'; in the event, it was a relief. At this stage he did not expect to make great progress, only to keep his soul alive by prayer and communion three times a week. The question whether he would go further in the religious life remained open: he hinted to Stead that his circumstances might *excuse* this. The hint is very delicately worded: he would not himself suggest that he abandon a marriage, but it would help if the Church urged him to do so. He liked Underhill but sometimes felt he needed the severer disciplines of a priest called Whitby. Nothing could be too ascetic, too violent, too 'Ignatian' for his needs. Violent, as Murry had foreseen. One of his first tasks was to come to terms with celibacy and to find it easy for the first time. In his poem 'Animula', he speaks of 'denying the importunity of the blood' and living solely for 'the silence' after the blessing.

Eliot's penitent in part I of *Ash-Wednesday*, turning and turning on the winding stair, acts out the two mental 'turns'

Andrewes prescribed for a conversion: a turn that looks forward to God and a turn that looks backward to one's sins, sentencing oneself for the past. In this sermon 'Of Repentance', preached on Ash Wednesday 1619, Andrewes gives an exhaustive analysis of the demands which conversion must make on the most developed and sensitive conscience – the weighing of motives, the *'hatred of sinne'*, the guard against hypocrisy.

Eliot was impatient to fix his identity. As a public figure he soon took it upon himself to call for the religious reform of society at school prizegivings and church conclaves. The private self lagged behind. It is a human weakness to write about things first and learn about them afterwards, Eliot admitted. In *Ash-Wednesday* and the Ariel poems, written between 1927 and 1931, Eliot wonders if he does not belong with those who espouse Christianity officially without being properly committed, whose ostentatious piety is 'tainted with a self-conceit'.

In 1927, just before his baptism, he had remarked that a great poet does not believe or disbelieve the system of belief available to him in his particular time or place. He simply makes use of it, or a fusion takes place between the poet's emotional needs and a given set of local beliefs. Eliot did not make it easy for his contemporaries to understand his conversion. In 1928 in a preface to a collection of essays, *For Lancelot Andrewes*, he announced rather stiffly that he was an 'Anglo-Catholic in religion'. It sounded absurd, coupled with solemn espousals of royalism and classicism. Eliot gave the impression that all these beliefs were of equal importance to him. He did not make it clear that his royalism and classicism were subsidiary to his Christianity and should be taken in a special way. By royalism Eliot did not mean King George V or any living ruler but an ideal similar to that of Sir Thomas Elyot, a hope that the majesty, propriety, and responsibility of a ruler would reform people from above. He believed that Church and King should work together. The King, he said later, 'had not merely a civil but a religious obligation towards his people'. Similarly, Eliot invoked classicism to uphold a Christian education. 'If Christianity is not to survive,' he wrote later, 'I shall not mind if the texts of Latin and Greek languages become more obscure and forgotten than those of the languages of the Etruscans.'

It seemed to many of Eliot's contemporaries that he wilfully averted his eyes from social problems between the wars and took refuge in obsolete institutions. The *Times Literary Supplement* called Eliot a kind of traitor. Edmund Wilson deplored 'the unpromising character' of the ideals and institutions he invoked and the 'reactionary point of view'. The *Manchester Guardian* said that only an American expatriate could go so far in the direction of the right.

Critics and friends like the Woolfs were baffled because, naturally, they assumed Eliot was allying himself to an institution whose appeal declined between the wars. But for Eliot belief was 'something detached from the temporal weakness or the corruption of an institution'. Like many religious thinkers he put together a faith which answered private needs and then attached that to an institution which, he believed, carried the living stream of Christianity, though it needed reform. Eliot's attachment to Anglicanism had this dual aspect. He saw means of support and self-correction within the English traditions; at the same time he brought something of himself to the Anglican Church, a spirit more vehement, more dogmatic and zealous. As Newman once remarked: 'It is not at all easy . . . to wind up an Englishman to a dogmatic level.' The average layman was more concerned with the demeanour of the vicar than with theology. Eliot's dogmatic orthodoxy, his concern with damnation, his intolerance in his earlier years for ordinary sinners, his sense of civilisation's decay and doom, his intuitions of a 'promised land beyond the waste' – all this suggests a lingering Puritan strain, rather different from the equable, mild-mannered temper of the gentlemen-clergymen with whom Eliot began to associate and to whose habits he wholly conformed.

Eliot's temperament craved an exacting moral code. Chastity, austerity, humility, and sanctity, he said he must have – or perish. This code did not, of course, conflict with the aims of Anglo-Catholics, but it was *sui generis*. To express his ideals of virtue Eliot fastened on an English institution that was particularly mild in its minimal demands, and set about reforming it from within. During the thirties he called upon Anglicans for a stricter theology, for discipline and asceticism, for a religion not 'watered down and robbed of the severity of its demands'.

A 'tireless Calvinist', Robert Lowell called Eliot, who 'harried his pagan English public' with godliness and austerity. As a New Englander with family ties to the Eliots, Lowell understood an 'almost sensual enjoyment of starch and morality' which Lowell defends as 'desperately precious' in its high-mindedness – flowering 'as something better than sensitivity, something heavily selfish – creation and faith.' The English served Eliot as the lost tribes, as the Indians had served the religious energies of the Puritans and as the Westerner had served the missionary zeal of Eliot's grandfather in mid-nineteenth-century St Louis and his uncle in late nineteenth-century Oregon. Lowell recognised in Eliot's attraction to Anglicanism the authentic colour of the New Englander who would preach a more rigorous code than that which prevailed and enjoy its proprieties of form and the introspective mood it induced. If Eliot's mask enacted England, his inbent eye recalled the New England divines.

Eliot's public was partially justified in its unfriendly reaction to his faith. He had misled it by defamiliarising the message of *The Waste Land* and then baffled it by his odd attachment to the Anglican Church. The hostility Eliot evoked, however, seems excessive and probably lay outside Eliot personally, in the age itself. Edmund Wilson deplored the forced mating of New England temper with Anglican mode, yet admitted at the same time the unfriendliness of their age to anything religious.

Eliot joined a church which, for him, retained the strength of the Elizabethan establishment, a national church reinforced by secular power. Beside support for his private life, he found strength also in a sense of community and tradition. Many groups in America are based on shared theory.

Whether it be a shared faith, a political ideology, or a professional bias, there is an emphasis on creed and jargon, a strictness within the ranks combined with intolerance for the uninitiated. The members share no past and, very likely, no future. What they have in common – and on this they insist – is the label. Eliot pinned on his Anglican label in the preface to *For Lancelot Andrewes*. He brought to the Church of England the American's capacity to commit himself to an idea with a fervour that seems at once strained and brave, wilful and yet attractive in its sheer vitality of moral passion.

Eliot discarded popular ideologies of social change – extremist politics and liberal optimism – as solutions to cultural despair, and offered as an alternative the idea of a community knit together by religious discipline. Liberal humanism, Eliot felt, could work only for a few highly developed individuals who lived in the aftermath of a strong religious tradition. Babbitt's doctrine of the 'inner check' was too subtle and private to be the masses' alternative to the encroaching chaos of the thirties. Men like Russell and the Huxleys, who believed in a civilised but non-religious mentality, have too naïve expectations of human nature. Eliot was not against liberalism or democracy *per se*; he feared that they would not work: 'It is not that the world of separate individuals of the liberal democrat is undesirable,' he wrote, 'it is simply that this world does not exist.' Eliot saw the masses, with their illusion of freedom, manipulated by a society organised for profit which would influence them by any means except their intelligence.

Eliot saw in the English Church decency, common sense, and a moderation that, he felt, might provide a corrective to the faddist modern mind. He deplored the kind of facile mind that leapt across all existing reality to some simplistic solution – communism; later, fascism – what he called 'the gospels of this world'. In 1910 already, Gide had prophesied that the weakness of the twentieth-century mind would be in 'locating the ideal of perfection not in equilibrium and the middle path, but in the extreme and exaggeration'. Eliot thought he found a responsible and rational answer in the *via media* of Elizabethan Anglicanism, and praised its flair for compromise. 'In a period of debility like our own,' he wrote later, 'few men have the energy to follow the middle way in government; for lazy or tired minds there is only extremity of apathy, dictatorship or communism, with enthusiasm or indifference.'

In the thirties Eliot was criticised for his refusal to turn the *Criterion* into a forum for writers with radical social ideas. It seemed to many that he was simply aligning himself with a crass, old-fashioned conservatism. Although Eliot did discount the sweeping ideologies for social change then current, his own 'scheme for the reformation of society' was not old-fashioned. He saw that the future lay with the lower middle class, who would be the most numerous and whose taste would be indulged. He assumed that the lower middle class would have inferior taste, but he did not kick against this. Instead he proposed a reformation of society set at a low level: 'a social minimum', he called it. There should be communities where Christian values would not be fervently upheld but assimilated into humdrum lives as behaviour and habit. He proposed communities small enough to consist of a network of relationships, so that people would watch over one another. He felt that a renewed sense of community would energise society, although he admitted that a rural ideal did not fit the urban-industrial scene of the twentieth century. Eliot also felt there should be a place for a spiritual élite, not to command or compel other people, but to preserve the best standards of thought, conduct, and taste so that people should have a sense of higher forms of life towards which they might, if they wished, aspire.

From a historical distance, Eliot's ideological position seems more reasonable than the sweeping ideologies fashionable in his day. His modest ideal was men's virtue and well-being in community for all, and, for a few, the divine beatitude. He wanted a community that would grant the individual a sense of dignity, and he was indifferent to twentieth-century political schemes in which the individual was of small worth.

*

It is difficult to distinguish what was innovative and original in Eliot's vision of the world from what was idiosyncratic and sometimes sick. William James pointed out how each temperament makes religion according to its needs. If people are humane, their religion tends to be comforting; if they are self-absorbed and obsessed with a darker life, their religion tends to exalt self-sacrifice and drastic cures. Eliot braced himself for 'scourges' and bloodshed. His nature, like that of St Narcissus, was drawn by martyrdoms and feats of asceticism more than by Christ's superior morality of compassion and non-violence.

Eliot was sensitive to the power of evil in human hearts and felt that his conception of sin, in a twentieth-century world dedicated to material, political, and sexual cures, was itself a triumph. He felt the devil not so much in social wrongs, but within, and believed that the chief purpose of civilisation was to cope with the notion of original sin.* Lust seemed to him the most corrupting of all sins and, as a young man, he wished the flesh could be denied, burnt away by that refining fire he so often invoked. Soon after his conversion he wrote savagely that those who 'suffer the ecstasy of the animals' may look forward only to death.

Eliot always acknowledged and derided the idiosyncratic element in his philosophy. Although he presented himself as an exemplary figure, he included his flaws. Eliot had an extraordinary drive for perfection, and in his early years hunted for signs that he had been singled out in a special way. He wished to be God's ambassador, but owned again and again that he could not honestly claim the credentials. Even in his light-filled moments he retained a degree of modesty or hesitation. Because of his distance from perfection – a distance reinforced by his times – he went at it doggedly and fundamentally alone. Eliot's mental isolation perhaps brewed

* 'La vrai civilisation', Eliot once quoted from Baudelaire, '... est dans la diminution des traces du péché originel.' SE, p. 381.

the dubious elements in his life – the prejudice, the distrust of women, and the narrow self-absorption. His character was self-centred enough to assume that the world and its vicissitudes – women, wars, seasons, crowds – existed as signals for his conduct. His isolation and the absence of surer signs brewed also a certain wilfulness. Eliot's poetic record did not concentrate on the beatific vision, but on himself, his will to be chosen.

Eliot passed his youth walled in by shyness and vast ambition. His early adult life may be seen as a series of adventures from the citadel of his self in search of some defining experience. He made expeditions across a perilous gap that divided him from the great world, and ventured into society, into marriage, into religious communion. He tried to maintain the polite, even curiosity of an explorer far from home, but each time had to withdraw – shuddering from the contact – to his citadel, where he would then labour to record, as precisely as possible, his strange encounters. It was soon apparent to Eliot that the religious encounter was the most commanding of his experiences but, ironically, with this perception the gap seemed to widen, to become even more difficult to cross. By 1925, it had become clear to him that if he were to cross the gap successfully he would have to abandon his citadel, and plunge into a journey of no return.

At each stage of his career Eliot defined his identity and measured his distance from perfection. There was, in his poetry, a persistent self-portraiture – from the languid, impeccable gentleman in 'Spleen', who waited impatiently on the doorstep of the Absolute, to Prufrock, whose impulse to assault the universe with a prophetic truth beat beneath his anxiously correct façade; and from the phantom pilgrim searching the city for a miraculous cure for depression to the penitent climbing the purgatorial stair. One developing personality redefined, in each poem, the position won in the previous poem. From the start, Eliot was preoccupied with his own special fate, but he was uncertain how to characterise himself. He sensed his identity as a 'shadow of its own shadows, spectre in its own gloom'. Eliot haunted his poems like an irresolute ghost seeking shape and form and visible role. When at length he was sure of his best self, he revealed a preacher, his outlines distinct, his feet planted on an Anglican platform.

Eliot took up a stance unlikely to charm the audience of his day, of pilgrim, prophet, and preacher. The models of manhood by which he measured himself – Augustine, Lazarus, Ezekiel, Elijah, Dante – were heroes of other, more religious ages. The 'lost' generation followed him willingly to the brink of despair, but wondered at his inclinations when he went beyond it. His exhortations sounded odd in their ears, dogmatic, irrelevant, as he went in search of higher love.

7

ENTER BEATRICE

WHEN EMILY HALE began to give Eliot's gifts away, she held back one for the rest of her life. It is a speech in which he revealed something vital to both of them: the power of love to make a new life. 'What every poet starts from', he said, 'is his own emotions', which may be 'his nostalgia, his bitter regrets for past happiness'. These regrets might become, for a 'brave' poet, the basis of an attempt 'to fabricate something permanent and holy out of his personal animal feelings – as in the *Vita Nuova* . . .'.*

These words, delivered before the Shakespeare Association on 18 March 1927, three months before his baptism, suggest that Eliot's renewed contact with Emily Hale was suffused with the impetus of his conversion. This prompted an attack on readers who, Eliot said, fastened on what was superficial in his work and invariably ignored 'my biography . . . in what I *did* write from personal experience'.

The tentative proposal in this talk was matched two months later by the arrival of a letter from Emily Hale on a spring day in May. As it happened, she was spending three months in Florence, the city of Dante and Beatrice. This was just about the time that Vivienne left England for treatment abroad. She was to be away nine months, which can only have been a relief. At lunchtime Eliot walked around Russell Square with William Force Stead. Looking at the sun on the

---

* Printed as *Shakespeare and the Stoicism of Seneca* (1927), repr. *SE*, pp. 107–20.

new leaves, Stead said impulsively: 'it would be nice to be in love on a day like this.'

'Perhaps it is the weather,' Eliot replied, 'but I had a letter from a girl in Boston this morning whom I have not seen or heard from for years and years. It brought back something to me that I had not known for a long time.' He remembered, perhaps, a girl singing 'May Morning' in a Boston drawing-room. Emily Hale was now thirty-six, but to Eliot she was still the 'girl' of his youth.

From now on, she became the focus of his growing nostalgia for his origins: shades who called and gestured behind the grey rocks of the New England shore. After his thirteen years of exile, she provided the relief of a common past from which she had never been diverted, as Eliot had been diverted by what Henry James would have called, in short, Europe. She remained always recognisably a Bostonian.

She was still at Downer College, now promoted to Assistant Professor of Vocal Expression in 1927 and granted half a year's leave of absence. At Downer, it was her custom to direct four or five plays a year, including scenes from Dickens (1925) with Miss Hale playing the affected dancing master, Gentleman Turveydrop (in *Bleak House*), *Twelfth Night*, and *A Midsummer Night's Dream*. She staged Shakespeare every June in an open-air theatre in the woods behind the college. When she had put on *Sherwood* by Alfred Noyes in 1926, an actress missed her cue, and Miss Hale had the presence of mind to burst into song, crooning a medieval ballad until the actress entered. (She noted on a programme that this was her most ambitious production with a cast of 125.) She saw her productions as a 'synthesis of the Arts' with colour, form, design, music, and dance as integral elements. Some choices were Yeats's *Cathleen ni Houlihan* (1924), Barrie's *Alice-Sit-By-the-Fire* (1924), Barrie's *Dear Brutus* (1928), Lady Gregory's *Spreading the News* (1928), and Galsworthy's *The Pigeon* (1929). She remained in Milwaukee through the twenties, taking charge of a red-brick dormitory, Johnson Hall, along Downer Avenue; teaching Midwestern girls how to cross their ankles in the approved Boston style;

chaperoning dances in her bright, flowing gowns; and walking with conspicuous aplomb across classrooms as she conducted courses on 'The Training of Voice and Body' (compulsory for First Years), 'Dramatic Reading', 'Stage Technique', and eventually, 'Literary Interpretation'. It was during her last two years at Downer, 1927–9, that she renewed contact with Eliot.

When she ventured to approach him in 1927, she asked no more than advice on what Modern literature to use in her classes. In 1929 she wrote again about a lecture she was to give on Modern poetry. Eliot sent her Hulme's *Speculations* and asked her to send him the text of her lecture. Her lecture notes on Eliot are brief and not, at this stage, admiring: 'Gifted, so much to say he falls down under it – *ironic incisive complex bitter.*'

On 4 April 1929, just before Miss Hale left the college to spend a long summer abroad (she would linger in London until early October), she staged the balcony scene from *Romeo and Juliet*, with herself as Juliet. On Eliot's part a 'Lady' was taking shape in *Ash-Wednesday* (1927–30) and *Dante* (1929).

While Eliot composed these works Emily Hale was visiting England during consecutive summers in Europe from 1927 to 1930. Their reunion was propelled by a dream that was given the space of long separation to unfold. To dream of meeting after many years and many trials was a replay of Dante's reunion with Beatrice on the verge of paradise; as Eliot saw it, the recrudescence of old passion in a new emotion, in a new situation which 'comprehends, enlarges, and gives meaning to it'. Like Beatrice, Eliot's Lady forgives the poet his defection. In the autobiographical essay on Dante, Eliot quotes and then translates these lines:

> Olive-crowned over a white veil, a lady appeared to me. And my spirit . . . without further knowledge by my eyes, felt, through the hidden power which went out from her, the great strength of the old love. As soon as the lofty power struck my sense, which already had transfixed me before my adolescence, I turned leftwards . . . to say to Virgil: 'Hardly a drop of blood

in my body does not shudder: I know the tokens of the ancient flame.'

Eliot is rather more discreet than Dante about the reason for the poet's abjectness before his Lady. 'He abandoned me,' Beatrice says explicitly, 'and gave himself to others.' Nor did it help Beatrice 'to invoke inspirations by which in dreams', she says, 'I recalled him'. Beatrice, directing her eyes at Dante from beyond the river (Lethe) between purgatory and paradise, is matched by judging eyes in Eliot's 'Dream Songs'.

Eliot once discussed with Stead the great beauty of the *Vita Nuova*, and the way that Dante's love for Beatrice passed over into love of God. 'I have had that experience,' Eliot said rather shyly, and then lapsed into silence. His own idea of love was disturbed from the first by the body's masturbations and defecations in his 'First Debate between the Body and Soul' leading to *The Waste Land*'s ruthless 'Burning burning burning burning' of polluted flesh. He rejected uncleanness with the New England rigour of Emerson, who said plainly, 'the sublime vision comes to the pure and simple soul in a clean and chaste body'. Eliot's obscene poems were an extension of this: a licence to think of sex so long as it's seen to be ugly and degraded. His hatred of women's physicality is dangerously close to the sex-criminal who fancies he's called upon to punish women for their allure. What saved Eliot – and what made women fall in love with him – was a capacity for absolute devotion. This capacity had been warped by the pervasiveness of squalid sex, but had surfaced in response to a minister's daughter, upright Emily of the straight back and dark, shining hair. Eliot's imagination dwelt again and again on a beloved woman's hair, the light on it in 'La Figlia' (1912), wet in *The Waste Land* (1922), loosened in *Ash-Wednesday* (1930), sweet brown hair blown over the mouth – feared now as a distraction.

The 1927 talk with its passionate resonance was Eliot's first confession of his dream. The second begins more directly: 'Lady, . . .'. The confession is startlingly intimate, all the more so for the fact that it is proclaimed in public. In this poem, called appropriately 'Salutation' and written later in

1927, immediately after Eliot's conversion, the first tentative impulse to convert memory and desire into holiness has become a definite programme; the woman a visible figure with an assigned role. She is to be a 'Lady of silences' who presides over a dead self, guardian of its demise. A memory of love – 'Rose of memory' – supports the end of a tormented life and concludes with a renewal of visionary power as the poet looks to a promised land. God speaks to him as to Moses: 'This is the land'. A poem that begins with a Lady and ends with the voice of God is the formula for the central imaginative drama of Eliot's mature years. In this, the woman has a helpmeet role: she is to be the initiating influence and prime listener.

In the imagined presence of the Lady, a penitent sheds his past with his flesh. He breaks himself down to the bare bones of a rudimentary existence. These are the sole remains of the old life: dry bones, scattered in the desert, waiting to be recomposed. The bones are not dismayed by the body's dismemberment. They 'chirp', content to put themselves in the Lady's power to make the man anew. For reverence has replaced diseased forms of love: frustration and, worse, the satiety of barren lust:

> Terminate torment
> Of love unsatisfied
> The greater torment
> Of love satisfied.

The only way that Eliot could admit a renewed love was on the basis of chastity. The recovered bond with Emily Hale preceded his separation from Vivienne and, even after, infidelity was unthinkable. Both were proper Bostonians of the utmost rectitude. In the savage, spectacular drama of 'Salutation' three white leopards devour the penitent's flesh, an imaginative complement to Eliot's vow of chastity in March 1928, while the Lady's purity makes her a modern avatar of the Virgin. As sequels to 'Salutation' followed, she is increasingly an object of worship.

'Salutation', published in December 1927, was originally

an isolated poem, then became the second part of the long sequence *Ash-Wednesday*. A rearranged order shifts the focus from the merciful Lady to the agonies of the penitent man. His ordeals of self-confrontation and fearful solitude are succeeded by a final ordeal: the temptation to erotic love. Looking out on the past, through the window of memory 'bellied like a fig's fruit', he recalls a woman's sweet brown hair in an enchanted 'maytime', but he must hold back from its appeal. A flute plays not to the senses but to the spirit ditties of no tone, while the 'silent' woman bends her head in assent. It is a sign of grace, a token of the Word to come, 'unheard, unspoken'. In her presence the fountain of the spirit shoots up. It is the Lady 'who made strong the fountains': of this power the poet is certain.

Eliot's idea of love does not fit our usual categories, sexual and romantic. 'The love of man and woman', he said in 1929, 'is only explained and made reasonable by the higher love or else is simply the coupling of animals.' Eliot wanted nothing less than perfect love, part of his longing for 'the impossible union'. This is how he explained it in 1935 in one of his numerous buried essays: 'I mean the turning away of the soul from the desire ... of drugged pleasures, of power, or of *happiness*. I mean "love", in the sense in which "love" is the opposite of what we ordinarily mean by "love" (the desire to possess and to dominate or the desire to be dominated by).' He wished to transform the energy of desire into something absolute and lasting, and had to go back to the late Middle Ages for a state of feeling which, he insists, we no longer experience, more thrilling than anything we know, as Dante said of Beatrice: 'imparadisa la mia mente.' But where Dante sees Beatrice as a person – for one thing, he names her; for another, she speaks – Eliot's Lady is nameless and mute. From her first appearances in 'La Figlia che Piange' and 'The Love Song of Saint Sebastian', character is subsumed in an image of purity.

In his mature years Eliot was more concerned with love than in his early years: love's essence in memory; divine Love; and, many years later, his discovery of marital love. The automatic disgust with many women in the early poems came from not knowing them as they might know themselves. They are slotted into place as rousers or prey of low instinct.

Emily Hale was exempt from low instinct. Though not ethereal herself, and not the least silent as a teacher of speech and drama, she became the source for silent, ethereal women who elevate the poet's spirit. To consummate such a love might tarnish the dream that made the art or, more accurately, art's climax. So Emily Hale was set to play the roles of Virgin and Beatrice. Hard, of course, on Emily Hale for, as no real woman fits Eliot's reductive image of rank temptress, so no real woman could approximate his dream of purity.

*

Emily Hale returned to England in the summer of 1930, attending a Shaw Festival at Great Malvern (which included the first performance of *The Apple Cart*), and lecturing for the Art Poetry Circle of the Lyceum Club and the American Women's Club in London. She stayed, at least some of the time, at Burford in the Cotswolds. Eliot wrote to her there in September, and once again on 6 October at an unknown address. In December, Eliot confided to Stead that he had found a certain happiness which made celibacy easy for the first time.

Emily Hale did not fail Eliot's dream of beneficence. She later told an ex-pupil: 'A very dear friend of mine was involved, early in life, with a weak and selfish and seriously unstable partner. For many years I observed the blighting effect of this marriage on my friend.' To Eliot, she had a kind way and a nice smile, as he described her in one of his unpublished Cat poems where Miss Hale is the one Old Morgan (the Faber office cat) would most like to see.*

* TSE sent two uncollected Cat poems to EH. The one referred to above is untitled. The other is called 'Morgan Tries Again'. He wrote another comic poem for her, called 'A Country Walk'. She dated the Cat poems about 1937 or 1938. All three are in Princeton University Library. A

In the summer of 1930, Eliot identified Massachusetts as his ancestral habitat. This assertion, made on 20 June, followed his completion of the final part of *Ash-Wednesday* where the scene moves to the New England shore. The poet's wings, which were collapsed in the opening section and then strengthened by the quiet presence of the 'life-giving' Lady, now fly seaward on course of Eliot's expeditions off Cape Ann, a scene he always associated with divine intimations. Across space and time, he hears the whisper of ancestral voices, New England divines who spoke God's Word – not individuals but the collective shades who beckon him from 'exile' to the promised land that is still, after all, his inheritance.

Eliot was brooding on the past after his mother's death in 1929 and two years before he took up the Norton professorship in 1932, a belated fulfilment of his family's wish that he return to Harvard. The dream of return entered Eliot's work for a decade, culminating in *The Family Reunion* in 1939. Ironically, it was during the very decade following his surrender of American nationality that his nostalgia was at its height. Yet Eliot's America was never the geographic United States; it was, as for the greatest American writers, a dream. The exile dreams of the granite rocks of the New England shore, the bent golden-rod, and the salt smell of sandy earth. Once more, he hears the distant call of ghostly forebears as they drift back into the fastness of their own time and, with that, his resolve hardens. He, too, must speak the Word everlasting. And over this resolve presides a woman who is nameless, faceless, known only in a series of subordinate clauses, 'Who ... / Who ...', who walks with 'the new years', who restores his power to write 'new verse', and who bends her head in silent acceptance and gives the all-important sign that the Lord's Word would come. Linked with the shaping scenes of his New England youth, she alone can bring him back to the New World. In *Marina*, written in

copy of 'A Country Walk' is amongst the Tandy Papers in the British Library. TSE also gave EH an inscribed typescript (1938) of *Old Possum's Book of Practical Cats*.

July 1930 and published in September, while Emily Hale was still in England, a voyager effects an imagined crossing. He resigns his stale life for 'the new ships' as he homes in hope, lips parted, towards a woman.

Marina ends with this rediscovery of a woman long-lost and dearly loved. She evokes a tender, almost tremulous longing, comfort, and hope. It is as though a bolt is shot back and a lost feeling stirs. It is not romantic love; it is a familiarity that brings a man back to his primal self. So grace comes to Eliot in a human form, no longer veiled, but close as family. A pulsing moment of approach gives way to a recognition of kinship.

The setting is not actually Massachusetts, but Casco Bay, Maine, with the fog in the fir trees that crowd the Maine shore. Eliot explained that he felt enough of a Southerner to be something of an alien in Massachusetts so that, even in his youth, the New England of his associations existed more in Maine, the destination of his most ambitious sailing ventures. It is there, in imagination, that his voyager is 'awakened' as the longed-for call comes through the fog, and suppressed emotion breaks out in a cry of greeting. Battered, almost broken as he crosses from one life to another, he comes at last to a woman who awaits him like a divine call.

Eliot said that there is 'almost a definite moment of acceptance at which the New Life begins'. This meant less the outward act, more the hidden life of conversion which, for Eliot, was a bid to discover, or rediscover, 'the unread vision in the higher dream'. The demands of the higher dream were twofold. It meant the retrieval of what Robert Lowell called 'that short moment when the New World and God were one'. This fused in Eliot's fancy with a retrieved Emily Hale who seemed, to all who remember her, the embodiment of old Boston, from the clear, precise diction of her old Boston accent to the conscious perfection of her manners and conduct. Eliot's poems of 1927–35 move towards a pulsating moment or a vision of radiant light in an English garden. Like Beatrice, Emily alone could stir the higher dream through her shared memory of unsullied love. Between 1930 and 1934 they developed some sort of understanding. First, through memory, then through meeting, Eliot hoped for a renewal of feeling that would help him recover a visionary gift. In youth there had been hints and guesses but, during long years of a wretched marriage, his life had been deadened despite its overt success.

'Where is the Life we have lost in living?' he asked. To recover a lost life meant not only to recover the power to dream but also to slough off the unwanted past, chiefly the wife who polluted the dream by her drugged proximity. As it turned out, Vivienne refused to be dismissed and, with this complication, the dream was all but destroyed.

This prolonged struggle gave another meaning to the new life, as Eliot put it: 'the recognition of the reality of Sin is a New Life'. It is as though counter-views fought for dominance: on the one hand, the higher dream associated with Emily Hale; on the other, the sense of sin associated with Vivienne. Out of this conflict came the great poems and plays of Eliot's maturity: *Ash-Wednesday*, *Murder in the Cathedral*, *The Family Reunion*, and *Four Quartets*.

In the course of the thirties, Eliot came to perceive that the vision he longed for, what he called 'reality', was blocked by his unworthiness and, worse, an inability to shake off contamination, sexual in origin, but deepened by the years of mental disturbance which Eliot had shared with Vivienne – and went on sharing, in a sense, during the subsequent years of separation during which Vivienne tried to tug Eliot back into a mental nightmare which, with even greater determination, he shut off as past. This trial of wills is, in biographic terms, a contest between the claims of past and future and, in religious terms, a contest between body and soul. It reappears in *The Family Reunion*, a play about a man who believes that he has destroyed his wife and must pay a lifelong penance if his soul is to be saved. It is transmuted yet again into the more abstract terms of *Little Gidding* in 1941–2, where the contest of past and future, body and soul, becomes a contest between the flames of hell and those of purgatory: 'to be consumed / By either fire or fire'.

This contest is central to Eliot's life, while the cool Eliot of the many masks, the gentleman joker, is peripheral. The external facts are now well known, but the interior struggles remain in shadow where profound events take place beyond record, reflected only in creative acts.

*

Eliot was honest about failure: lips that would – but can't quite – pray, the convert who declares his belief before the world but denies it 'between the rocks'. He had to accept a fissure or Shadow (as he called it) between form and content: on the one hand, a programme so grand that he could not state it and, on the other, a weak, hollow man waiting and waiting for a call, for the message of the thunder ('DA ... Datta ...'), or a fount of renewed feeling. Well before his conversion, Eliot foresaw the difficulties: the process of transformation might be painful and protracted, possibly, through the rest of his life. '*Life*', he sighed, '*is very long*'.

In each successive poem, Eliot told his conversion story from the vantage-point of a further stage as Providence led him, he said, from one point to another: irresolute in 'The Hollow Men' (1923–5); ill-at-ease in the 'old dispensation' in his first post-conversion poem, *Journey of the Magi* (August 1927); broken in 'Salutation' (December 1927); waiting in *Ash-Wednesday* (December 1927–April 1930); and, at length, some quickening sense of attainment in *Marina* (July–September 1930). A devout life would not suffice, only right feeling. Certain bits in Eliot's essays of this time seem to vibrate with private import, as in 1931 when he fastens on certain lines 'which surely no man or woman past their youth can read without a twinge of personal feeling:

> O God! O God! that it were possible
> To undo things done, to call back yesterday. . . .

He says of a degrading sexual tie, 'one becomes moral only by becoming damned. . . . The possibility of that frightful discovery of morality remains permanent.'

243

There was a telling controversy between Eliot and a Princeton theologian, Paul Elmer More, on the cruelties of hell. Paul Elmer More also came from St Louis, and followed a journey much like Eliot's in that, as converts, they arrived at their faith from 'somewhere else'. Both men emerged from American Calvinism, a journey, Eliot felt, no English theologian was in a position to understand. In the friendliest way, More accused Eliot of residual Calvinism, and Eliot, equally friendly, accused More of heresy. More had declared that God did not make hell. This shocked Eliot: to him, hell was *giustizia, sapienza, amore*, the words over the entrance to Dante's *Inferno*. More thought eternal damnation too cruel to be a divine plan. Is your God Santa Claus? Eliot demanded. He perceived something above morals and human happiness and worse than ordinary pain: it was the very dark night or desert. He spoke in June 1930 as though he had been or still was there. Then, in August, he wrote that people only stay in hell because they cannot change.

In the meantime, he hoped that a 'new life' would prompt the spoken word, but in no ordinary way. As he took up a stance of 'a man with a mission', he tried out the cry of the prophets Isaiah and Ezekiel. In his Bible, he marked God's call to Isaiah: 'Fear not: for I have redeemed thee, I have called thee by thy name; thou art mine.'

To assume such a stance was, of course, daunting in a secular age. 'CRY what shall I cry?'* was the refrain of 'Difficulties of a Statesman' (1931) as a leader tries to turn from power to prophecy. Riding away from the sycophantic throng who admire only the image and trappings of fame, he tries out Isaiah's voice: 'All flesh is grass . . .'. As early as 1923, Eliot had told one of his reviewers Richard Aldington

---

* Isaiah 40: 6–8:

   The voice said, Cry. And he said, What shall I cry? All flesh is grass, and all the goodliness thereof is as the flower of the field.

   The grass withereth, the flower fadeth: because the spirit of the LORD bloweth upon it: surely the people is grass.

   The grass withereth, the flower fadeth: but the word of our God shall stand for ever.

that he had 'an inherited disposition to rhetoric' from innumerable ancestors who had occupied themselves with the Church. But his most direct model came from his mother, from poems like 'Saint Barnabas. A Missionary Hymn', which begins:

> Let me go forth, O Lord!
> How burns within me the unuttered Word.

Eliot once said that 'the American writing in English does not write English poetry'. The difference does not lie fundamentally in local subject matter but in 'the different rhythm in the blood'. His own 'cry' came from the dominant genres of sermon and spiritual journey. His dream-passage to the grey rocks of the New England shore is like Whitman's passage to 'realms of budding bibles'. His kick against the Old World, where people tooth one another and vegetate in their sty of contentment, is like Whitman's exhortation: 'Have we not grovel'd here long enough eating and drinking like brutes . . . Steer forth'. There is some connection between the silent Prufrock, wondering if he dare disturb the universe, and the stabs of Eliot's voice at vacant commuters whose only monument will be a thousand lost golf balls: 'The desert is squeezed into the tube-train next to you.'

Eliot's old friend Sir Herbert Read said that one always had a slight uneasiness in his presence, in case he might at any moment assume the judicial robes. He stood in the same New England tradition of moral earnestness as his ancestor the Revd Andrew Eliot, who in 1765 had preached to Boston society on 'a generation of vipers', meaning his audience; and, a century later, William Greenleaf Eliot, the admired grandfather, of whom a classmate at Harvard Divinity School had said: 'His eye is single. . . . There is something awful about such conscientiousness. One feels rebuked in his presence.'

The grandson's 'cry' was the imminent decline and fall of civilisation. This is the classic American sermon, the jeremiad, developed by settlers in the seventeenth century in order to repossess their dream of perfectibility. *The Waste Land* had prophesied ruin: London Bridge 'falling down falling down falling down'. The morale of the speaker almost collapses with this fall. Eliot's stand against collapse was a lone voice keeping the faith alive 'through the dark ages before us'. Looking right into that dark future, he predicted a time 'of cords and scourges and lamentation', of war and 'maternal sorrow'. Only saints would prevail, holding to 'the ultimate vision'. To this vision, Eliot would not himself lay claim. He bore witness to its existence, but the reality of what exactly it was he witnessed must fade, he feared, amidst the clamour of secular society, fade into the flatness of record:

> ... set down
> This set down
> This ...

Hope, Eliot said in an obscure wireless talk, lay 'in the lives of prophets', those who not only keep the faith through dark ages but live through the mind of that dark age and get beyond it. Prophets, he went on, are not always recognised as such, 'but it is through them that God works to convert the habits of feeling and thinking ... to which we are all more enslaved than we know'.

The prophetic role was part of a larger programme. The two completed parts of 'Coriolan' were sketches for a progress that was to move from empty shows of power to a prophetic role and then on towards a state of mystical elevation based on St John of the Cross. The latter two stages remained unwritten.* It is as though Eliot were sketching possibilities without an assured sense of their outcome. This was the course of composition for all his long poems: he would write small pieces which, later, he would pull together with some dramatic resolution that depended, to some degree, on developments in his own life.

---

* Eliot told Middleton Murry on 20 October 1931 that he doubted that he could write the fourth part on the state of the saint, and on 17 February 1932 he wrote to More that he wished to discuss St John of the Cross when next they met. Of the third part he says no more than that it was writable. My guess is that it would have been about the recovery of spiritual power, still 'hidden' from the would-be prophet of part two.

The great man vacillates between embracing and escaping the prophetic role. There are times when his mind is diverted by thoughts that have no public importance, some Pipit of his past and the sounds of small creatures, the firefly, the dove, like some lost emotion tucked under the soft wing of memory. A line comes back from a fragment, 'Hidden under the heron's wing', which Eliot had written as a young man before he left Boston: a woman crossing the lawn towards the speaker. Eliot retrieves this memory, and repeats its exact terms, as Emily Hale advanced, once more, out of the past.

*

After ten years of teaching, she allowed herself an interim from 1929 to 1932. This, she said in July 1931, 'has given me an excellent opportunity to review the past, as well as to plan for the future, in my work'. For two winters, 1929–30 and 1930–1, she had offered lectures on 'The Early American Theatre', 'The Shaw Festival in England', on the Irish, English, and Parisian stage, and on 'Fantasy and Reality in Modern Poetry' at the Commander Hotel in Cambridge, Massachusetts. She also gave 'Readings from Contemporary Verse', and in April 1931 took the role of Judith Bliss in the latest hit of the London stage, Noël Coward's *Hay Fever*. That summer, her one-woman recital in Seattle drew an enthusiastic society audience – many standing at the back – as she entered (according to one review) 'very pretty in a white chiffon dress with a flower pattern in rose color' with 'a wide cream straw hat' and carrying lilies of the valley and gardenias – reminiscent of Eliot's La Figlia or 'the hyacinth girl', her arms full of flowers. Emily Hale's recital turned from the sophisticated repartee of *Hay Fever* to Edna St Vincent Millay ('The Harp Weaver'), and then to Oscar Wilde's fairy tale 'The Selfish Giant' with a piano accompaniment. Her audience was hushed for Wilde; laughing more and more over her impersonation of a 'Sociable Seamstress' as she pulled imaginary pins out of a cushion and talked with them in her mouth; and almost cried over her concluding choice: Amy Lowell's 'Patterns'.

By 1931 she needed to work full time again, and put out feelers to President Jaqua of Scripps College in Claremont, California. It was founded in 1926, one of two colleges for women west of the Mississippi. At first, she hesitated to leave her mother in the East; then in January 1932 accepted Jaqua's offer of a two-year appointment as Assistant Professor of Oral English (she insisted on 'professor', not 'instructor'). Her courses (she named them) were to be 'Dramatic Interpretation' and 'English Speech and Diction'. In preparation, she took a private course in phonetics. No sooner did she arrive in Claremont than she was playing in *Hay Fever* once more. 'Her breeziness, her drawl and pseudo-aristocratic manner', reports a review, were 'captivating'.

At this time Eliot was preparing to come to America for the first time since the rushed visit in 1915. He accepted the Charles Eliot Norton professorship at Harvard for the academic year 1932–3. He and Emily Hale planned to meet, for on 15 May she wrote rather apologetically to Jaqua for an advance college calendar for the fall of 1932 as 'others' plans beside my own, are dependent upon your dates'.

The two years at Scripps, 1932–4, were a high point of Emily Hale's life. For the first time administrative duties were peripheral to a drama post. She was Head of House at Toll Hall, a fresh white dormitory faced by tall palms under a blue sky. Gracious, immaculate in a V-neck white blouse, casual white skirt, shady hat, and a particularly elegant pair of white shoes threaded with ribbon tied neatly about her slim ankles, the mature Emily Hale (now forty-one) was admired by her students. They noticed how she made a ceremony of a refectory meal; they imitated her style and manners, and visited her constantly.

Laurabel Neville (Hume), recalled Emily Hale as 'a vivid interesting person who attracted a large following of stage-struck girls; I was one of them. Part of her charm was her dignity and gaiety, and her Bostonian accent. And the weekly letters that came to her in blue envelopes with British postage from the great poet. She had a leather folder in her room with two pictures of Mr. Eliot, autographed to her. . . . She lived on campus, and her living-room was a mass of color. She wore a black silk dressing-gown (you can see that we visited her informally and often) covered with gold brocaded Chinese dragons. Her many bookshelves were covered with photographs, some of her appearing in plays in Boston – *non*-professional productions, she assured us. Evidently her family had not approved of Emily going on the stage at all, but she persisted . . . anyhow. She was an excellent director.'

She maintained a firm balance between warmth and reserve. Margaret Ann Ingram remembered a certain look that said 'don't intrude further' which the girls respected.

Emily Hale made friends also amongst the faculty with English teachers Ruth George, a poet (Emily later sent her book to Eliot), and Paul Havens (a recent Rhodes Scholar). His intelligent wife, Lorraine, became one of Emily Hale's lifelong correspondents. In the 1980s several Americans, then in their seventies, eighties, and nineties, remembered her at this good time. One of her most perceptive students was Marie McSpadden ('McSpad'), who designed sets for her productions and came to know her well. She recalled a pretty woman who seemed young with soft features, but who could be authoritative as a director:

> She was a lonely person, highly sensitive and prone to attach herself to a few students. I think she considered most of us 'primitive', a viewpoint often held by New Englanders. Young Californians are prone to be active in the out-of-doors. My friends and I were absorbed in studies only fifty percent of the time. This confused and amused Emily but she liked to share our activities and meet our 'dates'. . . . I remember her directing a Molière play very successfully.
>
> I cannot remember her having men friends – perhaps because of her caring for Eliot, perhaps being shy and lacking the opportunity to meet other men on a women's campus.
>
> Financially she had to be careful. I don't think that she had independent funds, although her aunt in Boston was close to her. However, she did purchase a small Ford roadster and on one spring vacation she and I drove to Yosemite National

Park, the beauty of which deeply impressed her. She also was fond of attending concerts and plays in Los Angeles, a forty-minute drive from Scripps.

Drama began to take a more prominent place at the college. Under Miss Hale, the languishing Siddons Club sprang to life with her first production, *La Locandiera* (*The Mistress of the Inn*), an eighteenth-century comedy by Carlo Goldoni. The girls were soon abandoning themselves to grandiloquent bows and Italian oaths on a moonlit balcony. The *Scripture*, the college newspaper, reported hilarious rehearsals: a marquis trying to see through his pasteboard monocle, and the cast snorting at the line 'Illustrious, here are the eggs!'

Miss Hale, the report went on, broke 'three records and one heel hopping over the footlights. Miss Hale preserves equanimity even when teaching each actress to say "lit-tle" instead of "li-ul." Miss Hale is wonderful.'

Later that year she put on Lady Gregory's *The Dragon*, accompanied by weird music and magic whistles, carrying the audience 'through the world in a dream'. Another review praises Emily Hale as Lady Bracknell in the Padua Players' production of *The Importance of Being Earnest*:

> Miss Hale as Lady Bracknell dominated the play with one sweep of her lorgnette. She provided the motivating character, and combined social rapacity with a most imposing glare. Her make-up failed to give her the requisite years for the part, but her dignity of bearing compensated to some degree.

She spoke often of Eliot, always as 'Tom', and wore a ring he had given her. Faith McAllister recalled that she would say to her girls, 'Emily Hale speaks only to Eliot, and Eliot speaks only to God,' conveying to Californians the exclusive loftiness of Boston, where it was said that Lowells spoke only to Cabots, and Cabots spoke only to God. Her joke has a serious application to *Ash-Wednesday*, where the poet's 'I', aided by the subordinate 'who' of the Lady in the middle, approaches 'Thee' in the final part. (One of Miss Hale's special girls, later, in Concord, Massachusetts, remembered how she would intimate a private 'understanding' of this poem.) There was much excitement at Scripps when Miss Hale announced that the poet would actually arrive to see her in the winter of 1932–3 and would speak to the students on the Victorian nonsense poet Edward Lear. Early in December, in preparation for his visit, Emily Hale made Eliot the subject of the weekly book talk in the Toll Hall browsing room. It was noticed that she spoke more about the man, whom she knew, than about the poetry, but she did read some of his poems and spoke of 1922–8 as his 'bitter period'. She described him as 'a man of extremes, a man of undoubted faults and highest virtues'.

At this moment, Eliot was giving a sermon ('The Bible as scripture and as literature') on 1 December 1932 from her uncle's pulpit, the oldest pulpit (1717) in America, at the historic King's Chapel on Beacon Hill in Boston.* It has a graceful simplicity, filled with cool natural light through the clear panes of its Georgian windows, which look out on the bare branches of trees. 'I wait for the LORD, my soul doth wait, and in his word do I hope,' Eliot quoted from Psalm 130. 'My soul waiteth for the LORD more than they that watch for the morning: I say, more than they that watch for the morning.'

Then, he set out on a 3,000-mile train journey across the continent. Back in London, Vivienne lost touch at this point with the movements of a husband who had decided never to see her again. Only Virginia Woolf asked awkward questions.

'And you are now on the Santa Fe Railway,' she wrote. 'But why? Where are you off to?'

Emily Hale was waiting at dawn on the West Coast platform where, at 6.20, Eliot descended, unshaven, from the carriage. What made the next few weeks different from all the subsequent years of her attachment to Eliot is that, for once,

---

* King's Chapel was Boston's first Anglican church, founded in 1686. It was redesigned in 1749–54 with the idea of a building 'as plain as the order of it will allow'. It was closed when the British were evacuated from Boston in 1775. After the Revolution, it revised its liturgy and in 1787 became an independent church, the first Unitarian church in New England.

thousands of miles away from the centres of their lives in Boston and London, they relaxed their vigilance. In any case, everyone knew that Eliot had come all this way to see only one person. 'How else could he have been attracted to our campus?' said Margaret Ann Ingram. She recalled 'a flurry of undergraduate speculation of "something" between Emily Hale and Eliot'. It remained Emily's practice to share carefully selected excerpts from Eliot's letters with her pupils; inscribed copies of his books were in her room. On 6 September (at the very time he tried in vain to separate from Vivienne before leaving for Harvard) he had mailed Emily an advance copy of his *Selected Essays 1917–1932*; when he visited her in January 1933, he brought her a newly published volume of *Sweeney Agonistes*.

Her new friends were given shares in Eliot's entertainment. Some gave him tea. Mrs Havens drove him to church. With the determined pride of a young mother, she marched him upstairs to view the baby. Surrounded by so many well-wishers, there was little privacy, so one day McSpad took them to her mother's cottage on Balboa Island (between Los Angeles and San Diego). It was then a quiet place in winter, reached by a car bridge or small car ferry from Balboa Beach. McSpad sailed them round the harbour and then left them alone on a sandy beach called Corona del Mar at the harbour's mouth. Afterwards, Eliot sent McSpad a copy of *Marina*.

Back at Harvard, Eliot gave Pound strictly PRIVATE word that the United States had done him good, so much so that in the spring of 1933 he felt torn between America and England. From America he wanted, specifically, domestic affection; from England, something else he did not spell out, as well as a degree of anonymity impossible in America. In America he was still exasperated by the small-minded materialism of the virtuous; in England, though, there was the eighteen-year nightmare of his marriage – like a bad novel by Dostoevsky, he confided to Paul Elmer More. Drawn alternately to both countries, Eliot felt like Alice passing through the looking-glass of a two-sided life. Fortunately, the time of choice was long gone. Or was it? As he raced about, from New York to Princeton, Virginia, Haverford, Yale, Smith, Mount Holyoke, Bryn Mawr, Vassar (where *Sweeney Agonistes* had its first performance), Providence, Buffalo, Pasadena, Minneapolis, and St Louis, he tossed off jaunty letters to Virginia Woolf, describing the Cabots and Sedgwicks of Boston and a wild woman of Providence, the first ever to make eyes at him. She replied to every one of his remarks, 'My! What a line you've got!' He was amused by a restaurant shaped like a bowler hat, and picked up the latest popular songs. He liked to sing:

> I met you first at Spring Street,
>   And then upon my word
> I thought I'd known you all my life
>   When we reached 23rd.
> I won your heart at Harlem,
>   At the Bronx you murmured Yes:
> We lost no time
> On that ride sublime
>   On the Subway *Express*.

One person saw through Eliot's disguise as superior Englishman unbuttoning to people who thought themselves his intimates. When the Princeton critic Edmund Wilson saw Eliot give a reading in New York, he remarked to the novelist John Dos Passos: 'He gives you the creeps a little at first because he is such a completely artificial, or rather, self-invented character . . . but he has done such a perfect job with himself that you often end by admiring him.'

The true Eliot was not entirely invisible because of the impulse to confess. It came up in Virginia. 'I speak as a New Englander,' he told his audience in 1933, and, as such, tried to revive words like 'heresy', 'Original Sin', and the 'diabolic'. He believed that the disappearance of belief in Original Sin meant the disappearance of 'real' people who undergo moral struggle. For this reason, contemporary literature seemed full of unreal characters. So far, so good. But what made these

lectures notorious (Eliot never reprinted them) was intolerance for free-thinking Jews and certain writers. We see here
prophecy warped by some sickness in the prophet when
denunciation loses its aim and becomes dangerous. It is like
the warped judgements by the God-fearing men of Salem
(including Eliot's forebears, Andrew Eliott and Judge Blood)
who hung witches in the 1690s. As a rival prophet, D. H.
Lawrence was Eliot's arch-heretic with a religion of his own
making: 'Woe unto foolish prophets that follow their own
spirit, and have seen nothing!' Quite arbitrarily Eliot exempts
a genuine heretic, James Joyce, on the grounds that, in his
story 'The Dead', Joyce put the ethical weight on 'an intense
romantic and spiritualised love' rather than on a dead
marriage. This bears directly on Eliot's own life – at a critical
stage in the spring of 1933 – between a 'spiritualised' love for
Emily Hale and dread of his moves to end all further contact
with his wife.

On 14 March he had written to Lady Ottoline Morrell:
'For my part, I should prefer never to see her again; for hers, I
do not believe that it can be good for any woman to live with
a man to whom she is morally, in the larger sense, unpleasant,
as well as physically indifferent. But I am quite aware of
putting my own interests first.' F. Scott Fitzgerald, who met
him at this time, noticed that he appeared 'very broken and
sad & shrunk inside'. It was after he delivered his last set of
lectures in Baltimore from 10 to 12 May* that Eliot wrote
to his solicitor in London to request a Deed of Separation
from Vivienne.

He lingered in America into June. Here he was part of a
family again, near three sisters in Cambridge and surrounded
by affection. As soon as the spring semester was over, Emily
Hale returned to her aunt and uncle in Boston. Eliot was fond
of the Perkinses and called them, as Emily did, 'Aunt Edith'
and 'Uncle John'. They welcomed him to their home where,
in the hall, hung the portrait of Emily Hale as Eliot would

* The Turnbull lectures on 'The Varieties of Metaphysical Poetry' at
Johns Hopkins University.

have remembered her, a rather regal young woman. According to Eliot's brother, Henry, this was one of the happiest periods Eliot had known since childhood.

In the midst of family, in a bookish city where Eliot was a celebrity, he and Emily Hale were less free than in California. Dorothy Elsmith, a friend who lived at Woods Hole, provided a retreat, as she recalled: 'Emily and Mr Eliot made several visits to the anonymity of my home here [Ros Marinus], where they walked the beach, in quiet retreat from Cambridge publicity.' Mrs Elsmith also joined them, together with the Revd and Mrs Perkins, for a weekend in the Berkshires. Then, in early June, there was a family vacation, which included Emily Hale, at Mountain View House in Randolph, New Hampshire. Eliot's poem 'New Hampshire' is patently autobiographical. 'Twenty years and the spring is over': the poet 'grieves' for lost opportunity, but enjoys a blissful respite. He is 'Between the blossom- and fruit-time' and experiences, briefly, a domestic idyll as imaginary children 'Swing up into the apple tree'. Emily Hale was vital not just as the Beatrice-figure of his poetry, but because she returned him to his 'simple soul'. She had the power to restore, if only now and then, his capacity to feel. The final glimpse of Eliot and Emily Hale together at this time is on 17 June when, with Dorothy Elsmith and members of the Eliot family, she attended his address at his old school, Milton Academy.

Back in England, he went into hiding from his wife. According to Lorraine Havens, Emily Hale, too, was in England during that elusive summer of 1933. She returned to Scripps with an elkhound, a present from Eliot. There is no mention of her presence in Frank Morley's detailed account of this time, when Eliot stayed with the Morley family at Pikes Farm in Surrey, yet that dog does have the substance of fact.

When Eliot visited Virginia Woolf in early September, he appeared rejuvenated: 'He is 10 years younger: hard, spry, a glorified boy scout in shorts & yellow shirt. He is enjoying himself very much. He is tight & shiny as a wood louse. . . .

But there is well water in him, cold & pure.' She saw it bubble with unexpected life. When she asked about Vivienne, he replied with some asperity, resenting 'all the past waste and exaction'. For too many years he had seen 'nobody'. Now, at forty-six, he wanted 'to live, to love'.

*

Vivienne refused to accept their separation. In fear of her pursuit Eliot kept his address secret as he shifted from one hiding place to another. In September 1933 he stayed with Anglo-Catholic clergymen at Kelham Theological College at Kelham, Newark, Nottinghamshire, and when he returned to work in the autumn he lived near the office (at 24 Russell Square) in a Great Ormond Street flat with three homosexuals, Ken Ritchie (later chairman of the Stock Exchange), Richard Jennings, a bibliophile, and Clifford Kitchin, a novelist, who recalled that when Eliot went out of an evening he would often 'apply a bit of slap [theatrical makeup]'. After a short tour of Scotland and a jaunt to Paris, Eliot moved into a guest house in Courtfield Gardens (33 Courtfield Road), but Kensington proved too expensive: three guineas a week for one room. On 7 December, he was tramping the pavements of Clerkenwell looking for cheaper lodgings. The bathrooms were uninviting, but he could get a room at one guinea a week, with supper at one shilling and sixpence, and half-a-crown a week for coals. The new life was no longer a dream.

Eliot's pressing needs were to restructure his outward life and to evade Vivienne. Before his return to England he toyed with a policy of incognito, not without relish – it amused him to imagine meeting Pound, also incognito (shades of Eeldrop and Appleplex), at some sequestered spot like Cliftonville or Reigate; the actuality of hiding was rather less fun. He found a permanent hideout in a clergyhouse at 9 Grenville Place, off the Cromwell Road in the preferred area of Kensington, where he was a paying guest of Father Eric Cheetham, vicar of St Stephen's. His rooms were drab, with hideous purple covers in a small, angular sitting-room, and meagre dribbles from the hot tap (he shared a bathroom with the curates). It was not a home. He had only a few of his books, stood on top of one another, for the bookcases had shelves missing. The District Line ran under his bedroom, and sherry and glasses had to stand on the sill. The only light relief seems to have been provided by the unknowing Sisters of St Elizabeth, who washed for Cheetham and Eliot: they carefully took out their pyjama cords for ironing, but always forgot to put them back.

Behind these cheerless conditions lurked a fear that the years with Vivienne had scarred him permanently. There were times when he wondered if his present course, 'denying the importunity of blood', would destroy, not save him. He might lose all substance and become 'a spectre in its own gloom'.

Outside the clergyhouse, he sought containment in his club (the Oxford and Cambridge in Pall Mall) and, socially, in the Faber–Hayward circle. John Davy Hayward was to play an important role as adviser and flatmate in Eliot's later years. He was a young man who had made his first approach to Eliot when he was an undergraduate at Cambridge in the mid-twenties. The son of a surgeon in Wimbledon, he went to Gresham's School, Holt, and from there won an Exhibition to King's College, Cambridge, in 1922. By the time he came up in 1923 he was already disabled by the progressive paralysis of muscular dystrophy. His contemporaries thought that he had not long to live, but he defied fate with his wit, his bright eyes, his resonant bass voice in musical societies and, not least, his comic imitations of people and puffing trains.

For that generation of students, the seventeenth century was the favoured age: Donne was their poet and Webster their dramatist. George Rylands (who went to work for the Hogarth Press and then became a Cambridge don) recalled John Hayward as the Fourth Madman in *The Duchess of Malfi*, at once comical and macabre. He loved doing all the madmen, especially the line in Act IV Scene ii: 'I have found out his roguery: he makes an allum out of his wives urine, and sells it to Puritans, that have sore throats with over-straining.' In another play he acted behind the scenes a bevy of prisoners under torture, producing 'some of the most blood-curdling noises ever heard in Cambridge'.

While still an undergraduate, he edited Rochester for the Nonesuch Press. After he went down in 1927, he settled in London as a professional man of letters, editor, anthologist, critic, and bibliographer. In the twenties and thirties he published admirable editions of Donne and Swift (including the first correct recension of *Gulliver's Travels* since the eighteenth century) and also a short life of Charles II. In his wheelchair, he went about London with unconcerned ease. He would allow himself to be lugged up to the second floor of a London restaurant for a book collectors' dinner – he joined a dining club founded by Michael Sadleir called 'The Biblioboys' – and then pushed into a taxi to go home alone to his flat in Bina Gardens, off the Brompton Road (not far from the clergyhouse).

On Eliot's return to London, a group gathered round Hayward whose members had a passion for Sherlock Holmes and also exchanged light verse (privately printed as *Noctes Binanianae*). Identities of the Coot (Geoffrey Faber, who was bald), the Tarantula (John Hayward, at the centre of the web and having, as his friends were aware, a considerable power of stinging), the Whale (Frank Morley, who was large) and the Elephant (Eliot) were assigned. The mannered repartee between these characters has now dated. Their jokes had the after-dinner jollity of men who evade expressiveness. Their verbal play was a feeble emulation of the poetic star, Eliot, who was, at this low point, parodying himself.

He had temporarily dried up. At the end of 1933 Vivienne refused to sign a Deed of Separation, and it became obvious that she would never consent to her husband's freedom. It was like cranking a machine as he began to compose *The Rock*, his pageant history of the Church in Britain (performed at Sadler's Wells from 28 May to 9 June 1934). 'Nothing but a brilliant future behind me,' Eliot said in July 1934. 'What is one to do?' With the rise of a new generation of thirties poets, he feared that he would soon appear an old fogey, and began to play a caricature of that role: a man who tended to fall asleep in club chairs.

What was happening at Hayward's flat on 'Bina nights' was the formation of a court circle in which Eliot could be encased. His courtiers were tactful enough to make no demands. As gentlemen, they refrained from intruding on Eliot's private life and showed themselves content to engage with the limited persona of a jokey Old Buffer. At the publishing house, he liked to upset a board meeting by setting off a firecracker (on the anniversary of American independence) under Geoffrey Faber's chair. He sent obscene verses to male friends, about that Big Black Kween whose bum was as big as a soup tureen. As late as September 1932, when Eliot was forty-four years old, he sent off his latest effort about a fart that broke stained-glass windows. There was nothing spontaneous in this: the joker was another convenient mask, a way of keeping other jolly chaps at a distance. (If any presumed to allude to the verses at the wrong moment, Eliot's respectable mask would slide into place and, with frigid amazement, he would declare that no such verses existed.)

All of this was a strategy for dealing with a public world. It was a world of men without women. Emily Hale was directing and teaching 6,000 miles away. The wives, Mrs Faber and Mrs Morley, stayed quietly at home. No woman could hope for high promotion at Faber according to Brigid O'Donovan, an Oxford graduate who was Eliot's secretary from 1934 to 1936 and left the firm for this reason.

Within this male clique, Eliot now took up Henry James's mantle as the Master. When facilities at the clergyhouse broke down, Hayward conveyed to Morley the noteworthy fact that the Master had to shave and shit at his club. And the Master, no doubt aware of instant relay, said little beyond the banalities of his day-to-day activities. Any one entry in Virginia Woolf's diary, after one of her easy talks with Eliot, tells us more than Hayward's mountain of trivia. A devotee, hanging on Eliot's lips, Hayward seems not to realise the

Master's inscrutable distance. The new life was masked by Old Buffer routines; the extremist, by elaborate courtesies. Eliot's outermost casing was his formal public image of formidable authority. Beneath this was the outer casing of the Director's daily routine at Faber and the night-time jollities at Bina Gardens.

These were supplemented by domestic jollities down in the country, at Hope Cottage in Hampshire, with the Tandy family. Eliot came to know them through a drinking partner, Geoffrey Tandy, who worked at the Natural Science Museum and afterwards for the BBC, where he read a selection of Eliot's Cat poems on Christmas Day 1937 (two years before they were published). Tandy was the hopeless husband of Hope Cottage. He lived, Eliot quipped, between the devil and the BBC (small sums grudgingly paid – not what the Eliots and Harvard would regard as a manly job). Tandy drank and womanised and contrived disappearing acts that were hard to disentangle from war work after 1939, but in fact he abandoned his family. This was apparent to all only after the war, but Eliot's circuitous phrases to Tandy's wife, Doris (Polly) Tandy, show him well aware of her burden. Eliot visited Polly and her three children frequently in the thirties, taking up a role as domestic pet, while trying out his Cat poems and aspiring – he hinted – to a slot on 'Children's Hour'. The second child, Alison (known as Poony), was one of the dedicatees of Old Possum's Book of Practical Cats. Poony was the recipient of a humorous unpublished elegy for milk teeth, in which Old Possum consoles the child that though she must now feed on mushes, she soon would have new tushes to crack a nut or chicken bone; while poor Old Possum, losing his teeth two by two each year, would have to wait for something called a dental plate.

Poony's mother, Polly, was the very antithesis of Vivienne: she was a practical, religious, warm-hearted countrywoman who mothered Eliot, knitted him a Fair Isle pullover, posted on the worn slippers he left behind, bought him a new scarlet pair, and sent fresh produce, chickens, boiling fowls, pheasants, as well as posies tucked in moss at Easter. He liked her the better for not being a 'scholard'. For all that, there is something unfathomable in the persistent laughter of the 140 letters he wrote to Pollytandy from 1934 to 1963. These letters don't reflect Polly in any way except as a type of womanhood – so much so that Eliot was moved to adapt Tennyson's Victorian tag: he for the sword, she for the knitting needles. This is odd coming from a playwright who claimed (he told Polly in the fifties) to invent better roles for women than for men. For the Pollytandy of Eliot's letters is not a real person: she apparently has no interests or desires beyond her children; makes no demands whatever; is grateful for Eliot's largesse (school fees for the two girls); and never once protests when he ruins plans at the last minute because something Important has come up. Eliot projects a woman who cannot fail to be entertained by his comic grovelling, and will never question that relentless joking that controlled her, distanced her unvoiced drama, and willed attention to his own tedious performance as Tom Possum out of Uncle Remus, signed 'Tp'.

Most people who wrote memoirs of the Eliot they 'knew' seemed to feel a certain triumph to have got past the formidable façade to the comic performer, but they were nowhere near the hidden life. Its inner casing was another set of rituals: daily prayers at St Stephen's Church in the Gloucester Road and, from 1934, duties as Vicar's Warden. This was the visible chrysalis for the invisible life now in the making. When the saint-to-be enters in *Murder in the Cathedral*, he speaks enigmatically of 'the pattern'. Eliot believed there was an eternal pattern of action, but could even the highest intelligence perceive it through the veil of Time?

The first logical step must be to shed the illusions of Time and, with it, the temporal order: the deceptive schemes of sexual love, worldly ambition, and political power, all the vanities of all the fools under the sun. To replace these, Eliot needed a rigorous programme that would carry him across the perhaps impossible gap between time and eternity. The pattern for such crossings lies, of course, in the Bible, which resonates through Eliot's new verse.

In one way the new life was not new: in poem after poem, his mother had plotted the course from the wilderness of this world to the Celestial City; and not his mother alone but, generations back, his forebears had appropriated the journeys of the Bible as a model for their own journeys to New England to found a New Jerusalem, a city on a hill.

Eliot had a mock competition on ancestors with Virginia Woolf. He set against the numerical importance of her Venns (evangelicals, connected with the Clapham Sect) such weighty New England figures as the Revd Daniel Greenleaf, the Revd Obadiah Smith, and the Revd Dr Asahel Stearns (1774–1839), who served as state senator and became Professor of Law at the newly established Harvard Law School. His book *The Revised Statutes of the Commonwealth of Massachusetts* (1836) was a standard text. He was a descendant of Isaac Stearns, who migrated from England to Salem in 1630. For these home models of migrant and preacher Eliot found more prestigious parallels in Europe. Dante more than any other writer marked out the route from 'depravity's despair' to 'the beatific vision': a complete schema. What all Eliot's models have in common was the pattern of a life in which failure was linked to beatitude. He was attracted for this reason also to Pascal. 'His despair, his disillusion,' Eliot said, 'are essential moments in the progress of the intellectual soul; and for the type of Pascal they are the analogue of the drought, the dark night, which is an essential stage in the progress of the Christian mystic.'

*

The climactic scene of the new life took place in Gloucestershire in the late summer of 1934. Preparations began at Scripps College, California, on 19 February when Emily Hale asked President Jaqua for a year's leave to go to England. Jaqua (who was regarded by his faculty as a difficult, rather devious man) would not guarantee her post, but she went all the same. To take this risk, she must have been confident of Eliot's attachment or recklessly in love – or both.

In the meantime, she had scope for her dramatic talents as never before: her students' enthusiasm enabled her to put on four plays that year, apart from her courses. In November 1933 she staged an Indian legend, dramatised by Dr Alexander, a member of the Scripps faculty. The Christmas play was a Symbolist drama by Paul Claudel. In March 1934 she directed Shaw's satire *Great Catherine*; and finally, in June, *Comus*, in one of the college courts to mark the three-hundredth anniversary of its presentation at Ludlow Castle. She managed to procure the original music from England, and a string orchestra to play it. Lorraine Havens, one of the nymphs, could still, in her eighties, recall 'our song'. Visitors were invited from colleges and schools in the Pomona Valley, and the play was reviewed in the press, which had only praise for the staging and the expressiveness of the cast.

As departure drew near, there was a round of farewells. On 29 May, Toll Hall gave Miss Hale a farewell tea, accompanied by harp and piano. Early in June, the Siddons Club invited her to a barbecue, when the fresh air of San Dimas Park was defiled by burnt onions at a supper of hamburger and watermelon. Regrets were offered to their 'most honorable Directrice' that 'our riotous attitude may have hidden our true sentiments'.

On 15 July, Emily Hale sailed from Boston. On arrival in England she joined the Revd and Mrs Perkins, who were already installed at Stamford House, Chipping Campden, in Gloucestershire. Emily was to have the adjoining Stanley Cottage. Eliot went there at once: on 30 July, he wrote to thank Mrs Perkins.

He was a frequent visitor, according to Jeanette McPherrin, a Scripps student who stayed at Stamford House en route to France. Edith Perkins was a dedicated gardener and a keen photographer of local gardens. Sometimes Eliot accompanied these visits. When, in 1948, he presented her lantern slides to the Royal Horticultural Society, he recalled that Hidcote Manor was 'the one I loved the best'. His more tentative ventures with Emily Hale into the open countryside are recorded in an unpublished comic verse, 'A Country Walk:

An Epistle to Miss E— H— with the humble compliments of her obliged servant, the Author'. It is mainly about the Author's terror of cows. Emily Hale added at the bottom: 'we often took long walks in the country about Gloucestershire'.

The Perkinses had leased Stamford House from Mrs Sunderland-Taylor, who went to Yugoslavia in the summers. It is an early eighteenth-century house, with cottages on either side, built on a grassy bank towards one end of the High Street. The front bedrooms look out on the church tower. Downstairs, a Queen Anne fireplace graces the long wall of the sitting-room. That and the dining-room across the hall are well-proportioned and genial without being too grand. Eliot, coming there from the clergyhouse, told Aunt Edith in 1935 that he came 'to feel "at home" in Campden in a way in which I had not felt at home for some twenty-one years, anywhere'.

Emily Hale wrote to Scripps in August that she was 'optimistic' under the supervision of a doctor in London who was to make some decision in the autumn, and she describes her life in Campden with delight:

Stamford House,
Chipping Campden,
Gloucestershire.
August 27, 1934

Dear Dr. Jaqua:

Your very kind letter of over a month ago brought me very much pleasure and comfort: it happened to come on the morning when I was going up to London to see the doctor who is to supervise my care over here, and I left Campden feeling no matter what the doctor said your kind words and generous [statement] about my work at Scripps, would be the best tonic for me.

On the whole, his report was encouraging, although I can not know about his final decision until the autumn when further examinations will be made. I note with appreciation what you say of the year's appointment for Mr. and Mrs. Lange, and I shall hope that I can give you a definite statement about year after next in time enough for your own convenience in planning for that future day.

... Amid the beauty of these surroundings in which we are

living at present, I am bound to be optimistic, and optimistic I
wish to remain [as] to the final decision. If Mrs. Jaqua and you
could but come in for tea this afternoon, you would find your
way up the long curving street of Chipping Campden, which is
the one street the town has, and on which stand houses dating
as far back as the early 15th century, almost all of any
succeeding period as well, made from the beautiful Cotswold
stone, for which this region of the Cotswold hills is as famous
as its once far famed sheep and wool markets. . . . We live and
keep house in quite a modern building, 1705 being the date
over the door, and a fine type of dignified domestic architec-
ture which represented the house of the well to do farmer at
that time. . . . Back of the house lay originally the farmyard
and outbuildings – these are transformed into a very lovely
garden and garden sheds respectively, the garden rising in
three terraces – on one of which I now sit, looking thru' a
superb old pear tree, over the *stone tiled* roof of such warmth
of grey, to the famous church tower which rises in its glory at
the *top* end of the street – a landmark for miles around. We
live a very quiet – to some a too quiet life perhaps – as the
residents in a town of 2,000 citizens. . . . All marketing
purchases are delivered by hand, the bread comes out of a
large basket on the arm of a man too small to carry it, or the
milkman stands like a reincarnated Roman charioteer, in his
two-wheeled cart, driving his gay sage pony, who knows at
just which house door he shall wait, or the quiet voiced
butcher hands you a leg or a shoulder in a quite callous
manner! . . .

I walk two or three times a week to some spot of interest or
charm not too far away, and any stroll along these Cotswold
woods or even the wolds is its own reward.

Jean McPherrin joins us today until she goes to France. . . .

The political news in the papers is of course wholly centered
on Germany. . . . As yet we have no 'inside' news on German
affairs as there are few men who move in state circles here but
my uncle, Dr. Perkins, feels very sure much is going on in
Germany of which we know nothing. . . .

My kind regards to Mrs. Jaqua, please, and believe me
Very sincerely yours

Emily Hale

It is not known exactly when in 1934–5 Eliot and Emily

Hale paid a visit, so momentous for Eliot's poetry for the next eight years, to Burnt Norton, two miles outside Chipping Campden, but facts point to early September 1934. Eliot sent a postcard from Gloucestershire to Theodore Spencer at Harvard and on 4 September wrote to Aunt Edith: 'My weekend, apart from being twice the length, gave me still more happiness than the previous one.' In *Burnt Norton* (1935) it is a time of 'autumn heat', both literally – the roses in their second flowering – and as a metaphor for a mature love which recalled the lingering, regretful desires for 'La Figlia', where, long before, in 1912, Eliot had rehearsed an autumn departure from the garden of young love. The garden at Burnt Norton presented the temptation to replay that scene, that past, those other selves that might have been. 'Footfalls echo in the memory', wrote Eliot, 'Down the passage which we did not take / Towards the door we never opened / Into the rose-garden.' The light which had irradiated La Figlia's hair, the beatific light inspired by the hyacinth girl, reappears as miraculous 'water out of sunlight' in the garden's dry concrete pool.

Burnt Norton is owned by the Earls of Harrowby. Two years later, in 1936, the sixth Earl and Countess took up residence, but at the time of Eliot's and Emily Hale's visit it was mostly unoccupied. It was the garden, not the house, that they explored: a formal, timeless garden with box hedges and a processional path leading to two great pools set squarely in the centre of a sweeping semi-circle of lawn. The 'brown edge' of the pool in Eliot's poem is a covering of old green moss. The pools were empty (as they still are), the larger slightly shaded by overhanging gold-green branches, so that the light fell on it in dappled fragments.

When Eliot says that the roses had the look of flowers that are looked at, it was not poetic fancy. The straight path to the pools leads through two lines of rose-bushes (the present ones are red) which lean out along the path, in attitudes of attention, as one advances through an eighteenth-century arch or arrive, as Eliot and Emily Hale did, down a flight of steps, round the corner of the box hedge, to pass slowly down

266

the path, getting the heady scent of the full blooms. The faces of the roses, turned towards the walker and leaning slightly into the path, give one an extraordinary sense of advancing as in a procession through a divided crowd – like a marriage aisle – towards the arena of the pools. Birds call from the wild part of the estate below a brick wall to the right of the pathway.

To go to Burnt Norton is to discover a lost world, like the haunted garden filled with the voices of unborn children in Kipling's 'They'. The entrance is about three-quarters of a mile's walk from Chipping Campden along the Stratford road. It is easy to miss the unidentified turn-off to a private track, which bumps along and curves across several fields until you come to the arched entrance and, beyond that, a rose-garden, and beyond that, extensive other gardens laid out in the eighteenth century in the expensive taste of Sir William Keyt, a dissipated baronet who eventually became insane and burnt the house and himself in it – hence the name. The garden has remained as it always was, immaculate and silent, except for the birdcalls. This garden was the scene of Eliot's divergence into a lost world of experience.

According to a Boston friend, the few who knew what happened there were sworn to secrecy and are now dead. There is no way of verifying this, but a momentous encounter with a woman who brings back the past was reshaped three times in Eliot's writings: the 'Bellegarde' sketch, sent in the spring or early summer of 1935 to his brother in Cambridge, Massachusetts; *Burnt Norton* itself; and the rose-garden encounter in Eliot's subsequent play, *The Family Reunion*. Each work relates an experience of love from a different angle. 'Bellegarde', written first, is the most physical of the three versions: a man experiences 'leaping pleasures' that release him from a mood of futility and reach a 'matchless' moment; then fade all too fast, 'impaired by impotence'. There is a dramatic arousal and an even more dramatic collapse that seems psychological, not physical, for pleasure is almost at once eroded by a self-lacerating mind that worries over the experience until it is virtually destroyed. The poetry is so intensely self-absorbed that a reader might well wonder if there was any partner at all, but the title, 'Bellegarde', does imply the presence of a woman, both beautiful and good, as in the novel to which Eliot alludes.

It is *The American*, an early work by Henry James. The American in Europe, Christopher Newman, falls in love with a mature, aristocratic woman, Claire Cintré, who is guarded by her strict French family. Ruthlessly, to the visiting American inexplicably, they abort the love affair, virtually an engagement, just as it appears to succeed. As usual, Eliot swerves from his source (as in his 'Portrait of a Lady'). In James, the woman recedes into a convent, where she shuts herself beyond Newman's reach; in Eliot's 'Bellegarde', the object of love is again invisible (like the Lady of silences, behind her veil) but, here, more completely deprived of her agency. For it is the writer – stricter than the Bellegardes themselves – who silences and shuts off the woman.

Two details in 'Bellegarde' suggest that it was the germ of *Burnt Norton*. The woman is a not unwelcome apparition from the past, and there is, too, the matchless moment and afterwards. The opening and conclusion of *Burnt Norton* rework the rudimentary 'Bellegarde' material as an encounter with a first love. The rapport is so acute that the ghosts of their former selves seem to walk towards a moment that transcends love with a glimpse of eternal 'Love', the still point of the turning world, as literally they walk the aisle of roses towards a pool filled with sunlight. This moment fulfils Eliot's dream in 1921 of 'Memory and desire', of a girl who had once inspired a moment of unspeakable bliss 'looking into the heart of light, the silence'. In 1934, this same woman, now in the flesh, provoked once again that particular vision as the pool's unfolding lotus glitters 'out of the heart of light'. The man is drawn from 'un-being' into full being. Whatever actually happened at Burnt Norton, the poem claims some breathless, unforgettable bliss: 'Quick now, here, now, always – '.

Writing this about nine months after the event, the speaker addresses his now-silent companion with intimate certainty that she shared the rapport that called up the ghostly selves of their youth. As their footfalls continue to echo in their memories, so, now, 'My words echo / Thus, in your mind.' The experience was over – it seems they will never know such bliss again – but the poetry re-creates the experience, for her he tells her, as well as for others. His gift to her, was to re-create their experience with such verbal sublimity that it will outlast time, as when Shakespeare says that time will wither his beloved, but the record will remain:

> So long as men can breathe and eyes can see
> So long lives this, and this gives life to thee.

Eliot's final record of this scene in *The Family Reunion* (its scenarios go back to 1934–5) colours in the man and woman, and offers an explanation for fading emotion. Two women are associated with the sunlit moment. The virginal, waiting Mary is destined to become what the other, Agatha, is, a middle-aged college teacher. Mary brings Harry 'news' of a door that opens to 'Sunlight and singing', but it was, for Harry, 'only a moment, it was only a moment / That I stood in sunlight, and thought I might stay there.' Mary remains bereft and resigned. Her older counterpart, Agatha, has had an affair with Harry's father and awakens some replay of attraction in Harry. For Agatha, the feeling is simple nostalgia for love and unborn children, followed by solitary endurance:

> I only looked through the little door
> When the sun was shining on the rose-garden:
> And heard in the distance tiny voices
> And then a black raven flew over
> And then I was only my own feet walking
> Away, down a concrete corridor. . . .

For the man, Harry, it was a phantasmal union and in some way incomplete:

> And what did not happen is as true as what did happen
> O my dear, and you walked through the little door
> And I ran to meet you in the rose-garden.

Agatha replies that this 'is the beginning'. She means that having passed through this door, there is no going back. The silent woman of *Burnt Norton* is granted, here, her voice, and when she speaks of 'relief from what happened', she speaks for both. For her, the 'relief from that unfulfilled craving' is simply the release of natural love. For Harry the words apply differently: the mystical rapport fulfils a craving for visionary communion which had fed his dreams, until this moment to no apparent purpose. It is, at the same time, a release from his private nightmare.

Eliot explained this to his director, Martin Browne, in a letter full of superfluous confessions: Harry, he said, was partially de-sexed by the horror of his marriage. He could be 'stirred up' by a lovable woman but, because of his state of mind, was unable to develop this feeling into a stable commitment. His attraction to a particular woman warred with his general idea that all women are 'unclean creatures'. His solution is to find refuge in an 'ambiguous relation'.

Eliot was at ease with the familiar Emily of his Boston youth, and also at ease with the Beatrice–Emily of poetic fancy, but may not have known what to make of an offer of natural love from a virtuous woman. He once remarked to Paul Elmer More that the good were to him more bewildering than the bad for they have an easy and innocent acceptance of life that he simply could not understand.

Compared with the inevitability of Dante's approach to paradise through reunion with Beatrice (Eliot said that when they meet in the last cantos of the *Purgatorio*, Dante is already in the vicinity of paradise), his own reunion with Emily Hale in the paradisal garden left behind it a trail of uncertainty and introspection. Was it not impossible to recover the might-have-beens of the past? Had not all possibility of renewed love turned to dust in present marital circumstances? And then, there were the alternative attractions of martyrdom. In December 1934, when Eliot turned to this subject in *Murder in the Cathedral*, it was more pressing than a matchless moment.

*

Right action comes from right feeling. Eliot stressed the poet's commitment to emotion, 'precise' not sloppy emotion, and he tried to train it on a perfection beyond human limits. Only saints could aspire to such perfection. Eliot fixed on Thomas à Becket, a twelfth-century Englishman who became the most popular saint in Western Europe in the late Middle Ages.

In Becket, Eliot found a model who was not that different from Eliot himself. Here was a man to all appearance not born for sainthood, a man of the world, the able and all-powerful Chancellor of Henry II, who moved from worldly success into spiritual danger. Following his investiture as Archbishop of Canterbury in 1162 (a wholly political move on the part of the King), he at once resigned his chancellorship and declared allegiance to a Higher Power. So acrimonious was the dispute with an outraged Henry II, who stripped Becket of his office in 1163, that he fled England. For seven years he found refuge in a monastery in France. When, in 1170, he returned to reclaim his see, he came to face almost certain death.

The play stresses the fact that Becket's sainthood was not achieved without struggle. This was no noble-minded Thomas More (martyred by Henry VIII), but a man exalted out of a fair share of worldly dross and political ambition. Eliot said that a bit of the author may be the germ for a character but that, too, a certain character may call out latent potentialities in the author. *Murder in the Cathedral* was a biographic play that had its biographic impact on Eliot in shifting the balance of the new life from the shared course of love to the lone course of religious trial.

Eliot chose this subject despite the fact that the Canterbury Festival, for which the play was commissioned, had had (as might be expected) almost too many Beckets in recent years. But Eliot was determined. Martin Browne, who directed the play, said that not once did Eliot consider anything else.

The external action of the play is minimal: its focus is the last days of Becket's life, in December 1170, as he awaits his murder. His doom, and the dismay of his priests and people, set off the inward triumph of the saint in the making. The act of murder is no more than the occasion for this inward action. He must make perfect his will as he moves in measure towards a death that is God's will. When the abusive Knights arrive to kill him, drunk, stumbling, rowdy, what Thomas hears is the steady oncoming measure of his destiny: 'All my life they have been coming, these feet. All my life . . .'.

We, the audience, are privileged to witness that rarest of all actions, when a person crosses the gap between the human and the sublime, shedding the last temptations of his humanity and, at the last, living by a divine order. His defiance of his killers, there in Eliot's earliest pencil notes, is an unswerving intent to hold to his assigned role to give his life 'To the Law of God above the Law of Man'.

The novelty of this action is that Eliot dares to fix the spotlight, unwavering, on what is normally invisible: the inward moments of transformation. In his review, F. O. Matthiessen noted that the play's inwardness is 'of the sort that shows Eliot even more clearly than ever in the tradition of Henry James, and, more especially here of Hawthorne'. The temptations that beset Becket are like the evil whisperers in Hawthorne's eerie allegories. Virginia Woolf, more hostile, called the play 'the pale New England morality murder'. The one sees Eliot succeed, the other fail to solve the obvious problem: how on stage to make interior action visible? This was to be the problem of all Eliot's plays, and later on he tried to solve it by cutting short the reach of the interior action. In this play, though, he solved the problem boldly and effectively by embodying the whispers of Becket's past as four visible Tempters who play on him with increasing subtlety.

The last and most dangerous is the whisper of spiritual pride: to die for immortality on earth, to dream of the saint's tomb and pilgrims in the centuries to come or, even more insidious, to die to stand high in heaven. These dreams are the 'higher vices', and Eliot, projecting them through Thomas, the Archbishop, understands well that to seek glory is the route to hell. To want sainthood is to undercut it. This is the divide, narrow but plummeting, between saint and sinner. The closeness of the Fourth Tempter to the saint in the making must be shown in production as a mirror image. Eliot told his brother that this Tempter should be a man of the same stature and same type as the Archbishop and, like him, clad as a priest and tonsured. Eliot added that it was more important that this part be played competently than any of the others.

He himself considered and then refused the part of Becket in the film. He preferred the role of Fourth Tempter, which he did as a voice echoing in Becket's head. Spiritual pride is the temptation that lingers in the mind of the elect, who is vulnerable to it precisely because of his unavoidable awareness of that possibility. Given Eliot's gifts, this was the part of the drama that touched him closely. The way he went into Becket's head after a series of external Tempters, suggests the closest of self-encounters and, too, Eliot's own relation to the saintly model: a flawed other-self, left behind on the wrong side of the gap between frailty and perfection. The Fourth temptation was perhaps where Eliot stood in December 1934 to April 1935 as he wrote this play: still in danger of taking the right course for the wrong reason, still fighting the last temptation of success: glory. He certainly did fear damnation: he told Paul Elmer More that he walked in daily terror. And at the same time he was blessed just enough to be able to imagine the crossing Becket made. His own recent quickening in a shaft of sunlight, in a Cotswold garden in September 1934, made it possible to conceive the absolute conviction of Becket: 'I have had a tremor of bliss, a wink of heaven, a whisper . . .'.

Martin Browne contrived to suggest that Eliot did not think of Tempters until Browne pointed to a certain lack in the play. This is not borne out by Eliot's preliminary pencil notes. It is true that the label 'Tempters' did not appear in these notes, and nor did they appear in the first draft of Part I which Eliot showed to Martin Browne in March 1935, but, on the back of the fourth of the eighteen pages of notes, Eliot jotted down the names of certain contemporary authors, numbering them one to four. These were, I propose, the germ of four allegorical Tempters. It seems that Eliot (like Dante) worked from living models to frame his hierarchy of sin.

The first name that occurred to him was that of his ex-teacher, Bertrand Russell, with whom Vivienne had committed adultery, and next to this name he put a two: this was the Tempter to power who speaks with persuasive reason. In the twenties and thirties, Eliot had attacked Russell repeatedly. In a 1927 *Criterion* review of Russell's *Why I Am Not a Christian*, he had stated that Russell's Radicalism was merely a variety of Whiggery, as his non-Christianity was merely a variety of Low Church sentiment. Russell, he said in 1931, preached 'the enervate *gospel of happiness*', bolstered by popular catchwords of emancipation which may have been advanced in Russell's youth but were by now eminently respectable: 'What chiefly remains of the new freedom is its meagre impoverished emotional life.'

The second name was H. G. Wells, and against it Eliot put a one. A noted philanderer, Wells was the source of the first and most easily dismissed of the Tempters. He represents the facile charms of the senses and good-fellowship. In the first production, the First Tempter wore a top hat to show the man-about-town.

Number three was D. H. Lawrence, the blustering boor. In terms of social status, the Third Tempter, who is a restive baron, does not fit Lawrence's working-class origins, but what they share is rebellious heat. Becket is tempted to bring down the whole social edifice. 'Samson in Gaza did no more,' he muses, and then, abruptly, turns from what would be the 'desperate exercise of failing power'. If he breaks, he must break alone.

Next to number four are two curious names: Huxley and Babbitt. Their connection with the fourth and most dangerous Tempter is difficult. To which of the Huxley brothers, Julian or Aldous, did Eliot refer? Did they represent, for Eliot, a substitute religion, fake spirituality in the case of

Aldous* or the humanism of Irving Babbitt? In the *Criterion*, Eliot called Babbitt (another ex-teacher) a 'real' Atheist as opposed to Russell and, as such, to be taken more seriously. In a letter to the *Bookman* in 1930 Eliot wrote that his chief apprehension about Mr Babbitt was lest his humanism be transformed by disciples into the hard-and-fast dogma of an ethical church, or something between a church and a political party. Theodore Spencer, a colleague of Babbitt at Harvard and Eliot's main host in 1933, thought 'one must beware of taking his word literally and at the loss of one's own integrity. There seems to be [a] fatality which overcomes all Babbitt's disciples; they are a sad lot . . .'. But this isn't commensurate with the spiritual pride of the Fourth Tempter (for whom Eliot himself seems a more fitting candidate).

What all four numbers have in common is that they are writers. Eliot was pitting himself against rival opinion-makers a year before his *Primer of Modern Heresy*, which distinguished Lawrence as arch-heretic. 'I am concerned with the intrusion of the *diabolic* into modern literature,' Eliot had said. '. . . It may operate through men of genius of the most excellent character.'

The Tempters conduct Becket around his own past so that he becomes a spectator of himself. As a chorus of the Women of Canterbury watch Becket watching his life, so we, as audience, watch in turn as Eliot sets up before us an introspective structure of watching within watching: the visible form of the play exhibits the inner life as an act of detection. The audience is compelled to abandon its passivity as spectators. Goaded by the Knights, who come forward through time to justify their murder as it fades from our sight, we are tempted to deny what we have seen. Just as Thomas Becket faced his four Tempters, so the present-day audience is tried by four killers who tell us comforting lies, bolstered by

---

* See Julian Huxley, *Religion without Revelation* (London: Ernest Benn, 1927) and Aldous Huxley, *Do What You Will* (London: Chatto, 1929).

our favourite catchwords of common sense and by deft appeals to our insidious envy of superiority, our secret delight at its collapse. The killers regret it, they say politely, but violence is sometimes necessary. They were only doing their duty. Eliot wrote this play in a period of the rising duplicity and violence of fascist regimes. Just before the play went on in America in 1936, Eliot discussed with his brother the difficulty of conveying his intended satire on the totalitarian state to a country where the problem did not exist as in Europe.

Eliot gave here his clearest exposition of his essential political position, which was to attack all forms of political power and rhetoric. He implies that the only way the business of the world might be conducted with any safety is on the basis of moral principles that derive from strict belief. For the mass of people, the humanist dream of the nineteenth century, voluntary altruism, won't work. For altruism is, alas, not built into human nature. Eliot's view of human nature is like that of Hawthorne in their kinship to Puritan New England, their recoil from the optimism of latter-day America. Both share the Calvinist presumption – Hawthorne regretfully, Eliot savagely – that man's nature is fundamentally depraved. The Second Knight, the prime agent of power, veils his depravity (as did the Second Tempter) with the discourse of reasonable expediency.

The beguiling argument of the last killer, like that of the last Tempter, is the most difficult to resist. It is the excuse of psychology. Richard Brito puts it to us that Thomas Becket willed his death, actually provoked it and was, in fact, a suicide not a saint. Again, Eliot challenges the audience's immunity, for we know this to be the opposite of the truth, and yet it was just the sort of cleverness to which Eliot's age and our own has been particularly susceptible. It would be so much simpler to accept this glib, catchy interpretation that would relieve us from contemplating what is, anyway, beyond our compass. Should we let the saint recede to his usual hazy distance from modern memory? The poetic suggestiveness of the medieval drama is turned into our own blunt prose. The very language that attracts us with its comforting familiarity – hard, punchy, deceptively conclusive – is called into question. As witnesses – in our capacity as audience – we simply cannot swallow its lie. We are compelled to act, but what exactly should be our role? Jury? Sleuth?

The most challenging role is to become a sleuth of the inner life – Watson to Eliot's Holmes – and this will be the response of the active reader to all of Eliot's works. Sometimes, poor old Watson *is* rather thick; sometimes he's shoulder-to-shoulder on the scent. As Eliot spoofed the scholarly sleuth in his ostentatiously learned notes to *The Waste Land*, so Becket spoofs the empty rituals of power in his exchange with the Second Tempter, the Russell-figure, aristocratic scion of one of England's political families. Becket poses real questions like those of the Musgrave Ritual which, in the Sherlock Holmes story, an ancient family has bleated, uncomprehendingly, for ten generations. It takes the brain of a Holmes to break through the mumbo-jumbo which leads him to a crime, but a crime incidental to a treasure buried so long it is almost unrecognisable. In the same way, the murder in *Murder in the Cathedral* is *not* what we are there to detect. The title itself spoofs the act of detection as it invites us to it. Martin Browne presented the murder in a stylised way that swerved from historical fact, as Eliot was aware: he mentioned to his brother that, in actual life, Beckett, a powerful man, knocked the killers about a bit before they got him down. There were practical reasons for cutting down on the action – the stage in the Chapter House of Canterbury Cathedral was awkwardly shallow – but everything in the play points to a kind of sleuthing that shifts from murder to the inner life. The culprits themselves are obvious and not very interesting – Eliot called them pathetic – beside the moral crisis of their victim, and his sublime solution.

Murder in the Cathedral was written for a special audience of church-goers who could be relied on for what Poe called 'that moral activity which *disentangles*'. Eliot told his brother that, when he wrote the play, he thought its run would terminate with the Canterbury Festival in June 1935. But within a few months, in November, the play opened in a small theatre in London: the Mercury at 2 Ladbroke Grove in Notting Hill Gate. It was taken there by Ashley Dukes, who had acquired the theatre for the incipient ballet company of his wife, Marie Rambert.

Eliot never expected the popular success that the play at once achieved, and this because he underrated the popular audience. The chorus of Women in Canterbury reflects Eliot's regard for the select Canterbury audience for whom he wrote: sensitive to the Void beyond death and fearful of the momentousness of God's hand in a drama that comes so close to their own small lives. The advantage of writing for the select audience was that Eliot did not talk down, as in his subsequent West End plays. Conrad Aiken was struck by the women's language of humanity: 'That is perhaps the greatest surprise about it – in the play Eliot has become human, and tender . . .'. The chorus – partitioned between varied individual voices – represents all who confront the mystery of corruption and the mystery of holiness. Their humanity, which the saint's vocation precludes, draws the audience into the play in another way, through common feeling.

A young OUDS* actor, Robert Speaight, created the part of Becket. He was thirty-one where Becket was fifty-six, and of middle height where Becket was tall, but Speaight's elocutionary skills shone in a play that was mainly speech. He received immense acclaim for his restrained eloquence, and soon became a leading actor in the West End. Browne's production brought out the allegoric side to the play; he himself played the Fourth Tempter, stealing a seat on Becket's throne through the darkness cast over the stage. Browne presented the play as a medieval tapestry: we can imagine how the flexible exploratory verse would bring the tapestry to life.

After an American tour, where there were full houses but unfortunate mishaps in arrangements, the play reopened at

* Oxford University Dramatic Society.

the end of October 1936 at the Duchess Theatre, Aldwych, a few yards from the Strand. *The Times* hailed it as 'the one great play by a contemporary dramatist now to be seen in England'. Excerpts from the 1936 production were televised that December (when television was still in its preliminary stages) with an invited audience of three hundred, including Flora Robson, Robert Donat, Ashley Dukes, and the Revd Eric Cheetham.

As the years passed it became clear that *Murder in the Cathedral* was attracting a new audience for serious theatre. Queen Mary came to see it in February 1937 and, after nearly four hundred performances, it toured the provinces. In Leeds the audience sat silent for a full thirty seconds after the final curtain before breaking into rapturous applause. During the war, in March 1941, the Pilgrim Players, with Martin Browne as Becket, presented the play in an air-raid shelter to an earnest and attentive East End audience, mostly from Stepney and Bermondsey. Settings, props, and movements had, of course, to be simplified to the utmost to suit the shelter. They continued to play this emergency version for three years in shelters, cathedrals, and village schoolrooms. One performance was given in the basement of Lloyds Bank in Leadenhall Street to a deeply stirred audience, mainly from Hackney. The whole basement was fitted with bunks and held over two hundred sleepers. Henzie Raeburn (an actress with the Pilgrim Players and wife of Martin Browne) recalled that for the first ten or fifteen minutes the form and language of the play seemed strange to the audience; then it became 'one of the most "shared" performances I have ever known'.

After the war, the play became popular for school and college productions. Eliot's old school Milton Academy put it on in May 1948. It was also produced at Eliot's place of retreat, the House of the Sacred Mission at Kelham in Nottinghamshire. This was a training college for future Anglo-Catholic priests who could not afford a university education. The Kelham Brethren ate little and did their own housework. Their production of *Murder in the Cathedral* was rather bleak, to judge from photographs.

The full possibilities of the play were not realised until Helpmann's highly theatrical production in April 1953, which, as Brooks Atkinson observed in a superb review, proved that a play of poetic and spiritual distinction could be made to fit the commercial theatre. Robert Helpmann, an Australian who had made his name with the Royal Ballet (he was the first long-term partner of Margot Fonteyn), used his dance experience to keep the chorus in motion in a way that clarified its feelings: huddling in casual throngs, frightened, gossiping about the Archbishop, or sweeping lightly across the stage like withered leaves blown around the walls of Canterbury by the winds of political violence. Helpmann somehow managed to make the chorus dramatic and also brought out the contrasting tones and tempos of different characters. The blustering entrance of the killers shook the play out of its preoccupation with spiritual problems. Becket's Christmas sermon, when he perceives that he must act solely as God's instrument, was like a sweet interval in a storm. This was Robert Donat's great moment. Standing alone, downstage, outside the frame of the main drama, he delivered his intimate lesson with a simplicity that was very moving. 'He never intrudes on the part personally,' wrote Brooks Atkinson. 'He brings to it his own humility as an artist. He sees in the part the devout exaltation of Mr. Eliot's view.'

Eliot himself thought Donat the best of the three Beckets he had seen. He remarked to Mary Trevelyan, who accompanied him to the performance, 'Speaight was an actor being an Archbishop; Groser [in the film] was a priest trying to act; Donat is an actor failing to be an Archbishop, yet the only one who gives some idea – too much perhaps – of what the Archbishop and Chancellor was like.'

This production brought out the balance between different parts of the play: the lamentation of the Women; the anxious questions of the Priests; the belligerent assertions of the Tempters; the simplicity of the sermon; the barbaric hostility of the Knights and their whining appeals to the audience. It was, said Atkinson, 'a grand design'. Everything, he said, in

Mr Eliot's character and experience had prepared him for this work.

*

Here, then, was the given plan: a model life acting its part in a grand design. But where, exactly, did Eliot stand in relation to this design? Was he facing the difficulties of the fourth temptation? Or was he less advanced, still at the phase of waiting? I think he could imagine, but did not himself know, with the certainty of Becket, 'the moment that pierces one with a sense of God's purpose'.

Eliot's old avidity for the agonies of martyrdom was directed now through moral channels – he spoke repeatedly about the need to discipline one's emotions – but something idiosyncratic remained that was alien to the mildness of Anglican traditions. He was what Jean Stafford said of Robert Lowell, 'a puritan at heart' in his liking for certain aspects of Catholicism: fasting, retreats, penance. Both would have worn hair shirts if they could have found one. In the absence of Puritanism, both sought a religion of equal rigour. The *Church Times* did recognise in *Murder in the Cathedral* 'a smack of the Puritan temper'. It's noticeable in the pervasiveness of corruption. The Women of Canterbury smell a 'hellish' sweet scent in the woodpath, and feel a pattern 'of living worms' in their guts. Vileness floods their senses – rat tails twining in the dawn; incense in the latrine; the taste of putrid flesh in the spoon – until they recoil from all living things in a swoon of shame.

They say: 'We are soiled by a filth that we cannot clean, united to supernatural vermin.'

The poet Stevie Smith noticed, in the thirties, how Eliot's poetry mounts with each touch of contamination. This horror is private, she said briskly, peculiar to the author, who 'enjoys feeling disgust and indulges this feeling with the best of his poetry'. His state of mind is like some ascetics who stimulated contempt for the flesh by fixing their eyes on decaying bodies. Eliot had observed the skull beneath the skin.

To him, no ordinary life could be wholesome. To cleanse our vileness, martyrs must suffer extreme cruelties. Stevie Smith, a moderate Anglican, deprecates the way that Eliot touched 'that Christian nerve which responds so shockingly to fear and cruelty, which Dante touched most surely of all and one might have hoped for all time'. She questions the excitements of martyrdom and the tortures of hell – brutal scenarios that take the flatness out of life.

While Eliot pursued his trials, Emily Hale continued to wait. She could not give an answer to President Jaqua at the end of 1934, as arranged, and so lost her post. She remained in Europe through the summer of 1935 while, for Eliot, the exhilaration of the new life faded into a protracted ordeal. He had to atone for his abandonment of Vivienne and try to expunge the taint left by their marriage. There was an increasing conviction that nothing must impinge on this excruciation. What Emily perhaps did not grasp, or not fully, was Eliot's attraction to pain and his need, more pressing than the need to love, to recast pain as a dark night of the soul.

All through the thirties Eliot was meeting Emily Hale, and in his next, most autobiographical play, *The Family Reunion*, he posed his continued dilemma: should a man at the end of a tormenting marriage seek salvation through natural love or through a lone pilgrimage across a whole 'Thibet of broken stones' that lay, fang up, a lifetime's journey?

8

THE MYSTERY OF SIN

A NEW LIFE sheds the old. The problem for Eliot was that the old life, in the form of Vivienne, refused to go away. From 1932 to 1938 she haunted him: there were insistent attempts to see him at Faber and Faber; there was her continued presence in his memory; but worst was some obscure miasma of evil, the residue of years of wrong. He never solved what he called 'the Mystery of Iniquity'. It was, he said, 'a pit too deep for mortal eyes to plumb'.

A simple view endorsed by all his friends, was that, since Vivienne was (in Virginia Woolf's phrase) a 'bag of ferrets' around Eliot's neck, and a bar to further progress, he must leave her. But, in September 1932, when he had tried to separate, Vivienne ran 'amok' through London. Distraught, she had seen him off at Southampton when he sailed on 17 September to take up his year's post at Harvard. In the spring of 1933, he had sent a letter to his London solicitor to prepare a Deed of Separation. He enclosed a letter for Vivienne, and then had to face his return to England in June. He told a friend that the interim was like 'a phantasma, or a hideous dream'.*

That spring there arose a germ of a conflict that was to persist for some years. On the one hand was his renewed love for Emily Hale, sealed by the visionary promise that came to him in her presence in 1930, and was to come again in 1934. Yet Eliot retreated from this promise into a further period of

---

* Brutus in *Julius Caesar*, II. i.

moral agony. The plan to leave Vivienne was foiled, not in actual fact, but in Eliot's mind, by his own scruples, his fear that he had been, still was, and must continue to be implicated in Vivienne's destruction. As the years passed, he was drawn deeper into the mystery of sin through contemplation of the choices he had made. His wife's wreck made it unthinkable for Eliot to pursue what to an ordinary man would have seemed an obvious solution, and accept the comfort that Emily Hale offered. By the mid-thirties the new life was no longer directed by the Lady of the *Vita Nuova*; it was dominated by 'the reality of Sin'. He said in April 1933 that only when we are awakened spiritually are we capable of real Good, but the danger is that, at the same time, we 'become first capable of Evil'.

The need to explore, diagnose, and eradicate evil was the prime motive for several great works which all had their origin in the gravest moral crisis of his life from 1934 to 1938. There could be no pat conclusions of guilt or innocence, but there could be re-creations of Eliot's dilemmas, with the complex suggestiveness of imaginative works. From a social, legal, and even priestly view, Eliot did no wrong in leaving his wife. In fact, a common view was surprise that he had not left her long before. But Eliot's works explore feelings that preceded and accompanied his dismissal of Vivienne; feelings that were not only socially inadmissible, but beyond the usual limits of prose. The earlier years of Eliot's marriage were the background to the macabre, unfinished play *Sweeney Agonistes* (1926), and the later years of separation the background to the introspective nightmare of *The Family Reunion* (1939). These plays are complementary, for both expose a man's horror at the discovery of a capacity for violence. The strange feeling is not guilt, but a curious contamination that bonds Sweeney and Harry with their victims – or imagined victims. Even more curious is a certain pride that they should suffer so acutely for imagined crimes. Eliot described this more precisely in an essay where he says that it could be one's glory to be man enough for damnation. In April 1936 Eliot asked P. E. More if he could recommend a good treatise on Original Sin, and all his works from the mid-thirties to the mid-forties are preoccupied with hidden sin, the acute sense of which came to the surface during his prolonged struggle to be rid of Vivienne.

From late April to mid-May 1933, Eliot was in Charlottesville, Virginia, and it was there that his resolve hardened. 'Iron thoughts come with me / And go with me', he wrote as he waited to leave a wife who would certainly fight separation with all the weapons of the weak. He became determined to obliterate Vivienne from his life at whatever human cost.

This decision was sufficient basis for a disturbed future. Eliot had always feared that to leave Vivienne would destroy her, but his difficult position was that to go on with her would have damaged himself. In future, he would refuse any form of contact with his wife even when she appeared in extreme distress. He put himself beyond her reach; disappeared from view. To achieve this, he pitted his implacable will against her ingenuity, but in the end it was his withdrawal from responsibility that Vivienne was to find unbelievable. She was, in effect, under sentence, though its exact nature would not emerge until 1938.

Eliot's judicial nature came, he perceived, from the 'witch-hangers' of family history. 'We didn't burn them, we hanged them', he noted. In December 1933 he pictured his ancestor side by side with Hawthorne's ancestor, trying witches in the 1690s. Both inherited the need to inspect evil. Eliot told Pound that he just naturally smelt out witches, couldn't help it. But, as Hawthorne was aware, to venture on this activity is to risk misjudgement and worse. 'It shall be yours to penetrate . . . the deep mystery of sin,' the devil promises the impeccable Puritan in Hawthorne's most telling fable of the New England mind. As witness to acts of depravity, including his own, the Puritan then takes on a hypersensitivity to sin that will cut him off from human ties. For Eliot, too, the 'red' mood that took hold in Virginia was a strange, isolating state, beneath the rectitude of his manner.

Already, he was haunted by Furies. They lurk first in an

epigraph that Eliot chose for *Sweeney Agonistes* in October 1926 ('*You don't see them, you don't – but* I *see them: they are hunting me down . . .*'). As late as 1953, Eliot spoke of the poet 'haunted by a demon, a demon against which he feels powerless, because in its first manifestation it has no face, no name, nothing; and the words, the poem he makes, are a form of exorcism of this demon'. All through these fraught years of Eliot's middle age he seems to struggle against demonic possession, that disease of the soul that had so gripped early New England. Like *The House of the Seven Gables* (to Eliot, the finest novel in English),* where the family is haunted by 'the violent death . . . of one member of the family, by the criminal act of another', *The Family Reunion* (called at first 'Follow the Furies') turns on a curse which is a compulsion to murder. In Hawthorne, the curse emanates from a wizard and festers in a well, emblem of the inner life. In fact, a well appears in Eliot's drafts as a possible scene of murder, and here too the curse emanates from a witch. As Harry may be tempted to break away from the Furies through the natural love of the waiting Mary, so Eliot hoped to break out of the nightmare of his psychic bond with Vivienne through an emotional commitment to Emily Hale.

Hope Mirrlees was one of the few among Eliot's friends to take trouble with Vivienne. She had come to know them through Virginia Woolf, who described Hope as impulsive, ecstatic, odd. She was attentive to her thyroid gland and her dachshund but not too absorbed to be attentive also to Eliot's troubles. She recalled that any ordinary remark could provoke from Vivienne a barrage of questions, her eyes staring at some hobgoblin of the mind: 'She gave the impression of absolute terror, of a person who's seen a hideous goblin, a goblin ghost. . . . Her face was all drawn

---

* The English scientist Peter Medawar recalled in *Memoir of a Thinking Radish* (OUP, 1986) that, once, at a small dinner, he suggested to TSE that each would write down on a slip of paper the finest novel in the English language. Medawar chose *Middlemarch*; TSE surprised Medawar with *The House of the Seven Gables*.

and white, with wild, frightened, angry eyes. An over-intensity over nothing, you see. Supposing you were to say to her, "Oh, will you have some more cake?" she'd say: "What's that? What do you mean? What do you say that for?" She was terrifying. At the end of an hour I was absolutely exhausted, sucked dry. And I said to myself: Poor Tom, this is enough! But she was his muse all the same.'

Vivienne's feverish energy and Eliot's languor, what he called his *aboulie*, were short of manic and depressive extremes, yet brought together, they had formed a sick bond that Eliot had to escape but continued to use creatively. Theresa Eliot put it neatly when she said that 'Vivienne ruined Tom as a man, but made him as a poet'. The pair were strangely like the Ushers in Poe's tale of mental breakdown. The artistic Usher tries to bury his frenzied twin, the Lady Madeleine, in the vaults of the subconscious, but she returns to haunt him, recalled by a mind that cannot be whole without her. So, in *The Family Reunion* (1939) and *The Cocktail Party* (1949), the wish to be rid of a woman is countermanded by her hold from beyond the grave – the insidious, still-living tie of prolonged intimacy.

Through Sweeney, Eliot dramatised the prospect of spiritual fear. Desmond MacCarthy, at the first London production, saw 'a man under a lamp sitting at a table . . . speaking out of himself, out of his inner terror. He is addressing the girl opposite him, but he is also addressing us: it is half a sinister soliloquy, half a confession – or perhaps a threat to her.'

What is not explained is the motive for murder. Eliot's letters to Pound, with their undisguised misogyny, might help us to understand that the play was rooted in the peculiar circumstances of his own life. This kind of link, though, could easily become reductive, for the point of Eliot's career is how he managed to transmute almost maddening states of mind into a universal drama. The best commentaries are his essays, especially his record of the horror that is 'projected from the poet's inner world of nightmare'. This nightmare – and it is here that Eliot makes his dazzling leap to a spiritualised view of his career – 'is a triumph; for hatred of life is an important phase – even, if you like, a mystical experience – in life itself'. The essays also analyse a mind that becomes moral by becoming damned. Eliot was fascinated by Middleton's seventeenth-century play *The Changeling* about a strange sexual tie in which the unwilling partner becomes 'habituated' to the repulsive partner:

> Beneath the stars, upon yon meteor
> Ever hung my fate, 'mongst things corruptible.

Twice, Eliot's essay quotes these lines of the damned mate.

Eliot's friends – the Woolfs, Ottoline Morrell, and Hope Mirrlees – attended a masked performance of *Sweeney Agonistes* by the experimental Group Theatre in its upper studio at 9 Great Newport Street in November 1934. 'I sat by Tom,' Virginia Woolf reported in her diary. 'Certainly he conveys an emotion, an atmosphere: . . . something peculiar to himself; sordid, emotional, intense – a kind of Crippen in a mask.' It was a shrewd, almost prophetic dart, for Eliot chose to go as Crippen, the murderer of his wife,* to a fancy-dress party given by Adrian Stephen in 1939, six months after Vivienne was put away for life. When Vivienne saw *Sweeney*, revived by the Group Theatre on 2 October 1935, she wondered how she had managed not to faint at the 'absolute horror of the thing'.

Eliot once said that an author may put into a dramatic character 'some trait of his own' which may be 'some tendency to violence or to indecision, some eccentricity even, that he has found in himself. Something perhaps never realized in his own life, something of which those who knew him best may be unaware.'

Sweeney Agonistes is unfinished and baffling, and almost never produced. Eliot set it up on two distinct levels. Sweeney's state of spiritual terror was to address itself to what Eliot envisaged as a small receptive élite in the audience,

* The American-born Dr H. H. Crippen poisoned and cut up his wife in 1910. He was hanged.

while, theoretically, the 'literal-minded and visionless' sector would share the response of their counterparts on stage: for them, the fortune-telling games of the tarts, the party songs of the Jazz Age, and murder as mere thriller. This superficial action is a cover for the fact that the core of the play is non-dramatic or, rather, pre- and post-dramatic: foreboding and remorse.

The lack of visible action is often seen to be a flaw in Eliot's plays, but interior action can be dramatic in its own way. In his 1935 revival, Rupert Doone made all the characters projections of Sweeney's mind: they were his bogeys on a darkened stage. Even when they unmasked at the end, they were scarcely human. Sweeney alone did not wear a mask but appeared as a sinister clerk in pin-striped trousers and steel spectacles.

The real problem is the cover-action: the extensive card-game of the tarts and the boring high-jinks of Krumpacker and the Jew, Klipstein. In his poetry Eliot had dismissed Burbank and Bleistein with one lethal glance. It was an effort, now, to extend attention to the soulless – in later plays, to platitudinous aunts or cocktail natter – but Eliot prolongs these scenes as a sop to what he takes to be the thicker portion of a theatre audience.

'If the audience gets its strip-tease it will swallow the poetry,' he told Pound. 'IF you can keep the bloody audience's attention engaged, then you can perform any monkey tricks you like when they arent lookin, and its what you do behind the audience's back so to speak that makes yr play IMMORTAL for a while.'

Such a line was bound to be self-defeating. Eliot wanted to reach a popular audience, but looked down on it. Not even the thickest theatregoer is likely to be engaged by Krum-packer and Klipstein, whose pointless antics serve only to set off Sweeney from his milieu.

Still, there was one dramatic advantage to a play on two levels. Here, and again in *The Family Reunion*, Eliot jolts the audience from one level of reality to another, giving pre-eminence to psychic or supernatural horror. This jolt should be played up in performance to undercut the banalities of naturalistic action. Martin Browne, who directed all Eliot's subsequent plays, often missed the point when he begged for more action of the ordinary kind, and his predecessor, Rupert Doone, made the same mistake in his staging of *Sweeney Agonistes*. He set up a final scene of actual murder which is not in the text: Sweeney, armed with a razor, raised his arm, and Doris screamed off stage. A razor chase, done in slow motion, was retained in the Morley College production in the mid-fifties. Such crude action only obscures further the hidden life of penitential torture.

*

The Eliots' misery had been more or less hidden for the first ten years. Until his brother's visit in 1926, Eliot had kept Vivienne's addictions from his family, and later said that the worst of it was there being 'nobody to hold one's hand and nobody to tell about it'. There was the odd confidence to Bertrand Russell or the Woolfs, but to them, too, he never mentioned drugs. Vivienne herself was initially even more discreet. A veiled confession to Sydney Schiff suggests that she was disturbed by the violence of her husband's distastes. These, she thought, stemmed from a lack of vigour which he could not admit.

From 1925 to 1938 Vivienne allowed her fear to become public. The description of the wife in *The Family Reunion* is an accurate picture of Vivienne as others saw her at this time: an excited woman who would never leave her husband alone. A student called Wynard Browne, who came to see Eliot in 1930, had the door slammed in his face.

'Why, oh why, do they all want to see my husband,' Vivienne wailed.

In the play it is said that the wife wanted to keep her husband to herself to satisfy her vanity. She didn't want to fit herself to his relations or friends, but to bring him 'down to her own level'. As Vivienne became more fearful she would target this person or that, and drag Eliot into vendettas against the Sitwells or Marianne Moore. At this time, too, she began to complain of her husband.

'She used to go about a great deal with me,' Eliot recalled in 1954, 'and I was afraid of the dreadfully untrue things she said of me and afraid that my friends believed her. I couldn't say anything – a kind of loyalty perhaps and partly a terror that they would show me that they believed her and not me.... Happy? NO, I was never happy ...'.

It is only fair to say that Vivienne's anxiety was not groundless. There was a husband who never loved her, and doctors who never managed to diagnose her physical ills yet had no hesitation in pumping her with dangerous drugs, as a girl with opium, later with alcohol-mixtures for headaches and morphine in various forms. In 1932 both Edith Sitwell and Virginia Woolf, and later Miss Swan at Faber, noticed an overwhelming smell of ether as Vivienne entered a room. In fact she used to rub it all over her body, so that it is not surprising she often appeared to be half-dazed, fighting dim obstacles. Vivienne cannot be held responsible for behaviour that was largely drug-induced, and her husband suffered with her. Though he blamed himself, he did do what he could over very many years. His emotional withdrawal deepened Vivienne's distress, but he had to protect himself. No one else could bear her for very long. The worst of it was, I imagine, the endless uncertainty: the long episodes of illness; the odd hopes of recovery.

In 1927 two events had exacerbated the mental damage of the collapse in 1925. In March, Vivienne's father died at the Warrior House Hotel, at St Leonards in Sussex. In her diary she remembered 'how his dying eyes lingered on the sea & the sunsets, sitting up in bed in room no. 9. poor, poor darling Father. I remember how he always begged me to stroke his head ... & how I wish there were still *someone* who needs the touch of my hands which are the best part of me.' Deeply attached to her father, she returned to the hotel after Eliot left her, in 1934, and walked the beach with her memories:

... a lovely clear night, with a low sloop down in the East, &

the illuminated trams dashing up & down the front. It was cold & sharp & clean & very tempting to stay out. *Full* of memories, Father & Tom, Tom & Father – those two of my heart. *The sea is so much in it all.*

Vivienne broke down after her father's death. For nine months, she went from one sanatorium to another in France, ending up at Malmaison outside Paris. About a month after Vivienne's departure, the second and more far-reaching event took place: Eliot's conversion in June 1927, preceded in May by the overture from Emily Hale. With her quivering sensitivity, Vivienne at once perceived Eliot's rejection when he came to bring her back from Malmaison to London in February 1928:

> My dear Tom brought me back with him but he did not want to. I was *out of my mind*, & so behaved badly to Tom & got very excited. It seemed everything he said was a *sneer* & an *insult.* . . . My *first* night in England was a very *un*happy, lonely night, sick & *frightened.*

The following month, Eliot took his vow of celibacy. I've wondered whether, at this point, he conceived his plan to leave Vivienne which, perhaps for him, only a monastic code could justify. As Eliot detached himself, Vivienne never knew who would abet him. This was the reason for her suspicious scrutiny of Conrad Aiken, and her resistance to other visitors. There were times when she gave up and, like the tortured wife of *The Waste Land*, walked the streets at night. Sometimes she did not return and stayed the night in a hotel. Most of her actions between 1928 and 1932 were desperate, ill-judged claims on her husband's attention, literally plucking at his sleeve while he talked. These claims were always underlined by her frail health, and illness seemed to strike particularly at times of crisis, as in 1923 when Eliot tried to leave the bank. In June 1929 she had pleurisy when Eliot's mother was dying and he was on edge. 'A *terrible* time for my poor angel boy,' she recalled.

Vivienne's apprehensions that he would leave her led to wild accusations of other women, Lady Ottoline and Virginia

Woolf. She clung to her husband, listened to his phone calls, and insisted on accompanying him on visits to the Woolfs, who found her sinister. Her conversation was challenging, explosive. At Monks House, in November 1930, Virginia, proud of her honey, asked Vivienne: 'Have you any bees?'

'Not bees,' Vivienne answered. 'Hornets.'

'But where?'

'Under the bed.'

Vivienne's blasts of truth did not win friends; they aroused pity for Eliot. 'You're the bloodiest snob I ever knew,' she said loudly to him at a party. Conversation stopped. Eliot drank heavily. He was never sure how far she would go.

Once, when Eliot invited the Fabers, the Joyces, and Osbert and Edith Sitwell to dinner, Vivienne, coming in late with a twisted smile, picked an argument with her husband across the table.

'It's been lovely, Vivienne,' Enid Faber thanked her at the end of the meal.

'Well, it may have been lovely for you, but it's been dreadful for me.'

'Nonsense, Vivienne, you know it's been a triumph,' said poor Mrs Faber.

'A triumph! . . . Look at Tom's face!'

Eliot remained, for the most part, imperturbable. Only those who knew him well could detect the merest flicker of exasperation when he stressed the last syllable of her name: 'Vivi*enne*'. He treated her, Willard Thorp recalled, like a patient father with a fractious child. Evie Townsend, Faber's secretary, also noticed Eliot's patience when his wife would ring him soon after his arrival at the office, and demand his return. He would apologise for interrupting his dictation, and leave.

When Conrad Aiken came to lunch in the autumn of 1930, he saw a woman like a scarecrow on straw legs who embarrassed her husband in front of guests.

A high churchman called Gordon George spoke of 'pure intellect'.

'There's no such thing as pure intellect,' Eliot declared.

'Why, what do you mean?' laughed Vivienne. 'You know perfectly well that *every* night you tell me that there *is* such a thing: and what's more, that *you* have it, and that nobody *else* has it.'

'You don't know what you're saying,' Eliot retorted rather lamely.

At a poetry evening, arranged by Eliot in 1930, his droning voice was drowned now and then by Vivienne raging in the street outside. John Hayward exchanged glances with Lady Ottoline. Paying the Eliots a dutiful visit in November 1930, Ottoline found herself in the midst of a fight to the death – Vivienne speaking to Eliot as if he were a dog; Eliot 'grim' and 'horrid'.

Father Underhill took it upon himself to advise separation. Did he realise that this would mean the virtual extinction of Vivienne? Beneath the Eliots' repartee lay this issue of life and death, and Aiken sensed the violence of their emotion. Hatred, he thought it. Vivienne was 'shivering, shuddering' like the wife in *The Family Reunion*: 'A restless shivering painted shadow'.

Between 1928 and 1932 there must have been times when Vivienne's claim prevailed. She had, Eliot acknowledged, a gift for argument which he called coercive. His letters to Ada Leverson* present a domesticated couple, accepting middle age and loss of initiative. In 1930 he dedicated *Ash-Wednesday* to Vivienne. It must have been a placatory gesture, no more, for the poem looks away from her towards a promised land. With its longing memories of New England, it turns towards the idealised muse of Emily Hale.

Vivienne was Eliot's muse only so long as he shared her hell. There was no place for her in the purgatory of *Ash-Wednesday*, in the sainthood of *Murder in the Cathedral*, and in the introspective ordeals of *The Family Reunion*. As Eliot's works put aside the distractions of worldliness for self-contemplation, real women are replaced by abstractions,

---

* Mrs Leverson, known as 'the Sphinx', had been a loyal friend to Oscar Wilde. She was the sister of the Eliots' friend Mrs Schiff.

ideal beneficence or hellish torment. A new phase of religious poetry was contingent on Vivienne's dismissal. The conversion, in short, spelt her doom.

To Vivienne, this must have seemed the more threatening for not being at once clear. Her verbal assaults on Eliot all had to do with his façades and prevarications, as though she would force him to declare – something. When Virginia Woolf noticed that Eliot looked 'leaden' and 'sinister' in 1930, she blamed Vivienne, who was a 'torture'. But Vivienne's frantic scenes are not inexplicable if she did sense a future for Eliot that did not include her. Her scenes were not so much protests as, increasingly, try-outs for a doomed role, a reckless, perverse performance that contributed to her ruin, as though, in a strange, mocking way, she played – to the hilt – some scenario imposed upon her.

Edith Sitwell, meeting Vivienne by chance in Oxford Street in the summer of 1932, called out, 'Hullo, Vivienne.'

'No, no, you don't know me,' Vivienne replied. 'You have mistaken me *again* for that *terrible* woman who is so like me. . . . She is always getting me into trouble.'

Eliot's poetry repeatedly contemplates the end of a woman, and the earliest instances precede Vivienne's appearance in his life. Men in the early poems despise women as 'the eternal enemy of the absolute', and cope with inhibition by dreams of power, a godlike power to end women's lives. What is particularly disturbing is the unreality of the female victim. She is punished, it would seem, for her flesh. Veiled with irony, a delicious brutality slips through in 'Portrait of a Lady' ('Well, and what if she should die some day. . . ?'); unveiled, in 'The Love Song of Saint Sebastian', a man throttles a woman as a mode of possession.

On 4 March 1932 Eliot wrote a formal letter to Vivienne, promising to return to England following his Norton professorship at Harvard for the academic year 1932–3. Clearly Vivienne, fearing that he would remain in America, made him state that his appointment at Harvard was not renewable, and that he would return in May 1933.

Just before Eliot's departure in September 1932, they paid

their last visit, as a couple, to the Woolfs at Rodmell. A photograph shows Eliot standing beside Virginia Woolf, while Vivienne stands apart, drooping, her white hat pulled down over her eyes. Dressed in white satin in the rain, her handkerchief exuding ether, she behaved weirdly. Virginia saw her as a doomed Ophelia: 'alas no Hamlet would love her, with her powdered spots.' The Woolfs tried to be kind: Virginia gave her a jar of home-made raspberry jam, and Leonard some flowers. 'We had tea', Vivienne recalled, '& as I was *very nearly insane* already with the Cruel Pain of losing Tom . . . I paid very little attention to the conversation. . . . We got back to the Lansdowne [Hotel, Eastbourne] I felt *very ill & was in a fever.* Tom also *seemed very strange.*' As she wrote these lines, she toyed with the pathetic illusion that, if she had clung harder, he could not have left her. She berated herself for not having had the nerve to accompany him to America: '& so am damned for ever – .'

*

Two years later, Vivienne Eliot sat in the waiting-room at Faber and Faber, her hands screwing up her handkerchief as she wept. She asked for her husband, whom she had not seen since his departure for America. This was a routine visit, and there was a routine to deal with her. Eliot's secretary, Brigid O'Donovan (just down from Oxford and herself in love with the poet), would phone Eliot, who would slip out of the building. He was not in, Brigid told Vivienne, who then would leave. For the rest of the day Eliot would be distant and on edge, speaking with cautious slowness.

Vivienne was left alone in a flat decorated with pictures of her husband. Her diaries of 1934–6 resound with the shock of his abandonment, which she could never quite believe was voluntary. She made wild efforts to bring herself to his attention. At the same time she joined numerous clubs and began a career in music, but it became increasingly difficult to compose herself to undertake even trivial chores. The lined face that looked back at her from a portrait by a friend showed, she thought, 'all the blank expression of one who has learned to keep out of the way'. 'My face is yellow like parchment,' she wrote in July 1934, 'no colour, dead eyes – am as thin as a rat. Too restless to rest. Too tired to think constructively. NO hope, that I can see, in any direction.' A creature of unblunted sensitivity, she continued to fight against nameless obstructions, bruised again and again by the evasive politeness of former friends like Geoffrey Faber who had given their loyalty to Eliot and screened him, at any cost to Vivienne, from contact with her. Her sense of a nightmar- ish conspiracy sounds mad, but it is not unjustified – for everyone she knew conspired to keep Eliot out of sight.

Vivienne Eliot was cast off by those who aligned them- selves with her husband, and this meant almost everyone whom they had known as a couple. His friends considered her unbalanced. Eliot himself believed she was sane, but talked herself into an unbalanced state. In the mid-thirties she joined the Fascists, though her diary shows not the slightest interest in politics, simply a dim wish to belong to some form of social existence. She clung to formal ties, sending handker- chiefs to Eliot's sister Marian, who replied coolly. Everyone to whom Vivienne appealed took Eliot's part, refusing to make any move to bring them together. It baffled Vivienne that people behaved as though her husband hardly existed; they told her that they rarely saw him.

Virginia Woolf found her in September 1933 sitting 'under a crowned effigy', Eliot's photograph by Elliot Fry with a wreath of daisies. Vivienne gave out that her husband had unaccountably chosen to absent himself, leaving her in suspense and largely in the dark. That September, Eliot defended himself to Lady Ottoline (whom he had deputed to keep an eye on Vivienne while he was in America – no easy task as Vivienne became increasingly distraught). He said that his insistence on a permanent separation had been made clear to her. At the same time he did admit that he thought it fruitless and unnecessary to give her reasons for his decision. He refused – through solicitors – her plea for an interview at their flat. Instead, it appears that he wrote to her on 27

November 1933, and in December Vivienne acknowledged to Virginia Woolf that he would not come back to her.

'I would give a good deal to see him,' she wrote in her diary on 20 January 1934. She refused to sign 'any blackmailing paper relinquishing all rights to him for anybody', though she would put '*all* in Tom's hands, if he wld. honestly come back to me'. She felt unfit to live alone and care for herself: 'I look like a little *ghost* of a *street child*.' Slowly, that year, she packed up and sold household goods, sometimes blanking out on the day's activities. 'The rest of the day', she wrote on 11 August, 'must have been unspeakably wretched, for, I cannot remember anything at *all* about it.' Her ruin was not sudden; it was the slow accumulation of lost days:

> 17 September 1935
> ... I just slowly grope my way through Limbo, sometimes accelerated by a kind of artificial fury, which rages for a time, *during* which I can perform great tasks, & after which I am utterly spent & dry & sick. I think I feel more & more as *Tom* used to feel, & I suppose still does. I shd. understand him so much better now.

To follow the full story from 1933 to 1938 it is essential to allow the voice of Vivienne's diaries to sound freely so as to record a situation of maximum moral density. The mills of God, she wrote, had ground her to powder. Or had someone sinned against her? The sin, she adds, was *not* her husband's. She could not bring herself to believe that it was his free choice to have left his 'true champion'. Yet on 11 December 1934 five or six men forced their way into Vivienne's flat to remove Eliot's books and copies of the *Criterion*. They pulled shelves off the wall, damaged a clock, and went off with some of Vivienne's books. The raid left her in a 'state of nervous collapse'. A second raid followed on 15 July 1935 to get Eliot's files and photographs. She wrote to Dr Miller: 'It hurt me so terrible [*sic*] that they took away all those photographs of the Eliot family which I have had round me all the last twenty years, and of which many were sent to me.'

Despite recurrent collapses, Vivienne could rally. Her

imagination was formidable, which is why Eliot feared to meet her, feared even – in his work – that she would haunt him always. Her habitual role of woman in distress was interrupted by a more dashing one of woman to the rescue. She sallied forth in blue serge cape and waistcoat, flourishing a cigarette-holder, or in a black velvet coat and black angora turban, determined to pierce the mystery of her husband's disappearance. 'At last the *courage* had *come* to me . . .' she wrote in her diary. A daring and, for Eliot, humiliating phase of pursuit was initiated on 13 September 1934 when Vivienne placed an advertisement in the personal column of *The Times* for 17 September (though it was not printed):

> Will T. S. Eliot please return to his home 68 Clarence Gate Gardens which he abandoned Sept. 17th, 1932.

Her rationale was to check whether her husband was alive, but the real purpose was to test or, at least, expose barriers to communication. Another scheme was to offer to hand over to Eliot some silver and his deed box, and to ask the bank to secrete her in the room when he came to collect them. When she visited Faber and Faber, Miss Swan and Miss O'Donovan received her kindly, but told her that Eliot's presence was erratic.

'Tom never *was* erratic,' she mused. 'He was the most regular of men.'

In March 1935 she took courage to protest loudly at the office: 'It is too absurd, I have been frightened away too long. I am his wife.'

She toyed with the notion that Eliot was a prisoner of sorts, which sounds absurd, but he was, in fact, guarded by various stalwarts. To his wife his invisibility was a mystery. It was, therefore, a day of triumph when, on 18 November 1935, after more than three years, she finally faced him at the *Sunday Times* Book Exhibition at the Dorland Hall.

A friend sent Vivienne the newspaper announcement that Eliot was to talk at 3.30. She dressed as a Black Shirt – what she called in her diary her 'Fascist' uniform – with a black beret, a large black mackintosh cape, and a penguin pin that

Eliot had given her in 1927, and, armed with Polly, their dog, confronted Eliot as he arrived:

> I turned a face to him of such joy that no-one in that great crowd could have had one moment's doubt. I just said Oh *Tom*, & he seized my hand, & said how do you *do*, in quite a loud voice. He walked straight on to the platform then & gave a most remarkably *clever*, well thought out lecture. . . . I stood the whole time, holding Polly *up* high in my arms. Polly was very excited & wild. I kept my eyes on Tom's face the whole time, & I kept nodding my head at him, & making encouraging signs. He looked a *little* older, more mature & smart, much *thinner* & *not* well or robust or rumbustious at *all*. No sign of a woman's *care* about him. No cosy evenings with dogs and gramophones I should say.

During the applause, Vivienne pushed her way to the platform and let Polly off the lead. The dog tore round Eliot's feet, jumping for joy. Eliot took no notice, but Vivienne, undaunted, leapt up beside him on the platform.

'Will you come back with me?' she demanded quietly, leaning forward with her hands on the table.

'I cannot talk to you now,' Eliot said. He signed three books for her and left quickly with Richard Church.

'Come back' was the essence of Vivienne's plea. In this phase she entertained dreams of offering Eliot protection. She imagined giving him two rooms, with lock and key, so that he might work in the flat, unmolested. She would treat him, she planned, like a grown-up son. Another plan was to let him know that she would leave the door open from 10.30 to 11 every night. 'Here is your home,' she wrote, '& here is your *protection. Which you need.*'

To Vivienne, Eliot's few words at the Dorland Hall implied a promise of contact. 'Everything was perfectly allright between us,' she wrote to Messrs James & James, her solicitors. It seemed important to her that the large audience constituted 'many witnesses' to this promise.

Vivienne also sent letters to her bank manager and to Eliot himself, which initiated her last and fatal role: an accident, she fears, might befall her at any moment. She cast herself –

300

accurately – as a doomed wife, the living replica of the doomed wife of Eliot's next play. When the play opens, she has gone overboard during a voyage, and Harry, the husband, is not sure if he tipped her over. He is guilty, anyway, of wishing to do so.

Sir Herbert Read, whose friendship went back to the early days of the marriage and who could remember Vivienne as sweet and lively, thought that posterity would judge her harshly, but from the vantage-point of the next century the harshness, it seems, came from her contemporaries who aligned themselves with Eliot and deplored a woman who refused to be subdued. Her sketches show her powers of observation. In her good spells she could be fun, with a daring critical intelligence and a quick engagement that would be appealing. Towards the end of the twentieth century it became modish to back Vivienne against her husband, but to take one side in this story is to deny the ambiguities of the whole truth. Vivienne, like some pathetic people, was insensitive to others. It seems of less moment that she flouted decorum and embarrassed her husband, than that her own strong feelings were so compelling that she became increasingly unaware how others thought and felt.

Vivienne was also a snob. She was agog about royalty, and sent Eliot's poem *Marina*, about a spiritual journey, to Marina, Duchess of Kent. She fantasised descent from the houses of Carnarvon and St Germaine to the extent of using their crests. But in such silliness, and in her wilder moods, she was never dangerous; and these moods were, in any case, episodic. It is likely that Eliot was never quite sure whether she was mad or not, but did always know that, since no one else would look after her, he alone was in a position to save her. Curiously, in his play, the end of the wife is a side issue. What interested him was if the husband can save *himself* through confession and protracted penance.

Though Harry is not conceived as a likeable character – Eliot later called him a prig – the play does sanction self-absorption in the name of moral trial. Pride was the recurrent concern of Eliot's maturity, in the form of the final Tempter of Becket, in *Four Quartets*' need for humility, and in the humbling of the Elder Statesman. In *The Family Reunion*, though, pride is treated far less critically. It may be that Eliot identified too closely with Harry to judge him with customary detachment while he planned and wrote this play in the heat of marital crisis.

Edward Fox once played Harry looking exactly like Eliot, impeccable, reserved, but forced by inner necessity to fragmented disclosure. The play gains in urgency in the light of Eliot's life: it is the text of his public confession as part of his private bid for salvation. Formal confession in the Anglican Church was, for Eliot, rather too mild a ritual. His scrupulousness demanded more unflinching introspection, much like Harry who is condemned for his wife's end by no one but himself.

What was Vivienne's part in this drama? Did she, like the wife in the play, provoke her end? Her diaries show that the long-drawn-out process of separation was, for her, a drama of pursuit and escape, in which pursuer and victim could suddenly, terrifyingly, change places. On 19 June 1935 she expected something like an arrest. Though the day passed uneventfully, she set off for France with fears for her life. Was this wholly a deranged fantasy? In July she sent Eliot wild letters pleading with him to return. She visited Faber and Faber, and Miss Swan told her that Eliot was rarely there, a lie that Vivienne accepted, temporarily, with despair. Resentment alternated with fear, neither unreasonable in her circumstances. Effort after effort to reach her husband – through the Passport Office, through their dentist – was blocked. I don't believe that any battered wife was ever so protected as Eliot in his fear of meeting a wife from whom there was no actual danger. She, for her part, was physically afraid in the summer of 1935, perhaps an inkling of the asylum ahead: 'I am a fugitive. From whom, I know not (precisely, *yet*),' she wrote on 4 August. Between then and the middle of 1938, Vivienne's position changed from pursuer to pursued.

In June 1936, she pretended to have gone to America. She gave as her forwarding address 83 Brattle Street, Cambridge, Mass., an apartment block which was the home of Eliot's favourite sister, Marian Cushing Eliot, and also of a distant relative, Elizabeth Wentworth, who had been the only member of the family to meet Vivienne in London after Eliot left her, and who subsequently wrote Vivienne a few friendly letters. Vivienne gave out that she had gone to be with her husband's people – her own improbable family reunion – but there was another motive: to imitate Eliot's disappearance following his departure for America. She lost his track, she says, in December 1932, which was of course the time that he crossed the continent to see Emily Hale. Vivienne's Day Book states her motives:

> to reduce the strain on my brain, & at the same time to see if I could succeed in disappearing so completely & baffling all attempts to trace me as my husband has. And, at the same time I have in my mind such an undying resentment against all those who had any part in this business that I want them to know what it is like to suffer in the same way.
>
> *Tiresias*

At this point I became Daisy Miller.

She gave out that she had let her flat to a student at the Royal Academy of Music, called Daisy Miller, who would answer correspondence in her supposed absence. This was the self she now chose to be. *Daisy Miller*. The very name reverberates with unstated suggestion. There, amidst disheartened ramblings, Vivienne implied a brilliant reading of her position.

Daisy Miller is a tale by Henry James about a reckless woman who dies misunderstood. Her liveliness does not conform to the dictates of the correct but corrupt Roman society where she is placed. Accompanied by a shallow, neglectful mother and an offhand younger brother, she assumes a freedom of behaviour that brands her as ill-bred. This freedom becomes flamboyant in the face of the chill caution of Winterbourne, who pays her passing court.

Winterbourne, a Europeanised American, who is even more rigidly correct than Europeans, aligns himself with public outrage at Daisy's behaviour. We hear Daisy's story, after her death, filtered through the distorting consciousness of Winterbourne, and our challenge is to reconstruct it so as to perceive inexpressible emotion in Daisy's wildness and, more difficult, to discern the source of her tragedy in the peculiar character of Winterbourne: his withholding of the self. Hawthorne, who understood, said James, the 'deeper psychology', called this the Unpardonable Sin: a habit of spectatorial detachment, rooted in pride, which severs his New Englanders from the 'human heart'.

1936 is the last year of the records that Vivienne kept for posterity's judgement. I find it admirable that she never blamed her husband for his desertion. As the years went by, her passionate loyalty became her sole claim to dignity, and the ideal which she intended her diaries to publicise. It was her wish that they be published verbatim: she felt herself to be a victim of a 'fantastic' conspiracy to keep her husband beyond her reach. What she did not realise is that the papers show not only her pathos but the warping effect of protracted suffering: she was haughty and demanding to employees, quick to fault others, and the politically dim sort of Fascist who enjoyed the excitement of a rally where public denunciations provided an outlet for private fury. In judging Vivienne, it is tempting to focus on unpleasant aspects of the thirties – her politics, her snobbery, her cold instructions to her servant. To read her vituperative letters is to realise that Virginia Woolf was not far off when she exclaimed 'Vivienne! Was there ever such torture since life began! – to bear her on one's shoulders, biting, wriggling, raving, scratching, unwholesome, powdered, insane, yet sane to the point of insanity . . .'. Her mother alone sustained some fondness for 'my little Vivy', but late in 1936 the already ailing Mrs Haigh-Wood had a stroke. She became a helpless invalid, and Vivienne's last shred of support was gone.

Shortly before this, she made a valiant effort to take up a career in music. On 26 September 1935, she passed the pianoforte entrance examination and enrolled as a student at the Royal Academy of Music. She took up singing with Miss Gale, and exulted in her '*huge*' voice. She meant to work hard, but there were endless distractions. What kind of piano should she hire? A long, exhausting fuss followed. She went repeatedly to see *Murder in the Cathedral*; in January and February alone, seven times. She failed her Elements of Music examination that winter, and then in the spring had a 'poisoned' foot. That summer, when she had three more examinations, she kept up her round of grand receptions, and dashed about to furbish up her elaborate wardrobe. How could she practise when she had to think about her leopard coat and model gowns?

The public engagements, of course, filled a social gap. Daisy Miller was called upon to state that Mrs Eliot 'has had very great friends, & she prefers to mourn their loss, than to fill the gaps they leave'. Her thoughts turned to Bertrand Russell or to Osbert Sitwell: what had happened to those distinguished friends of the early days of her marriage? She reminded Geoffrey Faber that he had often been her guest, but he kept her at bay with the placatory notes of a busy gentleman. Vivienne also wrote to Theodora Eliot and the Henry Ware Eliots, and urged them, for form's sake, to keep in touch with her, but she wrapped this pathetic plea in resentful words.

On 5 August, Daisy Miller explained that Mrs Eliot was 'apt to lose her wits and go all to pieces'. A letter to her solicitor on 10 August hints that she will soon be dead. She was still brooding over Eliot's disappearance and in September hunted up the cables (to do with his return) that she had received in July 1933. That September she also wrote to 'The Literary Manager' at Faber and Faber to offer her own illustration for *Marina*. Eliot's secretary rejected the offer politely.

She still made her futile journeys to the office. She began to believe that she was being followed, and on 10 December wrote to Geoffrey Faber to protest, but he denied any knowledge of this. The last we hear of Vivienne's voice was her intention to send Christmas cards to Eliot and to her American sisters-in-law, Marian, Theodora, and Margaret. She insisted on this connection to the end, and refused to be addressed by any other name than 'Mrs T. S. Eliot'.

From the beginning of 1937 she fell silent, and there is a gap in her story. Then, on 14 July 1938, a letter from her brother to Eliot announced her doctor's recommendation to have her certified:

Dear Tom,

I am very sorry to have to write to you on your holiday but I am afraid I must.

V. was found wandering in the streets at 5 o'clock this morning and was taken into Marylebone Police Station. . . . The Inspector at the Police Station told me she had talked in a very confused and unintelligible manner and appeared to have various illusions, and if it had not been possible to get hold of me or someone to take charge of her, he would have felt obliged to place her under mental observation.

As soon as I got to the City I rang up Dr Miller . . . He got a reply from [Allen & Hanbury's, chemists] this morning in which they said that V. called every day for her medicine, that she appeared to be in a deplorable condition and that they had no idea of her address. Dr Miller was therefore on the point of writing to me because he feels that something must be done without much more delay . . . [He] feels V. *must* go either to Malmaison [the sanatorium near Paris] or to some home, and I am also inclined to think that, because there is no telling what will happen next.

V. had apparently been wandering about for two nights, afraid to go anywhere. She is full of the most fantastic suspicions and ideas. She asked me if it was true that you had been beheaded. She says she had been in hiding from various mysterious people, and so on.

I have made a provisional appointment with Dr Miller for 2.15 pm tomorrow (this was before I discovered you were away).

I really don't know whether to suggest your running up to town tomorrow and returning to Gloucestershire in the evening, or not. You will be able to decide that yourself, but I would be grateful if you would send me a telegram in the morning to say what you decide.

Yours ever,
Maurice

It is obvious that Maurice normally had no contact with his sister, that he made no effort to hear, really hear, what she feared, and that he was disturbed by what seemed to him and the policemen nonsense, though Vivienne's terror was in this instance intuitively accurate, as events would show: she was in acute danger of what amounted to life imprisonment, and her terror was all the greater from the facelessness of the enemy. As it turned out, her enemy proved to be unknown doctors who passed sentence on her after the briefest contact. An order for Vivienne's detention would have had to be signed by two relatives or close friends. Maurice Haigh-Wood was one of the signatories; there has been some speculation whether Eliot could have been the other signatory, but recent evidence makes it clear that Eliot stayed out of it. He was in Gloucestershire at the time, which means he was with Emily Hale; when Maurice asked him to come up to London, Eliot, it seems, declined to hold his hand. He may have felt that he alone had shouldered responsibility for Vivienne for seventeen years, and that now her kin should take over. Eliot's thoughts and actions during the following month – the critical month for his wife – are not known, but he was not directly involved in her committal. He did, though, take the view that it was done for Vivienne's own good. This was no doubt a view shared by all the men who ruled Vivienne's affairs at this point – and Eliot did rule one essential area. What seems still questionable is that though Eliot had washed his hands of Vivienne, he became an executor, with Maurice, of the Haigh-Wood estate, which means that he authorised the use of Vivienne's own money to pay the costs of a life imprisonment that was undoubtedly convenient for him.

Maurice wrote again to Eliot on 17 August 1938, to say that Vivienne had seen Dr Hart and Dr Mapother, who had sealed her fate:

Both doctors felt strongly that she should be put into a home. They handed me their certificates. I then had to go before a magistrate to obtain his order. I got hold of one in Hampstead.

I then went to Northumberland House [a private asylum in London authorised to take certified patients], saw the doctor there, & arranged for a car to go with 2 nurses to Compayne Gardens that evening. The car went at about 10 pm. Vivienne went very quietly with them after a good deal of discussion.

I spoke to the doctor yesterday evening, & was told that Vivienne had been fairly cheerful, had slept well & eaten well, & read a certain amount . . .

I gather . . . that Vivienne was in the habit of saving up her drugs & then taking an enormous dose all at once, which I suppose accounts for the periodical crises.

As soon as you get back I should very much like to see you . . .

> Yrs ever,
> Maurice

To say that Vivienne was fairly cheerful and reading a certain amount sounds suspicious, as though Maurice felt obliged to tell his brother-in-law only what he would wish to hear. Unless Vivienne were drugged, it is inconceivable that she should have accepted this tamely, particularly in view of her attempt to escape. The story of her attempted escape is told in an unexpected letter from a Londoner whose mother and cousin, both long dead, planned it:

> 18 Dartmouth Park Avenue
> London NW5 1JN
> 18 August 1993

Dear Dr Gordon

I write on the remote off-chance that I have a clue which might help in your further researches into Vivien Haigh-Wood. . . .

There was in the nineteen-thirties a Lunacy Law Reform Society, composed of volunteers aiming to befriend and help those who had been certified and confined. There may be some archives preserved somewhere. . . .

Many people had relatives certified because they were

tiresome and, quite often, to get hold of their money, when they may have been no more than eccentric.

One of those active in the Society was Louie Purdon, my mother's cousin and also her closest friend. I knew Louie well and remember her clearly. . . . My mother [Marjorie Saunders] died about ten years ago and Louie had died about five years before that. . . . [Louie, who worked at Allen & Hanbury's chemists, where Vivienne collected her daily doses of medicine] did do all-night duties on a rota with others but she was in fact a pharmacist. . . . One of Louie's stories, as told to me, was of going with 'Mrs Eliot' to a performance of Sweeney Agonistes. Viv had chosen to go in the uniform of the British Union of Fascists. They were hissed by the audience as they walked down the aisle to their front seats. This was embarrassing but Louie recounted it as funny.

Louie was a somewhat earnest spinster but she had plenty of humour. She needed it in her work with the certified. She said 'I didn't understand the play. It was all about birth, copulation and death. My only consolation is that at the time I did not know what copulation was.'

As I was given to understand, the law provided that if anyone certified could 'escape' and evade 'capture' for six weeks (I think it was) they automatically became de-certified and had a chance to resist re-certification.

This was the main style of help of the lunacy law reformers: sheltering individuals during these six weeks. I recall from childhood a glorious pianist-lady who made our pebble-dashed suburban semi-detached ring with Wagner. Louie herself was well-known for her 'befriending' work but the lady was not traced to our house. . . .

One evening my mother went up to a café near Allen & Hanbury's off Oxford Street to receive Vivien and take her home to stay. Instead she was told that 'Mrs Eliot' would not be coming and that the arrangement was off. I believe Vivien had been apprehended before she got to Louie.

Thereafter Louie was not able to communicate with Vivien. The 'home' she was in would not pass on telephone messages. Louie's letters were returned. . . .

Yours sincerely
Basil Saunders

The cruellest aspect of her imprisonment was that it cut

Vivienne off from her only friend, Miss Purdon, the last person to act on Vivienne's behalf and the only one at the time to see that she was wronged. After some years abroad, when Maurice saw his sister again in 1946, he acknowledged that she was as sane as he was. And then, a few years later, when Bertrand Russell was eighty-one, he wrote a story of 'Mrs Ellerker', based on Mrs Eliot, about a woman who is too courageously sane to lend herself to the artifice of emotional repression. She betrays her rather dull husband to embark on an affair with Mr Quantox, described by Russell as 'sparkling and witty, a man of education and wide culture'. After he has used her, Mr Quantox abandons Mrs Ellerker, leaving her embittered and tormented by her guilty secret. She tries to confess, but because Mr Quantox is socially above reproach, she is disbelieved and sent to an asylum. The narrator, committed likewise to the asylum, regrets that he 'failed to save' Mrs Ellerker. Eliot's guilt was more ambiguous.

Vivienne behaved, we recall, as though she saw a 'goblin ghost'. Harry, in Eliot's play, is also haunted by ghosts but, in the play, the family doctor is patently unfit to judge them. If Eliot really thought Vivien's committal was for her own good, he must have held an ambiguous attitude to doctors' judgements. For Vivienne, agitation led to the asylum; for Eliot's hero, agitation was a sign of superior destiny.

It is as though Eliot were living out a tale by Poe or James in which superficial order is forced upon terrible wrong which lurks beneath the surface becoming the ghosts of the mind. Vivienne receded into the background of Eliot's consciousness, a phantom of anguish and reproach. He put himself so totally beyond her reach that it was as though he had vanished or she were no more.

In 1936 Eliot wiped out the dedication of *Ash-Wednesday* 'To my Wife' from the new *Collected Poems 1909–1935*. After Vivienne was certified, she was made a Ward in Chancery, and Eliot never visited her in the asylum where she was held, incommunicado, for the rest of her life. That one moment when they shared the platform at the Dorland Hall in November 1935 was the last she saw of him. Soon after that meeting, she recalled with pleasure her husband's clean-cut mouth, his fine head, his keen deep eyes. She still loved him, the hopeless kind of love that feeds off exaggerated trust.

'I *trust* the man,' she told Louie Purdon. 'He has some very strong reasons. You do not argue with God, or question his ways.'

9

ENTER THE FURIES

ELIOT'S VOW OF celibacy was never irreversible, as his second marriage would eventually prove. Between 1928 and the end of 1934 the celibate course had been challenged by the alternative that Emily presented, and the possibility that grace might come through natural love. Helen Gardner (the prime Eliot scholar of his time) told me that Eliot's family believed he would marry her, and this might well have happened if Eliot had managed to sustain the bliss that came to him at Burnt Norton, but it had faded as swiftly as it came.

Soon, in the autumn of 1934, Eliot had to make a choice. He might make a firmer commitment to Emily Hale. On this she herself had staked her livelihood. On the other hand, there was Vivienne, not taking separation tamely, and making it clear that she would go on staking *her* claim to rights and attention as Eliot's legitimate wife: that way lay the dark ordeals of endurance. It may in fact have been this dark prospect that shut off the heart of light.

This conflict was going on invisibly between the politest of tea parties (on 3 November, Eliot told Virginia Woolf that he would give tea to Kensingtonian and ecclesiastical guests, including the Revd and Mrs Perkins) and a visit to Chichester Cathedral on 30 November with the Perkinses and Emily. Virginia Woolf, who knew nothing of Emily Hale for another year did, on 21 November 1934, discern Eliot's divided state with brilliant acumen:

Tom's head [she wrote in her diary] is very remarkable; such a conflict; so many forces have smashed against him: the wild eye still; but all rocky, yellow, riven & constricted. Sits very solid – large shoulders – in his chair, & talks easily but with authority. Is a great man, in a way, now: self-confident, didactic. But to me, still, a dear old ass; I mean I cant be frozen off with this divine authority any longer.

That winter, while Eliot composed his drama about the making of a saint, Emily was 'frozen off'. Something happened or, more likely, did *not* happen, so that, on 30 January 1935, she wrote to President Jaqua to ask if she might return to Scripps, her characteristic clarity clouded by cryptic words of dismay: '. . . The future holds no answer to the problem of the moment, and the question between East and West was indeed one of their never meeting as Mr. Kipling said long ago. But I am doing what seems to me the best thing now, and that is all any of us *can* do, I suppose.' But she had held on too long. Jaqua had given her post away. In her reply from Florence on 12 March she explained the delay: there had been 'problems' to settle.

By Easter Emily Hale had returned from Italy to Chipping Campden, and Eliot came at once to visit. It would have been soon after that he wrote *Burnt Norton*, which summed up his new position: it was impossible, for the time being, to recover the actuality of love. Though it was the essential matter of the past that must shape the future, it was at present fading with the fading light of the election in the rose-garden. He must 'Descend lower . . . / Into the world of perpetual solitude'.

There was no knowing how long the way down would take. *Burnt Norton* initiated, then, a phase of waiting to last through the years that Eliot composed the *Quartets*. The finale to the whole sequence repeats seven years later the memory of their visit to Burnt Norton: 'Quick now, here now, always – '. Though consummation was definitely postponed, nothing changed Eliot's recollection of that matchless moment.

Since Emily Hale had now no post for the fall of 1935, she stayed on in England till the end of the year. New details are revealed in a series of letters between Eliot and the young graduate student from Scripps College, Jeanette McPherrin, a modern linguist who eventually became a professor at Wellesley. While she was studying in France, Miss McPherrin had joined Emily in Rome during her winter vacation early in 1935, and Emily left London to join her in Guernsey for her next vacation in April of that year, at which time Miss McPherrin began to act as a confidante in a threeway friendship with Emily and Eliot. He called her 'Jeanie', and felt free enough to express his delight in a photo of Emily crouched smiling beside a pot of flowers in the summer of 1935. A masterpiece, Eliot insisted. *He* thought it charming, even if Emily did not, and was sending it off before she could stop him. That summer he offered to shelter both women in his lodgings, on condition, he told Jeanette, that Emily had a room to herself.

Eliot and Emily saw a great deal of each other in the course of 1935. Eliot came to Chipping Campden just before Easter, again in May, and once more during the latter half of July. On 25 July, the Morleys picked up Eliot at Chipping Campden to take him to Wales for ten days.* Early in September 1935 Eliot returned to Chipping Campden, and again at the end of the month when, as he pictured it to Virginia Woolf, he ran away from a bull into some black-berry bushes. That weekend he was celebrating his forty-seventh birthday: *The Yeomen of the Guard* at the Stratford Theatre on Friday night and a dinner on Saturday, arranged with great care by Emily, ostensibly in honour of her aunt, with healths and tasteful speeches and an Occasional Poem by the poet himself which he thought went down rather well. On 30 September he wrote to Aunt Edith about feeling more at home in Campden than anywhere: 'I want now to thank you for all your kindness and sweetness to me during the past two summers.' For Emily's sake, he courted her aunt's favour, though he disliked her managerial perfection; her husband,

---

* 'Usk', which resulted from that journey, was printed privately in October 1935 together with 'Cape Ann'. Emily Hale had a copy for Christmas, signed 'Tom', and she kept the gift until Eliot's second marriage in 1957.

an amiable schoolboy, given to woolly counsels, was no more than a pawn in her hands. Eliot, jealous of their claim on Emily, observed grimly how Campden suited the pair with its olde worlde atmosphere stinking of death.

When Emily's mother joined her in London for the autumn, they lodged near enough to Eliot to be called neighbours. Mrs Hale turned out to be rather terrible. Mentally broken, she now dabbled in spiritualism. When Eliot sat down to lunch she looked at him piercingly, and remarked that he was the image of her deceased husband; and before Eliot got over that, she added that very likely the dead man was now with them in the room.

The last notable event of that year was on 26 November when, at Eliot's insistence, Virginia Woolf invited Emily with Eliot to tea. Virginia Woolf, who was hard pressed with visitors, gave Emily Hale scant attention. She wrote the following account to Ruth George:

> 19, Rosary Gardens,
> South Kensington, S.W.7
> December 6, 1935.

Dearest Ruth,

. . . We sail for Boston the Friday of next week, arriving just before the Christmas week. I shall be with my old friend Miss Ware with whom I lived in Boston before, but how long I shall stay there I do not know. All my energies must be devoted to finding some sort of position for the coming year. Of course I feel I cannot return to Scripps, unless Dr Jaqua makes the first move and even if he did, I do not know that I could be confident of my future standing at the college. I grieve more over this forced severing of a possible return, than over the actual mess of last year. Should I find I had the money to come out, I should, on the pretext of seeing to my things, and I should come to you, dear Ruth, and ask for the unfulfilled visit to the Ranch also.

I can think of no Christmas greeting more to your taste, than for me to try inadequately to tell you of my taking tea with Virginia Woolf and Mr Woolf, last week Tuesday. Of course this was done in the company of Tom Eliot, who is one of a closer circle of friends, admitted to their life. They live in the upper floors of their press, the Hogarth, and in ample tree shaded Tavistock Square. We mounted one flight of stairs to the narrow door locked, till opened by a neatly dressed charwoman who led us up another flight, narrow and steep, at the top of which we removed our wraps. Taking breath, we ascended yet again, to the small, low-ceilinged dining-room, where our hosts had preceded us, with the other guest, young Stephen Spender. In the soft light of a small lamp on the square tea table, Mrs Woolf rose to greet me, and I thought of you even then, as I faced a very tall slender woman, dressed in a dark non-descript dress, over which was worn a short dark velvet coat. The simple dark clothes set off to advantage the small head carrying a wealth of greying hair, thick, but soft, which she wears simply off the forehead, and massed in a great Rossetti like coil at the nape of the very long slender neck. A narrow dark ribbon binds the hair accentuating the pre-raphaelite impression. The features are delicately modelled, if claiming no regularity of beauty, and although the face is lacking in mobility, as we think of the term, there appeared to me a sense of the mind's attentiveness and colour, (if I may so put it) traceable under the mask-like expression, mask-like except for the eyes, which register the reaction of each moment. A strong impression of cool detachment constantly contradicts itself by an equally strong impression of highly charged concentration. Her manner is not one to place people at ease, quite frankly speaking, though with Tom Eliot and Spender she was simple, friendly and responsive in an almost girlish way. I sat opposite her at the tea-table, an excellent place in which to listen (yes, listen, not chatter, Ruth) and to observe. Mr Woolf was at my right, as thin as she, but much less tall; the face is almost emaciated, the features very aquiline but not necessarily Hebraic, the expression warmer than hers, especially the eyes which to me revealed a number of qualities, as patience, weariness and isolation. He carries on his shoulder, not an atlas world of care, but a tiny marmoset, who lives on this human hill crest, all day long, peering out at one, first from one side, then the other; this tiny furry ball has a long tail which hangs down from his master's neck almost like a short queue, slightly confusing at first. I found myself getting on very well with Mr Woolf, who consciously or not puts one soon at ease. After an introductory theme of marmoset and affectionate spaniel Sally, who was at our feet, he took up a more serious note of conversation, asking thoughtful questions about America, question[s] almost naive, like an inquiry 'whether the American Indian mingled in our good society'. For the most part, the conversation was upon topics and personalities, known to the other four, Stephen Spender being very much at home with his hosts also, and by his very boyish open eyed, gentle manner, affording an interesting contrast to the profundity of his remarks. Tea was simple, but abundant, a comb of honey from the Woolfs' country place, receiving second place of honor with Mr. Ws. birthday cake which his very old mother never fails to send to each of her children on the anniversaries; there is a very odd assortment of furnishing in the dining room and in the larger drawing room below, whose walls are covered with decorative panels by Mrs Ws. sister, Vanessa Bell. There is a slight French flavor in this room, but I had the impression that their surroundings make little difference to either of the owners, or at best are artistic too unconventionally to be admired by the average visitor. Downstairs Mrs W. addressed several questions directly to me, suddenly but very carefully, so to speak, as if it really mattered what you answered her, and you found yourself wanting very much to make it matter and were curiously aware of your English as you answered. She sat quite gracefully, on a small sofa at the further end from S.S. and me (I had hoped she would be next to me) and smoked languidly but in a very practised way. The impression of cool, half mocking detachment began to lessen, it became a reserve, a shyness, a husbanding of fine abilities for the moments when they must be used and tested. As one felt the atmosphere warming and jollier, an interruption unwelcome to all of us, I believe, came in the shape of two French visitors, a man connected with the Revue des Deux Mondes, and his wife. Mrs W. began in French with him, which I am told she does not like to speak although she does it well. There seemed no need for us to stay, nor promise of a return to the earlier mood of the afternoon, so we said good-by. Since then I wrote to tell Mrs W. of how much I had enjoyed her books (I had no good chance to, you can see) and referred to you as

317

a lovely personality who admired her from far away California.

Now I must stop, although I have many many other things to relate, all making it very difficult to leave London. . . .

Yours,
Emily Hale

P.S. I read to Tom much of your letter and he loved it, too.

Emily was not a success with the Bloomsbury Group: it closed ranks against her in the same way it had shut out the Russian dancer Lydia Lopokova, when she had married the Bloomsbury economist Maynard Keynes. To Virginia Woolf, Miss Hale appeared too proper, an impeccable Bostonian. In a flight of inaccurate malice, Virginia Woolf wrote her off as rich, 'Eliot's rich American snob lady'. Eliot had told Ottoline Morrell in October 1934, 'She is quite an exceptional person, though it may not be immediately obvious.' Lady Ottoline claimed that she had tried to like Miss Hale but could not see what Eliot saw in her. By their second meeting at 10 Gower Street in October 1935, Emily had become 'that *awful* American woman Miss Hale. She is like a sergeant major, quite intolerable. However Tom takes her about everywhere . . .'.

Bloomsbury's hostility to Emily's rectitude was contradicted by Eliot's regard for a woman whose moral code was self-defeating: it did enrage him, but provoked, too, a protective concern for her pliability. Jeanette McPherrin shared this concern, unusually unguarded on Eliot's part. For once, he was not acting: there was genuine feeling, mostly exasperation that Emily did not stand up for herself. She was painfully respectful to her controlling Aunt Edith and her fool of a mother. Both drained Emily, and Eliot detected immediately the expense of spirit in Emily's efforts to save Aunt Edith from her mother, whereas, in Eliot's opinion, Mrs Perkins had the kind of gentle relentlessness that no one could stand up to – least of all Emily, who seemed to him haunted by her feeling that she ought to be a lot happier with Aunt Edith than she actually was. Eliot thought Emily partly responsible for her relatives' repressive manner, by treating

318

them with depressing abjection – she often spoke of her need for 'self-improvement'. Eliot tried to suggest that there was a wrong way of being humble as well as a right way. But when he observed, none too favourably, how certain members of her family took advantage of her sense of duty, she put him in his place. Here was someone whose conscience was even stronger than his own refined instrument of self-torture.

A little ruefully, realising he had to tread more carefully with someone so sensitive and proud, he turned to Jeanette to support his campaign. The heat of his anger suggests something more than sympathy for Emily's subordinate position: his own long years at Vivienne's beck and call – she used to call him away from the bank during working hours to make her hot carrot juice – alerted him to the futility of Emily's care for her disturbed mother. What upset him most was that he was not in a position, as he saw it, to rescue Emily – this made him want to rush out into her aunt's garden and pull up all her prize dahlias and whatnots. He foresaw the damage Emily's scrupulousness could inflict on herself combined, as now, with financial dependence. It was essential that she get a job, any job at this point, but preferably one as far from her mother and Boston as possible. It made him miserable, he said, to think of Emily far away, subduing herself to relatives instead of expanding.

And so it was: by 1936, Emily was back in Boston with the Perkinses (who returned for the tercentenary of King's Chapel), becalmed between her manipulative aunt and pathetic mother, and applying for one post after another (still handicapped by her lack of a college degree). Eventually, Emily found a position at Smith College for the fall of 1936. She was appointed Assistant Professor in the Department of Spoken English. Her schoolfriend Margaret Ferrand who taught at Smith, probably secured the post.* But by this time Emily had broken down.

In the spring she took refuge in a Unitarian retreat called

---

* In a letter to Margaret (14 July 1968), Emily Hale calls her 'my once upon a time employer!' (Sophia Smith Collection, Smith College).

Senexit at Putnam, Connecticut. Mrs Velma Williams, who ran it, stood quietly, half-shadowed in the hall to greet Miss Hale when she arrived through a grove of pines. The murmur of the great trees soothed her during the night, also an assurance of the 'ascent of the finite to the Infinite'. She recalled later 'the retreat from this little world of men to the great spaces of the Service'. Faith began to heal her when she turned beyond the doorway at the far end of the communal room, and found the chapel. 'I think I remember tears coming at once to my eyes. Whether at a communion service or daily homily, we worshipped a Spirit breathlessly close to us, and felt the presence of loved ones, whose spirit also was by us.'

She was still too ill to write, but the Perkinses kept Eliot informed. In a state of some alarm he booked a passage via Montreal in August. By the time he sailed, news came that she was a little better – possibly helped by the prospect of his arrival. Apart from one reading at Wellesley College (near Boston), this was not a public visit, and until Eliot's letters to Jeanie McPherrin came to light in 1992 nothing whatever was known about this visit to New England – beyond a stamp in a passport and a few photos. The Perkinses thought the breakdown came from Emily's daily efforts with her mother. Eliot doubted this, but did not articulate his own view. Obviously, Emily had lost hope in their future. She had been wearing his ring since about 1932, and after four years the problem of Vivienne and the aftermath of emotional horror that Vivienne trailed were still unresolved.

When Eliot arrived in Cambridge, Massachusetts, on 31 August, he found Emily much changed. She appeared numb to the external world, thinking only of her own shortcomings, wanting to be helped but too ready to agree with whatever he said to her. There was a spiritlessness he had never seen in her before, and he feared that a depression as bad as this must leave its mark. It was painful, he said, to see this in a person who normally gave so much to others.

He stayed with his eldest sister, Ada, at 31 Madison Street, Gray Gardens, Cambridge, near the Perkinses at 5 Clement Circle where Emily was convalescing: it would have becn easy to see her daily. He gave her a leather-bound Bible, and beside his inscription she always kept a small marker with the words 'The Lord make his face to shine upon you' (above a delicate flower print).

Eliot's aim was to give her enough support to see her through to a good start at Smith. She did pick up a bit when they went away to Woods Hole on the coast. When the semester started, he went to Northampton: she seemed to be coping, but still without her customary verve.

Eliot's visit in September–October 1936 was also the occasion of a family reunion. Photographs record a vacation in rural New Hampshire, Eliot in a cloth cap, his sisters in their rockers on the porch of Mountain View House. This might have been another time of decision. Eliot was, as he put it years later, very much in love with Emily Hale, and would willingly have sacrificed everything for the possibility of marrying her. A professorship at Harvard was on offer. It would have been logical for Eliot to consider a return to Massachusetts as an obvious solution to pursuit by Vivienne, who had always feared to cross the Atlantic.

In his play *The Family Reunion*, Harry looks into the possibility of returning to his old home after years abroad. There he meets Mary, who had shared his youth and is still 'Waiting, waiting, always waiting'. But return proves impossible, for Mary's appeal is blotted out by the pursuit of Harry's dead wife in the form of Furies.

'I cannot tell you when or whether there will be more of *Sweeney*,' Eliot had written to a producer, Hallie Flanagan, on 9 February 1934, 'but in any case I hope to begin something new of the same kind as soon as I have finished with a dramatic pageant [*The Rock*] . . .'. In 1936 he still thought *Sweeney Agonistes* the most original thing he had done, but ten years had made too great a difference for him to finish it in its old form. Eliot's most ambitious works gestated for several years, during which he tried out fragments or sections; then there would be an enormous effort to unify and complete. No work gestated longer than *The Family Reunion* with its roots in the *Sweeney* fragments of

1923–6. The first four of ten discernible layers of composition date back to 1934–5, and precede or coincide with *Murder in the Cathedral*. The commissions for *The Rock* and *Murder* interrupted a plan for a play which grew out of the facts of his life: a family who had disapproved of the hero's marriage, who had not attended it, and were glad it was over; a marriage linked with exile; a wife, possessive, shivering with nerves, doomed, closely modelled on Vivienne; and a waiting woman, no longer young, with close ties to the hero's family, who would have been the approved choice.

The timing of the play's composition forecasts events in Eliot's life with uncanny closeness. In the play Harry is said to be 'psychic' in that he knows in advance that his wife will be destroyed. Eliot completed his second Working Draft in the spring of 1938. On 7 June a letter from his secretary, Anne Bradby (later Ridler), to Ezra Pound implies that the play was nearly ready for performance. During the next two months, July–August, Vivienne was put away. The play was due to go on that autumn, though it was eventually postponed for a few months. Michael Redgrave, who played Harry in the first production, said that Eliot sat with his head down during rehearsals, revising until the last moment.

Writing at the very time of his wife's crisis, Eliot conveys the torment of the questions that gnaw at Harry. Did he push his wife off the deck? Or did she, as she had threatened, destroy herself? Harry is struggling to escape the shadows of his marital past. He is haunted, like Sweeney, by his own latent violence, except that the Hoo Ha's are now visible as Furies. No longer funny, they appear the essence of evil to the man at whom they look with terrible complicity. The problem for Harry, as for Eliot himself, was how to cope with two separate lives: the stained years abroad and the distant past at home.

The first scene that he worked out in any detail centred on the waiting Mary as she offers Harry new hope. The date of this scene, 1934–5, puts it exactly in the period that Eliot was most engaged with Emily Hale, then making prolonged stays in England. Mary urges Harry to open a door just to hand;

she pictures the smell of new-cut grass under sunlight. The door opening into a garden of love was to be the opening scene of *Burnt Norton*, but had its origin in this early, unfinished draft of Eliot's play, written soon after the actual visit of Eliot and Emily Hale to Burnt Norton in September 1934, which provided an initial impetus for both *The Family Reunion* and *Four Quartets*.

In *Burnt Norton*, the woman is faceless, subsumed in 'we'. Here she is the leader into new experience, with all the charm of assurance. Mary, in draft, may be closer to Emily Hale than the toned-down Mary of the final play. She is allowed to take a more diagnostic view of Harry than in the revised version of their exchange: a corrective, not flattering view. To her, Harry is a man who creates his own torment and prefers it. This torment is a form of pride which masks his fear of taking up a new role, in case he might not appear so well in it.

The next phase of composition, also 1934–5, was an additional scenario in which Harry explains the double nightmare that now became the central drama of the play. One nightmare is a state of possession which goes back to the ancestor who was cursed by a witch: in this state Harry cannot see his wife as human. The other nightmare seems to be a state of mental isolation in which he feels divided from the self he had been in his youth. This explanation is something of an answer to Mary's simple cure of natural feeling. Harry, if not mad, is on the brink of madness. 'O that awful privacy / Of the insane mind!' Harry exclaims in the play, and these are the very words Eliot himself was to use in describing his life with Vivienne, years later, to Mary Trevelyan. He said: 'I used to find that, once I got out of the atmosphere, I recovered normality surprisingly quickly. But at the time it seemed as though it would never end.' Harry needs another, more daring cure than natural love, which is offered by the other beneficent woman in the play, the older Agatha: her cure is a process of de-possession, what the play finally calls 'exorcism'. Harry must translate his isolation into the deliberate solitude of a special destiny: he must cross some frontier into another world. This brings Harry into line with Eliot's own states of extremity and religious trial.

Next come three pages of pencil notes for a scene between Mary and Downing, Harry's chauffeur, as watchers of Harry's fate. Downing tells Mary that Harry's is to be a lone journey, and he confirms the notion that it is destined in some way. His lordship's marrying was 'a kind of preparation for something else'. The three pages are on the same paper as the manuscript of *Murder in the Cathedral*, and were kept with it. This was the last of the fragments of 1935. There followed a gap of about eighteen months until 1936 when, on returning from an actual reunion with his family and Emily, Eliot began again.

The autobiographic basis of the earliest fragments give to this play the emotional intimacy of Eliot's early work, as though we were looking at a man with his back to us, who abruptly turns and speaks with low, confessional urgency, and then, as abruptly, turns away once more. This confessional manner is not very English, though Harry is made out to be an English lord. Martin Browne misconceived the play from the start when he praised the reality of the family and criticised non-realistic scenes (the Furies, and the trances when characters speak beyond themselves). The weakness, as with *Sweeney Agonistes*, lies rather in Eliot's naturalistic cover: the idle chatter of people he despises, who in this play are the obtuse members of the family. They seemed to Virginia Woolf stiff pokers. For the sake of a theatre audience that Eliot was to underrate for the rest of his career, he forced himself – and us – to attend to dullards' chit-chat. Their platitudes roll out, even from the wise Agatha in her (to Eliot) dull capacity as Principal of an Oxford women's college. As Helen Gardner noted, this aspect of Agatha is not convincing, especially when she complains of thirty years of trying not to dislike women. (In the 1950s, when Janet Adam Smith* was proposed as Principal of a women's college,

* Janet Adam Smith (afterwards Mrs John Carleton) was Assistant Editor of the *Listener* (1930–5), and then worked for the *New Statesman*

Eliot sent her a warning postcard of a stately hen, with the message: 'This card should help you to remember how to behave'. The card also refers to Agatha as 'a most tiresome woman'.)

The Family Reunion looks neither to past nor future except as they bear on a present agony of choice. Harry must choose the right course from three alternatives on offer: his family's drama of reunion; Mary's related drama of renewal through love; and the still-obscure drama of the Furies. In all the years that Harry remained abroad, he had come to think of family life as simple, but he discovers on his return that the simplification had taken place in memory. Most members of the family are rigid with lifelessness, and precisely because they have changed so little, the change in Harry is more manifest. Martin Browne told Eliot that he found Harry baffling. In reply, Eliot sent that long analysis of Harry that sounds like a confession. Eliot covered his tracks, characteristically, by telling Browne that he identified with Charles, an uncle of slightly modified dimness, but Harry is patently Eliot, as Virginia Woolf saw at once: 'the chief poker is Tom'. The letter reveals 'a horror of women'. What might well be a reasonable wish to be free of an impossible wife calls out an extreme pattern of feeling, an old pattern for Eliot that goes back to the murder of a woman in 'Saint Sebastian', revived in *Sweeney Agonistes*, and connected with a predisposition to see women as creatures of sexual sin who dare men to consort with them and so receive their ineradicable taint.

As this mind pursues itself, the external world comes unstuck. Harry talks past his expectant family, saturated with his awareness of something present to his mind but not visible. As a student, Eliot had noted that what appears as paranoia, delusional insanity, may be a diabolical mysticism. More than thirty years later, his play contrasts a state of demonic possession with the blinkered state of Harry's aristocratic family. The social setting is that of the English

and Nation (1949–60), in the last eight years as Literary Editor. Her first marriage, in 1935, was to Michael Roberts, a contributor to the *Criterion*, and Eliot was godfather to one of their three children.

country-house comedy of manners, yet the feeling of moral horror – Harry's alertness to incursions from the unknown – is pure New England. Harry, Lord Monchensey, has a stern sense of culpability – not in the eyes of the world, but in the privacy of his own superior conscience. In colonising England in this way, Eliot followed Henry James, whom he praised in 1933 for 'his curious search, often in the oddest places, like country houses, for spiritual life'. The play jolts us successively from the familiar to the strange, domesticating, as James does, dangers 'that look like nothing and that can be but inwardly and occultly dealt with, which involve the sharpest hazards to life and honour and the highest instant decisions and intrepidities of action'. The aunts and uncles are out of English detective fiction from Conan Doyle to Agatha Christie: the old buffer of the club, the retired Indian army officer, the spinster of the vicar's teas. The deeper drama is the mystery of sin and redemption explored with a strenuous rigour that came to Eliot most directly through his mother. All through the play, Eliot sustained this parallel of native core and English façade that derived, ultimately, from himself. Externally, he was an English gentleman; internally, as he now and then admitted, a Puritan – and all the more Puritan for not having been born in Massachusetts.

For the three generations that the Eliots had lived on the Mississippi, they had continued to look upon New England as their spiritual home, and after Eliot's father died the family all filtered back to Cambridge, Massachusetts. The exile often cultivates the spirit of place, which can be more real to him than the place where he actually lives. It gains imaginative wholeness through memory and distance, like James's Boston or Joyce's Dublin or Eliot's Cape Ann. Eliot's hold on ancestral destiny actually grew stronger after he relinquished his nationality, not just in his use of American locale in his later poems but in a more deep-reaching retrieval of the New England conscience. Eliot may have claimed English tradition but, it may be, English tradition cannot wholly claim Eliot, for he brought into English tradition not only a native habit of introspection but also a state of mind that survived and flourished in the relative isolation of New England in the seventeenth century: intolerance. 'It is as radical as any form of Calvinism,' wrote a reviewer of *The Family Reunion* after the first Edinburgh Festival production of 1947.

There was a rumour in America that when Eliot once gave a friend letters of introduction to certain Bostonians, he also identified them through their representations in *The Family Reunion*. A letter from Eliot's sister Margaret to their brother Henry expressed 'the family's anxiety, when Tom went back to England' after his brief visit in August 1915 to explain his actions. *Time* magazine reported that some of Eliot's relations regarded him as the black sheep, and quoted their saying 'his poetry still fuddles a lot of us'. Henry Ware Eliot retorted on 21 March 1938 that members of family considered themselves in a uniquely favourable position to understand the work, 'some of which is unintelligible unless you know the man'.

In returning to his family, Harry imagines an escape from one life to another. Mary offers the subtlest encouragement when she assures him that she remembers, and can return him to, the 'real' Harry. With her, he tries out the view that his marriage had been the 'accident of a dreaming moment' when he was someone else. The early unfinished draft gave more attention to Mary's offer of natural happiness, and the light, singing, and water that Harry glimpses through her are metaphors Eliot always uses for rare moments of renewal. Her voice sounds like a waterfall, and in her silence – always a potent word for Eliot – is the sound of nature, of ordinary life persisting between the two storms of marriage and Furies. In the unfinished draft, Mary urges Harry to stay in one place, and acquire the rhythms of recurrent seasons. The routine surface life wouldn't matter because there would be stillness in its depths. In all subsequent drafts, Mary counsels what Eliot was to consider again, in more abstract form, in *East Coker*: a life which would take its place in the ancestral round, in time's scheme, where there is necessary union of man and woman, and couples hold each other by the hand. For Eliot himself, as he conceived the play in 1934–5, the future hung in the balance. To go on with Emily could bring him a late spring of natural happiness, corresponding to the upswing of their time together in New Hampshire in early June 1933.

The Family Reunion was set in late March and, on one title page, Eliot jotted the words 'vernal equinox'. Could Harry accept the spring? The alternative, as Harry puts it to Mary, is to turn back into wintry darkness, a timeless dark night of the soul. Against natural love is Harry's horror of women which, Eliot explained to Browne, made Mary repulsive, though there remained a normal bit of Harry that was still attracted to her personally. In Mary's favour is her power to bring him 'a new world in the deep, the abyss of light, a *new* world'. The earlier drafts have this deep rhythm of emotion. Harry is quickened by her glimpse of new life, her repudiation of the shadows around him, but at the very point of accepting what she has to offer, the Furies claim him more completely than ever before. All else fades into unreality. Mary herself appears obtuse because she can't see them.

Furiously, he rejects her: 'You're of no use to me.'

This decisive moment is all the more dramatic in earlier drafts for the strength of the alternative emotion that precedes it. From this moment Mary is wiped out dramatically. When Martin Browne and Frank Morley questioned this, Eliot made a note to himself to fill out her role by having her arrange flowers. Morley said this was no solution, but the flower-arranging remained. Emily Hale, too, urged Eliot to make more of Mary. In 1938 he gave Emily his Working Draft, which contained, near the end, a long speech of protest from Mary, indignant that her feelings are never consulted, and saying that she wants her turn to live. The speech follows a suggestion that it is from Mary, specifically, that Harry's destiny takes him. Emily Hale wanted Eliot to intensify this idea earlier in the play. She advised him to shift the speech to the beginning. The effect, which she did not spell out, would have given more play to Mary's feeling. But though Eliot agreed to the shift, he would not be drawn into Mary's drama. He toned down all protest so that she comes to be

328

quiet and controlled, closer to the depressed Emily of 1936. When Harry is due to arrive, Mary fears that it won't be easy talking to him after all that has happened, and wonders how she can stand it.* As a single woman lingering (like Emily) at home, she feels a superfluous misfit, her troubles commonplace beside those of a man who has a place and a function and a life. Mary's revised role was to go on waiting in the uncertain space between the worldly routines of a women's college (parallel to Emily herself teaching at Smith) and the otherworldly, directed life reserved for Harry alone. Eliot's only real concession was to cut Harry's line about loathing the smell of women.

Emily Hale played her special part so long as Eliot's sense of two lives hung in the balance. She belonged to one of these lives, the family past. I think that she upheld, through memory, the innocent Eliot (as Mary, the 'real' Harry) but then, like Mary, had to accept a man damaged by his more recent past, and accept, too, the penitential 'lifetime's march' that took him away from her.

*

The Furies bring evil home with inescapable terror. They show Harry that there is no untarnished self to which he can return. The taint of his flesh has reached his marrow. Are the Furies (as in one draft) the origin of evil? Or are they divine messengers? The uncertainty comes from the obscurest recess of Eliot's mind, what he called the octopus or angel with which the poet struggles. Like Jacob, wrestling with the angel, Harry is 'chosen', but this means a lifetime of tests.

The crucial test is the Furies, who are real in the terms of a play in which real and unreal change places. The apparent reality of the family comes to appear precarious, and is finally extinguished when their clock stops in the dark of the last scene. The insubstantiality of reported phantoms should be confounded by a dramatic shock when they enter. The

* This bit was cut.

spectacle should be overwhelming, as in Michael Elliott's Royal Exchange production in 1979 (the most successful production to date), when they appeared at every entrance of the Roundhouse in Camden, London, at about twice the human size, hooded in white like the Ku Klux Klan, to a grinding noise unendurable to the ear. They loomed over the audience on every side in a sudden black-out, blocking all exits. Such terror was never achieved in Eliot's lifetime by all accounts of productions on both sides of the Atlantic. Reviews mention the Furies surprisingly little, which itself suggests their feeble impact. Most of these productions were constrained by Eliot's fear of a sceptical audience. In Martin Browne's productions, the Furies were safely contained in a side window. In fact, Browne's final view was that they should not appear at all, only their effect on Harry. But this solution would underscore the obtuse family view that Harry is mad. It is essential to persuade the audience that Harry is a man of destiny, and visible Furies point to this with maximum force.

On the other hand, it would be all too easy to raise a laugh. This Gielgud saw when he read the script in 1938 (to consider the part of Harry). If the Furies were crudely visible they might seem ridiculous. After a performance at the end of 1948 in Sweden, Eliot reported that the Furies had appeared as a sort of rugby team of fifteen huge leprous giraffes, swarming out when the bookshelves parted in a library that looked like St Pancras Station. In an Illinois production in 1949, the Furies looked like toy puppets or jacks-in-the-box: not scary, rather fun. In October 1958, at the Phoenix Theatre in New York, they had red pupils glaring from enormous white eyes, as they peeped coyly through the draperies of the living-room. The programme gave the cast list side by side with a large advertisement for 'MY SIN . . . a most provocative perfume'.

Hell must have real sins and sinners, Eliot told Pound, people like himself. (He advised Pound to put *him* into the *Cantos* if he wanted a proper hell, rather than mere types like the financiers Beaverbrook, Mellon, and Rothermere.) In the hell of *The Family Reunion*, Eliot has a man like himself, caught in moral problems like his own. The challenge for Harry is to move from hell to purgatory, and this depends on his courage to face the Furies who are projections of his changing state of mind.

On one level this is a ghost story like 'The Jolly Corner' by James, where an exile, returning to New York after years abroad, meets his deformed other self lurking in the old family home. As Agatha predicts from the start, Harry will have to face his ghost, down the corridor that led to the nursery, and 'it will not be a very *jolly* corner'. On a deeper level, Harry is moving according to a predestined pattern. Harry's wish to kill is not, he finds, his own wish only, but a 'curse' passed down the generations of his family. Deeper than individual, psychological drama lies this universal drama of innate depravity. Calvin said: 'we are so ... perverted in every part of our nature that by this great corruption we stand justly condemned and convicted before God, to whom nothing is acceptable but righteousness, innocence, and purity.' Harry comes to realise that if he faces the depravity in himself and his family (who epitomise the whole human family), he can play a part in a pattern of redemption.

This is the right drama. In taking up the moral burden of the family, Harry is to rescue its spirit, not preside over its daily doings. Obtuse members of his family see only the psychological drama, following the traumatic end of his marriage. To them, the Furies are signs of his disturbance. Eliot's sister Ada may have exemplified such a view when she feared that her brother's 'dramatism' would endanger his sanity. But, in the play, there is one member of the family, Agatha, who recognises the Furies as real. She tells Harry that his nightmare is a real purgatorial fire, and so sanctions his departure as an essential move in a predestined pattern. Eliot told Martin Browne that Harry follows the Furies* like the

---

* An early title for the play was 'Follow the Furies'. Another was 'Fear in the Way'.

Disciples dropping their nets. This, then, is a biblical pattern: to leave one's family for the religious life. Agatha and Mary bless his way: 'Follow follow.'

Eliot sent two drafts to Emily Hale for comment. Years later, the American poet Marianne Moore wrote to Emily saying she had often heard Eliot speak of her, and 'have thought of you almost as a collaborator in some of T. S. Eliot's plays'. One of Emily Hale's suggestions (on the second of the two drafts) was that Harry's mission be brought to a stronger climax. She wrote at the end of the penultimate scene: 'chance for Harry's explanation of Furies as he *now* sees them . . .'. The result was an important additional dialogue beginning with an aunt's question, 'But why are you going?', and ending with Harry's announcement of his 'election'. He means to purify himself through solitude, following the desert saints: the heat of the sun, thirst, the icy vigil. There is some talk of 'care over lives of humble people' who are ignorant and have 'incurable diseases', but this is unconvincing. Harry is no Father Zossima,* with compassion for the sufferings of the people. He is absorbed in his own soul and, through him, Eliot explored the nature of a hermit in the making.

Audience comments overheard at the end of the play suggest that some leave the theatre bewildered about Harry and, to some extent, disappointed. Aunt Amy's death on Harry's departure was Eliot's attempt to give such members of the audience a finale of an obvious sort, but the real end is the prayer of the two women who will imaginatively 'follow' Harry wherever his pilgrimage takes him, as we, the audience, should ideally 'follow'. In the end, Eliot did not accede to the pleas of Martin Browne and Emily Hale to close the play more explicitly. In Emily Hale's draft he tried to state Harry's sanctification, but this he cut. The play was so close to his own experience that it had to remain as open as his own fate.

Eliot's new life turned on choices he made in the mid-

---

* Father Zossima is the popular saint in Dostoevsky's novel *The Brothers Karamazov*

thirties: to turn from the path of renewed love and family reunion, choosing the lone path of religious ordeal. Specifically, this meant standing by the form of High Anglicanism which made divorce impossible. It meant that though, at some point, Eliot did wish to marry Emily Hale, their relationship would remain no more than an understanding – something more than friendship. This decision to hold back may have been reinforced by the fact that Eliot's closest friends in London did not take to Emily Hale. John Hayward dismissed her in slightly mocking tones, as though she were some fad of Eliot's, an unwelcome diversion from the male club. Eliot, though, was not a man to be influenced inordinately by his friends. It is more likely that his was a moral decision.

It may be that Emily's fate was sealed from the time that he first conceived the play in 1934–5. Mary, unlike the wife, is at least visible, but like the wife she is barely a character, and even less so in Eliot's revisions. It is a one-man show. The dead wife represents his polluted soul; Mary, a rather perfunctory temptation. The country house, with its decayed family, is a naturalistic front for what is really a morality play in which figures move in set patterns, as they try in different ways to free the house from the curse of its decline.

Eliot plays up the difference between this momentous drama and the paltry disaster of Harry's brother, John, who has drunkenly reversed his car into a shop window in Ebury Street and told the police, 'I thought it was all open country about here.' The Wodehouse-ish joke comes from the *Evening Standard* of 14 April 1937, which reported that Viscount Forbes (son of the Earl of Granard) of Halkin Street, S.W., drove at 52 miles an hour in Beddington Lane, near Croydon, on 4 February. When stopped, he said, 'I thought it was all countrified.' Eliot also kept the *Standard*'s May 1937 report on Robert Edgar, aged twenty-one, a graduate of Christ Church, Oxford, who was charged with drunken driving in the High Street on Coronation night. When arrested, he refused to be examined by a doctor. 'I have always refused to do so because I distrust their efficiency,' he told the court. This very English comedy of manners sets off the quite different moral drama where the Furies lead Harry 'across the frontier'. At the end, Harry fades out of clear-cut English society into the dim distance of a far frontier. The accidents of such as John are nothing to the danger that Harry is to face, of being alone with his flawed self.

The Family Reunion poses outward accident versus internal danger as a challenge to the audience: which matters? The one is patent; the other a mystery. The play teases us with the superficial mystery of murder, especially when a policeman arrives on the scene, but that drama is undercut by the profounder mystery of guilt. Harry did not push his wife overboard, but – as Eliot pointed out in a letter to Martin Browne – he didn't call for help, nor did he jump in after her. Is passivity culpable? Hawthorne said: 'It was the policy of our ancestors to search out even the most secret sins, and expose them to shame.' The repressed Puritan world of secrets and sudden breaches of decorum is half-concealed within the tame setting of English society. The shock comes when extreme containment is broken by disclosure: 'I pushed her.' The unexpected confession is the tactic of Eliot's early dramatic monologues: 'I have had a hundred visions' or the hope that an unwanted Lady 'should die some afternoon . . . / Should die and leave me sitting pen in hand'. These are the disclosures of a mind approaching some frontier of vision or horror.

Agatha's role is to direct Harry across that frontier. It was a difficult, perhaps impossible part, Eliot remarked to Mary Trevelyan after seeing Sybil Thorndyke in Peter Brook's production in 1956. She must be a soothsayer as well as a normal, warm-hearted woman. Agatha had to have a measure of spiritual power, and this was what was lacking, again, in Lilian Gish in New York in 1958. Agatha's formidable task is to make the frontier real, and this can happen only if the production prepares for it. The country-house setting has to seem by contrast increasingly unreal, so that we shift from watching a predictable drama of strains and manners to a drama that is beyond us.

Eliot's aim was what he termed the ultra-dramatic. In two unpublished talks in 1937 he said that poetic drama could awaken the audience to a hidden pattern of reality which may supersede what is ordinarily dramatic. He believed that an audience would accept this so long as there was something more ordinary to attend to. The characters in such a play have a double existence: they must appear living creatures like ourselves; at the same time, they must make us see through ordinary classified emotions into a world of emotion of which we are normally unaware, which comes from the depths of the playwright himself. A poet, once he has found his way into these strange lands of more than polar darkness and more than equatorial light, may gradually lose interest in the ordinary, and his characters may come to be, in the ordinary sense, less real. Such a poet has crossed the frontier from dramatic action to the spiritual action that transcends it. Eliot spoke repeatedly of a poet who has crossed into a world where we cannot follow him – somewhere *beyond* the dramatic.

Eliot had a rationale, then, for his unwillingness to be explicit about Harry's future actions. Under pressure, he told Michael Redgrave that Harry would take a job in the East End, but this was a sop to an actor: it was never in the script. The statement elicited by Emily Hale, 'I have this election', was as far as clarity could go.

Eliot moves beyond drama through his use of seasonal change. The greenhouse flowers that Mary brings on stage were not just to give her some feeble action: they bear out a precise time, late March, in the north of England: just too early for garden flowers. The metaphoric reach of the poetry – the strongest poetry in all Eliot's plays – suggests that the spring that is on the way is not to be a natural awakening but a time of pilgrimage that will take Harry outside time's scheme to the polar regions of extreme trial where the life of the senses will freeze.

The vernal equinox might be said to be the fulcrum on which Eliot himself moved and had his being, swinging into the 'cruellest' month of April or swinging back the other way into the dark night of winter when only the soul's sap quivers. The seasonal cycle at which the play stands poised is superseded when a man abandons all seasons to move in perpetual winter from pole to pole. Spring, to Harry, excites us with 'lying voices', and is, therefore, 'an evil time'. He repudiates the stir of the senses so as to see himself as part of some monstrous aberration of all men, of the world 'which I cannot put in order'. Order is the clue to his true mission – and to Eliot's. It is not to be a missionary in any literal sense, but to create order in the form of a perfect life. The autobiographical crisis of the play propels Eliot into the abstract order of the *Quartets*. The bridge between the two was what Mary called, in the early unfinished draft, perpetual exile.

*

Eliot abandoned the theatre for the next eight years. The reason he gave was the difficulty of putting on plays with the outbreak of war. Yet *Murder in the Cathedral* was revived successfully throughout the war in a variety of improvised theatres. It is possible that the failure of *The Family Reunion* daunted Eliot, for the first production at the Westminster Theatre closed after five weeks. But there may have been some more compelling reason: his need to retrieve the grace glimpsed at Burnt Norton five years before. 'I must follow the bright angels' is Harry's exit line, a difficult line for an actor to deliver with any conviction. Harry exits from the explicit medium of the theatre into the invisible drama of spiritual autobiography. For the only cure of demonic possession lay in further exploration of what *Burnt Norton* had called the way down. This slow, painful transformation of a flawed self had been the alternative to an immediate experience of bliss which Eliot had called the way up. In the two sequels that Eliot planned in 1940, bliss was to remain only a memory. The way down now took over, culminating in an imaginary journey across a vast and terrible sea. The only landmark was the treacherous rocks, the Dry Salvages, off the coast of Cape

Ann. In closing with this ordeal, Eliot meant to renew the crossing of Andrew Eliott, in 1669, to the New World. It meant distancing himself, at least temporarily, from the comfort of love and family. In a sense, he was exchanging the present-day reality for the dream of New England. The ancestral journey loomed out of the past, that crossing that was driven by the loftiest dream of a purified life and was, at the same time, a surrender to the severest of trials.

10

THE PERFECT LIFE

STARTING FROM 'ACUTE personal reminiscence' – reunion with an old love or 'things ill done and done to others' harm' – *Four Quartets* recounts Eliot's struggle to recast his lot during his years in the clergyhouse in Kensington. This is reflected in the original title, 'Kensington Quartets', which Eliot had always in mind until he completed the poems in September 1942. Looking back, he seemed to have lived on the edge of a 'grimpen', a dangerous mire.* The period of trial in Eliot's life from 1934 to 1938 then came to epitomise the ordeal of a nation under fire from 1940 to 1942. Yet in the midst of danger, both personal and public, there is a promise of renewal in an idea of the perfect life.

Although only one of the four poems is set in New England, the entire sequence revives the American Puritans' resolve to establish the perfect life on earth. In the seventeenth century they set out the signs of election as an exact sequence and, because communication of this took precedence over art, they eschewed more imaginative forms of writing for the plain style. Eliot, too, set out the inward sequence, and often in terms that were deliberately prosaic. 'The poetry does not matter,' he said in 1940.

In earlier days, Virginia Woolf had seen Eliot as 'a New

---

* Eliot derived 'grimpen' (*EC*: II) from Conan Doyle, *The Hound of the Baskervilles* (1902): 'Life has become like that great Grimpen Mire, with little green patches everywhere into which one may sink and with no guide to point the track.' Conan Doyle derived the word from Grimspound Bog, near Widecombe, on Dartmoor.

England schoolmaster', and Pound had complained about his blood, 'the thin milk of . . . New England from the pap'. His own unwillingness to acknowledge his native tradition until late in his career was fear of 'provincialism'. From the start he wanted to be a worldwide writer, not local like Hawthorne, with whom he actually had much in common. Yet, far from throwing off his native tradition, Eliot renews the idealism, the strenuousness and moral power of colonial New England as he brought to greatness its distinctive genres of sermon and spiritual biography. At the same time, through his use of parallels from Europe and the East, he rescued native tradition from 'provincialism'.

Andrew Eliott, who crossed the sea as an act of faith, is the ancestral exemplar. Eliot's parallel tradition came from books he had read first at Harvard, the *Upanishads*, *The Divine Comedy*, *Samson Agonistes*, and the mystics of the late Middle Ages, St John of the Cross and Dame Julian of Norwich, all of whom set out a similar progress towards perfection. This Eliot undertook to renew for his own time, the grim years of the Second World War. 'Now,' he said in 1940, 'under conditions / That seem unpropitious.'

The form of life that Eliot both inherits and renews is simple. His long poems often look formidable because of their bookish allusions, but these serve only to support, in different terms, a simple proposition, say the prevalence of sterility in *The Waste Land*, or the emotional demands of 'turning' or conversion in *Ash-Wednesday*. The epigraph to *Burnt Norton* proposed two equally valid ways to perfection: the way up and the way down are the same.

The 'way up' is a life directed by a visionary moment in which the mind perceives a timeless 'reality'. Eliot begins with his own intuition of the way up in the garden of Burnt Norton. Walking with Emily Hale through the rose-garden at Burnt Norton, Eliot experienced a startling access of emotion that awakened him momentarily to 'the heart of light'. It seemed no less than a miracle that he should be allowed to experience once again illumination through human love, and that this should not be reserved for the innocence of youth but should come in middle age to a man contaminated by marriage. As the speaker comes from the rose-garden, across the lawn towards an empty pool of dry concrete, it seemed to fill with water out of sunlight. He feels the same indescribable ecstasy as in *The Waste Land* where, rapt by a memory of the 'hyacinth girl' whose arms were full of flowers, a man had stared 'into the heart of light, the silence', only to collapse into the sterility of sexual relationships in a polluted London. So too, at Burnt Norton, the moment passes: a cloud shuts off the sun, the pool is dry once more, and the visionary is left with 'The waste sad time / That stretches before and after.' But the comedown is not the same. In *The Waste Land* a man is flung from sublimity to futility; in *Burnt Norton* he turns from sublimity to perceive an alternative course by which we may transcend our imperfect existence. The 'way up', then, provides the incentive to pursue the 'way down'.

Until *Burnt Norton*, Eliot aspired to the way up of the chosen, those who live perpetually in the light of grace, but after his imaginative encounter with the Furies of 1934–9, he aligned himself, in the later *Quartets*, with the other party, the flawed beings who must be remade. 'Sin is Behovely', Christ's words to Dame Julian of Norwich in the fourteenth century, confirm what was apparent to Eliot's conscience. The way down, which dominates the central two poems, *East Coker* and *The Dry Salvages*, is an operation on Original Sin, a radical excision of all one feels, knows, and is. Assuming the otherness of the divine spirit, a seeker must divest himself of all the attributes most precious to him if he is to come to know what is utterly beyond human nature and knowledge.

The initial publication of *Burnt Norton* as an isolated poem in 1936, the gap that followed while Eliot wrote *The Family Reunion*, and the separate publication of the subsequent three poems, encourage us to read the *Quartets* separately, but they are unified, not merely by the formal repetition of their five-part structure, but by a profounder strategy of repetition. It is the strategy of Emerson's essays, where each sentence is self-contained but repeats, in different terms, the same idea. It is also the tactic of the sermon: each unit, whether homely or poetic, is designed to awaken the audience in one way or another. Like any number of Americans, Eliot is writing a form of scripture. He draws on the cadence of the Bible with its long line, its rhythmic cumulation, its riddling, oracular language, its movement towards inexpressible revelation. The reader must launch into the chasm between Emerson's sentences or follow Whitman's trail of dots or fill the blanks on Eliot's page. Eliot emulates the repetition of the Bible and its alternation of prosaic and poetic that he saw as essential to a long poem.

Repetition is the very sermon of *Four Quartets*: to try again and yet again for the perfect life, and not to look for the fruits of action, an end to the pilgrimage. What appears to be the end – it may be a climactic effort, it may be the end to a poem – becomes, in the model life that Eliot devised, a new beginning, as the moment in the rose-garden, which might have seemed a *Paradiso* at the end of the 1936 *Collected Poems*, turns out, in the course of continued existence, to be only the beginning of a longer poem that demands recurring effort. Each subsequent poem repeats the effort in new scenes of self-surrender and acute risk: in *East Coker* the way down is a submission to surgery; in *The Dry Salvages* it is to 'fare forward' across a battering sea.

Although the beginning of effort repeatedly succeeds the end, Eliot does suggest the possibility of progression: 'In my beginning is my end.' In one sense he means simply the inexorable course of the lifespan which ends in death. But then, to a Christian, death is the beginning of eternal life: 'In my end is my beginning.' A seeker lives in time with an eye to eternity: that supreme possibility of progression is implied when he longs for 'the unimaginable / Zero summer', for a fullness of being that lies outside the round of the seasons, outside time's scheme.

Eliot sets himself the question: how do we live in time so as to conquer time? Each of the *Quartets* explores a point of intersection of time and timelessness which Eliot draws initially from his own life. In *Burnt Norton* there is the moment of love, but love turns to 'dust on a bowl of rose leaves'. To Emily Hale it remained a 'mystery' for the rest of her life. Yet Eliot's commitment to the solitary burden of the soul is not out of line with an American plot where the Jamesian New Englander, awakening to life, renounces love out of a finer moral passion 'to be right', or where Melville spurns the ease of the shore to confront the nature of creation, or Huck Finn lights out for the Territory ('there is no more solitary character in fiction', said Eliot), or the Lone Ranger turns his back on the homestead and rides into the sunset to confront dangerous facts that lie beyond the limits of domesticity. The frontier for Eliot is that of time and eternity.

To consort with his own kind was only a respite from this lone journey. For most of his life Eliot was a solitary who yet saw it as his duty (as public figure or as a Christian performing acts of charity) to partake in the world. Love did not come easily, for, until the last eight or nine years of his life, he reserved emotional energy for a higher object than woman, as Aeneas abandoned Dido for a higher destiny to found Rome. Eliot identified with the moment when the gods call Aeneas, urging a further voyage, and promising him *imperium* without end, and Eliot cultivates also the *pietas* of the classical hero when, in the wake of old Andrew Eliott, he renews the ancestral voyage in *The Dry Salvages*: 'Fare forward, voyagers.'

'Destiny' resounds with unmistakable import in the essays Eliot wrote while he composed *Four Quartets*. The woman who confers the heart of light remains a shade from the past who is allowed to impinge on the hero's consciousness only in so far as she renews his destiny. For here, in the first *Quartet*, he is a hero orchestrating a private future, not as yet an exemplar who speaks to us. We may overhear, but cannot share, his exclusive moment. Nor is it explained why love must turn so entirely to 'dust'. The same abrupt denial recurs in the midsummer night when couples dance, holding each other by the hand, feet rising and falling in rhythmic concord. For a time, the poet lends an eye to this recurrent festival of coupling and earth's fertility, but then, like a shot, comes his dark judgement that it amounts to nothing but 'dung and death'. The stern voice of denial is like that of the Puritan killjoy in Hawthorne's tale who rebukes and breaks up nuptial frolics at Merry Mount. Hawthorne was more aware of the moral ambiguity of the killjoy position: that so grave a sense of corruption, of 'dust' and 'dung', is itself corrupting. For it warps bonds of feeling.

Not love but art is one certain point of intersection with the timeless: a Chinese jar, created at some point in time, which 'still / Moves perpetually in its stillness'. As a schoolboy at Milton Academy, Eliot used to envy a room-mate whose grandmother had collected Chinese jars brought home by the Salem clippers. Here, the jar comes to represent the classic art to which Eliot now aspires. As the jar epitomises the achievements of Chinese civilisation, and as the garden, blending formality with mystery, epitomises the achievements of English civilisation, so Eliot seeks to fulfil his own tradition of New England divines who tried to convey the Word. Ordinary words 'slip, slide, perish, / Decay with imprecision, will not stay in place', but against the perpetual decay of language in the course of time Eliot has as his model 'The Word in the desert', language that has the permanence of scripture, as though graven on tablets of the law.

The initiating impulse for this enterprise comes from a silent, faceless companion at Burnt Norton: not the woman as a person, but love's transforming power. It starts as 'we', a shared experience, but Emily Hale's power to generate this came largely through memory and imagination. It did not depend on frequent meetings, and may have flourished the more with partings. So, the public face of Eliot's poetry obliterates Emily Hale, not only by an appropriate conversion of life into art, but by subsuming her unvoiced appeal in the 'voices of temptation' at the end of *Burnt Norton*. Temptation, for Eliot, meant love's sensual dross. From his earliest juvenilia, he showed a distrust of sensuality, a belief that love was too delicate to be enjoyed.

Eliot expected of Emily Hale an extraordinary feat: that her feeling should match his own need to transmute love into

'Love', a distilled concentrate that would never evaporate. Language cannot convey this feat: 'I can only say, *there* we have been; but I cannot say where.' The moment in the rose-garden, in the arbour when the rain beat, or in the draughty church in the November mist – such scenes point to place, and affirm that infinity was shared. If he etherealised her presence in verse, letters record the substance of the ordinary: she wore sturdy shoes for country walks; he met her trains; he went with her to Cook's to buy tickets for her holiday in Guernsey with Jeanie McPherrin. Yet, through poetry, Eliot was asking for 'freedom' from desire, from the obligations of the usual 'action', from all 'outer compulsion' in order to live 'by a grace of sense'.

It is impossible as yet to know if Emily Hale understood this challenge and, if so, how she met it. My guess is that she was exalted by Eliot's ideal in the way that Emerson's listeners were intoxicated by his offer of spiritual power. One of her pupils at Smith College reported that she read aloud an advance typescript of the second poem, *East Coker*, 'as if it were a love-letter from God'. She gave a copy to a pupil, inscribing it 'From Emily Hale, a friend of T. S. Eliot'. Some time later, she retrieved the copy when she was going to meet Eliot, and returned it with a further inscription: 'From T. S. Eliot, a friend of Emily Hale'. She was, understandably, not quite content with beautiful friendship and hoped, even expected, that they might one day marry.

The Word, Eliot says, is most attacked by 'voices of temptation'. These were, the draft shows, a 'circling Fury' (derived from Vivienne) and a 'sweet' temptation (derived from Emily, in her marriageable aspect). To have yoked these together may seem as reductive as the note to *The Waste Land* which asserts that 'all the women are one woman'. But here, I think, he owns to fear. To succumb to sweetness as he had once succumbed to Vivienne – now 'the crying shadow in the funeral dance' – would distract the poet from his duty to assume the Word.

So Eliot wove unrelated strands of his existence together 'in

344

an emotional whole', he told Anne Ridler. The fear of Vivienne, the love of Emily, the aims of art, and the endless reach of the religious life were brought together and cohere within the formal structure of the quartet. Outside poetry, the strands remained disparate, which is why we get such varied and sometimes conflicting reports of Eliot's behaviour: humorous, pious, domestic, distant. This leads to the common assumption that Eliot was a theatrical trickster, a deployer of masks in the sophisticated game of public manipulation, but such a view does no justice to the emotional unity of the poetry. For it is only through the poetry that we see the whole man, for whom the important ties were those that served to generate some feeling – it might be horror, it might be ardour – strong enough, extreme enough, to open him to 'vibrations beyond the range of ordinary men'.

Eliot's fascination with the extremities of the religious life came to him early, in his poems of 1914–15. 'The Burnt Dancer' and 'The Death of Saint Narcissus' show the origin of the refining fire of *Four Quartets* in which you 'move in measure like a dancer'. In 1935 Eliot revived the burning and dancing – dance as the precise, controlled movements of classical ballet (Eliot became a patron of ballet). The discipline of ballet is like the discipline of the religious life as Eliot began to understand it through the extreme demands of St John of the Cross.

This saint revealed the way down. The way up is now closed to the seeker, but its memory is to remain 'always' a high point of attainment. A draft of *Burnt Norton* ends with the divine light in repeated flashes that pulsate beyond the poem:

> Light
> Gone.
>
> Light
> Light of light
>
> Gone

*

Eliot could not hope to repeat that spontaneous intuition. Ridden by guilt in the four years between the first and second *Quartets*, he had now to begin the long ordeal of self-transformation. Beginning – this word reverberates through *East Coker* – once more from the bedrock of temporal existence, he set out to find the pattern of the perfect life.

The model for this life came to Eliot in earliest childhood through his mother's poems and her image of the Pilgrim Fathers. Her son's New World voyage takes off at the end of *East Coker*. Eliot had rehearsed it back in 1930, where a pilgrim approaches the New England shore as a promised land after the seventeenth-century ordeal of the sea. *Marina* had described the 'Bowsprit cracked with ice', the weak rigging, the rotten canvas, the leak, and the seams that needed 'caulking' in the same detail as Bradford's history of the voyage of the Pilgrim Fathers, written between 1630 and 1650: '. . . the ship was shroudly shaken, and her upper works made very leakie; and one of the maine beames in the midd ships was bowed and craked, which put them in some fear that the shipe could not be able to performe the voiage.' Some wished to go back, but others heartened them: 'And as for the decks and uper workes they would calke them as well as they could. . . . So they committed them selves to the will of God . . .'. For they were convinced, as another early historian, Edward Johnson, put it, that they were destined for 'the place where the Lord will create a new Heaven, and a new Earth in, new Churches, and a new Commonwealth together'.

Eliot's dream-voyage, too, makes for heaven, and East Coker is the point of departure. East Coker is the village in Somerset from which Andrew Eliott set out. In the poem his voyage is impelled by his rejection of the earthly life and its oblivious pleasures; he leaves behind him merrymakers who dance in their communal ring from time immemorial. A condemnation of them to 'Dung and death' repeats the Judge Blood force of *Marina*: Death to those 'who suffer the ecstasy of the animals', and Death to vanity in bright clothes, and Death to pigs 'who sit in the sty of contentment'. (Was this the holy Word, Hawthorne might have asked, or did the ancestral shade of Salem hover over Eliot's lips?)

It is from sexual union that Eliot recoils most violently, with an intolerance alien to Anglican tradition. He hastens couples to 'death' with a finality that suggests his own abortive marriage: the one dead end in his life. His first visit to the pretty village of East Coker, on foot, in June 1936, from an inn called The Three Choughs in Yeovil, Somerset, was at a grim time in his private life, with Vivienne, that month, threatening to go to America or, alternatively, to end as Daisy Miller, and at the same time Emily's breakdown. John Hayward, the first to read a draft of *East Coker* in February 1940, found it poignantly self-revealing. Its mood of 'disturbance' arises from pangs of love, rejected, unwanted, but forcing their way to the surface.* As in 'The Love Song of Saint Sebastian', sexual turmoil is magnified as the dissolution of the universe into chaos. Eliot feared this as the embrace of the Devil. The youthful would-be 'saint' denies sexual need; the ageing poet – exaggerating his age – deprecates 'the disturbance of the spring'. To belong to another is to become a 'creature' of 'summer heat'. Eliot had in mind the New England figure of Goodman Brown, who discovers sin in a dark wood when he stands with his bride 'beneath the canopy of fire', menaced by devilish enchantments.

In August 1937 Eliot went to stay with Sir Matthew Nathan at a manor house in West Coker, and from there re-explored East Coker. The poem retraces his approach that late summer day, looking down the lane in the haze of heat. The dahlias sleep. And then, as he hears a faint pipe, the present dissolves in a dream of the past: ancestors lift clumsy,

---

* There is some suggestion of a parallel with Yeats, but the alignment is forced. Eliot appears to draw on Yeats's terms in 'An Acre of Grass' – Yeats's denial of autumnal, wise serenity of age with folly and frenzy – but Eliot twists the allusion to fit his own more idiosyncratic case: an ageing man's fear of belonging to another (*EC*: II).

loam-clogged feet as they dance in a ring. Eliot will not 'keep time'. He maintains a spectatorial distance that is not only distance in time but a refusal of the rounds of temporal life. What alerts him is the dawn wind that beckons the emigrant to the New World. At this point Eliot joins in.

'I am here,' he says suddenly. 'In my beginning.'

Early in 1939 Eliot searched out his beginnings in the *Sketch of the Eliot Family* in the British Museum. There was, he discovered, an earlier phase of the family in Devon, where they had been respectable squires in the fourteenth and fifteenth centuries. One had been a knight of the shire for Devon in about 1430. In the poem, though, Eliot chose to ignore this and concentrate on the two centuries when the family lived at East Coker. He identified himself with the grave Tudor moralist Sir Thomas Elyot, grandson of Simon Elyot of East Coker, and Andrew, the cordwainer who left East Coker in 1669. Bold in their piety, both fulfilled the family motto, *Tace aut face*, 'Act or be silent'.

It was Eliot's view that family fortunes had declined from about 1914. By the 1930s and 1940s his brother and unmarried sisters lived in modest apartments compared with the large house that their father had built on Cape Ann. Eliot never returned to that house after 1915 – the family must have lost it – but he had it nostalgically in mind when he described the long-deserted house, left to the field mouse, at East Coker.

As the New World journey broke the pattern of generations, so Eliot broke with family expectations in 1915 to steer a lone course – the course that would ultimately revive family distinction as well as its boldest tradition of moral or spiritual frontiering. Eliot was past fifty when he launched a new course in *East Coker*. 'Old men ought to be explorers', he said, and though, in a sense, he was making an interior journey all his life, the course he set himself in 1940 was more dangerous and demanding than anything he had done before.

Despite previous efforts at change – marriage in 1915, conversion in 1927, the change of nationality, the vow of celibacy, and the termination of his marriage – Eliot seems to have felt early in 1940 that true inward change had yet to begin. It had, in fact, already begun, with the declaration of war, which broke a pattern of existence from 1933 to 1939: the regular spring or summer reunions with Emily Hale. The upheaval that followed her departure in September 1939 was the signal for a new and fiercer discipline of asceticism.

In this discipline Eliot was consciously following others in earlier centuries whom, he adds modestly, one cannot hope to emulate. It was still as untested as the 'vast waters' and infinitely remote farther shore must have seemed to those who ventured to colonise America. The English houses vanish and, in their place, the sea stretches. The explorer is determined to break the mould of the worldly life, to see its scenes recede behind him and hear its voices fade. He will be alone: this much he knows. So he goes forward into 'the dark' to be remade: 'O dark dark dark.' Cut off from all light (the visible world, the senses), he enters the mysterious dark night of the soul.

St John of the Cross speaks of the 'fortunate night' in which there is no light but 'that which burned in my heart'. It guides him 'more surely than the light of noon'. Samson, the other model, also waits in blind darkness 'amid the blaze of noon'. Such was to be Eliot's future in the forties and fifties, as he moved through the blaze of publicity that came with fame. In the central sections of the first two *Quartets*, he distinguishes one sort of darkness from another. There is the darkness of tube trains, where oblivious commuters shuttle to no purpose along the metalled rails of their lives; but descending lower (Eliot told his brother that he was thinking of the lift at Gloucester Road station – at rush hour it's hard to think of anything less spiritual) and lower yet, there is a different darkness: a conscious stripping of the self's props, knowledge, emotions, and, most risky, identity itself. The idea is that if divinity is unutterably other, remote, and hidden beneath a cloud of unknowing, it is necessary to strip oneself of everything one knows in order to encounter it.

Eliot said that this dark night was analogous to 'the drought' which is an essential stage in the progress of a mystic.

Throughout his career, he explores it in the urban waste, the desert, the jagged stair, the disturbing journey of the Magi, the grim voyage, and here Samson's period of abasement – betrayed by his wife, a prisoner of the Philistines – on his way to becoming God's agent. Eliot follows Milton in his focus on the period of waiting in darkness that was, for Eliot, so clearly the route to the perfect life that in his poetry (where there is little attainment) it comes to be the perfect life itself.

All these physical and psychic ordeals demonstrate a single condition, a state of trial, with its strains of terror, emptiness, and patience. The state is dramatised with increasing subtlety until, in *East Coker*, Eliot is able to speak the riddling language of St John of the Cross which contains the secret of transformation:

In order to arrive at what you do not know
    You must go by a way which is the way of ignorance.
In order to possess what you do not possess
    You must go by the way of dispossession.
In order to arrive at what you are not
    You must go through the way in which you are not.*

This method abjures soul-searching – no clamouring self-hatred – for a quiet nonentity: 'where you are is where you are not'.

The monk Thomas Merton has described St John of the Cross as the 'most hidden of saints', and 'the patron of those who have a vocation that is thought, by others, to be spectacular, but which, in reality, is lowly, difficult, and

* When Eliot uses the words of St John of the Cross they are not twisted as are many other allusions in Eliot's earlier poetry. The words are taken from *The Ascent of Mount Carmel*, I. xiii, in the translation of E. Allison Peers which was in Eliot's library:

In order to arrive at that which thou knowest not,
Thou must go by a way that thou knowest not.
In order to arrive at that which thou possessest not,
Thou must go by a way that thou possessest not.
In order to arrive at that which thou art not,
Thou must go through that which thou art not.

obscure. He is the patron . . . and the Master of those whom God had led into the uninteresting wilderness of contemplative prayer.' Uninteresting? The word defies us to understand this neutral state far removed from overt holiness.

So, Eliot set himself to negate the senses and all worldly notions of success in order to become a vacuum for grace to fill. The *via negativa* demands a new and more extreme surrender, as Eliot phrased it, 'inoperancy of the . . . spirit'. The saint's chart of the narrow way to perfection is marked with the words 'Nothing – nothing – nothing – nothing.' To do nothing is not a passive state, explained Father Bede Frost in *St John of the Cross*, which was reviewed in the *Criterion* in April 1938, 'it is the highest activity of which the soul is capable, the deliberate and sustained effort of the soul to suffer, in the sense of allow, all that God may will to effect in it'. *East Coker* records Eliot's attempt to put this into practice:

I said to my soul be still, and let the dark come upon you
Which shall be the darkness of God.

Eliot had earlier imagined drastic attempts at transformation through violent death in his 'saint' poems and in the many death-fragments of the *Waste Land* manuscript. The way down of the *Quartets* is a more gradual process. Its main challenge is patient 'waiting'. The Catholic mystics stress the length of the undertaking: usually it takes years. *The Cloud of Unknowing* insists that nothing must be forced: no flogging to bring on a glow, no excess fasts to induce hallucinations, no staring eyes, no humble bleats, if you please. The Rule of the Reformed Carmelites, which St John of the Cross joined, was severe but not fanatical. The saint warned monks and nuns not to perform any penance because it gave them satisfaction. This would be 'animal penance', and would gain them nothing by its mechanical extravagance. The ascetic stunts favoured by the deluded 'saints' in Eliot's student poems would not do by these exacting standards. Nor, too, the strained philosophic vigils in Paris in 1911. In 1940 he preaches an opposite course: 'Wait without thought, for you are not ready for thought', repeating the fourteenth-century dictum that 'interior work proceeds through lack of knowing, patience, and love'.

The discipline does include love. Eliot has not forgotten Burnt Norton, but is now determined to rid himself of 'Undisciplined squads of emotion'. He must retrain love to serve his solitary search for perfection. 'The Lover', he jotted in his notes, is 'ill of love', so ill that an operation is necessary. Eliot told Anne Ridler that the operation was 'the heart of the matter'. It's a strange heart, bleak and obsessed with pain. The scene switches from a patient under ether 'conscious of nothing' to a patient awake to surgery. The surgeon with 'bleeding hands' (Christ) plies his steel knife to the patient's 'distempered part'. Eliot would have us witness this in slow motion. A reader with no taste for torture feels like a reluctant voyeur.

The treatment involves an agonising freeze of the fevered senses. 'I faint with heat', Eliot's manuscript notes explain, ' – must be frozen in the lonely North.'

The patient quakes as 'the chill ascends from the feet to knees'. The fever 'sings' – it issues in poetry – as it is extinguished. At length, an ice cap 'reigns' over destructive fire. Triumphant, the now 'frigid' lover shows off the briars of his punishment. The briars hint at a parallel with Christ's crown of thorns, but the claim seems untenable. The insistence on blood and pain is too like the repellent masochism in Eliot's 'saint' poems.

He admitted that this was 'very un-English' and, when George Every called it 'Jansenist', he seized the label. Jansenism was a movement in seventeenth-century France which seems interchangeable with Puritanism in its insistence on the degraded and helpless state of man. Eliot argued that in certain men of intense penetrating power, there is 'a Jansenism of the individual biography'.

While Eliot explored these ordeals of the inner life, he continued to conduct a life of outward conformity as he shuttled to the office on the Underground in his bowler hat. Perhaps this was his own form of uninteresting neutrality.

William Force Stead pictured him at this time: his hair, still dark, was parted on one side and sleeked down, perhaps with a dab of brilliantine. His expression behind his spectacles was earnest, a little pensive or wistful, with a hint of humour at the corners of the mouth. He continued to play the Old Buffer, particularly with Virginia Woolf, who could be relied on to see through the mask. On 16 February 1940 she saw the 'great yellow bronze mask all draped upon an iron framework. An inhibited, nerve drawn; dropped face – as if hung on a scaffold of heavy private brooding.'

Such private extremity in 1940 matched public extremity at the time of the Blitz. Eliot offered to those undergoing the war an acceptance of a process of suffering. He wrote on 8 February 1940: 'We can have very little hope of contributing to any immediate social change; and we are more disposed to see our hope in modest and local beginnings, than in transforming the whole world at once. . . . We must keep alive aspirations which can remain valid throughout the longest and darkest period of universal calamity and degradation.' *East Coker*, with its long view of history and deeply felt sense of place, its feeling for the antiquity of England and for the contemporaneity of the past, gave assurance that the age-old routines of the English village would survive the disasters of the present. For all its rigour, *East Coker* is the most optimistic of the *Quartets*. Helen Gardner recalled the extraordinary impact of this poem at the darkest moment of the war. Published as a supplement to the *New English Weekly*'s Easter number (21 March 1940) it had to be reprinted in May and June, and within a year sold nearly 12,000 copies.

At this time the thirties poets – the 'Pylon Boys' as the Faber poets were called – declined in public favour. Maynard Keynes, writing to the *New Statesman and Nation* in October 1939, noted that the intelligentsia of the Left had been loudest in demanding that the Nazis be resisted, but 'scarcely four weeks have passed before they remember that they are pacifists and write defeatist letters to your columns, leaving the defence of freedom to Colonel Blimp and the Old School

Tie'. John Hayward reported with his usual acidity that a poet called Barker was moving heaven to be sent to Japan. With other writers doing a bunk (Auden and Isherwood to America; MacNeice to Ireland), the recent death of Yeats, and the success of *East Coker*, Eliot became from this time pre-eminent in England.

As he completed the poem, he told John Hayward that he spent the weekend playing chess, eating large meals, and reading the detective novels of Peter Cheyney. How does this comfy Eliot fit the tormented penitent whom Virginia Woolf glimpsed at the time he was writing *East Coker*? I don't think it a blind, but that his antithetical sides were interdependent, the domestic cat of regular habits and the daring pioneer on the frontiers of consciousness. The two sides worked together most effectively in the special circumstances of the war when there was less interference with their balance: fewer office demands and no social ones. As an air-raid warden, Eliot had to visit houses in his area, and talk to people about stirrup pumps and incendiary bombs, and he spent two nights a week fire-watching, but he saw almost nothing of intellectuals. The Woolfs were more often marooned in Rodmell, and stayed there permanently after their home in Mecklenburgh Square was bombed later in 1940. The Hayward circle had broken up. Frank Morley was working at Harcourt Brace in New York. John Hayward himself was evacuated from Bina Gardens by Lord Rothschild, and carried off as his guest to Merton Hall, Cambridge. It is clear from Hayward's bulletins to Morley that Eliot kept Hayward's feelers at bay with lengthy reports of air-raid practice in the basement in Russell Square and comic accounts of his experiences in the black-out. Hayward had to try hard to squeeze a drop of juice out of him. William Force Stead said that Eliot's address in 1940 was still something of a secret: 'I believe', he adds, 'he is an introvert living mostly in himself and only now and then seeking distraction.'

Eliot's two greatest poems, *The Waste Land* and the *Quartets*, seem to speak directly to their times, yet both draw on private, sometimes strange experience, to generalise for all

1. (*above left*) William Greenleaf Eliot (1811-87). 'The standard of conduct was that which my grandfather had set'.

2. (*above right*) Eliot's mother, Charlotte Stearns. Her poetry mapped the states between loss and recovery of faith.

3. (*above*) Eliot in St Louis, 1892-3, aged about four.

4. (*right*) Eliot with his father in 1898. Henry Ware Eliot, Sr died in 1919 convinced that his son had ruined his life.

5. A late child. Aged eight at the gate of his birthplace, 2635 Locust Street, St Louis, with mother, cousin Henrietta, (left) and sisters Margaret and (obscured) Marian.

6. Eliot as a boy

7. Aged nineteen (1907). A student at Harvard, he was writing poems about the fragility of emotional experience.

8. The outer harbour and porch of the Eliot house, Eastern Point, Gloucester, Mass., (1909) 'What seas what shores what grey rocks...'

9. (*left*) Eliot graduated in 1910. That summer with his favourite sister, Marian, at Eastern Point.

10. (*right*) The all-sail fishing fleet in Gloucester harbour. The fishermen's dangers at sea became the emblems for spiritual daring.

11. (*above*) Eliot the sailor c. 1911-13.

12. Emily Hale, at twenty-three, as Eliot would have remembered her when he left for England in 1914. Her favourite photo.

13. Vivienne Eliot in London. 'I owe her everything', Eliot wrote to his father soon after their marriage in 1915.

14. 'He laughed like an irresponsible foetus'. Bertrand Russell with Lytton Strachey and Lady Ottoline Morrell at the time he toyed with Vivienne, 1916.

15. Vivienne at Garsington, 1920: 'My nerves are bad...Yes, bad. Stay with me'. (*The Waste Land*)

16. Eliot with his mother, who visited England in the summer of 1921.

17. 'Eliot will be there in a four-piece suit'. Visiting his publisher, Virginia Woolf.

18. Across London Bridge, spire of St. Magnus the Martyr, whose 'inexplicable splendour' provides momentary relief in *The Waste Land*.

19. (*left*) In 1925 Eliot joined the publishing firm of Faber and Gwyer.

20. (*above*) Vivienne, December 1930. Sent to Eliot's sister Marian.

21. (*above*) Eliot on the Massachusetts shore in 1932-3, with Professor Theodore Spencer of Harvard.

22. (*right*) 'Twenty years and the spring is over' ('New Hampshire'): Eliot at Mountain View House, Randolph, NH, June 1933.

23. (*above*)
Sweeney: 'Any
man might do a
girl in'. Rupert
Doone's *Sweeney
Agonistes* (1935
revival)

24.(*right*) John
Hayward: friend,
bibliographer, and
adviser on *Four
Quartets*.

25. (*right*) Burnt Norton:
'And the pool was filled
with water out of sunlight'.

26. (*below*) The rose
garden at Burnt Norton in
Gloucestershire.

27. (*below*) 'And the deep lane insists on the direction / Into the village'. Eliot's photo (1937) of the road from West Coker to East Coker in Somerset.

28. (*above*) 'The granite teeth' of the Dry Salvages offshore from Cape Ann.

29. Little Gidding, Huntingdonshire: 'You are here to kneel where prayer has been valid'.

30. The temptation of spiritual pride. *Murder in the Cathedral*, Canterbury, 1935 (with Robert Speaight as Becket).

31. (*left*) Eliot with Helen Hayes (Agatha) and Ruth Lodge (Mary) in *The Family Reunion*.

32. (*below*) Eliot on the set of *The Family Reunion*, 1939, watches a perplexed Mary (Ruth Lodge) with the haunted Harry (Michael Redgrave).

33. (*above left*) Eliot called this 'a masterpiece': Emily Hale with flowers 1935.

34. (*above*) Emily Hale – recovering – with Eliot at Woods Hole, 1936

35. (*left*) Eliot at Woods Hole, 1936

36. Eliot at 'The Shambles' in Surrey where he wrote the last two *Quartets* 1941-2 from left to right: Constance Moncrieff, Lina Mirrlees, Hettie James (back), Ellen James (holding wool), Hope Mirrlees, Eliot.

37. (*right*) Mary Trevelyan.

38. (*above left*) Eliot and Emily Hale in Vermont, 1946. He came to see her perform in Noel Coward's *Blithe Spirit*.

39. (*above*) Eliot at Woods Hole, 1946.

40. (*left*) Emily, after Eliot declined to marry her, 1950.

41. Eliot on vacation with his wife, Valerie.

time. In *East Coker* private turmoil is reflected in a world war, which is reflected in turn in cosmic disorder. Eliot takes these Transcendentalist leaps from one order of existence to another to the outermost reaches of the universe, but then, lapsing into prosaic terms, admits that this exercise has its origin in the pangs of love. His advisers, Hayward and Faber, missed the comic point when they deplored the lapse from high style. The bathos was deliberate: 'That was a way of putting it – not very satisfactory.' Poetry or philosophy is undercut as an absurd elaboration of private truth. The blunt truth is the struggle in middle age to cope with disturbing emotions, and at the same time to break the deadening round of habit.

Middle age, Eliot found, was a time of choice, not the retrievable choices of youth, but those that risk the soul. The worst danger is to avoid choice, to lapse into 'autumnal serenity', to 'cover yourself in forgetful snow', the death-in-life that Eliot had always feared: in the round of Boston tea parties of 'Prufrock', in the London work-routines of *The Waste Land*, and now in the tube trains of *East Coker* which carry eminent men of letters, merchants, civil servants, chairmen of many committees, Directors, and readers of the *Stock Exchange Gazette* to Hampstead, Putney, and Ludgate. Eliot was one of these Directors, on his way to Hampstead (to bath at the Fabers' since his landlady could provide only one jug of water). In his capacity as Director, he was the heir of those old English Eliots who went round and round in a ring. *East Coker* rebels not only against the social round, but against all pointless recurrence: the recurrent lifespans of passing generations, and the repeated destructions of history. Mere physical existence in the opening line, 'In my beginning is my end,' finds its alternative in the final triumphant claim to eternal life: 'In my end is my beginning.'

Each person must apply the formula for transformation to his own experience. In *East Coker*, the formula comes to life as St John of the Cross gives way to the American progenitor who had the nerve to make the crossing. Eliot must follow. He must undertake a voyage, not of course in actuality (though he does draw on sailing memories), but in spirit. This will be the trial of the next *Quartet*. He must renew the ancestral state of mind: venturesomeness ('Home is where one starts from') and more: a willing, almost reckless exposure to the unknown.

Eliot switches back and forth from English to American perspectives. *Four Quartets* is thought of as an English work with some reference to America, but the reverse may be true. The very notion of an Old World implies a New World perspective from which 'the old world may be seen, made explicit'. The sequence of poems, as it evolved early in 1940 when it was to conclude with the third *Quartet*, had at this point a plot that was essentially American: a recoil from civilisation to cast oneself into the wilderness, in this case the sea. The 'three quatuors' would move from the civilised enclosures of the English garden with its box hedge, straight walk, and concrete pool, to the wild ocean; from the predictable routines of the English village to encounter

> Through the dark cold and empty desolation,
> The wave cry, the wind cry, the vast waters
> Of the petrel and the porpoise.

The waterway beckons the American – Ishmael, Huck, Arthur Gordon Pym – as a mysterious and terrible power. Eliot's sea is strewn with treacherous rocks and drowned men; his Mississippi in spring flood carries its usual 'cargo' of bodies and chicken coops. This nature is not English. It is not the nurse, the guide, the guardian. It is alien to man; he cannot interfuse with its moods. He might pit himself against it, like Ahab or Gloucester fishermen, or he might beat obedient to its control. Poetry must explore the frontiers of the spirit, Eliot wrote on 27 April 1939, but 'these frontiers are not the surveys of geographical explorers conquered once for all and settled'. He imagines rather a perpetual frontier, a perpetual mystery on the borders of the known world.

The end of such a voyage is a divine call. *Marina* sketched a complete scenario for a task which the *Quartets* undertake only in part. For they show with admirable honesty that, in practice, the voyager can't make it, or not in the same way. Too flawed now for the planned approach to grace, the voyager can hope only for a haven, an orderly life of prayer and observance. In the course of writing *East Coker* Eliot changed plan. It was part of the exercise in humility to put off hope of attainment to a fourth poem, and so prolong the trial by water with a further trial by fire.*

If in 1940–1 Eliot was unfit as yet for grace, he could still hold to love. Distanced from Emily by the war which kept him in England and her in the States, Eliot defines love as an emotion that is truest when here or there do not matter. Love survives with its promise of a further 'intensity'. It is a dream love letter saying in public what Eliot possibly could not say in private. It is love cherished like a vision across the sea, to be reached by a most gallant venture. This dream stirred Eliot more than the actual presence of Emily Hale.

Separation and chastity: these were the conditions of continued love as Eliot jotted pencil notes for the conclusion:

> Alone – the ice cap
> Separated from the surfaces of human beings
> To be reunited in the communion

The first draft set it out clearly: one must 'be separated' for 'a further union, a deeper communion'.

*

Where does one's beginning start? Is the beginning somewhere along the line of forebears? Or is one shaped, unaware, by some scene of childhood? When he was homesick, at first, in London, Eliot wrote to his mother: 'I always think of

---

* Eliot told Hayward that he began at this point to see four poems on the basis of the elements: air, earth, water, and fire. This is a late and superficial organising idea. Eliot wrote to Professor William Matchett on 19 Jan. 1949: 'Certainly by the time that poem [*East Coker*] was finished I envisaged the whole work as having four parts which gradually began to assume, perhaps only for convenience sake, a relation to the four seasons and the four elements.'

return to St Louis as meaning Concord grapes on the table in the blue fruit basket.' Now, in December 1940, Eliot turned to his beginnings in St Louis, where the rhythm of the Mississippi beats inside him in the nursery bedroom, in the backyard where he plays, and in the gaslit nights of the early 1890s. The river is present even in 'the smell of grapes on the autumn table'. The Mississippi, Eliot said, 'made a deeper impression upon me than any other part of the world'. He remembered it as 'a treacherous and capricious dictator' which in flood 'may obliterate the low Illinois shore to a horizon of water, while in its bed it runs with a speed such that no man or beast can survive in it. At such times, it carried down human bodies, cattle and houses. At least twice, at St. Louis, the western and eastern shores have been separated by the fall of bridges.' A native does not merely see the river, he experiences it: he accepts the river god as his god.

In the third *Quartet*, Eliot took up the challenge of autobiography: to make sense of one's life. This was his climactic effort to fuse past and future in a single pattern. To do so, he must once more sink back into the past to extract the defining scenes: the childhood on the longest river; the ten-year-old peering into a rockpool on Cape Ann; the youth sailing his precarious course through the granite teeth of the rocks. There, far off in the past, were intuitions of the divine nature: the power and terror of the Mississippi in flood, an implacable destroyer, a 'strong brown god', and the sea with its 'Many gods and many voices'.

A group of three rocks called the Dry Salvages was the last landmark when the young Eliot had sailed from Cape Ann to Maine. Four and a half miles offshore from Rockport, the farthest mainland of Massachusetts projecting out into the Atlantic, the Salvages consist of two great ledges. The Big Salvage is always out of water, but the Dry Salvages are hidden at high tide. The name, it is said, derived from the fact that the dangerous, partly hidden rocks reminded settlers of the red men, the 'savages'. The ledges, which have been the scene of many shipwrecks, extend far under water; big seas break over them, and only seamen who know the channels

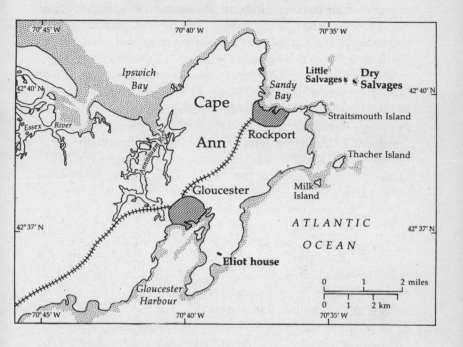

can make the passage safely. In a fog, Eliot and his classmate Harold Peters would hear the 'groaner', a whistling buoy east of Thacher's Island, scene of a famous shipwreck in the seventeenth century. Once, in a nineteen-foot knockabout, Eliot and Peters rounded Mount Desert Rock in a fog and heavy sea. They took refuge on Duck Island, and after a rough night and with a gale still blowing, made it to the little harbour at Somesville, Maine. The logbook shows a sketch of Eliot unmooring in the wind with the caption: 'Heroic work by the swab.'

This forbidding sea with its hidden rocks, its 'sea howl', its warning foghorn, and multitudes of drowned fishermen, opens up the farthest horizon of the *Quartets*. The sailor, exposed to a force beyond human control and a time beyond history, feels 'the ground swell, that is and was from the beginning'. The sea is in touch with its genesis, and to be adrift there is like moving on the face of creation.

At first Eliot planned a 'sea picture' only, then approached the sea by way of the river. The river is tamed to some extent by human history, its commerce and bridges. The sea is untamed, unchanged, eternal. At the land's edge the sea (eternal time) and the land (historical time) encroach upon each other. The sea's salt is on the briar rose; rocks, the farthest point of land, jut out to sea. These rocks are a point of departure for the poet who, from his place in time's scheme, sets out on the timeless sea.

Eliot's own experience at the edge of time – as sailor, as poet, as pilgrim – provides the live matter for generalisation. A poem about time and how to conquer time appears, to many readers, philosophical, but Eliot was not, he insisted, a philosopher. He was not concerned with abstract thought but with states of feeling. He once said, 'I suspect that what is often held to be a capacity for abstract thought, in a poet, is capacity for abstract feeling – something much more properly the poet's business.' *Four Quartets* gives to such feelings a sequential order that would hold good at any time, in any place, for those who demand more of themselves than a routine life. Illumination is followed by the darkness of humility, which is followed, in turn, by an almost reckless daring, and finally by a resolute calm. Such feelings are too rare for conventional statement. They are explored through four landscapes, each of which provides only a starting-point for the complex interior landscape of each stage of the soul's progress. Each is at the edge, what Eliot calls 'the point of intersection of the timeless'. And although he says that to be there is 'an occupation for the saint' and not, he adds modestly, for 'most of us', in fact this is exactly where the poem proves Eliot to be as he frames an ideal order from the turbulent feelings of the private life.

It is not before the world but out of sight 'between the rocks' that a convert must test the reach of his faith. And farther out, in the lap of creation, where there is nothing else – no human or intellectual distraction – is some naked confrontation of which Eliot can speak only indirectly. His venture is always to confront 'reality', his word for whatever lies beyond the 'Unreal city'. He believes that 'reality' exists – it comes to him in the silence that obliterates the twittering world – but he is never sure if he can meet it. Eliot despised a watered-down Christianity of sweet promises. He looked to the havoc of the sea.

Eliot first rehearsed this voyage in the long narrative which Pound cut in its entirety from the *Waste Land* manuscript. The hardy Gloucester fishermen who sail through winter seas to the Grand Banks were Eliot's boyhood heroes, and their journey, terrible as it is, does turn its back on the urban waste. Eliot did, at one stage, counter London with the venturing nerve of his native tradition. The draft was like a scene from Melville or, more likely, Poe's 'Narrative of Arthur Gordon Pym' in its visionary horrors and approach to the ice. This native strain remained part of Eliot in all the fraught journeys in his poetry that find a final expression in *The Dry Salvages*.

In 1921 he foresaw disaster: the ship strikes an iceberg, and goes down. Can this be God's will? 'If Another knows, I know I know not'. In 1940–1 a voyager again braves the sea, conscious of the menace to all who venture from their natural habitat. He is in a 'drifting boat', at the mercy of winds and currents, yet there is a vein of optimism. The urge to 'Fare forward' echoes Whitman and, through him, Columbus, voyagers with inextinguishable visions in their heads. 'Sail forth,' urges Whitman, 'bound where mariner has not yet dared to go.' The daring in *The Dry Salvages* recovers the recklessness of Whitman's pioneer: 'And we will risk the ship, ourselves and all' seeking 'You, strew'd with the wrecks of skeletons, that, living, never reach'd you.' Eliot, too, has seen the bone on the beach. Stretched on the far-flung mesh of the sestine,* to which he clings as he moves on, he takes in the terror of an ocean littered with the wrecks of those who were not strong enough to survive the alien element.

Going to sea is itself an act of faith. The sailor drifts in a state of unattached devotion when, suddenly, he hears a bell that warns of death and judgement. Appalled by the destruction and 'silent withering' of all life, accompanied by 'the soundless wailing', he asks the overwhelming question: 'Where is there an end of it'? There is no bitterness, only surrender to a reality he cannot fathom. The repeated 'There is no end of it' finds an answer in what appears an afterthought: there is no point to existence except, he adds, the divine spirit that sustained the life of Christ. Death no longer appals, and Eliot sinks into massive repose, content now to lie near his ancestors in St Michael's Church at East Coker.

The quiet end is taken by some to be a poetic failure. But the greatness of Eliot's conception lies in the integrity with which he backs down from dreams of attainment in favour of modest expectations – modest, in view of the glimpse of divine light at Burnt Norton, the call in *Marina*, and, going back, the 'Silence' in the Boston street. Progress will not, in his case, follow the perfect sequence. After the third repeated effort, he must acknowledge his mere human status and his mortality. He must return to the once-despised earth, and nourish the soil. He is now convinced that earthly life can be 'significant' even if not inspired with visionary light. The final notes of the third *Quartet* play out his acceptance of life on these restricted terms, an acceptance hard won, and itself a measure of moral progress. He is not, after all, one of the saints. This very recognition is an advance in the difficult exercise in humility.

The Waste Land concludes with a dramatic progression into the mountains. There are no such peaks of attainment in *Four Quartets*, no thunderous message. Eliot owns that for

---

* The sestine or sestina (as in *The Dry Salvages*: II) is 'a poem of six six-line stanzas, in which the line-endings of the first stanza are repeated, but in a different order, in the other five' (*OED*).

him, as for other people, the most to be looked for is the odd hint or guess that comes in rare 'unattended' moments when he drifts into the interface between time and the timeless. Part of the exercise in humility was not to play up, or even expect, progression. Eliot was bent on accuracy, not drama. The later *Quartets* are a corrective to the self-absorbed heroics of Harry when he exits to follow the bright angels. What drama remains lies in a renunciation so subtle that it seems, even to astute readers, to fall flat. Such readers do not see that drama is a consolation that Eliot has refused. It is braver, and certainly more realistic, to face one's sheer ordinariness, to expect no divine call, to write (as Hopkins put it) letters to 'dearest Him who lives alas! away', and still to go on trying to perfect existence. That is what Eliot now meant by 'action'. The desperate valour of the voyager gives way to unseen action that might go on in the obscurest of lives.

So it was that Eliot finally renounced an ambition which, in early years, sent Narcissus out of town to avoid the common press of thighs and knees in order to become 'a dancer to God'; sent the pilgrim of *The Waste Land* to the far-off mountains to surrender to divine control; and sent the 'turning' convert of *Ash-Wednesday* into the desert to cry 'unto Thee'. The impulse to turn from a contemptible society was reversed in the winter of 1940–1, when Eliot came to concede an interdebtedness with his kind without which he must forfeit the very religious hopes that, for so long, had seemed to set him apart. The terror and isolation of the sea turned him back, full circle, to the timebound land he had left, 'to know the place for the first time'. It is there, not at the extremity of the sea's jaws, that he must live and act and find matter for future poems and plays.

This was not a retreat, but a new challenge. He had to find a way to use what he knew of the perfect life of the spiritual élite to improve the life of ordinary people. The injunctions he offers – 'Prayer, observance, discipline, thought and action' – are not as mysteriously thrilling as '*Datta, Dayadvam, Damyata*', but, like the Ten Commandments, they have the distinct advantage of being plain and attainable.

The Dry Salvages is about the frontiers of action where a significant life is made. There are two struggles, first with the ghosts of the past, then with the ghosts of the future. Memories, expectations: these must dissolve in the timeless pattern of spiritual autobiography.

The memory of Burnt Norton, which might have led another man into 'affection' and the 'security' of family bonds, came to be for Eliot the basis of a quite different life which seems always to have hovered on his horizon. He must switch biographic plots, as Harry, his portent, had switched to the plot of salvation. Leave father and mother and follow me, Christ said. Eliot had planned at one point to explore the 'meaning of "mother" & "father" ', but abandoned this, retaining an invocation to the Virgin. Looking back to Burnt Norton, he now decides: 'We had the experience but missed the meaning.' It had been an alert. The miraculous light and the children's voices (like the children's voices that brought on the conversion of St Augustine): all signs point one way.

Looking back at his life from the timeless perspective, Eliot discounts biography. The past, he says categorically, is not mere 'sequence' or even 'development', and to see it in this way would be as bogus as to spell out a life from palms, tea leaves, entrails, or psychoanalysis. Character composed by such routines, said Eliot (thinking of Freud), 'has all the defects of the synthetic substitute; its actions are tediously predictable; it is always unconvincing, and usually false'. For the significant life is an imaginative act. A man like Eliot becomes significant precisely because he conceives a shape to his life as opposed to a ready-made formula imposed upon it. Eliot's distrust of biography made it inevitable that he should forbid it for himself. It was not only reserve, but a distrust of the fullness of the genre as practised in his century, crowding the 'unattended' moments which form the dominant figure in the carpet of our existence.*

* Eliot said after completing *The Dry Salvages*: 'We look in a poet as in a novelist, for what Henry James called the Figure in the Carpet.' Essay on 'Rudyard Kipling' in *A Choice of Kipling's Verse*, ed. T. S. Eliot (London: Faber, 1941), p. 15.

These transforming moments lie 'unattended' beneath the trivia of the external action, as Eliot put it explicitly: '. . . our own past is covered by the currents of action.' In a draft he uncovers the 'essential moments' of his own history: the vigils in Paris and the emotional quickening that came to him as a young man as he sailed off the coast of Cape Ann:

> Remember rather the essential moments
> > That were the times of birth and death and change
> > The agony and the solitary vigil.
> Remember also fear, loathing and hate,
>
> .   .   .   .
>
> The fresh new season's rope, the smell of varnish
> > On the clean oar, the drying of the sails,
> > Such things seem of least and most importance.
> So, as you circumscribe this dreary round,
> > Shall your life pass from you . . .

It seems to have been harder to integrate the 'moments of agony' that were as lasting as the moments of happiness. In his notes he jotted: 'problem of permanence of past pain.' He cannot, and must not, forget 'the ragged rock in the restless waters', torment like Vivienne's, not visible but there. On a calm day the rock appears merely a monument to past danger, but in the 'sudden fury' all the menace of the past returns, Harry haunted by Furies, and the 'circling fury' in a draft of *Burnt Norton*. Eliot's own life goes on like the longest river, bearing its carrion away, the remains of things done to others' harm: this moral burden will be there always.

From the past he turns to a future that is blighted by this past, and touched by nostalgic regret for sensations of love that must wither with time: the faded songs, 'Ecstasy' and 'May Morning', that Emily Hale sang in 1913 in a Boston drawing-room where young Tom Eliot sat applauding with his Hinkley cousins. Love will become a memory, like a spray of lavender pressed in a book yellowing with time. This future he foresaw even before he experienced love, and from the start it gave him a detachment that is not to be confused with worldly cool. It is an absolute detachment from time itself.

Eliot resolves to look to the future with 'an equal mind'. It is an idea that he derived first from the *Bhagavad-Gita*, studied at Harvard. He learnt disinterestedness from the Indian scriptures, not to be concerned with the fruits of action. In the third *Quartet*, he points to a battle scene where the god Krishna justifies the killing of kin to Arjuna, who shrinks from this outrage. Krishna urges Arjuna, as a member of the warrior class, to fulfil his *dharma*, to play his appointed role in a cosmic drama, and says that the slayer and the slain cannot comprehend the Lord's will. This is a sanctification of murder – we quite can see why Eliot adopts it to quiet his guilt, but sanctimonious self-interest is jarring in a poem of this calibre. We may be insects beside his intelligence, yet we can say no, most definitely no, by the standards of the Ten Commandments (Thou shalt not kill, which Eliot, as a Christian, might be expected to uphold). How can the command to fare forward regardless of the destruction of others be 'right action'?

At this time Eliot refused to concern himself about Vivienne during the bombardment of London. The practical Mary Trevelyan ventured to suggest that he move her to a place of safety. Though Eliot himself had now settled outside London, he replied that, in his wife's case, he had no authority to contravene court orders.

Eliot's characteristic form of action turns away to inward excruciation, as one draft shows: 'And Atonement makes action possible'. He must still fare forward, but as a flawed man, one of those who try but may not succeed. He belongs with those who have no definite vocation, and who still risk the journey into timelessness. The risk is to relinquish one's self in the vain hope of transformation. That way lies mental wreckage, to be washed up like the bone on the beach. The only hope is not to hope at all, which is to surrender all sense of personal future to those, in generations to come, who will make the same effort at perfection. He sees his future always in suspension between the flawed and the perfect life, like a traveller who has left one shore and has not reached the other, moving uncertain through the space of his lifespan.

In October 1940 Eliot moved out of London to become a paying guest of Hope Mirrlees, her mother, and aunt in their house at the top of a steep hill in Shamley Green, near Guildford in Surrey. After the bachelor quarters of the last six years, as Leonard Woolf put it, 'surrounded by curates', he was now surrounded by women. He read Uncle Remus aloud to them. The household was filled with evacuees from Wandsworth and Barking, between eighteen and twenty-two women and children, with a few husbands on Saturday nights. In the cosy overheated atmosphere of the 'Shambles' Eliot enjoyed his position as prize domestic pet amongst women who cherished numerous cats and dogs. Someone in the house called Cocky believed they would meet up with pets in the next world. Eliot would have relished the comic discrepancy between his venturesome inner life and the upholstered setting where conversation centred on the importance of the vet (constantly needed for the overfed dogs), and the nightly ventures of the Field Marshal (Margaret Behrens) hunting for her peke who took to chasing rabbits by moonlight. The only other male about was a decrepit gardener, Mr Turner, who was afraid of mice and a writer of letters of condolence to the royal family (he used the acknowledgements as testimonials). Eliot's letters from the Shambles carry his comic note of content in soothing female company. There was the regular German parade overhead each night, Eliot wrote to Polly Tandy on 3 November 1940, but so far no crumps nearer than a mile or so. A further comfort was a private cow, so no shortage of milk and butter. Enid Faber noticed that Eliot took on the comfortable look of a practical cat, by which she concluded that life at the Shambles must suit him. It was, Eliot told Virginia Woolf, the healthiest life in years.

This was the improbable setting in which Eliot dreamed up his most daring imaginative enterprise. The writing of The Dry Salvages was interrupted by weekly forays to a bombed

London. He usually went up on Wednesdays (driven by Sir Philip Gibbs), got through a few brief duties, and stayed either at the Belvedere Hotel in Kensington or with the Fabers, who had a reinforced basement shelter. On Thursdays and Fridays he did his fire-watching, playing patience to pass the time, and recuperated at Shamley Green over the weekend. He wrote on Mondays and Tuesdays. In the winter of 1940–1 he saw almost no one, and was free as never before to give his prime effort to poetry. He was always able to write plays intermittently, but for poetry he needed sustained concentration.

Eliot's most elusive self who disappears across the horizon of *The Dry Salvages* is not, he says, the same person who disembarks. The cosy Eliot of Shamley Green and the public Eliot of the many masks is superfluous to this hidden man, not to be known outside his work and, even there, vanishing into silence. Faceless, he relaxes to 'the sleepy rhythm' of the voyage or the poem as it wells in the mind. He is inchoate, carried along, always in the making. The passage, the poem itself, represents Eliot's homelessness in the Kensington period and during the war years. It is impossible to fix him through his past, or even through the saintly life of his ideal future. He is kin only to those who experience the fading of personal emotion, and fear defeat en route to the perfect life.

Eliot lacked the assurance of his Puritan fathers that the promised land lay ahead. Writing at a critical stage of the Second World War, he was more conscious of the likelihood of defeat. Each week he went up to a London that was partially destroyed, its continued existence more threatened than at any time in its history. At the very time that Eliot came to take action, to make the imaginative crossing to the New World, he found that his allegiance to the Old World had taken too deep a root. So Eliot's way forward turned out to be the way back. He jotted in his notes: 'To get beyond time & at the same time deeper into time.' He must now reconcile himself to a continual suspension in time, on the verge of 'hints and guesses'.

To keep the verge open is to retain the native posture of the

American: the openness of mind implied in the persistent 'Fare forward, voyagers'. He is urged on by a disembodied voice, like the alien pulse that beat in the arm of the voyager in *Marina*. This voice warns him to think of the lives of others. Future action must lie in his power to affect other lives, especially lives to come. The voice descants in the rigging, like the eerie quickening of the strings in the finale of Beethoven's A Minor Quartet, which Beethoven composed when he was deaf and which, Eliot said, had a sort of heavenly gaiety. The voice descants 'not to the ear' but to the spirit. It speaks 'not in any language', as Eliot himself wished to get '*beyond poetry*, as Beethoven, in his later works, strove to get *beyond music*'. Out at sea, at the farthest verge of time, there is a renewed intimation of immortality that was to bring him, in the final *Quartet*, into unison with the timeless poets of the past.

*

Eliot now set himself to imagine the 'unimaginable'. The last *Quartet* reaches for a sublimity that Eliot knew to be beyond him, beyond everyone. God has said: 'Thou canst not see my face, for there shall no man see me, and live.' Christ and the saints have faces. This unimaginable divinity is more remote, the unnameable creator. Eliot said that the poetry of the Bible (at its height in Psalms and Isaiah) was secondary to religious experience. The Bible must not be read as literature but as an experience of the Word. The problem for the religious poet, Eliot went on, is that he is dependent on the experience but cannot command it. He can speak the Word only if the divine spark enters him.

This would be the ideal conclusion to spiritual autobiography. In the middle two *Quartets*, Eliot had undertaken the descent into the dark night of humility. Now, he set before himself the possibility of ascent, but it would depend upon the yield of his own life.

Eliot had created a framework into which God-given life might be breathed. That breath had flitted through the garden at Burnt Norton. Then, between the first and second *Quartets*, came what, in Eliot's eyes (though not in any public view), was the prime sin of his life, and hope of beatitude was put aside for a Thibet of penitence. His solution to sin was to recall the design of a life in which abasement was essential to the holy scheme of recovery: the pattern given in Exodus, and repeated in the lives of prophets, Christ, and the Christian saints and mystics. One reason why Eliot turned from the theatre back to poetry may have been the need to explore the design of spiritual autobiography again, and again, and yet a fourth time, in order to wring from his life that classic pattern.

This life, in past centuries or in the present of 1941–2, always has a single aim: to recover the divine. It might well not happen at once, or in the space of *Four Quartets*, but it was to happen at some stage in the future, even if that event lay beyond life itself. That consummation Eliot forecast from the 'Shantih', the peace which passeth understanding, echoing on after *The Waste Land*.

A muted longing for renewal breathes through the opening of the last *Quartet*. If only it would come now. He imagines how it would be: how the sun would flame the ice of his body. For Eliot it was late middle age; the senses were frozen; and as he looked now to the winter of his being, he wondered if the divine fire that seemed so remote would ever quicken him.

The private struggle goes in tandem with the set pattern of spiritual autobiography. The tension between private tumult and set form, found in the classic arts, was demonstrated for Eliot's generation most stunningly by the Russian Ballet. The abandon of Nijinsky's leap in *Le Spectre de la rose* – Nijinsky said that he would simply forget to come down – was contained within the strict decorum of the classical positions. Eliot had this particular ballet in mind as he wrote the last *Quartet*. On 10 December 1941, when Hitler was at the gates of Moscow, Eliot blithely wrote to *The Times* to urge that the Ballet be invited for a season in London.

The danger of an additional *Quartet*, as he realised, was that the individual struggle might not hold its own. If the formula became too dominant, the poem would lose its life. By the end of the third *Quartet* the formula and the poet were pulling in harmony, set for unambitious but continuous action. In the fourth *Quartet*, Eliot took an enormous risk. Poised over the turning rim of the wheel, he now went for the hub, the still point. This was his Nijinsky leap. Could he achieve that sustained height or must he fall back into the repeated round of purgation? An honest reading of the scale of perfection would indicate his final state: would it be purgatory or beatitude?

Eliot's initial notes, as well as his first typescript of July 1941, suggest that his first impulse was to look to beatitude. The dumb spirit, he imagines, would stir. The high points of his past are answered by a burst of light from the rising sun.

The initiating scene is this flaming light, and a pilgrim kneeling in a secluded church, the site of a devout community in the seventeenth century. Little Gidding is the only one of the four places that had no autobiographic association, nor is it mentioned in Eliot's plan. It could have been, he admits, any of a number of holy places. This was simply the most convenient, 'Now and in England'. There, deliberately, he placed himself in his imagination, in the icy brilliance of the winter light, in prayer. Would the divine spirit descend 'now' in a place where 'prayer has been valid'?

Eliot had to find a place to come to rest, and it had to answer certain needs. He wished to reaffirm the devotional life as practised long ago at Little Gidding, where two brothers and a sister, Nicholas, John, and Susanna Ferrar, developed a unique blend of the domestic and monastic. Their community (of about forty people) had gone off to a lonely part of Huntingdonshire to found their own way of life which conformed, at the same time, to the strict rules of their faith. It may be the closest phenomenon in Anglican history to the American Puritan impulse to go into the wilderness to found a 'city on a hill'.*

The word 'now' is crucial to *Little Gidding*. Now – when Eliot planned the poem some time in the first half of 1941 – was the Blitz. On 16 May 1941, 3,000 civilians were killed or injured in one air-raid. The rest of Europe had fallen to Hitler, and England was in imminent danger of invasion. Little Gidding was particularly appropriate because it, too, had suffered damage in time of war, and had survived it. After the community gave refuge to Charles I, Cromwell's soldiers ransacked the church in the winter of 1646.† They ripped out the organ and the pulpit, which they burnt outside, and threw the font, lectern, and engravings into a nearby pond. Nicholas, the deacon, had died in 1637, but John and Susanna sustained their pattern of life until 1657 when both died.

The other attraction of Little Gidding was that, like Burnt Norton, it is one of England's hidden places. Hard to find, down an obscure track, the civilised beauty and order of Burnt Norton is hidden from the world. So, too, the minute church at Little Gidding is buried in the still sparsely populated rolling countryside between Huntingdon and Oundle. As you approach it down a 'rough road', on the left is the site of a medieval village which was deserted after the Black Death in the fourteenth century. When Nicholas Ferrar arrived there in 1625, the local manor house and medieval church were derelict, and for the next five years he and his family restored them. They are there, intact, 'when you leave the rough road / And turn behind the pig-sty'. Like the garden at Burnt Norton, it is still as Eliot described it. For him it is in the secret places that meaning 'breaks'.

Eliot was escorted to Little Gidding by the Revd Hugh Fraser Stewart, a Pascal scholar, and his wife, Jessie, on the afternoon of 25 May 1936, after Eliot had participated in a

---

* The phrase appears in a *Criterion* review of Oct. 1938. Bernard Blackstone reviewed A. L. Maycock's *Nicholas Ferrar of Little Gidding*, 154–7. Little Gidding appears again in the *Criterion* in Jan. 1939 when Charles Smyth reviewed Blackstone's edition of *The Ferrar Papers*, 366–71 (he notes that Ferrar was called 'a saint of the Church of England').

† The church was rebuilt in the eighteenth century, and added to in the nineteenth.

viva in Cambridge at the request of Maynard Keynes. In the sequence of Eliot's visits to the four sites of the poems, Little Gidding followed Burnt Norton. Imaginatively the two are linked: the evanescent light and the rising sun; the evanescent rose of human love and the everlasting rose of divine love. The nostalgia for 'the passage which we did not take / Towards the door we never opened' recalls the poet's lingering thought of La Figlia, 'how they should have been together'. There is, again, a slight stir of the maytime-playtime of the senses in the first draft of *Little Gidding* as Eliot goes back to the actual May of his only visit to this place. It recalls the 'voluptuary sweetness' of that May, the 'playtime' of the wakened senses which gives 'human joy' but no 'greater rapture'. When Hayward questioned 'playtime' Eliot said that he was referring back to the rose-garden of *Burnt Norton* and the children in the apple tree of 'New Hampshire'. The web of private cross-reference also links the voluptuary sweetness with the 'sweet disconsolate chimera' that lingered in the mind at the end of a draft of *Burnt Norton*. Later in 1936 Eliot crossed to America to help Emily Hale over her depression.

The years in which Eliot visited the scenes of *Four Quartets* – Burnt Norton in September 1934, Little Gidding in May 1936, the crossing to New England in August–October 1936 and, finally, a second visit to East Coker in 1937 – were the years of upheaval, torn between nostalgia for unfulfilled love and the fury of tormented conscience. At the core of *Four Quartets* are the compacted memories of four years during which Eliot's new life was taking a decisive shape. The *Quartets* gestated in Eliot's mind for about as long as *The Waste Land*: seven years in all. While *The Waste Land* grew out of a rag-bag of fragments that, for some years, had no focus, *Four Quartets* grew in concentric layers around the core of private memory, which continues to nourish the poems from well below the surface.

In 1940–1 the core was overlaid with the freezing asceticism of Eliot's chosen way. The remembered ecstasy in the rose-garden and the remembered maytime of the senses were subdued to the dark night of the soul. This was the substantial central layer of *Four Quartets*: the body's punishment, the soul's trial, its progress and (a still-remote possibility) its reward.

The final layer, no more than an outer casing, is the public point of reference: the war. The fire of bombs comes, in turn, to overlay the ice. Ideally, there would have been a divine fire. Instead, Eliot settles for what is more common, a punitive fire. Fire-watching during the air-raids, Eliot saw 'the dark dove with flickering tongue'. The bomber brings home once again the intolerable question of the waste of life, a question repeated in each quartet: in the rose of love that turned to dust; in the family that flourished and fell and lay buried in earth; in the black bodies brought down by the flooding water of the Mississippi. The elements that sustain us also destroy us. The fourth *Quartet* speaks of the victims of war who too might ask 'Where is there an end of it?'

Superimposed upon the bomber is the dove of the holy spirit. The refining fire – pain that is God-given and, as such, accepted – may redeem what Eliot called (in his outline) the 'daemonic' fire of war. To this pain Eliot was drawn by temperament as much as by identification with his adopted country in time of trial. When Forster reread *Little Gidding* his enthusiasm was tempered by justifiable dislike of Eliot's 'homage to pain': 'What animal except the human could have excogitated it? Of course there's pain on and off through each individual's life. . . . You can't shirk it and so on. But why should it be endorsed by the schoolmaster and sanctified by the priest until the fire and the rose are one when so much of it is caused by disease and bullies? It is here that Eliot becomes unsatisfactory as a seer.'

There are times in the final *Quartet* when Eliot reaches for a loftiness that cuts him off from the impact of others' feelings. He told the Greek poet George Seferis that, in a shelter, 'I would feel the need to get out as quickly as possible, to escape all those faces gathered there, to escape all that humanity'.

To Eliot war, as a historical event, was peripheral to its

private moral meaning, as the First World War had been peripheral to the private wasteland. London Bridge 'falling down falling down falling down' was a token of private collapse on Eliot's return to London in January 1922 from his breakdown in Lausanne, and only tangentially a wartime hallucination that happened to Bertrand Russell when he saw the jammed troop trains of the doomed depart from Waterloo. In the same way, for Eliot, the historical event of the Blitz was, in Emersonian terms, a token of his being and becoming. He saw in the bombs the curative possibilities of purgatorial fire and wrote in the manuscript:

> Fire without and fire within
> ~~Expel~~
> Purge the unidentified sin . . .

In the aftermath of air-raids, the accumulated debris would be suspended in the London air for hours and then would slowly descend, covering people in a fine, white ash. This was the fire 'without'. But the fire 'within' would outlast the war, a sign that he was chosen, if not for bliss, at least for endurance. Eliot's ARP* duties, watching 'firecrackers' from a rooftop in South Kensington (a fairly safe post between the bombing points of Earls Court and the Museums) provided the setting for the culminating scene of the *Quartets*. He gazed down on a London much of which had turned into smouldering heaps of rubble. After a raid there would be an eerie silence. There was no traffic, since most of the streets were blocked by fallen buildings, and hardly any pedestrians, only a pall of smoke and everywhere an acrid smell of burning. Eliot was animated, not harrowed, by this horrific scene as he chatted to other fire-watchers, mostly retired Indian majors.

If the feat of Eliot's greatest poetry was to convert urban reality to nightmare or vision, here was the vision ready-made. From the charred and smoking ruins, a shade rises, a 'familiar compound ghost', who speaks from beyond time in

---

* Air-Raid Precautions.

Eliot's own voice. This is the poet's climactic encounter with his other self: a ghost of the immortals who bears a promise of immortality to the still-living Eliot.

Self-judgement turns on the ghost's prophecy. In the first version the ghost brings a promise of the 'eternal': 'it is here'. Forget the modish theories, the ghost tells him, and the modish language that sustained them. Modernism is already fading, the fate of fashions. Joined with the ghost, Eliot watches his life pass in sequence, all he loved and all he hated, the moments that would link him with generations gone and generations to come. He watches his own past dissolve into the mists of time. Now to draw nearer to the 'dead and the unborn': he must detach from the living, 'the voices and the faces that were most near'.

It is 'autumn' in the first draft. It was autumn at the poet's imagined parting with La Figlia; and autumn here, he told Hayward, was 'to throw back to Figlia che piange' (as the chatter of unborn children at Burnt Norton was a throwback to the dream children of 'New Hampshire'). In this wartime autumn he must again resign 'the last love of earth'. It is a test of his purpose. Can he relinquish her memory as the lover of La Figlia had done so many years before?

> She turned away, but with the autumn weather
> Compelled my imagination many days.

It is Eliot's private trial to repeat this scene, resigning love again and yet again, till it becomes an emblematic gesture of his journey. The youth who parted from the garden-girl had been destined to join the company of the timeless even before Eliot's departure for Europe in 1914.

This is all he can do, the ghost assures him in 1941. 'The rest is grace'. With this resonant promise, the sound of an explosion wakes the poet to the present: 'At which I started: and the sun had risen.' The sun may confer the longed-for radiance; it also signals a return to time.

Eliot's adviser John Hayward said oddly little when he read this ambitious part in the summer of 1941. He said it was 'all right', as were parts I and V. There were limitations to

Hayward. He was a stickler for language, and certainly, in many places, pushed Eliot to clarify. But, like Pound, he was blind to religious experience. He had no idea what was meant by 'Zero summer'. Too clever by half, he thought it had something to do with the absolute zero of physics. Nor did he grasp the import of 'silence'. Hayward's failure to respond to the ghost's visitation unnerved Eliot. He took the failure upon himself, and put the poem aside for a year. Then he struck through the passage in heavy pencil. He said later that it 'cost me far more time and trouble and vexation than any passage of the same length that I have ever written'.

Some time between the summer of 1941 and the summer of 1942, Eliot decided that greatness would come not through sublimity, as he had hoped, but through savage honesty. He was still consciously aiming at his highest reach as a poet, still walking shoulder to shoulder with the compound ghost of the immortals, Yeats, Shelley and, above all, Dante, whose verse form he still adopts. But in the drastic revision that Eliot undertook in August–September 1942, it was as though he recognised that he could not touch the ultimate heights of the *Paradiso*, so settled instead for searing confession. A rough draft for the ghost's revised speech owns that 'old rooted sin puts forth again' after all his straining to subdue it, and 'the starved unflowering growth shows still more foul . . .'.

He told Hayward that he intended to inject 'some acute personal reminiscence', and the emotional impact of the revised speech came from Eliot's exposure of guilt, obviously about Vivienne. He now began to cultivate the 'rending pain' of recall, of 'motives late revealed' and 'things ill done and done to others' harm'* in all assurance of virtue. He

---

* Eliot echoes lines from Yeats's 'Vacillation', which he had quoted before in *After Strange Gods*:

> Things said or done long years ago,
> Or things I did not do or say . . .
> Weigh me down, and not a day
> But something is recalled,
> My conscience or my vanity appalled.

Eliot used sin, as Yeats used the foul rag and bone shop of the heart, to spur

explained this carefully to Hayward on 7 September 1942: 'I mean not simply something not questioned but something consciously approved.' The backing of friends now served only to deepen guilt: 'fools' approval stings.'

It took a grim moral courage to let go the visionary moments with their latent promise, and let judgement fall, with the utmost severity, on what he most wished to forget. We recall that Eliot had confided to Virginia Woolf that what he feared above all was humiliation. But the reward of honesty was what is probably the greatest passage of poetry he ever wrote, as he turned away from the plot of attainment to his habitat of pain.

Though Eliot intended to sharpen the 'personal' element in the revised version, both versions are personal in different ways. The first is more autobiographical; the second, more confessional. The first distils the shape of a life that calls the poet out of himself into eternity. The second takes a hard look at the flaws he will share with other ageing men: the cold craving of the senses for what they no longer enjoy, and stale sneers that fail to amuse. The first version singles Eliot out as heir to the immortals. The second version thrusts him back in place as ordinary stained creature. And yet it points the stains with such unerring brilliance that, in another way, it, too, breaks through the veils of existence, exchanging introspective clarity for visionary power.

*

Eliot did more drafts of *Little Gidding* than of any other quartet. The first three he wrote quickly and with ease; the last took eighteen drafts in all (if we count working carbons

new poetry. He pulls out the same ugly emotions as Yeats, the lust, the rage, the remorse, but in Yeats the compunction is short-lived: he is the wild, wicked old man. Eliot's compunction will go on. For Yeats the fire refines art; for Eliot it is the remedy for sin. The absence of any real affinity with Yeats is obvious in Eliot's familiar solution when he redrafts the speech in prose: 'there is only the one remedy, pain for pain, in that purgative fire which you must will . . .'.

as well as top copies). Why was it so immense and prolonged a struggle? Of course, *Little Gidding* had to be the summation of the preceding poems and, as such, of Eliot's whole career. But could there be another reason? Could he have been waiting for some yield from his life that did not, in the end, come? In disclaiming the life of a saint, Eliot was performing an act of humility essential to the life of a saint. He would wipe out pride and spiritual ambition – and yet, could he have embarked on a series of religious ordeals without some sort of ambition or, we may prefer to call it, hope?

The survival of all these drafts makes it possible to see the evolution of *Little Gidding* as the logic of its emotions changed. There were three main layers of composition: a brief handwritten plan, the first complete typescript of July 1941, and the revised poem of August–September 1942. The initial plan set out the sequence of a transfigured life in four stages, each with some intimation of immortality. The first two stages are familiar: a wintry state shot through with heavenly light, superseding the play of the senses, and then a stage of destruction by 'daemonic fire' ('The Inferno'). Following this, the plan looks forward to detachment from human ties, and then, finally, all life absorbed into a 'central fire'. It concludes with an Invocation to the Holy Spirit.

Central to this plan is an exercise in detachment: 'They vanish, the individuals, and our feeling for them sinks into the flame which refines.' There is nothing, initially, about communal feeling: that came later. The underlying wish is to cut ties. This risky action, I imagine, is what Eliot undertook in 1941–2, and here is the clue to his problem with the last stage of the *Quartets*: his failure to reach the divine fire.

It was through detachment that Eliot would follow the mystics into their state of grace. For this reason he clung to detachment throughout the period of revision – the passage remains unchanged from the first to the final draft – despite just criticism from Hayward that his idea was 'uncompromising' and 'rather laboured'. Hayward was not the first of Eliot's friends made uneasy by his assumption that the divine is to be found through withdrawal from human ties. There had been the dismayed response to his epigraph to *Sweeney Agonistes* to this effect, taken from St John of the Cross. Unquestionably, the precedent is there in monastic tradition. *The Cloud of Unknowing* urges a pupil to 'forget all created things . . . so that your thought and longing do not turn or reach out to them'. So, too, the *Imitation of Christ*: 'See that you are inwardly free and purified, unattached to any created thing.' You must find the grace to send others 'right away and then when you are left alone, be joined to God alone'. Eliot naturally set his sights lower. For him the end of detachment is only 'the purification of the motive'. In private terms, he could justify his severance from Vivienne only by a purer motive than attachment to another woman.

Eliot's curt exposition of detachment is curiously flat, not because his aim is less lofty than the mystics', but his feeling is different. Genuine mystics show concurrent love for fellow-beings, which is a sign of their state of grace; Eliot's detachment is more rigid. He seems oblivious (like Harry) to the effect that detachment, even of the purest kind, will have on other people. For all his commitment to a Christian community, he still did not extend his imagination, in practice, to people lower than himself in the social scale; extend it, that is, beyond the demands of duty (he willingly spent August 1941 editing the *Christian Newsletter*) and the more superficial demands of courtesy and kindness. Many have testified how Eliot would unbend and show consideration, but time and again we detect at a more private level that withholding of imaginative energy that is perhaps the greatest danger of the spiritual life: I mean self-obsession. Although Eliot stuck by 'England' through the war, his 'love of a country' seems a thought-out, almost theoretic alignment, not deeply felt (as in, say, the wartime England of *Between the Acts* by Virginia Woolf).

In the plan, detachment was to precede the coming of 'Love', but in the first draft this is where the poem broke down. In a first, scrawled manuscript, it began at a high point with the descent of Christ and the poet's speaking 'in tongues' of the 'culmination of desire'. Then, in the second stanza, comes the collapse of confidence as Eliot finds sin in place of grace. A 'sign that brands' is straight out of *The Scarlet Letter*: a dire, puritanical sense of pervasive sin from which there is no escape. He speaks dully of a gambler who has lost the game of salvation. This man staked all for heaven, but will moulder in the grave, like the despised revellers in East Coker.

Here was serious failure. The feeling was dead. Eliot was simply not possessed by the central fire of his plan. Since he could not meet the demands of transfiguration, he deflects energy into heavy denunciations of '*Unprofitable Sin*' and '*Sundry Pleasures*'. Hayward, reading this in late July 1941, told Eliot candidly on 1 August that it did not fit the rest of the poem. It was 'obfuscating', he said. The sad fact was that the 'eternal' promised by the ghost was not, after all, at hand.

Eliot's immediate diagnosis was that the flaw (in part IV) lay with the ghost's prophecy (in part II). To presume to name Love as the outcome of the process, he had to climb down and, once more, try to purify his poetic instrument with self-laceration. This would fit the stanza that Eliot retained from part IV, where redemption comes 'from fire by fire'. It did have to be the old stand-by, pain – not vision – that would bring the poem to life.

There is a way of suffering, Eliot argued, that has in it 'already a kind of presence of the supernatural and of the superhuman'. Because the sufferer 'cannot adjust himself to the actual world he has to reject it in favour of Heaven and Hell, or because he has the perception of Heaven and Hell he rejects the present world'. This explanation helps us understand his position, but it falls short of the sublime pain to which part IV aspired and which St Bernard, the twelfth-century abbot of Clairvaux, described with confident acumen. A burning compunction can be a mystical grace, he says,

> which consumes but does not affect. It burns sweetly, it produces a delightful desolation. It acts at the same time as fire upon our vices and as ointment upon our souls. . . . When you

experience this power which totally changes you, and the love which sets you on fire, understand that the Lord is present in your heart. (Sermon 57)

In probing the problem of *Little Gidding* I don't mean to suggest that the first draft was without the poem's final greatness. Much of the final draft was already there in July 1941. What makes the first draft so interesting is evidence of an underlying schema that was loftier, potentially, than the final one, and which might have provided a heaven-sent climax to Eliot's earlier work, but which he could not (for reasons we can only guess) fulfil.

I have wondered whether, had Eliot delayed longer, his life might have caught up with his initial conception and, if so, whether *Little Gidding* could have succeeded equally well as a rather different finale. But he was impatient to finish. With other jobs in the offing, he allowed far less than his usual yearly space between quartets. The third *Quartet* was published in February 1941, and by June he had a draft for the fourth. After his bout of revision a year later, he told Hayward in September 1941 that 'to spend much more time over this poem might be dangerous. After a time one loses the original feeling of the impulse, and then it is no longer safe to alter. It is time to close the chapter.'

The introspective mind of the last *Quartet* remains, as always, the votary of 'Solidad' (solitude) waiting, a trifle less patiently, for the incursion of divine fire. Behind this act of attention, a community comes into focus. During the long wait, it is a prop, and if the worst should happen – spiritual defeat – it would be a haven, as once the community at Little Gidding gave refuge to Charles I, a 'broken king' at night, after his crushing defeat at the battle of Naseby.

People who lived through the Battle of Britain remarked on extraordinary fellow-feeling and resilience during the shared danger. It was under these unique conditions that Eliot was trying to feel his way into that sense of community. Although he judged the English as 'not wholly commendable', and although, too, they were of 'no immediate kin', he could share their endurance and indomitability in the face of defeat.

When Allen Tate invited Eliot to Princeton, he replied in March 1943 that he could not leave London during the war.

Three scenes of this time show Eliot feeling his way into the English community – not the intellectual élite, who had always welcomed him, but groups of ordinary people. There were the chats with retired Indian majors through the long night hours at the Air Raid Post. There was his life amongst the women at the Shambles where he absorbed the English tone of affectionate humour, the domestic flair for comic drama as a kind of resourcefulness. One day in September 1942 old Mrs Mirrlees got herself locked in the bathroom: the lock was jammed. The whole population of the Wood congregated outside the door as Eliot – the only other male was the ancient gardener – climbed a ladder. When the rescuer reached the window he found Mrs Mirrlees placidly reading a thriller. Anyway, he could do nothing that way. Holmes and Watson, he thought, would have put their shoulders to the door and burst through. Eliot and the gardener only got sore shoulders. The gardener tried a crowbar in vain, the dogs barked, and everyone implored everyone else to keep cool. Finally a servant shook the door, and it opened.

The third scene was on a train in August 1941, when Eliot took on the character of the lovable English eccentric as he read over the first typescript of *Little Gidding*:

> . . . re-reading the poem in the train yesterday (with a Three Nuns Vicar peeping over my shoulder: I wonder what he made of it, together with the Giant Umbrella and a volume of Kipling – he probably thought I was what is now euphemistically called an Anglo Indian) . . .

At this time he was putting together a selection of Kipling's verse. It was through Kipling, the insider who was also an outsider, that Eliot found his position in relation to England. Kipling, Eliot said in his Introduction, had 'a universal foreignness', and yet could see more clearly because he was 'alien'. He had 'a sense of the antiquity of England, of the number of generations and peoples who have laboured the soil and been buried beneath it, and of the contemporaneity of the past'.

Records of the past tend to follow the lines of victory. Eliot counters this with a record of historical figures in their times of defeat. His drafts cite Richard III (defeated on Bosworth Field in 1485)* and the Duke of Wellington, not as the victor of Waterloo but as the unpopular politician in 1831, when a mob, believing him the major opponent of the Reform Bill, broke his windows. In each case, Eliot extracts a pure moral emblem from its murky historical context. The courage to go on in the face of defeat had its public meaning at a time when England stood alone against Hitler, but Eliot's persistence in wearing a white rose in his lapel on the anniversary of Bosworth, for years after the war, suggests that for him the private sense of defeat was pre-eminent. When Eliot sees history as a pattern of 'timeless moments', he extracts arbitrarily certain scenes that bear on the peculiar history of his own soul. He implies that the private individual may create the past, as Emerson put it: 'it is part of the business of the critic to preserve tradition – where a good tradition exists . . . but this is eminently to see it *not* as consecrated by time but to see it beyond time.' This idea is reinforced by Hegel's *Philosophy of History*, which Eliot owned and marked as a student. Hegel saw history as a manifestation of the Spirit which is eternally present: 'Spirit is immortal; with it there is no past, no future, but an essential *now*.' For Eliot it is the spirit in the face of defeat that is 'now and England'.

*

As he wrote the wartime *Quartets*, Eliot began to take on the aura of fame that remained for the rest of his life. He was from then on in constant demand, broadcasting and lecturing

* 'Richard seems an odd companion for Charles I,' Helen Gardner comments (*CFQ*, p. 209), and explains that they were brought together by Mr George Every in a play about King Charles's visit to Little Gidding, which Eliot read in 1936.

abroad for the British Council, as well as talking on Shakespeare (in autumn 1941, in Bristol), on 'The Music of Poetry' (in February 1942, in Glasgow), and on 'The Classics and the Man of Letters' (in April 1942, to the Classical Association). Eliot told Martin Browne that all this public activity was a 'drug' as opposed to the 'solitary toil' of *Little Gidding*, which 'often seems so pointless'. He was invited to Iceland in the autumn of 1941 (cancelled due to illness), and to Sweden in the spring of 1942. At a time when semi-official relations with Sweden were being established, he flew to Stockholm with Bishop Bell for five weeks. Bell made contact with two Germans, Hans Schönfeld and Dietrich Bonhoeffer, representatives of an organised opposition to Hitler who wished to make contact with the British Government. Bishop Bell duly contacted Anthony Eden, the Foreign Secretary, on their return, but the Foreign Office failed to respond to this initiative.

Eliot had hoped to revise *Little Gidding* in the winter of 1941–2, but had to put it off till the following August, when he redid the ghost's prophecy and the defective part IV. He sent the final poem to John Hayward on 2 September. The success of the 1942 version lies in Eliot's acceptance of the fact that he was not a candidate for the divine spirit. He would not fudge this with a verbal 'smoke-screen'. He had, at least in theory, the dove's descent. And, in theory, he names God as 'Love'. The poetry of 'Love' came late in the evolution of *Little Gidding*, only in September 1942, in the last stage of revision, when a penitent approaches the 'unfamiliar Name' through the fires of purgatory. It is as though Eliot had to put himself through excruciating torture to name this emotion. He did try, at this last stage, to infuse warmer feeling by reverting to Burnt Norton ('Who heaped the brittle rose-leaves? Love.') but his final revision turns from what he calls 'brittle' love to a higher love born of torture as he puts on the 'intolerable shirt of flame'.

The poem still lacked something, a note of attainment, and Eliot's last additions were the voices of two fourteenth-century mystics: Dame Julian of Norwich's *Revelations of*

Divine Love, and the 'Calling' of the anonymous writer of
The Cloud of Unknowing which draws Love into him. The
compassionate uneducated woman and the learned man
represented, to Eliot, 'the two mystical extremes'.

Except for the voices of the mystics and the opening
intuition, when the sun flamed the ice, the final *Quartet*
became wholly purgatorial. This balance between ephemeral
intimation and ongoing endurance was Eliot's judgement of
his own condition. The conclusion, in one sense, remains
provisional. Spiritual autobiography is always in the making.
Little Gidding, like all Eliot's poems, resonates into a future
beyond the poem which is our future as much as the poet's.
This may be less triumphant than his initial plan, but its
advantage is to make the poem moving to those of us whose
lives are imperfect and who can make no claim to beatitude.

Little Gidding recounts 'the end of the journey': 'end',
'purpose', 'fulfilment' are the words in the air. The 'end' is to
come to rest in theological orthodoxy. It does not matter,
though, if we do not share Eliot's precise belief, since the
greatness of the work has been the authenticity of the
search.* Eliot does not state truth. He points towards it by
arriving at places where truth is manifest.

The 'end' is also to sum up a pattern of experience inherent
in the preceding *Quartets*, which inheres also in Eliot's life. In
his early poetry, he had perceived the move from divine
'reality' back into ordinary life as a jolt across a vast gap
because, in early years, he had seen ordinary life as corrupt, in
opposition to the life of the spirit. One triumph of *Little
Gidding* was to close this gap. After the air-raid the two

* In Eliot's 1929 essay on Dante he said that 'there is a difference . . .
between philosophical *belief* and poetic *assent* (*SE*, p. 218). In Dec. 1932, in
his unpublished address in King's Chapel in Boston, he reminded the
congregation that it was not necessary to believe what Dante believed in
order to enjoy the poetry, although to enjoy it fully one ought to understand
what he believed. Eliot repeated this idea yet again, in 1945 in Paris, in
another unpublished lecture. Lucretius and Dante, he said, do not try to
persuade readers of their beliefs but to convey what it feels like to hold
certain beliefs ('Le Rôle social des poètes'; an English translation is part of
the Hayward Bequest in King's College, Cambridge).

worlds of time and timelessness become alike, and the poet treads between with an 'ease' that 'is cause for wonder'.

The implied question – it may go back to the overwhelming question that Prufrock was too locked up in time to frame – is how to rescue ordinary life from its worthless banality. The answer is now quite simple: to pare away the agitations of the present – the tug of the senses, the modish sneers, and all the nonsense of fame – and hold fast to a timeless judgement, like the Word in the desert. The very appearance of Eliot's timeless ghost in the Cromwell Road, speaking in Eliot's own prophetic voice, demonstrates the incursion of the timeless into time – if we had the wit to see it.

In *Little Gidding*, Eliot is doing it all for us: in each part, the timeless pierces the familiar façades of ordinary life. It is behind the pigsty in the English countryside and it is on the ash-strewn London pavement and it is in the silence between the waves, a permanent presence as Eliot knew it, already, as a child, on the Cape Ann shore. Given this awareness, an ordinary life can be transfigured. This is the 'end' of *Little Gidding* and of *Four Quartets* as a whole: nothing less than to re-create our existence.

Eliot re-creates an actual place, Little Gidding, as a model of the transfigured life, much as his ancestors dreamt of a godly society that would be a model to all the world. Little Gidding itself is subsidiary to the icy fire which Eliot projects upon the memory of his visit on 'a really lovely day' at the end of May, the only good day in the spring of 1936, he wrote to Mrs Perkins in Boston.

Little Gidding was just one instance of a way of life that could absorb the timeless. It projected from past to future the shape of a life that might be a perfect vessel for the divine spirit to fill. As the ritual repetition of the devotional life was to be Eliot's valid alternative to a lifetime burning in every moment, so the rhythmic words of poetry must be an alternative to God's burning Word. A classic language, precise, ordered, wide open to both old and new, receptive to subtleties of thought and feeling, might become (like the life) a perfected vessel for timeless content.

*

In an unpublished lecture in 1937, Eliot spoke of a pattern of emotion in which a man acts beyond character, according to a hidden and mysterious order. *Four Quartets* follows emotions beyond those we ordinarily know as human, though we may have hints and guesses. The drafts show the personal source of these emotions; the revisions, Eliot's control of the personal matter, allowing just enough to enliven the poem with the urgency of private struggle, yet subduing it to the ideal pattern. Eliot did not dwell on struggle for its own sake: he extracts the permanent import swiftly, almost ruthlessly, shedding his life like a husk so that it is the perfect life that remains before us.

In the course of this experiment, three forms of life are superimposed one upon another. First, there is the parallel: the repetition of lives that have gone before, and the ritual repetition of the observant life. This coexists with the aspiring line of progressive development: it would fit the linear form of the converted life which leads through the ordeals of the wilderness to a vision of the promised land, the Grail, or the Celestial City. Eliot's journey, though, ends where it began. Its final form is circular. After the effort at transformation, Eliot realises that he has become what was always implicit in his origins. In so far as he has been true to his child's sense of being, he has not changed. The wheel which seemed to suggest the dull repetition of meaningless existence fades into the circle, a singleness of being, self-contained, complete, as Eliot returns at the last to his American childhood to recover simplicity and innocence. This biographic circle is intact also from the opposite angle: Eliot's 'way back' to England completes the 'way forward' of Andrew Eliott to the New World. Eliot planned that his life should end, even more neatly than his poem, in the ancestral earth of East Coker where his ashes do, in fact, now lie. The parallel, line, and circle compose an abstract design, but one distilled from actual life.

To read *Four Quartets* as a whole is to experience a

cumulative effect, like a great piece of music. As in music, there is a set form: each *Quartet* begins with an actual experience in Eliot's life; at the centre of each is some action or journey; at the end of each some struggle with language that parallels the effort at the perfect life. Yet, cumulatively, the *Quartets* convey a profounder unity than the repetition of set form. This is the ultra-human pattern to which he wished to give the accuracy of a formula. The successive poems tell the story of Eliot's gradual discovery of this formula, starting from a flash of intuition. With painstaking care, he goes on to test intuition against experience: the experience of his own life; the experience of others in other ages. The essential intuition was there in childhood, not looked for but (as a first draft put it) 'heard, half-heard, in the silence / Of distant lands and seas.'* Exploration takes him back to this past to repossess the intuition, and behind it the dead, the line of ancestors who strove to purify their lives:

> We are born with the dead;
> See, they return, and bring us with them.

When Edith Sitwell wanted to select one of the *Quartets* for an anthology, she wrote to Eliot: 'I am now tearing myself to pieces about which of the *Quartets* I am going to ask for (the moment I choose one, I want the others too . . .)'.† Although the poems were published separately – the last also on its own in October 1942 – they are, as Sitwell felt, a unit. The complete sequence was published first in America on 11 May 1943, and eighteen months later in England. Eliot said that the poems got better as they went along: 'the fourth is the best of all.' In an interview, he told Helen Gardner that of all his poems *Little Gidding* best stood the test of saying exactly what it meant. And, as she said, this satisfaction was unparalleled in Eliot's comments on his work. 'The *Four*

---

* This was the original conclusion. When the phrase 'distant lands and seas' was changed to 'between two waves of the sea', literal-minded John Hayward queried if there could be 'silence' between waves. Eliot then exchanged this important word for the less dramatic 'stillness'.
† She chose *Burnt Norton*.

Quartets: I rest on those,' Eliot continued to state in his last important interview in 1959, and he said the same in conversation: 'I stand or fall on them.'

In Eliot's early years a gap yawned between body and soul, between the wasted land and the white towers of Wren's churches. His polar oppositions seemed irreconcilable as the poetry rocked from scene to scene. In *Four Quartets* the opposition of time and eternity is resolved as Eliot found points of intersection in art, in the life of Christ, and in the Church.

On 28 March 1931 Eliot had written to Stephen Spender:

> I have the A minor Quartet [of Beethoven] on the gramophone, and I find it quite inexhaustible to study. There is a sort of heavenly or at least more than human gaiety about some of his later things which one imagines might come to oneself as the fruit of reconciliation and relief after immense suffering; I should like to get something of that into verse before I die.

In his youth Eliot had dared to hope for heavenly bliss ('your heart would have responded / Gaily . . . beating obedient / To controlling hands') but in maturity had to content himself with reconciliation and relief. In the final lines of *Four Quartets* he reaches towards – though cannot himself attain – reconciliation of pain and divine love. The fire and the rose are one. Here the 'unimaginable' is stated: the coexistence of opposite, God-given sensations. Eliot dared to formulate this longed-for 'reality' of feeling that, some day, it might once more call out a perfect life – not necessarily his own. The true artist, he quoted, 'knows that he is but a vessel of an emotion whence others, not he, must drink'.

The last lines are a finale not only to *Four Quartets* but to Eliot's poetry as a whole, which seeks repeatedly to formulate a pattern that would give meaning to our ephemeral existence, and to reconcile that existence with whatever lies beyond our compass. For it is the function of art, he said, to give us some perception of an order in life by imposing an order upon it.

This order, though, remains a mere formula unless it

touches the life of the reader. Mary Lee Settle, an American novelist who did war-service in London, recalled the impact of *Four Quartets* when there really was 'dust in the air' and the ruined rows of houses stood like empty husks, their wallpaper stained with rain. At a time when people queued for rations and suffered loss and privation, Eliot 'had somehow refined what he had to tell us, beyond the banality of disappointment and hopelessness, into a promise like steel'. That first generation of readers responded to a promise of recovery made with 'a miraculous effrontery of spirit' in the face of years of wrong. He became, she remembered, 'our lay priest'.

For other readers, at other times, *Four Quartets* makes its mark when we come alive to feeling 'which we can only detect . . . out of the corner of the eye and can never completely focus. . . . At such moments, we touch the border of those feelings which only music can express.' The rhythm and order of the artist bring us to a condition of 'stillness and reconciliation', and then, Eliot adds, must 'leave us as Virgil left Dante to proceed towards a region where that guide can avail us no farther'.

Eliot did himself enter some new region after the autumn air-raid, presumably in 1940 when London was bombed every night from 7 September to 2 November. '. . . It *was* autumn,' he told Hayward on 5 August 1941. In that eerie silence, the still-living poet envisaged the compound ghost of the immortals whom he now knew he would join. Together they patrolled the ruined streets in defeat and purgatory beyond Eliot's own time. So he passed beyond private trial towards a transcendent calm that he took from a wise woman, Julian of Norwich, in another, distant century of disaster:

> And all shall be well and
> All manner of thing shall be well.

II

LADY OF SILENCES

ON THE MORNING of 23 January 1947, Eliot had a phone call from Maurice Haigh-Wood. It was to say that Vivienne (aged fifty-eight) had died suddenly of heart failure in the night. John Hayward took the call, and it was he who broke the news.

'O God! O God!' Eliot said, and buried his face in his hands.

In the years following *Four Quartets* the growing eminence of Eliot's public character seems to obliterate the private man. The more visible he became, the more invisible the self that sought what he called 'reality'. The next chapter will follow Eliot's public course, but this chapter will explore what is harder to know, that elusive private life. From 1927 to 1956, Eliot's private life was centred on Emily Hale, and the more that is known about his relation to Emily Hale, the stranger and more complex he appears. This tie remained the secret of Eliot's life because Emily agreed to play out the role he assigned: a 'Lady of silences'. He wrote about a thousand letters to her, vastly more than to any other person, an average of between one a week and one a fortnight over the thirty years of their attachment. According to their agreement, the letters were sequestered for fifty years after the death of the survivor – until 12 October 2019. No other letters of Eliot were sealed from public view for anything like this length of time.

Half the correspondence – Emily Hale's letters to Eliot – vanished. She wished her letters to be read after her death and, at some stage, Eliot thought of leaving them to the Bodleian Library. But when Emily Hale made enquiries, of Eliot himself in 1963 and of the library in 1965, she drew a blank. She concluded that Eliot had destroyed her letters, and told herself that he did it 'to protect me'. In 1986 Peter du Sautoy, Eliot's fellow-director at Faber, told me that, in 1963, Eliot gave him a fairly large, old-fashioned metal cash-box with gilt embellishments. It contained a good many letters, tightly packed, which, he said, he had long meant to destroy. Mr du Sautoy duly burnt them, at Eliot's request, without looking at them. These were probably the Hale letters.

Luckily, a letter of 1947 to a close friend, Lorraine Havens, has survived, and also a batch of letters to Willard Thorp, written between 1957 and 1969 (mostly to do with her bequest of Eliot's letters to Princeton). These do give some idea of her relation to Eliot from her point of view. They are the letters of a woman of integrity: an old-fashioned woman whose depth of feeling is contained by absolute standards of conduct. Without her letters to Eliot, much of the truth will never be known. I am content that there should be some mystery; it is more truthful to leave a gap than to pretend to fullness of documentation, for there is no end to the nuances of a relationship. Yet there is a tale to be told, and though facts are few, it won't do to trip past on the usual trail of Eliot's public appearances with their train of anecdote, as when Eliot put on his connoisseur act over the cheeseboard at his club in order to fob off a visiting academic, Hugh Kenner. If we shut out the anecdotes of people who knew Eliot only through his array of façades, and see him from an unfamiliar angle, that of a woman who loved him, we might find the Eliot who is simply not there in friends' reports of the later years.

Dimly, it is possible to make out, between the bare facts of dates, meetings, partings, a Jamesian story of old Boston: high-minded people, caught in their own web of intricate morality. The foil for this hidden love is Eliot's public friendship from 1938 to 1956 with Mary Trevelyan, his escort at parties, the theatre and, most often, church. Her story is part of the next chapter. Suffice to say now that the tone of the friendship with Mary Trevelyan was as different as national character, conducted with candour rather than intimacy, jollity and, on her part, tolerant good sense. Like Polly Tandy, the homey countrywoman with whom Eliot continued to correspond, Mary had the English relish for the comic phrase, which may have helped Eliot find a voice for the comedies he now tried to write. False teeth, he joked, made him speak like Winston Churchill, but his dentist said he would overcome it. Mary Trevelyan was the kind of confident Englishwoman who could handle thousands of men with ease, as she proved in her relief station for troops, just behind the front line, towards the end of the war. It was all too easy for her to plan Eliot's life, and her organisational energy was sometimes intrusive. Though Eliot saw more of Mary than he ever saw of Emily Hale, it was for him less significant. In the forties and fifties, his distance from all friends, even the fearless Mary, was so firmly governed by what he called 'rules', that he seems harder to know in this period than any other. The other obscure period is 1911–14, the graduate years at Harvard which were a time of upheaval. It now appears that in the late forties he had another upheaval for, on 27 April 1949, two years after Vivienne died, he told Mary that he had experienced some sort of psychological change of life.

He was shocked by his wife's death, but even more by its consequences. For now, unexpectedly, he was free to marry Emily Hale, which, for the last fifteen years, she and his family had believed was what he wanted. Yet at once he realised that he had no emotions or desires to share. This, he later told Mary, was his tragedy. 'I have met myself as a middle-aged man,' says the hero of Eliot's new play, *The Cocktail Party*, when he discovers, after his wife departs, that he has lost his wish to marry the shining, devoted Celia. The worst moment, he adds, is when you feel that you have lost the desire for all that was most desirable.

In 1950 Eliot told Mary Trevelyan that it now seemed to him impossible to share his life with anyone. It seemed to him that his life was effectively over: the rest would simply mark time.

The ending of crucial relationships with women, in the late forties and early fifties, counterpoints some decline in emotional vitality in Eliot's lectures and plays. He was always drawn to women of great vitality who, in different ways, energised his writing. The death of Vivienne meant the loss of Eliot's focus of torment. His rejection of Emily Hale finally broke the dream that had given the rare moments of radiance to his poetry. So Eliot lost at once the two women who had stirred his greatest work. Instead, they preyed on his conscience.

*

In the crises of their marriage, Vivienne used to declare herself unfit to live. Eliot would then promise anything, and she would drown in tears. He described these scenes to Mary Trevelyan, who was *not* fascinated. She was a bracing person who did not encourage self-pity. Her memoir passes over these confidences a little briskly.

Eliot had never quite believed in Vivienne's threats of death, and had feared more the nakedness of her emotional demands. No woman in his family, daughters of genteel New England, would have behaved with such appalling abandon. Eliot never visited Vivienne in the asylum, not, I imagine, out of callousness, but because he feared the compelling power of her strong 'Welsh shriek'. The fact that he had not been able to love her would have been, in any case, a denial of her cries for help. Through Emily Hale, he had retained a capacity for love – love as recovered innocence – yet the fact remained that, throughout the marriage to Vivienne, he had loved someone else. Because, during the early forties, he had disciplined this feeling by asceticism, he had still hoped to redeem himself by extravagant rectitude. Vivienne's death exploded this scheme.

Eliot told E. W. F. Tomlin (a writer on philosophy who had contributed reviews to the *Criterion*) that feelings of guilt and horror haunted him daily. 'I can never forget anything,' he said. 'The horror! the horror!' of a wasted life came back, draining hopes of salvation. In *The Cocktail Party* (drafted in 1948), an estranged wife, Lavinia, returns to possess her husband, Edward, in the worst way. For she confers on him a character he dreads, that of a hollow man, incapable of feeling. This is the 'death of the spirit' which, in the original acted version, Edward declares is even worse than fear of madness: a solitary mental prison from which there seems no escape. That this should be a permanent condition is Eliot's definition of hell:

> What is hell? Hell is oneself,
> Hell is alone, the other figures
> Merely projections.

In this scene, the husband calls his wife the 'angel of destruction'. At her touch, he tells her, there is nothing but ruin:

> O God, what have I done? . . .
> Must I become after all what you would make me?

In *The Cocktail Party*, Eliot transmutes the powerplay of his marriage – which partner's image of the other will prevail? – into a fictitious comedy which resolves their impasse. Lavinia, a sharp-tongued woman, is too efficient and unspectacular to derive from Vivienne, and yet there is the odd line that recalls her power, as when Edward speaks of

> The whole oppression, the unreality
> Of the role she had almost imposed upon me
> With the obstinate, unconscious, sub-human strength
> That some women have.

'I cannot live with her', he goes on, but also 'cannot live without her'. She has made him incapable of any existence of his own. There is an awakening to psychological horror here, as though Poe's Roderick Usher were to analyse the lifelessness that descends upon him once his frenzied twin, the Lady Madeline, is buried, for she continues to exist in the vaults of the subconscious, and within a few days returns to haunt and destroy the dwindling life of Usher.

In a strange way Vivienne's wild cries that she could not live and Eliot's macabre fantasies of the death of women were complementary, and came true in her premature end. She was the dark mirror of her husband's imagination, for she held up to him her unforgettable degradation. During those frightful nights with Vivienne, he had only to see the 'face that sweats with tears' to realise the torments of hell. Though his experiences with her had validated the poetry of 1915–26, he had feared that she would contaminate his soul, and possess it wholly. For Eliot felt his primal self to be pure – a purity he associated with memories of childhood, the New England shore, and Emily Hale. The great effort of his mature years had been to shake off degradation (and Vivienne with it) so as to recover, through the vigilant practice of virtue and prayer, a pristine beatitude. In *Four Quartets* he had ventured to look towards blessedness, but here was denial. Was he to live out his life shackled to the shade of Vivienne, the memory of her physical prison the mirror of his mental prison, her denial the mirror of his? Was his guilty soul to be forever irredeemable? It was natural to Eliot to take extreme measures. Christopher Sykes said that he thought of retiring into complete seclusion, but was dissuaded by John Hayward. Mary Trevelyan had an idea that, following Vivienne's death, he committed himself to ten years of penitence.

Eliot said that he felt more 'disintegrated' now than if Vivienne had died fifteen years earlier. There was now less resistance, he added by way of explanation. In 1947 he was fifty-eight, and showed signs of ageing. In America that spring he was seen to be gaunt, pallid, 'and tensely withdrawn from anything reminiscent of the flesh'; in July, on his return to England, he had two operations for his hernia; in October he had most of his remaining teeth extracted. An ebb might seem reasonable, and yet we cannot forget that Eliot assumed the mask of age all his life. Like Lambert Strether, in *The Ambassadors*, he sometimes played up age to avoid the demands of involvement. As always, the truth is as subtle as

James's fiction: motives lurk behind motives in the recess of conscience. And nowhere is Eliot more mysterious than in his shifting relations to women. If he gave the impression of a remorseful man, one who seemed to an old crony, Sir Herbert Read, to have 'some secret sorrow or guilt', it was possibly not so much guilt for his wife as for Emily Hale. This, he eventually told Mary Trevelyan, was the deepest cause of his disturbance.

The stories of Vivienne and Emily Hale belong together, extreme counterpoints, like hell and heaven, of Eliot's creative life. When Eliot told Mary Trevelyan that he would have been less upset if Vivienne had died in 1932, he did not, as yet, reveal to her his tie with Emily Hale. Fifteen years earlier, when he had left Vivienne, Emily had been the counter-dream in the ascendant. If Vivienne had died then (as she had often threatened), could the new life have taken the form of marriage to Emily Hale? On one level, Eliot did believe that this is what he wanted. And yet, his work invariably tells us more than what he declared in person. The profounder introspection of *The Family Reunion*, which explores Eliot's situation so closely, suggests that there was in 1934–8 a shift in which potential love was subdued by a state of sin. It suggests that were Eliot, like Harry, legally free, he would still not marry the waiting woman but would choose, rather, to pursue the solitary ordeals of penitence. In a curious way, his work foretold the events of his life.

In the winter of 1940–1, Eliot spoke of the 'emotionless' years of living among the breakage of what was most reliable, and therefore fittest for renunciation. This was the frozen state he cultivated in *Four Quartets*, his extreme remedy for sin, modelled on the asceticism of the saints. The result of the subjugation of the body was not an access of divine love but 'failing powers'. It is not surprising that, when he was free to marry, he found no desire. The anticlimax, after so many years of waiting, seemed to him a catastrophe.

*

Emily Hale never claimed, like Vivienne, to have been Eliot's muse. She was concerned more with the man than the poet: the Eliot of their family circles. Of the latent monk, and of the heights of a destiny that would exclude any close human contact until it was fulfilled, she saw, perhaps, not enough. With her, the comfy family aspect of Eliot would have been to the fore, as during the weekends in Chipping Campden in the thirties when Eliot had shared a family feeling that he found soothing after years of exile.

Eliot's light verse to Emily Hale, with its details of country walks and visits to Faber, shows the playful ease and suddenly erupting humour of his verse for children. Eliot figures as the cowardly grown-up child, town-bred, who is a great nuisance on country walks because he fears the prongs of a bull lurking behind every tree. Emily Hale is the admirably composed companion, in her tweeds and brogues, who puts up with all the fuss. Eliot appears also as a Cockney cat, the office cat called Morgan, who tries once again to put paw to paper to extol Miss 'Ile on her birthday: 'Now you jist try your paw – let it come from the 'art – '.

Where Emily Hale saw Eliot in terms of this playful familiarity, Eliot saw Emily Hale also as the material of religious poetry. And when his private searching came to an end, so too the interest in her. In the final *Quartet*, Eliot spelt out a 'detachment' from individual ties. Although he pictured his psychological change as a sudden event of the late forties, his poetry suggests a more gradual and inexorable process of mental separation. *The Cocktail Party* has a rejected woman take off on a spiritual venture of her own, but if this was a fantasy for Emily Hale it was not an appropriate scenario. As a Unitarian, she was not given to the extremities of the religious life. She wanted marriage, not immolation. Marriage, she said, would have been 'so perfect a solution' to years of waiting.

For so long a relationship, there were relatively few meetings. Most of the time the Atlantic divided them. It was an attachment nourished on letters. For Emily Hale, the letter was a form that gave her pleasure: her surviving letters have the warmth and range of tone – affection, irony, honesty, restraint – of a woman adept at friendship. Eliot tended to be more cautious in the overtly personal form of the letter, and to Emily he was never explicit, it appears, about his position. For this was part of her sense of loss later when he died. Not to explain would have been entirely in character. But there are implicit explanations in his poetry, so subtle that it is hard to imagine that actual letters could surpass them. If Emily Hale read *East Coker* as 'a love-letter from God', may there not have been other such communications buried in Eliot's published works in which Eliot allowed himself, under the effective cover of poetic licence, to explore a profounder and more changeable understanding of what love meant to him than he would have permitted himself in person? We might, then, with careful delicacy, read back from the work to the life to find, as Emily Hale found rereading *The Cocktail Party*, 'many a passage which *could* have hidden meaning for me and for him'.

So long a bond is not a mere sequence of biographic facts. There remains the search for meaning: what the relationship meant to Eliot as the material of art, and what it meant to Emily Hale, who would have read his poems and plays in the light of their attachment. What the 'catastrophe' of 1947 brought out was that, over the course of many years, they had developed divergent views of their relationship.

Miss Hale had the gift, her pupils said, for bringing out the gifts of others. She had the strength that comes from imaginative generosity not, like Eliot's, from the will. As she became the presiding 'Lady' of Eliot's poetry, he would lay down will and pride before what he pictured as the purest altruism. This Lady, withdrawn in her 'white gown', is continuous with a lady in a white gown in 'The Love Song of Saint Sebastian' whose role was to witness the lover flogging sexual desire to death.

In the depths of Eliot's waste, Emily Hale had visited his memory as a lost dream of love untarnished. It had induced in the speaker of *The Waste Land* a revelation which blots out sense ('my eyes failed') and language ('I could not speak')

400

as he looks into 'silence'. To this he holds ('I remember / The hyacinth garden'), as to a lifeline, in the claustrophobic marital chamber where the wife's words beat against him.

Renewing the tie with Emily, Eliot had invented a momentous drama, partly on the model of Dante and Beatrice, partly a Jamesian drama of buried involvement. How is it possible that James seems almost to create Eliot, to forecast him? James imagined a sensibility so highly developed that it did not as yet exist, but might evolve, particularly in the context of the high-minded New England in which both James and Eliot spent their formative years. In his *Notebook*, on 5 February 1895, James set out a 'little formula' for a strange love story that is strangely like the fancy evolving in Eliot's work between 1927 and 1930:

> . . . the man of genius who, in some accursed hour of his youth, has bartered away the fondest vision of that youth and lives ever afterwards in the shadow of the bitterness of the regret. . . . The fancy of his *recovering* a little of the lost joy, of the Dead Self, in his intercourse with some person, some woman, who knows what that self was, in whom it still lives a little. This intercourse is his real life. . . . *She is his Dead Self: he is alive in her and dead in himself.*

Eliot's 'Lady of silences' presides over a dead self, guardian of its demise. There is this consolation in her existence, for the bare bones of the lost self live still through her watchful fidelity.

It is always a woman who is the recipient, or potential recipient, of poetic confession, which makes women matter to Eliot in quite a different way from their appearance as Laforguian butts of ironic dismissal or allegoric butts of a sense of sin. The confessional content of these encounters with women is a brooding sense of fate: a man whose life marks time for some overwhelming experience, something rare and strange, possibly horrible. In the view of society women, who come and go, this conviction would seem absurd, and Prufrock finds no woman in the Boston of 1911 in whom he can confide. But between 'Prufrock' and 'Gerontion', in 1919, Eliot came to know, trust – and leave

Emily Hale. In 'Gerontion' a listener is there to hear a low-voiced confession: 'I would meet you upon this honestly. / I that was near your heart was removed therefrom. . . . / I have lost my passion.' Willard Thorp, husband of Emily Hale's confidante, Margaret Thorp, suggested that 'you' is a woman with whom the speaker had known some moments of passion and beauty. She has urged him to relive these moments, at least in memory, an antidote to his barren existence, but he would be honest with her: he has lost the acuteness of his senses. 'How should I use them for your closer contact?' Astonishing candour irrupts through the stale crust of disillusion.

When Emily Hale met Eliot again after many years, she was rather awesome, with straight dark hair swept back from a face that appeared immobile until she became expressive. She had a formality, even primness, belied by a glint of humour. She was disciplined, with a clear idea of how she would live. Her manners had the impeccability of Boston, not England, where politeness is more casual. She was formal even in the way she moved: straight, controlled; then her eyes would crinkle, and she would be mischievous. Like Eliot, her formality would relent with intimates, but she had a warmer feeling for people with whom she enjoyed staunch attachments. These remained unbroken as she moved from post to post across the States. Though she lived on harder terms than women of their background, earning her living, she aged well. Her care for a mentally ill mother also brought her and Eliot together: two mature people, each with a secret burden.

She typified New England to which she was always returning. In 'Cape Ann', written on the eve of Emily's departure from England in December 1935, Eliot's mind follows her back to scenes of his youth where, more than twenty years before, he used to bird-watch, and that memory provides the focus for the quickening of more immediate emotion: 'O quick, quick, quick . . . Sweet sweet sweet.' In *Marina* and 'Cape Ann' Eliot was projecting himself over the heads of his associates in London into the waiting life that came to him as a far-off reverberation from the depths of the past that was, at the same time, the other life that might have flourished for him, had he not abandoned it for art and fame.

So, from the dream, came actuality, what Emily called the 'flowering'. It began when she was forty-one and Eliot forty-four. Some bond was established in 1933, sealed by a ring and reinforced by the frequency of Eliot's letters and the climactic visit to Burnt Norton.

The source of all this goes back to 'Hidden under the heron's wing', the poem Eliot wrote at the time that he was first drawn to Emily Hale. A beloved brings a whisper of hidden revelation, hidden under the heron's wing or enclosed in lotus-buds before daybreak. At this time, Eliot was studying Indian philosophy, which makes frequent reference to a thousand-petalled lotus that enfolds enlightenment. It is associated in the *Kama Shastras* with the most desirable of women, the lotus-lady or *padmini*. Though, usually, Eliot tended to separate body and soul, he derived from Eastern thought the image of a woman where such a distinction is not made. The traditional connotations of the lotus-lady range from sensual to spiritual. In *Burnt Norton* the lotus that once sang to the young lover in Boston, now unfolds its hidden vision: 'And the lotos rose, quietly, quietly . . .'.

In the end this is all that Eliot wanted from Emily Hale. Once he has the heart of light, human love is left to turn to dust. There is a startling ruthlessness about this reach for ultra-human bliss, reminiscent of St Augustine or Abelard, men who were capable of passionate devotion yet were avid for purity. For such men, purity was counter to human fidelity, which they came to perceive as temptation. This state of mind, alien to our time and, possibly, to women in all ages (there is none of this ruthlessness in Héloïse), is what makes Eliot the most elusive of poets. Christianity has recognised the danger of religious emotion, the temptation to pride, by attempting to guard it with the virtue of humility, but the ultimate danger is that humility should coexist with pride and even mask it. Hawthorne explored this state of mind in the figure of the Puritan minister, Dimmesdale, who acknowledges himself to be a sinner both in private and finally in public, but sins more than he knows in the self-absorbed extravagance of his humility and in his denial of the natural bond with his lover, Hester Prynne. To freeze the senses does not necessarily exonerate Eliot from the bond that, by 1935, had been established. How could the woman who had shared the heart of light be detached from its import for the life ahead? It is easy to justify a solitary religious position in the case of monks and nuns who have incurred no other obligation; less easy where the solitary path cuts through trust. It has then to be self-serving, and the denial of obligation implies a belief in the exclusiveness of the soul's superior instants. This state of mind is heroic, that is, not wholly moral, though often clothed in rectitude.

There is something of this ferocity in Eliot's aspiration – heroic, exclusive – beneath his masks of conformity: the English gentleman, the churchwarden, the self-deprecating man of letters, and not least the transformation into doting husband in the last eight years of Eliot's life, all of which present an image of normality.

Emily Hale continued to teach and, at the close of each academic year, would arrive in England. Over the years it became a ritual for Eliot to meet her boat train, a ritual that went on into the fifties, through his years of great fame when Mary Trevelyan noted the priority of this commitment with some surprise. For the amount of time Emily Hale was in England, there is an odd dearth of information. It is as though a veil of silence covered her. The 'Lady of silences' was not herself a silent person; she was, on the contrary, as friends remember, distinctly articulate. The silences emanate from Eliot: 'silence' as his word for an experience of unspeakable bliss, and silence, it would seem, also as a practical policy, accepted by his friends and by Emily herself. She never embarrassed him by any public disclosure of their understanding.

Still, a few facts of their meetings filter through. Emily joined the Perkinses as usual, at the end of her first academic year at Smith College. She had recovered effectively enough for Smith to reappoint her. Eliot visited Chipping Campden in August and September. That summer she accompanied Eliot to Edinburgh for his honorary degree. At the last minute she discovered that a long dress was obligatory, sped out, and returned in a dress splashed with a dramatic print. Eliot teased her about her brightness at so sober a gathering. Emily herself liked to tell of being snubbed. She was admiring a private garden when Lady Drummond, looking pointedly at the floral colours of her guest's dress, said: 'I see that Miss *Hale* has brought her garden with her.'

When she arranged the Christmas service back at Smith College on 16 December 1937, she included Eliot's 'O Light Invisible'.

In July 1938 Eliot was once again in Chipping Campden, and the same month Emily Hale may have been the woman who accompanied him to a poetry reading at a Student Christian Movement conference at Swanwick in Derbyshire. Mary Trevelyan, who first met Eliot here, thought the woman was his wife. When in London, Emily used to visit Cat Morgan at Faber, where Eliot's secretary, Miss Swan, made her welcome. She was known to Faber colleagues, but clearly there was some agreement to keep her under wraps, possibly because Vivienne (until she was institutionalised in July 1938) would not have been averse to scandal. It could not have been an unforeseen danger that the two women might cross paths on their visits to Faber. Eliot put something of their conflicting emotional claims into *The Family Reunion*, staged in February 1939.

In July 1939 Emily Hale went off to stay with Janet Adam Smith's mother in an uncomfortable castle in a marvellous setting on the west coast of Scotland, where she performed in a play. On 30 August, with war imminent, John Hayward reported to Morley that Eliot was trying to embark Æmilia with her uncle and aunt on anything seaworthy sailing westward.

Three years of separation followed. Eliot completed the wartime *Quartets*, and Emily Hale continued at Smith. She understood that only by unremitting atonement could Eliot hope to transform the Furies of conscience. A Campden friend said that she believed that 'if she were patient for long enough, her moment of glory would assuredly arrive', but she was more generous than this implies, more like Alice Staverton, the mature woman in 'The Jolly Corner' (the James tale to which Eliot referred in *The Family Reunion*), who hopes to heal a man haunted by the hideous ghost of his other self, through the comfort of her acceptance.

In the autumn of 1942 Eliot returned to America. Nothing so far is known of this visit except that his sister, Ada, the eldest and cleverest (the Mycroft to Eliot's Sherlock Holmes), was seriously ill. In the same year, Emily Hale left Smith College abruptly, without an alternative post. Some disagreement preceded her departure, but it was so minor that I have wondered if something else disturbed her. Had she hoped, with the completion of the *Quartets*, for a resolution to her own long trial of patience? Eliot's brother once complained that she used to kiss the family as though she were a prospective member. Eliot replied that there was a commitment, but the understanding was that he would not marry Emily so long as Vivienne lived.

There followed a difficult time. She continued to feel handicapped by lack of formal credentials, and in the summer of 1941 had returned to the University of Wisconsin for some course work, including a graduate essay on 'Criticism and its Function for the Teacher of Interpretation'. For a short while, in 1943, she taught at Bennett Junior College in Millbrook, New York, then moved on to teach in high schools. She never held an academic post again. Later in 1943 she had a temporary position at Concord Academy in Concord, Massachusetts, and managed to stay on. At the beginning of the new school year in 1944, the headmistress, Miss Josephine Tucker, announced that Miss Hale had 'returned to spend the entire year on dramatics and speech training'. On 31 May 1944 Eliot came to give the Commencement address. One pupil, Sarah ('Fanny') Tomaino, was bored and disappointed by his 'cool dry tone' – she had wanted him to sound like a poet. But she remembered his 'praying-mantis' handshake and his studied pronunciation of 'po-et-treh'.

In November 1944 Emily Hale directed *Quality Street* by James Barrie, with Fanny Tomaino in the lead. She recalled: 'Miss Hale's presence during that short time in my life has always remained with me – every detail – how she costumed me in her own Empire-cut, satin peignoir. How, after the performance, when the material was hopelessly stained with perspiration, she said "of course it can never be worn again." Then seeing the anxiety on my face either said something or smiled in a way that said "Never mind, it is worth it to *both* of us." ' Because her teacher seemed old to the teenage girl, she called her 'Mrs' Hale until she was taken aside and told: '*Miss* Hale if you please, Fanny. As yet I have not accepted the hand of any man in matrimony.' Another time, the girl shared a seat with her on a train from Concord to Boston, and recalled (more than forty years later) that Miss Hale 'looked more dressed up than I had seen her, in a blouse with a ruffle. She said, "I am going to the zoo with Tom." What a thrill to have her share this confidence! The school grapevine had it that Miss Hale had some secret connection with the famous poet T. S. Eliot. Also, I was the only member of my English class who felt that she "understood" *Ash-Wednesday*. Thus my fantasy connection with Mr Eliot was already in place. And there, as the train pulled into the platform, stood "Tom" himself, in his dark clothes, leaning on an umbrella. The train passed him before it stopped and I heard Miss Hale's voice calling "Taum, Taum" down the platform.'

Her post may not have been secure, for she put her furniture and books in storage and lived in one furnished room after another. In 1945, she spoke of 'my wretched way of living in the last three years'. This continued all through her years in Concord until the end of 1947.

Meanwhile, in London, the wartime separation from Emily Hale had brought Eliot closer to Mary Trevelyan. Through Emily Hale, Eliot had lived a life of memory vital to his poetry, but he was not above taking pleasure in the jolly company of Mary, who mattered not a whit to his poetry but was eminently agreeable – partly for the very reason that there was, as yet, no basis for any emotional claim.

Mary was what the English call a good sort. She was reliable without being dull. She had the English blend of sturdiness and humour, with the confident determination of women like Mary Kingsley, whose *Travels in West Africa* she read aloud to Eliot. Janet Adam Smith recalled how she always talked to a man, and ignored his little wife. Where Emily had the elegance and subtle shades of the past, Mary was the type of the moment: a woman in the uniform of the Armed Forces, hearty, back-slapping, her very Englishness propping Eliot's commitment, at the end of *Four Quartets*, to a particular destiny, 'now and in England'.

In 1945 Eliot sent Emily Hale another of those literary 'letters' that she kept to the end of her life. In *What is a Classic?* he spoke of an obligation to resign love for a higher 'destiny'. His model was Aeneas, 'the man in fate' who must abandon Dido as the gods command. Eliot, though, does not consider, as Virgil did, the woman's anguish. Aeneas justifies himself on the ground that he made no formal commitment: 'I have never held the wedding torches as a husband; I have never entered into such agreements.' Eliot's account skirts the confrontation, to dwell on the hero's burden of guilt, as though suffering were his exclusively. Later, Aeneas descends to visit the shades of the dead, and there encounters his lost love. Eliot sees her agonised withdrawal not for its own pathos but as a 'projection' of the hero's conscience. Aeneas, he added in 1951, 'felt a worm', and then, more warmly: such a destiny 'is a very heavy cross to bear'.

To Eliot, Dido in the Underworld is a model woman who behaves just as a man would have her behave: she does not rail; she does not say a word; just takes herself off. He finds in this dreamlike scene of parting 'a refinement of manner, springing from a delicate sensibility, ... in that test of manners, private and public conduct between the sexes'. Parting, he goes on, must be 'civilized' in the style of Henry James. Eliot's concern for manners – his appreciation of what he calls Dido's 'snub' – belies the emotional tension of the woman's flight into the forest of shadows, 'burning' and 'fierce-eyed' as she 'tears herself away'. Aeneas, too, is not quite so refined and wormish as Eliot suggests. He is 'stunned' and 'follows at a distance with tears and pity for her as she goes'.

What is a Classic? reveals Eliot's own concern with destiny. The voyager of his poetry was a contrived identity: the gods never quite distinguished him, as they did Aeneas, with explicit command, but he denied love all the same. Crucial to Eliot's dream of destiny was its burden of guilt. The fated man, he said, 'does not forgive himself – and this, significantly, in spite of the fact of which he is well aware, that all he has done has been in compliance with destiny', with 'a greater inscrutable power'. He projects himself through a Jamesian version of this exile, whose destiny it was to be the link between two great nations. A. Walton Litz has said that *Four Quartets* was the last poem of this century to speak to English and American alike. For Eliot, the two peoples were not only allies in war but united in a common culture, embodied in his own person. His praise for the exile's 'absence of provinciality' speaks for his own ambition to carry the best of his native tradition – the venturesome moral energy of America – beyond its frontiers. That voyage back to provincial origins in *The Dry Salvages*, to the Mississippi and the New England shore, retrieves a native spirit that Eliot would implant 'now and in England'.

*

In March 1946 Emily Hale directed Noël Coward's *Hay Fever* in aid of the American Friends for European Relief. It played to packed auditoriums in Concord. In the summer she acted in *Blithe Spirit* with the Dorset Players, in Dorset, Vermont, and Eliot was in the audience. This comedy about a husband whose dead wife's spirit returns to trouble his relationship with his new wife may have provided the germ for Eliot's first comedy, *The Cocktail Party*, where a wife disappears into a sanatorium, leaving her husband to his affair with another woman, and then returns to take possession of him. According to Dorothy Elsmith, Eliot 'used to follow Emily in her summer theatrical appearances. She was a clever, excellent actress' with an animation that surprised people who knew her only as a rather conscientious and disciplined elocution teacher. There is a rare photograph of Eliot and Emily Hale together in Vermont: she, slim in her simple shirtwaist with her hands in her pockets, looks at the camera with charming grace; Eliot beside her looks oddly formal in the summer setting, in his dark suit with the usual handkerchief in his breast-pocket. Another photograph was taken in Dublin, New Hampshire, where the woman beside Eliot has been cut out of the picture. What remains looks a bit like the Vermont photo which has been kept safely at Princeton. The New Hampshire photo, which is in one of the family albums at Harvard, could well have been cut at Eliot's wish.

That summer of 1946 Eliot's base was his brother's apartment at 84 Prescott Street, Cambridge, Massachusetts. At the end of July he sailed back to England, taking a present of maple sugar from Emily Hale to Janet Adam Smith, who had known Eliot from the time that she started her career as literary critic in the early thirties and married Michael Roberts, who wrote regularly for the *Criterion*. Her family knew Emily Hale quite independently through its connections with the Boston élite.

Between 1933 and 1946 Eliot's relation to Emily Hale would have established a settled pattern of occasional meetings, fondness, and jokes, all of which sustained their understanding. From the time of Eliot's conversion to the time of Vivienne's death she provided a chaste love that could be sustained, it seemed, indefinitely.

The unexpected death of Vivienne challenged the stable bond. Eliot retreated at once from the possibility of action, asserting that it was too late.* He told Mary Trevelyan, on 15 April 1947, that he dreaded the coming visit to America so much that it would be a relief to get started so that he could look forward to his return. He sailed on 22 April, and soon

---

* Like Lambert Strether in *The Ambassadors*.

after his arrival his brother, Henry, died of leukaemia. While he stayed with his sister Margaret at 41 Kirkland Street, Cambridge, Emily Hale was not far away in Concord where, that spring, she put on one of her most ambitious and successful productions, *Richard II*. Henry's widow, Theresa, invited Emily to her apartment, meaning to bring her together with Eliot on the assumption that they would both wish to marry. But when Eliot arrived he turned on Theresa in a white fury which she remembered to the last months of her life.

Still, sooner or later, it was necessary to make his psychological change of life known to Emily Hale. They met privately two or three times. One meeting took place in June when Eliot went, at her instigation, to Concord Academy to give another address at its twenty-fifth anniversary Commencement. On 3 June he sat in the school hall like an aged eagle, with stooping shoulders and forward-thrusting head, but spoke with 'the wry Yankee wit; he might have been Emerson himself, except for the cosmopolite suavity'. He told the girls that he had written *The Waste Land* 'to relieve my emotions'. Otherwise, he appeared at his most withdrawn, applauding automatically, but looking up only with effort. A letter from Emily to Lorraine Havens reports exactly what happened between them:

> with the Dorset Players
> Dorset. Vt.
> August 7 '47

Dearest Lorraine,
   ... His visit here was a sort of public nightmare of events – his only brother died soon after he arrived – and from that strain he had spent himself thro' lectures and readings plus the *three* commencements when he received honorary degrees. ... I am going to tell you, dear friend, that what I confided to you long ago of a mutual affection he and I have had for each other has come to a strange impasse whether permanent or not, I do not know. Tom's wife died last winter very suddenly. I supposed he would then feel free to marry me as I believed he always intended to do. But such proves not to be the case. We met privately two or three times to try to sift the situation as

thoroughly as possible – he loves me – I believe that wholly – but apparently not in the way usual to men less gifted i.e. with complete love thro' a married relationship. I have not completely given up hope that he may yet recover from this – to me – abnormal reaction, but on the other hand I cannot allow myself to hold on to anything so delicately uncertain.

I am very much at a loose end at present, having resigned from the Academy in Concord, and given up the rented house. I want dreadfully to have some little place of my own – and be free to follow my interests as I lead them or they lead me. I have even thought of trying for dramatic work seriously since I love it so and know I can do it. I am here acting with a small summer group as I did last year – had one excellent part and another promised which has had to be given up for another production. . . . I value your and Paul's friendship so very much. Perhaps you will have a brilliant idea as to what I can do another year.* Love to Paul and yourself in full measure –

Yours
Emily Hale.

Eliot kept his stay in New England as short as possible. He left in mid-June (after at last getting a doctorate from Harvard). He was shaken. He later told Mary Trevelyan that he had experienced a catastrophe which he could not reveal because it involved another person. Emily Hale called it a 'miscarriage': emphatic words from such restrained people.

Eliot's evident ageing in 1947, which, it has been implied, was an outcome of Vivienne's death, more likely followed his discovery that he had lost his passion. After his minor operations, Eliot spent August and September convalescing in the country. Across the Atlantic, Emily Hale soothed herself with the luxury of three unfurnished rooms at 9 Lexington Road, Concord. There she arranged her own things and nursed plans for a new start in the theatre until, in the spring of 1948, she took up another teaching post. Meanwhile, hope of Eliot's 'recovery' faded. When he was due to return to America to the Institute for Advanced Study at Princeton for

---

* Paul Havens was now President of Wilson College, Pennsylvania. This was a hint that he might find a post for her.

the fall semester of 1948, she steeled herself to his withdrawal in a sad sentence at the end of another letter to Lorraine Havens:

[90 Commonwealth Ave]
Boston.
September 12th 48.

Dearest Lorraine,

. . . You may well ask about me, dear friend. I . . . remained in Concord, very happily living in a small but attractive apartment made out of one floor of a really old house. From my so-called life of leisure I was suddenly called to Abbot Academy, Andover . . . to fill a sudden vacancy in speech & drama for the rest of the year, having half the week in Andover and half the week in Concord, putting on two plays and teaching long hours on the two [?] days I was at Andover. But it was all so happy mutually, that Miss Hearsey, who knew me years ago when we were girls, asked me to return permanently – which offer I could not refuse, tho' I hesitated to give up certain indulgent ways of life I enjoyed so much. But I am committed now to a very fine school I think, and best of all, the school has made over some part of a house they own into a very fine apartment – repapered, repainted, etc – into which I am moving this week, tho as there are two stories, I really have more rooms than furniture to put into them. But little by little something new will be added perhaps and I *love* having my own dear possessions about . . . me after years of absence from them. . . . T. S. Eliot comes to Princeton this winter to the Institute of Higher Education – as guest visitor – but I expect I shall see him only occasionally. Dear Lorraine –

My love as ever to you –
Emily Hale.

At this very time, before Eliot left for Princeton, he was drafting *The Cocktail Party*, the work which Emily Hale selected for its 'hidden meaning'. She did not specify what it was, so that to read the play for this meaning can be done only with the utmost caution. This play does yield the most subtle explanation of Eliot's new position, and at the same time remains intact as a work of art. Eliot said that a play is less personal than a poem, yet the complete cover of dramatic

413

form actually gave him the freedom to expose, more directly than anything since *The Family Reunion*, a private crisis. It is not hard to see how he transmutes the crises of 1947 – the death of Vivienne and the rejection of Emily Hale – into drama. There are obvious parallels with Lavinia, the wife who is 'impossible' (as Eliot told the first cast) and vanishes without warning, and the other woman, Celia, who now expects to marry the husband, Edward. But the interest of this sort of identification is trivial. What brings the play to life is the emotional charge of Eliot's feeling working, as ever, well below the surface. At this buried level there is a word of consolation as well as rejection. It would have told Emily Hale that it was 'too late' now for marriage but that, all the same, she had been the saving grace of his life.

For the first and last time in his career, Eliot creates in this play a woman who acts in her own right, not as a foil or prop to a man's realisation as artist, convert, or sinner. Celia is not a bodiless Virgin or a Lady of silences. She states her surprise at Edward's defection with brave distinctness, and is the focus for sympathy in the play. Edward is a self-confessed mediocrity beside her. It is his destiny to recognise that his mediocrity lies in his inability to love; and it is Celia's destiny to discover in her slighted depth of feeling the altruism of a potential saint.

In so far as Emily Hale was the source for Celia, it was Eliot's imaginative farewell: in the course of the play, Celia's fate moves off-stage. Yet, through her, Eliot expounds a very rare form of love. Never did he create so lovable a woman, assured and sensitive. In the first two acts, she is lovable in the ordinary way yet, to the talented man, she is also extraordinary. Two men have loved her, the middle-aged husband with whom she has had a long affair, and the young film director, Peter Quilpe, the artist who has loved her platonically. Of the two it is Peter who has a clearer understanding of Celia's distinction. She did not arouse the usual excitement or desire for possession, but a feeling at once more intense and more tranquil. Peter speaks of 'moments in which we seemed to share some perception, / Some feeling, some indefinable experience / In which we were both unaware of ourselves.' Here Eliot explores the matchless 'moment' that he owed to Emily Hale. Peter declares it to be his only experience of what he, like Eliot, calls 'reality'. Celia, like Emily, opens the route to reality – so long as she remains physically unattainable. Edward advises Peter against consummation. In six months, he warns, you would find that she was 'another woman' and you 'another man'. Eliot's sexual prejudice shows in this banal cynicism. The 'fever', Edward asserts, must eventually cool; a couple must jolt on to the sterile ground of their innate difference. This is to be expected in marriage, which may be redeemed by goodwill, but such a solution would be too humdrum for Celia's gifts. It would be, Edward assures her, 'the ruin of loveliness'. Marital 'tedium' must not be the 'residue of ecstasy'.

There lies behind this Eliot's fear that to enjoy love is to destroy it. Inhibition tortured passion until it atrophied. In *The Family Reunion*, in *Burnt Norton*, and finally in *The Cocktail Party*, Eliot speaks of love as a door. In *Burnt Norton* he can peer through the door into a rose-garden. In *The Cocktail Party* the door is shut: 'There was a door / And I could not open it. I could not touch the handle.'

When Edward seems free to marry the woman he had professed to love, he discovers that he simply doesn't want her as a wife. The confrontation of Edward and Celia in the second scene of the play seems to correspond so exactly with Emily Hale's report of her exchange with Eliot in June 1947 that the dialogue may re-create the substance of their very words.

Celia confesses to Edward that, for her, 'the dream was not enough'.

For Edward, the loss of his wife 'only brought to light the real difficulties'. He wants to be alone to 'understand'.

Celia, puzzled, wonders if it is just panic and a wish not to make an effort, a moment of fatigue. Edward replies that it is not only that.

Celia then wonders if he is on the verge of a breakdown, but Edward doesn't feel that his reaction is treatable.*

Celia begs him to assure her that 'everything is all right between us'.

Then Edward rejects her. You are a very rare person, he tells her. 'But it was too late.' He acknowledges that he should have known that it wasn't fair to her. His line of defence is that she should have assumed that the continued existence of his wife would have prevented their marriage. 'What future had you ever thought there could be?'

Celia declares that she had abandoned the future to live in 'a private world of *ours*' in which happiness had a different meaning. 'A dream. I was happy in it till to-day.'

In the dialogue that follows, Eliot implies that it was the woman who betrayed the dream when she wanted 'this world'. When she breaks the dream with her wish for marriage, the man becomes aware that, for him, the dream was an escape from a given course of existence, a mere 'make-believe' which his 'tougher self' now refutes. Eliot is speaking in Emersonian terms of the integrity of the self which, in a typescript version, he calls 'the *daimon*, the genius'. It is to this intransigent self that Emerson in 1841 had addressed his heady message of self-reliance. The claim of this self is more radical, more absorbing, potentially more excluding than in other civilisations, as de Tocqueville shrewdly observed: American individualism was such that a man might be shut up in the solitude of his own heart. Eliot would not permit any social tie to invade his solitude. He could not love, he told Emily Hale, as did less gifted men. It was a claim which she was bound to accept.

Eliot's consolation for Emily Hale is, I think, the 'hidden meaning' of Edward's words to Celia: 'If I have ever been in love – and I think that I have – / I have never been in love with anyone but you, / And perhaps I still am.' Emily Hale

---

* Mary Trevelyan immediately thought of this exchange when, on 5 June 1950, Eliot said that he didn't suppose the woman he had loved 'will *ever* understand what it was all about. She, and others no doubt, would say I ought to have seen a psychologist.' This Mary reports in her diary.

had understood this from Eliot: 'he loves me – I believe that wholly', she had told Lorraine Havens. This is further confirmed on Eliot's part in a letter to Mary Trevelyan in 1950: he said that though he did not wish to marry the woman he had loved, he believed himself to be still in love with her. As Edward confides to Peter Quilpe, he must 'do nothing', and content himself with the woman he remembers. To live through memory was, Eliot once remarked to Mary Trevelyan, '*my* way of thinking'.

Eliot's tribute to the rarity of Emily Hale's character comes in the first two acts, where we see Celia in her human aspect. The sacrificial Celia of the final act is Eliot's invention based on the tragic end of Charles de Foucauld.* Born to wealth and social position, Foucauld found his vocation as a missionary priest at Tamanrasset in the Hoggar Mountains of the Sahara Desert. His aim, Eliot saw, 'was not primarily to convert by teaching, but to *live* the Christian life, alone among the natives'. He lived in a stone hermitage and gave medical aid to tribesmen, and then was killed suddenly in 1916 by a marauding band. Celia's end is equally sudden. Her crucifixion by hostile tribes near an anthill (in the script for the first performances at the Edinburgh Festival, in 1949, her body is eaten away by ants) is reminiscent of the dismemberment of a woman in a lysol bath in *Sweeney Agonistes*. The script dwells on how the heathens have some very nasty ways of cooking Christian natives – cooking that begins before they are dead. Though traces of Celia's body are found, it is difficult to tell what has happened to it at such a stage of decomposition – bodies do, of course, disintegrate quickly in Kinkanja. Before crucifixion, her body has been smeared with a juice attractive to ants – so that she would have been devoured with brutal slowness by ants as she died. Eliot always wishes to jolt us with some incursion of actual

---

* In a letter of 30 May 1935, Eliot had recommended to Jeanette McPherrin the *Vie de Charles de Foucauld* by René Bazin. He was a much greater man, Eliot said, than Lawrence of Arabia. Again, on 10 April 1941, Eliot referred to the biography of Foucauld in a wireless talk. It conveyed, he said, the extraordinary 'spiritual quality' of this life.

horror, actual pain, and yet the distaste of the Edinburgh audience and of the producer, Harry Sherek, was justified. The director, E. Martin Browne, warned Eliot that the distaste was as much for the flippancy with which the cruelty to Celia was introduced, and that he lost his audience when her death had no active impact for the listeners – nothing, said Browne, developed from their hearts. Even minus the sensational lines, another Edinburgh production in 1997 provoked a reviewer to write: 'The ending is . . . repugnant, condemning an inconvenient girlfriend to a grisly death . . . which is represented as a moral triumph.' The priestly psychiatrist who brings this about 'is cravenly unquestioned'.

This reviewer was a woman, and as women's voices grow stronger Eliot's 'bullying' is rightly questioned. Bodies are women's creations; we don't want to see them killed or tortured or throttled. Here is more than a little residue of the sadism of 'The Love Song of Saint Sebastian'. In both, a woman is idealised, then mutilated so that nothing but memory remains. 'The Love Song of Saint Sebastian' was written in 1914; *The Cocktail Party* in 1948–9: these were the two dates when it would have been appropriate for Eliot to marry Emily Hale. Both times Eliot fixed on an alternative to physical possession, her idealised image, a far more powerful form of possession because it is godlike. If he stops creating her, she stops existing. This is what Emily Hale had to endure, whether she knew it or not.

Celia's sacrifice is seen from the perspective of party-people. In *Murder in the Cathedral* and *The Family Reunion*, the martyr or penitent was centre-stage; in *The Cocktail Party*, she is moved aside as the focus settles on the unconvincing accommodations of Edward and his returned wife, Lavinia. Eliot expected a West End or Broadway audience to identify with Edward and Lavinia, as though we were the same kind of unpromising material. John Dexter, in his 1986 production at the Phoenix in London, breathed life into the finale by having Lavinia and Edward bathe their words in the warmth of demonstrative gestures, and the curtain came down on marital play. Lavinia's very visibly swelling belly bore out the fertility of marriage. Their psychiatrist, Sir Henry Harcourt-Reilly, played with messianic vehemence by Alec McCowen, shouted 'it's a good life' with a bang on the desk.

With less assertion than in this production, the play falls down on its insistence that a patched-up marriage is the best we can make of relations between the sexes. Geoffrey Faber, writing to Eliot on 25 August 1949, protested: 'The lines where [the psychiatrist] Reilly speaks of parents who don't understand each other and neither understand nor are understood by their children are not true of marriage and parenthood as I have been fortunate enough to experience these states...'. Eliot's cold reply on 29 August denies human love: '... In the universe of discourse in which Reilly is moving during that speech there are two primary propositions: 1. nobody understands you but God, 2. all real love is ultimately the love of God.'

There is another problem, less easy to solve. In Act III Eliot moves his best character, Celia, out of sight so that her story comes to us like an echo from afar. The problem is that so much more is made of the sadistic details of her death than of the good life that led to that death. Celia is more interesting for her indomitable character than for her death, and some image of her work should dominate the scene. This would be simple on film. On stage, it would be difficult, though not impossible, to open up the drawing-room to some glimpse of the real Celia, like the glimpse of the real Odette behind the ballroom in Act III of *Swan Lake*.

The Cocktail Party is worth rescue if only for its most memorable scene, Celia's interview with the psychiatrist or 'guardian' in Act II. At this point, Eliot drops the Noël Coward comedy of manners for exploration of the inner life. Helen Gardner once said that in his plays Eliot was writing to some extent against the bent of his natural genius. 'Essentially he was an explorer, not an expounder, discovering truth of feeling, and the truths that feelings point to, in the process of exploration.' It was always difficult for him to stage the invisible life of the spirit. It is not surprising that *Hamlet*, the play *par excellence* of the inner life, was the model to which he clung. 'I have that within which passes show' is true for Harry in *The Family Reunion* as for Celia in *The Cocktail Party*. But where Harry remains mysterious to the audience, Celia does clarify her discovery of her surprising vocation. Eliot achieves this clarity by distancing himself, to some degree, from the saint in the making. Celia is not tormented by the tempters and Furies of Eliot's heroes with their flawed pasts. Celia also has the advantage of genuine humility. She is the victim of Edward's change of heart but has no high sense of her own drama. She has a woman's modest expectations – assuming quite ordinary needs for love, marriage, friendship – so that her transition, in one scene, from ordinary to extraordinary is absorbing.

Celia's disappointment with Edward does not crush her. She retains her capacity for high moments of love, the memory of which she will carry into her new life:

> For what happened is remembered like a dream
> In which one is exalted by intensity of loving
> In the spirit, a vibration of delight
> Without desire, for desire is fulfilled
> In the delight of loving.

Here Eliot sums up what I think he felt for Emily Hale: she evoked a sense of exaltation without the fret of desire. Her extraordinary gift was to make him into a person capable of the delight of loving. Reilly, the authoritative voice of the play, explains that knowledge of love might be used by the saint but equally by those who must reconcile themselves to the human condition. This second course is the one that Eliot chose at the end of the *Quartets* and attempts to realise in this play. Such people

>   . . . may remember
> The vision they have had, but they cease to regret it,
> Maintain themselves by the common routine,
> Learn to avoid excessive expectation,
> Become tolerant of themselves and others . . .

This programme is the antithesis of the solitary journeys of Eliot's earlier years, the pilgrimage into the mountains, the journey of the Magi, the reckless voyages. As the dream of purity receded over Eliot's horizon, he turned to confront common life which the theatre must reflect if it is to gain the wider audience to whom he hoped to speak.

*

For ten more years Eliot sustained the outward pattern of his friendship with Emily Hale. Twice, in 1948 and 1952, he travelled to Andover, where she taught at Abbot Academy from February 1948 until June 1957. As she predicted, she saw little of him during his stay at Princeton, New Jersey,* in 1948, when he went north to Boston three times. In June 1953 she went with Eliot, his sister Marian, and Dorothy Elsmith, to St Louis to hear him reminisce about his family in the town of his birth. When Emily was due to arrive in London in mid-August, Eliot cancelled an annual outing to Windsor with Mary Trevelyan in order to meet the train. Both women went to Edinburgh later that month for the opening night of Eliot's next play, *The Confidential Clerk*, and took turns to visit him where he sat with his niece, Theodora, in the royal box. Theodora thought that Emily should not have come: she was 'a pale shadow of her former self'.

Though Eliot still loved Emily Hale, he preferred not to see her and felt embarrassed and unhappy when he did. He was irritated by 'a man's sense of being in the wrong', and decided that they now had little in common. It was, he repeated, 'too late'. He had become 'fixed', however much he rebelled against this fixing. He was 'burnt out', a 'haunted man'. The self-image is unmistakably Jamesian. In the *Notebooks*, James had the idea of 'some friendship or passion or bond – some affection long desired and waited for, that is formed too late? –

* Eliot remarked that Princeton's Center for Advanced Studies was like a Jamesian 'Great Good Place' for elderly celebrities.

I mean too late in life altogether. . . . They but meet to part or to suffer. . . . They may have been dimly conscious, in the past, of the possibility between them – been groping for each other in the darkness. It's love, it's friendship, it's mutual comprehension. . . . It's a passion that *might* have been. I seem to be coinciding simply with the married person encountering the *real* mate, etc.; but that is not what I mean.' The issue of marriage is peripheral to their waiting 'too long – till something else has happened'. What happened was 'the wasting of life'.

Meanwhile, Emily Hale went on with her work. She had a good post at the oldest girls' school in the U.S., where she was appreciated. Ever loyal to J. M. Barrie, she put on *Dear Brutus* (a third time) and *The Admirable Crichton*; also Shaw's *Candida*, and *Antigone* by Jean Anouilh. One pupil, Ann Kennedy Irish, said that 'Eliot's loss was Abbot's gain. Miss Hale nurtured and expanded our love for and understanding of the theatre.' Her skill in casting resulted in admired performances, and she worked as carefully with girls in minor roles as with the stars. She also showed a sympathetic concern for the girls as individuals. When Eliot arrived at the school for an impromptu talk in 1952, the rumour flew round that he was a 'very special' friend of Miss Hale. They still corresponded, and Eliot still sent copies of his works as they came out: 'The Three Voices of Poetry' in 1953, and in 1954 'The Cultivation of Christmas Trees'. She took comfort in their old habits, and in the fact that no other woman had meant as much. For thirty years, as Barbara Burwell put it, 'her whole life and world were bound up with Mr Eliot'.

She was therefore devastated when Eliot married again in January 1957. She retired from Abbot Academy, and then collapsed. She went into the Massachusetts General Hospital in Boston complaining of dizziness, and was investigated for a brain tumour, but the doctors found nothing. It was an emotional breakdown. Barbara Burwell remembered her coming to recuperate at Woods Hole, unsteady, leaning on a cane, and looking as though she had aged ten years. She never fully recovered, never got back her vivacity. What she retained was the inner core of conduct, a stoic centre, but she withdrew from her wider circle of contacts. Caroline Willington, a family connection, said: 'When Tom married a second time, Emily really went into seclusion. We lost track of her for many years.'

This reaction was not just to the shock of his marriage, but to the fact that Eliot now broke completely with her. During the course of their correspondence between 1932 and 1947, Eliot (Valerie Eliot reports) 'liked to think that his letters to her would be preserved and made public fifty years after they were dead.' He was 'shocked and angry' when she informed him in 1956 that she was giving the letters to Princeton University Library during her lifetime. 'It seemed to him "that her disposition of the letters in that way at that time threw some light upon the kind of interest which she took, or had come to take, in these letters. *The Aspern Papers* in reverse." '* On 24 January 1957, two weeks after Eliot's marriage, the Librarian wrote to state that the letters would remain sealed until fifty years after the death of the survivor.

Mrs Burwell remembered her mother's mention of an 'unappreciative letter from Mr Eliot'. Its substance was to rule Emily Hale out of his life: he wanted, from then on, no more to do with her. The breach was such that Janet Adam Smith felt, as Eliot's friend, that she should not accept an invitation from Emily Hale when she visited the States in the early sixties.

From 1957 Emily Hale turned her attention to what she called 'my memoirs'. Silenced by Eliot's wish in her lifetime, she resolved to speak to the future. On 20 July 1957 she refers in a letter to Willard Thorp to an Introduction she had written to Eliot's letters which she was now turning over to Princeton. She read the Introduction to Professor Thorp (whom she called 'my tutor in Public Affairs') and his wife, Margaret,

* In *The Aspern Papers* by Henry James, the aged lover of the great American poet Aspern secretes their correspondence, and holds off a 'publishing scoundrel'. Her niece, Tina, eventually burns the papers – see below how Eliot follows this idea through in his own actions.

and it had their approval. That July, she sent to Mr Dix, Princeton's librarian, a new copy of the Introduction which, she told Thorp, 'I made even *more* personal and detailed than earlier – also I enclosed the last of T.S.E.'s letters – with the exception of one – which relates directly to the disposition of the letters to the University. I am especially glad I felt like finishing off the correspondence, because Mr Dix could read for himself T's reaction and be relieved of his own sense of having brought difficulties upon me.'

Emily Hale had now to vacate the rooms belonging to Abbot Academy. Her future was uncertain. She still hoped to pick up a half- or full-time post. Then, in October, she went to 'live' in England, in Chipping Campden. It was a return to the hallowed ground of memory, the Campden of the thirties, and it could not be the same. She appeared disturbed to locals, and did not stay long; by February 1958 she was back in Boston. In March she went to teach at Oak Grove School in Vassalboro, Maine, and after one semester retired finally. In the last decade of her life she returned to those places – the Cotswolds, Smith College, Concord – where she had been happiest. Between September 1958 and 1963 she lived at 83 Crescent Street, Northampton, Massachusetts, but at Smith, as in Campden, she no longer had a place. She was lonely. The faculty kept to its own circles, and she was not invited by those she would have liked. She told the Thorps, 'I miss the real exchange and stimulus of worthwhile ideas and people.' In May 1963 she moved back to Concord, and settled at 9 Church Green, a little house built during the Revolution.

That summer she had another impulse to speak to the future. In July she made a recording of Eliot's letters to her, and gave it to Princeton. As a professional speaker, she had often read Eliot's poems aloud on formal occasions or in class, and this had been her only legitimate voicing of what meant more to her than anything else. For more than thirty years she had been careful not to expose to the public her relationship with the great poet. But in the summer of 1963, she did raise her voice in a new way: she put on tape a spoken memoir.

On 18 August 1963 she wrote to Willard Thorp: '... I had suddenly felt almost a revulsion against the whole story – so personal – so painful in many ways – of T.S.E. and E.H. – becoming public property in years long after we both are gone. ... I haven't had the courage yet to read the good secretary's transcript, but may do so to-night to one close relative I have who knows the story. For M[argaret]'s very good suggestions – biographical data etc – personal references in poems – more later.'

Emily Hale tried the spoken word, her particular *métier* because, Willard Thorp explained, she had trouble putting her memories together on paper. Obviously, she had not been entirely satisfied with the Introduction of 1957. A transcript was made from the tape, and sent to the Thorp. Margaret now suggested that her friend might pick out the personal references in Eliot's poems. On 18 August, Emily suggested that she might do still better if she were to respond spontaneously to questions from Professor Thorp. She told him that she wanted to put on tape, and then to have transcribed, 'a conversation with you – question & answer – ... I feel that *you* can get from me the material which scholars will want fully, as much as my personal memoirs.'

A week later, on 24 August, she sent the Thorps a newly edited transcript. In her covering letter, she was now anxious to secure this document for the future, and praised the 'discreet secretary' for getting so much 'from my garbled wandering words as she did'. At the same time, she admitted, she was 'appalled at the fact as you put it – "I came through" at all in the midst of the confusion'. She was torn between a sense of public duty and reticence. She said deprecatingly that she could hardly flatter herself that the changes in the transcript made the story more valuable. She shrank from Margaret's idea that she identify personal details in Eliot's work: 'Later I shall try to write out what M. suggested – tho' there is *mighty little* of me in any poetry!'

After a holiday with a ninety-year-old friend of the Perkinses in Seattle, she came to a bold decision: she would break another form of silence she had come to accept. After six years, she would write to Eliot, who was now nearly seventy-five, in order to secure her side of their correspondence. It is a painfully correct letter, written with brave composure:

September 12, 1963

Dear Tom,

It is difficult to break the silence which has existed between us for the last several years, but you would be the first to admit I think that the changing circumstances of our lives and increasing years necessitate that we both face certain facts and problems with courage and objectiveness.

. . . [Professor Thorp and Mr Dix] asked me to ask you if you cannot reconsider the time limit set by you for public access to the letters to a much shorter period than the one you have already named. I concur wholly to this request myself. . . .

Closely connected to the disposition of the Princeton letters are my letters to you which long ago you planned to place in the Bodle[i]an at Oxford. The question has also been asked in Princeton if these two collections should not be under the same roof. . . . It would seem to me if you are still preserving my letters, that your consent in placing them in this country would be the only correct practical solution, don't you think? And do you or I have legal claim on them? ·

Remembering your scrupulous attention and care in all legal aspects relating to literary material, writer's rights, etc. I am sure I can count upon you to leave specific directions in all matters regarding our past correspondence which assumes very different implications today than earlier. I think you will be aware that for me to consider my life as important because of its relationship to you – a noted world figure – is very difficult. I must as now act impersonally for the sake of the future in raising these questions, equally difficult for both of us but wholly professionally and historically correct. I do hope you will accept what is thrust upon us – shall we say – because you are you.

Further, I hope your health is better than I know it to have been lately. I learn of you from time to time from the Cambridge relatives.

In the thought of past friendship,
Emily Hale

Eliot did not reply. By November, she began to think that something had changed his mind about keeping her letters. It occurred to her that he might be ill. Another possibility was that 'he as of old – can't disturb the present, to stir up past memories and plans'.

On 26 December Willard Thorp discussed 'this strange impasse with your letters to T.S.E. His silence, after your careful (and gentle) letter of last September, is incredible, unless, as you suggest, he may not be well. As you know, under the law, the letters belong to him and he can dispose of them as he wishes. But the right to quote from them or to publish any or all of them belongs to you and your legal heirs – forever, so far as we know. One would think, therefore, that he would like to know what your wishes are in the matter . . .'.

She replied on 5 January 1964: 'I have *almost* a suspicion that my letters have been destroyed!'

By February 1964 Emily Hale had dotted all the 'i's, as she put it, in her collection. This largest, by far, of all collections of Eliot's letters was only part of what she had. From 1927 she had amassed a vast and valuable array of typescript drafts and first editions, all sent by Eliot, most of them with inscriptions. This collection was equalled at the time only by that of Henry Eliot in Cambridge, Massachusetts, and John Hayward in London. Emily Hale repeatedly refers to her collection as 'personal', whereas Hayward saw his more impersonally as an archive with himself as 'keeper'. Henry Eliot made his collection as head of the family, to be part of the Eliot family collection at Harvard. These last two collections have been preserved intact, but Emily Hale, forced by the loss of her post at Smith to live in a furnished room, began to make gifts (none of these were sales). The first that I can trace is a typescript of Eliot's essay on Pascal, which she gave to Harvard in 1944. As she made her offers to Scripps, Harvard, and Princeton, she always declared that she would retain certain of Eliot's works that were, for private reasons, precious.

There is a pattern to Emily Hale's bequests: the big gifts

were made in the wake of shock: in 1948–9 following the catastrophic encounter in 1947, and in 1957 after Eliot's marriage. The bulk of the first editions went to Scripps College, in honour of Ruth George, the English teacher for whom Emily always expressed great affection. President Hard made chill responses to Emily Hale's repeated suggestion that she herself should be brought out to Scripps with the books. She sent off the first two packages, together with a photograph of Eliot, in the spring of 1946. On 3 June she got a note from the president's secretary, Marion Winne, to say that Hard was unable to acknowledge the gift himself because he was busy elsewhere. Hard's behaviour remained graceless, the indifference of a man of affairs to a middle-aged female of no importance. Emily Hale did indulge, just once, in a send-up of his blurry jargon: 'Our plans for the . . . presentation [of her Eliot collection] having been put off, by the consent of the interested "parties" . . .'.

On 8 January 1948 she approached Hard once more. To defray the cost of travel to California, she offered to give a reading of Eliot's poems for the College or a public audience: 'I do this sort of thing professionally,' she wrote, 'and as I am not attached to any teaching staff this year, I am freer to give my own programs. I have read aloud a good bit of Eliot in all his phases . . .'. The spoken word helped people, she said, to understand the poetry. Future generations would give a good deal to hear the woman Eliot had loved reading poems which she in some part inspired but, of course, to all appearance, she was nothing more than a high-school teacher. Hard replied on 23 January 1948:

Dear Miss Hale,
I appreciate the suggestion that you have made concerning the lecture-visit to the campus, and I wish that it might be possible. I ought to tell you, however, that we are pretty fully committed this year, owing to the fact that we have stretched our lecture fund resources in inviting Marjorie Nicolson. . . .
Sincerely yours,
Frederick Hard, President

She did not answer 'as there seemed nothing to say.' But

she remained confident and quite determined that Scripps did owe her this visit. In March she suggested that the College might find some funds in the autumn. Meanwhile, she sent a good 'public' photograph of Eliot taken before the war when he was 'looking far healthier than the poor man does now'. She also offered to send *Sweeney Agonistes*: 'I call to your attention that the "Sweeney Agonistes" volume has particular significance as it was inscribed to me when Mr Eliot visited Scripps in the early 1930s.' She was disappointed by the lack of notice. There was no account of her gift in the alumnae bulletin. A friend, Mrs Volkmann, who visited Scripps library, reported that the librarian in charge had no idea where the Eliot books were. Hard's reply of 27 March ignored all this. He filled the sheet with bland comments about the weather.

In 1957 another set of packages went off to Scripps, including the typescript of *The Cocktail Party*, an early typescript of *Cats*, and an address of 1947 'On Poetry'. In the early sixties, she sent Alexander Jackson of the Houghton Library, Harvard, 'unusual personal memorabilia' including a draft of *The Family Reunion* with her own marginal comments to Eliot and their correspondence relating to the play, a postcard from Eliot dated 18 October 1955, a carbon copy of the typescript of his Shakespeare lectures of 1937, the address that Eliot gave on that frightful occasion when Vivienne intercepted him at the book fair in 1935, a broadcast with many corrections on 'A Christian Britain', and his address to the English Literary Society at University College, Dublin, in 1936.

She gave six 'special' items to the Thorps, including the loosely bound first editions of 'Song for Simeon' (November 1928) and *Two Poems* ('Cape Ann' and 'Usk') signed by 'Tom' at Christmas 1935. She also gave some papers to Smith College and to Miss Porter's school in Farmington.

From 1963 she heard reports from Eleanor Hinkley of Eliot's failing health, but did not know how serious this was. On 4 January 1965, he died. At once memory took control, and she was able to retrieve the Eliot of their long attachment. Her concern for future scholars took second place to her allegiance to Eliot and, by extension, his wife, for whom she could now feel sympathy. She was, said Mrs Burwell, always magnanimous. She decided that Princeton should return her memoir so that she might destroy it.

9 Church Green
Concord, Mass. 01742
17 Jan 1965

Dear Willard,
... I feel that the letters alone give enough evidence of so abnormal (or is it normal) a story – and for the sake of my caring for him, as friend and a loved one – I should not underline the miscarriage, so to speak of what seemed to be so perfect a solution to the long years of waiting for happiness.

It might *not* have been happy, or right, had the relationship been consummated, and I must always remember I was unaware of the complexities of both the situation* and his nature – or ready to believe in a side I knew so well of his nature. Be what it may, I hope you and M[argaret] can realize I shrink from the intimacy of the personal disclosure. ...

Willard Thorp urged her to reconsider, but for the time being she was firm. On 31 January she replied: '... there are other elements in life which I think equally as important as the objective literary professional point of view you both have.'

Then Mr Dix suggested, as a compromise, that she edit the more intimate details out of the text. She felt she should do this, not only for Valerie Eliot's sake, 'but from *my own* feeling for shielding the association with a man I loved, and who *I* think, did not respond as he should have to my long trust, friendship and love'.

She put off a final decision about the memoir: 'I shall wait', she said in February 1965. Her last comment on the collection, in November, does not include a decision. In this letter an ambivalence about publicity remained: she owns to

* Crossed out.

curiosity about the future's response to Eliot's letters, and tries not to regret that he had probably destroyed her own:

Nov 27th [1965]

Dear Willard,

... This changing of T.S.E.'s mind about my letters shows how terribly secretive he was about our 'affair' and I am more grateful than hurt – which I think I am a little that friendship through difficult years as well as love – is thus wiped out for the record. But on the whole, gratitude is uppermost as he probably meant to protect me, not himself or Valerie alone. Who can say?

How are you both?

Always affectionately
Emily H.

All happiness ended with Eliot's marriage, but she continued to live her dauntless style. Her aunt left her some money, and she used it to travel to Grand Manan Island in the Bay of Fundy, to Scandinavia, and South America. She endowed a building in a college for Blacks in North Carolina. One year before her death, in 1968 when she was seventy-seven, she played Mrs Higgins in a Concord production of *My Fair Lady*. 'I did have a *very* happy, rather remarkable "come back" in this last rôle,' she told Margaret Thorp, 'and it gave me a warmth of friendliness each night from all the scene-stage hands and actors!' As one watcher recalled: 'When Mrs Higgins, in her picture hat, long flounced gown and parasol made her entrance, with ease, style and aplomb, to the manner born, she took over the stage and received an ovation.'

*

The love story of T. S. Eliot and Emily Hale is not the usual tale of waiting: waiting until love on the man's part died; the woman faithful to her death. That is only superficially true. A stranger story lurks in Eliot's poetry, essays, and plays. In *The Cocktail Party*, when the empty-hearted husband rejects the woman he has loved, she asks him if she had been merely a passing 'distraction'. He denies this. Emily Hale, too, believed that her attachment to Eliot had been as momentous for him as for her. When, after knowing him forty-four years, he broke with her in 1957, she did not conclude that she had been negligible. She was baffled – when Eliot died she said that a past mystery was now a future mystery – but she clung to her conviction that this 'affair' had given some importance to her life. This, in a tone of muted sadness, is convincing. Her letters are otherwise modest and restrained. She was not like the Countess Tolstoy or Alma Mahler, who basked in reflected fame: that kind of woman, distorted by the sacrifice of her own lesser talents, seems now a curiosity of history. Emily Hale's triumph is to come through the veil imposed upon her – as 'hidden', as 'Lady of silences' – wonderfully undistorted. There are, as yet, few facts, few letters, but all give out the same clear note of a woman who could sustain a balance of sense and feeling, who was willing to risk her livelihood for the sake of love, and when it was not to be, could begin again: at the end of 1935 when she returned to Boston and started to hunt for a new post, and again in 1947, and yet again ten years later. The breaks in her career – 1934–5, 1947–8, 1957–8 – coincide exactly with decisive dates in Eliot's life. There was, for her, a repeated pattern of demoralisation, followed by spirited renewal. She managed this renewal because she had the talent to 'create' others: she did this for her actors, and she must have done it for women friends, all of whom felt themselves to be special. Above all, she did it for Eliot: how exactly, we shan't be sure without her letters. My guess is that because she had known him almost always, as his family did, not as the construct of fame, she was able to rescue him, in a critical phase of his life in the early thirties, from the 'unreality' that is the condition of 'hollow men'. Years later, during another phase of hollowness, his second wife was to rescue him too, a young woman rejuvenating an old man. By then it was almost too late for creativity, so that story, for all its happiness, will tease posterity less than the more mysterious tie to Emily Hale.

This mystery, as she said herself, was buried with Eliot: the strangeness of an attachment that was, for many years, bound up with the fate of his soul. Such an attachment does not fit our categories (like romantic love), and to imagine it is to risk a fiction. Some answer lurks in Eliot's poetry, a figure in a carpet, aesthetically intact yet, by virtue of repetition, inviting discernment: the lover of 'La Figlia', who prefers to construct a memorable figure of a beautiful girl, literally a statue on a pedestal, to the disturbing alternative of coming together; the wretched Gerontion, who laments that he has lost his passion, and asks pitifully how should he use atrophied senses 'for your closer contact?' Later on, the virginal Lady props Eliot's vow of celibacy, defusing desire in the longed-for reunion. Emily Hale seems to have played a curious role in the de-sexing of Eliot, despite her own wish for 'consummation'. It was not a role she chose, but one designed by Eliot's imagination, and played out until it was, as he said, 'too late'.

It is difficult, particularly for a woman, to set aside an impression that Eliot distorted women's actuality in feelings warped by fear. But so distant a judgement cannot absorb the whole truth. To get even a glimmer about this 'affair' it is vital to let go our usual terms of sex, love, friendship. As Eliot went 'beyond poetry', so his relationship with Emily Hale, closely associated with his poetry, also defies definition. Agatha and Mary in *The Family Reunion* understand that they are to be 'watchers and waiters'. It may be that the passive role of waiting was subordinate to the more interesting role of watching. Emily Hale watched over Eliot's new life in the thirties and forties, or they were watchers together.

Watching meant abstaining from action until it was too late. It seems impossible to escape the self-serving involvements of perfect gentlemen in the late novels and tales of Henry James: Lambert Strether and John Marcher, whose earlier incarnations were men like Winterbourne and Robert Acton. Marcher spends nearly his whole life marking time for a destiny more remarkable than love, for some rare and strange distinction. In maturity he recovers a relationship with a woman, May, who agrees to watch with him. Marcher convinces May that it would be worth waiting for: 'I think of it simply as *the* thing.' Eliot used exactly the same term when he spoke of the notion of some infinite 'thing'. Love wouldn't be 'it', Marcher thinks, because love isn't strange enough. And you couldn't take a lady on a tiger-hunt. 'Something or other lay in wait for him, amid the twists and turns of the months and years, like a crouching beast in the jungle.' This is what Eliot meant by 'Christ the tiger'.

So Eliot, like Marcher, refrained from love and carried his burden of suspense quietly, giving others no glimpse of its effect on his life. He used good manners as Marcher does, as the cover of the hidden life: 'He hadn't disturbed people with the queerness of their having to know a haunted man. This is why he had such good – though possibly such rather colourless – manners.' He was on guard not to let this lapse, yet, said James, he was quite ready none the less to be selfish, just a little, when he found a woman who would let him. His destiny was not a privilege he could invite her to share. Her privilege was to stand with him 'against the rest of the world'. Their relationship was one of lightness overlying what the woman calls 'the real truth about you', and she had 'a wonderful way of making it seem . . . the secret of her own life too'. She was in the secret of the difference between the public forms he went through and the detachment that reigned beneath them, that made of all behaviour 'a long act of dissimulation'. He wore a mask painted with an expression of social decorum, but out of the eyeholes there looked eyes with an expression that did not match. The woman, alone of all the world, met those eyes, just as Emily Hale met what she saw to be 'a man of extremes'.

As they grew old she still watched with him, the guardian of his promise, and let the association give shape and colour to her own existence. Such a course of existence awaits a climax, but nothing happened. The years ebbed. The story of Emily Hale was like a trailer that Eliot towed so far behind him that it was almost out of sight, bearing his fragile hope of perfection. When that hope faded in the later forties and early fifties, the trailer was detached and the story of Emily Hale put aside for a quite different story of marital fulfilment.

As a wife, Emily would have shared the publicity that came to Eliot with the Nobel Prize. As a watcher she had shared, instead, the hidden core of his life, what was pure, passionate, creative. There must have been some exhilaration in the shared moments. Naturally she wished this recognised, but accepted that it must wait fifty years after her death. She did regret, she owned, that she would not be here when Eliot's letters 'burst upon the world'.

12

FAME AND FRIENDS

IN 1950 ELIOT suggested to Mary Trevelyan that they drink to The Guardians. After his rejection of Emily Hale in 1947, this was the role that he assigned to John Hayward and Mary, his two closest friends from the late forties to the mid-fifties. Their proven loyalty was to protect Eliot, and their social astuteness guide him, through the public phase of his career.

At the end of the war, Eliot left the seclusion of the Shambles to settle again in London. He and Hayward took a flat, 19 Carlyle Mansions, the block of flats in which Henry James had lived, in Cheyne Walk in Chelsea. Eliot attempted no great work after *Four Quartets*. He turned from the private search for salvation to public life, to the lecture platform and the popular theatre. *Four Quartets* projects the final stage of a moral cure: to enter into a sense of community. This move was not a spontaneous need but a mission conducted from the centre of what Eliot continued to see as a blighted civilisation.

From 1940 (with the success of *East Coker*) until 1956 Eliot was in great demand and spoke everywhere, at universities, school prize-givings, and the London Library (where he joined a line of distinguished presidents including Carlyle, Gladstone, and Leslie Stephen). When he arrived in Princeton in 1948 the whisper 'TS . . . TS . . . TS . . .' rushed like a wind through a town agog with expectation. Eventually, in 1956, he spoke in a basketball stadium in Minneapolis to 13,700, the largest crowd that has ever gathered to hear literary

436

criticism. After he won the Nobel Prize in 1948 he was treated as a star, though his gravity and tensely withdrawn expression seemed to deprecate adulation. His silences gathered weight. He used to stand with his hands against his back, his arms akimbo. With his tall frame, now slightly stooped, he looked like a benign crane in horn-rimmed glasses. Rapt and reverent audiences listened to the slow procession of scrupulously selected words, rather toneless, but carrying the breath of godlike authority. Listeners came for the real thing, not a spurious god of the media. His poetry had certified that he was one of the great souls. He already had the stamp of the timeless upon him.

The trumpets of fame are predictable, sycophantic, reductive; the public figure locked in the expected image. It was, Eliot told Mary Trevelyan, 'the most desperately lonely business'. At a party in 1950, when he was asked to perform Sherlock Holmes from memory, he began softly, as if to himself: 'at a time when Europe was ringing with his name, and when his room was literally ankle-deep with congratulatory telegrams, I found him prey to the blackest depression.' In 1950 he said that he had not known till then what it was like to be famous: 'No-one thinks of me as a poet any more, but as a celebrity.'

Eliot's contemporaries had seen the man, not the celebrity. Sir Herbert Read had witnessed moods of depression that, on occasion, had left Read 'utterly depleted'. Compared with this, the thinness of what younger associates tell us suggests that, in this phase, Eliot was most inscrutable. He confided to Mary Trevelyan that he hid behind impenetrability. His gestures of weariness and his appointment book kept admirers at bay. Although in the early 1950s he used to see Mary once, twice and sometimes even three times a week, he preserved a fiction that minimised the relationship. She must agree, he insisted, that over all the years they had met only once a fortnight. His letters to her show that, even to a constant companion, he was guarded and changeable. In time she learnt to read the simpler signals – his fingers drumming on the table spelt bad weather – but he remained after twenty years still incomprehensible. As companions, in later years, he seemed to choose either proven fans (whose devotion would have been tested over many years) or undemanding friends like Christopher Sykes, with whom he watched football on Saturday afternoons. Sykes, nineteen years younger, was a writer and diplomat who joined the BBC in 1948. From about 1941, with the deaths of Joyce and Virginia Woolf, Eliot was no longer associated with contemporaries of equal genius – with darting insights on Virginia Woolf's part, sudden intimacies on Eliot's: that kind of engagement came to an end. Eliot's letters in the late forties show that he avoided Desmond MacCarthy, another member of Old Bloomsbury. There is bafflement in MacCarthy's letters as Eliot complained variously of minor ills, his servant's absence, and his unwillingness to offer poor food at his club. There is superficial cordiality, a crumb or two of literary criticism and, behind that, the gap left by Eliot's insistent retreat. Almost all accounts of these years sound curiously empty, as we are regaled with the anecdotes of people who 'knew' or interviewed Eliot. The man is simply not there. Did he go dead in the late forties, as he saw himself in relation to Emily Hale, or did the prophetic soul live on, burning, inscrutable, behind the façades?

To a new generation untouched by his presence, yet informed of his prejudice and the sad fate of Emily Hale, Eliot is not likeable. In his last years he softened to his second wife, but valiantly as she defended him, this can't obliterate the preceding decade. Exposés, on the other hand, also falsify the truth. The whole truth depends on holding a balance of two almost antithetical selves. There is the man who often failed to control his contempt for ordinary people, who was burnt out, and courting fame to the further depletion of his vitality; and there is a public hermit who recognised that the time had come to take up, once more, the task foreseen in 'Coriolan' in 1931: to sound a genuine message that could pierce the chatter of the sycophantic throng. To command its attention he did need fame, yet to live as a celebrity cut him off still further from the human heart. Although he took pains to be kind and attentive, he also indulged in merciless comments on people of whom he did not approve. He had a crowing, rather mocking laugh, as if he found much amusement in the follies of the world.

If the public hangs on your lips, it is difficult not to make solemn pronouncements. This Eliot began to do, on lesser occasions. Called on too often, his platform statements had sometimes the drone of set positions. Many letters to Mary Trevelyan or to William Turner Levy, a priest in New York, suggest that sensations now tapped their beaks in vain against the hardening shell of the elder statesman of letters. To look past this public figure is to see a sealed-off man who was, at the same time, an emissary of sorts, pursuing an unswerving course, apocalyptic, alone, still racked by the evil of secular existence.

As Eliot's fame grew on the permanent scale, he became unknowable. His manner remained modest and genial, but he was as invisible to his unknowing friends as the famous writer James exposed in 'The Private Life', whose public image gives no clue to the unapproachable life behind the shut door of the writer's study. One of Eliot's characters, Sir Claude (in *The Confidential Clerk*, 1953), speaks of 'the private door / Into the real world' of the artist. Art has 'this . . . remoteness I have always longed for'.

Eliot's work itself reveals – less often, but still intermittently – a character who never appears elsewhere, except when he allowed Emily Hale to look through the 'door' at Burnt Norton. The memoirs of his friends were skimpy and unsatisfying, but Mary Trevelyan left a sustained record, entirely gripping and at the end of the century still unpublished. In 1958 she combined extracts from Eliot's 221 letters with extracts from her diary of their meetings and conversations which she had begun to keep in 1949. 'The Pope of Russell Square' is the fullest record we shall have of what it was like to be Eliot's companion during his most invisible years of fame. This Eliot is continuous with the Eliot of the anecdotes – mischievous, joking, generous with presents – but less guarded. Mary alone, apart from Eliot's sisters and John

Hayward, saw a difficult, moody man. 'O dear me', 'O La! La!' she exclaims at intervals in her diary. '*Tiens!*'

When they met, in 1938, Mary was a brainy woman of forty-one, with bracing energy. She was Warden of the Student Movement House in a spacious Georgian house with curving staircase, mirrored walls, Adam fireplaces, and painted ceilings in Russell Square (later, during the war, they moved to 103 Gower Street). She had a long, intelligent, horse face (slightly pointed towards the chin), with a charming, faintly lopsided smile. Her voice was low and throaty, with a rich nuance of tone well adapted to her jokes. She could say the outrageous with the matter-of-fact aplomb of the intellectual (upper-middle) class, as when she told a younger friend, Ann Stokes, that 'she *loathed* the Student Christian Movement who regarded her running of the Student Movement House as lacking in gravitas & fervent efforts to convert the many students from umpteen countries & religions, & who eventually sacked her. Accordingly, every Ash Wednesday she made a rule to pray during Lent for what she wickedly & delightfully called her "SCUM List".'

Hers was humour rather than wit: a tone of high enjoyment, mature and tolerant. She liked people; liked foreigners. The Student Movement House was mainly for foreigners, and Eliot saw her as a mainstay for her 'waifs'. At the time they met, she was keeping a diary about the exploits and trials of her charges, which, to amuse herself in shelters during the Blitz, she turned into a book called *From the Ends of the Earth*. In the summer of 1941 she offered it to Eliot, and it was published by Faber early in 1942.

Mary had been born in 1897 into the professional élite, a distinguished family of churchmen, academics, writers, and diplomats. After leaving Grovely College, Boscombe, she became a scholar at the Royal College of Music, and her first posts were as organist and choir-trainer at St Barnabas' in Oxford, and as a music teacher at public schools for boys, Radley and Marlborough. After travelling in Ceylon and Kashmir in 1930–1, she was struck on her return by the lost look of groups of young Indians in the London rain. So, she took up the post of Warden in 1932, and became increasingly interested in the problems of Eastern students migrating to the West for study, and its effects on their return home.

She had a relish for record (her uncle was the eminent English historian G. M. Trevelyan). As a natural diarist, her attention turned outwards to ordinary lives: students and, later, soldiers. Her letters, too, take in multiple lives. She was an observer – she saw, for instance, that Eliot didn't look quite natural when dressed up because he tried too hard to be correct – but she was not attuned to subtler vibrations. It is doubtful if Eliot ever revealed to her the side reserved for his poetry. It is fitting that their friendship was at its height when Eliot was writing comedies, *The Cocktail Party* and *The Confidential Clerk*. The absurd play of manners with undercurrents of feeling – but not the rarefied feeling of earlier plays – was complemented by Mary's familiarity with social currents. She had the range of awareness of a born nurse of the Florence Nightingale sort, with an organisational flair based on the intelligence to grasp priorities, and she was quick to pick up the more obvious disturbance of people in difficult situations. This is what made her so effective with displaced students and soldiers on active service. Her memoir of Eliot shows no sign of 'frontier' intuitions; nothing of the 'silence' that Eliot had shared with Emily Hale. Their friendship was based on talk: fairly humdrum talk of church politics, Eliot's new overcoat, and whether the Rondabouts (Lady Rhondda and friend) should be invited to lunch at the Shambles – would rations stretch to a larger party? What attracted Eliot was Mary's fearlessness: she teased him, as Virginia Woolf had done in earlier days, daring to prod the outer bulwarks of his reserve.

In July 1938 Mary had been asked to look after Eliot when he came to read at the Student Christian Movement conference in Swanwick, Derbyshire. He had arrived with a cold and a stiff neck, and read *The Waste Land* and 'The Hollow Men' in a harsh voice, with his head on one side. After he left, Mary staged a parody of this reading – harshness and stiff neck included – and suspecting Eliot of a sense of humour, she sent him a copy. He sent an amused reply and, later that year, agreed to read at the Student Movement House. Crowds came: young men in corduroy trousers and floppy ties, carrying Eliot's poems under their arms and looking intense. Mary noticed that Eliot seemed 'terrified' after the reading, when he had to meet some of them.

She initiated a regular correspondence with Eliot when she was appointed to the Anvil, a religious Brains Trust which broadcast on the Home Service once a week. Mary was the sole woman amongst clergymen and theologians (she was supposed to represent 'the ordinary person') who were to answer questions sent in by listeners. She submitted some of these questions to Eliot, and was undaunted by his ponderous replies. She said that, once she was on the air, she could not recall anything he had said – thankfully, because she could not have passed it off as her own.

'What were you like as a child?' Mary asked Eliot at their first lunch, at Viani's in Charlotte Street, in the spring of 1941.

Eliot, who had just completed *The Dry Salvages*, began promptly: 'Born on the Mississippi . . .'. When they parted, he held her hand a long time. Mary was 'amused and flattered'.

What gave Mary her sense of a special friendship was that she was permitted to witness Eliot's transformations from distant politeness to informal chatter, jokes, and eventually confidences about his family and the trials of his marriage. To Mary, this meant intimacy; to Eliot, only the exchange of masks, formal for informal. The switch was utterly disarming to all who found themselves favoured in this way, but the informal Eliot who was witty with colleagues, domestic with women, and a story-telling godfather with children, loaded with expensive and carefully chosen gifts, still guarded an Eliot who remained unreachable. One of the maxims in which he delighted was 'always suspect everybody' (the maxim of 'Old Foxey' in *The Old Curiosity Shop*). Life was a grander version of mystery fiction, Dickens, Poe, Conan

Doyle; Eliot, a master detective, the incarnation of Holmes: aloof, solitary, trusting no one but the faithful Watson. Mary was an ideal Watson: the uninspired but worthy confidante, rather worldly in outlook, to whom could be trusted the more mundane details of a great enterprise. Mary–Dr Watson would urge him not to strain his health; would cheer and console; above all would listen. Unfortunately, Mary Trevelyan came from the governing class and had decided opinions of her own. When, in the mid-fifties, she presumed to censure Eliot, the friendship came to an end.

Mary was a mannish woman, tall, dark, with a high-handed, even bossy manner. She dominated younger friends, but was considered a 'good pal', generous with help, kind and sensible. Her advice was not necessarily comforting, but always right. She knew everyone; she was fun; and she always had loads of friends, like Rose Macaulay, but no romance until, at the age of forty-four, she found her hand in Eliot's.

She realised that she was in love with Eliot in 1942. It was irrevocable, but controlled. Her hearty manner gave no hint of her feelings, so that when, in 1944, she took off for the Normandy beaches in the wake of the troops, Eliot bade farewell to her as 'a Man of Action'. Mary said that she was never sure what he felt for her. He certainly enjoyed her company and came to depend on her practical propping, but there was, I think, a warning to her in a letter of 19 December 1944 in which he talks of wishing to spend the Christmas season in a monastery. The deliberation with which he signed himself her affectionate and well-meaning friend laid down the limits of their association.

As Eliot grew older, entrance to his inner circle depended on the strictest loyalty and discretion. Eliot put Mary Trevelyan through a test. At the beginning of 1942 he asked her to take on a disturbed poet from the East, a disciple and imitator of Eliot, who had also made a wretched marriage with an English girl. Mary, provided with funds from Eliot, was to rescue him when he set fire to his clothes, or drove into a lamp-post under the drunken impression it was his wife. When, on this last occasion, Mary collected him from a casualty ward, he lay back in the taxi with his feet on the opposite seat, reciting yards of *The Waste Land*. This was the sort of situation where Mary excelled: she was patient and attentive to Eliot's protégé. When she phoned to make her report she could not resist telling Eliot one episode. The young poet had lain back in her office chair, his eyes closed, remarking: 'I had a fantasy last night. I dreamed that you were my mother and Mr Eliot my father.'

Eliot's laugh came back: 'I really think we might have done better than that.' Mary had passed the test as a trusty nurturer of waifs. It may well have been as needy waif that Eliot had held her hand.

Mary Trevelyan complemented Eliot in their main difference. He sheered away from people; she was gregarious. She told him shrewdly that when he spoke (as he often did) of 'fear' of people, he was really avoiding disturbance. Then, too, there was Mary's Englishness. During the war, when Eliot wished to partake in the mood of national commitment, she helped to place him more firmly 'now and in England'. The solidity of her connections would have appealed to him: G. M. Trevelyan was Master of Trinity (Cambridge); her brother-in-law Warden of Keble, and later Bishop of Oxford. Another brother, Humphrey, was in the Indian Political Service. Eliot enjoyed introducing her to his sister Marian as 'the Vicar's daughter': she was, indeed, the devout eldest daughter of the Revd George Philip Trevelyan, who had built various churches of his own High Anglican persuasion, and whose family had been connected with St Stephen's in the past. She may have epitomised, for Eliot, the Anglican community. Without much spiritual imagination, she was an appropriate companion for the less ambitious regimen Eliot had prescribed for himself in 1941 of 'prayer, observance, discipline, thought and action'. She was welcome to accompany him to all services.

Love does not blur Mary Trevelyan's picture of Eliot. He was 'creepy' at times, at times enraged, as unpredictable and moody as the weather. Her tone is not unsympathetic; it is humorously tolerant, using humour in the English way to

melt awkwardness. She pictures how Eliot would sing
tunelessly in a harsh low voice, on the way home after
dinners: music-hall songs of his youth, or Negro spirituals.
Mostly, she makes fun of his clothes. When bishops came to
preach at St Stephen's, he wore his City clothes, and looked
uncomfortable in a stiff collar. He was still devoted to his
bowler, which was too small and, Mary thought, didn't suit
him. He used to wear a black tie on the anniversary of St
Bartholomew and a red tie for Charles, King and Martyr.
Sometimes an old overcoat (inherited from his brother and
too large) would cover the impeccable outfits: it had
misshapen pockets in which he might have stuffed a manuscript. So Mary created a lovable eccentric, and left out – she
duly records the omission – his wounding comments on
almost everyone, and her own 'deep distress'.

Her memoir offers a unique view of Eliot, a view as
impossible for his contemporaries as for his younger devotees. His artistic contemporaries, breaking with Victorian
convention, had welcomed strangeness of all kinds. They had
liked Eliot for it. The next generation, the trusty ones, tell us
that, on the contrary, Eliot was not strange: he was kind and
considerate. This is not, of course, untrue, but it simply
doesn't tell us about the man who wrote some great works
which were not striking for their kindness and almost savage
in their 'hatred of life'. Mary Trevelyan came exactly between
these two generations – she was ten years younger than Eliot
– and she preserves a useful balance. She had more distance
than Eliot's contemporaries and less devotion than his later
adherents. Her intellectual and social aplomb made it
possible for her to like and admire Eliot without idolising
him. He was sufficiently at ease with her not to disguise his
rages, as he called them. Later, when he permitted himself to
fall in love with a younger woman, he became different, wholly
lovable. But to Mary he was often fussy, hypochondriacal,
self-obsessed, capricious. She was appalled by the suddenness
of his fury, and would beg him to control it for both their
sakes. He would get out of her car, and slam the door. Few
saw Eliot from that closer perspective. He would relax his

extreme formality, take off his jacket, and even (in very hot weather) his waistcoat, and they held hands before parting for their respective vacations (always apart, against Mary's wish), but it was no more than the clasp of chums. And like old chums, they put up with their tiffs.

This looks ahead to their habits of the late forties and early fifties, but even in the early phase of their friendship Eliot gave conflicting signals. He would propose lunch, then vanish for three months. This was not initial shyness, but consistent with a curious habit of their later association. Mary said that he would 'disappear' after they had a particularly happy time together. She got to expect it. It was as though he had to take cover from the claims and fatigues of friendship, in the same way, perhaps, that Hawthorne and Thoreau would dive into the woods if they sighted each other – a potential fellow – on the Concord horizon. If Mary Trevelyan and John Hayward were useful to Eliot, that was incidental to their love for him. For Eliot, their usefulness was the *raison d'être* of the ties. He withdrew from Mary whenever the tie exceeded its uses, delimited after 1950 by 'rules'. He told Mary that it would get on his nerves to see *anyone* more than once a fortnight. He never enquired into her own needs.

Mary became Eliot's prop at a time when he was detaching himself from Emily Hale. She had no inkling of Emily Hale's existence until 1950, when Eliot did not tell her much more than that he had been in love with one woman all his life and could find no words to explain the nature of that love. Because Emily Hale represented for Eliot New England, the past, his youth, and visionary powers, to drop her was to become, emotionally, a hollow shell. This is what he meant, I think, by his cryptic reference, in 1949, to a psychological change of life. It was Mary Trevelyan's misfortune to have tried to engage in a closer relationship with Eliot at this time. In the early forties everything had seemed to point to lifelong friendship – the frequent meetings, the ease and laughter – but a peculiar hollowness echoes through Mary Trevelyan's memoir which is not there in her other books. The hollowness is not from her side but, at second hand, from his: his leaden comments on Culture seem to be given out at a remove from himself; his humour is often rather forced. It sometimes took the form of a pile-up of cryptic references to possibly non-existent people who beset the great man with demands for his attention, the point being Eliot's covert plea to leave him alone. He also delighted in a torrent of bogus excuses, shading into the genuine which was the dictum from the book of Possum the Wise that one only achieves something by neglecting something else.

The lurking hollowness in the memoir lies, above all, in Eliot's relation to Mary herself. She had so secure a sense of self that it never occurred to her that Eliot's remarks and letters reflect back a limited caricature of a woman as guardian. Her books show that she was more than a kindly companion to a great man, tough enough to cope with his moods; she had pluck, an adventurous resilience, and a determination of her own.

Eliot did give Mary fair warning as he warmed to her, if we read between the lines of the memoir. In 1942 he warned her of his native Calvinism, which he described as a handicap he could not overcome: this slipped, characteristically, into a cascade of light-hearted trivia. The grave, stern man could relax in a fashion, though his strangeness came out as distinctly in his relaxation as in his religion. On 29 June 1942 he sent Mary an explanation of his nature. Hedged with wild fictions, the letter at once conceals and reveals his awareness of alternating acts: he would involve himself, then drop people. The letter speaks in terms of committees, but what he says is true of his pattern of withdrawals from closer attachments – Conrad Aiken, Emily Hale and, eventually, John Hayward and Mary herself. The dismissal of Vivienne, though understandable in itself, was part of a pattern which is there throughout his life. Towards the women in this group, different as they are, he behaved in the same way: as though an inexorable and godlike Judgement had annihilated them from the face of the earth. It was the less binding business-colleague kind of relation that tended to survive the years: Sir Geoffrey Faber, Sir Herbert Read, Allen Tate, Peter du Sautoy.

Pound is the one exception: despite his ridicule of Eliot's faith, despite his crazy, exhausting, unreadable letters in the twenties and thirties, and despite his broadcasts for the Fascists during the war, Eliot never forgot what he owed to Pound. He visited him at St Elizabeths (the Washington institution for the criminally insane),* and worried over Pound's funds as, in the early London years, Pound had worried over him. In the late fifties and early sixties, Eliot sent Pound soothing final letters in which he praises Pound's achievement and plays down his own.

*

From 1944 to 1948 Mary Trevelyan was mostly abroad on war and post-war missions. This second phase of her friendship with Eliot was a period of correspondence in which Mary shone: her letters to Eliot from the Army in Belgium in 1944–5 show her finest hour. Eliot's replies were small beer by contrast, as he admitted. While she ploughed between shell-holes across the Normandy beaches and waded through battlefield mud that submerged her wellingtons, Eliot was wrapped up in the overheated house at Shamley Green, amidst old ladies, dogs and cats, turning over his theories about Culture and worries over a choice of successor to Archbishop Temple. While Mary Trevelyan marshalled 50,000 Front Line men in and out of the relief hostel that she set up in Brussels, Eliot was asking why she had not replied to his query whether he should or should not write to *The Times* about some minor issue of church politics.

Her seventeen long letters to Eliot, relaying wartime experiences in France, Belgium and Germany, were published in 1945 (with Eliot's name omitted) as *I'll Walk Beside You*. The title came from a popular song, sung to the troops

* Pound was incarcerated after the Second World War, having been found mentally unfit to stand trial for treason.

nostalgic for girlfriends or mothers or, as Mary recognised, apprehensive of reunions. It was Mary, herself, who was 'beside' these men, who listened to their stories, tended the wounded in transit, and met British prisoners of war as they were released. Her exploits in the six months from September 1944 to May 1945, as she presents them in letters to Eliot, are part of their story, for they show the kind of woman to whom Eliot was drawn as he put into practice *Little Gidding*'s principle of detachment, but found, at the same time, some need for a woman's support.

On Mary's first night in France, she slept in a house which until recently had been headquarters of a German brigade. Huge swastikas adorned the walls, and Hitler's sayings: 'THE WILL TO CONQUER IS GREATER THAN THE WILL TO LIVE.' The ceiling of her room was down in three places, there was a pile of rubbish at one end, and no sanitation. The mud got worse as she drove north in September 1944: the rain came down, the windscreen wipers would not work, and one small side lamp gave out every few yards. 'I found the only way to get along was by holding my torch out of the window,' she wrote to Eliot. After landing periodically in ditches or, once, up a bank, she arrived at one destination covered in mud from head to foot to find no water in which to wash. A white-haired Yorkshireman remarked: 'Eh, lass, think of that five inches of hot bath-water we used to grumble about – what wouldn't we give for it now?'

The British Liberation Army had entered Brussels on 3 September, and Mary arrived at the beginning of October. At once, she requisitioned the Albert, a hotel which could provide hot baths and clean sheets for troops now fighting on the German front. They arrived in batches for forty-eight hours' relief after months of appalling strain. None had had leave since the Normandy landing. They arrived weary, hungry, and dirty from daily tank and trench warfare and long nights in 'foxholes' or slit trenches, often knee-deep in water, with 'Moaning Minnies' overhead. At night, they alternated two hours sleep and two hours on guard. All had seen friends killed or wounded.

Mary knew that she had to raise morale fast, 'for 48 hours is so short', she wrote to Eliot, 'that we must make them feel at home as quickly as possible'. She sent them morning tea in bed, and put together a library on the first floor so that men could get away from the crowd. She set up a barber's shop, and got a photographer who would develop shots in forty-eight hours. Two women artists sat in the lounge making quick pencil sketches of the men for them to send home. Classical record recitals were popular, also a dance held every other night to a Belgian swing band with partners from the Belgian Red Cross and YWCA.

Two attitudes pervade her letters written from 21 Army Group HQ (Rear) near Brussels. First, she thought carefully about the state of mind of the troops who, after a brief taste of what some called, in her visitors' book, 'heaven', had to go back to killing. Some confided to her their 'fear and horror of being turned into murderers'. One evening in the chapel Mary fell into conversation with a miner who said: 'For the last four years I have been trained to kill men, now I am killing them. I hate it and I can't get away.' Military discipline forced such men to kill women and, when the fighting stopped in the early months of 1945, not to give chocolate to famished German children: this was called 'fraternisation'.

Somehow Mary could hearten men when they expressed their horror at themselves. She allowed them to relieve their minds, yet prevented the collapse that horror could bring on. She never allowed herself to forget for one moment that there was no way to save these men from climbing back on the lorries to go back into the nightmare of bringing another country to its knees. She was concerned that the break should give them relief without unfitting them for their terrible task. She saw it as 'mental rehabilitation'.

Secondly, an admiration for the men pervades her letters. Where Eliot looked down on ordinary men as 'termites', she found them uncomplaining, humorous, and amazingly appreciative. Her liking was the secret of the Albert's success.

In November 1944 she obtained permission to go to an air-evacuation centre, four miles outside Brussels, where she tended the wounded as the first batches arrived from Arnhem. She fed one boy who had refused to respond to the orderlies and stared at the ceiling with almost sightless eyes. Eventually, very slowly, he began to talk about his life as a bank clerk in Manchester, and by the time she saw him off, even managed a little joke. She was matter-of-fact, like a good nurse with patients on the brink of demoralisation. She could normalise men: this was her gift on which Eliot was to draw. In the meantime, he wrote to her that his masseuse, Mrs Millington, would have to pound his neck a lot more before he might be like other people.

In April 1945, with Berlin almost fallen and the end of the war near, Mary began to receive huge numbers of newly released prisoners of war, 'the most tragic and pitiable body of men'. Many had been prisoners since Dunkirk five years before. They arrived from Germany at the rate of fifteen hundred a day, and stopped at the Albert for twenty-four hours before they went on to England.

Mary was writing an epistolary form of historical record for eventual publication, and these letters to Eliot were not personal. He read them aloud to the women (and pets) at the Shambles, before sending them on to Mary's mother in Oxford. In the most moving of her letters to him, she wrote:

> I wish you could see the daily procession. Many of the men are skeletons, all are hollow-cheeked with sunken eyes. Some are wounded, nearly all find walking a difficulty. They wear all kinds of garments, German tunics and Service caps, torn shirts, ragged old battle-dresses, even pyjama tops. For the most part they have had no change of clothing for months. . . . Many are dazed and still cowed. While they wait in huddled crowds to be documented we go and talk to them. They are at first amazed to hear an Englishwoman talking, they are timid and uncertain. As I talk, making a little joke about some particularly outlandish garment, perhaps, I can see them beginning to relax a little. Then suddenly they begin to talk – and it seems as though, once started, they can't stop. They crowd round like children, trying to tell what happened to them, words pouring out, sometimes quite unintelligible. . . . They are not hungry, they are quite literally starving. The

evening is spent in the Canteen. It is a strange sight, for every man has his hair, clothing, hands covered with white de-lousing powder and, at first glance, they give the impression of being very frail old men.

Mary felt that even though they passed through her hands only briefly, something must be done towards restoring them. Many ex-prisoners seemed stunned and unresponsive: they did not clap the vocalists as the troops did, and the local clowns seemed too quick for their dulled perceptions. Nor did they respond to communal singing. Never one to give up, Mary organised a band to play old tunes of five years before: at this, they began to hum and whistle a bit. Their problem was that they had been out of the normal world so long and been so degraded by imprisonment that they were, she saw, afraid of not knowing how to behave. One colonel, sitting with Mary in a Brussels café, managed to articulate this in a low voice when his companion colonel wasn't listening.

'I wish I didn't feel such a fool. I don't know how to behave or what to do. I do hope it will all come back soon.' Such officers feared they had become peculiar. The fact that such men, with their stiff-upper-lip training, could speak so directly to Mary suggests, again, that she was more than a good sort. They could trust her with the truth. She was not too dismayed by the uglier aspects of the active life. She was just sensitive enough to be effective: she would not have seen, like Eliot, 'The horror! the horror!', for to see that is to become so disheartened with human nature that it takes an exhausting effort simply to keep on.

It was precisely because Eliot was often debilitated by 'the horror' that he needed a prop like Mary Trevelyan. All the women in his life were strong, with the exception of Vivienne, and even she had a certain useful strength in the power of her macabre imagination. Eliot's mother was strong in her principles; Emily Hale was gallant; Mary, strong in her fearless management; and finally, Valerie Eliot was to be strong in her loyalty, which would protect Eliot for a generation beyond his lifetime.

Mary thought the best thing in her life was her friendship

with Eliot, but she mattered to him rather little as it turned out. Her best thing was, arguably, these six months behind the Front Line. All her best qualities were to the fore. Nursing Eliot was too minor a job for her vigorous talents, and her busyness came to be mildly irritating, like the guardianship of the bossy Julia in *The Cocktail Party*. 'Oh it's YOU again, Julia,' Eliot greeted her in 1949 in a chemist's in Southampton Row. After the dress rehearsal for the London opening, which Mary attended with Eliot in April 1950, he said on the drive home: 'Julia can now show compassion.' Mary herself recognised that much of the good-hearted but rather managerial Julia 'is me'. In short, she was better with thousands of ordinary men than with one genius.

In 1947 Mary Trevelyan went off to war-devastated countries, northern France, Greece, and then Burma, Malaya, North Borneo, and Thailand, to make the first surveys of priority needs in education for UNESCO. Eliot pictured her sailing in a sampan down the Irrawaddy to lower Burma, the intrepid woman traveller responsible for little brown men called Buz Saw and Go Bang. Their letters play out the old fantasy of the white man's (now woman's) burden, but without the old earnestness and hypocrisy. Mary reported efforts that were comic in their futility, and Eliot was not surprised to hear that the future of the East was not going according to *Christian Newsletter* plans. He put an element of Mary into Celia's intrepid mission to the East, the Mary who recounted her adventures among the wilder tribes of Burma. He even asked her for tips for his East Indian island: whether there were monkeys; whether the jungle people tied up their victims and smeared them with sticky stuff to attract insects. He complained that there was no information on these vital points in her reports.

In Celia Copplestone, he conceived a character who could encompass the disappointed love that derived from Emily Hale and the dauntless mission to the East that derived from Mary's letters of 1947–8. I have wondered if these letters had some innocent part in detaching Eliot from Emily Hale. Emily was a woman to whom he owed a lot: he felt the obligation of her years of faithful love. Mary, on the other hand, had the attraction of the carefree adventurer, ready to help him from her bounty of organisational energy, the heat of which was, mercifully, turned elsewhere. Eliot may have contemplated their friendship with most satisfaction in those years when Mary was being energetic thousands of miles away.

Although she was only six years younger than Emily Hale, Mary was more the type of the moment, made fashionable in wartime by the square shoulders of mannish costumes in plain, dark colours. Already, in 1941, in *The Dry Salvages*, Eliot saw ties of the past fading, like the faded song that Emily had sung before the First World War. 'Ecstasy' of 1913 was now replaced by 'I'll Walk Beside You', a new sort of song, associated with a new sort of woman, not the Jamesian 'lady' watching and waiting, but the tough activist, shoulder-to-shoulder with men of action. Hers was not the inward ordeal of rectitude, the moral refinement of the native New England habitat, rather the robust candour of English friendship. Humour preserves it from heaviness but also slants the truth, so that what predominates is the style of candour rather than candour itself, and the laughter that avoids the demands and dangers of intimacy.

What Mary Trevelyan offered Eliot was this kind of joking relationship that could just touch the border of intimacy. He did tell her that he could not speak so freely to anyone else, nor permit anyone else to return such forthright comment. Once he sent her one of his rebukes by mail and, aware that this rocket was on its way, took her out for a companionable dinner. Mary had the nerve not to let this pass. After they had it out, they held hands in Mary's car, a trifle 'emotioné' as Mary put it. Strong in her self-assurance, less malicious than professional intellectuals (John Hayward, for instance), Mary Trevelyan invited Eliot to a more benign kind of laughter, not the lethal derision of his early years, but a more relaxing exchange of anecdote, like her account of her disconcerting dance with an enormous Guardsman at the Albert. He was so silent that she wondered if it was possible to fall asleep while dancing. 'After a few rounds,' she said, 'I risked a crick in the neck and looked up at him. He said with extraordinary dignity, "Excuse me, madam, I am trying not to hiccup." '

*

While Mary Trevelyan was coming and going, Eliot settled into his new arrangement with John Hayward in February –March 1946: the shared flat on the third floor overlooking the Thames in Carlyle Mansions. Hayward had proposed such an arrangement as early as 1935, but at that time Eliot had been too harassed by Vivienne's pursuit to have an address of his own. Hayward saw himself as Eliot's *très-loyal serviteur*. Like Mary, he was a guardian in the late forties and early fifties, though he served Eliot in a different way, as literary adviser and self-styled Keeper of the Eliot Archive. Together they saw Eliot through a difficult stage of his life in which he felt, more completely than ever before, bored with all living that had no religious meaning.

Eliot's arrangement with John Hayward was not really a home. In a sense, Eliot was homeless from 1914, with the exception of interludes in the thirties when he had felt 'at home' in Chipping Campden. Otherwise he had simply shared houses with Vivienne, with the Revd Eric Cheetham, with Mrs Mirrlees, and now with Hayward, in a way that sustained his interior solitude. This solitude he did not expose even to his confessors, to whom (he told Mary) he spoke of sins the confessors would understand. He saw it as an act of consideration not to mention sins too subtle or too complicated to explain. These remained unresolved. In a furious moment when he was bent on pushing Mary into conformity with new 'rules', he asked that it be understood that he was an old man with an uneasy conscience and bad dreams. He appealed not on the grounds of genius (as to Emily Hale) but as a sinner. His moodiest moments with Mary Trevelyan were not personal; they had to do with private 'horror', which he projected, once, on a pair of American tourists dining at a nearby table while he was at the Edinburgh Festival in 1953, or, another time, in 1951, on a down-home

American sing-song in Hampstead. Suddenly, he felt himself in a cage with wild beasts, and, going white, burst out: 'Do you know the Song of the Reconstructed Rebel?' He began to sing in a loud, raucous voice, with extreme violence, until Mary got him into a taxi. That alert to 'horror', compounded by a private burden of atonement, lay behind Eliot's habits in the eleven years that he lived with John Hayward.

Despite the inexorable progress of muscular dystrophy, Hayward remained the most sociable of men: the flat was the centre of Tarantula's web of bibliographical contacts that extended now across Europe and America. His visitors were continuous: as one left, the next would arrive. Hayward would be sitting in his front room, half-slewed round in his wheelchair to face his guest, dominating his world so that the dim hootings outside seemed less important. His world was dispensing judgements and stings, hilariously funny if you were not the victim. His hand would fumble for a small cigarette which he would somehow manage to light, 'his eyes widening as some horrid but delightful thought formed itself to be uttered'.

Hayward was a keen adviser. He was known never to say no to a request for guidance, and so the network grew larger, the immobilised figure at the centre more empowered. Eliot, with Hayward's compliance, evaded this web. The two men lived quite separate lives.

The arrangement was built around Eliot's privacy. Hayward gave him the outer structure of a normal life shared with others, and sanctioned, at the same time, the withdrawal of a solitary. It was a way of life carefully laid down as a set of habits. Eliot visited Hayward's room once a day, in the evening, for a brief talk, and on Saturday afternoons took him for a walk. Sometimes Hayward would help Eliot to entertain visiting celebrities – say Adrienne Monnier and Sylvia Beach* – at King's Road restaurants. Sometimes

* In 1919 Sylvia Beach, an American, opened a bookshop called Shakespeare and Company on the Left Bank in Paris. It became a meeting-place for expatriate writers, and in 1922 published Joyce's *Ulysses*.

Eliot might accompany Hayward to the literary parties of the capital: in the fifties it would create a stir when he arrived, pushing Hayward's chair. But then again, he might do nothing. He was free to shut the door of his room. Only once, at Easter 1955, did Eliot's withdrawal make for visible strain. John and Mary decided that he was making minor ailments an excuse for staying in his room, and John went so far as to hint that he was indulging in a degree of hypochondria that might affect his reputation.

The problem, of course, was Eliot's need for privacy: the excuses, the shut door, the broken arrangements with Mary were all understandable if Eliot had to balance the contradictory claims of his life as public hermit. For Eliot, as for Sir Claude, the private door is an 'escape into living / Escape from a sordid world into a pure one'.

Winter and summer, Eliot went by bus at 6.30 every morning to kneel on the cold stone floor of St Stephen's Church. After early mass, he wrote in the morning, standing up at a kind of lectern, typing three or four pages of a play or lecture. At about noon he would take the giant umbrella (specially made, with a large handle) and catch a bus, sitting on the top deck, to Piccadilly Circus, and from there went by Underground to Russell Square. At night, he usually had his meal on a tray in his bedroom, though occasionally he would dine with Hayward, or join him for tea at weekends. On Saturday afternoons, he would push Hayward across the bridge to Battersea Park or to the gardens of the Royal Hospital. It must have meant a certain amount of domestic responsibility to live with a disabled man, for they employed only a daily housekeeper, a sympathetic Frenchwoman called Mme Amory. She could not pronounce Eliot's name, and called him 'Monsieur le Professeur'. When Madame was not there, Hayward must have depended on Eliot for morning coffee and letters that had to be posted. Eliot was always punctilious about duties to the unfortunate – Mary noted how assiduously he visited a dying White Russian, Tereschenko, at Wandsworth – but the solitude prevailed. It was simply not 'done', Mary said, to visit Eliot and Hayward together, and they had few friends in common. The exceptions were Christopher Sykes, who accompanied them on the Saturday walks, and increasingly, as the years passed, Mary herself. From 1952 Mary and John began to compare notes and commiserate when Eliot was snappish with John or evasive with Mary.

'He can't help hurting us,' she said to John, and John added: 'He has a streak of sadism which he fights against.'

Mary's forthrightness made her relation to Eliot unmatched in this period of fame. Even John of the barbed tongue was his devotee, and in any case John's domestic base depended on Eliot, as well as some part of his prestige in literary circles.

For Eliot to live with so ill a man as John Hayward seems an act of charity, but the benefit was in Eliot's favour. Hayward guarded him from the outside world: for some years he took all phone calls. Like Mary, he was at the centre of the intellectual establishment, Mary by inheritance, Hayward by his precocious achievements as editor and 'man of letters' (as he liked to call himself, regretting that the phrase had come to sound affected). Eliot, the 'resident alien' ('Metoikos', as he once signed himself), depended on Hayward, who had a passion for accurate English, to oversee his drafts.

During the war Hayward, like Mary, had passed the test of loyalty. From Merton Hall, Cambridge, where he was evacuated, he had advised Eliot, with great verbal acumen, on the wartime *Quartets*. Later, he told Helen Gardner that, of all his activities, his share in *Four Quartets* gave him the most satisfaction. On 27 June 1940 he wrote from Cambridge to assure Eliot that the Eliot Archive was with him for safe-keeping. It was at this point that his role as mentor, successor to Pound, was added to his role as 'Keeper' or 'Clerk of the Works'. As the drafts of the later *Quartets* came in, he had them bound in order. After the war he mopped up other drafts of poems, talks, and plays.

Hayward was ideally suited to serve Eliot in this dual capacity. He was always there, and he was prodigiously well versed in English poetry. He told Kathleen Raine with justifiable pride, 'I have read the whole of English poetry, *twice*.' In 1947 he was behind the National Book League's exhibition of first and early editions of English poetry, the first attempt ever to present at one time in one place the whole range of English poetry from Chaucer to the present. His illustrated catalogue was variously described as 'exemplary' and 'a permanent landmark in bibliographical scholarship'. In 1951 he organised another exhibition, *Le Livre Anglais* at the Bibliothèque Nationale in Paris. In the postwar years he edited *The Penguin Book of English Verse* (1956), as well as Penguin selections of Donne and Herrick, and prose selections of Swift and T. S. Eliot. In 1952 he also became editor of the *Book Collector*, which he ran brilliantly as a dictator until it became the pre-eminent journal in its field. Colleagues would turn the pages of a new issue, trembling at Hayward's commentary, and powerful institutions fretted under his censure, which could be intemperate.

Hayward was committed, like Eliot, to the purity of the English language. He once took the Distillers Company to task for allowing an advertisement in which three whisky bottles were photographed standing on a volume of Scott. He urged Kathleen Raine that, as she put it, 'a poem should never appear which had not been perfected in accordance with those old rigorous standards of the language whose custodian he knew himself to be'. Eliot was only one of a large number of writers who submitted their drafts or proofs to his meticulous 'carpentry', who had to endure his frank, sometimes chastening comments, and who had to admit that he was almost always right. In 1949 Mary Trevelyan noted that Eliot's experiment of sharing a flat with Hayward was a success: 'Besides a strong personal affection, he depended greatly on John as his literary critic and seldom felt quite easy in his mind about anything he had written unless John approved.'

In the post-war period, Hayward was still mobile in his wheelchair, presiding over bookish society in London with his frightfully clever and cruel remarks. He feared nobody, said a King's College fellow. 'If there was trouble – well, let there be trouble. He rather liked a row.' Eliot shared his friend's acerbity, but their tactics were opposite. Eliot's was to withdraw; Hayward's to engage with a satire that was withering on a first encounter.

Gwen Watkins, wife of the Faber poet Vernon Watkins, recalled being introduced to John Hayward as 'a witty woman'.

'*Be* witty,' said Hayward shortly, through his bulbous lips.

Graham Greene remembered how he would throw back his head and draw in 'a loud long breath (his left arm waved like a tentacle of an octopus, and captured his silver cigarette case), as I asked him a direct and indiscreet question about some writer whom he did not regard with unmixed friendship. A pause and out came the atrocious anecdote.' His aim was to amuse. His friends, vastly entertained by these whiffs from the Underworld (as Virginia Woolf had called the literary marketplace), forgave him the malice: it was a compensation, they said, for his disease.

Hayward's powerful head, his knowing, bright eye, waving, half-paralysed left tentacle, and blubbery lips gave him the appearance of fairy-tale wickedness – a wicked godfather, said Janet Adam Smith – reinforced by his mix of banter and learning. He had a way of provoking confidences, sometimes indiscrete confessions. He relished scandal. This may be one reason why Eliot kept some protective distance. Their friendship ran on the smooth sophisticated routines of the joking relationship that the Tarantula and the Elephant had established in the thirties at Bina Gardens.

Both Hayward and Eliot cultivated personae. 'I shall wear, I think, my admirable red waistcoat to your party,' Hayward said to Mary Hyde. She noted how he used clothes – his cummerbunds and waistcoats, needlepoint slippers, and checked summer suit – to divert attention from his infirmity. So, too, Eliot used City neutrality to distract attention from his extreme antipathy to the paganism of the age. These were his antinomies of night and day. John, like Mary, helped to create Eliot's daily life; neither approached the Eliot of the night, who slept under a large crucifix (rescued by Mary from a devastated town in Germany), and whose reconstructive mission was briefly revealed when he chose the alias of Nehemiah, the rebuilder of Jerusalem. This identity he declared on the phone to Mary during one of his stays at the London Clinic, where he wished to remain incognito.

Eliot and Hayward had also the unspoken link of suffering: not only the obvious suffering of Hayward's body and Eliot's penitence but the strain of protracted celibacy. Hayward was paralysed from the waist down; Eliot had willed his own freezing since 1940 when he showed how 'the chill ascends from the feet to knees'. Neither was a natural celibate. Hayward's torment was that desire remained alive, and he was brave enough to express openly his attraction to women. At one party, when Caitlin Thomas (wife of Dylan) asked if he would lick the ice-cream off her arm, he said he would lick it off any part of her body but not in so public a place. Graham Greene, who shared a taste for erotica with him, said that he had a strong appreciation of physical love. Hayward's frustration is easier to understand than Eliot's denial of a physicality that was, to him, unclean. Though he felt crippled in the late forties when he made the decision not to marry Emily Hale, his renewal ten years later suggests that this was only a phase, consequent perhaps on his guilt for the broken lives of two women. 'Atonement' was the watchword of this time. Taken off-guard one night by a visit from the writer Julia Strachey (niece of Lytton), he appeared in his dressing-gown looking, she said, weird, ghostly, Strindbergian.

Despite all that they shared, there was a huge temperamental divide between Eliot and Hayward, epitomised by their rooms. Hayward's had soft green walls, a green bookcase and bed, invitations on the mantelpiece, and a wide window where he sat, back to the room, looking out at the *comédie humaine* enacted on a single bench on the Chelsea Embankment. He often asked Kathleen Raine to pull it more into his view after she left. In contrast, Eliot chose two small dark rooms at the back of the flat, looking down into the well of the building. There he lived, I imagine, like Jeremiah in the pit or St John of the Cross in the dark prison. There, under the crucifix, he observed religious rules, some given, some of his own devising. He memorised passages from the Bible, said the rosary every night, and kept the fasts. During Lent he denied himself gin, and limited his favourite game of patience to one pack. Hayward thought that behind the closed door he played innumerable games of patience. It was a convenient and suggestive alibi. His life was as emblematic as a tale by Hawthorne: the closed door; the dark well; the game of patience – or was it endurance of the dark night of the soul? Their first housekeeper, a young Irishwoman who soon left to be married, refused to believe that Eliot was a distinguished writer. It was Hayward sitting at his desk who was 'the writing man'. Eliot, she insisted, was 'a holy man'.

Writing of the 'neutrality' of St John of the Cross, Thomas Merton said that, at its height, the holy life does not impose itself on the attention of others. If Eliot was invisible it was not because he enjoyed merely the sophisticated game of masks. At his highest reach, his aim was the invisibility that guards a life of invisible devotion. Eliot contemplated the virtue of unremarked devotion in particular in 1952–3 while he wrote *The Confidential Clerk*. The retired Eggerson, a clerk entirely without charisma – some would say entirely without interest – is a 'confidential clerk' in the sense that he is, really, a divine agent.

In 1955 Eliot pretended to Mary Trevelyan that he would like to change his name; he would become obscure again as Bonsir. This might translate, he mused, as Goodchild. Alternatively, he might turn out to be Badboy. And so, behind the studied neutrality of the arbiter of the literary world, this allegorical drama, touched with faint, Hawthornian mockery, went on. Bonsir was another alias thought up at the London Clinic. Eliot was inordinately happy there, Mary Trevelyan observed, and it occurred to her that he was malingering. But in the inaccessible privacy of the clinic he was dreaming up new identities. The obscure Bonsir was the other face of Nehemiah. 'Bonsir Nehemiah,' he announced on the phone.

*

Eventually, in 1955, Eliot came to see Bonsir as Mary Trevelyan's adoptive nephew. The third and longest phase of their friendship began in 1949 when Mary returned from the East to work for London University as its first Advisor to Overseas Students. Her flat and office in Brunswick Square were only a few minutes' walk from Eliot's office in Russell Square, and they began to meet more frequently than before her departure. He used to sing snatches of American songs: 'Say, gal, I'm certainly glad to know you . . .' or 'Come on my Houseboat with me . . .'. Eliot held Mary's reassuring hand all through a conversation with the Vice-Chancellor of London University after he was given an honorary degree in 1949. In parting also, he would hold her hand for a long time, even though they were to see each other quite soon. She thought it a sign of growing attachment but, more likely, he was grasping a new lifeline after his rejection of Emily Hale.

Unlike Emily, Mary Trevelyan was always visible as Eliot's escort. Their friendship went through three distinct phases: the testing phase; the wartime and post-war correspondence; and now a long phase with Mary in pursuit and Eliot backing away but increasingly dependent on her as Guardian. His dependence gave her the illusion of control, which was compounded by his unwillingness to be explicit about his feelings. Marriage, he did eventually make clear, was out of the question. Instead, he devised a relationship in which he had some of the benefits of a wife – caring, companionship, the domestic pleasure of long Sunday evenings with eggs and bacon, followed by records, at Mary's flat.

He worried about the frequency of their meetings and phone calls and, periodically, tried to counteract it with his rules. But frequency crept back, and established a hundred small traditions over the years: a net of habit in which he felt comfortable. There were the casual suppers on Sundays, the drives before or after church, and the notes on Mary's car, simply to say 'Good-morning'. Once, he leapt unexpectedly into her car as she stopped at a traffic light. Mary drove him to his appointments – soothing his nerves en route – or deposited him on time at the station when he left on vacations which she had planned for him. In return, he plied her with gifts, including a new car.

Mary's abundant activity complemented Eliot's arrangements with Hayward. Together, these two practical, decisive people preserved the outer structure of Eliot's life from 1949 to the end of 1956. Once, when Mary suggested to John that further help was needed, John replied that there was no one else: they were Eliot's sole close friends. John welcomed Mary's co-operation. In April 1950, at a party with the Shereks, the Martin Brownes and the Kenneth Clarks at the Savoy after the London opening of *The Cocktail Party*, John, affable in his flowered waistcoat, said to Mary: 'I look on you as part of the family.'

It was an odd family: a paralysed man with a barbed tongue; an independent single woman; and a hermit doing penance in his back room, his health flagging as he forced himself through public duties. It was, all of it, duty, Eliot told Mary. Nothing, certainly not the fourteenth honorary degree, gave him the slightest pleasure. Just plain nonsense, she thought in her brisk, slightly impervious way, but he spoke the truth.

In 1949 Mary began to record her times with him. 'I set myself this task', she wrote, 'because I have an unreliable memory and it seemed a waste to have so close a friendship with our greatest living poet and not to record some of his conversation.' She wrote immediately after seeing him. The random form of a diary, recording week-to-week events, is counterbalanced by Mary's fixity of focus: it is always Eliot before her eyes, once looking pitifully old as she sees him from a distance trying to pick up his walking-stick on Chelsea Bridge; always Eliot's voice interrupting her when she holds the floor; and Eliot's singing, like an out-of-tune bassoon, 'Swing Low, Sweet Chariot', on the car journeys home. Her diary looks at him consistently with the attentiveness of a woman in love with her subject but unable to fathom him. She was astonished by the odd furious letter, accusing her of

impertinence. Her fairly controlled explosions of exasperation ('Poets!') and her surprise at his tendency to 'disappear'
after their good times, see so far and no farther: 'he seemed to
take fright and going away was his instinctive defence.' She
was so much the social being that she had no understanding
of the solitary; an oblivion to Eliot's inner life goes hand-in-
hand with her observation of his switches from a sunny face
to what she calls a refugee face. It was a refugee who met her
next move.

Two years after Vivienne's death, Mary hoped that Eliot
would be ready to settle their relationship: she wanted to
know where she stood. Her words were plain, practical,
unromantic: she called marriage a 'working arrangement'.
Her moderate expectations were, of course, the opposite of
Eliot's notion of heavenly love, and it was inconceivable for
him to think of Mary in that way.

He replied on 27 April 1949 that the thought of sharing his
life with anyone was a nightmare. He explained this by
mysterious reference to a tragedy which Mary naturally took
to mean Vivienne but which, as Eliot was to explain a year
later, meant what had happened to him and Emily Hale. Eliot
remained 'frightened' of women (he used this phrase often in
conversations with Mary Trevelyan). To unbend, he needed
the reassurance of many unthreatening contacts. Lots of
church-going, Mary prescribed for their friendship after it
was shaken by her proposal. Over the next year, she nursed a
hope that Eliot would recover, and on 29 May 1950
proposed again. This time it was a case of love's blindness to
Eliot's unmistakable signals of withdrawal.

'Will you be looking in this week?' Mary asked on 26
March, on their way home from church.

'Not unless it's really necessary,' Eliot replied.

'It's not at all necessary,' said Mary shortly, and there was
a pause while he got out of the car. Then he turned, contrite.

'I *would* like to come round this week and hear some music
if it is possible.' That evening he brought Mary many
presents.

A few weeks later he remarked: 'I never see ANYONE for pleasure.' Mary didn't believe it.

'You're an unusual friend,' she said guardedly.

'And in the end, unsatisfactory,' he warned.

Mary mistook Eliot's need to be safe from molestation as a plea for more protection. She saw the same plea in his uneasiness at receptions, and in his fears of falling ill, alone, as he grew old. Once again, she offered marriage as a practical solution – to her own loneliness as well as his, she ventured to say.

This time, in his reply of 2 June, Eliot took pains to make his position clear. He was driven to expose to Mary, as to no one else, what he called the most agonising experience of his life. Concealing only Emily Hale's name, he said that he had been in love with someone else for a great many years, and that it would be too simple to say that love had faded. It was much more than that, more than he could find words to express. He had never wanted to marry anyone but this one woman. His failure to fulfil the promise of this love was felt to be an index of the state of his soul: physical exhaustion was a sign of a profounder spiritual depletion, perhaps a sense that forgiveness had not come and might never come. He told Mary, in conclusion, that there remained a pain that gnawed at his liver, and which he expected to go on till his death.

She responded to his confession with ready sympathy. She saw Eliot not as a hermit tormented by his dream of divine love but, in her more prosaic way, as a man in a prison, largely of his own making. On 5 June they had a talk which, she hoped, opened the prison a chink. She assured Eliot that what he had told her would make no difference to feelings for him which could not be killed. Poor Mary needed this relief of expression but, rather deftly, Eliot deflected her back from the role of lover to her customary one of guardian. Again, Mary misunderstood. Still hopeful, she thought that Eliot's toast to The Guardians referred to the future guardians of their relationship.

Eliot's romantic loyalty to the memory of his bond with Emily Hale could only enhance Mary's respect. He was a man capable of a great love. In the light of this, she could understand his not wanting her, or anyone, to share his life. Did he shrink from inflicting pain on her, with the consoling half-truth that he no longer enjoyed his love's company, so that, by implication, Mary was, in present day-to-day terms, first in his life? It was reasonable for him to believe, in his depleted state in 1950, that he would never again wish to marry. And he did wish to retain Mary's friendship. He could not deprive himself of the help that supported his bouts of nerves, the jollity that cheered his gloom.

Soon after the exchange, on 23 July, Mary heard that Eliot was to give lunch to an American, Miss Emily Hale. Mary jumped to the fact that this was 'THE lady'. Eliot appeared gloomy at the prospect, and Mary was not at all cast down. He had the imaginative power to project his policies on others so that, in general, they accepted them, as Mary accepted the limitations of a demanding friendship. But there were occasional crises when his powers of projection met with resistance or dismay. Vivienne's protracted refusal to be dismissed became a nightmare; Emily Hale's confidence that he still wished to marry her and, failing that, her continued faithfulness became an embarrassment. A man, Eliot told Mary, doesn't like to be made to feel *guilty*.

Mary's proposals must have changed the friendship. The memoir does not acknowledge this, but it does show Eliot's increasing irritability from 1950. Mary was too sturdy to take this personally and, on the face of it, their habits resumed as though nothing had happened: the dinners, the drives, the anxious confabs about such subjects as the see of London. Eliot might say, 'you always expect the worst and you are always right'. With Mary he could be mildly indiscreet about his 'mediocre' contemporaries. Shaw was 'a mischievous child'; F. R. Leavis was 'disgruntled and sneering', resentful that when the *Criterion* had been in its heyday Eliot had not supported his magazine, *Scrutiny*. Pound was perhaps 'never really sane. Oh yes, as a young man I swallowed him whole . . . I think he has become gradually, increasingly, insane through a long period of years. He only liked *good* poets and had no compassion for, or interest in anyone else. He could never laugh at himself – nor could he be laughed at – he has always been egocentric.' He thought that the best English poet was Edwin Muir (Auden, whose greatness was undisputed, he no longer regarded as English). Day Lewis he thought mediocre, and also a mediocre adulterer. Edith Sitwell was too much of an exhibitionist, but he admired Marianne Moore: '*quite* outstanding and way above most of the men of her generation. She has invented a new idiom, hitherto unused.'

He also enjoyed mild indiscretions about the Church. The Pope, he told Mary, compared favourably with our dear Archbishop (Fisher)* in being less like a headmaster. He even told her that when he made his confessions (three times a year) there were limits to what he could say, and that he accepted lunch from his confessor as part of the penance.

Eliot seemed to find what lurked in his soul incommunicable outside poetry. Just once, on 22 January 1953, he let it out to Mary in a long fiery speech which she recorded with care:

> I believe in hell, yes, I do. I live in constant fear of it myself. If there is a Heaven there must be a Hell. But it's all *outside time* and therefore beyond our earthly comprehension. Yet I *know* I have always known hell – it is in my bones. I don't believe this is common – perhaps I am abnormal.

A few months later, he said that his religious life was 'the *whole* of me, yet too many people think it is irrelevant'. Often their talks touched the borders of intimacy, but rarely went further. Eliot would touch on Vivienne or reminisce about his childhood with elderly parents or describe his sister Marian, whom now, in his loneliness, he felt to be his very flesh and blood. He recalled, too, his visit to London in 1911 and his time at Lloyds Bank.

Mary took him on nostalgia-drives to the *Waste Land* area

* Once a headmaster, he was known to a generation of schoolboys as 'Flogger Fisher': he had a reputation for pausing between cuts to make sure the pain of each cut was fully felt.

of the City, past Lloyds, down King William Street, along Lower Thames Street, where in his lunch hours Eliot had visited St Magnus the Martyr and watched the fishermen at Billingsgate market, and from there they drove on to the Tower and over Tower Bridge with a great red sun sinking behind the cargo ships. Eliot, quoting Shelley, prowled the byways of the City. They once went to Moorgate to find Bunhill Fields, the cemetery, and explored Islington and Canonbury. Driving to Putney, where Eliot liked to pick out odd names on little shops, was a revival of the Eeldrop explorations of the dingy-respectable South London suburbs of Eliot's early years and, going back further, the *fin de siècle* slumming in Paris in 1911 and in the Roxbury area of Boston in 1910. One drive took them past Crawford Mansions in Paddington, the cage in which Eliot had lived with Vivienne, and another to Victoria Grove, the home of cats Mungojerrie and Rumpelteazer. But Eliot's favourite drive was in the purlieus of Paddington, and his idea of a 'splendid exploration' in 1955 was to drive the whole length of the Portobello Road, a world of 'fantasy' compared with the respectable charms of Chelsea.

The equivalent treat on Saturday afternoons with John Hayward and Christopher Sykes was to watch football games in a winter drizzle in the Chelsea Hospital Gardens. The first time they went it was a match between the Marylebone Dustmen and a team from the Chelsea Municipal Maintenance with one spectator, a melancholy old man raising his voice to chant, 'Come . . . on . . . the . . . Maintenance!' This forlorn scene fascinated Eliot, and it became a regular excursion.

His network of habits formed a cocoon for the invisible life that, I imagine, stirred rather feebly between the need to atone and a more insidious hollowness of heart which neither Mary nor John could dispel. Mary, who saw its symptom – that there was almost no one whom Eliot found himself able to like – was alarmed, at times, at his air of weariness, and wary of sudden plunges into moody darkness; but he never spoke to her about atonement. Shut out, without quite knowing why, she had moments of impatience when she thought him evasive, even 'deceitful'. When he reasserted his distance, she assumed the inexplicable aberration of a great poet who was, at the same time, a 'silly old boy'.

Yet, for a long time, the cocoon of their habits remained, so immediate and visible that Mary never imagined it could ever become brittle. And for a long time Mary's cocoon did protect an unhappy creature who had little hope of transformation. With her he had not domestic happiness, but a semblance of domestic stability. When they arrived at her flat (first in Brunswick Square, later at 23 Embankment Gardens), Eliot would work the lift, take in the milk, put his hat, coat, and umbrella in Mary's bedroom, and cook supper with his sleeves rolled up. His help in the kitchen was not altogether appreciated. Afterwards they would listen to records: the *Coriolan* Overture; Beethoven's A Minor Quartet, op. 132 (which had inspired *Four Quartets*); and Eliot's favourite, the Mozart clarinet quintet ('I love the *economy* of Mozart,' he said). He also enjoyed Haydn's trumpet concerto, Mozart's oboe quartet, and the slow opening crescendo of the second movement of Beethoven's Seventh Symphony.

They sometimes went to the theatre to see, say, Cicely Courtneidge in *Gay's the Word* in 1951 or, in October 1952, Emlyn Williams as Dickens, starting off with the Veneerings and Podsnaps, and going on to Paul Dombey's death. Mary liked to be taken to dine at the Garrick Club, with its long table lit by candles, surrounded by Zoffany pictures. Otherwise they dined at the more anonymous Russell Hotel, or the more expensive Écu de France, or with Margaret Rhondda and Theodora Bosanquet (who had been amanuensis to Henry James). Another habit was an annual visit to Windsor Castle, where they were entertained by Sir Owen Morshead, the King's Librarian.

All this time Mary saw to Eliot's comforts, advised, and worried over him. Should he take legal action over a 1952 article on his supposed homosexuality? 'After all, that does NOT happen to be my temperament,' he said. How kind she was to bring him rhubarb and country eggs. The eggplant had made a nice pie. He had bought himself a new coat, exactly like the last. When he returned from his jaunts to America, he turned the pages of his diary, recounting to Mary the events of every single day he had been away.

His dependence on her reached its height in the summer of 1954, when Eliot broke his rule about separate vacations. He was taking his sister Marian to Farringford (once Tennyson's home, now a hotel) on the Isle of Wight. Uneasy about managing this alone, Eliot invited Mary (and her car) to join them. With alacrity she organised their days. She drove them to Osborne to see Queen Victoria's Durbar Hall and State Apartments, and after tea she and Eliot climbed Tennyson's Down to look at the Needles. They walked two miles, and on the way back picked wild flowers and lay on the grass on the top of the down (not too near the edge, in deference to Eliot's fear of heights). A heavy sea-mist descended, so they climbed down again, and walked through the fields to Freshwater Bay and along the beach. In the evening they ate in the huge hotel dining-room, with a portrait of the Poet Laureate and early portraits of Victoria and Albert, elderly couples speaking in whispers, and Eliot, his back carefully turned to the room. After dinner, he taught Mary the game of 'petunia', a variety of patience.

Mary was happy enough to discount the odd gloom. Marian admitted to Mary that her brother could be trying, and asked her not to leave him. She and a niece, Theodora, who had become Mary's friends, suggested that she might marry Eliot, but Mary told herself that she was too sensible to nourish this hope.

The next summer, Eliot, on vacation in Sussex, again summoned Mary for a weekend before she was to drive him back to London. Again, from Mary's point of view, it was idyllic. On the way home, they drove past Julian and Juliette Huxley, the ex-Director-General of UNESCO and his Swiss wife, whose patent curiosity left Mary with the complacent conviction that they had 'thought the worst'.

13

A Prophet's Mission

MARY DARED TO confront Eliot about aloofness. She did this through his plays.

'Your people are mere puppets, speaking what you want them to speak,' she said in February 1950. 'They don't really come alive at all – and what often puzzles me is that although, in some ways, you seem to know so much about people, in other ways you seem quite blind – perhaps because you don't like them.'

Eliot put up no defence except to say 'you mustn't want to know too much about people'.

He set a standard that cut off idle or destructive curiosity, but Mary detected also a limiting self-protection in the phase following the heights of the *Quartets*. If we compare Yeats or Virginia Woolf after the highest flights of maturity, the Byzantium poems or *The Waves*, there was in both a continued willingness to expose themselves to reciprocal knowing. Virginia Woolf's friendship with Ethel Smyth may have disrupted her privacy, but it did compel a new phase of outspokenness in the cause of women. Yeats, too, dared more as he exposed the 'lust and rage' of an old man, staring into 'the foul rag and bone shop of the heart'. Both could say 'What then?' and ride the crest of a new wave as it rolled across the timeless sea. Their readiness was all. Eliot, in contrast, seemed to back away from emotional risk. His withdrawal from Emily Hale in the summer of 1947 may be the biographic marker for a new degree of self-protection at the very time that he embarked on a mission that meant constant exposure to people. Did his self-protection work against the mission? Or did his remoteness actually enhance the status of judgements that came, it seemed, from on high? Emerson, who walked 'on stilts', was 'patient' of his remoteness, 'inasmuch as it makes my solitude dearer & the impersonal God is shed abroad in my heart more richly & more lowly welcome for this porcupine impossibility of contact with men'.

Eliot's American predecessors, Emerson, Whitman, Pound, had assumed the platform posture of a poet who is a spokesman for public destiny. The American scholar, said Emerson, disseminates principles born from the private life, and in doing so looks to 'the conversion of the world'. No less. These Americans do not write literature in the European sense of the word: their rhetoric does not terminate in aesthetic form, but in the conversion of the reader. Whitman called for a poet to assume the status of Judgement: 'He judges not as the judge judges but as the sun falling around a helpless thing. As he sees the farthest he has the most faith.' The greatest poet, Eliot said in 1954, may not belong to his age 'not only by being behind or ahead of his age, but being above it'. Such a poet shares the problems of his age and the language in which its problems are discussed, but 'may repudiate all the current solutions'.

Eliot saw that the war had brought the sickness of civilisation to a crisis without curing it: the sickness was raging everywhere. He saw the prospect of 'centuries of barbarism' which, in an interview in 1945, he related to the coming dominance of technology. His *Notes Towards the Definition of Culture* (begun in 1943 and published in 1948) rise to 'prophetic gloom' as he elaborates on a vision of a degraded society which will destroy 'our ancient edifices to make ready the ground upon which the barbarian nomads of the future will encamp in their mechanised caravans'.

Eliot's *Notes* and speeches repudiate conventional efforts, political, international, educational, as well as the futility of Christian conferences. He sees the core of the problem in the corruption of language, the basis of thought, which is, in turn, the basis of integrity. This he spelt out in a speech at Aix-en-Provence on 6 December 1947. His target was those who use words for base purposes, to manipulate the masses who suffer passions but do not think. The profoundest effect, he warned in 'The Social Function of Poetry', is that feelings are blunted: '. . . our own ability, not merely to express, but even to feel any but the crudest emotions, will degenerate.' The poet was the main bastion against this abuse: without his renewal of language, civilisation will decline.

The *Notes* warn of a decline already visible in every department of human activity, proceeding towards, he repeats, 'a period, of some duration, of which it is possible to say that it will have *no* culture'. In a letter to Desmond MacCarthy, he complained of films, popular writing, Hemingway, newspapers, and the corruption of the language, a result of debasing people to the decadent-barbaric. 'We live in an *impossible* age,' he lamented to Mary, 'a world of thugs.' Most days he could not bring himself to look at the newspaper until teatime. He spoke of Gomorrah and of Nineveh: our cities were doomed, like those of the Bible. He prayed in the Underground. It might not be good for one's prayers, he said, but one's prayers might be good for the Underground.

Eliot's contempt for his age was fanned by private horror. At the time he began the *Notes*, back in the middle of the war, he explained this to Mary Trevelyan. It was 1944, the flying-bombs were overhead, and they were discussing fear of death. Eliot said there was something else which he couldn't get to the bottom of, 'disgust, horror, physical nausea, the *nightmare* of evil'. As self-styled Master of the Heresy Hounds he hunted evil, and now and then identified it, privately, in a particular person – surprising targets like the artist Roger Fry, the biographer Lytton Strachey, and the novelist Charles Williams – all of whom had been friends in earlier years. We can't separate Eliot's greatness as a poet from his strain of virulence that from time to time went off the rails – the same Eliot who in 1933 had felt able to share with his Virginia audience his view that a spirit of tolerance was to be deplored, as was 'any large number of free-thinking Jews' in a society.

Unassailable as Eliot was as the greatest living poet from 1940 on, there was the odd protest against his anti-Semitism. In 1950, at the time of *The Cocktail Party*, an article appeared in New York which astonished Eliot – he was aggrieved, not sorry. The best-known incident was at the Poetry Society in London in about 1950 when a writer called Emanuel Litvinoff read a poem 'To T. S. Eliot' in Eliot's presence: 'Bleistein is my relative,' he read, 'I share the protozoic slime of Shylock', and 'underneath the cities, / a billet somewhat lower than the rats', recalling the 'protozoic slime' of Bleistein's eyes in Eliot's poem, and its racial hatred:

> The rats are underneath the piles.
> The jew is underneath the lot.

Litvinoff links the verbal target with acts of extermination: 'Pieces of our flesh / float with the ordure on the Vistula.' Most of the audience began to clap; Spender (a quarter Jewish) shouted, 'Tom isn't anti-Semitic'; while Eliot, head down, muttered, 'It's a good poem, it's a very good poem.' Retelling this incident to an audience in Oxford on 9 May 1996, James Fenton (as Professor of Poetry) noted that Eliot never withdrew opinions that were commonplace in 1919 but offensive after the Holocaust. For the evil of that event could not be entirely unconnected with thinkers who fuelled hatred. Fenton ended his lecture with the statement, 'Eliot was a scoundrel.' After a shocked moment, people clapped. I did not. Exposés of Eliot are sharpened by his supremacy as moral arbiter, but we can't forget his vision of perfection. Hatred is common; perfection rare. In him, the two were interfused.

As the voice and embodiment of Culture, Eliot addressed audiences ostensibly about practical measures in a period of reconstruction, but he spoke from a point of reference beyond his time, against the worldly life in all times. In a wireless talk in 1946 he called for 'spiritual organisation'. In April 1955, when asked to give a luncheon talk to the

Conservative Union, with Anthony Eden* in the chair, on the subject of literature and politics, he planned to stump them with the question: 'What is man, that thou are mindful of him?' Afterwards, he told Pound that he thought Eden had not understood the talk, nor noticed an implied criticism of himself.

Eliot's monumental judgements and warnings slide unobtrusively into his talks, social ideas, and plays. The tactic was to get an indifferent, largely atheist audience to take in a moral message without realising it. Reilly, who is more like a priest than a psychiatrist, tells his patient:

Half of the harm that is done in the world
Is due to people who want to feel important.
They don't mean to do harm – but the harm does not
    interest them.

This appears incidental to the cure of a disrupted marriage. In the next interview, which will elicit the buried vocation of a potential saint, Celia says apologetically:

I don't hear any voices, I have no delusions –
Except that the world I live in seems all a delusion!

Again, the judgement slides past as if it were an afterthought, as Eliot later dropped the same passing thought into 13,000 minds in the Minnesota stadium: the pursuit of normality, he said, is an adjustment to a 'deranged society', instead of to the fundamental Order of Things.

To extract the sermon is to realise that, in this period, Eliot was a man with a mission, sent to warn of 'chaos', the last days of civilisation. If he was remote between 1947 and 1957, there is the possibility that he had to be alone as a voice crying in the wilderness. Auden saw that his *Notes Towards the Definition of Culture* was not about society in the usual English sense of the word: 'Whig? Tory? All flesh is grass. Culture? The grass withereth.'† Eliot was speaking not in

* Foreign Secretary, future Prime Minister.
† In Isaiah 40:8 the grass is contrasted with the Word which shall last forever.

the political terms of his time but as 'a voice in Ramah weeping, that will not be comforted'.*

The prophets of the Old Testament are cast down by pervasive iniquity. Their style and message – the promise of renewal conditional on extended trial – has been central to American speech from the New England divines down to their greatest descendant, Eliot. Where Christ offers being through the incarnation of the spirit, the prophet has no being. The spirit is given through the Word, through language alone. Eliot took up this task in the forties and fifties when, repeatedly, he craves purity of language.

'In the year that King Uzziah died,' Eliot began a plaintive rhyme in which Rumpuscat feels bad inside. The bathos looks back to Prufrock, who had a hundred visions but felt insecure at a tea party. It both conceals and reveals the poet's model, here the scene of Isaiah's verbal purification as part of his call *c*. 740 BC. Isaiah laments that he is a man of 'unclean lips' who lives in the midst of a people of 'unclean lips'. Then a seraph takes a live coal from the altar,

> And he laid it upon my mouth, and said, Lo, this hath touched thy lips; and thine iniquity is taken away, and thy sin purged.
> Also I heard the voice of the LORD, saying, Whom shall I send, and who will go for us? Then said I, Here am I; send me.

This emissary offers himself not as a person but as a channel for a message: he is to be God's instrument. This is how Eliot's Becket defined his vocation in his Christmas sermon. And this may be the closest we can get to the mission that lies behind the studied neutrality of Eliot's appearance. The unassuming demeanour, the quiet manner, the measured, neutral voice were designed to outlive personality.

To address a whole society, Eliot had to relinquish his richest poetic material, the private agony. At earlier stages in his career his character infiltrates the poetry, and it does resurface in 1958 in Eliot's final play. But in the forties and

---

* The voice is that of Rachel, who foresees the vision of Isaiah: her children's children going into exile.

early fifties he took up a task that went against the grain of
his searching genius. He relinquished the outposts of experience, sublimity and degradation. The sinner, central to the
earlier plays, disappears; the saint moves to one side; and the
main action sorts out a middle-class marriage of no great
promise. Following this course even further in *The Confidential Clerk*, Eliot turns to business people of relentless banality.

The elect amongst them is the retired clerk, Eggerson,
whose obscure goodness plants itself in a suburban garden
where he grows vegetables for 'Mrs. E'. Eggerson is a
believable person – he was based on a real clerk, Mr
McKnight, who had been Eliot's first colleague at Lloyds
Bank – but because Eggerson's language is locked in con-
tented cliché there is no chance of expressive depth. Eggerson
is mentor to his successor, a second-rate organist turned
businessman under pressure from his presumed father, the
financier Sir Claude. In the course of the play it is revealed
that the young clerk is an orphan, and is therefore free to
devote himself to the organ in Eggerson's parish church and,
eventually, to take orders. He is a man in search of identity,
abjuring father, mother, and the inviting Lucasta, so that he
might fulfil a devotion to God alone. None of Eliot's
prospective saints is quite as humble as this second-rate
organist whose very name, Simpkins, proclaims his nonentity.
To be God's instrument one must become nothing. Only
from nothing can new being emerge.

Eggerson is the fixed point of integrity in a play in which
the other characters seek their true selves: the financier turns
out to be a frustrated potter; his bossy, classy wife, Lady
Elizabeth, turns out to be – marginally – less stupid than she
at first appears; his illegitimate daughter, Lucasta, turns out
to be – marginally – less flighty than the female construct she
adopts. Salvation for these routine types is limited to dim
perceptions of the fact that they have assumed 'unreal' lives.
In his youth, Eliot had satirised the collector of porcelain (Mr
Silvero) and the bogus medium (Mme Sosostris). In *Four
Quartets*, he had ridiculed the devotees of pentagrams,
tea leaves, and psychoanalysis, the pastimes of the hopeless,

and in 1948 he had endorsed the exclusion of a Jew (identified in coded language as a lady of the usual foreign origin) from the Eliot Collection at Harvard, on the grounds that her approach was psychoanalytic. (He said that he particularly wished to exclude psychoanalysts, casters and horoscopes, and other practitioners of magic.) Now, striving for charity, Eliot acknowledges that Lady Elizabeth's woolly obsession with *The Light from the East* and Sir Claude's collection of pottery are their only possible substitutes for religion.

Art, Eliot allows, can rouse us to identify with a maker of forms, the likeliest approach for the secular mind to the Maker. In the rare case of Simpkins, art – organ music – will take him further, into religious commitment, but for Sir Claude, the prototype of worldliness, art will provide only an intermittent 'escape' from his life of 'make-believe' – though, since he is not creative, the escape is itself, he owns, only another mode of make-believe. For the women in the play, there is not even this escape: their salvation, if we can call it that, lies in assent to motherhood and marriage, the family structure that provides a bedrock of order for the secular life.

To hold an audience it is essential to reflect it. Yet there are times when Eliot bends over too far, when he sees us, his audience, as more vulgar, obtuse, and soulless than we are. In early plays, in *Sweeney Agonistes* as in *The Family Reunion*, Eliot had jolted his audience from the social round into unknown modes of being. *The Confidential Clerk* kindly protects us from such useless disturbance. The elect slide smoothly into their secret rites, and have nothing to communicate beyond obedience to a given destiny. The audience is cheered along by heavy, now-dated farce.

Many prefer to end their consideration of Eliot with *Four Quartets*. The present consensus is that his work declined from that point. The odds would seem to have been against his mission to speak to a vast public. Yet it succeeded, and to a degree not measurable by the tedium of certain speeches nor the flaws of certain plays. Eliot's achievement in this phase cannot properly be judged in aesthetic terms, and this may be the very secret of his mass appeal. For his pronouncements attained an authority that was heard with awe. How this authority came to be, in so cynical a century, is still a mystery. It was backed but not explained by mere fame. He was a figure on a platform, a voice on the wireless, a presence that made itself felt as a standard of judgement which looked beyond its time.

*

After the Second World War came a second wave of cultural despair, less fertile in its literature than the first which took its rise in the works of Flaubert, the French Symbolists, Dickens, and Conrad, and reached its crest after the First World War in *The Waste Land*. The second wave was more predictable. Below the froth of its black humour is the automatism of jaded opinion. In 1958 Eliot spoke of the monotony of nihilism, which can't be kept up indefinitely: 'Nihilism itself becomes boredom.'

Eliot's comedies do refute nihilism, but their redeeming characters, Celia and Simpkins, are not allowed to display their strength. They recoil from society and business into hidden vocations: Celia joins an austere nursing order and goes off to the wilds; Simpkins will disappear into a dim future beyond our understanding. We are not permitted to follow them as, say, Sylvia Plath tugs us with her into the pure trajectory of her gallop into the red Eye of the morning. Eliot turns us firmly to face what his great souls reject. As he sees it, the 'indomitable spirit of mediocrity' is our destiny, and our only relief, dear reader, is to make the best of a bad job.

Helen Gardner predicted in 1965 that Eliot's comedies would come back one day. In time, the drawing-room manners and clichés of the late forties and early fifties will take on a period quaintness. But if there is enduring substance in *The Cocktail Party* and *The Confidential Clerk*, it lurks in places where Eliot slips in lines which he does not expect his audience to grasp. At certain points, characters speak beyond the audience what Eliot called '*transparent*' words. When the psychiatrist refers to his 'sanatorium' he remarks – as though it were an aside – that it is not for ordinary people but for potential saints. 'You will forget this phrase,' the psychiatrist goes on to Edward Chamberlayne, the ordinary patient, 'And in forgetting it will alter the condition.' He defies the West End or Broadway audience to conceive the transformation of saints.

The opening of the play is even more mystifying:

> ALEX. You've missed the point completely, Julia:
> There *were* no tigers. *That* was the point.

Our task is, once again, to play Watson. Directed by the all-knowing Holmes, we must do our blundering best to solve the mystery. Julia drives this challenge home later in the first scene when she says: 'There's altogether too much mystery / About this place to-day'. Eliot's first plays were all mysteries of sorts. In *Murder in the Cathedral* there is the question of who killed the Archbishop, and in *The Family Reunion* the question of whether Harry killed his wife. In *The Cocktail Party* there is the mystery to which Julia refers, the strange disappearance of a woman who had invited her friends to a party. But all these mysteries are blinds (rather like the pat conclusions that Hawthorne dealt out to the despised gift-book readers of his enigmatic tales), sops to an audience incapable of divining the true mystery which is the recess of consciousness: the haunted men of the first plays; the hidden destinies of *The Cocktail Party*. These are interior mysteries, hard to stage, hard to voice (and perhaps, like James, better suited to the small screen than to the theatre).

'You've missed the point completely . . .'. We are told this before the drama has even begun. We Watsons are bound to miss the point – unless we have read 'Gerontion', and know that the tiger is Eliot's image of revelation ('Came Christ the tiger'). So the fact that there *were* no tigers is the opening premise for a new interior drama: how does one live without revelation? The lines recall Holmes's insistence on the dog in the night. 'The dog did nothing in the night-time,' protests a mystified inspector. That, Holmes replies, was the point.

Eliot starts without hope that the tattle of the cocktail hour can accommodate the coming of Christ or the immortal hand that framed the Tyger in the forests of the night. At the very outset of his intercourse with the worldly audience of the commercial theatre, he shuns the world; as he invites our attention, his teasing obscurity shuts us out from the only mystery that really matters: the meaning of existence under clouds of unknowing.

Eliot spoke most forcefully beyond the audience of his age when, in 1944, he isolated a new menace: a provincialism not of space but of time. All the peoples of the globe can be provincials together in so far as they are preoccupied with the issues of their newspapers in a way that blocks out the timeless questions of existence. Eliot seems to be muttering to himself alone when he adds: 'Those who are not content to be provincials, can only become hermits.'

Provincialism was an issue throughout Eliot's critical prose from the time that he published 'The Three Provincialities' in 1922. For Eliot, provincialism was not simply a justification for leaving America, as it was for Henry James. 'Provinciality of point of view is a vice,' he asserted as early as 1918 and repeated, 'a positive literary vice', in Dublin in 1936. Writers must 'disturb the provincialism of their particular place and time'. His models were Babbitt and P. E. More, who were 'emancipated' from the prejudices of place and time, and above all Dante, the 'least provincial' of poets. Dante's universality of content and precision of language crossed national boundaries with greater ease than any other writer. This is the rationale behind Eliot's international frame of reference. To be too nationalistic, he said at the time *The Waste Land* came out, is to become 'insupportable to posterity'.

Dante, Eliot said, was the most '*European*' of writers, and this was his own insistent image. This might appear a repudiation of America, but for Eliot the notion of the 'European' was not a matter of locale but a state of mind that overpassed all frontiers. It actually had a native connotation which, we recall, he spelt out in his essay on Henry James: 'It is the final perfection . . . of an American to become . . . a European – something which no born European, no person of any European nationality, can become.' The benefit of transplantation was to gain a sense of the uniformity of human nature, as well as its superficial local variations. It was also to have a horizon beyond St Louis, Boston, or London. Wherever Eliot stood, part of him was not there – he had something in reserve. His self-imposed distance from home, his detachment, took on the authority of a Modernist position, but this was not an end in itself, because he was also detached in time. From that vantage-point he saw a biblical plot: the recurrent destruction of a corrupt society. His private horror – 'the *nightmare* of evil' – was like that of the prophets, for whom, alone in their time, 'history had meaning'. His other model was Aeneas, whom he saw as the prototype of Christian pilgrim: his crossing from one culture to another had its real meaning as an act of obedience to the timeless gods. He is obedient to the destiny they impose. 'For he is humbly, a man with a mission; and the mission is everything.'

In summing up the careers of Aeneas, Pascal, and Dante, Eliot looks back on his own: the private import is there in unobtrusive asides. This retrospective note sounds more often and with increasing authority in later talks, where Eliot lays down his guidelines for posterity. He said that his best criticism was a by-product of his private poetry workshop. In essays on the writers who influenced him – Dante (1920, 1929, and 1950), Baudelaire (1930), Pascal (1931), and Virgil (1944 and 1951) – as well as in more general guides – 'Poetry and Drama' (1951), 'The Three Voices of Poetry' (1953), 'The Frontiers of Criticism' (1956), and 'To Criticize the Critic' (1961) – Eliot suggests how we might read and assess his work. The later essays were dismissive of the popular theories of his early years: 'impersonality', 'objective correlative', and 'unified' or 'dissociated sensibility'. A hundred years on he predicts, these phrases will survive only as curiosities of the mind of his age. The same goes for the tradition which he made fashionable in his time – the upgrading of the Metaphysicals and wits; the downgrading of Milton: all this, he admits, was a matter of subjective feelings. Eliot's public quibbles with Milton on rhetorical grounds obscure his indebtedness (in *Sweeney Agonistes* and *East Coker*) to the great predecessor whose dramatic account of the dark trial of the soul was unsurpassable, who could speak the Word with vast eloquence, and whose story of the beginning of all creation was on a grander scale than Eliot's more personal beginning in East Coker.

'I'm surprised we were allowed *Milton* this afternoon,' Dylan Thomas said to Eliot after a poetry reading; 'I thought he was dead.' He was the first to protest with any vehemence: '*Dislodging* Milton with very little fuss,' he fumed at Eliot during a dinner which Edith Sitwell gave at the Sesame Club. (Dylan Thomas was then learning passages of *Paradise Lost* by heart for a Third Programme reading in which he took the part of Satan.) Eliot at once put the blame on Leavis, but it no longer matters. Half a century later, his Who's Who of literary importance is out of date.

In 1929 Eliot wrote E. M. Forster that remarkably honest letter acknowledging the element of 'bluff' in his early critical strategies. Forster had been right, of course, in guessing that there were private motives underlying the doctrine of 'impersonality'; nor was it more true as a doctrine, though on the other hand no more false, than its opposite. In his early essays Eliot aimed for an 'icy inviolability' and strict doctrine as an antidote to the sloppy impressionism of his critical predecessors who had engaged in 'that parlour game, the Polite Essay – which consists in taking a tiny point and cutting figure-eights around it'. With swift reversals or refinements of statement, Eliot forged a disembodied voice of one 'called to the seat of judgement'. He canonised and excommunicated at will until he came to be called 'the Pope of Russell Square'.

How did the English come to accept an American as supreme authority for half a century (from 1940 to about 1990)? Possibly the success of his influence, and the failure of

Pound's, lay not in their message, which was similar, but in Eliot's tone. His tone was the master-stroke of his strategy: it became more English than the English. The turning-point was in 1920, when Richard Aldington introduced Eliot to Bruce Richmond, editor of the *Times Literary Supplement* from 1902 to 1937. Eliot said that Richmond taught him to edit out 'unseemly violence', and to write in a temperate, impartial way. The precise Englishness, though, was more the style of self-deprecation with its clever deployment of 'merely': 'I merely want to say . . .'. I am not making any particular claims, he told his audiences – and so they accepted everything he said. They may even have enjoyed their bafflement. Scholars certainly relished the futile source-hunting that Eliot's notes to *The Waste Land* invited. It was only decades later that Eliot declared at Minnesota that this sort of academic exercise was a waste of time unless it was secondary to 'understanding'. He confided to Helen Gardner that hers was the only criticism of his work that he could recommend to anybody. He had a thicket of reservations about Matthiessen's study of *The Achievement of T. S. Eliot* (1935) and (he repeated) the kind of criticism that goes hunting for recondite sources.

Eliot also criticised the 'lemon-squeezer' approach of close critical analysis. He thought that readers might take in a little information, but should be left alone with a poem. His later essays undercut the reductive categories of academe. In 'Yeats' (1940) he made it clear that a poem is neither wholly personal nor wholly impersonal, but 'transmutes' the life of the writer into art. Nor has the reader controlling licence as he had earlier implied: 'The fact that a poem can mean different things to different persons . . . must, however paradoxically, be reconciled with the assertion that it has an absolute and unalterable meaning.'

Eliot's early essays set the fashion for the rest of the century that elegant writing was ironic and detached, and, partly for this reason, his earlier essays were more famous. It may be, though, that Eliot's later, less ironic criticism was a portent of a time yet to come, when we shall tire of irony and welcome, instead, the breath of feeling. In Eliot's later essays he repeatedly owns to feelings as the source of his ideas.

The later essays give five guidelines to his career. Firstly, they acknowledge the personal basis of his art. In 1940, explaining the superiority of Yeats's later work by 'the greater expression of personality' in it, he found it necessary to revise his doctrine of impersonality. What he now understood by 'impersonality' was that of a poet 'who, out of intense and personal experience, is able to express a general truth; retaining all the particularity of his experience, to make of it a general symbol'.* In the fifties he became even more explicit: 'A poet may believe that he is expressing only his private experience; his lines may be for him only a means of talking about himself without giving himself away; yet for his readers what he has written may come to be the expression of their own secret feelings and of the exultation or despair of a generation.'

What begins to emerge, here, is a poet preoccupied with self who, as it were by accident, intersects with his age. It's less chancy than Eliot implies: his scenes – from urban bedsits to the country house – appear to reflect a range of the lives of his day, but for the poet they are part of the interior landscape, emblems of vice or unreality projected from his inner world of nightmare. His art of omission protects us from the full glare of its intolerable revelation: that every scene, every person – with the exceptions of the Lady of silences and the saints in the making – is worthless *sub specie aeternitatis*, and that we, his audience, are part of the 'deranged' world. That is perhaps why Eliot shuts us out. His attention to society is laboured because it is peripheral to his

---

* Eliot expounds the same idea in 'A Note on War Poetry':

Where is the point at which the merely individual
Explosion breaks

In the path of an action merely typical
To create the universal, originate a symbol
Out of the impact? This is a meeting
On which we attend. . . .

attention to the self and the permanent Order of Things. As a graduate student, and for the rest of his creative life, Eliot pursued an elusive sense that he was, in the words of his Harvard dissertation, 'the adjective of some transcendental self'.

Another guideline for posterity is Eliot's repeated insistence on the coherent career. He spoke of the capacity of a great poet to suffuse a body of work with a significant thought, as Wordsworth did: 'there is something integral about such greatness'. The unity in variety came from an 'inner compulsion'. A sense of unity in his own career strengthened with age as he came to value 'a consistent view of life' that comes with the 'maturing of a man as a whole, the development and co-ordination of his various emotions'. Eliot may have feared that posterity would divide his career and plump for the early years, ignoring the new life and the later drama. He insists that one can grasp no one work or phase without seeing it in the whole pattern formed by the sequence of works, so that the full meaning of any one of Eliot's works is not in itself alone, but in that work in the order in which it was written.

A third guideline is Eliot's declaration in 1959 that his poetry came from America. This was ignored for too long because of the prestige of Eliot's internationalism, and understandable ignorance of the American implications of his stance as 'European'. Only Edmund Wilson, reviewing *Poems 1909–1925*, perceived at that time that Eliot's 'real significance is less that of a prophet of European disintegration than of a poet of the American Puritan temperament'. He went on to align Eliot with Marcher, Strether, and the Hawthorne of the Notebooks. Eliot himself provides a further clue to these affinities when he finds in James and Hawthorne a distinctive sense of the past. For them, as for Eliot, the present becomes pressing just as the past dominates with its ghostly presences. Eliot wrote this in 1918: it foretells the visitations of the hyacinth girl, the ghosts of the rose-garden, the Furies and, still to come, the guilty past of the Elder Statesman. The settings are English, but the disturbed and haunted sense of the past is American.

In 'American Literature and the American Language' (1953), Eliot recalled the early stimulus of what a man said 'long ago or in another language' which 'corresponds' to what he wanted to say. He had found remote models safer because they could not be copied. He had looked to Laforgue for *vers libre* rather than to Whitman, and to Baudelaire for psychic decadence rather than to Poe, Baudelaire's source of inspiration. So, too, he had looked to Dante for the extremities of 'depravity's despair' and 'the beatific vision', not to his own Puritan heritage, or to the Jansenism of Pascal which, as Eliot had described it, was 'morally a Puritan movement within the Church', whose 'standards of conduct were at least as severe' as the Puritanism of his own forebears. At the end of his life, Eliot said that he had been profoundly influenced by the style of F. H. Bradley, the English idealist philosopher on whom he wrote his dissertation. Bradley believed that what we really observe are fragments of a greater Reality: this idea, central to Eliot's poetry, corresponds to the Transcendentalism of Emerson, who wrote that 'fractions are worth more to me because corresponding fractions are waiting . . . that shall be made integers by their addition'.

Who were Eliot's real models? Was there a native tradition? Auden once remarked that no genuine European could have made Eliot's celebrated statement that tradition is not inherited but acquired by great labour. It has been assumed that Eliot's acquired tradition is to be found in the historical or literary parallels by which he attempted to universalise private states of mind. But it is increasingly recognised that there is an inherited tradition, none the less, obscured by the international frame of reference: some residue of many New England divines or Judge Blood, who made himself conspicuous in the punishment of witches. Hawthorne was prepared to recognise that 'strong traits of their [Puritan] nature have intertwined themselves with mine'. The Dimmesdale nature pervades Eliot, the excruciation of a sinner of high spiritual gifts, gazing absorbed into the mirror of election with its associated dangers of pride and despair:

> To the high mountain peaks of faith and sanctity he would have climbed, had not the tendency been thwarted by the burden, whatever it might be of crime and anguish, beneath which it was his doom to totter. It kept him down, on a level with the lowest; him, the man of ethereal attributes . . . .

Yet it is this very secret burden that gives to the minister the Tongue of Flame.

Early on, in 'The Three Provincialities', Eliot believed that Americans had not produced works of the calibre of the best European writers: the measure was Shakespeare and Dante. The high-flown allusion, developed in the quatrain poems written in 1917–19 at Pound's direction, was a strategy that placed him at once in the international league. Yet Pound himself noted the correspondence between sophisticated and native traditions. The quatrain form was said to derive from Théophile Gautier's *Emaux et Camées* (1852), but it also came, Pound pointed out, from the Bay State Hymn Book of the colonial settlers of Massachusetts.

There is another, less obvious motive for Eliot's use of the prestigious parallel. He was a loner in the American tradition of cranky loners. He wished to express feelings that were savage and strange like the mystical hatred that is close to madness. He was determined to expose readers to feelings they had not experienced before. He said that the difference between a madman and an effective writer is that the former has feelings which are unique but cannot be shared, and are therefore useless; the latter discovers new variations of feelings which can be appropriated by others. Eliot used the classic parallel to point acceptability, to claim a semblance of normality, though he often twisted allusions to accommodate an inertia and horror of his own. Only very occasionally did he discover an exact equation in another writer. This is why he was unusually reluctant to let go, at Pound's insistence, 'The horror! the horror!' from *Heart of Darkness* as the preferred epigraph to *The Waste Land*. In such rare cases of equation he does not twist the allusion for his usual comic effect – and this is where Eliot really is: with the unholy loves of Augustine's youth ('To Carthage then I came . . .'); with

Arnaut Daniel in Dante's refining fire, purging the sin of lust; and yearning towards the scriptures' promise of the peace that passeth understanding. These allusions helped to preserve Eliot's sanity as they established the legitimacy of his content. His appeal to tradition was another master-stroke of his early years, for under its cover he could deviate from norms of feeling and, at the same time, establish states of being that might otherwise appear too rarefied or misanthropic.

Eliot's fourth critical guideline is to confound the usual polarisation of conformist and revolutionary. The rebel, he argues, may appear the most perfect social conformist. 'When a man takes politics and social affairs seriously the difference between revolution and reaction may be by the breadth of a hair.' For Eliot, to invoke the Order of Things in the midst of twentieth-century chaos, to insist on self-discipline in the face of a permissive society, to be in short a Critic (in poetry no less than in speeches), was to take a revolutionary line. 'Reaction' was, to him, a necessary act of social regeneration, not the stale conservatism of the mindless reactionary. To take politics seriously was to repudiate politicians in favour of poets like Wordsworth, 'the first, in the unsettled state of affairs in his time, to annex new authority for the poet, to meddle with social affairs, and to offer a new kind of religious sentiment which it seemed the peculiar prerogative of the poet to interpret'. He saw in Wordsworth 'a profound spiritual revival' which had its social sequels in the Oxford Movement and Victorian humanism. Once again, a European writer is used in a way that 'corresponds' with American tradition, the revolt against deadness in a pattern of religious revivals: in the 1740s the Great Awakening led by Jonathan Edwards; in the next century the revivals of Emerson, Thoreau, and Whitman; and in the next – the link is inescapable – *The Waste Land*.

Eliot's final guideline, now the most popular, was his concern for language. The classic poet serves his language by leaving behind him a language more precise, subtle, and capable of expressing a new range of experience. In Eliot's best critical finales he connects this linguistic challenge with the frontiers of consciousness: the poet must make people 'see and hear more at each end [of the ordinary range] than they could ever see without his help'. He feels 'the obligation to explore, to find words for the inarticulate, to capture those feelings which people can hardly even feel because they have no words for them'. Language is always dying; its categories become reductive; its emotional terms stale. It is the poet's duty to alert us to the moments when language fails, as when Eliot points to the infinitely gentle, infinitely suffering 'thing'. The gaps in his poetry alert us to 'a fringe of indefinite extent, of feeling which we can only detect, so to speak, out of the corner of the eye and can never completely focus'. These are the 'unattended' moments at the beating heart of Eliot's poetry when he invites us to look with him into the silence at the still point of the turning world. Eliot injects silence into the early poetry with blank spaces on the page. In his later poetry, words are potentially the Word; the power to write, potentially a sacred power. 'The Word in the desert', language as authoritative and durable as scripture, remained a mirage of perfection. Towards this Eliot set his course in obedience to his belief in a given task. As the fifties wore on there seemed no prospect of personal reward.

*

The outer casing of this mission began to erode in the mid-fifties.

Mary Trevelyan hinted to Eliot that he hurt her and John Hayward.

Eliot replied that if this were true perhaps he had better sever his connection with them.

Anyone less confident would have been crushed by one of Eliot's rebukes for impertinence in September 1956, but Mary was prepared to have it out.

'I refuse', she said, 'to be put in the corner for something I have not done.'

'I think my stomach is a little disordered,' said Eliot plaintively on the phone.

'I should think it *is*,' retorted Mary and invited him to tea, thinking 'jolly d . . . of me to ask you.'

Eliot once told her that she had a terribly ingenious way of putting him in the wrong, and he didn't like it. The annoyance would last some time (because, he explained, his reactions were slow), then he would climb down bearing gifts. After one of their earlier tiffs, in October 1953, he produced a peace offering after church with a shy smile, a battered tin of Breakfast Sausage.

Their refuge of habit was fortified by daily prayers for each other, but there was increasing friction. When Mary confided to her friend Ann Stokes her unrequited love for Eliot, she added: 'All genius is, by its very nature, selfish.' She became impatient with Eliot's fuss over minor ailments, pills, and potions, but more likely resented the excuses and demands that went with these complaints. Eliot was, in fact, enfeebled in the mid-fifties, his main problem being 'a lesion between the left and right compartments of his heart'. From about 1954 his heart would speed up to 120 or 140 beats a minute, and he would be rushed to the London Clinic for several weeks at a time. But he would go there, too, for nothing more than athlete's foot. Mary thought he worried so much about himself that he made himself iller than he was. He needed cosseting, he protested, and gave Mary the name and address of a priest to summon to his deathbed. She noted with irritation that he rather enjoyed the clinic, cut off there from all obligations, from human contact – from her. This was the nub of it: Eliot wanted to be left alone. And as a friend, Mary had no rights. She did persuade him that, for the sake of his sisters, for whom she was the sole source of information, she must be at least allowed details of his condition, but Eliot held back. He was always afraid she would presume too far.

Mary never quite fathomed his detachment, and never foresaw the intransigence of his withdrawal. Three times,

Eliot retired into the citadel of the self and shut the door: in 1932 it shut on Vivienne Eliot; in 1947 on Emily Hale; and now, in 1956, it was closing on Mary Trevelyan. When, in August, she proposed a drink one Sunday evening 'if you'd *like* to see me', Eliot replied: 'You know quite well that I *never* want to see *anybody*.' Was he too feeble, or was he forming another chrysalis, from which he might burst out, a new being?

But what was he to be? As he listened to his heart bumping and racing in the night, he feared that he was coming to his end, feared loss of creativity, even loss of mind. He was disappointed by the reception of 'The Cultivation of Christmas Trees' in 1954, the first straight poem he had published in years.

'As for poetry,' he told Mary, 'well, it doesn't come.'

What she saw as an 'abnormal' fear of death was perhaps a fear of death without redemption. All his adult life, Eliot had waited for a sign: in earlier years a sign of grace; latterly, a sign of forgiveness. Then, in 1956, as he felt his strength ebb, came the unexpected offer of a young woman's love. Even more surprising was his response, a new-found vindication of his capacity to love which seemed to assuage all the years of guilt.

From 1950 through the mid-fifties, Eliot was reading the Harvard theologian Paul Tillich, who argued that forgiveness is not wrung through the rigours of self-punishment, self-accusation, and self-humiliation. There is no condition for forgiveness, said Tillich, except the need for it. He offered a theology based on love rather than one based on penitence; on 'the creative abundance of the heart' rather than the solitary's withholding of the self: 'Do not greedily preserve your time and strength . . . Keep yourselves open for the creative moment which may appear in the midst of what seemed to be waste.'

There came a moment, perhaps a fearful point of illness, when Eliot at last found himself ready for forgiveness. Horror, gloom, and penitence came to an end with his discovery of the unconditional love of a young woman.

Eliot's effortless superiority had been, in a way, his cross: it set him apart, so that to love or sympathise was not simple as for most. He could be genial, jokey, painstaking, but these had been acts of deliberation, duty not pleasure. His studied kindness had masked his detachment, his mature alternative to youthful contempt. He was torn between duty to God and duty to man. Duty to God might be to fast on a saint's day, but then he had a cold which the fast might worsen and so prevent his duty to dine with the vicar. He *preferred* to do his duty to God and risk the duty to man but, being an Eliot, one's duty was to do the thing one least wants. So the vacillation went on, the fasting hermit deferring, unwillingly, to the public man. And when the public tug was too prolonged, he retired to the London Clinic. Mary sensed that these retirements were not wholly a matter of health: they were a relief from adulation, from people who wished to know him because he was famous, people who were exhausting like – she could not admit it – herself.

There, in the clinic, as he read theology, identities passed before him: Nehemiah, Badboy, Bonsir, or was he a neurotic depressive? Or would some other being emerge? In the darkest recess of his chrysalis, Eliot was shedding a lifelong recoil from contact for a new readiness, a need to be forgiven. In his Bible, he marked the words, 'I, even I, am he that blotteth out thy transgressions for mine own sake, and will not remember thy sins.' By January 1956 Eliot was imagining an agent of forgiveness in his last play, 'a peach of a girl' who, he said, was almost too good to be true.

*

Eliot often remarked to Mary Trevelyan or John Hayward that he was frightened. He was frightened of travel, phone calls, and above all of having to talk to a woman, as once during the war when he was left to dine alone with Jean Kennerley, the wife of a Faber director. The threat of contact was defused when a woman became a Guardian, as Mary Trevelyan had been for nearly twenty years. The caring women in Eliot's late plays offer consolation as they look after a battered man: Julia practically, Monica in *The Elder Statesman* healing his conscience so as to release the comfort of natural love.

Although Eliot froze for some years, he did harbour a residue of feeling that could be kindled. He was not a cold fish: there were buried emotions, intact but undirected so that, even as he aged, women found him attractive, fell in love, proposed. In *Four Quartets* he spoke of the 'unattached devotion which might pass for devotionless'. Almost all his life Eliot seems to have waited to confer this love, and at last it happened in a way that changed him completely.

14

LOVE: THE UNFAMILIAR NAME*

THE TALKING-POINT OF 1957 was Eliot's secret marriage
to his secretary, Valerie Fletcher, and his transformation
on honeymoon in the South of France. The wedding was a
surprise to Eliot's closest friends, John Hayward, Mary
Trevelyan, and Geoffrey Faber. A letter delivered by Eliot's
solicitor notified Faber that the marriage had taken place.
Eliot gave advance notice only to his solicitor, Mr Higginson,
and his fellow-director at Faber, Peter du Sautoy, who was to
engage a new secretary. Eliot was sixty-eight and Valerie
Fletcher was thirty. They were married at 6.15 a.m. on 10
January, not at St Stephen's, where it was known that Eliot
went every morning, but at St Barnabas' in Addison Road.
There, Eliot discovered, Laforgue had also married an English
girl in 1886. Eliot's second wife found him a man 'made for
marriage'. He was, she declared, 'a natural for it, a loving
creature'.

Complete understanding of the change that took place in
1956 must remain a mirage. Why was it in 1956 – not some
other year – that Emily Hale disposed of Eliot's letters? Could
there be any connection between this act, the anger it aroused
in Eliot, his visit to America that year, his collapse on ship
home, and his turn to his secretary? Until the fifties, Eliot
believed himself incapable of loving another woman: at some
point, then, he made up his mind to withdraw the guard on a
capacity for natural love. Falling in love is, anyway,

---

* *Little Gidding*: IV: 'Love is the unfamiliar Name.'

impossible to explain. Eliot spoke of 'thoughts without need of speech' and 'speech without need of meaning' in the attunement of lovers who make a private world. On the other hand, it would falsify the last stage of Eliot's life simply to record the fact of change. For it took place in the context of nearly a whole lifetime that now stretched behind Eliot, and although we cannot know what was private, we might ask how he worked this up in his imagination. For he presents a story of emotional release in his last play, which he began in October–November 1955: another confessional play, about a great public figure who has become hollow at heart, and is 'saved', at the end of his life, by the steadfast love of a daughter.

'*Do* make them human beings this time,' Mary Trevelyan urged Eliot in January 1956 after he drafted the first act.

'Don't I always?' he protested. 'They seem to *me* human – but perhaps I don't know much about human beings.'

'How can you?' Mary said. 'You dislike them so much.'

'I'm sorry for them. They seem to me pathetic.'

'You only like them at a distance,' Mary persisted, 'so long as they don't come near you.'

He seemed to take this in while she played some Mozart on the gramophone. Was nearness after all possible? Looking back on his life, there had been two attitudes to women: contempt and reverence. Eliot's late turn to natural happiness seems a new thing, but the possibility is latent, as far back as 1930, in the final line of *Marina*. A great denouncer of the hateful world, a man battered after his life's journey, finds comfort in a woman who is his kin: 'My daughter,' he greets her.

Eliot came to recognise in his secretary the absolute dedication of an ideal heir. Valerie Fletcher, at the age of fourteen, had experienced a conversion of sorts on hearing John Gielgud's recording of *Journey of the Magi*. Its steady, questing rhythm changed her life. While the rest of the world saw a baffling man, she appeared with complete simplicity to know him at once. 'I was bowled over. It just hit me,' she said. 'The whole feeling of Tom in it – and the impression I formed then – was borne out right throughout marriage and everything. After that I tried to find out everything I could about him. It was something very sympathetic. His confessor once said of him in old age that he had a childlike heart. I think that was very true.'

From that moment, she 'had to get to Tom, to work with him'. She was born in 1926 in Headingley, Leeds, the daughter of an insurance manager with a taste for reading. Like many who fought in the First World War, his knapsack had been crammed with poetry. His daughter inherited his love of poetry: until she discovered Eliot, her favourites were Spender and MacNeice. During the war she travelled all the way from Leeds to hear Eliot read at the Wigmore Hall in London. 'It was very disappointing. Tom kept his head down throughout the reading and I went back very flat.' Another time, she went to a service at St Stephen's for the thrill of putting money in a collection box brought round by Eliot himself.

She attended a girls' public school, Queen Anne's in Caversham, Reading, a school which did not, in the forties, send its products to university. Nor did its sporting ethos invite the expression of the intellectual passion suggested by the girl's dramatic response to Eliot's poem. When she left school, she told the headmistress that she was determined to be Eliot's secretary, and wrote to Faber and Faber asking if there were a vacancy. There wasn't. So in the meantime Valerie Fletcher went to work for six months at the Brotherton Library of the University of Leeds and, after that, as a private secretary to the novelists Paul Capon and Charles Morgan. Then, in 1949, aged twenty-two, the vacancy she had waited for came up. She was recommended by W. Collin Brooks, a magazine editor and friend of her parents who, like Eliot, had joined the Burke Club when it was formed in the late thirties, a serious Tory dining-club made up of MPs and journalists.

The night before her interview she was so nervous that she cut her hand in the kitchen, and she approached Faber and Faber in a bandage. For two hours she walked up and down in Russell Square trying to calm herself. Even before she met Eliot she was sure that she understood him. 'I felt I knew him as a person,' she said, 'and evidently I did. I even knew a lot of things about Vivienne, I don't really know how.' This is how she described their meeting:

> He was just everything I had ever imagined him to be. He was in this little Dickensian office and he was as terrified as I was. He smoked and smoked ... We talked about 17th-century poetry [including Herbert] and so on and, as I was leaving, he put his chin round the edge of the door and told me he had to see all the applicants before he made a decision. I knew there were a lot of other girls – one of them had a double first from Oxford. But then he paused, looked at my hand and said: 'But I hope you'll be able to type in about 10 days' time.'

Two days later a letter arrived asking her to begin. For eight years 'Miss Fletcher' was self-effacing and reserved.

'I can't get to know her at all,' Eliot told Mary Trevelyan in 1955, 'she shuts up like a clam'.

Once, in those years, she surprised him. During one of his visits to America, she dined out with an Indian protégé of Eliot's. When he heard of this, his sudden impulse to violence revealed some strong, as yet unacknowledged feeling.

All this time she was amassing a vast collection of Eliot's publications, an even better collection, it is said, than his own. She worked for a man wrapped in immortality who was afraid of women and would dodge into the lavatory to avoid having to walk out of the building with anyone working late at the office. She did often, he noticed, work late. Tall, fair, fresh-faced, the new secretary still looked like an athletic schoolgirl. When the Welsh poet Vernon Watkins arrived to see his editor, her arms swung back and forth in her need to protect him. This was the one legitimate way that she could express her devotion, and this is the daughter's primary role in the first draft of Act I of Eliot's new play. She is at one with the need of the public man, a 'prestige item', to shy away from people who would stare, gossip, and fall upon him. Their talk is all of plans to preserve his privacy: a table in a private alcove and coffee in a private sitting-room. He has come to take her rather for granted as his protective environment. At the same time, she is aware that he depends on her in a more subtle way, for she is the only one who believes in an unknown self behind the public face. She feels that she comes nearer than anyone, nearer than Claverton himself, who has lost touch with his real being. His success conceals a deep failure. Recently, the first draft tells us, he had become, for some reason, not wholly successful; rather like Eliot, whose most recent play had been received with the politeness due to a man known to have had brilliant gifts.

Eliot had already drafted the first two acts of the new play when he became seriously ill in February 1956. A severe attack of bronchitis brought on coughing and choking, which revived his cardiac trouble. Digitalis failed to help and he was in the French Hospital for five weeks. In March, when he was crawling to life again, he had to turn to his Minnesota lecture on 'The Frontiers of Criticism'. He was due to leave for America in April, and at that point did not expect to go back to the play until September. The lecture was 'sticky': he felt, in March, that he had nothing to say. He was still like the ailing Claverton of the first act: a man whose power seems gone.

Eliot continued on the verge of existence for the next six months. On the return voyage, he took ill three days out of Southampton, and was carried off the *Queen Mary* on a stretcher. Then, a week later, came the news that his sister Margaret had died suddenly and alone in her home in Cambridge, Massachusetts. People remembered Eliot looking 'sere', 'stricken', and 'cadaverous'.

'How does one set about *dying*?' he asked E. W. F. Tomlin.

In September he returned early from a holiday in Switzerland. He was wheeled from the plane by a nurse, and taken back to the London Clinic with a return of tachycardia and an abscess on his hip. Mary noticed a nervous spasm of the leg which he seemed unable to control.

During each period of illness, Valerie Fletcher looked after his affairs, and, imperceptibly, his dependence on Mary shifted to her as his need deepened. In Eliot's second scenario for his play 'the ELD[ER] ST[ATESMAN] begins to unburden his heart to DAUGHTER'. Valerie Fletcher's response, I would guess, fitted Eliot's scenario: '. . . instead of condemning him, as he expects, she exhibits a new protective affection. He is still further affected by her response.'

At this point Margaret Behrens, a wartime occupant of the Shambles and now friend to both Eliot and Miss Fletcher, invited them to spend the winter in Mentone. Miss Fletcher could stay with her, and Eliot next door at a hotel. This proposal brought on a declaration of love on both sides. By December 1956 they were engaged, Valerie wearing a finger-guard over her ring but noticeably radiant to Hope Mirrlees when she visited the office. The situation offered Eliot another opportunity to indulge his taste for secrecy – he and his fiancée would meet behind a pillar in the Russell Hotel across the square from Faber and Faber.

The second draft of *The Elder Statesman* introduces a love scene between the girl and a man who, in the first draft, had been a shallow mirror image of her father, a public man in the making. In this new scene, the girl finds herself saying words of love which can 'never be retraced'. She is numbed by the momentousness of these words and says, 'they stand for something / That has left me, is lost to me, given up forever.'

Eliot showed unexpected sensitivity to a woman's feelings: he understood the shock of abandoning her reserve, the loss of self in the surrender, the daring of that moment of lifelong commitment which is too great to absorb.

The man replies as though he, too, spoke beyond himself, taken over by a voice in his head, *her* voice: 'Is it you or I who speak?' Her words seem to come from far away, yet very near. This is the very moment of transformation. 'You are changing me,' he says, 'And I am changing you.'

Eliot was concerned, at first, that a young woman shouldn't do this. 'Ah, my deare, / I cannot look on thee,' Herbert put it in his poem 'Love', a favourite of Eliot's. The poet draws back, guilty 'of dust and sinne', but love is persuasive:

You must sit downe, sayes Love, and taste my meat:
So I did sit and eat.

The ease with which Eliot took up this offer of love was unprecedented. I think it had to do partly with the easing of guilt as love opened up the possibility of complete honesty, like the daughter in his play whose entire confidence invites the public figure to make his first genuine confession. All his life the public man has been fixed behind his masks; now, he longs to break out, but fears to show himself to the woman whose idol he has become. Could her innocent love survive knowledge of things ill done and done to others' harm?

Like Eliot himself, and like Harry in *The Family Reunion*, Lord Claverton is a man of 'morbid conscience'. Again, there has been no crime punishable by law but what they call sin. Claverton, as a young man, once ran over a dead person, and did not stop. This repeats, in a different setting, Harry's guilt for his wife's death. Eliot said that he began his plays with an 'emotional situation'. Both times he transmutes into drama his own long-held guilt for his unresisting part in Vivienne's end.

There is a boon companion-in-guilt in *The Elder Statesman*. Gomez is a successful scoundrel, a comic type, not drawn from life, but two aspects of his career have parallels in that of Vivienne's brother, Maurice Haigh-Wood: the fact that Maurice, too, did not resist Vivienne's committal, and the fact that, fairly soon after, he went abroad for some years. Alternatively, this may be yet another encounter with an alter ego, for in January 1918 Eliot had signed himself 'Enrique Gomez' in a review of *The Sense of the Past* by Henry James.* In the late fifties a resurrected Gomez embodies Eliot's fear that the truth, known only to a secret self or to a companion-in-guilt, would come out some day in distorted form – as exposé – as, in fact, it did in a mid-eighties play and in a lavishly inaccurate biopic in the mid-nineties.

---

* An amusing note adds that 'Señor Gomez wishes to thank [an equally fictitious] Miss Anna Louise Babson of New York for revising the English version of this review.'

The other ghost from the past is an actress who has become a talkative old woman. Years ago, Lord Claverton had been her first love and she had sued him for breach of promise. This was settled out of court, but now, late in life, Maisie lets him know that she has kept his letters. To her, it was no trivial affair and the letters will prove it. He had touched her soul, as she had touched his, and she has thought about him all her life. Maisie, too, is a comic type, a low-life caricature of a sentimental singer – her famous number was 'It's Not Too Late For You To Love Me?' – but the situation of a broken understanding does look back to Eliot's guilt over Emily Hale, while the evidence of the letters is a quite literal enactment of his fury at losing control of his letters to her.

Eliot once said that a character might speak 'in unison' with the author, even call out his latent potentialities, and through Claverton he returned to the most intractable material in his life. He had said in 1940, in a rough draft of poetry, that the past is 'a pit for us still to explore'. Advancing now to this pit, Eliot revived something of the grimness of *The Family Reunion* as an old man explores the depths of his conscience. Its Furies appear this time as unwelcome visitors who press him with emotional blackmail. Both see him as a dodger: with Gomez he has dodged responsibility for his actions; with Maisie he has dodged responsibility for an emotional tie. Mock humility, she says, is one of his dodges. Claverton must face each on close terms, and in so far as he does face them, in mind as well as in person, their menace fades, and they become what their limited characters imply, negligible.

Claverton admits the truth of his past only in the last act, written after Eliot's marriage. A year later, in January 1958, he commented: 'I can only say that it is a very different play (and I believe a better one) for so much of it having been written during this last year, than it would have been if I had finished it before our marriage.' The changes in the play make its synopses and drafts more interesting than those of the preceding, more brittle comedies. Composed as Eliot fell in love with Valerie Fletcher, it looks towards their union.

At first, in October 1955, Eliot had only a title in mind: 'The Rest Cure'.* He told Mary that it was like going with his seven characters through a long, dark railway tunnel, and that when they emerged he would know them. In November –December 1955, when he drafted the first act, he did not as yet quite know the young woman. She was, at this stage, no more than a model of filial piety, potentially a guardian angel (Eliot's first name for her was Angela†). In this first draft the father is waiting in a vacuum for death, and Eliot adds in pencil to the typescript that the blankness of the walls mocked the blankness of the mind. As Eliot made his way through that dark tunnel with his characters-to-be, I think he began to hope that there might be someone who would understand his true self, and who could be trusted to defend and continue it beyond his lifetime. In Act II, after Claverton has endured the visitations of his contemporaries, he is shaken and bruised but, in the curtain line, hopeful of a cure – and the hope is directed to the young woman.

'But have I still time?' he asks her. 'Is it too late for me?'

Some time between Act II, drafted by 1956, and Act III, written in 1957–8, I would guess that Eliot opened his heart to his wife, as Claverton confesses to his daughter in the certainty of her unshakeable love. What has made the difference, he tells her, is not 'the heinousness of my misdeeds / But the fact of my confession. And to you . . . / To you, of all people.' As he exorcises the spectres from his past, he emerges from his 'spectral existence into something like reality'. Reality, now, is not transcendental: it is human contact. It is enough to confess the truth to one person even if it must remain concealed from the rest of the world. Then his 'soul is safe', and then 'he loves that person, and his love will save him'.

This private confession takes place through the public

---

* At some point Eliot made an isolated note that nothing was wrong except a mind diseased, ('Miscellaneous Essays', n.d., Hayward Bequest, King's College, Cambridge.

† Martin Browne said that Eliot changed it because it was too much like Lucasta Angel (in *The Confidential Clerk*).

medium of the theatre: it must be repeated, nightly, before a large audience. In this Eliot harks back, once again, to the New England trial of the soul by public confession. At the same time, as Eliot put it in a dedicatory poem to his wife, the play represents his words to her. As his confession to one person, it is the basis of their union, which is to be the most complete and intimate bond, as the dedication takes care to describe.

During their courtship, Eliot had typed several pages of Act II in late November 1956. Act II had put Valerie Fletcher – at least in Eliot's imagination – through a test of confidence when the actress deplores the great man's 'shabby behaviour' in private: 'he doesn't understand women,' she declares. 'Any woman who trusted *him* would soon find that out.'

Eliot's wife-to-be had to face his ghosts. The words of the actress tell of another bond that might outlast their lives – as, in fact, Eliot's letters to Emily Hale will survive for centuries to come. The actress tells the public man that she reads his letters every night.

'Were they very passionate?' he asks uneasily.

'They were very loving,' she answers. In her view, 'we're still together', and Eliot added in pencil to the first draft: 'And more frightening to think that we may *always* be together.'

This claim precedes the confession in Act III which stirs in the old man a saving tide of feeling, sweeping fear away. In this last play, Eliot spelt out the danger of his own later years, that feeling denied deadens the soul. His carapace had thickened; his will had hardened as the years of penitence rolled away without apparent gain. His public masks had become so habitual that they had dried up the very sources of feeling they were designed to protect. During the early fifties, Mary never quite dispelled his impenetrability, and her proposals only made him more guarded. By the mid-fifties he was fading, when he found the daring to strip the mask.

Eliot surprised people. His reckless first marriage surprised his family. His conversion in 1927 startled his contemporaries, as his conversion to natural happiness in 1957 startled a younger generation of admirers. Until at least 1953, Eliot expected to retire to an abbey. 'One day I will go there to stay, permanently,' he told William Turner Levy, the priest in New York. 'It suits me. I would have no guests then . . .'. Was Eliot's new marriage, after a thirty-year attempt at celibacy, the one act that broke the inexorable pattern of the religious life? Or was it the consummation of that life?

At a party on Eliot's return from honeymoon, he appeared knit together with his wife, arms and hands enfolded. He looked as though a lifetime's barriers to emotion had been dissolved. When Mrs Eliot was borne off to be introduced, Gwen Watkins sat down next to Eliot and said: 'You look as if, like Dante, you'd passed into paradise.'

'Exactly,' he said, pleased. For him, paradise followed purgatory with the same logic that purgatory had followed the hell of his first marriage.

This transformation is forecast in the first draft of the second act of 'The Rest Cure', the writing that immediately precedes Eliot's second marriage. Angela discerns that the old man is going through pangs of change from one kind of life to another. She urges him to 'burst out, become a butterfly!' The words go back to 1911 and Eliot's '2nd Debate between the Body and Soul', which dreams of a condition in which the soul might 'burst out at last, ingenuous and pure'. If, from 1911 to 1956, Eliot was a creature in a chrysalis, testing his power of transformation, his late marriage completed a lifelong process.

The play, written extraordinarily close to unfolding events, dramatises the self-confrontation of a man waiting for death. It is when the public figure stops performing and comes to rest in a sanatorium (like Eliot's rest-cures in the London Clinic) that he faces his whole past. The sanatorium in *The Cocktail Party* had been a place for the transformation of an appointed martyr. Claverton's position is humbler: his cure is not to become God's agent but to accept the forgiveness that comes to him through a young woman. The complex emotional situation suggests that what happened to Eliot in 1956 was not only a simple matter of falling in love but a coming to 'rest' in a changed conception of existence in relation to God. The God of fire, the intolerable shirt of flame that Eliot put on at the end of *Four Quartets*, became a God of blessings. Love, an 'unfamiliar Name' to the Eliot of 1942, made itself known to the elder Eliot of 1957.

This final position was one that Henry James, Sr, had put to Emerson. All that men value as religious progress, he said, going alone, renouncing, self-mortification, was the way *from*, not the way *to* what they seek 'for it is only as our existence is shared, not as it is self-hood, that it is divine'. Emerson, the New England prophet of self-hood, copied the admonition into his journal.

Eliot's transformation through phases of hope, courtship, secret commitment, and, finally, secure public love, is charted in the evolution of the last play from synopses, to the drafts, to the stage, to the triumphant dedication of the published work to his wife. In the third act, written after marriage, the young woman turns out to be not as passive as she appears in the drafts of the first two acts. She is certainly not one of the puppets of whom Mary had complained. The name, Angela, was changed to Monica, the name of St Augustine's strong mother, who urged the transforming experience of his life. Monica may not actually speak other than conventional loving words, yet a subtle actress could convey that her loyalty, put to the test, is deeper than language. She has the staunchness of Antigone upholding her aged father at Colonus. As far back as March 1938, Eliot had told Martin Browne that one way to complete Harry's career would be an *Oedipus at Colonus*. In other words, the old man who finds peace of mind should succeed the middle-aged man haunted by Furies. We might plot a line from the young savagery of Sweeney, to the mature guilt of Harry, to the loving serenity that comes like grace to Claverton as he passes through the 'door' at the end of life.

'I am only a beginner in the practice of loving,' he says. 'Well, that is something.'

Eliot broke into love poetry in his revisions to Act I (completed on 9 February 1958) and in Act III which introduce love-duets between Monica and her fiancé, Charles.

Charles was now reconceived as a sensitive man who finds it difficult to express love, but tries:

> ... like the asthmatic struggling for breath,
> So the lover must struggle for words.

More rewriting and cutting went on in the new love scenes than in any other part of the play.

It was first produced at the Edinburgh Festival from 25 to 30 August 1958, with a young Anna Massey in what was only her third part as Monica. Alec McCowen as the errant son, Michael, was more riveting to the audience, wheeling round on his heel to flash his accusation at the old man. It must have been a weakness of that production that Martin Browne did not think much of Monica as a dramatic character: he found the accusers dramatically more interesting. This dated response mistakes the point of the play, which turns on an extraordinary maturity of feeling in a young woman who sheds grace on awkward men of power.

In Eliot's original version of Act III for the Edinburgh production, Monica explored the process of falling in love. It is a pity that these speeches were cut from the published play, because they manifest the woman's emotional vitality. The emotional engagement of this original scene is Eliot's first writing after his marriage. What remains of it in the published version is swamped by the twaddle of his earlier comedies. In the original, Monica, I think, speaks not only for herself but 'in unison' with the Eliots in their new-found bond. 'You've no idea how long I've been in love with you,' Monica confesses, 'long before the words came.' She cannot trace its beginning for 'one's whole life has been the preparation for its advent'.

The scene also brings up the long appearance of coldness in the lover who was slower to acknowledge the bond. Here, I think, Eliot speaks through Monica to his wife words which, as he put it in his dedication, 'have a further meaning / For you and me only':

It's very frightening, falling in love:

So frightening, that one refuses to recognise it,
For to recognise it is to face the terror of it.
And the terror aroused by the sight of the belovèd
Freezes the blood.

For a moment, the strangeness of Eliot comes back, as he
approaches marital love with the old power to imagine – and
fear – the unknown. This is not great poetry, but it is
touching that the poet of sublime agonies should now try to
articulate simple things lovers say to each other, that they
'belong together' and 'feel alone' in company. The man
speaks in wonder of the birth of 'a new person' who is 'you
and me together'. The woman, more expressive, speaks of
'the certainty of love unchanging'.

*

There was a cost to all this: the loss of the Guardians of the
preceding phase. Neither Mary Trevelyan nor John Hayward
remained part of Eliot's changed life, and many felt that
Hayward's dependence warranted more consideration. It was
felt by his friends that it would not have been inappropriate
for Eliot to have seen him regularly, or even occasionally, for
old time's sake, and they said too that it would have been
fairer to have warned a flatmate in advance of the wedding.
When Eliot did not return from church, as usual, on the
morning of 10 January, Hayward thought of calling the
police. Later in the day he phoned Peter du Sautoy and spoke
rather grimly about '*il matrimonio segreto*'.*

Eliot shrank, too, from telling Mary Trevelyan. He saw her
according to their routine – church, drives, teas – up to a
week before the wedding. In August 1956, while Eliot was on
holiday in Geneva and Mary in Herefordshire, he sent her a
postcard almost every day for a fortnight. Then, from
September, Mary noticed an increased edginess. 'My *dear*
lady . . .' Eliot would stop her, and lapse into silence. Forms
of kindness remained. When Mary was ill in mid-October, he

---

* Cimarosa's opera of that name had recently been in the news.

brought her whisky through the drenching rain and, in the course of one day, phoned three times. In late November he continued to oblige Mary with a reading for her newly formed Goats Club for local and overseas students, which she started, she said, as an experiment in race relations. The club was a huge success, with Eliot for its first president. A photograph shows him seated, pale and old, amidst newcomers to London.

In mid-December (by which time Eliot was secretly engaged) he dined with Mary, her brother Humphrey Trevelyan, the Ambassador to Egypt, and his wife, Peggie, to hear of their flight during the Suez crisis.* Eliot also invited himself to tea on consecutive Sundays, and on 16 December he stayed from 3.30 to 7 p.m. talking of presents. He always gave Miss Swan a present, he said, starting years ago when she was kind to Vivienne.

'But I don't give Miss Fletcher anything,' he went on (relishing the private joke). 'I don't think it suitable to give one's secretary presents.'

Then he picked up *Bleak House*, a present to Mary, and read his favourite bits aloud for an hour.

On 23, 27, and 29 December Mary went to tea with Eliot, who had a cold. On the 29th he looked better. She noted with approval that there were not so many medicines as usual. The last time they met was on 2 January, when they spent two hours in their old haunt, the Russell Hotel, drinking Tio Pepe and talking of Vivienne. As they parted, Eliot held Mary's hand a moment, saying: 'As you know, I always mention you in my prayer.'

Mary was away from London from 3 to 9 January. A letter from Eliot awaited her return. It said that on Thursday the 10th he would marry Valerie Fletcher. It was not a sudden decision: they loved each other very much. He added that he had prized Mary's friendship, and would be loth to lose it.

---

* Humphrey Trevelyan was Ambassador to Egypt from 1953 till 1956. He later became Ambassador to the USSR and, in the late sixties, was made a life peer.

Mary, opening this letter on the morning of the 10th, was stunned. Unbelieving, she phoned Hayward again and again.

Both naturally fell back on their manners. Mary wrote a note of good wishes to Eliot's office. 'My dear chap,' Hayward said disarmingly on Eliot's return from honeymoon, 'why didn't you tell me?' This was on one of two occasions when Eliot went back to the flat to collect his belongings. Hayward felt no resentment but, as the months passed, grew bewildered at Eliot's withdrawal. 'I thought that everything was all right,' he said to friends in May. Now on his own after ten years, he felt his helplessness anew. His morale never recovered.

It is not difficult, though, to understand Eliot's need for secrecy. Hayward was a notorious gossip, and Mary was bound to be put out, not only as Eliot's escort, but in view of the now-embarrassing excuse which Eliot had given, in kindness in 1950, that he did not wish to marry anyone. In that letter of 2 June 1950, he had made the revealing comment that the desire not to inflict pain can often approach very near to cowardice. This might be a more subtle explanation of Eliot's actions, as Graham Greene saw precisely when he spoke of 'the moral cowardice of the sensitive man'. More obviously, Eliot feared ridicule. To neither John nor Mary could he hope to explain the idyllic nature of his attachment. He was not just a doting old man, or avid, like Yeats, for excitement. His capacity for love was bound up with intellectual respect and deep trust. He had, thus late, made the discovery that there are different kinds of pure relationship, not only the impossible purity of sublime love but a realisable union of mind, body, and soul.

And yet an element of strangeness does still remain. It echoes in the stupefaction of Mary Trevelyan in the last pages of her memoir: 'Have John and I known and loved the real man?' She says exactly what Emily Hale said, that after years of knowing Eliot you found, suddenly, that you did not know him. He could leave relationships and pass on. Eliot was most in his element in the act of memory. He chose as his totem the elephant* who never forgets. After his marriage, he designed a joint bookplate (beautifully executed by David Jones in black and green), an elephant's head (drawn by Eliot himself) with an upraised trunk that encircles an arrow, derived from the name Fletcher, meaning 'maker of arrows'. But the elephant could forget when he chose. He denied writing obscene verses. He denied Conrad Aiken's memory of two incidents that showed 'a streak of sadism' in his nature. He would not be pinned by others' memories. Mrs Morley, who had harboured Eliot during the summer of 1933 when he broke with Vivienne, found, when she met him some years later, that he hardly seemed to know who she was. He had a capacity, not to forget in the ordinary way, but to wipe out what did not fit the model of existence as he devised it. In old age he was concentrating on the paradise of natural love, so John Hayward, who patently had no place in paradise, was left behind.

Of course Eliot did the proper thing. He paid his contribution to the Hayward flat for another two years. After six months he issued invitations to John and Mary, but he was not going to see them alone. Intimacy, such as it had been, was over. John did once come to lunch with Robert Frost and Rosamond Lehmann, and the Eliots did once return the visit, but John felt that Eliot avoided him, and contact lapsed. In his 1963 edition of the *Collected Poems*, Eliot removed his acknowledgement to John Hayward, originally printed before *Four Quartets*.

With Mary, politeness broke down almost at once. When she had no reply to her note, she wrote to Eliot again saying in her forthright way that, despite her initial shock, her affection for him would not change. This gave quick offence. She was, Eliot replied, impertinent; Mary recoiled; and soon another long friendship came to an end. Emily, too, had her 'unappreciative' letter, terminating a tie of forty-five years.

* The elephant was a family crest. Its origin is recorded in *The Oxford Guide to Heraldry* by Thomas Woodcock and John Martin Robinson (OUP, 1988): 'the *Elephant's head proper* granted in 1492 by ... John Writhe, Garter, to the brothers Thomas and John Elyott'.

There is a curious defence of the Elder Statesman in one (later) draft, to the effect that he was compelled to 'sacrifice others' for higher ends, a sacrifice justified by the sacrifice of himself. In *The Cocktail Party*, Edward hesitates to rebuild his life on another's ruin, but the priestly psychiatrist reassures him that it's all right so long as he suffers enough in private:

Your business is not to clear your conscience
But to learn how to bear the burdens on your conscience.

Eliot's morality of penitence dwells on a solitary excruciation that excludes full awareness of one's effect on others. Claverton's moral agony would move us more if he did not see sin so exclusively 'in relation to the sinner'.

This is the minister Dimmesdale speaking. When his secret explodes before the Puritan throng, he excludes from this high drama the partner of his past. The fact that this partner is a woman of rare distinction deepens the moral ambiguity of Dimmesdale's salvation. Eliot, though, simplifies the moral position by making the partners of Claverton's past negligible. He transcends them with ease to find his glory in the act of confession.

The loftiness of Eliot's moral stance provokes extreme reactions of allegiance or resistance, but neither leads to truth. The whole truth is, of course, unattainable, but some of it lies in the New England trait of moral reflection, in the search for moral positions, and in the authority of the spiritual frontier. 'Explore your own higher latitudes,' Thoreau urged. 'If you would learn to speak all tongues and conform to the customs of all nations, if you would travel farther than all travellers, be naturalized in all climes ... Explore thyself.' Frontiering of this kind is a radical act. It cuts loose, and moves on. It shakes off the dust of the previous frontier. So Eliot spat out the butt-ends of past days and ways, en route to paradise.

*

'Love reciprocated is always rejuvenating,' Eliot said in 1958. 'Before my marriage I was getting older. Now I feel younger at seventy than I did at sixty. . . . An experience like mine makes all the more difference because of its contrast with the past.'

All at once, he seemed to shake off a lifetime's habit of introversion. Though he and his wife were almost never separated, he wrote to her once a week. They liked to stay at home, drink Drambuie, eat cheese, and play Scrabble. He used to leave a message for her on their magnetic set, for the next time she opened it. (In 1994, nearly thirty years after his death, she said in an interview that she had yet to read the last message – as though his words still hung in the air on their way to her.) He was *fun*, she said, and his own repeated declarations of happiness broke our convention that it is not seemly to show off married bliss, a convention that coexists with the platitude that marriage palls. 'None of my books are fitted to be wedding presents,' Hardy remarked to Virginia Woolf when she visited him in 1926. Hardy's pessimism had reversed the platitude of his own time, the domestic sentiment of the Victorians. In 1958 Eliot, in turn, reversed pessimism with his poem 'To My Wife'. It breaks the formality of the usual dedication, with its public announcement of 'the leaping delight' that quickens the senses of the husband, and the joined sleep of lovers whose bodies smell of each other. Such directness from a man, old and austere, is even more startling than Yeats's admission of his 'old man's frenzy'. The old Yeats exults in the return of vitality; the old Hardy is disturbed by 'throbbings of noontide' which shake his fragile frame; but the old Eliot tells us something more subtle and unexpected. Poets speak, usually, of the frenzy of love, of its transience and loss; Eliot tells of an experience that is sustained. Faithful lovers breathe in unison as they sleep with a sense of union that will infuse their life. By contrast, the passing affair saps feeling. Eliot's early poems describe the push-button sex of the female jaguar whose bust promises 'pneumatic bliss', and the apathetic automatism of clerk and typist who couple like 'crawling bugs'. Eliot set out such scenes shortly because they are in truth boring, mere variations of emotional sterility. The alternative had been renunciation: Prufrock's inactivity in the presence of women's arms 'braceleted and white and bare', the parting with La Figlia, and decades later the withdrawal of Simpkins from the seductive Lucasta. This pattern reflects Eliot's own withdrawal until marriage redeemed love itself.

In 1958 Eliot introduced his wife to the United States. In Texas he opened an exhibition of his first editions and papers, and accepted a Deputy Sheriff's badge and a ten-gallon hat which he sported amongst his relatives in Boston and at church in New York. Mrs Eliot told a reporter from the *Boston Globe* that they had enjoyed Texas, but felt most at home in Cambridge. Eliot's expression of happy pride as he held his wife's hand was unprecedented. His face split into unaccustomed smiles as he faced photographers. Jovial, joking over Prufrock's lack of love-life, he seemed to enjoy the impact of his new image. The man who, at twenty-one, had written 'I grow old ... I grow old...', now told reporters that he might take dancing lessons 'as I have not danced at all for some years'. Sure enough, when some Harvard students got up a dance at a boathouse and sent an invitation to Eliot, who was dining that night with the Master of Eliot House, John Finlay, together with the I. A. Richardses, the Harry Levins, and the Archibald MacLeishes, the Eliots alone went to the boathouse – Eliot rather shyly – while the other guests made their excuses and went home.

Throughout his life Eliot could unbend unexpectedly. He had unbent in the early twenties to Virginia Woolf, when she had dared to laugh in his white marble face. He had unbent to Mary Trevelyan when, in 1938, she had sent him her parody of his stiff-necked reading. In 1949 he had unbent to Iowa students who, by way of congratulations on the Nobel Prize, had sent him a record of 'You've Come a Long Way from St Louis'. His reply was that he took note of the line: 'But, Baby, you've still got a long way to go.'

He responded, each time, to a sense of humour. With Valerie Eliot, humour became his constant note. He began to

T. S. ELIOT

write fan letters to Groucho Marx and was not put out by the brashness of the replies. When they exchanged photographs (Eliot put Groucho on his office mantelpiece beside Yeats and Valéry), Groucho commented: 'I had no idea you were so handsome. Why you haven't been offered the lead in some sexy movies I can only attribute to the simplicity of the casting directors.' One letter from Groucho begins daringly:

> Dear Tom:
> If this isn't your first name, I'm in a hell of a fix! But I think I read somewhere that your first name is the same as Tom Gibbons', a prizefighter who once lived in St. Paul.
> My best to you and your lovely wife, whoever she may be.

To this, Eliot replied graciously: 'My lovely wife joins me in sending you our best.' He enclosed another photograph from an oil portrait done in 1961, and added: 'It is very good-looking and my wife thinks it is a very accurate representation of me.'

Groucho responded, in turn, with a further meditation on Eliot's name: 'The name Tom fits many things. There was once a famous Jewish actor named Thomashevsky. All male cats are named Tom – unless they have been fixed. . . . So when I call you Tom, this means you are a mixture of a heavyweight prizefighter, a male alley cat and the third President of the United States.'* He went on as one writer to another: 'I have just finished my latest opus, "Memoirs of a Mangy Lover." ' . . . I doubt whether it will live through the ages, but if you are in a sexy mood the night you read it, it may stimulate you beyond recognition. . . . I would be interested in reading your views on sex, so don't hesitate. Confide in me.'

Eliot, who was seventy-five and ailing, delayed his reply for eight months, when he wrote to invite Groucho and his wife to the Eliots' flat in London in June 1964. Groucho gave a hilarious account of their meeting to Gummo Marx:

* Thomas Jefferson.

516

Last night Eden and I had dinner with my celebrated pen pal, T. S. Eliot. It was a memorable evening.

The poet met us at the door with Mrs. Eliot, a good-looking, middle-aged blonde whose eyes seemed to fill up with adoration every time she looked at her husband. He, by the way, is tall, lean and rather stooped over; but whether this is from age, illness or both, I don't know.

At any rate, your correspondent arrived at the Eliots' fully prepared for a literary evening. During the week I had read 'Murder in the Cathedral' twice; 'The Waste Land' three times, and just in case of conversational bottleneck, I brushed up on 'King Lear.'

Well, sir, as the cocktails were served, there was a momentary lull – the kind that is more or less inevitable when strangers meet for the first time. So, apropos of practically nothing (and 'not with a bang but a whimper') I tossed in a quotation from 'The Waste Land'. That, I thought, will show him I've read a thing or two besides my press notices from Vaudeville.

Eliot smiled faintly – as though to say he was thoroughly familiar with his poems and didn't need me to recite them. So I took a whack at 'King Lear' ...

That, too, failed to bowl over the poet. He seemed more interested in discussing 'Animal Crackers' and 'A Night at the Opera'. He quoted a joke – one of mine – that I had long since forgotten. Now it was my turn to smile faintly.

Groucho persisted with *King Lear*; Eliot, equally determined, asked Groucho, if he remembered the courtroom scene in *Duck Soup*. Groucho, in turn, dismissed the subject – he had forgotten every word – but resigned himself to the end of the literary evening. Instead they talked about what they actually had in common, an affection for good cigars and cats. Groucho admitted a weakness for puns, and found that Eliot was 'an unashamed – even proud – punster'. Groucho thought him 'a dear man and a charming host'.

Marriage brought out a sense of fun that was always there, in the child on a St Louis street-corner, smiling mischievously with his nurse, Annie Dunne; in the middle-aged Eliot who entertained Janet Adam Smith's children with readings from *Uncle Remus*, so much so that one or two phrases – 'Jest loungin' aroun' and worryin' – passed into their family language. There was a homey side to Eliot: the man who 'interfered' in Mary Trevelyan's kitchen, who sent a recipe, 'Mrs Runcie's Pudding', for inclusion in the *St Louis Symphony of Cooking* in 1954, and who now discussed cake shops, fishmongers, and greengrocers in the Gloucester Road with Ivy Compton-Burnett in a shared taxi after a Knightsbridge party. Valerie Eliot brought out this humorous domestic pet, like one of his Cats who represent, in caricature, some aspects of Eliot himself. Macavity, the monster of depravity, vanished in this period, but Gus the theatre cat remained, and Jennyanydots, the domestic purrer.

He now went to the office only three days a week. His chief interests were the London Library and the revision of the Psalter. Most evenings he and his wife read aloud to each other: Boswell, Coleridge's letters, *Kim*, and poetry (not much from younger writers). Eliot praised his wife's very good mind and passionate love of poetry. He was, he told Violet Schiff, madly happy to be her husband. 'It is a wonderful thing', he wrote to Levy, 'to be happily married, and a very blessed state for those who are called to it, even at my age. I have a very beautiful and good and sensitive wife . . . – she has everything to make me happy, and I am humbly thankful.'

Vivienne Haigh-Wood had been frail and helpless; his second wife had sense and humour, and cared for him with all the generous love that he could have desired. His married happiness restored the self-confidence his turbulent years with Vivienne had undermined. 'Without the satisfaction of this happy marriage,' he wrote in 1960 in the fiftieth anniversary report of Harvard's class of 1910, 'no achievement or honour could give me satisfaction at all.'

Eliot's earlier women, Vivienne and Emily Hale, had been transmuted into figures in a morality drama. In Conrad Aiken's view the Eliot he had known in their youth was a man who put art before life: '. . . art and love – that was the primary order, for if one could sacrifice love for art . . . one could never – could one? – sacrifice art for love – or only momentarily, and with an eye over the shoulder, the unsleeping knowledge that this, like all experience, but more than most, was the indispensable raw material of art.' Valerie Eliot was not to be transformed in this way. In the last play and the dedicatory poem, Eliot celebrates her as she was: Monica's line 'unchanging the certainty of love' was the real-life motto of their marriage, encircling the head of the elephant on their bookplate.

By this late stage, art was, in fact, no longer an issue. The impulse to write poetry had long since faded, and *The Elder Statesman* had been conceived as the last play. A surge of vitality following the marriage did awaken the possibility of further writing. Eliot told Henry Hewes in 1958 that he now planned another verse play and more poems in a new style. 'I reached the end of something with the *Four Quartets*,' he said, 'and anything new will have to be expressed in a new idiom.' This would presumably be the love idiom of the last revisions to *The Elder Statesman*. But Eliot's health flagged again in the early sixties, and he wrote only one more scrap of verse: an extra stanza to the dedicatory poem 'To My Wife' for inclusion in the last edition of *Collected Poems*. He went back to the thirties for the image of the rose-garden, to open that door to love which, with Emily Hale, 'we never opened'.* In *Burnt Norton* the speaker is dismissed from the garden: 'Go go go . . .'. All he has is a glimpse of a paradise never to be possessed. But now, in 1963, Eliot took possession of this garden:

> No peevish winter wind shall chill
> No sullen tropic sun shall wither
> The roses in the rose-garden which is ours and ours
>   only . . .

In the autumn of 1964 Eliot wrote to Cyril Connolly to thank

* *Burnt Norton*: I (1935):

> Footfalls echo in the memory
> Down the passage which we did not take
> Towards the door we never opened
> Into the rose-garden.

him for a kindly review: 'You were the first sympathetic reader and critic to call attention to the unusual fact that I had at last written a poem of love and happiness. It would almost seem that some readers were shocked that I should be happy.' Neither advanced age nor the months of tedium in the West Indies which doctors prescribed each winter, could dim this.

He said: 'This last part of my life is the best, in excess of anything I could have deserved.'

*

Mary Trevelyan noticed that this marriage took place exactly ten years, to the month, after Vivienne's death, as though a set period of penitence had come to an end. Whether this is true or not, Eliot did fit his life to a pattern. A life that would pass through the ordeals of the waste and penitence in search of perfection absorbed Eliot until his last eight years. It called out his greatest poetry. Then came a certain hollowness in the early fifties, as though the Eliot of the great poems was no longer there. And then, in 1956, there appeared the possibility of a different pattern of redemption: not through the heights of divine communion – those heights of the mystics were now closed to Eliot – but through a human solace. As Tillich describes this experience in *The New Being*, in the midst of despair there is the certainty of forgiveness, and the fire of love begins to burn. It is a breakthrough: 'it transforms everything'. The love that Eliot's wife brought him would have been a sign that he was, at last, blessed.

The more obvious benefit of the marriage was nurture. Eliot's health remained delicate. He was ill on honeymoon in February 1957, and in September had a long bout of Asian flu which lasted into October, when he caught another chill in Paris. 1958 was a better year – he travelled in America and put on *The Elder Statesman* – but the November fogs were trying to his bronchial weakness. By the winter of 1959–60 he told Pound that he had to put most of his energy into breathing. In February 1960 he went to recuperate in

Morocco, but dust from the Agadir earthquake brought on asthma. In January 1961 the Eliots took a leisurely cruise to Jamaica, where they stayed at Ocho Rios until March. In 1961–2 they went to Barbados for the usual regime of swims and sunbathing. Eliot told Vernon Watkins that he found nothing to attract him to the tropical islands except the climate.

By then, Eliot had aged. He was bent over a cane, his colour ashen, his features softened and his voice weak. At the end of 1962 he collapsed after a four-day smog in early December. It was the memorably cold winter of 1962–3 (the coldest January on record since 1838) when people's bones ached from the blizzards. Instead of a projected journey to the Bahamas, Eliot spent five weeks in the Brompton Hospital under continuous oxygen. His wife never left his side, determined to be there when he came round from his coma. She fobbed off the press with a statement about bronchial trouble while she nursed him through this crisis.

In March, when he recovered, he asked Peter du Sautoy to destroy the box of letters. Eliot must have known that he was close to death; as he had said of his friend Paul Elmer More in February 1937: it would be surprising if a man of so much wisdom were quite unaware of the coming of such an important event. In 1949 he had confided to Mary Trevelyan that he was afraid of death, but now he faced it calmly.

'Death is not oblivion,' he said in 1958. 'People who believe that are not afraid of death.'

In these last years Eliot was taking retrospective views of his career. The most candid are in letters to Pound, who was now released from St Elizabeths and back in Italy. In these letters, Eliot speaks harshly of his sense of failure, of doubt, disgust, despair. This may have been as much a gesture of empathy with Pound's broken state as a self-judgement. He cabled Pound on 31 October 1959 that he would never forget his own great debt to him to whom all living poets were indebted, that Pound's criticism had been immensely helpful, and his work epoch-making. Two months later he wrote how he had envied Joyce his apparent self-confidence, and went on to slight his own prose, particularly *After Strange Gods*, which expressed, he owned, his disturbed state in 1933. Nor was he pleased with *The Use of Poetry and the Use of Criticism* except for a few paragraphs. On 29 January 1960 he went on to confess that there was much in his life that he still could not bear to think about for long at a time, but *The Waste Land* and the three last *Quartets* did seem worthwhile.* Now, it was hard to accept a diminution of creative power, and Valerie had to work hard to snap him out of his gloom. As late as November 1961 he still spoke of things he wanted to do.

Eliot gave his last public lecture at the University of Leeds, in July 1961, with an eye to posterity. In 'To Criticise the Critic', he spoke past the predictable adulation of his present-day audience in order to set up the judgement of the future. It is an extraordinary exercise in detachment, for he looks back on himself, the pre-eminent critical mind of his age, from a hundred years on. His foresees and assents to the fading of theories that had captured his time. Taking the opposite position to the doctrinal impersonality of his early criticism, he confessed repeatedly to a criticism based on subjective 'feeling', a kinship with certain writers as opposed to others, 'emotional preferences' that gave vehemence to the generalisations which, in turn, shaped the taste of an age.

His enduring essays, he predicted, will be on particular writers who fed his emotions and influenced his writing: the verbal clarity and emotional extremities of Dante; the horror of the seventeenth-century English dramatists (Webster, Tourneur, Middleton, Ford); the rigorous sermons of Bishop Lancelot Andrewes; and the personality of F. H. Bradley, combining scepticism with a search for the Absolute, which gave international philosophic status to a paradox native to the New England mind (as Eliot saw it in Emerson, and as Emerson himself saw it in his aunt Mary Moody Emerson,

---

* Curiously, he excludes the first quartet, *Burnt Norton*, which inspired the whole sequence, and will be for many of us the most captivating. We may wonder if the exclusion has to do with Eliot's current mistreatment of Emily Hale, whom he associated with its landscape.

the purest exemplar of that Yankee fusion of scepticism and passionate piety). In short, Eliot's last message is to disregard the preference of his own time for his early, more aesthetic essays in favour of his mature, more 'judicial' essays. Although Eliot does 'shyly' intrude himself into the company of the foremost English poet-critics, Johnson, Coleridge, Dryden, and Arnold (in order of preference), Eliot's real claim is to go beyond criticism as he wished to go beyond poetry to speak from on high, not words but the Word, everlasting truth.

In old age he felt a change and narrowing of his tastes. The devotion to Dante remained, as ever, constant ('the comfort and amazement of my age'), but now he turned more often to Shakespeare rather than Shakespeare's contemporaries, and to Herbert rather than Donne. George Herbert was the subject of Eliot's last critical work, a British Council pamphlet published in 1962.

With Herbert, as with Pascal, Eliot fixed on a religious figure so congenial that he could speak in unison with his chosen model. In 'Pascal' (1931) Eliot had marked a particular 'sequence which culminates in faith', rational scepticism transformed into religious fervour. *George Herbert* is another such exercise in spiritual autobiography, and in this sense is Eliot's last view of his life.

His portrait is of a devotional poet guided in his formative years by a mother of bookish tastes, piety, and exceptional gifts of mind; a man well-born, proud, and snobbish, meticulous of dress and ambitious of worldly position who, in his thirties, turned aside from the world. At that point 'the pride of birth natural to Herbert was transformed into the dignity of the Servant of God'. With a powerful intellect and by nature not meek, Herbert underwent unsparing self-examination and self-criticism. His poems show 'ample evidence ... of the cost at which he acquired godliness'. There was no steady progress: he falls, he rises. Herbert avoided what Eliot tells us is the great temptation to the religious poet: to set down not what he actually feels, but what he would like to feel. It is here that Eliot is most entirely in unison with

Herbert, in his scrupulous honesty about failure or limitation, and also in a proud man's struggle for humility.

Unlike his friend Donne, who drew crowds to hear the oratorical sermons at Paul's Cross, Herbert turned away from fame. A close friend was Nicholas Ferrar of Little Gidding. For a time Herbert was prebend at Leighton Bromswold, five miles south of Little Gidding, and later took an equally modest post as rector in the village church of Bemerton in Wiltshire. Eliot's Herbert is not a mild man in a charming pastoral retreat. Quick-tempered, given to moods of rebellion, his poems set down 'the fluctuations of emotion between despair and bliss, between agitation and serenity, and the discipline of suffering which leads to peace of spirit'. Eliot's phrases sum up his own career. Herbert was able to say, he quotes: 'And now in age I bud again.' Like Eliot, he had a happy marriage in his last years that promoted a final picture of religious serenity. Eliot closes by quoting in full the poem 'Love', in which every line suggests a parallel with Eliot's own life:

> Love bade me welcome: yet my soul drew back,
>   Guiltie of dust and sinne.
> But quick-ey'd Love, observing me grow slack
>   From my first entrance in,
> Drew nearer to me, sweetly questioning,
>   If I lack'd any thing.
>
> A guest, I answer'd, worthy to be here:
>   Love said, You shall be he.
> I the unkinde, ungratefull? Ah my deare,
>   I cannot look on thee.
> Love took my hand, and smiling did reply,
>   Who made the eyes but I?
>
> Truth Lord, but I have marr'd them: let my shame
>   Go where it doth deserve.
> And know you not, sayes Love, who bore the blame?
>   My deare, then I will serve.
> You must sit down, sayes Love, and taste my meat:
>   So I did sit and eat.

To a man who has known much illness there is, in such surrender, a 'convalescence of the spirit'. Such convalescence sustained Eliot until his death on 4 January 1965. Allen Tate's report of his last visit confirms this serenity: 'The last time I saw him was in September, 1963, at his house in London. He had been seriously ill the year before and he had trouble walking. As we were leaving, he stood at the drawing-room door, leaning on two canes. I had put on my coat and I turned to wave a second good-bye. He couldn't raise his hands from the canes, but he smiled as he moved the fingers of one hand to acknowledge my gesture.'

In the last months of Eliot's life John Hayward asked after him tenderly, as if there had been no breach. He admitted how much he missed Eliot, and wished that he could see him again.

'He was – my dear – friend,' Hayward said brokenly on the telephone to Helen Gardner on the day of Eliot's death.

John Hayward died later in the same year, on 17 September, aged sixty, and a wit to the end. When he telephoned Kathleen Raine to say that he was not well enough to see her, she asked:

'Is there anything I can send you?'

'A wreath, I think, my dear,' was his reply.

At Eliot's Westminster Abbey memorial service, the absence of John Hayward and Emily Hale, two people who were central to Eliot's mature works, went unnoticed, while the press duly recorded a great crowd of publishers, ambassadors, and family: Martha and Abigail Eliot, play-mates from the New England summers of Eliot's childhood, Pound, Dr Thomas Faber who, as a child, had heard Eliot read *Cats*, and two people whom Eliot himself would have preferred not to see, Maurice Haigh-Wood and Mary Trevelyan.

In 1949 Eliot had chosen the second movement of Beethoven's Seventh Symphony for his funeral, rather than his favourite *Coriolan* Overture, which he had feared might sound too grand. The service included also Stravinsky's setting for 'The dove descending' from *Little Gidding*; a reading by Alec Guinness from Eliot's later works; and a hymn of Herbert's, one of relief not trial:

> Thou hast granted my request,
> Thou hast heard me:
> Thou didst note my working breast,
> Thou hast spar'd me.

Far away, in Massachusetts, Emily Hale recorded her grief privately in a controlled letter to Margaret Thorp:

> 9 Church Green
> Concord, Mass 01742
> January 11, 1965.

Margaret my dear,

Your short note after the event of last Monday, was very welcome on Saturday. I thought naturally, a great deal of you, Willard and Bill Dix, since we four are so very intimately concerned with what is now a future – as well as a past – mystery and remarkable personal story.

I had not known until last autumn – and then not in great detail from E.H.H. [Eleanor Hinkley] how terribly ill he has been for two or three years – the old bronchial weaknesses, plus many complications, so an oxygen tent seems to have been in constant attendance, Poor Man. The family report that Valerie has been *very* remarkable in her nursing as well as other wifely duties – : her life has indeed been devoted to his wants – perhaps I could not have filled this requirement as she has done – perhaps – only perhaps – the decision to marry her was the right one.

I had gone unexpectedly from New Bedford to Woods Hole – the doctor's appointment being postponed – so that I was with Dorothy E[lsmith] who knew both T.S.E. and our relationship as intimately as anyone. I can't answer you very closely as [to] how I 'feel' – some of it has come back so vividly, it has not been easy; and having the public know *nothing* is at once a blessing and a burden . . .

I try hard to take this all dispassionately but it is a little hard . . .

> Lovingly
> Emily

526

An additional letter to Willard Thorp, on 17 January 1965, shows a growing kindness to the widow: 'I am happy I can very honestly say I am thankful she was his so devoted companion these last years. I have no feeling of anything else towards her – nor any feeling about T[om] except to *accept* it all without any bitterness or unkind thoughts.' On 20 January, in heavy snow, she attended a service for Eliot in the Memorial Church at Harvard. Harry Levin was there, also Robert Fitzgerald and Walter Bate. She found the academic occasion 'uninspiring'.

Emily Hale continued in her poised style to act and travel, and died in Concord in 1969.

Mary Trevelyan lived until 1983. She was awarded an OBE in 1956 and a CBE followed in 1967.* She founded the International Students House in London and, as governor, 'had little brown people to tea', as one Indian recalled. According to her nephew Humphrey Carpenter, 'she never recovered from the shock of Eliot's marriage, and spent a great deal of the remainder of her life mulling over what had happened. Their friendship had been the centre of her life, and she was crushed by his rejection.'

Valerie Eliot continued to live in the flat she had shared with Eliot in Kensington, surrounded by his books and photographs and tending, according to her trust, the altar of the dead. It is curious how Eliot projected Jamesian dramas on the women who loved him. Vivienne played the wild Daisy to his shocked Winterbourne. Emily played the companionable May, watching with Marcher for a spring that was not to be. Finally, Valerie Eliot had the happier task of the beneficent Alice Staverton, in whose arms Spencer Brydon comes back to life, purged from his encounter with his frightful other-self in the haunted house of the past. A latecomer to her husband's life, Valerie Eliot has given her own life to his memory, editing his *Letters* and the manuscript of *The Waste Land* with scholarly acumen and observing his wishes – no mean task in a later, more critical

---

* Order of the British Empire. Commander of the British Empire.

age when questions of what happened before her time raise their heads. She has defended him strongly, and done her utmost to promote the image of the Eliot whose heart was pure in her presence.

In Eliot's last work the spurned actress predicts that the Elder Statesman will be playing a part even in his obituary. In most of Eliot's obituaries he was, predictably, the Nobel prizeman, the international writer, the Anglican churchman, the jolly joker. But C. Day Lewis, helped by Hayward, did break through these roles to the agonised introspection of the sombre-clad son of the Puritans who stooped, lined and bowed by a sense of sin, around Russell Square. This one obituary did recognise that 'the fastidiousness, the moral taste, and the intellectual severity, which were a legacy of New England ancestors, merged with the Anglo-Catholic tradition to direct his poetry ever farther in the exploration of spiritual awareness . . .'.

Some time after Eliot's arrival in England, he had acquired a photograph of Poets' Corner in Westminster Abbey, with Dryden in the foreground. On the second anniversary of Eliot's death his own plaque was placed in Poets' Corner, next to Tennyson and Browning and at the feet of Chaucer. Reynolds Stone, a descendant of Sir Joshua Reynolds, engraved on it those lines where Eliot speaks explicitly from beyond the grave:

And what the dead had no speech for, when living,
They can tell you, being dead: the communication
Of the dead is tongued with fire beyond the language of
the living.

With death, the acts of his life fall into perspective, and we see its inward coherence.

'Though our outward man perish, yet the inward man is renewed day by day,' read Peter du Sautoy at Eliot's memorial service. Eliot did not wish his outward man to be preserved in biography. He called, rather, for an imaginative grasp of the inner life as expressed through works of art, 'for

528

the things which are seen are temporal; but the things which are not seen are eternal'.

*

'Can a lifetime represent a single motive?' Eliot asked in a pencil note in 1941.

To him the 'life of a man of genius, viewed in relation to his writing, comes to take a pattern of inevitability, and even his disabilities will seem to have stood him in good stead'. If we apply this to his own life, its inner coherence is obvious. If we follow, say, his relations with women, it is curious to see how they were absorbed into what seems a predetermined pattern. Emily Hale prompted the sublime moments; Vivienne, the sense of sin, and, throughout the first marriage, the living martyrdom. Later, sensible, efficient Mary Trevelyan served her long stint as support during the years of penitence. For her their friendship was a commitment, for Eliot quite peripheral. His passion for immortality was so commanding that it allowed him to reject each of these women with a firmness that shattered their lives.

The shape of Eliot's life is one of paring down, concentration. Much had to be discarded to make his life conform to the pilgrim pattern. His early years turned on his acceptance of this pattern, his later years on the question of its fulfilment. Throughout his life we find the tension between an idiosyncratic nature and an ideal biography. Its drama lay in efforts to close the gap between nature and perfection at whatever personal cost, revelling to some degree in that cost, and inspecting his suffering as the distinguishing brand of his election. To be chosen, he had to purify the very ambition that set him going. And so the moral drama of the later years, from *Murder in the Cathedral*, centres not on the earlier festering of lust and primitive violence, but on the pride and subtler taints of public dignitaries. Eliot always calls for judgement, but, we can never forget, for divine not human judgement.

At best a life of Eliot can be but a complement to work

529

which speaks for itself. He reminds us that lives turn on 'unattended moments' of humiliation and triumph that happen now and then, but rarely at times of official crisis or celebration.

In Sweden in 1948 to receive the Nobel Prize, Eliot was shaving one morning when a procession of six girls, dressed (it seemed to him) in nightgowns and wearing crowns of lighted candles, marched into his room. Hastily wiping the suds from his face, he stretched an arm around the bathroom door for his overcoat, which he put on over his underclothes, and then bowed to them as they sang. He shared publicity with the Harringay Rangers, a visiting hockey team composed mostly of Canadians who chewed highly scented mint gum. The celebrations of the Nobel Prize were peripheral to the dramas of the inner life, like the moment in 1926 when he fell on his knees before the *Pietà* in Rome. His first marriage was peripheral to 'the awful daring of a moment's surrender'. And Harvard was peripheral to the Silence in the streets of Boston, that 'ultimate hour' in June 1910 when, it appeared to him, 'life is justified'.

Where the centre of interest lies in the inner life, we diverge from the schema of historical or political biography where the centre of interest lies in public action. With writers, we wish to know the source of creativity, which may be unknowable or incommunicable, buried in the solitude of the artist's life. And here is the almost insuperable challenge: not formal obstacles to Eliot biography, nor his masks, but the silent spaces of the writer's life. He, alone, can reveal them. In this sense, Eliot will always remain master of his biography, revealing and concealing with the utmost calculation.

What he does tell us repeatedly is that there were feelings beyond the nameable, classifiable emotions of lives directed towards action. On 31 March 1933 he spoke of 'the deeper, unnamed feelings which form the substratum of our being, to which we rarely penetrate; for our lives are mostly a constant evasion of ourselves . . .'. This might touch on the experience of the saints, though he was careful not to claim that. Yet to ignore the presence of this model, as it came to him initially through the poetry of his mother and then through his reading as a student, would be to miss a singleness of purpose to which life and art were both subordinate. With Eliot, writing was not an offshoot of the life; the life was an offshoot of the writing. The work forecasts the life, even determines it, as, say, the dream of parting in 'La Figlia che Piange' forecast Eliot's actual parting from Emily Hale, or as the drafts of the last play spell his own discovery of human love. It is not enough to see, as Henry James put it, that 'art *makes* life, makes importance', for, with Eliot, it was an exemplary pattern that made the art that made the life. So the parting at the start of Eliot's career and the love that closed it were, in a sense, dictated by the biblical pattern of renunciation and blessedness.

It would falsify the dominance of this pattern to recount Eliot's life in the usual compendious form. For this reason, the present impossibility of authorised biography may be, not a handicap, but an advantage, because of the chance to invent a more appropriate form. For full-scale biography is unsuited to an understanding of Eliot's life. And this may be one reason why he forbade it. He made it clear that whatever is worth recording would not be found in wills and legal papers presided over by the lean solicitor, nor in well-intentioned recollections, the webs woven over the career by beneficent spiders. The single force of the career is contained in the awful daring of a moment's surrender: 'By this and this only, we have existed.'

Eliot surrendered to a form of life to fit an ideal order which we can never directly know, but may, at moments, apprehend. At such moments he burnt with the nearness of the infinite 'thing', but it slipped away and the rude clamour of the city returned to blunt his senses. His achievement was to redefine the perfect life in the uncongenial conditions of the twentieth century, aware all the while that its marking points – moments of light and horror – were not the markers of his own life only, but those of many generations, past and future.

Eliot was only superficially a man of his time. His affinities were with spokesmen for the perfect life in other centuries, the Catholic mystics of the Middle Ages and the American Puritans of the seventeenth century. He said in 1954 that he combined 'a Catholic cast of mind, a Calvinistic heritage, and a Puritanical temperament'. His was not the cultural despair, the dead-end alienation of Modernity but the purposeful withdrawal of one who passed through his age as a hermit, refusing its debasement. Displaced, as it were, in time, he derided his contemporaries' political solutions, their smug rationalism, their meaningless toys – horoscopes and porcelain collections – their boring parties, their magazine-style romances. Eliot saw the children of the twentieth century as aliens clutching cheap gods. Like a prophet he denounced those who sat 'in the sty of contentment' and, above all, those who backed predatory commerce. He had seen in his youth in America the hypertrophy of the motive of profit and the gross misuse of money. In 1939 he foresaw that this evil was more tenacious than those that provoked the Second World War. In 1939, in the context of totalitarian dictators, his rhetoric seemed irrelevant; now, with the increasing dominance of global economic masters, far more powerful in their invisible pervasiveness, it could not be more pertinent:

> Surely there is something wrong in our attitude towards money. The acquisitive, rather than the creative and spiritual instincts, are encouraged. The fact that money is always forthcoming for the purpose of making more money, whilst it is so difficult to obtain . . . for the needs of the most needy, is disturbing to those who are not economists. I am by no means sure that it is right for me to improve my income by investing in the shares of a company, making I know not what, operating perhaps thousands of miles away, and in control of which I have no effective voice. (Appendix, *The Idea of a Christian Society*)

He criticised the exhaustion of natural resources by unregulated industries ('exploiting the seas and developing mountains') and warned that 'a good deal of our material progress is a progress for which succeeding generations may have to pay dearly. . . . For a long enough time we have believed in nothing but the values arising in a mechanized, commercialized, urbanized way of life: it would be as well for us to face the permanent conditions upon which God allows us to live upon this planet.'

Eliot had no hope that politicians, deferring to money masters, would listen to his exhortations. He wrote that God commanded him to 'prophesy to the wind, to the wind only for only / The wind will listen.'

So, he accepted the solitude of a man of 'destiny', and for much of his life put love aside as a distraction. Denouncing the chaos of his century, he pointed to a vision that he was not himself to enjoy. His move from America to Europe gave him a peculiar detachment, a universal foreignness. He remained somehow alien to Englishmen and the Anglican Church, to everything with which he identified. He devised an anti-self not, like Yeats, to extend the self, but to guard it: the jokey clubman was a cover for the solitary; the mild gentlemanliness a cover for the extremist; the impersonality a cover for confession; the acquired European tradition a cover for native roots. Eliot cut from the draft of his last play two telling lines on the exile who must exchange

The loneliness of home among foreign strange people
For the loneliness of home which is only memories.

His youth was interred in another land, its shadow moving with the shades behind the grey rocks of the New England shore. Hope Mirrlees perceived something of this when she said: 'He wasn't a bit like an Englishman,' though he could feel 'most violently English', as when he sported his white rose on the anniversary of the death of Richard III. 'I once said to him: "You know there is this indestructible American strain in you." And he was pleased. He said: "Oh yes, there is. I'm glad you realised it. There is."'

In his last years, he stressed his origins. His life sprang from the New World with its flair for spiritual frontiering and its unique demand, in the words of Increase Mather, 'That persons should make a Relation of the work of Gods Spirit upon their hearts'. Eliot set down such a 'Relation' from 'The

Hollow Men' to the confession of the Elder Statesman. His 'deeper failure' was analysed more intimately in a draft where it is recognised that the public man

> . . . who's been successful
> Isn't the real self – or that he has been striving
> All these years, for success, to conceal from himself
> Some deeper failure – or something he's ashamed of.

In the seventeenth century, public confession was compelled by a church which saw itself as the farthest outpost of ecclesiastical holiness. It was quite beyond the requirements of entry into the mild Anglican Church of which Eliot actually had little immediate knowledge at the time of his conversion. It was conversion itself that drew him, for, through that experience he revived the strenuousness of the New England divines for whom it was not enough to profess faith. For Eliot too it was not enough to repeat 'For Thine is the Kingdom'. Those words must pierce the convert, must annihilate his rotten self. Whimpering, he must submit to the terror of an Almighty hand. In New England, each person who would join the exclusive company of visible saints must experience and declare saving grace. Grace, though, must come unsought to a soul wrestling with sin as Eliot wrestled with the devil of the stairs.

Eliot was an expert on election. Like the divines, his forebears, no one knew better the stages and signs of salvation, but he had, himself, limited spiritual gifts. He had diagnostic self-insight, strength of will, endurance, and a readiness to recognise the reality of the unseen, but though he craved a lifetime burning in every moment, he had to accept a lesser course of 'trying'. Yet it was this acceptance of the common lot that made his mature poetry more accessible than the merciless clairvoyance of the early verse. He strove to content himself with right action, and not to hope too hard that grace would come to fill the waiting vessel of perfected conduct. But Eliot's was a God of pain, whose punishment, until the last eight years, was almost the only sign of the absolute paternal care. He certainly knew, after his conversion, moments of bliss; he did, late in life, meet the comforting face of his faith; but most of his life was spent in the shadow of its torments rather than its blessings.

He was simply too clever to be a saint. In his duality as warped saint, Eliot was the epitome of twentieth-century extremism. Yet his struggle to subdue intellectual pride, fury, and hatred proved fertile matter for poetry. There remains the paradox of a man who wished to be saint above poet but who became all the greater as poet for his failure to attain sainthood. He fell back on another goal, to be God's agent. As public spokesman, he achieved an extraordinary authority, his pronouncements echoed as truths from on high. The prophetic role, like the Puritan rigour of introspection, came most directly from America, as well as the challenge of a terrifying nature where man measures himself in the face of an immeasurable power that is and was from the beginning. Intimations of that power came to him from Cape Ann and the Mississippi. Despite his adaptation to England, his adoption of English religion, manners, and clothes, and despite his marriages to English women, his poetry led him back to 'the source of the longest river', and to the silence the child heard between two waves of the sea.

Moments of vision were few – the silence between the waves, the silence in the streets of Boston, the ring of silence in Paris, the rose-garden at Burnt Norton – but they restored the moral dimensions of a world in which visions belonged. Some 'obstruction', it seemed, was 'momentarily whisked away'. Although the vision dictated his course, Eliot chose to concentrate on the doubts and struggles that followed. These were easy to communicate, while the vision was essentially incommunicable. Habitual barriers re-formed very fast.

After moving in intellectual circles he experienced, in his spiritual venture, an exhilarating sense of isolation. When he was awarded the Emerson–Thoreau medal in 1959, he was hailed heir to a line of 'come-outers', New Englanders who spoke out for their private convictions, who braved misunderstanding and welcomed the solitude of original insight.

Eliot set himself to rediscover modes of experience absent from the world into which he was born: religious fear and hope, leading to the perfect life. If he could not live the perfect life himself, if he could not speak directly to his contemporaries, he still hoped his story would tell with generations to come, 'in a world of time beyond me'. He consigned his deeds to oblivion, and spoke to choice souls of the future, 'the posterity of the desert' who would re-enact his lone watch. Denied perfection, he lived to perpetuate its possibility for other lives.

APPENDIX I
ELIOT'S READING IN
MYSTICISM (1908–14)

SOME OF ELIOT'S student notes survive from his years at Harvard, about forty cards in the Houghton Library, recording his reading in philosophy. The majority of the cards show his interest in mysticism and the psychology of religious experience. In the following selected list I have omitted numerous journals of the day and asterisked those books from which he took more than brief notes.

AMES, E. S. *The Psychology of Religious Experience*. Boston, 1910.

BOURIGNON, ANTOINETTE. (She was a Franco-Flemish Quietist, 1616–80. Eliot cites the title as 'Vie'. Possibly this was Von der Linde's edition of *Das Licht der Welt*, 1895, or a biography by MacEwen, 1910.)

BURNET, J. *Early Greek Philosophy*. London, 1908.

CALDECOTT, A. *The Philosophy of Religion in England and America*. London, 1901.

CUTTEN, G. B. *The Psychological Phenomena of Christianity*. London, 1909.

DELACROIX, H. *Essai sur le mysticisme spéculatif en Allemagne au XIVe siècle*. Paris, 1910.

DUMAS. *L'Amour mystique*. Rev. ed., 1906.

INGE, W. R. *Christian Mysticism*. London, 1899.

— *Personal Idealism and Mysticism*. London, 1907.

— *Studies of English Mystics*. London, 1906.

JAMES, WILLIAM. *The Varieties of Religious Experience*.

London, 1902. (Eliot's notes are from the chapter on Mysticism.)

JANET, PIERRE. *Neuroses et idées fixes.* Paris, 1898.

— *Obsessions et psychasthénie.* Paris, 1903.

JEFFRIES, RICHARD. *The Story of My Heart.* 2nd ed. London, 1891.

JEVONS, F. B. *An Introduction to the History of Religion.* London, 1896.

JONES, RUFUS M. *Studies in Mystical Religion.* London, 1909.

LADD, G. T. *The Philosophy of Religion.* 2 vols. New York, 1905.

LEUBA, J. H. 'Les tendances fondamentales des mystiques chrétiens'. *Revue philosophique,* juillet 1902.

MURISIER, E. *Les Maladies du sentiment religieux.* Paris, 1901.

NORDAU, MAX. *Degeneration.* London, 1895. (Eliot notes that this book seeks to undermine mysticism.)

PATRICK, G. T. W. *Heraclitus of Ephesus.* Baltimore, 1889.

POULAIN, A. *Les Grâces d'oraison.* n.d.

PRATT, J. B. *The Psychology of Religious Belief.* New York, 1907.

RAUWENHOFF, L. W. E. *Religious Philosophy.* n.d.

RÉCÉJAC, E. *Essai sur les fondements de la connaissance mystique.* Paris, 1897.

ROUSSELOT, P. *Les Mystiques espagnols.* Paris, 1867.

STARBUCK, E. T. *The Psychology of Religion.* 2nd ed. London, 1901.

SUSO, H. *Life of Henry Suso, by Himself.* Trans. T. F. Knox. London, 1913.

UNDERHILL, EVELYN. *Mysticism.* London, 1911. (Eliot took copious notes.)

WOODS, J. H. *Practice and Science of Religion: A Study of Method in Comparative Religion.* New York, 1906.

— *The Value of Religious Facts.* n.d.

APPENDIX II

DATING THE *WASTE LAND* FRAGMENTS (1914–22)

THE MANUSCRIPT OF *The Waste Land* is a hoard of fragments accumulated slowly over seven and a half years. Only in the seventh year were the fragments transformed into a major work. In order to trace the growth of *The Waste Land* through all the stages of its composition, I first grouped the fragments according to the different batches of paper Eliot used and then established a chronological order by means of a variety of clues, many of which are provided by Valerie Eliot's clear and well-annotated facsimile edition of the manuscript. Further clues were provided by her edition of Eliot's letters, again with invaluable notes.

When Eliot was still at Harvard in 1914 he wrote three visionary fragments on the same (American) Linen Ledger quadruled paper, punched for filing: 'After the turning . . .', 'I am the Resurrection and the Life . . .', and 'So through the evening . . .'. Valerie Eliot dates the handwriting '1914 or even earlier'. These fragments should be read in conjunction with other poems of that time which were not included in the *Waste Land* manuscript but which presage *Waste Land* material: 'The Burnt Dancer', 'The Love Song of Saint Sebastian', 'Oh little voices . . .', and a religious poem of 1911, 'The Little Passion', which Eliot revised in 1914 and copied into his Notebook (all in *Inventions of the March Hare*).

In the autumn of 1914 Eliot went up to Oxford to read philosophy and there, a few months later, he wrote 'The Death of Saint Narcissus'. His first draft has the watermark

'Excelsior Fine British Make', the same paper used for 'Mr. Apollinax'. Both poems must have been written by January 1915, for on 2 February Eliot alluded to them in a letter to Pound ('I understand that Priapism, Narcissism etc are not approved of . . .').

No more fragments were written until some time after Eliot's marriage to Vivienne Haigh-Wood in June 1915, but in January 1916 Eliot wrote to his Harvard friend Conrad Aiken that he had '*lived* through material for a score of long poems in the last six months'.

Between 1916 and 1919 Eliot wrote another batch of fragments introducing new themes – the threatening wife and London. It might be possible to be more specific about the date of 'The Death of the Duchess' by matching the paper with that of non-*Waste Land* manuscripts but, in the absence of other clues, the paper evidence is inconclusive. The paper matches that of an unpublished 1916 review of HD's translation of choruses from *Iphigenia in Aulis*. It also matches a draft of 'Gerontion', which Eliot sent to John Rodker in the summer of 1919. Possible evidence for an earlier date is a 1918 reference by Pound (on a draft of 'Whispers of Immortality') to a Duchess who is outraged by Grishkin's animality. But there is no doubt that the poem was done by 1919: Valerie Eliot has found a letter written to Eliot in 1919 expressing admiration for it and referring also to Mr Bleistein in 'Dirge'.

A phrase from the 'Duchess', 'bound forever on the wheel', links the poem with 'London', whose inhabitants are bound on the wheel. 'London', 'Dirge', 'O City City', 'The river sweats . . .', and 'Elegy' were all written on Hieratica Bond small notepad sheets. The form of 'Elegy' points to Eliot's quatrain period, 1917–19; also the theme of death by water and the name Bleistein appear in other poems of 1918 and 1919. A drowning, similar to Bleistein's, involving the disembodiment and transformation of a Phoenician sailor, appears in 'Dans le Restaurant' (1918), which was later translated with alterations and added to *The Waste Land*. It is impossible, so far, to date the Hieratica cluster exactly, but

1918 seems a reasonable guess. The earliest date would be the spring of 1917 when Eliot began his career as a bank clerk in the City, for 'O City City' and 'London' are associated with that experience.

The turning-point between a hoard of fragments and a unified poem comes about through 'Gerontion', which was written in May–June 1919. Eliot did not include 'Gerontion' in the manuscript, and I shall not discuss it here except to say that Eliot saw 'Gerontion' as a prelude to *The Waste Land* but submitted to Pound's advice to exclude it. Towards the end of 1919 Eliot wrote to his New York benefactor John Quinn and to his mother in Boston that he wished to write a long poem he had had in mind for some time.

We now approach the sequence of *The Waste Land*'s composition during 1921. An unpublished letter of 7 February in the British Library, from Wyndham Lewis to Eliot's mentor of the time, Sydney Schiff, reports that Eliot had shown Lewis a substantial poem in four parts which Lewis thought remarkably promising. This is clear evidence that Eliot had put some sort of poem together by the beginning of 1921. There is no documentary proof, but it seems likely that he did his first drafts of parts I and II in the first half of 1921. Mme Sosostris's wicked pack of cards is a unifying device, an attempt to draw the fragments together with a parade of the poem's characters (including a merchant who would appear eventually in part III and a sailor associated with the phrase 'death by water'). The name of the bogus medium, Mme Sosostris, may seem to challenge a spring date for part I: it comes from 'Sesostris the Sorceress', acted by a Bertrand Russell character, in Aldous Huxley's *Crome Yellow*. Since this novel was published only in November 1921, could Eliot have written part I before then? Even if *Crome Yellow* was circulated in manuscript prior to publication, it was completed only in August. We might suppose that Bertrand Russell disguised as 'Sesostris the Sorceress' was a joke already circulating in his circle, perhaps deriving from an actual charade that took place at Garsington. They were always dressing up and performing.

On 2 May Eliot mentioned to Robert McAlmon and on 9 May to Quinn that he was reading the latter part of *Ulysses* in manuscript. The original opening scene of part I of *The Waste Land* is a Boston version of the visit to Night-town. The name 'Krutzsch' in this scene recalls the recent 'Song'.

There is no doubt that 'Song to the Opherian' (eventually discarded) was written by this time, for it was published in April in the *Tyro* under the pseudonym Gus Krutzsch. Eliot used his Harvard typewriter and British Bond paper for the *Waste Land* copy. Parts I and II of *The Waste Land* use the same typewriter and paper, though the paper of 'Song' is slightly yellower, perhaps a different batch. On 9 May 1921, Eliot wrote to Quinn that he had a 'long poem' in mind and 'partly on paper' which he wished to finish. More significant in this letter is the remark on Vivienne's absence at the seaside. Vivienne and Eliot would have been separated when he wrote part II as the top copy was mailed back and forth. (Vivienne wrote 'wonderful wonderful' next to her husband's graphic description of the tormented couple and 'Send me back this copy and let me have it' on the verso of the second sheet.)

Over the summer of 1921 Eliot saw the Russian Ballet and did a suggestive piece on Stravinsky's *Sacre du printemps (Rite of Spring)* for the *Dial*. It is unlikely that he pressed on with the poem on paper, since his American family was visiting from June to late August. After they left, Eliot saw a leading nerve specialist in September: he was having a breakdown, and was given three months' leave from the bank – providential freedom to complete his poem.

Pound visited London briefly in October. His letter to John Quinn, on approximately 22 October, makes no mention of the first two parts of a major poem, only a comment on Eliot's health. Evidently, Eliot was not yet ready to show Pound what he had.

On 12 October Eliot went to Margate with the old fragments, 'Song', and parts I and II – he must certainly have done these parts by then because in a letter of the time he mentioned as 'III' the part done in Margate. Using a different typewriter – presumably the newer typewriter his brother had left behind for him in late August – and yellowish paper with a 'Verona' watermark, Eliot typed his title-page with the epigraph from *Heart of Darkness*, a short lyric, 'Exequy', and, in duplicate, a long episodic section (III) which combines the old City fragments with further images of degraded Londoners: a Smyrna merchant, the clerk, typist, and the abused Thames daughters. The point is the city's contamination, focusing on degrading sex. Eliot called it 'The Fire Sermon' because he planned to assault these worldly sinners with the Buddha's sermon at the end of a Hieratica fragment, 'The river sweats . . .', to be appended to 'The Fire Sermon' as a finale. Again, Eliot wanted his wife's opinion: she would tell him if what he had done was publishable.

On 12 November Eliot left Margate, spent a week in London with his wife, then passed through Paris on 18 November, when presumably Pound jotted pencilled comments on the Verona sheets and 'Song'. Eliot spent the rest of November and December at a sanatorium in Lausanne, where he wrote two new sections, parts IV and V, a rough draft of 'Venus Anadyomene', and a fair copy of 'Dirge', all on the same quadruled paper. It would appear that Eliot did not take a typewriter to Lausanne. As Helen Gardner pointed out, in Lausanne Eliot does something unusual. He carefully transcribes his fair copies ('Dirge' and part IV) by hand. Further evidence that Eliot did not take his typewriter is that when he stops in Paris on his way home, part IV is typed on a borrowed (unidentified) machine, and part V on Pound's machine (taking out the full stop at the end of his pencil draft).

When Eliot returned to Paris early in January 1922 he showed part II to Pound for the first time – for Pound pencilled '1922' in exasperation next to Eliot's anachronistic reference to a closed carriage. (It is worth noting the pencil since Pound habitually used pencil for a first reading of Eliot's manuscript, and ink for a second reading.) Pound corrected part I only once, whereas he corrected 'The Fire Sermon' on two occasions, 18 November and early January. Eliot must have had British Bond paper with him for, when Pound cut the line '(Those are pearls that were his eyes. Look!)' from Mme Sosostris's prophecy, Eliot – reluctant to let it go – scribbled a late fragment, beginning with the same line, on British Bond.

His last fragment, 'The river's tent is broken' (the opening of part III), was written after Eliot's depressed return to London, replacing the Fresca couplets Pound had criticised. Pound's excisions in January 1922, transforming a manuscript of 800–1000 lines into a poem of 450 lines, are set out in chapter 5.

APPENDIX III

A NOTE ON *THE WASTE LAND* (1922) AND *ULYSSES* (1922)

ULYSSES BY JAMES JOYCE was published in book form in the same year as *The Waste Land* (1922), but it had been coming out in instalments, greatly admired by Eliot and influential for his poem. Eliot published the earlier chapters of *Ulysses* in the *Egoist* in 1919, and in the spring of 1921 read the later chapters in manuscript. It is easy to point to Eliot's specific borrowings, to the parodies of different English styles in imitation of 'Oxen of the Sun', and to Eliot's tamer Boston version of the visit to Night-town, but I don't think that Eliot was profoundly influenced by Joyce.

Eliot's specific borrowings, almost always from the 'Proteus' and 'Hades' episodes of *Ulysses*, reinforce his own sense of horror at the prospect of decay and death. They are essentially embellishments to the poem and came, with one exception, only late in the history of *The Waste Land*'s composition. From 'Proteus' came the dog vulturing the dead in Part I of *The Waste Land*. Like Joyce in 'Hades' Eliot aligns the living with the dead. Flesh interfuses with dead matter in the suburban gardens of Eliot's London as in Joyce's Dublin graveyard, and the decomposition of miserable people becomes part of everyday consciousness. Eliot adapts Bloom's thoughts as he walks about the graveyard ('How many! All these here once walked round Dublin') to the Dantean 'so many, / I had not thought death had undone so many'. Bloom thinks of a corpse planted rather than buried, and of the gardener digging the weeds which represent the body's sole form of revival. 'That corpse you planted,' Eliot's observer asks one of the mechanical workers sarcastically, 'has it begun to sprout?'

The funeral procession in 'Hades' passes the canal with the gas-works. Joyce's words 'rattle his bones', referring to the body in the coffin, are picked up by Eliot in 'The Fire Sermon':

> But at my back in a cold blast I hear
> The rattle of bones, and chuckle spread from ear to ear.

In the drowning of Phlebas the Phoenician in part IV, the sea current which 'picked his bones in whispers' is a new addition from Joyce's graveyard where the obese rat nibbles corpses: 'One of those chaps would make short work of a fellow,' Bloom observes. 'Pick the bones clean no matter who it was.' In a similar drowning scene in the manuscript fragment 'Dirge', Eliot like Stephen Dedalus resists having to share humanity with the dehumanised drowned object. 'Five fathom out there,' Stephen muses. 'Full fathom five thy father lies. . . . Bag of corpsegas sopping in foul brine. . . . God becomes man becomes fish becomes barnacle.' Eliot's corpse becomes a sea-object, in time indistinguishable from the life of the sea.

The rejection of history in part V of *The Waste Land* may be aligned with Stephen Dedalus's distaste for history as a tale too often heard or a nightmare from which one tries to awake. 'I hear the ruin of all space,' thinks Stephen, 'shattered glass and toppling masonry, and time one livid final flame.' The difference is that when Eliot contemplates the ruins of time, he conceives of an alternative timeless realm which he later calls the 'other Kingdom'.

Eliot imitates the kind of polluted, rat-ridden, decomposing modern city he found in Joyce's Dublin. But whereas for Eliot this means hell and nothing else, Joyce's imaginative exuberance allowed for multiple responses. In *The Art of T. S. Eliot*, Helen Gardner deftly summed up the differences between Eliot and Joyce, and the publication of the manuscript bears out her view that *The Waste Land* moves in the opposite direction to *Ulysses*. The earliest source material for *The*

Waste Land shows Eliot consistently leaning towards an escape from the sordid reality of daily life through 'aetherial rumours'. When Eliot discussed *Ulysses* with Virginia Woolf in 1922, he said that there was no 'great conception' and that Joyce's stream of consciousness often did not tell as much as some casual glance from the outside.

Vivienne Eliot met Joyce several times in December 1921 (at the time Eliot was completing *The Waste Land* in Lausanne, she was in Paris at 59 rue des Saints-Pères). She found Joyce 'a most unsympathetic personality. Vain!! egoist! Unseeing.'

APPENDIX IV

THE 'BELLEGARDE' SKETCH AND *MURDER IN THE CATHEDRAL* (1934–5)

IN THE HOUGHTON Library, Harvard, there are eighteen pages of pencil notes for *Murder in the Cathedral*. Eliot's brother, Henry, rearranged the order of Eliot's notes when he made a typed copy that would dovetail with the final text of the play. Fortunately, he kept a record of the page numbers in the original order, so that it is possible to reconstruct the sequence of ideas for the play and, significantly, the poems that Eliot associated with it, as the play evolved in his mind between December 1934 and May 1935.

Page 1: The manuscript of 'Rannoch by Glencoe' (published in Oct. 1935), which was clipped together with the following three pages of outline. The manuscript of 'Rannoch' shows very little change: the poem seems to have come remarkably whole. Eliot used one line about the starved crow in the final text of *Murder*.

Pages 2–3: Eliot jotted an outline sequence of scenes. Its brevity is unlike Eliot's more detailed scenarios for his other plays. Initially, there was to be less of the Chorus; there were two other characters, Herbert of Bosham and John; and, most interesting, no Tempters as yet.

Page 4: Outline of time scheme for each scene. On the back of page 4 Eliot jotted five names of contemporary writers, numbered one to four. These, I think, provided the germ of the four Tempters: Wells, Russell, Lawrence, and (conjoined) Huxley and Babbitt.

The 'Bellegarde' Fragment: One page of pencil manuscript is on the same paper as the other seventeen pages of the

Murder manuscript but, Henry Eliot notes, it was received separately about two months later. It contains six lines which were a revised extract from a separate typescript which Eliot called 'Bellegarde'. Henry Eliot included the two typescript pages of the original 'Bellegarde' fragment with the *Murder* manuscript. Though not aesthetically significant, the 'Bellegarde' fragment may be the earliest germ of *Burnt Norton* and, therefore, of *Four Quartets* (in the sense that the 1914 fragment 'So through the evening' might be said to be the germ of *The Waste Land*). If so, 'Bellegarde' is important not only as a link between two major works but as a suggestive autobiographic statement, with its Jamesian sense of lost love (Christopher Newman losing the daughter of the Bellegardes in James's *The American*), and the lover's own sense of impotence when the moment of love fades: a strange quick switch from leaping delight to loss. Over-analysis reads into delight the thin, illicit snatching at the pleasures of imaginative self-aggrandisement.

Pages 6–8: A tryout of some lines for the Chorus beginning 'Seven years and the summer is over'. It seems that as soon as he put pencil to paper, the Chorus came easily.

Pages 9–10: The words of the second [Tempter]. The word 'Tempter' does not itself appear. These men are still represented solely by their numbers.

Page 11: Plan for the fourth [Tempter]. The complete idea is here.

Page 12: Eliot then worked on the scene between Becket and the Knights, leading to murder. He started with the climactic moment of the scene: Becket's last defiant and submissive words.

Pages 13–14: Chorus, reacting to murder with its sense of a land defiled.

Page 15: Eliot tried out here the voices of the Knights as yet unnamed: taunting voices, tipsy voices, chanting in quatrains, just before Becket's climactic defiance.

Page 16: The defences of what are called, at first, Chairmen (not Knights). Eliot practises the tone of the voice, the style of talk, in the case of the first Chairman, a bland, disarming after-dinner style. Shocking mischief, he says easily. This is the verbal guise of the decent chap. I think he got this easy-going tone through the Chairman before creating his medieval parallel, the First Tempter.

The second Chairman assumes the style of reason. His audience is assumed to be prejudiced in the Archbishop's favour. The insidious appeal is to fair-mindedness: put yourselves in our place.

The third was to be young, tipsy, noisy. His self-defence is that murder was unpleasant, and he got nothing out of it.

The fourth is subtle, as befits the Fourth Tempter. 'Who killed the Archbishop?' he will ask.

Page 17: Becket's declaration that the Law of God is above the Law of man. Here Eliot grasped the essential polarities of the play. This came to him, logically, after the Chairmen's defence of the temporal order.

Page 18: Eliot planned a coda of adoration of God, thanksgiving for the blood of martyrs which creates holy places, and acknowledgement of responsibility for all the evil in the world. This was to be followed by the Chorus's prayer for mercy.

This manuscript outline shows that Eliot went straight into the words of the play. He was thinking, from the outset, in the rhythm of the play's poetic line.

APPENDIX V

THE HISTORY OF *THE FAMILY REUNION* (1934–9)

THERE ARE AT least ten discernible layers of composition following Eliot's first reference to a new play, along the same lines as *Sweeney Agonistes*, in a letter to director Hallie Flanagan in February 1934. The layers suggest that the play was brewing in the mid- rather than late thirties, and that Eliot struggled with it much more than *Murder in the Cathedral*, where he got quickly into the vein of the verse, and which seems to have needed only a sketchy scenario. In the case of *The Family Reunion*, Eliot types draft after draft. The smooth look of the typescripts can be deceptive: there are many telling changes. Eliot submitted drafts to five people for comment: E. Martin Browne, Ashley Dukes, Emily Hale, John Hayward, and Frank Morley.

1. Typescript scenario (Houghton). There are no names for the characters. The Furies are to be one man and two women in evening dress. The play ends when the hero decides to seek his purgation.
2. Unfinished draft (King's) with no names. Here Eliot first works out the scene between Harry and Mary.
3. Additional scenario, with names (Houghton). One type-script page on Part I, and two fascinating pages of rough but detailed pencil notes for Part II. The central idea is the process of de-possession. When Harry goes to pack, the ending trails off in uncertainty.
4. Three pages of pencil notes for a scene between Mary and Downing near the end of the play (Houghton).

These notes were filed with the manuscript of *Murder in the Cathedral*, and are on the same paper as Eliot's preliminary pencil notes for that play. It is probable that these first four stages of composition are much earlier than has been supposed, between February 1934 and the time that Eliot wrote *Murder* (winter–spring 1935).

5. After a gap of about eighteen months, Eliot began to give full attention to the play on his return from New England late in 1936. There is a typescript draft of Part I, dated 1937, with notes by Hayward. (Houghton: called 'Typescript A').

6. A complete typescript draft was given to Emily Hale (who presented it to the Houghton Library in 1960: 'Typescript B'). He considered as titles 'Follow the Furies' or 'Fear in the Way'. Here Agatha speaks of Harry's possible sanctification.

7. Complete typescript draft, with notes by Hayward, and dated 1937–8 (Houghton's 'Typescript C'). In this draft, Eliot struggles with Harry's speech about his divided self (II. ii, *Plays*, p. 102) that went back to early notes (see 3). He changes all the verbs from present to past tense, possibly to distance Harry's emotions of contamination and dissociation. It was probably to this draft that Eliot refers in three letters to Pound of 19 Dec. 1937, 17 Feb. 1938, and 21 Feb. 1938. In the first of these he says that the play is three-quarters written, and will be finished by Easter. At this point he declines to say more about it, glossing his family motto (*tace aut face*) as 'say nothing and saw wood'. By February he was prepared to say that he thought *The Family Reunion* a lot better than *Murder in the Cathedral*, and in the last of these letters announces that he has finished and will let the draft rest a while.

Typescripts A, B, and C seem very similar, which suggests how patiently Eliot retyped and revised the play.

8. Hayward's draft (King's), dated 28 September 1938, is called the 'first' draft. It is really a fairly late draft.

9. The Working Draft, dated 1938 (Houghton). This draft

is the same as 8, but with comments by Emily Hale, Martin Browne, and Frank Morley. Two marginal suggestions from Emily Hale led to two major changes.

First, she suggested that Mary's rebellious outburst came at the wrong point in the play, too late. Eliot shifted the speech to the second scene of the play. Since the speech was, in its original form, more insistent, the effect of the shift would have been to give to Mary's fate an importance which Eliot clearly did not wish to develop. He cut down her speech, making her tamer, less vocal, more polite: a woman who would submit to the waiting-and-watching role. Martin Browne and Morley had also urged Eliot in vain that Mary should be developed, or that the relation to Harry should have more substance. Following Browne's criticism, Eliot made a memo to himself to get Mary to arrange flowers, which, Morley was quick to point out, was far too feeble a gesture, but Eliot kept it. Emily Hale's more tactful pressure, later in 1938, led Eliot in effect to play her down rather than up.

Emily Hale's other major suggestion (endorsed by Martin Browne) was that Harry's mission be brought to a stronger climax. She wrote on the script: 'chance for Harry's explanation of Furies as he *now* sees them and to strengthen scene between Amy and himself.' The result was an additional dialogue in II. ii. beginning with Amy's question, 'But why are you going?' and ending with Harry's announcement of his 'election' to 'follow the bright angels'.

The Houghton Library has a sequestered correspondence between Eliot and Emily Hale about the play.

10. Finally, there is the play published at the same time as its first performance in March 1939.

ABBREVIATIONS

* Editions used in text. In the footnotes and source notes, when both English and American publishers of a book are cited, the first cited is the one used in this book.

ASG	*After Strange Gods: A Primer of Modern Heresy.* The Page-Barbour Lectures at the University of Virginia, 1933. London: Faber, 1934; New York: Harcourt Brace, 1934*.
AW	*Ash-Wednesday,* 1930 (see *Collected Poems*).
Beinecke	Beinecke Library, Yale University.
Berg	The Berg Collection, New York Public Library.
BN	*Burnt Norton,* 1935 (see *Collected Poems*).
CC	*To Criticize the Critic and Other Writings.* London: Faber, 1965; New York: Farrar, Straus, 1965, repr. Noonday-Farrar, 1968*.
CFQ	Helen Gardner, *The Composition of Four Quartets.* London: Faber, 1978.
CP	*The Collected Poems of T. S. Eliot 1909–1962.* London: Faber, 1963; New York: Harcourt Brace, 1963*.
CPy	*The Cocktail Party,* 1949 (see *Plays*).
DS	*The Dry Salvages,* 1941 (see *Collected Poems*).
EC	*East Coker,* 1940 (see *Collected Poems*).
EH	Emily Hale.
EMB	E. Martin Browne.
EMB	E. Martin Browne, *The Making of T. S. Eliot's*

554

Plays. Cambridge University Press, 1969; revised 1970.

ES   *The Elder Statesman*, 1958 (see *Plays*).

facs. WL *The Waste Land: A Facsimile and Transcript of the Original Drafts Including the Annotations of Ezra Pound*, ed. Valerie Eliot. London: Faber, 1971; New York: Harcourt Brace, 1971*.

FQ   *Four Quartets*, 1943 (see *Collected Poems*).

FR   *The Family Reunion*, 1939 (see *Plays*).

HM   'The Hollow Men', 1925 (see *Collected Poems*).

Houghton The Houghton Library, Harvard University.

ICS   *The Idea of a Christian Society*. London: Faber, 1939; New York: Harcourt Brace, 1940, repr. in *Christianity and Culture*, Harvest-Harcourt, 1960*.

IMH   *Inventions of the March Hare: Poems 1909–1917*, ed. Christopher Ricks. London: Faber, 1996*; New York: Harcourt, 1996. For over thirty years following Eliot's death, his Notebook and folder of miscellaneous manuscripts in the Berg Collection, New York Public Library, remained unpublished. Eliot dated many of these poems. In 1971–2, I, dated the undated poems (including fragments of the *Waste Land* manuscript), and reconstructed a chronology of composition essential to the story told, originally, in *Eliot's Early Years* (1977). What was paraphrased there, may now be quoted.

JH   John Hayward.

KE   *Knowledge and Experience in the Philosophy of F. H. Bradley*. London: Faber, 1964*; New York: Farrar, Straus, 1964.

King's   King's College Library, Cambridge University.

L   *The Letters of TSE*, i, ed. Valerie Eliot. London: Faber; New York: Harcourt Brace, 1988.*

LG   *Little Gidding*, 1942 (see *Collected Poems*).

MC   *Murder in the Cathedral*, 1935 (see *Plays*).

MT   Mary Trevelyan.

NDC   *Notes Towards the Definition of Culture*. London: Faber, 1948; New York: Harcourt Brace, 1949, repr. in *Christianity and Culture**.

NEW   *New English Weekly*.

NY   New York.

OPP   *On Poetry and Poets*. London: Faber, 1959; New York: Farrar, Straus, 1957, repr. Noonday-Farrar, 1969*.

Plays   T. S. Eliot, *Collected Plays*. London: Faber, 1962*; New York: Harcourt Brace, 1962.

PRS   Mary Trevelyan, 'The Pope of Russell Square'. Unpublished memoir of a twenty-year friendship with Eliot.

SE   *Selected Essays*. London: Faber, 1932; New York: Harcourt Brace, 1932, repr. 1960*.

SW   *The Sacred Wood: Essays on Poetry and Criticism*. London: Methuen, 1920; New York: Alfred A. Knopf, 1920. Repr. London: Methuen University Paperbacks, 1967*.

TLS   *Times Literary Supplement*.

Texas   T. S. Eliot Collection, The Humanities Research Center, Austin, Texas.

TSE   T. S. Eliot.

UPUC   *The Use of Poetry and the Use of Criticism: Studies in the Relation of Criticism to Poetry in England*. Charles Eliot Norton Lectures for 1932–3 at Harvard University. London: Faber, 1933; Cambridge, Mass.: Harvard University Press, 1933, repr. New York: Barnes & Noble, 1970*.

VMP   *The Varieties of Metaphysical Poetry: The Clark Lectures at Trinity College, Cambridge, 1926 and the Turnbull Lectures at The Johns Hopkins University, 1933*, ed. and intr. Ronald Schuchard. London: Faber*; New York: Harcourt Brace, 1993.

VW   Virginia Woolf.

WL   *The Waste Land*, 1922 (see *Collected Poems*).

NOTES

Chapter 1 Early Models

1 *Virginia Woolf.* (19 Sept. 1920). *The Diary of VW*, ii, ed. Anne Olivier Bell and Andrew McNeillie (London: Hogarth, 1978), p. 67.

1 *'this self'.* Lord Claverton in *ES.* Act II, *Plays*, p. 317.

1 *no biography.* Letter to Alfred Kreymborg (30 May 1925). Alderman Library, Univ. of Virginia at Charlottesville.

1 *'the sequence that culminates in faith'.* 'The *Pensées* of Pascal', *SE*, p. 360.

2 *spiritual autobiography.* Eliot to William Force Stead (9 Aug. 1930). Osborn Collection, Beinecke Library, Yale.

2 *'poet who . . .'; 'all the particularity'.* 'Yeats'. The first Yeats lecture at the Abbey Theatre in Dublin, repr. *OPP*, p. 299.

2 *Anthony Julius.* T. S. Eliot, *Anti-Semitism, and Literary Form* (CUP, 1995). Anti-Semitism, he argues, is 'an inseparable part of his greater literary undertaking' (p. 29).

3 *'things ill done . . .'.* LG:II in *FQ*. Discussed in detail in ch. 10.

3 *Notebook and MS poems. Inventions of the March Hare: Poems 1909–1917*, ed. Christopher Ricks (London: Faber; NY: Harcourt Brace, 1996).

3 *'Eternity's disclosure'. The Complete Poems of Emily*

Dickinson, ed. Thomas H. Johnson (London: Faber, 1970), no. 306: 'The Soul's Superior instants', p. 144.

3 *'There is nothing else . . .'*. 'Silence', *IMH*, p. 18.

4 *bluff*. A bold enquiry from Forster blew TSE's cover. See 'Forster, Eliot, and the Literary Life', *Twentieth-Century Literature*, xxxi (Summer/Fall 1985), E. M. Forster issue.

4 *'transfusion . . .'*. 'Ben Jonson', *SW*, p. 118.

5 *'never the bundle . . .'*. 'A General Introduction for my Work', *Selected Criticism*, ed. A. Norman Jeffares (London: Macmillan, 1964), p. 255.

5 *'the Saint of the West*. R. L. Rusk, *The Letters of Ralph Waldo Emerson*, iv (New York, 1939), pp. 338–9.

5 *'. . . in its sources . . .'*. *Paris Review* interview with Donald Hall, repr. *Writers at Work*, ed. Van Wyck Brooks, 2nd series (NY: Viking, 1963).

5 *'Eliots, non-Eliots . . .'*. TSE in conversation with MT (2 Apr. 1951), reported in her unpublished memoir, 'The Pope of Russell Square, 1938–58'. Owned by her nephew, Humphrey Carpenter and niece, Kate Trevelyan.

5 *'. . . the most one could possibly achieve'*. Ibid. (16 Nov. 1942).

5 *never 'whacked'; 'spoilt'; parents like 'ancestors'*. Ibid. (Apr. 1950).

5 *Henry Ware Eliot, Sr. and his daughters' handkerchiefs*. Valerie Eliot's note, *L*, i, 3.

6 *Henry's autobiography*. Sixty-page typescript, Olin Library, Washington Univ., St Louis. I should like to thank the Archives Supervisor, Beryl H. Manne, for her prompt help.

6 *faces on boiled eggs*. Frank Morley, 'A Few Recollections of Eliot', *Sewanee Review*'s T. S. Eliot memorial issue (1965), repr. *T. S. Eliot: The Man and His Work*, ed. Allen Tate (NY: Dell, 1966), pp. 90–113.

6 *'mournful'*. TSE in conversation with MT (Apr. 1950), PRS.

6 *'little Tailor'*. TSE to Charlotte Eliot (3 Oct. 1917), *L*, i. 198–9.

6 *'to make the best . . .'*. Charlotte Champe Eliot,

William Greenleaf Eliot (Boston: Houghton Mifflin, 1904), p. 336.

6 *'I am very well satisfied . . .'.* Address, Washington University (1953), repr. 'American Literature and the American Language', *CC*, p. 45.

6 *'the river is within us . . .'. DS, CP*, p. 191.

6 *steamboats.* 'From a Distinguished Former St. Louisian' (part of a letter from Eliot to M. C. Childs), *St Louis Post-Dispatch* (5 Oct. 1930).

6 *dates of floods*: Eric Sigg, 'Eliot as a product of America', *The Cambridge Companion to T. S. Eliot*, ed. A. David Moody (CUP, 1994), p. 23.

6 *'with its cargo . . .'. DS, CP*, p. 195.

6 *Annie Dunne and existence of God.* TSE, 'Why Mr. Russell is a Christian', *Criterion*, vi (Aug. 1927), 179.

6 *'I liked it . . .'.* Cited by Janet Adam Smith, 'Tom Possum and the Roberts Family', *Southern Review* (Oct. 1985), 1060, repr. *TSE: Essays from the Southern Review.*

7 *photograph.* All photographs mentioned in this chapter, mostly by Eliot's brother, Henry Ware Eliot, Jr, are in the Eliot Collection, Houghton Library, Harvard Univ.

7 *Jim Jum Bears.* The manuscript (n.d.) is in Special Collections, Butler Library, Columbia Univ.

7 *boys laughed.* TSE in conversation with MT (26 Dec. 1952), PRS.

7 *girl whispered.* Ibid. (12 Apr. 1956).

7 *'I walked . . .'.* Ibid. (6 Aug. 1953).

7 *location of the Eliot house; ragtime era.* Eric Sigg, 16–17.

7 *WL and jazz.* Ronald Bush, 'T. S. Eliot' in *American Writers: A Collection of Literary Biographies (Retrospective Supplement I)*, ed. A. Walton Litz and Molly Weigel (NY: Scribners, 1998), pp. 51–67.

8 *to ensure he did not get too wet.* H. W. H. Powel, Jr, 'Notes on the Life of T. S. Eliot 1888–1910' (MA thesis, Brown Univ., 1954), p. 28.

8 *accepted mother's domination.* St Louis letter from 'Margery' to Mary von Schrader and Randall Jarrell (n.d.). Berg.

8 'I hope . . .'. To TSE (3 Apr. 1910), *L*, i, 13.

9 'though the heavens fell'. Obituaries. Eliot Coll., Houghton.

10 'desert waste'. 'The Three Kings', Scrapbook. Houghton.

10 'the dying year'. 'Charade of the Seasons'. Houghton.

10 'April . . .'. WL: I.

11 like Lot in Sodom . . . . TSE to Pound (19 Dec. 1934), Beinecke.

11 'The Infuence of Landscape upon the Poet'. *Daedalus*, 89 (Spring 1960), 421–2.

11 *Cape Ann.* Robert Giroux, 'A Personal Memoir', in Allen Tate (ed.) *T. S. Eliot*, pp. 337–44.

12 *Gloucester.* Preface to James B. Connolly's *Fishermen of the Banks* (London: Faber, 1928). Eliot had Faber reprint this book, one of his favourites as a child, originally called *Out of Gloucester* (1902).

12 'Remember . . .'. Ibid., p. 267.

12 'Gentlemen and Seamen'. *Harvard Advocate*, 87 (25 May, 1909), 115–16.

13 great-grandfather. Sigg, 32.

13 algae. TSE to Pound (22 Oct. [1936?]). Beinecke.

13 'not so simple . . .' UPUC, pp. 78–9.

13 'faring forward'. FQ: 'Fare forward, voyagers'. Discussed in ch. 10.

13 'I was brought up . . .'. CC, pp. 43–60.

14 'How can one be familiar . . .'. Quoted by Herbert Howarth, *Notes on Some Figures behind T. S. Eliot* (London: Chatto & Windus, 1965), pp. 1–2.

14 self-denial. William Turner Levy and Victor Scherle, *Affectionately, T. S. Eliot* (London: Dent; NY: Lippincott, 1968), pp. 53–4.

15 grandfather's opposition to slavery. Sigg, pp. 24–5.

15 'a sumptuous church . . .'. Rusk, op. cit.

15 'All history . . .'. Ralph Waldo Emerson's essay, 'Self-Reliance'.

15 strong missionary hand. Letter to Middleton Murry (6 Nov. 1931). Berg.

15 *Tudor Eliots.* Pearl Hogrefe, *The Life and Times of Sir Thomas Elyot, Englishman* (Iowa State Univ. Press, 1967).

15 *Andrew Eliott.* See *EC, CP,* pp. 182–3 for TSE's recreation of the ancestral voyage. For facts, I am indebted to Eric Sigg, 'T. S. Eliot and the New England Family' (1992), pp. 3–4. TS lent to me by Ronald Bush. It contains fascinating detail of the Eliots' interrelations with numerous American writers. Sigg cites Walter Graeme Eliot, *A Sketch of the Eliot Family* (NY: Livingstone Middleditch, 1887), pp. 19–20. The Dickinson connection is from Jay Leyda, *The Years and Hours of Emily Dickinson* (New Haven: Yale, 1960), i, xliv, 304, 310; ii, 368.

17 *Andrew Eliot's temper.* Ephraim Eliot, *Historical Notices of the New North Religious Society in the Town of Boston, with Anecdotes of the Reverend Andrew and John Eliot* (Boston: Phelps and Farnham, 1822).

17 *'The primary channel of culture . . .'.* NCD, p. 115.

17 *'The Arts insist . . .'.* SW, p. 32.

18 *indifferent to the Church.* Eliot's cousin Frederick May Eliot told this to Powel: 'Notes on the Life of T. S. Eliot', p. 25.

18 *grandfather's rejection of miraculous conversions.* Sigg, *Cambridge Companion to TSE,* p. 15.

18 *'done' and 'not done'.* Levy and Scherle, op. cit., p. 121.

18 *'so far as we are human . . .'.* SE, p. 380.

19 *'Force and God'.* Published in *The Unitarian* (Aug. 1887).

19 *'outside the Christian fold'.* Letter to Bertrand Russell (22 June 1927). Russell Archive, McMaster Univ. See also review of Middleton Murry's *Son of Woman: The Story of D. H. Lawrence, Criterion,* x (July 1931), 771.

19 *belief in the Incarnation.* Introduction to *Revelation,* ed. John Baille and Hugh Martin (London, 1937).

19 *perfection.* Letter to Murry (6 Nov. 1931), Berg.

19 *William Greenleaf Eliot on Milton. Discourses on the*

Doctrines of Christianity (Boston: American Unitarian Association, 1881), p. 97. Cited by Sigg, *Cambridge Companion to TSE*, p. 15.

19 *Unitarians and the Jews*. TSE's telling letter to J. V. Healy (10 May 1940), Texas, is quoted substantially in Christopher Ricks, *T. S. Eliot and Prejudice* (London: Faber, 1988), p. 44.

20 '*intellectual and puritanical rationalism*'. A Sermon Preached in Magdalene Chapel (Cambridge, England, 1948), p. 5.

20 '*in a chilling void . . .*'. H. B. Parkes, 'The Puritan Heresy', in *The Pragmatic Test: Essays on the History of Ideas*, ed. Henry Bamford (San Francisco: Colt, 1941).

20 '*Nothing quieted doubt . . .*'. *The Education of Henry Adams* (Cambridge, Mass.: Riverside, 1961), p. 34.

21 '*onward and upward forever*'. 'The Relationship between Politics and Metaphysics', a talk to Harvard's Philosophical Society, quoted by John Soldo in *The Tempering of T. S. Eliot* (Ann Arbor, Mich.: UMI Research Press, 1983).

21 '*The great cities . . .*'. 'Democratic Vistas', repr. *Leaves of Grass and Selected Prose*, ed. John Kouwenhoven (NY: Modern Library, 1950), pp. 467–9.

21 *monotony*. ASG, p. 16.

21 '*a family extension*'. Letter to Herbert Read (1928), quoted in Allen Tate (ed.), *T. S. Eliot*, p. 15.

22 '*What a debt . . .*'. 'The Method of Nature' (1841). I am indebted to Faith Williams for pointing this out in her dissertation, 'Young Emerson as a Religious Writer' (Columbia University, 1973), p. 9.

Chapter 2 A New England Student

23 '*Silence*'. IMH, p. 18.
23 *unable to put into words. Listener* (19 Dec. 1946), 895.
23 '*You may call it . . .*'. SE, p. 358.
24 '*glad to the brink of fear*'. 'Nature', *Ralph Waldo*

Emerson: Selected Prose and Poetry, ed. Reginald L. Cook (NY: Holt, Rinehart, 1950, repr. 1964).

24 'old Boston'. Henry James, *The American Scene* (1907; repr. ed. Leon Edel, Indiana Univ. Press, 1968), p. 232.

24 'I regret'. *Selected Writings*, ed. Jacques Barzun (NY: Minerva Press, 1968), pp. 135–7.

25 'a nervous . . .'. Richard Hofstadter, *Anti-Intellectualism in American Life* (1962; repr. NY: Vintage, 1966), p. 191.

25 'I loathe mankind'. Henry Adams, *Letters*, ii, ed. W. C. Ford (London, 1930), p. 466.

25 'serious poetry'. 'The Genteel Tradition in American Philosophy', *Selected Critical Writings of George Santayana*, ii, ed. Norman Henfrey (CUP, 1968), pp. 95–6.

25 *Back Bay*. Henry James, *The American Scene*, p. 246.

26 'I yearn . . .'. Adams, *Letters*, ii, 466.

26 *related*. See Eric Sigg, 'T. S. Eliot and the New England Literary Family', op. cit. See also Eric Sigg, 'Eliot as a product of America', in *The Cambridge Companion to T. S. Eliot*, op. cit., pp. 14–30.

26 *caricatured Bostonians*. These poems were written in Oxford in 1915. CP, pp. 20–2.

26 'quite uncivilized'. 'Henry James: The Hawthorne Aspect', *Little Review* (Aug. 1918), repr. in *The Shock of Recognition*, ed. Edmund Wilson (repr. NY: Random House, 1955; London: W. H. Allen, 1956), p. 860.

27 'we looked through each other . . .'. Adams, *Letters*, ii, 414.

27 'the contemplation of the horrid . . .'. 'Dante', SW, p. 169. This was the first of three essays on Dante.

27 'the modern metropolis'. 'What Dante Means to Me', CC, p. 126.

28 *probation; 'loafed'*. Valerie Eliot, 'Biographical Commentary 1888–1922', L, i. xix.

28 'icicle'. Linda Simon, *Genuine Reality: A Life of William James* (NY: Harcourt Brace, 1998), pp. 89, 136.

29 *society a faculty meeting. The Education of Henry Adams* (Cambridge, Mass.: Riverside, 1961, p. 307).

29 '*My pupil Eliot . . .*'. Part of this letter (May 1914) is published in *Memoirs of Lady Ottoline Morrell*, ed. Robert Gathorne-Hardy (NY: Knopf, 1964; London: Faber, 1963), p. 255.

29 *room-mate*. H. W. H. Powel, Jr, 'Notes on the Life of T. S. Eliot 1888–1910' (MA thesis, Brown Univ., 1954) p. 61.

29 *Eliot at Harvard*. These memories above and below, are from Conrad Aiken, 'King Bolo and Others', in *T. S. Eliot: A Symposium*, ed. Tambimuttu and Richard March, (London: Editions Poetry, 1948), p. 20. (Hereafter called 60th birthday coll.)

30 *exercised*. TS by Leon Magaw Little, Houghton, and letter to Mrs 'Polly' Tandy (4 Sept. 1935), Tandy Papers, British Library.

30 *read Yeats. Paris Review* interview, repr. *Writers at Work*, ed. Van Wyck Brooks, 2nd series (NY: Viking, 1963).

30 '*this is up your street*'. Valerie Eliot, *L*, i, xx.

31 '*not a man's work*'. *Harvard Advocate*, 89, no. 5.

31 *Copeland*. Eliot's relationship with Copeland is described by J. Donald Adams, *Copey of Harvard* (Boston: Houghton Mifflin, 1960), pp 153–4, 159–64.

31 *pragmatism*. A holograph address on Politics and Metaphysics (1914) read before Harvard's Philosophical Society. Houghton.

31 '*never shocked*'. Cited by Simon, p. 166.

31 *highest good*. Eliot's philosophy notes. Houghton.

32 *had not liked Santayana*. TSE to MT (28 Sept. 1952), PRS.

32 *TSE on Santayana's philosophy*. TSE to Sydney Schiff (4 Aug. 1920), *L*, i. 395.

32 Three Philosophical Poets. Published 1910. Noted by Ronald Schuchard, *VMP*, pp. 2–3. The other two poets were Lucretius and Goethe.

32 *'the most comprehensive...'*. Cited by Schuchard, *VMP*. *SW*, p. 168.

32 *'before we can have...'*. Theodore Spencer, 'Miscellaneous Journal Entries' (29 Mar. 1929). Harvard Archives HUG 4806.35, with thanks to Mrs Bender.

32 *'a Catholicism of despair'*. 'The Humanism of Irving Babbitt', *SE*, p. 426.

33 *'very often right quite alone'*. *TLS* (29 Dec. 1927), 981–2.

33 *title.* later cancelled.

33 *'Towards any profound conviction...'*. BBC talk (1932). Eliot gave a series of weekly talks in March and April entitled 'The Modern Dilemma'.

34 *'The First Debate'*. *IMH*, pp. 64–5.

34 *'loose the spirit...'*. Charlotte Champe Eliot, 'Not in the Flesh, But the Spirit', Scrapbook. Eliot Coll., Houghton.

35 *first poems in* Advocate. Two 'Songs' and 'Before Morning', *Poems Written in Early Youth* (London: Faber, 1967), pp. 10, 18, 19.

35 *woman's wreath.* 'Song', first published in the *Advocate* (24 May 1907).

35 *'ghost of youth'*. *IMH*, p 17.

35 *'– I have seen...'*. 'Prufrock's Pervigilium', *IMH*, p. 44.

36 *Circe.* 'Circe's Palace', *Poems Written in Early Youth*, p. 22.

36 *Fiedler. Love and Death in the American Novel* (1960; repr. NY: Dell, 1967, London: Secker, 1961), p. 292.

36 *pale white woman.* 'Song', *Poems Written in Early Youth*, p. 22.

36 *girls staring.* Eliot recalled this scene in an address to the Mary Institute in St Louis in 1959. Published in *From Mary to You* (St Louis, 1959), p. 135.

37 *'Beyond the circle...'*. *Poems Written in Early Youth*, p. 21.

37 *Aiken recalled.* 60th birthday coll., pp. 21–2, and *Ushant* (Boston: Little, Brown, 1952), pp. 173–4.

38 *Tristan.* 'Opera'. *IMH*, p. 17.

38 *'Conversation Galante'*. CP, p. 25.
38 *'Nocturne'*. *Poems Written in Early Youth*, p. 23.
39 *'emasculate our children'*. Autograph letter to Thomas Lamb Eliot (7 Mar. 1914). Reed College Archives, Portland, Oreg. Quoted by John Soldo, *The Tempering of T. S. Eliot*.
39 *TSE on sex*. SE, p. 380.
40 *Laforgue's short life*. Details from David Arkell's excellent informal biography, *Looking for Laforgue* (Manchester: Carcanet, 1979), reviewed in the *London Review of Books* (24 Jan. 1980), 25.
42 *'I puzzled . . .'*. TSE to Robert Nichols (8 Aug. 1917), *L*, i, 191.
42 *'personal enlightenment'*. Turnbull Lectures (1933), VMP, p. 287.
42 *'a feeling of profound kinship'*; *'unshakeable confidence'*; *'personal intimacies'*: 'Reflections on Contemporary Poetry [IV]', *Egoist* (July 1919), quoted in *IMH*, pp. 399–400. See Helen Vendler's review of *IMH*, *LRB* (31 Oct. 1996), 8–9.
42 *'always himself'*. 'Modern Tendencies in Poetry', *Shama'a* (April 1920). I am grateful to A. Walton Litz for finding this rare article and passing on a copy when we team-taught Eliot one Michaelmas term at Oxford.
42 *Laforgue 'was the first . . .'*. 'What Dante Means to Me' (1950), CC, p. 126.
43 *'Souffrir . . .'*. 'Pour le livre d'amour'.
43 *something cooler*. Francis Scarfe, 'Eliot and Nineteenth-Century French Poetry', in *Eliot in Perspective*, ed. Graham Martin (London: Macmillan, 1970), pp. 45–62.
44 *'fort correctes . . .'*. Quoted by Arthur Symons, *The Symbolist Movement in Literature* (1899; repr. NY: Dutton, 1958), p. 56.
44 *'urbane dandysme'*. Herbert Howarth, *Notes on Some Figures behind T. S. Eliot* (London: Chatto & Windus, 1965), p. 105.
44 *'Manners . . .'*. Aiken, in *Life* (15 Jan. 1965), 92.
44 *'First born . . .'*. IMH, p. 35.

44 'And Life ...'. *Poems Written in Early Youth*, p. 26.

45 *1912 Ziegfeld Follies*. Sigg, *Cambridge Companion to TSE*, p. 19.

45 *'something of the actor'*. Aiken, in *Life* (15 Jan. 1965), 92.

45 *first batch of poems*. 'Conversation Galante', 'Nocturne', and 'Humoresque'.

46 *'not one older poet...'; 'status of poetry'*. 'The Last Twenty-Five Years of English Poetry' (1940), draft lecture for a cancelled British Council tour in Italy (Hayward Bequest), cited *IMH*, pp. 388–9.

46 *'Our people ...'*. Adams, *Letters*, ii, 313.

47 *'I suppose ...'*. *L*, i, 13.

47 *manliness at Harvard*. Kim Townsend, *Manhood at Harvard: William James and Others* (NY: Norton, 1996), especially pp. 15, 22, 28.

47 *Commencement that year*. The graduation ceremony and the Orator's speech are described in the *Boston Evening Transcript* (24 June 1910).

48 *'Essence ...'*. Subtitle to the 'Goldfish' sequence of four poems, and a line in the third, *IMH*, pp. 26–30.

48 *'Mandarins'*. *IMH*, pp. 19–22.

48 *'very sure'*. Following last line of section 1, and deleted.

49 *metaphysical*. *Listener* (19 Dec. 1946), 895.

49 *'And thou, Silence ...'*. Quoted by Symons, p. 58.

Chapter 3 Beyond Philosophy

51 *'La France ...'*. *La France libre*, viii, no. 44 (15 June 1944), 94–9.

51 *'scrape along'*. *Paris Review* interview with Donald Hall, repr. in *Writers at Work*, ed. Van Wyck Brooks, 2nd series (NY: Viking, 1963), pp. 91–110.

51 *'exquisite refinement'*. Valerie Eliot cites this (*L*, i, 25) from *The Quest of Alain-Fournier* (1953) by Robert Gibson, p. 159. The factual details of TSE's encounter with Dostoevsky come from Mrs Eliot.

51 *TSE on Dostoevsky's treatment of humiliation. Egoist* (Sept. 1918), 106.

52 *Verdenal on TSE's 'nonchalance', etc.* Verdenal's letters to TSE are given in full *L*, i, 20–36.

53 *'nervous sexual attacks'*. TSE to Aiken (31 Dec. 1914), *L*, i, 75.

53 *'when I was living there...'*. Conversation (2 May 1921), recorded by Robert McAlmon, *Being Geniuses Together 1920–30*, ed. Kay Boyle (NY: Doubleday, 1968), pp. 8–9.

54 *'No! I am not...'*. TSE to John C. Pope (8 Mar. 1946) about the latter's article 'Prufrock and Raskolnikov', *American Literature*, xvii, no. 3 (Nov. 1945), 213–30. Beinecke. TSE mentions that this passage showed the influence of Laforgue. This letter was printed in *American Literature*, xviii (Jan. 1947), 319–20.

54 *excised. IMH*, p. 31 and App. A. Since this is on the verso of bits of 'Portrait of a Lady' it is possible, though far from certain, he wrote this in Paris.

54 *the world 'imagined...'*. *The Wings of the Dove* (1902; repr. London: Bodley Head, 1969), p. 115.

55 *Bergson lectures*. Eliot's notes from the Bergson lectures are in the Eliot Coll., Houghton.

55 *Bergson 'most noticed'*. Syllabus for TSE's 1916 course on Modern French Literature, Lecture VI, cited in *IMH*, p. 409.

55 *'the mondaines'*. 'The French Intelligence' in 'Imperfect Critics', *SW*, pp. 45–6. Cited *IMH*, p. 410.

55 *temporary conversion. A Sermon Preached in Magdalene Chapel* (1948).

55 *Discard intellectual supports*. Henri Bergson, *An Introduction to Metaphysics* (1903), trans. T. E. Hulme (1912; repr. NY: Liberal Arts Press, 1955), pp. 49–50.

56 *hard to please*. Holograph poem, 'Fourth Caprice in Montparnasse' (dated Dec. 1910).

56 *'curl upward' and 'ring of silence'. IMH*, p. 68.

57 *'wind that breathed...'*. First draft.

57 *'He said: this universe...'*. *IMH*, p. 71.

57 *slumming*. See holograph poem, 'Interlude: in a Bar' (dated Feb. 1911).

58 *streets at night*. See 'Rhapsody on a Windy Night', *CP*, pp. 16–18.

58 *'I perceive . . .'*. Bergson, *An Introduction to Metaphysics*, p. 25.

59 *'What would we really know . . .'*. 'The American Scholar', *Ralph Waldo Emerson: Selected Prose and Poetry* ed. Reginald L. Cook (NY: Holt, Rinehart, 1950, repr. 1964), p. 65.

60 *hidden attunement of universe*. BN: II, *CP*, p. 177: 'The dance along the artery / The circulation of the lymph / Are figured in the drift of stars.' See Thoreau's *Walden*.

61 *fragment*. The second part of 'He said: this universe is very clever . . .', an untitled, two-part, holograph fragment on the verso of the debate of the constellations (dated Mar. 1911). *IMH*, p. 71.

61 *'Entretien . . .'*. dated February 1911. *IMH*, pp. 48–9.

61 *Eliot in London, 1911*. recounted by TSE to MT (2 Apr. 1951) and recorded in PRS.

61 *'Interlude in London'*. Holograph poem (dated Apr. 1911), *IMH*, p. 16. TSE uses the same phrase about hibernating in a letter to Eleanor Hinkley (26 Apr. [1911]), *L*, i, 18.

61 *excursion to Cricklewood*. details and conversation, *L*, i, 18.

62 *TSE's Baedeker*. 1908 edition. See p. 124. Hayward Bequest, King's College, Cambridge.

62 *vision*. 'Dante', *SW*, p. 170.

63 *had to return to Harvard*. Conrad Aiken, *Ushant* (Boston: Little, Brown, 1952), pp. 157, 186–7.

63 *new poems*. Third 'Prelude' and 'Prufrock's Pervigilium'.

64 *horrible vision of life*. See 'Cyril Tourneur', *SE*, p. 166, and discussion of hatred of life below, ch. 8, p. 288.

64 *'disorder . . .'*. 'Pascal', *SE*, p. 368.

64 *'Do I know . . .'*. *IMH*, p. 80.

65 *'brain'; 'something . . .'*. Ibid.

65 *'that superstition . . .'*. 'Faith', Scrapbook. Houghton.

65 *'The truth . . .'.* 'Giordano Bruno in Prison' (1890), Scrapbook.

66 *Prufrock in part . . . .* Interview, *Grantite Review*, xxiv, no. 3 (1962), 16–20.

66 *'Crapy Cornelia'.* Grover Smith notes the link with Prufrock in *T. S. Eliot's Poetry and Plays* (Univ. of Chicago Press – Phoenix, 1956), p. 15.

67 *'so much less violent . . .'. Vanity Fair* (USA) (Feb. 1924).

67 *Prufrock's confession.* 'Prufrock's Pervigilium', *IMH*, pp. 43–44.

68 *'To live . . .'.* Bergson, *An Introduction to Metaphysics*, pp. 25–6.

68 *exploit own weakness.* Eliot, 'London Letter', *Dial*, lxxiii (Sept. 1922), 331.

68 *spring 1914.* Eliot confirmed Aiken's date (1914) – spring 1914, he said – in a letter to John C. Pope (8 Mar. 1946), *American Literature*, xviii (Jan. 1947), 319–20.

68 *ravings of madman.* See reviews of the *Catholic Anthology* (1915).

69 *'Oh little voices . . .'. IMH*, pp. 75–6.

70 *upheaval.* VW, *Diary* ii (20 Sept. 1920), p. 68.

70 *'the nightly panic . . .'. FR*, I, ii, *Plays*, p. 80.

71 *Eliot on Realists.* See Eliot's introduction to Josef Pieper, *Leisure: The Basis of Culture* (1952; repr. NY: Mentor-Omega, 1963; London: Collins, 1965), p. 12, and 'Views and Reviews', *NEW* (June 1935), 151–2.

71 *'anything to do with reality'.* Quoted by Brand Blanchard, 'Eliot in Memory', *Yale Review* (Summer 1965), 637–40.

71 *Bradley on need for religious point of view.* Eliot, review of *Ethical Studies*, TLS (29 Dec. 1927), 981–2, repr. 'Francis Herbert Bradley', *SE*.

71 *'sweetness and light . . .'.* 'Commentary', *Criterion*, iii (Oct. 1924), 2.

71 *'agony of spiritual life'. Vanity Fair* (USA) (Feb. 1924), 29, 98.

72 'we justify . . .'. F. H. Bradley, *Appearance and Reality*, repr. intrn. by Richard Wollheim (OUP, 1969), p. 486.

72 'whether the universe . . .'. Ibid., p. 487.

72 commonly observed objects. 'Interlude: in a Bar', *IMH*, p. 51.

72 'nature of reality'; 'no province . . .'. *Appearance and Reality*, p. 431.

72 'appearances exist'. Ibid., p. 114.

72 'infection'. Ibid., p. 217.

72 'As an object . . .'. Ibid., p. 408.

72 'My mind . . .'. *KE*, p. 145. (Eliot's dissertation was eventually published under the title *Knowledge and Experience in the Philosophy of F. H. Bradley*.)

72 'palpable community'. *Appearance and Reality*, p. 229.

73 'it would not follow . . .'. Ibid., p. 228.

73 'my experience . . .'. Ibid., p. 229.

73 'What is subjective . . .'; 'All significant truths . . .'. *KE*, pp. 24, 165.

74 'lived' experience 'mad and strange'. *KE*, p. 143.

74 'half-object'. *KE*, pp. 147, 148, 162, 163, 164. I am indebted to A. Walton Litz for drawing attention to Eliot's 'half-objects', a term not found in Bradley.

74 *Eliot's Harvard classes*. Harry Todd Costello, *Josiah Royce's Seminar 1913–1914*, ed. Grover Smith (New Brunswick, NJ: Rutgers Univ. Press, 1963), pp. 121, 138, 173–5.

74 half-object; 'Any object . . .'. *KE*, pp. 110, 148. Eliot rejected personality in his essay 'Tradition and the Individual Talent' (1919).

75 'we are led'. *KE*, p. 31.

75 'diverge'. *KE*, p. 143.

75 'essentially vague . . .'. *KE*, p. 144.

75 fell apart. *KE*, pp. 143, 163.

75 'lived with shadows'. *KE*, p. 55.

75 'figments'. *KE*, pp. 147, 120.

75 'agony'; 'crazed by fear'. *KE*, pp. 31, 53–4.

76 'His philosophy . . .'. *Vanity Fair*(USA) (Feb. 1924).

76 sophisticated. 60th birthday coll., p. 20.

76 *dancing and skating lessons.* Receipts are in the Eliot Coll., Houghton.

76 *'pulled . . .'.* TSE to Pound (2 Feb. 1915), *L*, i, 86.

77 *regretted.* TSE to Pound (2 Feb. 1915), *L*, i, 86.

77 *'Ending in . . .'.* Lewis to Pound (before July 1915), noted *IMH*, App. A, p. 305.

77 *address.* Holograph, 'The Relationship between Politics and Metaphysics', written in 1913 or shortly after (it discusses Walter Lippman's *A Preface to Politics*, 1913). Eliot Coll., Houghton.

78 *'Stunt Show'.* The programme is in Houghton.

79 *like another son to Edward Everett Hale.* EH to Ricardo Quinones (2 Aug. 1965), who reported it in a letter to the present author (29 Sept. 1986).

80 *portrait of EH.* I am indebted to C. E. Dexter Morse for a photograph.

80 *dark brown hair* . . . Her looks were recalled by Marie McSpadden Sands (Scripps College '31), who became close to EH in 1932–3 when she designed sets for EH's productions. Letter to the present author (8 Sept. 1986).

80 *EH acting* A Backward Glance. T. S. Matthews, *Great Tom* (NY: Harper & Row, 1973), p. 146.

81 *'La Figlia che Piange'.* CP, p. 26. JH dated the poem 1911 (Helen Gardner, *The Art of T. S. Eliot* (London: Cresset, 1949), p. 107), but TSE, whose memory was excellent, dated it 1912 in a letter to Evdo Mason (21 Feb. 1936). Texas.

81 *'Hidden . . .'.* IMH, p. 82. This fragment is added to 'Do I know how I feel? Do I know what I think . . .'.

82 *Minny 'pure and eloquent vision'.* See Leon Edel, *Henry James: The Untried Years 1843–1870* (London: Rupert Hart-Davis, 1953), pp. 330, 332, 335.

82 *'I remember . . .'. facs.* WL, p. [12].

82 *'in any degree whatever'.* Valerie Eliot, 'Introduction', *L*, i, xvii.

83 *'Saint Sebastian'.* L, i, 46–7. Enclosed in letter to Conrad Aiken (25 July 1914), from Marburg, Germany.

84 *irrelevance of Emily Hale.* In retrospect, Eliot said that in a

youthful experience of love 'we do not so much see the person as infer the existence of some outside object which sets in motion these new and delightful feelings in which we are absorbed.' *UPUC*, p. 34.

85 *Eliot's objection to department.* Eliot's introduction to Josef Pieper's *Leisure*. Also, *NEW* (6 June 1935), 151–2.

85 Upanishads *by Phansikar.* This book from TSE's library is now part of the Hayward Collection, King's.

85 *different beliefs.* TSE, *George Herbert. Writers and Their Work*: no. 152 (British Council, 1962), p. 24.

85 *memorised Dante.* Eliot told this to Kristian Smidt, *Poetry and Belief in the Work of T. S. Eliot* (London: Routledge, 1961), p. 11. The date 1911 comes from a note by Valerie Eliot in her edition of the *Letters*.

85 *Dante's influence. Adelphi*, xxvii, no. 2 (1951), 106–14.

86 *Royce.* Josiah Royce, *The Problem of Christianity* (repr. Univ. of Chicago Press, 1968), p. 215.

86 *paper on 9 Dec. 1913. Josiah Royce's Seminar*, pp. 76, 78.

86 *paper on 16 Dec.* Ibid., pp. 83, 85.

87 *paper on 24 Feb.* Ibid., p. 119.

87 *'One tortured meditation . . .'. facs. WL*, p. [112].

88 *'The Burnt Dancer'. IMH*, p. 62.

88 *'a lifetime's death . . .'. DS*: V.

89 *'Priests . . .'.* From 'Pro Peccatis suae Gentis' (published in the *Christian Register*).

89 *study of saints and mystics.* Holograph index cards, 'Notes on Philosophy'. Houghton. See Appendix I.

89 *'If we would cease . . .'.* Evelyn Underhill, *Mysticism* (1911; repr. London: Methuen, 1945), p. 271. The quotation is from the chapter on 'Voices and Visions'.

89 *'to construct . . .'. AW*: I, *CP*, p. 85.

90 *'there's nothing homosexual . . .'. L*, i, 44.

91 *'I am one . . .'.* Letter to Paul Elmer More. Special Collections, Princeton.

91 *Hulme.* 'The Complete Works of T. E. Hulme' (about five poems) were printed as an appendage to *Ripostes of Ezra Pound* (London: Stephen Swift, 1912), p. 64.

Grover Smith points out the connection between 'Conversion' and 'The Death of Saint Narcissus' in *T. S. Eliot's Poetry and Plays*, p. 34.

92 *warning*. Holograph index cards and *Mysticism*, pp. 279–81.

93 *'strained'*. Letter to Aiken, quoted in 60th birthday coll., p. 23.

93 *Dimmesdale. The Scarlet Letter*, Centenary Edition of the Works of Nathaniel Hawthorne, vol. i (Ohio State Univ. Press, 1962), pp. 142–5. See also 'The Minister's Virgil', pp. 147–58.

94 *'exceptional awareness . . .'*. Unpublished lecture on Henry James at Harvard (Spring 1933), quoted by F. H. Matthiessen, *The Achievement of T. S. Eliot*, 3rd ed. (NY: OUP, 1958), p. 9.

Chapter 4 Eliot's Ordeals

95 *'type'*. Kim Townsend, *Manhood at Harvard* (NY: Norton, 1996), p. 12.

95 *Sheldon travelling fellowship*. There is a letter, dated Feb. 1914, from C. R. Lanman about the possibility of a travelling fellowship. Houghton.

96 *matrons in British Museum*. 'Afternoon', *IMH*, p. 53.

96 *shopgirl*. 'In the Department Store', *IMH*, p. 56.

96 *old woman*. Letter to Henry Ware Eliot, Jr (8 Sept. 1914), *L*, i, p. 55.

96 *'disengaged'*. Brand Blanchard, 'Eliot in Memory', *Yale Review* (Summer 1965), 637–40.

96 *the Heretic society*. TSE to Eleanor Hinkley (21 Mar. [1915]), *L*, i, 92.

96 *Karl Culpin*. Eliot, letter to the Secretary of the Merton Society (24 June 1963). Merton College Library, Oxford.

97 *'mystical experience'*. E. R. Dodds, *Missing Persons: An Autobiography* (OUP, 1977), p. 40.

97 *'O Conversation . . .'*. 60th birthday coll., pp. 22–3.

98 *'funny stuff'*. Ezra Pound, *Paris Review* interview (1962), repr. in *Writers at Work*, ed. Van Wyck Brooks, 2nd series (NY: Viking, 1963), p. 47.

98 *'extant milieu'*. Ibid., p 48.

98 *best poem*. Ezra Pound, *Selected Letters 1907–1941*, ed. D. D. Paige (1950; repr. NY: New Directions, 1971), p. 40.

98 *'worth watching'*. Ibid., pp. 40–1.

98 *Pound argued*. From the apologia TSE asked Pound to write to Henry Ware Eliot, Sr (postmarked 28 June 1915) stating the reasons for TSE's staying on in London. *L*, i, pp. 99–104.

99 *'He would cajole . . .'*. Introduction, *Literary Essays of Ezra Pound*, ed. T. S. Eliot (NY: New Directions, 1968; London: Faber, 1954), p. xii.

99 *'almost impersonally'*. 'Ezra Pound', *NEW* (31 Oct. and 1 Nov. 1946), 27–8, 37–9, repr. *Ezra Pound: A Collection of Critical Essays*, ed. Walter Sutton (Englewood Cliffs, NJ: Prentice-Hall, 1963), pp. 18–19.

99 *feelings and productivity*. Letter (20 June 1922). Quinn Collection, Manuscript Division, New York Public Library.

99 *American posture*. Wyndham Lewis, 'Early London Environment', 60th birthday coll., pp. 24–32.

100 *'dolts'; 'greasy vulgus'; 'born to the purple'*. Statements in March 1913 and 16 Feb. 1914, cited by Humphrey Carpenter, *A Serious Character: The Life of Ezra Pound* (Boston: Houghton Mifflin; London: Faber, 1988), p. 199.

100 *monopolisation; Evil Influence*. TSE to Pound (15 Apr. 1915), *L*, i, 96.

101 *Pound old-fashioned. Paris Review* interview, repr. in *Writers at Work*, p. 95.

101 *'Suppressed Complex'*. *L*, i, 87–9. *IMH*, p. 54, notes on title p. 208.

101 *'intellectual and emotional complex'*. 'A Retrospect' (1913), the leading essay selected by TSE for his edition of *Literary Essays of Ezra Pound*, p. 4.

101 *'unique success'*. Pound, *Selected Letters*, p. 40.

101 *Pound borrowed money*. Pound to Quinn (11 Apr. 1917). Quinn Coll.

102 *'an ass'*. Pound to Wyndham Lewis (July 1916), *Selected Letters*, p. 86.

102 *discipleship*. TSE to Quinn (Oct. 1923). Quinn Coll.

102 *'blood poison'; 'thin milk'*. Pound to William Carlos Williams (1920), *Selected Letters*, p. 158.

102 *'morbid . . .'*. Graham Martin drew attention to this comment from 'Four Meetings', in his Introduction to *Eliot in Perspective* (London: Macmillan, 1970), p. 22.

102 *'claim our property'*. Letter to Perry, quoted by Leon Edel, *Henry James: The Untried Years 1843–1870* (London: Rupert Hart-Davis, 1953), p. 264.

102 *caricatured himself as a Burbank more at ease with literature than life*. Ronald Bush, 'T. S. Eliot 1888–1965', in *American Writers: A Collection of Literary Biographies: Retrospective Supplement I*, ed. A. Walton Litz and Molly Weigel (NY: Scribners, 1998), p. 52.

102 *'born in Boston'* Henry James to William James from Venice (25 Sept. 1869), *The Correspondence of William James*, ed. Ignas K. Skrupskelis and Elizabeth M. Berkeley (Charlottesville: Univ. Press of Virginia, 1992), i, 92.

102 *'Henry James: In Memory'*. *Little Review* (Aug. 1918), repr. in *The Shock of Recognition*, ed. Edmund Wilson (repr NY: Random House, 1955), p. 855.

102 *identical conclusion*. Letters to Grace Norton (9 Aug. 1877) and to his father (11 Oct. 1879), *The Letters of Henry James*, ii, ed. Leon Edel, pp. 134–5, 258. Eliot, of course, would not have known of these letters in 1918 – it's extraordinary clairvoyance on his part.

103 *influence discussed in the* Egoist. Quoted by Ronald Bush, op. cit.

103 *'Christianity . . .'*. Pound to H. L. Mencken (1916), *Selected Letters*, pp. 97–8.

103 *'I consider . . .'.* Pound to Harriet Monroe (1922), ibid., p. 183.

104 *'Organized religions . . .'.* Editorial, *Little Review* (May 1917).

104 *fairy-lore and superstition.* Pound to Quinn (15 Nov. 1918). Quinn Coll.

104 *'diagnosis is wrong'.* Review of *ASG, NEW* (1934).

104 *'new and diverting verses'.* Pound to Quinn (Apr. 1918), *Selected Letters*, p. 134.

104 *'suspicious' and 'cowardly'.* TSE to Mary Hutchinson ([11? July 1919]), *L*, i, 318.

104 *Anthony Julius. T. S. Eliot, Anti-Semitism and Literary Form* (CUP, 1995), p. 35.

104 *most brilliant at prejudice.* See Christopher Ricks, *T. S. Eliot and Prejudice* (London: Faber, 1988), and Anthony Julius, pp. 28, 33: anti-Semitism in Eliot is 'creative'; it shows 'rare imaginative power', 'empowering his art'.

104 *'Money in furs'; 'Semite'; 'slime'.* 'Burbank with a Baedeker: Bleistein with a Cigar', *CP*, pp. 32–3.

104 *beaver hats.* Eric Sigg, *Cambridge Companion to TSE*, p. 23.

105 *prostitute.* 'Sweeney Erect' (1919), *CP*, pp. 34–5.

105 *'shit'; 'kuk'; 'a-pissin'.* TSE to Pound (31 Oct. 1917), *L*, i, 206.

105 *'Sweeney Among the Nightingales'.* *CP*, pp. 49–50.

106 *attack on Katherine Mansfield as 'Scheherazade'.* TSE to Pound (13 Aug. 1935) (Pound Papers, Beinecke), recalling the compound libel on Katherine Mansfield and another of Eliot's acquaintances, Brigid Patmore, an Irish literary hostess of the time, married to a grandson of Coventry Patmore and presumably a source for the rather nebulous Mrs Howexden, with her passion for experience, in the fiction. By 1935, Eliot regards 'Eeldrop' as juvenilia and out of date. 'Eeldrop and Appleplex', *Little Review* (May 1917), 7–11.

106 *'dangerous* WOMAN*'.* TSE to Pound (3 July 1920), *L*, i, 389.

106 *TSE, K. Mansfield, and Lady R.* TSE to Pound (7 Nov. 1922), *L*, i, 592.

107 *'deal'.* TSE to Richard Aldington. Information from Valerie Eliot, cited by Claire Tomalin, *Katherine Mansfield: A Secret Life*, (Viking, 1987), pp. 240–1.

107 *published review.* In the *Criterion.* Discussed by Julius, 167–71.

107 *Trilling's review of TSE's* Kipling. Ricks, pp. 25–8.

107 *'Shitwell'.* TSE to Pound (31 Oct. 1917), *L*, i, 206.

108 *'I struggle . . .'.* (31 Oct. 1917), *L*, i, 204.

109 *French cigarettes.* TSE's corrections of William Force Stead's unpublished reminiscences (29 Apr. 1940). Osborn Coll., Beinecke.

109 *'Philosophy . . .'.* Review, *International Journal of Ethics*, xxvii (July 1917), 543.

109 *'anarchic'; 'certain saints . . .'.* Review, ibid., xxvii (Oct. 1916), 112.

110 *Lévy-Bruhl.* Review, ibid., 115–17.

110 *Fred Eliot 'an ass'.* TSE in conversation with MT (26 Jan. 1948), PRS.

110 *'prodigies of wickedness'.* Election sermon (1765). Eliot Coll., Houghton.

111 *blasphemy. SE*, p. 373, and *ASG*, p. 56.

111 *Hulme's theory.* See Ronald Schuchard, 'Eliot and Hulme in 1916', *PMLA* (Oct. 1973), 1083–94.

111 *'neighbourhoods of silence'.* 'Eeldrop and Appleplex', op. cit.

112 *'doubt is inevitable'. Granite Review*, xxiv, no. 3 (1962), 19.

112 *life poor without religion.* Review, *Int. J. Ethics*, xxvii (July 1917), 542.

112 *'silence from the sacred wood'.* 'Ode' (dated July 1918), published in *Ara Vos Prec* (1920).

112 *'merry'.* Byron, *Don Juan* IV.v. l. 7: 'But the fact is I have nothing planned,/Unless it were to be a moment merry'.

112 *'practical side.'* TSE to Aiken (30 Sept. 1914), *L*, i, 59.

112 *'How much more self-conscious . . .'.* TSE to Aiken (31

Dec. 1914), *L*, i, 75. See quotation from same letter above, ch. 3.

113 *'For the boy . . .'. Int. J. Ethics*, xxvii (Oct. 1916), 127.

114 *poetry and prose sketches.* Vivienne lists '12 unbound poems by V.H.E.' in a 1934 inventory of her possesions. These are not among her manuscripts in the Bodleian Library, Oxford. Eliot published the best of her sketches and one poem, pseudonymously, in the *Criterion.*

114 *relationship of TSE and Vivienne.* Impressions based on Vivienne's diaries and manuscripts in the Bodleian Library, Oxford. I am also indebted to comments by Sir Herbert Read, Conrad Aiken, Aldous Huxley, and Bertrand Russell. (See Allen Tate's collection; Huxley's *Letters*; Russell's *Autobiography*, ii; and *Life* magazine, 15 Jan. 1965.)

114 *Powell's* Journals *1982–1992.* 3 vols (London: Heinemann, 1995–8).

115 *EH's family connections.* Letter from Caroline Willington (n.d.). Scripps College Archives.

115 *high-flown notion.* This notion was presented to Scripps students during a talk on Eliot in Dec. 1932 and repeated in the college newspaper.

115 *Harvard academics.* 'Mr. Apollinax'.

115 *ex-President Eliot's advice.* (25 July 1919), *L*, i, 322–3.

115 *'amusing'. L*, i, 97.

116 *'That Shakespearian Rag'.* Music by David Stamper. Words by Gene Buck and Herman Ruby. Published by Stern & Co., 102 West 38th Street, New York City. I'm grateful to A. Walton Litz for bringing a photocopy of this discovery to me. Until the late 1980s, we thought it was made up by TSE.

116 *'quite different'.* TSE to Eleanor Hinkley (24 Apr. [1915]), *L*, i, 97.

116 *not the custom to associate with women students.* See autobiography of the philosopher Sir Alfred Ayer, about Oxford in the twenties. *More of My Life* (London, 1984).

117 *'No one in London'.* Pound to Henry Ware Eliot, Sr

(28 June 1915), *L*, i, 102. I'm assuming that Pound put forward the same arguments to TSE as to his father at this time.

117 *'It seems just possible . . .'*. 'A Note on War Poetry', *CP*, p. 215.

118 *'I can't tell you'*. TSE in conversation with MT (Apr. 1950), PRS.

118 *obscure letter*. TSE to Doris ('Polly') Tandy (9 Sept. 1946). Tandy Papers, British Library.

119 *still in love with EH*. Valerie Eliot, Introduction, *L*, i, xvii.

119 *less 'suppressed'*. *L*, i, 104.

119 *Paolo and Francesca*. 'Dante' (1920), *SW*, pp. 165–6, and *Dante* (1929), *SE*, pp. 207–8.

120 *'At least we exist'*. *SE*, p. 380.

120 *'There are always some choices'*. *Milton Graduates Bulletin* (1933), p. 8.

120 *Russell on Vivienne and TSE*. Letter to Ottoline Morrell (July 1915), *The Autobiography of Bertrand Russell* (Boston: Little, Brown, 1967–9; London: Allen & Unwin), ii, 61.

120 *'the mind deserts the body . . .'*. 'La Figlia che Piange'.

121 *sexual beast*. See 'Circe's Palace' (1908) and 'Portrait of a Lady': III (1910–1).

121 *the affair of Vivienne Eliot and Russell*. Ray Monk, *Bertrand Russell: The Spirit of Solitude* (London: Cape, 1996), ch. 15 ('Mrs E') and pp. 469–516.

123 *TSE's letter to Russell*. *L*, i, pp. 115–6.

123 *'She has been ready . . .'*. *L*, i, 110.

124 *clean-cut mouth etc.* Diary (26 Dec. 1935).

124 *'very attractive'*. Wyndham Lewis, 60th birthday coll., pp. 24–32, and *Blasting and Bombardiering* (London: Eyre & Spottiswoode, 1937), p. 284.

124 *sexual problems*. Bernard Bergonzi comments on the sense of erotic failure in Eliot's early poetry in *T. S. Eliot* (NY: Collier, 1972), p. 22.

124 *bridegroom*. 'Ode'.

124 *'female stench'*. facs. *WL*, p. [22].

124 *'Now dance...'*. 'Thé dansant', *Criterion*, iii (Oct. 1924), 78.

124 *'most awful nightmare'*. TSE to Henry Ware Eliot, Jr (6 Sept. 1916), *facs. WL*, p. xi, and *L*, i, 151.

125 *'Vivien says...'*. *L*, i. 127.

126 *'any permanent entanglement'*. Russell to Ottoline Morrell (20 Aug. 1916). See Ray Monk, 470, 475, 482, 483.

126 *proof of the affair between Vivienne and Russell*. Robert H. Bell, 'Bertrand Russell and the Eliots', *American Scholar* (Summer 1983); discussed in more detail in Ray Monk, op. cit.

128 *'Fresca!...'*. *facs. WL*, p. [26].

128 *'admiring...'*. Katherine Mansfield to Violet Schiff (May 1920), British Library, quoted by Claire Tomalin, *Katherine Mansfield: A Secret Life* (Viking, 1987), p. 197.

129 *hyacinth*. Vivienne Eliot, 'Letters of the Moment – I', *Criterion*, 2 (Feb. 1924), 220–2.

129 *prematurely old*. VW, *Diary*, i (10 Apr. 1919), p. 262.

129 *heroic struggle*. TSE to Quinn (12 Mar. 1923). Quinn Coll.

129 *Vivienne's childhood operations*. TSE told Osbert Sitwell, who records this in his memoirs, cited in John Pearson, *Façades: Edith, Osbert and Sacheverell Sitwell*, (London: Macmillan, 1978), p. 238.

129 *Vivienne offered to live alone*. Pound to Quinn (4–5 July 1922). Quinn Coll.

129 *'nervous' collapses*. Vivienne Eliot, Diary (3 Oct. 1934). Bodleian Library.

130 *started to take drugs innocently*. Statement by Theresa Garrett Eliot (28 Mar. 1970). Eliot Coll., Houghton.

130 *Russell considered*. Letter to Robert Sencourt (28 May 1968). Bertrand Russell Archive, McMaster University, Hamilton, Ont.

130 *ether*. Footnote by Grover Smith, *The Letters of Aldous Huxley* (London: Chatto & Windus, 1969), p. 232.

130 *Haigh-Woods in 'very straitened circumstances'*. (23 July 1915), *L*, i, 110.

130 *'I think . . .'*. (8 Aug. 1917), *L*, i, 192.

130 *starvation; 'I opened . . .'; 'Tom knows . . .'; 'shove'; need for clothes, etc.* Vivienne to Henry Eliot (11 Oct. [1916], *L*, i, 154–6.

132 *rules of New England thrift.* Recited to me by David Hartwell, science fiction editor at Simon & Schuster, when we were graduate students at Columbia University in the late 1960s.

133 *Veneering.* The Veneerings (in Dickens's *Our Mutual Friend*) are nouveau-riche social climbers.

133 *cage.* 'Letters of the Moment – I'.

133 *'terrible'.* 'The Death of the Duchess', *facs. WL*, p. [104]. The title of a later version was 'In the Cage'.

133 *posterity.* Sir Herbert Read, Allen Tate's coll., p. 23.

133 *sick at night.* Diary (1 Sept. 1934).

133 *'black silent moods'.* Vivienne to Charlotte Eliot (8 Apr. [1917]), *L*, i, 173.

133 *'full of nerves'.* Vivienne to Mary Hutchinson ([16 July 1919]), *L*, i, 320.

134 *'life is so feverish'.* Vivienne to Henry Eliot (22 Oct. 1918), *L*, i, 245.

134 *'Vivien's assistance'.* TSE to Henry Eliot (2 July 1919), *L*, i, 311.

135 *'I had never seen . . .'. L*, i, 334.

135 *Dostoevsky novel; 'have seen other strange things'.* TSE to Eleanor Hinkley (23 July 1917), *L*, i, 189.

136 *reckless touch of madness.* I owe this phrase to Robert McCallion, whose letter (29 Mar. 1998) arrived opportunely as I revised this paragraph.

136 *'off our heads'.* Vivienne to Henry Eliot (21 Nov. 1918), *L*, i, 259.

136 *'knife edge'.* Russell to Ottoline Morrell (Nov. 1915), *Autobiography*, ii, 64.

136 *Russell's strange observations.* Ibid., ii, 7.

136 *'In the winter . . .'. Kangeroo* (1923; repr. NY: Viking, 1970), p. 220.

136 *'army of workers'. The Years* (NY: Harcourt; London: Hogarth Press, 1937), pp. 300, 340–1.

137 *Pound opposed TSE's enlistment.* Pound to Quinn (10 Aug. 1918). Quinn Coll.

137 *one of his poems.* 'Gerontion', *CP*, pp. 29–31.

138 *'in a little noisy corner....'.* Vivienne to Charlotte Eliot (28 June 1917), *L*, i, 186.

138 *'all I wanted to do...'.* *Milton Graduates Bulletin* (1933).

138 *'To hold...'.* William Turner Levy and Victor Scherle, *Affectionately, T. S. Eliot* (NY: Lippincott, 1968), p. 26.

139 *bend.* Charlotte Eliot, Poem. Eliot Coll., Houghton.

139 *'like putting Pegasus into harness'.* Charlotte Eliot, letter to Russell (18 Jan. 1916). Bertrand Russell Archive, McMaster Univ.

139 *'Europeanized American.* Aldous Huxley to Julian Huxley (29 Dec. 1916), *Letters*, p. 117.

139 *'bewildered'.* Recalled by TSE in conversation with M (22 Dec. 1953), PRS.

139 *'rather ill...'.* Lytton Strachey to Carrington (May 1919), Michael Holroyd, *Lytton Strachey: A Biography* (Baltimore: Penguin, 1971), p. 364.

140 *'Jack tied...'.* Quoted by David Bradshaw, 'Those Extraordinary Parakeets: Clive Bell and Mary Hutchinson', *Charleston Magazine* (Autumn/Winter 1997), 5–12.

140 *Vivienne's winsomeness with Ottoline.* Miranda Seymour, *Ottoline Morrell: Life on the Grand Scale* (London: Hodder, 1992), p. 425.

140 *'isn't Tom beautiful'.* Diary (26 Dec. 1935).

140 *'to be as brilliant as possible'; 'dress parade'.* TSE to Henry Eliot (2 July 1919), *L*, i, 310.

140 *'a savage'.* TSE to Mary Hutchinson ([11? July 1919]), *L*, i, 318.

141 *TSE and the Schiffs.* See 55 letters in the British Library Add MS: 52918, and TSE's obituary for Violet Schiff in *The Times* (9 July 1962). Her husband had died in 1944.

141 *'natural sincerity'.* Schiff to Vivienne (9 Dec. 1921), *L*, i, 492.

142 *one of 'us'. The Diary of Virginia Woolf*, iv (20 June 1935), p. 324.

142 *'the shadow'*. 'The Old Order' (1917), *The Essays of Virginia Woolf*, ii, ed. Andrew McNeillie (London: Hogarth; NY: Harcourt, 1986–1990s), 168. See also Henry James to Grace Norton (21 Dec. 1879), *The Letters of Henry James*, ed. Edel, ii, 261, for his liking for London's 'crepuscular' midwinter.

142 *'Come to lunch'*. Clive Bell, 'How Pleasant to Know Mr. Eliot', 60th birthday coll., p. 15.

143 *Pound wrote from Paris. Selected Letters*, pp. 166–7.

143 *readings by TSE, Sitwells, etc.* A. Huxley, *Letters*, p. 141.

144 *Aztec carving. Laughter in the Next Room* (Boston: Little, Brown, 1948; London: Macmillan, 1949), p. 38.

144 *'The* intelligent *Englishman . . .'*. Review of Wyndham Lewis's novel *Tarr* in the *Egoist* (Sept. 1918).

145 *Leonard Woolf's proposal. Letters of Leonard Woolf*, ed. Frederic Spotts (London: Weidenfeld, 1989), p. 279.

145 *'small and select public'*. L, i, 280.

145 *so rootedly established . . .'*. Conrad Aiken, *Ushant* (Boston: Little, Brown, 1952), p. 215.

Chapter 5 'The Horror! The Horror!'

147 *'his Inferno'*. Aiken to Theodore Spencer ([1930?]). Spencer Papers, Harvard Archives Pusey Library.

147 *'grouse against life'*. Epigraph to *facs. WL.*

147 *'It's interesting . . .'*. TSE to Aiken (30 Sept. [1914]), *L*, i, 59.

147 *'give the pattern'*. 'John Ford' (1932), *SE*, p. 180. I am indebted to Ronald Schuchard for pointing this out.

148 *'some rude unknown psychic material'*. 'The Three Voices of Poetry', *OPP*, pp. 110–11. The quotations below are from this essay.

149 *'For my people . . .'*. Jeremiah I:13.

149 *'And your altars . . .'*. Ezekiel 6:4–6. I am indebted to Elizabeth McClenaghan for the prophetic quotes, used in an essay on Eliot while she was at St Hilda's College, Oxford.

150 *three fragments. facs. WL*, pp. [108–14]. The three are written on the same quadruled paper, punched for filing, and with a 'Linen Ledger' watermark (used by several paper companies in America). Valerie Eliot dates the handwriting '1914 or even earlier', p. 130.

151 *Michael Wood*. In conversation, Columbia University, 1975.

151 *upside down*. For the religious significance of the upside-down posture, see Jonathan Smith, 'Birth Upside Down or Right Side Up?', *History of Religions. An International Journal of Comparative Historical Studies*, ix (May 1970), 281–303.

152 *'a psychological habit . . .'*. *SE*, p. 204.

152 *spiritual autobiographies*. Paul Delaney, *British Autobiography in the Seventeenth Century* (NY: Columbia Univ. Press, 1969.

153 *'I understand . . .'*. Quoted in *Ezra Pound: Perspectives*, ed. Noel Stock (Chicago, 1965), pp. 110–11 and *L*, i, 86.

153 *Narcissus*. Peter Anson, *The Call of the Desert* (London: SPCK, 1964), cites as his source Eusebius, *Historia Ecclesiastica*, vi. 9.

155 *essay on Dante*. (1929), *SE*, pp. 216–17.

156 *desert*. See George Williams, *Wilderness and Paradise in Christian Thought* (NY: Harper, 1962), for a detailed study of the biblical desert experience and its imaginative re-creation by various individuals and groups through history.

156 *'into a desert land . . .'*. John Higginson's preface to Cotton Mather's *Magnalia Christi American . . .* (1702), ed. Thomas Robbins (Hartford, Conn., 1833–5), i, 13–18.

156 *Dante walking over bodies. Inferno*, vi.

156 *unholy loves*. Augustine, *Confessions*, III. See *WL*: III for the same allusion: 'To Carthage then I came'.

157 *dried up. Paris Review* interview. repr. *Writers at Work*, ed. Van Wyck Brooks, 2nd series (NY: Viking, 1963).

157 *'a swan-song'*. TSE to Henry Eliot (6 Sept. 1916), *L*, i, 151.

157 'lived *through material'*. Part of letter quoted in *facs. WL*, p. x. *L*, i, 126.

157 *belittled private suffering.* Part of letter quoted in *facs. WL*, p. xiii.

159 *health-bulletins.* TSE to Russell ([14 and 16 Jan. 1916]), *L*, i, 128–9.

161 'Our sighs . . .'. draft C, final stanzas, *IMH*, p. 368.

161 'Elegy'. *facs. WL*, p. [116].

162 *'The river sweats . . .'. facs. WL*, pp. [48–52]. The river is again associated with an injured woman in a later poem which describes a man haunted at night by the reproach of 'a face that sweats with tears' looking up from the surface of a blackened river ('The wind sprang up at four o'clock', *CP*, p. 134). 'The surface of the blackened river / Is a face that sweats with tears' recalls 'The river sweats . . .'.

163 *Fire Sermon. The Teaching of the Compassionate Buddha*, ed. E. A. Burtt (NY: Mentor, 1955), pp. 96–8.

163 'Purge . . .'. 'The Present Hour', published in the *Christian Register*. Eliot Coll., Houghton.

163 *two new manuscript fragments. facs. WL*, p. [36].

164 'ghastly hill'. *facs. WL*, p. [34].

164 *empty naves.* London letter to the *Dial* (June 1921).

164 'London'. See *facs. WL*, p. [36] for the first draft and p. [30] for the second draft which Pound cut. Valerie Eliot provides a most useful note on Eliot's allusion to the City of God, *facs. WL*, p. 127.

165 'What's the use . . .'. Quoted by Henry Eliot in letter to his mother (12 Dec. 1921). Houghton.

165 'among the termites'. (1 June 1919), *L*, i, 299. Extracts from Eliot's letters to Strachey are also to be found in Michael Holroyd, *Lytton Strachey: A Biography* (Baltimore: Penguin, 1971), pp. 775–6.

165 *'Gerontion' May–June 1919.* In an autograph letter to

John Rodker (1 June 1919) Eliot says that 'Gerontion' is half finished (Alderman Library, Charlottesville). I should like to thank the reference librarian, Kendon Stubbs, for useful information.

166 *long poem.* Noted by Valerie Eliot, *facs. WL*, p. xviii.

166 *review.* 'A Sceptical Patrician', *Athenaeum* (23 May 1919), 361–2. Eliot rightly considered this one of his best essays (letter to Quinn, 9 July 1919).

167 *artist as Eye.* 'The Preacher as Artist, *Athenaeum* (28 Nov. 1919), 1252.

167 *sermon as 'form of literary art'.* Ibid.

167 *confessional-instructive.* See Daniel B. Shea, *Spiritual Autobiography in Early America* (Princeton, NJ: Princeton Univ. Press, 1968; London: OUP, 1969): ch. 3, 'Traditional Patterns in Puritan Autobiography'.

168 *Divine Calls.* Quoted in Newman's *Apologia Pro Vita Sua*, ed. M. J. Svaglic (Oxford: Clarendon, 1967), p. 111.

168 *pale and ill.* See Leonard Woolf, *Downhill All the Way* (London: Hogarth, 1967), p. 111.

169 *'engaged'; 'a new long poem'.* Schiff Papers: 52919. British Library.

169 *revising; by June.* TSE to Schiff (3 Apr. 1921) *L*, i, 444.

169 *May, more on paper.* Letter to Quinn (9 May 1921), quoted by Valerie Eliot in *facs. WL*, p. xxi: '. . . He was "wishful to finish a long poem" (as he still described *The Waste Land*) which was now "partly on paper".'

169 *tarot pack in 1921.* TSE in conversation with MT (March 1955), PRS.

169 *'a part of me . . .'.* Vivienne to Schiff (16 Oct. 1922), *L*, i, 584.

170 *Vivienne to Henry Eliot, L*, i, 465–6.

171 *'I have a feeling . . .'.* Henry Eliot to Charlotte Eliot (30 Oct. 1921). Houghton.

171 *'I really feel very shaky'.* (3 Oct. 1921), *facs WL*, p. xxi, and *L*, i, 473.

171 *'impossible'.* TSE to Henry Eliot (3 Oct. 1921), *L*, i, 472.

171 *horror and apprehension.* Eliot to Quinn (21 Sept. 1922). Quinn Coll.

171 *'unreal as death'.* TSE to Henry Eliot (3 Oct. 1921), *L*, i, 472.

171 *'not nearly finished'.* (13 Oct. 1921), *L*, i, 478. She was doing her husband's correspondence, and writing to say he could not do the next London Letter for the *Dial*.

171 *'I am afraid . . .'; 'the strain . . .'.* Henry Eliot to Charlotte Eliot (12 Dec. 1921). Houghton.

172 *Dr Vittoz.* Cleo McNelly Kearns, *T. S. Eliot and Indic Tradition: A Study in Poetry and Belief* (CUP, 1987), 152–7.

172 *'I do not know . . .'.* ([4? Nov 1921]), *L*, i, 484–5.

173 *seemed to like Margate.* Vivienne to Russell. Russell Archive, McMaster Univ.

173 *purposeful letters.* TSE's letters to Julian Huxley (26 and 31 Oct.) and to Aldington (6 Nov.) are quoted by Valerie Eliot, *facs. WL*, p. xxii.

173 *enlivened.* Pound to Quinn from Paris (22 Oct. 1921), Quinn Coll. Pound habitually reported on Eliot's literary progress to Quinn, and if he had seen any of *The Waste Land* he would surely have mentioned it in his letter.

173 *Chisholm.* 'Nancy and *The Waste Land*', *Nancy Cunard* (London: Sidgwick & Jackson, 1979), pp. 87, 339. See also p. 331 for her 'tryst' with Eliot at the Eiffel Tower in 1922.

174 *'caesarian Operation'.* Included in letter to Eliot [24 Jan? 1921], Ezra Pound, *Selected Letters 1907–1941*, ed. D. D. Paige (1950; repr. NY: New Directions, 1971), p. 170. *L*, i, 498–9. Valerie Eliot dates this letter 24 Dec. 1921 and TSE's reply [24? Jan. 1922]. I don't think TSE would have waited a month to respond, especially as he saw Pound in Paris in the intervening time. We can't be certain, but it is likely that the whole exchange took place in late Jan 1922.

174 Mauberley. Ezra Pound, *Collected Shorter Poems* (1958; repr. London: Faber, 1973), pp. 203–22.

175 *'the other figures . . .'*. I should like to thank Gillian Smee for pointing out these words in *CPy*, I, iii, *Plays*, p. 169.

175 *'SOVENIIA VOS . . .'*. *facs. WL*, p. [100]. Eliot uses Arnaut Daniel's words from the *Purgatorio*, XXVI.

175 *Russian ballet*. The influence of the Russian Ballet was suggested by Herbert Howarth in *Notes on Some Figures Behind T. S. Eliot* (London: Chatto & Windus, 1965), pp. 306–10.

176 *TSE on Diaghilev's ballets*. See Eliot's 'London Letters' in July and October to the *Dial*, lxxi (July–Dec. 1921), 214, 452–3, and 'A Commentary', *Criterion*, iii (Oct. 1924), 5.

176 *'no importance . . .'*. *Josiah Royce's Seminar 1913–1914*, ed. Grover Smith (New Brunswick, NJ: Rutgers Univ. Press, 1963), p. 89.

177 *'Ring out . . .'*. 'Easter'. Eliot Coll., Houghton.

177 *'somewhat elucidative'*. TSE to Pound ([late Jan 1922]), *L*, i, 504.

178 *recognisably Eliot's life*. Hugh Kenner noted the 'sequence of personal pasts' in *Eliot in His Time*, ed. A. Walton Litz (Princeton Univ. Press, 1973). p. 38.

178 *Sesostris and Russell*. Noted by Grover Smith in 'The Making of *The Waste Land*', *Mosaic*, 6 (Fall 1972). 136.

179 *'Those are pearls . . .'*. *facs. WL*, p. 13.

179 *voyager or pilgrim*. See *WL*: IV and V.

179 *'wonderful'*. *facs. WL*, pp. 11, 13.

179 *'original exuberance'*. Michael Foucault, *Madness and Civilization: A History of Insanity*, trans. R. Howard (London, 1967), p. 69.

180 *'thrown like an assegai . . .'*. VW, *Diary*, iv (10 Sept. 1933), p. 179.

180 *'As to Tom's mind . . .'*. Draft or copy (8 Dec. 1935) in Vivienne Eliot's Day Book (1935–6). Vivienne Eliot's papers are in the Bodleian Library, Oxford.

180 *hair stretched out tight*. See *WL*: V.

180 *'Hysteria'*. Eliot put the place and date of composition

on both JH's copy of his poems and on Harold
Monro's.

180 'Ode'. In *Ara Vos Prec* (1920).

180 'horror of life'. 'Cyril Tourneur', *SE*, p. 166.

180 'dying to propagate . . .'. 13 Apr. 1936 in Day Book,
1935–6.

180 red-eyed scavengers. 'A Cooking Egg'.

181 *Vivienne's nightmares*. Letter to Sydney Schiff (c. 1924).
British Library.

182 *preferable to death-in-life*. I owe this observation to
Fiona McArdle.

183 *part V only part 'that justifies . . .'*. The Autobiography
of Bertrand Russell (Boston: Little, Brown, 1967–9;
London: Allen & Unwin), ii, 254.

184 'Than sir Galahad . . .'. Malory, *Works* (London: OUP,
1973), p. 531.

184 'I carry the keys . . .'; 'angel-whispering'. 'Experience',
Ralph Waldo Emerson: Selected Prose and Poetry, ed.
Reginald L. Cook (NY: Holt, Rinehart, 1964) pp. 234,
242.

185 'in a trance'. The Diary of Virginia Woolf, iv (11 Mar.
1935), p. 288.

185 'It is a commonplace . . .'. According to Valerie Eliot
(*facs. WL*, p. 129), this statement, which Eliot made in
his essay on Pascal, was autobiographical and referred
to his writing of 'What the Thunder Said'.

185 disinherited prince. From Gérard de Nerval, 'El Desdi-
chado'.

186 'deploring action'. Pound, *Selected Letters*, p. 170.
Pound's two January letters and Eliot's one reply repr.
here with omissions pp. 169–72. In full in *L*, i, 497–9,
504–5.

186 'I John . . .'. facs. WL, p. [8].

186 '(Those are pearls . . .)'. Ibid., p. [6].

186 'DOLOR'. See *facs. WL*, p. [100]. Pound wrote in
January that 'the sovegna doesn't hold with the rest'.

186 three times through sieve. The letter is paraphrased by

590

Nicholas Joost, *Scofield Thayer and 'The Dial'* (Carbondale, Ill., 1964), p. 159.

186 *doubts on cutting of fisherman's voyage*. The doubts are half-phrased and abruptly dismissed in the taped interview (1959) with Donald Hall. Eliot Coll., Houghton.

187 *Quinn would not have cut*. Letter to Eliot (26 Feb. 1923) in B. L. Reid, *The Man from New York: John Quinn and His Friends* (NY: OUP, 1968), p. 580; and *facs. WL*, p. xxvi. Eliot sent the *WL* manuscript as well as those now published in *IMH* to Quinn as a gift in gratitude for the latter's help with publication and legal advice.

187 *'The river's tent is broken . . .'*. The rough draft is scribbled on the back of the discarded Fresca fragment, *facs. WL*, p. [24].

187 *'catastrophic'; 'mistakes'*. ([15 Nov. 1922]), *L*, i, 598.

188 *'excessively depressed'*. Pound, *Selected Letters*, p. 171.

188 *'torpor or deadness'*. London Letter to the *Dial*, 72 (Apr. 1922), 510–13.

188 *lunches with Aiken*. Aiken, Prefatory Note, 'An Anatomy of Melancholy', Allen Tate's coll, p. 194. There may be some confusion as to the date of these lunches. Aiken says that they took place *before* Eliot went to Lausanne but also says it was the winter of 1921–2. I think his 'winter' date is correct. He mentioned one of these lunches in a letter dated 15 Feb. 1922 in the Chapin Library, Williams College, Mass. I should like to thank the Custodian, H. Richard Archer, for useful information.

188 *sequel to WL*. Eliot's idea for a sequel is cited in a letter from Charlotte Eliot to her brother-in-law, Walter Lamb Eliot (7 May 1923): 'He has had for some time the plan for another poem in his mind.' Eliot Coll., Houghton.

189 *'My present ideas . . .'*. Letter, dated 12 Nov. 1922, repr. Casebook Series on *WL*, ed. C. B. Cox and A. P. Hinchliffe (London, 1968), p. 85. (This letter does not appear in *L*, i.)

189 *TSE told VW.* Quentin Bell, *Virginia Woolf: A Biography*, ii (NY: Harcourt; London: Hogarth, 1972), p. 173.
189 *'As for the poem...'.* 'A Note on Poetry and Belief', first published in Wyndham Lewis's *Enemy*, i (Jan. 1927), 15–17.

Chapter 6 Conversion

192 *'an expansion'.* Preface to the 1928 edition of *SW*, p. vii.
192 *Father Hillier.* Interview (Dec. 1974).
193 *TSE to Aldington.* From his home at 9 Clarence Gate Gardens (n.d.). Texas. I am grateful to Peter Ackroyd for his transcript.
193 *TSE touching up Vivienne's sketches.* 'The Two Mrs Eliots', interview with Valerie Eliot, by Blake Morrison, *Independent on Sunday* (24 Apr. 1994). Although Vivienne's diary (27 Mar. 1935) confirms collaboration between TSE and Irene Fassett, Vivienne's manuscripts in the Bodleian Library show that she conceived and wrote almost everything.
193 *Vivienne on her pseudonyms.* To Schiff (n.d.). British Library.
193 *'jailbirds'.* TSE to Pound (28 July 1922), *L*, i, 553.
193 *'getting recognised...'.* *L*, i, 392.
193 *'parvenu'.* 'A Sceptical Patrician' *Athenaeum* (23 May 1919), 361–2. TSE contrasts Henry James with Henry Adams with whom, in this instance, he identifies.
193 *'Westminster Abbey' and 'walk the plank'.* Carpenter, *A Serious Character: The Life of Ezra Pound* (Boston: Houghton Mifflin; London: Faber, 1988), p. 413. *L*, i, 586.
193 *Gunpowder Plot; phalanx.* I'm indebted for this information to Kieron Winn, of Christ Church, Oxford, who has written a doctoral thesis on Sir Herbert Read, including the Eliot–Read correspondence at the University of British Columbia, Vancouver.
194 *'cipher'.* (27 Apr. 1920). Houghton.

194 *Squire on WL. T. S. Eliot: The Critical Heritage*, i, ed. Michael Grant (London: Routledge, 1982), p. 192.

195 *'He is not a poet at all.'* Beatrix Walsh, *Oxford Magazine* (Eighth Week, Trinity Term, 1998), p. 21.

195 *I. P. Fassett's review. Criterion*, iii, 330.

195 *'Necesse est Perstare?'. Criterion*, iii (April 1925), 364.

195 *block*. Eliot mentioned his inability to write in a letter to Mark Van Doren (Jan. 1925). Special Collections, Butler Library, Columbia Univ.

195 *'Isn't he wonderful? . . .'*. 'Fête Galante', *Criterion*, iii (July 1925), 557–63.

196 *'in a state . . .'. The Wings of the Dove* (London: Bodley Head, 1969), pp. 119–20.

196 *'always wrestling . . .'*. Cited by Carpenter, p. 261.

196 *'Diary of the Rive Gauche'. Criterion*, iii (Jan. 1925), 292.

197 *'continually consults'*. Leonard Woolf to Margaret Llewelyn Davies (22 Feb. 1923), *Letters of Leonard Woolf*, p. 224.

197 *'the prospect . . .'*. TSE to Pound ([15 Nov. 1922]), *L*, i, 597. Cited by Carpenter, p. 411.

197 *Pound sent funds*. Carpenter, p. 412.

198 *stock*. Henry Eliot to Charlotte Eliot (16 Feb. 1920). She had resolved to give each of her children 200 shares.

198 *'as we once supposed'*. Henry Eliot to Charlotte Eliot. Fragmentary second half of letter, probably 1926 since he talks of seeing the Haigh-Woods – he was in England on honeymoon in 1926.

198 *considered leaving bank*. Cable to Quinn (2 Apr. 1923). Quinn Coll.

198 *'a hell of a time'*. Carpenter, p. 415.

198 *Vivienne and Mirsky*. Miranda Seymour, *Ottoline Morrell*, p. 519.

198 *uncanny astuteness*. TSE to Russell, Letters. McMaster Univ., Hamilton, Ont.

198 *'He is a Prophet'*. Diary (2 Oct. 1935).

198 *'a sort of super-being'*. ibid.

199 *thousand times worse.* Letter (7 May 1925), quoted in Russell's *Autobiography*, ii, 174.

199 *'abyss'; 'helpless . . .'.* Vivienne Eliot, Diary (Nov. 1934).

199 *Eliot burst out to Virginia Woolf.* VW, *Diary*, iii (29 Apr. 1925), p. 15.

199 *'drown . . .'.* VW, letter to Lady Ottoline Morrell (22 June 1932), *The Letters of Virginia Woolf*, v, ed. Nigel Nicolson and Joanne Trautmann (London: Hogarth; NY: Harcourt, 1975–80), p. 71.

199 *began in about Sept. 1923.* In Sept. 1923 TSE told Arnold Bennett that he wanted to write a contemporary drama about furnished flat sort of people. In the same month he wrote to Wyndham Lewis to thank him for encouragement over it. (Peter Ackroyd, *T. S. Eliot: A Life*, London: Hamish Hamilton; NY: Simon & Schuster, 1984, pp. 120, 129.) TSE later said that *Sweeney Agonistes* was written in two nights between 10 p.m. and 5 a.m. (A. Walton Litz, *Southern Review*, Oct. 1985, repr. *T. S. Eliot: Essays from the Southern Review*, ed. James Olney, Oxford: Clarendon, 1988, p. 10).

199 *'Am ill . . .'.* Letter (n.d.). Beinecke.

200 *approached Leonard Woolf for advice.* Letter (n.d.). Berg. The address (9 Clarence Gate Gdns) proves that it was not later than 1925, when the Eliots moved to Chester Terrace.

200 *draft of a letter.* The addressee is not legible. It may not have been sent, or even meant to be sent. Her writing books are in the Bodleian Library.

200 *Eliot defined Vivienne's case.* Letter to Leonard Woolf, (n.d.). Berg.

200 *Henry James and Head.* Lyndall Gordon, *A Private Life of Henry James: Two Women and his Art* (London: Chatto, 1998; NY: Norton 1999), p. 348.

201 *'rather brusk'.* Leonard Woolf to TSE (30 Apr. 1925), *Letters of Leonard Woolf*, p. 228.

201 *'a very violent treatment'.* Vivienne to Pound (27 June 1922), *L*, i, 523.

201 *'Is West alrite?'*. Four-page letter to Pound (n.d.). Beinecke.

201 *'took to' trances*. Ibid.

201 *might turn vampire*. Letter to Pound (27 Dec. 1925). Beinecke.

201 *Little Nell*. This was her signature to a note to Pound (n.d.). Beinecke.

201 *'anxious to die'*. Letter to Pound (n.d.). Beinecke.

201 *early TS of* Sweeney Agonistes. King's. 'The Superior Landlord' (an early title was 'The Marriage of Life and Death: A Dream'). The exact date is uncertain but TSE notes: 'My typing probably precedes the fragments themselves'.

202 *a dream*. Part of the original title was 'A Dream'.

202 *Sweeney*. The name may derive from Sweeney Todd, the murderous barber, or from the name of two men in the Harvard class of 1910, both respectable: Albert Matthew Sweeney and Arthur Sweeney.

202 *accept the roles assigned by fate*. In a contemporary essay on Dickens (1927) TSE wrote of characters who seem fated by some supernatural force to enact a given role. Ronald Bush has noted in a ground-breaking essay that 'Fragment of an Agon' is a work steeped in Hawthorne. He sees Sweeney as a descendant of Miriam (in *The Marble Faun*), who provokes murder only to find herself 'remote' from 'all that pertained to [her] past life' and living in moral seclusion. ('Nathaniel Hawthorne and T. S. Eliot's American Connection', *Southern Review*, Oct. 1985, repr. *Essays from the Southern Review*, pp. 65–74.

202 *contemporary essay*. 'Thomas Middleton' (1927), *SE*, p. 142. He adds: '. . . The possibility of that frightful discovery of morality remains permanent'.

203 *'Dream Songs'*. 'Doris's Dream Songs', *Chapbook*, 39 (Nov. 1924), 36–7: I.'Eyes that last I saw in tears'. II. 'The wind sprang up at four o'clock'. This uses several lines from 'Song to the Opherian', which Eliot published

in April 1921, and retained as part of the *WL* manu-script. III. 'This is the dead land' became part III of 'The Hollow Men'.

203 *EH in London in 1923*. Phil Hanrahan, 'T. S. Eliot's Secret Love', *Milwaukee* (November 1989), 81–5. I am grateful for the detailed research into a period of EH's life that was unknown to scholars. How splendid that he interviewed pupils from this early phase of her career.

203 *a post*. Information from Megan Sniffen-Marinoff, College Archivist, The Colonel Miriam E. Perry Goll Archives, Simmons College. Information on EH's vari-ous posts also from Abbot Academy, where she taught from the late 1940s to 1957. I am grateful to Margaret F. Couch, Librarian at Phillips Academy, Andover, Mass.

204 *'I have written to Emily'*. L, i, 305.

204 *EH's drama courses*. Archives of Concord Academy, Concord, Mass., where EH taught in the mid-1940s. I am indebted to the English teacher, Philip McFarland, for these facts.

204 *collection of photographs*. Emily Hale Papers, Sophia Smith Collection, Smith College Archives, Northamp-ton, Mass.

205 *sent EH* Ara Vos Prec. William Baker, 'Bibliographical Notes & Queries: note 420', *Book Collector*, xxxviii, no. 2 (Summer 1989). The Dantean inscription comes from the *Inferno* canto xv. The speaker is Brunetto Latini, Dante's teacher, who is amongst the sodomites. TSE marked the canto in the pocket edition he used at Harvard, and he would draw on this canto again in his first draft of *LG*: II.

205 *golden foot*. 'Song', *facs. WL*, p. 99.

205 *'golden vision'*. 'Eyes that last I saw in tears', op. cit.

205 *'between two lives'*. 'Song'.

205 *broken image*. I am linking broken stone in 'The Hollow Men' with the statue of La Figlia.

206 *'The important fact . . .'*. 'Eeldrop and Appleplex', *Little Review* (May and Sept. 1917), repr. *The Little Review*

Anthology, ed. Margaret Anderson (NY: Horizon, 1953), p. 104.

206 *'that frightful discovery . . .'. SE*, p. 142.

207 *'I don't think . . .'.* Letter to Bonamy Dobrée (1936), quoted in Dobrée's 'T. S. Eliot: A Personal Reminiscence', Allen Tate (ed.), *T. S. Eliot: The Man and His Work* (NY: Dell, 1966), p. 81.

207 *on verge of breakdown.* See VW's letter to Lytton Strachey (23 Feb. 1923) mentioning Eliot's becoming 'desperate', *The Letters of Virginia Woolf*, iii, p. 14, and Pound, *Selected Letters*, pp. 172, 173, 196.

207 *'I have not even time . . .'.* Letter (12 Mar. 1923), B. L. Reid, *The Man from New York: John Quinn and His Friends* (NY: OUP, 1968), p. 582.

207 *whisky bottle and Alida Monro.* Seymour, 519.

208 *VW on Eliot.* Letter to Vanessa Bell (18 May 1923). Quoted by Ronald Bush, *T. S. Eliot: A Study in Character and Style* (NY: OUP, 1983), p. 104.

208 *'crowskin'.* HM: II.

208 *'Let me also wear . . .'.* HM: II. See also *AW*: II: 'And I who am here dissembled . . .'.

208 *Hawthorne's Holgrave. The House of the Seven Gables*, ch. 12, 'The Daguerrotypist'.

208 *'I was still the same . . .'. LG*: II.

208 *Eliot's City clothes.* William Force Stead's reminiscences (29 Apr. 1940). Osborn coll., Beinecke.

208 *'I grow old . . .'.* 'The Love Song of J. Alfred Prufrock', *CP*, p. 7.

209 *'The Captain'; face tinted green.* Osbert Sitwell's memoir, cited by John Pearson, *Façades: Edith, Osbert and Sacheverell Sitwell* (London: Macmillan, 1978), p. 239.

209 *'no women worth printing'.* (7 Nov. 1922), *L*, i. 593.

209 *Vivienne's title for the* Criterion. Carpenter, p. 412.

210 *'For thine is . . .'.* See HM: V. I've taken the liberty of imaginative rather than factual truth: TSE described this habit to MT much later. PRS. See ch. 12 below.

210 *'The horror! the horror!'* This was the original epigraph to *WL*. See *facs. WL*.

210 '*I am afraid . . .*'. Pound, Cantos XXIX and LXXVIII, *The Cantos* (London: Faber, 1975), p. 145, 481. I am grateful to A. Walton Litz for identifying Eliot here.

211 *rational progress*. 'The *Pensées* of Pascal' (1931), *SE*, pp. 360–1.

211 *had never seen people on their knees*. M. B. Rickett recalled this comment made by Eliot at the Anglo-Catholic summer school of sociology at Keble College, Oxford (July 1933). Taped by the Revd Peter Mayhew in 1974.

212 '*Do you kneel down . . .*'. Quoted by Barbara Tuchman, *The Proud Tower* (NY: Macmillan; London: Hamish Hamilton, 1966), p. 146.

212 '*but sure . . .*'; '*ecstasy of assent*'. Quotation and comment from 'Lancelot Andrewes', *SE*, pp. 305–6.

212 '*pure*', '*medieval*'. *SE*, pp. 306–7.

213 *about 1923 or 1924*. The date stamp is obscured, but the envelope is among Vivienne's manuscripts of about 1923–4 in the Bodleian Library.

213 '*Must not the Lord . . .*'. 'Charade of the Seasons'.

213 '*Milton's celestial . . .*'. 'Blake', *SW*, p. 157.

214 Liturgical prayer book. Houghton.

214 *ejection*. Letter to Leonard Woolf (17 Dec. 1925). Berg.

214 *Orestes*. Epigraph to *Sweeney Agonistes*, *CP*, p. 111.

214 *deteriorated*. Implied in a letter to Russell (21 Apr. 1925), *Autobiography*, ii, 173.

214 *Anthony and Ellison*. MS in Bodleian Library.

215 '*This is my affliction*'. 'Eyes that last I saw in tears', *CP*, p. 133.

215 '*Sybilla*' *and the Sybil*. Cyril Connolly pointed out the connection in a *Times* review. The *WL* epigraph is from the *Satyricon* of Petronius.

215 '*The Paralysed Woman*'. (1922). I am indebted to Sandra and Eliot Gilbert for a dramatic reading they gave at a centenary conference on TSE (28 Sept. 1988) at the California Institute of Technology. Bodleian Library (New Library, Room 132): holograph (pencil)

in MSS. Eng. misc. d. 936/1–4, and TS in MSS. Eng. misc. c. 624.

216 *'curse out'*. Four-page letter to Pound (n.d.). Beinecke.

216 *notes for 'Au Revoir'*. Bodleian Library: MSS. Eng. misc. d. 936/1–4.

217 avalanche. to Schiff (n.d.). British Library.

217 *tea with the Woolfs. The Diary of Virginia Woolf*, ii (17 July 1923), pp. 256–7.

217 *rheumatism*. Letter (n.d.). Berg. (Leonard Woolf misdated this letter 1937: Eliot left Vivienne in 1933.)

217 *'EXTREMELY well'*. Letter to Russell (7 May 1925), *Autobiography*, ii, 174.

217 *'By the way ...'*. Vivienne to Conrad Aiken (n.d.). Huntington Library, California.

218 *'temporary aberration'*. (2 Apr. 1924). British Library.

218 *'living with me ...'; 'I find her ...'*. Russell, *Autobiography*, ii, 174.

218 *Lady Ottoline's warning to Vivienne*. Henry Eliot to Charlotte Eliot (21 Mar. 1926). Houghton.

218 *'perfectly well'*. Henry Eliot to Charlotte Eliot (1926?). Houghton.

218 *no longer quite normal*. Eliot to Russell (5 Oct. 1927). Russell Archive, McMaster Univ.

218 *fellow-patient*. Robert Sencourt, *T. S. Eliot: A Memoir* (NY: Dodd Mead; London: Garnstone Press, 1971), p. 124.

219 *Chester Terrace*. Henry Eliot to Charlotte Eliot (1926?) Houghton.

219 *making poetry pay* .... Note TSE added to Stead's reminiscences, op. cit, in 1955.

219 *TSE to Pound on allusions*. (12 Jan. 1934). Beinecke.

219 *Stead once witnessed*. Stead's reminiscences.

219 *TSE's 1935 report*. Copy in Eliot Collection, Houghton.

220 *TSE's letters of rejection; handling of general submissions*. Recalled by Brigid O'Donovan (his secretary from 1934 to 1936) in 'The Love Song of Eliot's Secretary', *Confrontation* (Fall/Winter 1975).

220 *a standard of civilisation*. Kathleen Raine to Leonard Clark (14 Feb. 1965). Berg.

220 *Clark lectures*. I am indebted here and below to Ronald Schuchard, the editor of *VMP*, for facts in his excellent introduction.

221 *'new words'*. *AW*: IV (1930).

221 *love in* VMP. Eric Griffiths, 'Boundaries of Love', a review of *VMP* in *TLS* (8 July 1994).

222 *battle between TSE and Murry*. This is the topic of an Oxford thesis by David W. S. Goldie, 'John Middleton Murry and T. S. Eliot: Tradition versus the Individual in English Literary Criticism, 1919–1928' (1991), to which I am indebted for most of the details below. Dr Goldie made use of the Murry Archive at Edinburgh University.

222 *'Mr. Muddleton Moral'*. 'F.S.F', 'Foreign Periodicals', *New Criterion*, iv, no. 3 (June 1926), 625.

222 *Murry's attack and draft*. 'The Classical Revival', *Adelphi* (Feb.–Mar. 1926). David Goldie discovered the draft in the Murry Archive.

223 *'the one veritable transitory power'*. *AW*: I.

223 *'teach us to sit still'*. *AW*: I.

223 *'humility . . .'*. Remembered by M. B. Rickett and recorded on tape by the Revd Peter Mayhew.

223 *confirmed*. I take the details of Eliot's entry into the Church from Sencourt, *T. S. Eliot*, pp. 127, 131, 132, and from Eliot's letters to William Force Stead in the Osborn Collection, Beinecke Library, Yale.

224 *Stead felt embarrassed*. Diary (29 June 1927). Beinecke.

224 *Stead recalled*. Reminiscences (29 Apr. 1940). Osborn Collection, Beinecke.

224 *should 'pass'*. 10 Aug. 1954 TSE recalled details for MT. PRS.

224 *first confession*. TSE to Stead (15 Mar. 1928). Osborn Collection, Beinecke.

224 *surrender and gain*. TSE to Stead (15 Mar. 1928).

224 *circumstances might* excuse *this*. TSE to Stead (10 Apr. 1928).

224 *'Ignatian'*. Ibid.

224 *celibacy.* TSE to Stead (2 Dec. 1930).

224 *Animula. CP*, p. 103.

224 *'turns'.* Lancelot Andrewes, *Sermons*, ed. G. M. Story (Oxford: Clarendon, 1967), pp. 122–3.

225 *demands of conversion.* Ibid., p. 129.

225 *admitted.* TSE to Pound (2 Apr. 1936). Beinecke. He's referring to his 1926 essay on Andrewes.

225 *'tainted . . .'. The Cultivation of Christmas Trees, CP*, p. 107.

225 *Church and King. Monthly Criterion*, vi (July 1927), 73.

225 *'not merely a civil . . .'.* 'John Bramhall', *SE*, p. 316.

226 *'If Christianity . . .'.* 'Modern Education', *SE*, p. 459.

226 *Edmund Wilson deplored. Axel's Castle* (NY: Scribner, 1931), p. 126.

226 *institution whose appeal declined.* Roger Lloyd, *The Church of England 1900–1965* (London: SCM Press, 1966), p. 457.

226 *'something detached . . .'.* 'The Church as Action', *NEW*, vii (19 Mar. 1936), 451.

226 *'It is not at all easy . . .'.* Newman, *Apologia Pro Vita Sua*, ed. M. J. Svaglic (Oxford: Clarendon Press, 1967), p. 185.

226 *chastity etc., or perish.* 'Christianity and Communism', *Listener* (16 Mar. 1932), 382–3.

227 *not 'watered down'.* 'The Church as an Ecumenical Society', address to the Oxford conference on Church, community, and state, 16 July 1937. (Typescript in Houghton Library.) See also 'Thoughts After Lambeth', *SE*, pp. 328, 329.

227 *'tireless Calvinist.'* Robert Lowell in *Harvard Advocate* (Dec. 1938), 20. Written when Lowell was a freshman. Repr. *Harvard Advocate: Centennial Anthology*, ed. Jonathan D. Culler (Cambridge, Mass: Schenkman, 1966). Statements by various people on TSE, pp. 63–81.

227 *Wilson deplored. Axel's Castle*, pp. 126–7.

228 *masses manipulated by profit motive. ICS*, p. 32.

228 *Gide. Journals*, i, ed. Justin O'Brien (repr. NY: Vintage, 1947), p. 136.

229 *'In a period . . .'.* 'John Bramhall', *SE*, p. 316. See also Eliot's essay on Bishop Andrewes (1926) and his 'Thoughts After Lambeth' (1931).

229 *reasonable.* See John Carey's indictment of Modernist extremism in *The Intellectual and the Masses: Pride and Prejudice among the Literary Intelligentsia* (London: Faber, 1992).

230 *William James. The Varieties of Religious Experience*, pp. 368–9.

230 *'scourges'. Song for Simeon.*

230 *'ecstasy of the animals'. Marina, CP*, p. 105.

231 *'shadow . . .'. Animula, CP*, p. 103.

Chapter 7 Enter Beatrice

233 *gifts.* See William Baker, 'T. S. Eliot and Emily Hale: Some Fresh Evidence', *English Studies* (Oct. 1985), 432–6.

233 *'What every poet starts from . . .'. SE*, p. 117.

233 *'Shakespeare and the Stoicism of Seneca.* Published 22 Sept. 1927. It was Helen Gardner who suggested to me that this essay marked the revival of contact. Conversation at her home in Eynsham, Oxfordshire, late March 1985. Dame Helen Gardner was the author of *The Art of T. S. Eliot* (London: Cresset, 1949) and *The Composition of Four Quartets* (London: Faber, 1978) as well as many other distinguished works. She was Professor of English at Oxford and edited the *New Oxford Book of English Verse*. She died in 1986.

233 *EH in Florence in 1927.* Phil Hanrahan, 'T. S. Eliot's Secret Love', *Milwaukee* (Nov. 1989), 80–5. This has useful details from EH's records at Milwaukee-Downer College in the 1920s. She wrote a travel piece about her visit to Florence for the Downer College literary magazine.

233 *with William Force Stead.* Reminiscences (29 April 1940). Unpublished holograph memoir of TSE in response to

questionnaire by Dr Osborn. Osborn Coll., Beinecke. Because some of this memoir is incorrect, Helen Gardner refused to edit it, but she did believe and like this particular anecdote.

234 *'May Morning'*. See above, ch. 3.

234 *EH's productions.* Emily Hale Papers, Sophia Smith Collection, Smith College, Northampton, Mass.

234 *'synthesis of the Arts'*. College bulletin, EH Papers, Smith College.

235 *EH's lecture notes on TSE*. EH Papers, Smith College.

235 *formal exchanges*. These letters were not sequestered with the bulk of the letters at Princeton, which are not to be unsealed until 2019. EH did not class these with the main body of TSE's letters because, for her, they preceded their understanding. For a fuller discussion of this correspondence see below, ch. 11.

235 *Dante's reunion with Beatrice. Purgatorio*, cantos xxx and xxxi.

235 *'comprehends, enlarges . . .'. SE*, p. 223.

235 *autobiographical*. Letter to Pound (29 Dec. 1929). Beinecke.

235 *'Olive-crowned . . .'. SE*, p. 224.

236 *discussed with Stead*. Stead, Reminiscences, op. cit.

236 *'First Debate'. IMH*, p. 64–5. Eliot dated this poem 1910. See above, ch. 2.

236 *'the sublime vision . . .'*. 'The Poet' in *Ralph Waldo Emerson: Selected Prose and Poetry,* ed. Reginald L. Cook (NY: Holt, Rinehart, 1950, repr. 1964), p. 331.

236 *sweet brown hair. AW*: III. For a perceptive reading of the sequence as a pivotal love poem see Carl Schmidt, 'Speech, Silence, Words and Voices', *UNISA English Studies* (Pretoria, 1983), pp. 17–22.

236 *'Salutation'*. This became part II of *AW*. The title comes from the *Vita Nuova*: IV, where Dante calls Beatrice 'the lady of the salutation'. 'Salutation' was first published 10 Dec. 1927 in the *Saturday Review of Literature*.

237 *'Rose of memory'. AW*: II.

237 *God speaks*. Deuteronomy 34: 4; Numbers 26: 52–6.

238 *ditties of no tone.* Keats, 'Ode on a Grecian Urn'. Soundless music is heard also in *DS*: III, where a voice descants in the ship's rigging 'not to the ear'. See below, ch. 10.

238 *'The love of man and woman . . .'. Dante, SE*, pp. 234–5.

238 *'the impossible union'. DS*: V, *CP*, p. 199.

238 *'I mean the turning away . . .'.* 'Views and Reviews', *NEW*, vii: 8 (6 June 1935).

238 *'imparadisa la mia mente': Paradiso*, canto XXVIII, l. 3: *'quella che'mparadisa la mia mente'.* I am grateful to Gwen Watkins for locating this quotation.

238 *love's essence in memory.* The phrase is lifted from the *Vita Nuova*: xx.

239 *at Burford*, TSE wrote to her c/o Mrs R. H. Gretton, 'Calendars', Burford, in Sept., and again on 6 Oct. to an unknown address. Princeton.

239 *confided to Stead.* Letter (30 Dec. 1930). Osborn Coll., Beinecke. All subsequent references to TSE's correspondence with Stead are to letters in this collection.

239 *'A very dear friend of mine . . .'.* Quoted in T. S. Matthews, *Great Tom* (NY: Harper & Row, 1973), p. 148.

240 *final part of* AW. *AW* was published on 24 April 1930.

240 *'life-giving'. AW*: II.

240 *divine intimations.* See *WL*: V, *Marina*, and *DS*: III.

240 *'exile'. AW*: V.

240 *golden-rod. AW*: VI.

240 *'Who . . .'. AW*: IV.

240 *sign.* 'We would see a sign!' TSE took these words from a sermon by the seventeenth-century Anglican Lancelot Andrewes. *CP*, p. 29.

240 Marina. *CP*, p. 106. A draft of this poem is in the Bodleian Library, Oxford. TSE's title *Marina* derives from Shakespeare's *Pericles*, which ends with a blissful reunion of a long separated father and daughter. Marina is a figure of absolute purity. See TSE's discussion of Shakespeare's late heroines Perdita, Miranda, Imogen, and Marina in an

NOTES

unpublished talk, 'The Development of Shakespeare's Verse'. King's College, Cambridge.

241 *bolt.* From Matthew Arnold, 'The Buried Life'.

241 *Casco Bay, Maine.* TSE to McKnight Kauffer (24 July 1930). Grace Schulman, 'Notes on the Theme of "Marina" by T. S. Eliot', in *T. S. Eliot: Essays from the Southern Review*, ed. James Olney (OUP, 1988), pp. 205–11.

241 *enough of a Southerner . . .* TSE to Stead (20 June 1930).

241 *'almost a definite moment of acceptance . . .'.* Dante (1929), *SE*, p. 237. Dante said, 'I have set my feet in that region of life beyond which one cannot go with intent to return.' *Vita Nuova*: XIV.

241 *the 'unread vision . . .'.* AW: IV.

241 *Robert Lowell. Collected Prose of Robert Lowell*, ed. Robert Giroux (NY: Farrar, Straus & Giroux, 1986), p. 181.

241 *embodiment of old Boston.* Confirmed by Isabel Fothergill Smith and Margaret Ann Ingram, colleagues in 1932–4 at Scripps College. See also *The Diary of Virginia Woolf*, iv (27 Nov. 1935), ed. Anne Olivier Bell (London: Hogarth: NY, Harcourt, 1982), p. 355, and her *Letters*, v, no. 3084, ed. Nigel Nicolson and Joanne Trautmann (London: Hogarth; NY: Harcourt, 1979), p. 446.

242 *'Where is the Life . . .'.* The Rock: Chorus I, *CP*, p. 147.

242 *'the recognition of the reality of Sin . . .'.* 'Baudelaire' (1930), *SE*, p. 378.

242 *'reality'.* BN: I.

242 *'to be consumed . . .'.* LG: IV.

243 *events beyond record.* I have lifted the phrasing of Carolyn Heilbrun, who, in *New York Times Review of Books* (10 Feb. 1985), understood precisely this problem and possibility in biography.

243 *lips that would pray.* HM: III.

243 *'between the rocks'.* AW: V.

243 *fissure.* I draw here on Eliot's correspondence with a Princeton theologian, Paul Elmer More, who explained a sense of a deep fissure in TSE's work between what More called actuality of form and actuality of content. In a letter

of 20 June 1934 TSE asked More if the fissure was less evident in *The Rock*. Princeton.

243 *Shadow*. HM: V.

243 *'DA . . . Datta . . .'*. WL: V.

243 *fount*. AW: IV.

243 *'Life is very long'*. HM: V.

243 *Providence led him*. TSE said this to Stead, who watched him become 'a man with a mission'. Unpublished autograph memoir of Lady Ottoline Morrell (dated 1 May 1938). Beinecke. Stead notes here that TSE made his remark about Providence more than once.

243 *'which surely no man . . .'*. 'Thomas Heywood', *SE*, p. 158.

243 *'one becomes moral . . .'*. 'Thomas Middleton', *SE*, p. 142.

244 *'somewhere else'*. TSE describes his affinities with More in 'Paul Elmer More', *Princeton Alumni Weekly* (5 Feb. 1937), and in a letter to More (11 Jan. 1937). More Papers, Princeton.

244 *More accused Eliot of Calvinism*. TSE refers to this in a letter to More (10 Aug. 1930). Princeton.

244 *Eliot accused More of heresy*. TSE to More (17 Feb. 1932). Princeton.

244 *Eliot's view of hell*. TSE to More (2 June 1930). Princeton. *Inferno*, canto III.

244 *August*. TSE to More (10 Aug. 1930). Princeton.

244 *'a man with a mission'*. Unpublished autograph memoir of Lady Ottoline Morrell (1 May 1938). Beinecke.

244 *Isaiah and Ezekiel*. TSE to More (7 Nov. 1933). Princeton.

244 *TSE's Bible*. King's College, Cambridge.

244 *'Fear not . . .'*. Isaiah 43: 1.

245 *'an inherited disposition . . .'*. TSE to Aldington (8 Oct. 1923). An extract from this letter was printed in the Univ. of Texas Exhibition pamphlet (1961).

245 *'Let me go forth, O Lord!'* Charlotte Champe Eliot. Hayward Bequest, King's.

245 *'the American writing in English'*. 'Tradition and the

Practice of Poetry', a talk given in Dublin in Jan. 1936, published in the *Southern Review* (Oct. 1985), 837–88, with Introduction and Afterword by A. Walton Litz, repr. *Essays from the Southern Review*.

245 *'realms of budding bibles'.* 'Passage to India', stanza 7, in *Complete Poetry and Collected Prose* (NY: The Library of America, 1982), p. 537.

245 *tooth one another. Marina.*

245 *'Have we not grovel'd . . . '.* 'Passage to India', stanza 9, p. 539.

245 *golf balls. The Rock*, Chorus III.

245 *'The desert is squeezed . . . '. The Rock*, Chorus I.

245 *Sir Herbert Read.* 'T.S.E. – A Memoir', Allen Tate's coll, 30.

245 *Andrew Eliot on 'a generation of vipers'.* Easter Day sermon, 1766. Copy in Eliot Collection, Houghton. TSE recalled this phrase in a letter to MT (26 Jan. 1948), PRS, and in a letter to Pound (4 Dec. 1936).

245 *admired grandfather.* TSE mentioned his admiration to MT (26 Jan. 1948). Letter quoted in PRS.

245 *a classmate.* James Freeman Clarke, in his Journal (May 1839). Quoted in obituary in Hayward Bequest, King's.

245 *the classic American sermon, the jeremiad.* See Sacvan Bercovitch, *The American Jeremiad* (Univ. of Wisconsin Press, 1978).

246 *'the dark ages before us'.* 'Thoughts After Lambeth' (1931), *SE*, p. 342.

246 *'scourges'. Song of Simeon* (1928), CP, pp. 101–2.

246 *'. . . set down . . . '. Journey of the Magi* (1927), CP, p. 100. See Alan Weinblatt's stimulating ideas on language in 'T. S. Eliot: Poet of Adequation', *Southern Review* (Oct. 1985), 1118–37, repr. *Essays from the Southern Review*.

246 *'lives of prophets'.* 'Towards a Christian Britain', *Listener* (10 Apr. 1941), 524–5.

247 *vacillates.* I owe this to John Mayer's talk at Cal Tech (Sept. 1988).

247 *Pipit.* Pipit is not mentioned by name in 'Coriolan', but the

poem is linked with 'A Cooking Egg' through the recurrent phrase 'eagles and trumpets'.

247 *'Hidden under the heron's wing'. IMH*, p. 82. For further discussion, see chs 3 and 11.

247 *'This has given me . . .'*. EH to President Jaqua. Scripps College Archives.

247 *review of EH's Seattle recital*. Cutting does not include name of newspaper, EH Papers, Smith College.

248 *Scripps College*. Information from Lorraine Havens, whose husband, Paul Havens, was an early member of the English faculty.

248 *made a ceremony . . . .* Recalled by Margaret Ann Ingram (Scripps '31), who was Assistant Registrar while EH was at Scripps. Letter to me (1 Sept. 1986).

248 *Laurabel Neville Hume's recollections*. Letter, Scripps College Archives.

249 *Marie McSpadden Sands's recollections*. Letter to me (8 Sept. 1986).

250 *Goldoni*. Report on rehearsals in the *Scripture* (7 Nov. 1932). Scripps College Archives.

250 *Lady Gregory*. I am indebted to Mrs Hume for sending a copy of her write-up on the Siddons Club for 1932–3 in *La Semeuse*.

250 *review of EH as Lady Bracknell. Scripture* (15 May 1933).

250 *Faith McAllister on EH*. Recalled for an audience at the Denison Library, Claremont, California, during the discussion after a talk which I gave on TSE and EH (Sept. 1988). The library was holding an exhibition of Emily Hale Papers and photographs on the occasion of Eliot's centenary.

251 *'understanding'*. Sarah F. Tomaino in a letter to me (13 Nov. 1988, following the publication of *Eliot's New Life* in September) with fascinating memories of TSE and EH in the period when she taught at Concord Academy in the mid-forties. See below, ch. 11.

251 *on Edward Lear*. His talk on Lear is reported in the *Scripture*. See also William Baker's reconstructed account

in 'TSE on Edward Lear', *English Studies*, lxiv (1983), 564–6.

251 *'bitter period' and 'man of extremes'*. Scripture (12 Dec. 1932).

251 *TSE's sermon in King's Chapel*. Unpublished. Houghton. Bequest of the Revd John Carroll Perkins. TSE was addressing the Women's Alliance. I am grateful for Valerie Eliot's permission (in 1975) to see this exceptionally fine work.

251 *Psalm 130*. Ibid. This psalm was eventually read at Eliot's funeral.

251 *Vivienne lost touch*. She recalls this date some years later in her diary. Bodleian Library.

251 *Virginia Woolf to TSE*. Letter (15 Jan. 1933), *The Letters of VW*, v, pp. 150–1, in reply to a letter from TSE in Nov. 1932.

251 *EH waiting*. Lorraine Havens heard these details from her husband, who went to the station with Emily Hale. He had once met Eliot at Oxford and had offered to drive him to the home of Mary Eyre which had been lent to Eliot for his stay.

252 *visit to Balboa Island*. Described by Marie McSpadden Sands in letter to me (8 Sept. 1986).

252 *the US had done him good*. TSE to Pound, dated Vigil of Ascension Day, 1933. Beinecke.

252 *From America he wanted . . . .* TSE to P. E. More (18 May 1933). More Papers, Princeton.

252 *felt like Alice*. Ibid.

253 *describing the Cabots*. Recalled in VW's letter to TSE (15 Jan. 1933), *The Letters of Virginia Woolf*, v, 150–1. Richard Clarke Cabot was Professor of Clinical Medicine and Professor of Social Ethics at Harvard. Ellery Sedgwick (who married Mabel Cabot) was editor of the *Atlantic Monthly*. They belonged to the élite of Boston society.

253 *a wild woman of Providence*. TSE to VW (March 1933). Berg.

253 'I met you first at Spring Street'. Copied out for VW in letter dated Twelfth Night 1935. Berg.

253 'He gives you the creeps . . .'. Edmund Wilson, *Letters on Literature and Politics 1912–1977*, ed. Elena Wilson (NY: Farrar, Straus, 1977).

253 'I speak as a New Englander'. ASG, p. 16. TSE repeated this self-characterisation as a New Englander in a letter to Pound (dated Childermass, 1937). See the outstanding article on Eliot's criticism by Ronald Schuchard: ' "First-Rate Blasphemy": Baudelaire and the Revised Christian Idiom of T. S. Eliot's Moral Criticism', *ELH*, xlii (Summer 1975).

254 *exempts Joyce*. ASG, p. 32.

254 *TSE to Lady Ottoline*. (14 Mar. 1933), Texas. Cited by Ronald Schuchard in *VMP*, p. 242.

254 *Fitzgerald's impression of TSE*. Fitzgerald to Edmund Wilson (March 1933), Beinecke. Quoted by Matthew J. Bruccoli, *Some Sort of Epic Grandeur* (NY: Harcourt, 1981), p. 345.

254 *Deed of Separation*: VMP, p. 242.

254 *Eliot lingered*. Vivienne expected him back in May according to a signed statement she extracted from him a year before. Bodleian Library.

254 *portrait of EH in the hall*. Recalled by C. E. Dexter Morse in a letter to the author.

255 *happiest*. Henry Ware Eliot to Marianne Moore (6 June 1936), cited by Ronald Bush, *T. S. Eliot: A Study in Character and Style* (NY: Oxford Univ. Press, 1983) p. 183.

255 'Emily and Mr Eliot . . .'. Dorothy Elsmith, letter to me (1 Aug. 1977).

255 *weekend in the Berkshires*. Ibid.

255 'New Hampshire'. Published April 1934 together with 'Virginia'. CP, p. 138.

255 'simple soul': *Animula*, CP, p. 103.

255 *attended his address*. Mrs Elsmith's letter to me. (1 Aug. 1977).

255 *Frank Morley.* 'A Few Recollections of Eliot', Allen Tate's coll., pp. 103–7.

255 *'He is 10 years younger'.* (10 Sept. 1933), *The Diary of Virginia Woolf*, iv, p. 178.

256 *shared flat with homosexuals.* Francis King, *Yesterday Came Suddenly: An Autobiography* (London: Constable, 1993), p. 197. I am indebted to Ronald Bush for passing on an article which footnotes this: James F. Louks, 'The Exile's Return: Fragment of a T. S. Eliot Chronology', *ANQ*, ix:2 (Spring 1996), 16–39.

256 *Kensington.* TSE to VW (31 Oct. 1933). Berg.

256 *7 December.* TSE to VW. Berg.

256 *incognito.* TSE to Pound (Vigil of Ascension Day, 1933). Beinecke.

256 *Eeldrop and Appleplex.* See above, ch. 4.

256 *TSE's rooms.* Described by VW, *Diary*, iv (31 Mar. 1935), p. 294.

257 *the Sisters of St Elizabeth.* TSE told MT years later. PRS.

257 *'denying the importunity of the blood'.* *Animula* (1929), CP, p. 103.

257 *'a spectre . . .'.* Ibid.

257 *John Hayward.* Many of the following biographical details come from a vivid obituary in the *Annual Report*, King's College (Nov. 1965), pp. 30–3.

257 *his voice and puffing.* Francis Meynell, obituary in *The Book Collector* (Winter 1965).

257 *the favoured age.* Desmond Flower, obituary, ibid.

257 *George Rylands.* Obituary, ibid.

258 *acted a bevy of prisoners.* King's *Annual Report*, op. cit. The details that follow are lifted almost verbatim.

258 *joined 'The Biblioboys'.* A. N. L. Munby, obituary, *The Book Collector* (Winter 1965).

258 *light verse.* The verses were privately printed in 1939 in a volume entitled *Noctes Binanianae* (referring to JH's flat in Bina Gardens). Copies in King's and Houghton.

258 *Vivienne refused.* Vivienne Eliot, Diaries, Bodleian Library.

258 *'Nothing but . . .'.* Letter to Bonamy Dobrée, quoted by

Dobrée in 'T. S. Eliot: A Personal Reminiscence', in *T. S. Eliot: The Man and His Work*, ed. Allen Tate (NY: Dell, 1966), p. 79.

259 *Old Buffer of the clubs.* He joined a good many: the Oxford and Cambridge Club; the Burke Club, a Tory dining club; The Club, an eighteenth-century foundation mainly for peers, but including John Betjeman and Desmond MacCarthy; later, the Garrick Club and the Athenaeum.

259 *obscene verses.* May be sampled in *IMH*.

259 *the fart and the stained-glass window.* Sent to Professor Theodore Spencer at Harvard in Sept. 1932, just before TSE arrived to take up the Norton professorship for 1932–3. Looking through Professor Spencer's papers in the Harvard Archives in Pusey Library, it is not my impression that he would have welcomed puerile drivel, but as TSE's host he would not have been in a position to refuse it.

259 *O'Donovan left.* Brigid O'Donovan, 'The Love Song of Eliot's Secretary', *Confrontation* (Fall/Winter, 1975).

259 *Hayward to Morley.* Hayward–Morley Correspondence, Letter XI (Feb. 1940). King's. Quoted *CFQ*, p. 32.

261 *Tandy letters.* Discovered in Hampshire in 1991 by Lesley Roberts in a gardener's crate, ready to be thrown out. Her neighbour, Edward Kidner's late wife, Anthea (Poppet), was the last of the Tandy children and Eliot's godchild: she had inherited the correspondence and some cat, pig, and parrot poems. Lesley Roberts, who works for the BBC, brought the papers to me in carrier bags, put them on the kitchen table, and sheaves of Eliot letters just tumbled out. She did a splendid job of ordering them. The papers are now in the British Library.

261 *'the pattern'.* MC, I, *Plays*, p. 17.

262 *competition on ancestors.* TSE to VW (Apr. 1934). Berg.

262 *'depravity's despair'.* 'What Dante Means to Me' (1950), CC, p. 134.

262 *'His despair . . .'.* 'The *Pensées* of Pascal' (1931), SE, p. 364.

263 *a barbecue.* Reported in the *Scripture* (5 June 1934).

263 *Eliot wrote to thank Mrs Perkins.* CFQ supplies the dates of TSE's letters to Mrs Perkins and also quotes from this correspondence owned by Donald C. Gallup, Eliot's bibliographer.

263 *according to Jeanette McPherrin.* Letter, Scripps College Archives.

263 *Hidcote Manor was 'the one I loved'.* Letter to Mrs Perkins, quoted *CFQ*, p. 36.

263 *'A Country Walk'.* Princeton.

264 *'to feel "at home" . . .'.* Letter to Mrs Perkins (30 Sept. 1935), quoted *CFQ*, p. 35.

266 *EH wrote to Scripps in August,* Scripps College Archives.

266 *postcard from Gloucestershire.* (Undated but the postmark says 4 Sept. 1934.) Theodore Spencer Papers, Harvard Archives, Pusey Library.

266 *'My weekend . . .'.* Quoted *CFQ*, p. 35.

266 *'autumn heat'.* TSE was always precise about seasons. If he wrote 'autumn' it is likely that it *was* autumn. See his letter to JH about a line in the first draft of *LG*: ' "Autumn weather" only because it *was* autumn weather . . .'. He goes on to say that autumn also provided a link with *BN*, 'La Figlia Che Piange', and 'New Hampshire'. It is significant that the latter, which is a poem of spring or early summer, not autumn, was linked by TSE with other Emily Hale poems.

266 *'Footfalls echo . . .'.* *BN*: I. All subsequent references to *BN* come from this opening section, unless indicated.

267 *'They'.* Acknowledged as a source for *BN* in a letter from TSE to JH (5 Aug. 1941), *CFQ*, p. 39.

267 *The garden has remained as it always was.* I first visited Burnt Norton with Helen Gardner and a group of her students in June 1974, in brilliant sunshine, and again with my husband on a mellow autumn day in early September 1986. The former visit was much in mind as Dame Helen had died and I was writing an obituary. The garden had not changed and was, still, deserted.

267 *'Bellegarde' sketch.* 'Sketch' is TSE's word in a letter to his

brother. Henry Eliot placed the fragment, together with 17 pages of MS jottings for *MC*, in Houghton. The fragment is on the same paper, but he notes that it was sent to him some two months later. It consists of one page with six lines (which TSE tried in vain to work into the play) and two other pages, the unfinished 'Bellegarde' sketch itself. See App. IV below.

267 *rose-garden encounter in* FR. Part II, ii, *Plays*, pp. 106–8.

267 *'leaping pleasures'*. Quotations come from the six lines that TSE tried to adapt for *MC*, quoted *EMB*, p. 44.

268 *'Memory and desire'*. *WL*: I. This section was written in 1921.

268 *'looking into the heart of light . . .'*. Ibid.

268 *'un-being'*. *BN*: V.

268 *'Quick now, here, now, always –'*. *BN*: V.

269 *'So long . . .'*. Sonnet 18: 'Shall I compare thee to a summer's day'.

269 *its scenarios go back to 1934–5*. See ch. 9 and App. V.

269 *'news'*. *FR*, I, ii, *Plays*, pp. 82–3.

269 *'I only looked . . .'*. FR, II, ii, *Plays*, pp. 106–7.

270 *Eliot explained to Martin Browne*. Letter quoted in full, *EMB*, pp. 107–8.

270 *TSE remarked to P. E. More . . . .* Letter (Shrove Tuesday, 1928).

270 *when they meet . . . . Dante* (1929).

270 *December 1934*. In December TSE discussed the play during a weekend visit to EMB. *EMB*, p. 55.

271 *'precise'*. 'Shakespeare', *SE*, p. 115.

271 *no noble-minded Thomas More*. *Church Times* review (June 1935), donated to the Houghton Library by the Revd John Carroll Perkins.

271 *a bit of the author as germ for the character*. 'The Three Voices of Poetry', *OPP*, p. 102.

271 *Martin Browne, EMB*, p. 35.

272 *'All my life . . .'*. MC, II, *Plays*, p. 43.

272 *earliest pencil notes for* MC. Houghton. See App. IV.

272 *'To the Law of God . . .'*. MC, II, *Plays*, p. 46.

272 *Matthiessen's review*, 'TSE's Drama of Becket', *Saturday Review* (12 Oct. 1935).
272 *'morality murder'*. VW, *Diary*, iv (Dec. 1935), p. 356. I am indebted to Ursula Werner for pointing this out in her Oxford thesis on the literary relationship of TSE and VW (1987).
273 *To want sainthood* . . . . I have lifted this felicitous and accurate sentence from Roger Lewis's winning essay for the Chancellor's English Essay Prize at Oxford University (on 'The world is but a school of inquiry').
273 *Eliot told his brother* . . . . Letter (28 Apr. 1936) when MC was to come to the US. Henry Eliot includes an extract from this letter with a typescript of MC in the Houghton Library.
273 *TSE told P. E. More.* Letter (2 June 1930). Princeton.
273 *shaft of sunlight.* MC, I, *Plays*, p. 12.
273 *'I have had a tremor of bliss'.* Part II, *Plays*, p. 44.
274 *1927 Criterion review.* (Aug. 1927), 177–9.
274 *'the enervate* gospel of happiness'. 'Thoughts After Lambeth', *SE*, pp. 323–4.
274 *'What chiefly remains* . . .'. *SE*, p. 324.
274 *'Samson in Gaza* . . .'. Part I, *Plays*, p. 24.
275 *TSE on Babbitt.* Review, *Criterion* (Aug. 1927), 177–9; and letter to the *Bookman* dated 31 Mar. 1930 (copy enclosed in letter to P. E. More).
275 *Theodore Spencer.* 'Miscellaneous Journal Entries', Harvard Archives: HUG 4806.35. I am grateful to Eloise B. Bender for permission to quote.
275 *A Primer of Modern Heresy.* This is the subtitle of *ASG* (1934), based on lectures at the University of Virginia in 1933.
275 *'I am concerned* . . .'. *ASG*, p. 56.
275 *'. . . It may operate* . . .'. *ASG*, p. 57.
275 *The Tempters conduct Becket* . . . . From Roger Lewis, op. cit.
275 *Just as Becket faced his Tempters* . . .'. D. E. Jones showed the parallels between Tempters and Knights in *The Plays of T. S. Eliot* (London: Routledge, 1960), pp. 61–2.

276 *Eliot discussed with his brother.* Letter (28 Apr. 1936). Extract included with a typescript of *MC*, Houghton.

276 *Eliot challenges the audience's immunity.* From Roger Lewis, op. cit.

277 *Holmes. MC* alludes to Conan Doyle's tale 'The Musgrave Ritual', one of Sherlock Holmes's early cases related by his friend Dr Watson. Grover Smith discovered the allusion in *T. S. Eliot's Poetry and Plays: A Study in the Sources and Meaning* (Univ. of Chicago, 1950, repr. 1971), p. 194.

277 *TSE mentioned to his brother.* Letter (28 Apr. 1936). Houghton.

277 *pathetic.* TSE to Sydney Schiff (4 July 1935). Schiff Papers, British Library.

277 *'that moral activity which* disentangles'. Edgar Allan Poe, 'The Murders in the Rue Morgue'. I am grateful to Roger Lewis (op. cit.) for this apt quotation and its application to *MC*.

277 *Eliot told his brother.* Letter (28 Apr. 1936).

278 *the Mercury.* This and the following details about the subsequent history of *MC* come largely from *EMB*.

278 *'That is perhaps the greatest surprise'.* 'London Letter' to the *New Yorker* (13 July 1935) from 'Samuel Jeake, Jr'.

278 *partitioned.* This is not like a Greek chorus.

278 *the mystery of corruption* . . . . I owe these phrases to Sarah Edworthy when she was an undergraduate at St Hilda's College, Oxford, in the 1980s.

279 The Times. There is a large collection of reviews of all TSE's plays in Houghton.

279 MC *in an air-raid shelter. EMB*, p. 154.

279 MC *in the basement of Lloyds Bank.* EMB to TSE (3 July 1941), quoted in *EMB*, p. 155.

279 *'one of the most "shared" performances'.* Ibid.

279 MC *at Kelham.* 1947. Photographs in Houghton.

280 *Brooks Atkinson's review. New York Times* (26 Apr. 1953). Copy in Houghton.

280 *TSE thought Donat the best* . . . . MT's diary for Apr. 1953, PRS.

281 'the moment that pierces one . . .'. Plays, p. 43.

281 'a puritan at heart'. Eileen Simpson, Poets in Their Youth: A Memoir (1982; repr. London: Picador, 1984), p. 131.

281 'a smack of the Puritan temper'. Review (June 1935). Donated to the Houghton Library by the Revd John Carroll Perkins.

281 'hellish'. Plays, p. 42.

281 'We are soiled . . .'. Plays, p. 48.

281 'enjoys feeling disgust'. 'History or Poetic Drama?', Me Again: Uncollected Writings of Stevie Smith, ed. Jack Barbera and William McBrien (London: Virago, 1981), pp. 148–52.

282 'that Christian nerve'. Ibid.

282 most autobiographical play. Agreed in discussion with Richard Ellmann in the 1980s.

282 'Thibet of broken stones'. FR, II, ii, Plays, p. 104.

Chapter 8   The Mystery of Sin

283 'the Mystery of Iniquity'. The Rock (London: Faber, 1934), p. 84, repr. CP, p. 169.

283 a 'bag of ferrets'. VW, Diary, iii (8 Nov. 1930), p. 331.

283 tried to separate. VW to Lady Ottoline Morrell (6 Sept. 1932) The Letters of Virginia Woolf, v, 99: 'I hope the separation is complete and final, as it promised to be when I last had news.'

283 sent letter. It is still unclear whether TSE sent this letter in February or after 14 May (the latter date is given by Ronald Schuchard in VMP). Miranda Seymour notes in her biography of Lady Ottoline Morrell that Vivienne did not appear to hear of the intended separation until June, though she was increasingly distressed by her husband's silence. The June date seems to be confirmed by Virginia Woolf's diary. This might well be cleared up when Eliot's letters of this period are published.

283 a friend. Roger Sencourt, A Memoir of T. S. Eliot (NY: Dodd, Mead, 1971), p. 151.

T. S. ELIOT

284 *'the reality of Sin'*. 'a recognition of the reality of Sin is a New Life' ('Baudelaire'). *SE*, p. 378. See above p. 213.
284 *'become first capable of Evil'*. *ASG*, p. 60.
284 *in an essay*. 'Baudelaire', *SE*, p. 380.
284 *Eliot asked P. E. More*. Letter (28 Apr. 1936). Princeton.
285 *in Charlottesville*. TSE was giving the Page-Barbour lectures at the University of Virginia.
285 *'Iron thoughts . . .'*. 'Virginia' (published 1934).
285 *'witch-hangers'*. Letter to Pound (8–10 Dec. 1933). Beinecke.
285 *'we hanged them'*. *Literary Essays of Ezra Pound*, ed. TSE (NY: New Directions, 1968), editorial footnote on p. 391.
285 *'red' mood*. 'Virginia'.
285 *Hawthorne's fable*. 'Young Goodman Brown'.
286 *'You don't see them . . .'*. Orestes in *Choephoroi*. The first scene was published in the *Criterion* (Oct. 1926) and the second in Jan. 1927 with the epigraphs repeated, *CP*, p. 111. On 9 Dec. 1932 TSE's audience at Harvard was given a picture of a poet with 'ghastly shadows at his back' (*UPUC*, p. 69). TSE refers here to Coleridge, but his repeated use of such shadows suggests its personal import.
286 *'haunted by a demon . . .'*. 'The Three Voices of Poetry', *OPP*, p. 107.
286 *Eliot and Hawthorne*. TSE said that *The House of the Seven Gables* was his favourite amongst the novels in 'The Hawthorne Aspect' (of Henry James), *Little Review* (Aug. 1918).
286 *'the violent death . . .'*. *The House of the Seven Gables*, ch. 1.
286 *witch*. According to the drafts, a witch passed a curse on Great-Uncle Harry. Houghton.
286 *Hope Mirrlees recalled*. BBC TV programme 'The Mysterious Mr Eliot', *Listener*, lxxxv (14 Jan. 1971), p. 50.
287 *Theresa Eliot*. She said this to Peter du Sautoy. Theresa Eliot was married to TSE's brother, Henry Ware Eliot.
287 *Desmond MacCarthy*. Review reported by Michael Sidnell, *Dances of Death: The Group Theatre of London in the Thirties* (London: Faber, 1984), p. 106.

287 *'projected . . .'.* 'Cyril Tourneur', *SE*, p. 166.

288 *becomes moral by becoming damned. SE*, p. 142.

288 *'Beneath the stars . . .'.* TSE quotes from Beatrice Joanna's magnificent death speech in *The Changeling*, *SE*, pp. 143, 148.

288 *'I sat by Tom'.* VW, *Diary*, iv, 260–1.

288 *fancy-dress.* VW to Elizabeth Bowen (29 Jan. 1939), *Letters of Virginia Woolf*, vi. 313.

288 *Vivienne seeing* Sweeney Agonistes. Diaries, Bodleian Library.

288 *'some trait of his own'.* 'The Three Voices of Poetry', *OPP*, p. 102.

288 *unfinished.* TSE added an ending for Hallie Flanagan's Vassar production in 1933. But, as Carol H. Smith has pointed out (*T. S. Eliot's Dramatic Theory and Practice*, Princeton, 1963) this ending doesn't quite fit the play. TSE never chose to publish it.

288 *on two distinct levels.* TSE, writing on John Marston (1934), suggested that 'what distinguishes poetic drama from prosaic drama is a kind of doubleness in the action, as if it took place on two planes at once.' Repr. *Elizabethan Dramatists* (London: Faber, 1963), 161.

289 *'literal-minded and visionless'.* TSE gives this theory, specifically in relation to *Sweeney Agonistes*, in *UPUC*, p. 153.

289 *1935 revival.* Details from reviews. The best is Desmond MacCarthy's for the *Listener* (9 Jan. 1935).

289 *Krumpacker.* Like the name Sweeney, the name Krumpacker may derive from a respectable man in the Harvard class of 1910, Walter Krumbeck, who became an educator.

289 *'If the audience gets its strip-tease . . .'.* TSE's facetious 'Five Points on Dramatic Writing' in a letter to Pound (19 Dec. 1937) is quoted by Carol H. Smith, op. cit., p. 53. Although TSE refers here to *FR*, the same theory would apply to *Sweeney Agonistes*.

289 *popular audience.* See 'Marie Lloyd' (1923), *SE*, pp. 405–8.

290 *A razor chase.* Described by Michael J. Sidnell, *Dances of Death: The Group Theatre of London in the Thirties* (London: Faber, 1984), p. 106.

290 *Vivienne's drug-addiction.* Statement by Theresa Garrett Eliot (28 Mar. 1970). Houghton.

290 *'nobody to hold one's hand . . .'.* Said to MT, PRS.

290 *discreet.* See *diary kept during marriage* (1919), referred to above, chs 4 and 7.

290 *description of the wife in FR.* Given by the chauffeur, Downing. *Plays*, p. 71.

290 *'Why, oh why . . .'.* Stephen Spender, 'Remembering Eliot', in Allen Tate's coll., p. 51.

290 *it is said.* By Agatha, *Plays*, p. 62.

291 *'She used to go about . . .'.* TSE to MT (28 Oct. 1954), PRS.

291 *alcohol and morphine.* Ackroyd, p. 190.

291 *Edith Sitwell.* See John Pearson, *Façades* (London: Macmillan, 1978), p. 277.

291 *'how his dying eyes lingered . . .'.* Diary (15 Sept. 1934).

291 *'. . . a lovely clear night'.* Ibid. (1 Sept. 1934).

292 *About a month after.* Since Vivienne returned in Feb. 1928 and was away nine months, it is likely that she left England in May 1927.

292 *'My dear Tom . . .'.* Diary (16 Feb. 1935).

292 *plucking his sleeve.* E. W. F. Tomlin, 'T. S. Eliot: a Friendship', *The Listener*, xcvii (28 Apr. 1977), p. 541. Cited by Ackroyd, p. 189.

292 *'A terrible time . . .'.* Diary (31 Jan. 1935).

293 *found her sinister.* VW to Quentin Bell (26 July 1933), *Letters*, v, 207. According to VW, Vivienne gave out that she and Ottoline Morrell had been TSE's mistresses. There was no truth in this.

293 *the Eliots' dinner.* Pearson, *Façades*, p. 242.

293 *like a patient father.* The Thorps dined with the Eliots in 1931. In conversation, Princeton, August 1985.

293 *Evie Townsend.* Recalled by Janet Adam Smith, 'Tom Possum and the Roberts Family', *Southern Review* (Oct. 1985), repr. *Essays from the Southern Review*, 213–26.

293 *Conrad Aiken.* To Theodore Spencer (5 Oct. 1930), Harvard Archives, Pusey Library. Quoted in *Selected Letters*, ed. Joseph Killorin (Yale, 1978), p. 162, but misdated as 31 Oct.

294 *poetry evening, and 'grim'.* Miranda Seymour, *Ottoline Morrell*, p. 520.

294 *Father Underhill.* TSE to Stead (2 Dec. 1930). Beinecke.

294 *'shivering, shuddering'.* Aiken's letter to Spencer, op. cit.

294 *'A restless shivering . . . shadow'.* FR, I, i. *Plays*, p. 62.

294 *letters to Ada Leverson.* Berg.

295 *'leaden' and 'sinister'.* VW, *Diary*, iii (8 Nov. 1930), p. 331.

295 *Edith Sitwell meeting Vivienne.* Osbert Sitwell, unpublished memoir on TSE, cited by John Pearson, *Façades*, p. 277–8.

295 *'eternal enemy'.* 'Conversation Galante', *CP*, p. 25.

296 *white satin and ether.* VW to Ethel Smyth (7 Sept. 1932), *Letters*, v, 100.

296 *'alas no Hamlet would love her'.* VW, *Diary*, iv (2 Sept. 1932), p. 123.

296 *'We had tea'.* Day Book (1 April 1935). Bodleian Library.

296 *a routine to deal with her.* Brigid O'Donovan, 'The Love Song of Eliot's Secretary', *Confrontation*, xi, ed. Martin Tucker (Fall/Winter 1975), 3–8.

297 *'all the blank expression . . .'.* Diary (10 May 1934). Bodleian Library.

297 *TSE believed Vivienne sane.* 'In conversation with VW, *Diary*, iv (10 Sept. 1933), p. 178.

297 *'under a crowned effigy'.* VW to Francis Birrell (3 Sept. 1933), *Letters*, v, 222.

297 *TSE to Lady Ottoline.* (20 Sept 1933). Texas. With thanks to Peter Ackroyd for his notes.

297 *on 27 November 1933.* VW had a letter from Vivienne on that day, she reported to Lady Ottoline Morrell (31 Dec. 1933), *Letters*, v, 266.

298 *'I look like a little ghost . . .'.* Diary (9 July 1934). Bodleian Library.

298 *The mills of God.* Diary (24 Aug. 1934).

298 *'state of nervous collapse'*. Diary (12 Dec. 1934). She had been served a court order to warn her in late Nov.

298 *'It hurt me . . .'*. Letter (16 July 1935). Copy in Day Book.

299 *'At last the* courage . . .'. Diary (Mar. 1935).

299 *Another scheme.* Diary (9 Jan. 1935).

299 *'It is too absurd . . .'*. Diary (13 Mar. 1935).

299 *Eliot was to talk.* He spoke on 'What in the practice of a particular art, such as poetry, do we mean by tradition?' He gave a copy of the text to Emily Hale.

300 *offering protection.* 1 Jan. 1935, entered into 1934 Diary.

300 *Another plan.* 7 Feb. 1935.

300 *'Everything was perfectly allright . . .'*. 28 Nov. 1935, copy in the Day Book, Scrapbook for 1935. Bodleian Library.

301 *Sir Herbert Read.* Allen Tate's collection.

302 *Edward Fox as Harry.* In the London production, 1978.

302 *public confession as bid for salvation.* There is a detailed analysis by Patricia Caldwell, *The New England Conversion Narrative: The Beginnings of American Expression* (CUP, 1983). In England in the seventeenth century this test was used by a relatively small number of sectarians. But New England's Puritans, led by John Cotton, adopted it widely.

302 *Eliot and the Anglican Church.* See above, ch. 6.

303 *Vivienne gave out . . .* The following details come from her 'Notes to Broad' (Mr Broad was her bank manager) in her Day Book, 1936. Bodleian Library.

303 Daisy Miller. Vivienne had ordered a copy from the Times Book Club on 1 Aug. 1935.

304 *'Vivienne!'*. VW, *Diary*, iii (8 Nov. 1930), p. 331.

305 *seven times.* In Feb. she went on the 1st, 8th, 11th, 19th, 22nd and 28th.

305 *'has had very great friends'*. 'Notes for Broad'.

305 *'apt to lose her wits'*. Copy of letter. Bodleian Library.

305 *cables.* Though Vivienne persists about a mystery, her diary records (29 Nov. 1935) that she actually met TSE on his return on 12 July 1933.

306 *Maurice Haigh-Wood, TSE, and Vivienne's certification.*

Valerie Eliot, letter to *TLS* (10 Feb. 1984), 139. The two quoted letters were printed as part of Blake Morrison's interview with Valerie Eliot, 'The Two Mrs Eliots', *Independent on Sunday* (24 Apr. 1994). TSE told Valerie Eliot about not holding Maurice's hand, and impressed on her that committal had been for Vivienne's own good. He took the view that had it not been done, Vivienne would have had an earlier grave.

308 *attempt to escape.* TSE recounted this to MT, MT's diary (2 Jan. 1957), PRS.

310 *'Mrs Ellerker'.* I have drawn on the deft wording of Ray Monk, *Bertrand Russell: The Spirit of Solitude* (London: Cape, 1996), pp. 431–2. The story is called 'Satan in the Suburbs' (1953).

311 *recalled with pleasure.* Diary (26 Dec. 1935). Bodleian Library.

311 *'I trust the man'.* Diary (14 Dec. 1935).

Chapter 9 Enter the Furies

312 *Helen Gardner.* March 1985. She didn't say how she came to know this.

312 *visit to Chichester Cathedral.* CFQ, p. 35.

312 *'Tom's head . . .'.* VW, *Diary*, iv, 262–3.

313 *EH wrote to President Jaqua.* Scripps College Archives.

313 *Kipling.* See *A Choice of Kipling's Verse*, ed. T. S. Eliot (London: Faber, 1941; repr. 1963), p. 111.

313 *Eliot came at once.* CFQ notes (p. 35) that TSE wrote on Easter Sunday to thank Mrs Perkins.

313 *time of* BN's *composition.* My dating is conjectural. It could not have been written before 24 March 1935 when Martin Browne read Part I of *MC*. Soon after this, possibly after rehearsals began on 7 May, Browne asked TSE to write the additional lines that were eventually to become the opening lines of *BN*. (See *EMB*, p. 56, and *CFQ*, p. 39.)

313 *'Descend lower . . .'.* BN: III.

313 *'Quick now . . .'.* BN: V.

313 *'Quick now . . .'. LG*: V.

313 *consummation postponed*. After Eliot's death, EH said in a letter to Willard Thorp (17 Jan. 1965) that the relationship had not been consummated. Thorp Papers, Princeton.

314 *ran away from a bull*. TSE to VW. Berg.

315 *EH to Ruth George*. Letter in the Denison Library, Claremont, Cal.

318 *impeccable Bostonion*. VW to Ethel Smyth (26 Nov. 1935), *Letters*, v, 446.

318 *'Eliot's rich American snob lady'*. VW to Clive Bell (4 Dec. 1935), ibid., p. 451.

318 *'quite an exceptional person'*. TSE to Ottoline Morrell (29 Oct 1934), Texas. With thanks to Peter Ackroyd for his transcription.

318 *'that awful American woman Miss Hale.'* Lady Ottoline Morrell (22 Oct. 1935), quoted by Miranda Seymour, *Ottoline Morrell: Life on the Grand Scale* (London: Hodder, 1992), 521–2.

319 *Unitarian retreat*. EH left a holograph ms, 'For Senexit' (5 Nov. 1941). EH Papers, Smith College.

320 *causes of Emily Hale's breakdown, etc*. In 1992, the Ella Strong Denison Library, Claremont, California, acquired 13 letters from TSE to Jeanette McPherrin (1934–54). The significant letters are 1935–6. Interesting photographs included. I am grateful to the curator, Judy Harvey Sahak, for her promptness in alerting me to these letters and sending photocopies.

321 *TSE gave EH a Bible*. Photocopy from C. E. Dexter Morse, who inherited the Bible from EH.

321 *autumn 1936*. In an interview with the *Star* (3 Nov. 1936), TSE said that he was working on a new play. In Nov. 1938 he told VW that *FR* had taken him two years off-and-on to write. A draft was read to EMB in Nov. 1937, which means that the first draft was done roughly between Nov. 1936 and Nov. 1937. Newspaper cuttings

attached to a draft of the play are dated April–May 1937, which may be one time when he worked intensively on it.

321 *very much in love.* Recalled in letter to MT (2 June 1950), PRS.

321 *A professorship at Harvard.* Offered by Professor Theodore Spencer in 1933. (Sencourt, *A Memoir of T. S. Eliot*, p. 153.)

321 *'Waiting . . .'.* FR, I, ii. *Plays*, 77.

321 *'I cannot tell you . . .'.* Sidnell, *Dances of Death*, pp. 100, 323.

321 Sweeney Agonistes *the most original thing . . . .* TSE to P. E. More (28 Apr. 1936). Princeton.

322 *ten discernible layers of composition.* See App. V below.

322 *date back to 1934–5.* The fourth layer is on the same paper as the MS of *MC* and was kept with it.

322 *'psychic'.* According to Downing, the chauffeur, I, i, *Plays*, 72.

322 *stained.* TSE to EMB (19 Mar. 1938), *EMB*, 108. Harry 'is aware of the past only as *pollution*'.

322 *the waiting Mary.* As yet she had no name in the King's College TS. See App. V for dating and a sequence of composition.

323 *additional scenario.* App. V:3.

323 *nightmares.* See Ronald Schuchard's account of other moments of horror, at Marlow in 1919 and Périgord in 1920, in his spot-on article 'T. S. Eliot and the Horrific Moment', *Southern Review* (Oct. 1985), repr. *Essays from the Southern Review*, 191–204.

323 *divided.* The 1938 Working Draft speaks of Harry's two lives.

323 *de-possession.* This word is used in the draft.

323 *'exorcism'.* FR, II, i. *Plays*, p. 101.

324 *three pages of pencil notes.* Houghton.

324 *marrying was 'a kind of preparation'.* This draft is explicit. Later, TSE made it deliberately vaguer: 'Whatever happened was a kind of preparation . . .'.

324 *Martin Browne praised.* TSE read the first complete draft to him on 14 Nov. 1937.

324 *stiff pokers.* VW, *Diary,* v (22 Mar. 1939), p. 210.

324 *Helen Gardner on Agatha. The Art of T. S. Eliot* (London: Cresset, 1949), ch. 6, p. 156.

324 *Janet Adam Smith.* In *Southern Review* (Oct. 1985), repr. in *Essays from the Southern Review,* pp. 213–26.

325 *'the chief poker'.* VW, *Diary,* v (22 Mar. 1939), p. 210.

325 *'a horror of women . . .'.* EMB, p. 107.

325 *present to his mind.* Phrases recalled from an article by Alfred Kazin on the ghost sense in American literature (Poe, Hawthorne, James) in the *New York Times Book Review* in about 1969.

325 *delusional insanity.* 'Notes on Philosophy': a set of index cards. This is a note under Richard Jeffries's *Story of My Heart.* Houghton.

326 *'his curious search . . .'.* 'Commentary', *Criterion* (Apr. 1933), quoted by Ronald Bush, *T. S. Eliot: A Study in Character and Style* (NY: Oxford Univ. Press, 1983), p. 183.

326 *dangers 'that look like nothing'.* Henry James, Preface to *The American* in *Literary Criticism,* ed. Leon Edel (NY: The Library of America, 1984).

327 *'as radical as any form of Calvinism'.* 'The Church in the Festival', *Life and Work* (Oct. 1947).

327 *Edinburgh Festival production.* At the Church of Scotland's Gateway Theatre. It was presented by the Pilgrim Players as part of a season of Eliot's plays. Henzie Raeburn (wife of EMB) was a success as Agatha. The *Scottish Daily Mail* suggested that TSE might be the greatest British playwright since Shakespeare.

327 *letter from Margaret Eliot.* Cited by Theresa Garrett Eliot, (28 Mar. 1970). Houghton.

327 *rumour.* It is related in an article on *CPy* by Geoffrey Parson in the *New York Herald Tribune* (12 Feb. 1950).

327 *letter from Margaret Eliot.* Cited by Theresa Garrett Eliot, (28 Mar. 1970). Houghton.

327 Time. 28 Feb. 1938.

327 *Henry Eliot retorted. Time.*

327 *'the accident . . .'.* I, ii, *Plays,* p. 83.

327 *early unfinished draft.* King's.

328 *upswing in New Hampshire.* Scc 'New Hampshire' and ch. 7 above.

328 *'vernal equinox'.* Quoted in *EMB*, p. 111.

328 *'a new world . . .'.* Quoted in *EMB*, p. 98.

328 *Emily Hale.* See App. V.

328 *A long speech of protest.* Working Draft, II, ii.

328 *the shift.* It was moved to Part I, ii.

329 *'lifetime's march'.* Agatha's words, *FR*, II, ii.

329 *origin of evil.* In one draft it is said that the origin of evil lay behind Harry's particular childhood. In the final draft TSE changed it to 'the origin of wretchedness' (II, ii).

329 *divine messengers.* TSE uses the phrases 'divine instruments' and 'divine messengers' in letter to EMB (19 Mar. 1938), *EMB*, p. 107.

329 *the octopus or angel.* 'The Three Voices of Poetry', *OPP*, p. 110.

329 *'chosen'.* Agatha, *FR*, II, ii. *Plays*, p. 105.

330 *Swedish production.* TSE gave this hilarious account to MT, PRS.

330 *advised Pound.* Letter advising Pound on the *Cantos* is dated Michaelmas 1933. Beinecke.

331 *'jolly corner'.* *FR*, I, i. *Plays*, p. 60.

331 *Calvin. Institutes of the Christian Religion* (2.1.8), ed. John T. McNeill (Philadelphia: Westminster, 1960), p. 251.

331 *'dramatism'.* Frank Morley in Allen Tate (ed.), *T. S. Eliot*, p. 110.

331 *the real purgatorial fire.* JH's draft. King's.

331 *like the Disciples.* Letter (19 Mar. 1938), *EMB*, p. 108.

332 *'Follow . . .'.* *FR*, II, iii.

332 *Marianne Moore's letter*, (27 Sept. 1959), EH Papers, Sophia Smith Collection, Smith College.

332 *the second draft sent to Emily Hale.* The Working Draft of 1938. See App. V: 9.

332 *the heat of the sun. FR*, II, ii. *Plays*, p. 111.

332 *sanctification.* TS.B. Houghton. It follows Agatha's 'Harry has crossed the frontier' speech. This was the first

of the two drafts that TSE sent to Emily Hale. She kept it until 1960, when she gave it to Harvard. See App. V: 6.

333 *polluted soul*. TSE used the word 'pollution' to EMB, op. cit.

333 Evening Standard *reporting*. TSE's cuttings were pasted on to the flyleaf to Part II of *FR*.

334 *'across the frontier'*. Agatha, *FR*, II, iii. *Plays*, p. 114.

334 *'it was the policy of our ancestors . . .'*. 'Endicott and the Red Cross' in *Twice Told Tales* (1837).

334 *'I have had . . .'*. 'The Love Song of J. Alfred Prufrock', *CP*, p. 4.

334 *'should die . . .'*. 'Portrait of a Lady', *CP*, p. 12.

334 *Eliot remarked to Mary Trevelyan*. PRS.

335 *two unpublished talks*. 'The Development of Shakespeare's Verse', King's. The talks were given in Edinburgh in 1937 and repeated in Bristol in 1941. In speaking of Shakespeare's late plays, TSE was theorising about the play that he himself was writing at the time.

335 *ordinary classified emotions*. Some of this went into 'Poetry and Drama' (1951) in *OPP*.

335 *strange lands of more than polar darkness*. This forecasts *FR*, I, ii, where Harry speaks to Mary of moving from pole to pole in the early Unfinished Draft (App. V: 2). And both talk and play forecast 'the unimaginable / Zero summer' in *LG*: I (1942).

335 *told Michael Redgrave*. EMB, p. 137.

335 *the life of the senses will freeze*. These polar regions forecast the deliberate freezing of the body in *EC*: II (1940).

335 *'cruellest' month*. WL: I.

336 *the soul's sap*. LG: I.

336 *'lying voices'*. *FR*, I, ii. *Plays*, p. 81.

336 MC *during the war*. EMB, p. 154.

336 *failure of* FR *daunted TSE*. Suggested by Bush, *T. S. Eliot*, p. 209.

336 *Harry's exit line*. II, ii. *Plays*, p. 111. Harry reappears once more, but only cursorily.

336 *The way up and the way down.* Epigraph to *BN*, from Herakleitos.

336 *vast and terrible sea.* In 1940 TSE planned a sequence of only three poems. *EC* and *DS*, planned together in 1940, are closely connected.

Chapter 10 The Perfect Life

338 *'acute personal reminiscence'.* TSE to JH (5 Aug. 1941). All quotations from this correspondence, now at King's College, Cambridge, are cited in *CFQ*.

338 *'things ill done . . .'. LG*: II.

338 *'Kensington Quartets'.* TSE to JH (3 Sept. 1942). This letter is bound with the typescripts of *LG*. The manuscripts and typescripts of *FQ* are mainly at King's College, Cambridge. There is also material at Magdalene College, Cambridge, and a typescript of *BN* at the Houghton Library.

338 *grimpen.* The source was pointed out by Helen Gardner, *CFQ*, p. 103.

338 *'The poetry does not matter'. EC*: II.

339 *books read at Harvard.* There is a collection of TSE's books in the Houghton Library, as well as his student notes. See App. I.

339 *'Now . . .'. EC*: V.

341 *alternation of prosaic and poetic.* In 'The Music of Poetry (1942), *OPP*, p. 25, he says that 'no poet can write a long poem unless he is a master of the prosaic'.

341 *'In my beginning . . .'. EC*: I.

341 *'In my end . . .'. EC*: V.

341 *'the unimaginable . . .'. LG*: I.

342 *'mystery'.* EH to Willard Thorp. Thorp Papers, Princeton.

342 *New Englander.* Lambert Strether in Henry James, *The Ambassadors*.

342 *TSE on Huck Finn.* Introduction to the Cresset Library's edition of *Huckleberry Finn* (1950).

342 *the midsummer night. EC*: I.

343 *the Puritan killjoy.* 'The Maypole of Merry Mount'.
343 *'still / Moves . . .'. BN:* V. This is Eliot's parallel to Keats's Grecian Urn.
343 *'slip, slide . . .'. BN:* V.
344 *'Love'. LG:* IV.
344 *a distilled concentrate.* '. . . concentration / Without elimination'. *BN:* II.
344 *'outer compulsion'. BN:* II.
344 *love-letter from God.* T. S. Matthews, *Great Tom* (NY: Harper & Row, 1973), p. 144.
344 *Emily Hale's gift of* EC. Ibid., p. 147.
344 *Emily Hale not content with friendship.* More detail in ch. 11 below.
344 *'in an emotional whole'.* (10 Mar. 1941), *CFQ,* p. 109.
345 *'vibrations . . .'.* 'What Dante Means to Me', *CC,* p. 134.
345 *'The Burnt Dancer'.* Dated June 1914. See above, ch. 3.
345 *'move in measure . . .'. LG:* II.
345 *'always'. BN:* V: 'Quick, now, here, now, always –'.
345 *draft of* BN. Houghton. TSE sent this carbon copy of his typescript to Frank Morley in New York. The first 'Gone' is added in pencil. These final lines were deleted on Morley's (marginal) advice. TSE gave the other extant draft to JH, and it is now in King's College Library, Cambridge, England. It contains two final lines of two words (similar to the Morley draft): 'Light', followed by a space, and then 'Gone' indented on the next line. 'Gone' is added again in pencil as though it were an afterthought. Both lines are cancelled.
346 *seventeenth-century.* The voyage appears to take three months: 'between one June and another September'.
347 *first visit to East Coker.* TSE to Polly Tandy (18 June 1936). Tandy Papers, British Library.
347 *poignantly self-revealing.* Tarantula's Special News Service, letter XII (Feb. 1940). King's.
347 *feared the embrace of the Devil.* TSE to EMB (Shrove Tuesday 1935), quoted in *EMB* (1970 reprint), p. 349.
347 *'disturbance'. EC:* II.
347 *'creature'. EC:* II.

347 *figure of Goodman Brown.* Hawthorne's tale 'Young Goodman Brown', is recalled by certain phrases in *EC*: 'in a dark wood . . . / And menaced by monsters, fancy lights, / Risking enchantment.'

347 *discovers sin in a dark wood.* Melville said that the tale was 'as deep as Dante'. *EC*, too, makes the connection, linking the opening of the *Inferno* ('In the middle . . .') with the dark wood of 'Young Goodman Brown'.

347 *'canopy'.* 'Young Goodman Brown'.

347 *approach to East Coker.* See illustration.

347 *dissolves in a dream.* Barbara Everett, in an interesting BBC talk in 1983 on *EC*, 'The Village of the Heart', said that 'entry to East Coker, in the poem, is the beginning of a dream'. In *T. S. Eliot: Man and Poet*, ed. Laura J. Cowan (US National Poetry Foundation, 1988).

348 *TSE and the* Sketch of the Eliot Family. TSE mentions in a letter to his brother (7 Feb. 1939) that he had looked it up. Their father, he recalled, had owned two copies.

348 *Sir Thomas Elyot.* Author of *The Boke Named the Governour* (1531). See above, ch. 1.

348 *family motto. EC*: I speaks of 'the tattered arras woven with a silent motto'.

348 *family fortunes had declined.* Mentioned in letter to Pound. Beinecke.

348 *had Cape Ann house in mind.* TSE to JH (27 Feb. 1940).

348 *'Old men . . .'. EC*: V.

349 *'O dark dark dark'. EC*: III alludes to Milton, *Samson Agonistes* (l. 80), *The Poems of John Milton*, ed. John Carey and Alastair Fowler (London: Longman, 1968, repr. 1980), p. 349.

349 *'fortunate night'.* 'Stanzas' (verses 3–4) preceding *The Ascent of Mount Carmel.*

349 *'amid the blaze of noon'. Samson Agonistes* (l. 80), op. cit.

349 *'the drought'.* 'The *Pensées* of Pascal', *SE*, p. 364.

350 *In order . . .'. EC*, III.

350 *'most hidden of saints'.* 'St. John of the Cross', *Perspectives*, iv (Summer 1953), 52–61.

351 *'inoperancy of the . . . spirit'. BN*: III. TSE here sums up briefly the two 'nights' of St John of the Cross: a dark night of sense, followed by a dark night of the spirit.

351 *saint's chart.* The chart accompanies *The Ascent of Mount Carmel.*

351 *'it is the highest activity . . .'.* Quoted in review by M. C. D'Arcy, *Criterion* (Apr. 1938), 538–9.

351 *'I said to my soul . . .'. EC*: III.

351 *The Rule was severe . . . .* E. Allison Peers, the Rede Lecture for 1932, collected in *St. John of the Cross* (London: Faber, 1946). TSE would have been responsible for Faber publications in theology.

351 *'animal penance'. The Dark Night of the Soul,* Book I, ch. 6.

351 *'Wait without thought . . .'. EC*: III.

352 *'interior work . . .'. The Cloud of Unknowing* (Harmondsworth: Penguin, 1961).

352 *'Undisciplined squads . . .'. EC*: V.

352 *'The Lover . . .'.* MS notes for *EC*: IV, *CFQ*, p. 95. There was no MS of *EC* except for part IV (TSE to JH, 23 June 1940).

352 *'the heart of the matter'.* 10 Mar. 1941, quoted in *CFQ*, p. 95. *EC*: IV.

352 *'conscious of nothing'. EC*: III.

352 *'I faint with heat'. CFQ*, p. 95.

352 *'reigns'. EC*: II.

352 *'un-English'.* TSE to Anne Ridler, *CFQ*, p. 95.

352 *'a Jansenism of the individual biography'.* 'Pascal', *SE*, p. 366.

353 *William Force Stead pictured him.* Holograph notes on TSE's character (1940). Beinecke.

353 *'great yellow bronze mask . . .'.* VW, *Diary*, v, 268.

353 *'We can have very little hope . . .'. NEW.* At this very time TSE was writing *EC.*

353 *thirties poets declined in favour.* JH's News Service to Morley. See letters IV, XXVIII.

354 *Barker.* JH, letter IV to Morley (Oct. 1939).

354 *playing chess etc.* TSE to JH (27 Feb. 1940).

354 *had to visit houses in his area* .... TSE to McKnight Kauffer (23 May 1940). Pierpont Morgan Library, New York.

354 *lengthy reports of air-raid practice.* Tarantula's News Service, letter II (Sept. 1939).

354 *Hayward had to try hard.* Letter III (Sept. 1939).

354 *'I believe . . .'.* Stead, holograph notes (1940). Beinecke.

355 *'That was a way . . .'.* EC: II.

355 *'cover yourself in forgetful snow'.* WL: I.

355 *to bath at the Fabers'.* VW, *Diary* v (16 Feb. 1940), p. 268.

356 *'the old world . . .'.* TSE is imagining Kipling's perspective on the English and, at the same time, speaking in unison. Introduction to *A Choice of Kipling's Verse* (London: Faber, 1941).

356 *'three quatuors'.* TSE planned 'three quatuors', JH told Morley in letter XI of Tarantula's Special News Service (Feb. 1940), *CFQ*, pp. 16–18.

356 *'Through the dark . . .'.* EC: V.

356 *the nurse* .... Wordsworth, 'Lines written a few miles above Tintern Abbey'. *Lyrical Ballads*, ed. W. J. B. Owen, (OUP, 1967), p. 115.

356 *Ahab.* Herman Melville, *Moby-Dick.*

356 *beat obedient.* See WL: V.

356 *'these frontiers . . .'.* 'A Commentary: that poetry is made with words', *NEW* (27 Apr. 1939), p. 27.

357 *the planned approach to grace. Marina.*

357 *TSE to William Matchett.* Quoted in *CFQ*, p. 18.

357 *here or there does not matter.* Eliot explained in a letter that this was an abbreviation of 'whether here or there'. *CFQ*, p. 113.

357 *'Alone – the ice cap . . .'.* *CFQ*, p. 111, has not transcribed correctly the pencilled holograph D2 (back of p. 5).

357 *'I always think . . .'.* TSE to Charlotte Eliot (14 Oct. 1917), *L*, i, 199.

358 *'the smell of grapes . . .'.* DS: I, *CP*, p. 191.

358 *'made a deeper impression . . .'.* (1930), quoted by

Anthony Thwaite, *Twentieth-Century English Poetry* (London: Heinemann; NY Barnes & Noble, 1978), p. 45.

358 *TSE's memory of the Mississippi in flood.* Introduction to Cresset Library *Huckleberry Finn*, (1950).

358 *rockpool. DS:* I and *UPUC*, pp. 78–9, which recalled an experience 'not so simple for an exceptional child as it looks'.

358 *power and terror.* TSE's phrase from the Introduction to *Huckleberry Finn* (1950).

358 *The Dry Salvages.* Information from *Alluring Rockport*, Sawyer Free Library, Gloucester, Mass.

359 *Eliot and Peters.* Leon Little's reminiscences for the *Harvard Advocate's* TSE memorial issue. Typescript in Houghton Library.

360 *'the ground swell'. DS:* I.

360 *'I suspect . . .'.* Talk on 'Tradition and the Practice of Poetry' in Dublin (1936), ed. A. Walton Litz, *Southern Review* (Oct. 1985), 883, repr. *Essays from the Southern Review.* This is a restatement of Eliot's position in *Shakespeare* (1927): 'To express precise emotion requires as great intellectual power as to express precise thought' (*SE*, p. 115), and again, more explicitly, 'Poetry is not a substitute for philosophy or theology or religion . . . it has its own function. But as this function is not intellectual but emotional, it cannot be defined adequately in intellectual terms' (*SE*, p. 118).

360 *'the point of intersection . . .'. DS:* V.

360 *'an occupation for the saint'. DS:* V.

361 *'between the rocks'. AW:* V.

361 *the long narrative which Pound cut.* See above, ch. 5, and App. II.

361 *'If Another knows . . .'.* facs. *WL*, pp. 68–9.

361 *'Sail forth . . .'.* 'Passage to India'. The Library of America's *Whitman*, op. cit., 539. This and the following quotations are from stanza 9.

362 *'significant'. DS:* V.

363 *fall flat.* Helen Gardner calls the ending 'lame' (*CFQ*, p.

149). It has been criticised also by Donald Davie and Ronald Bush.

363 *'dearest him ...'.* 'I wake and feel the fell of dark, not day', Gerard Manley Hopkins, *A Selection of his Poems and Prose*, ed. W. H. Gardner (Harmondsworth: Penguin, 1953), p. 62.

363 *'a dancer to God'.* 'The Death of Saint Narcissus' in *facs. WL*, 90–1.

363 *'to know the place ....'. LG*: V.

363 *sea's jaws. LG*: I.

363 'Datta, Dayadhvam, Damyata'. *WL*: V.

364 *the timeless pattern of spiritual autobiography.* Bunyan's words, quoted by Linda Peterson, 'Newman's *Apologia pro vita sua* and English spiritual autobiography', *PMLA* (May 1985), 300–14.

364 *the 'meaning of "mother" ...'.* Scheme for *DS*. MS (Magdalene College Library). *CFQ*, p. 118.

364 *'We had the experience ....'. DS*: II.

364 *entrails.* 'haruspicate', *DS*: V.

364 *Eliot on Freud.* 'A Commentary: that poetry is made with words' in *NEW* (27 Apr. 1939), which notes, further, that the 'dramatist must study, not psychology, but human beings' and also himself: 'to what he observes, dissects and combines he must add something from himself of which he may not be wholly conscious.'

365 *'... our own past'. DS*: II.

365 *In a draft Eliot uncovers ....* First draft of *LG*: II. *CFQ*, p. 228.

365 *'moments of agony'. DS*: II.

365 *notes. CFQ*, p. 118.

365 *'the ragged rock ...'. DS*: II. In draft this rock immediately follows the 'torment of others'. Bush (*T. S. Eliot: A Study in Character and Style*, p. 219) suggests a reference here to Vivienne.

365 *'circling fury'.* Draft of *BN*: V. *CFQ*, p. 88.

365 *carrion.* TSE's last thought of the Mississippi, in the drafts, is the line (added last) about the river bearing dead Negroes, cows and chicken coops.

365 *things done to others' harm.* TSE alludes to Yeats's lines (from 'Vacillation') in *LG*: II.

365 *a future.* 'Now about the future', wrote TSE at the end of his first draft of *DS*: II. This was cancelled in the second draft (*CFQ*, p. 134).

365 *foresaw even before he experienced love.* See ch. 2 above.

366 *'an equal mind'. DS*: III.

366 *Mary Trevelyan's suggestion.* PRS.

366 *'Atonement'.* Drafts of the ending of *DS*: V at King's, Magdalene, and Texas. *CFQ*, p. 146.

367 *Oct. 1940.* The date of TSE's move is mentioned in a letter to VW (28 Oct. 1940). Berg.

367 *household.* Janet Adam Smith, 'Tom Possum and the Roberts Family'.

367 *Cocky.* TSE to MT (29 Jan. 1945), PRS. Probably Constance Moncrieff.

367 *Margaret Behrens and her Peke.* TSE to MT (30 Oct. 1944), PRS.

367 *gardener.* TSE to MT (29 Jan. 1945).

367 *TSE to Polly Tandy.* His wartime letters (1940–1) give interesting details. Tandy Papers, British Library.

367 *Enid Faber noticed . . .* JH to TSE (7 Jan. 1941). King's.

367 *healthiest life.* TSE to VW (28 Oct. 1940). Berg.

368 *defeat.* See *LG*.

368 *'To get beyond time . . .'.* Notes for *DS*: V. Magdalene College Library, Cambridge. *CFQ*, p. 118.

369 *TSE on Beethoven's A Minor Quartet.* Letter to Stephen Spender (28 Mar. 1931), 'Remembering Eliot', *Encounter*, xxiv (Apr. 1965), 3–14, repr. Allen Tate (ed.), *T. S. Eliot: The Man and His Work* (NY: Dell, 1966).

369 *'not to the ear'.* Like the piper on Keats's Grecian Urn: 'Heard melodies are sweet, but those unheard / Are sweeter . . . / Pipe to the spirit ditties of no tone.' Helen Gardner (*CFQ*, p. 139) links the voice with the siren women in the *Waste Land* manuscript: IV whose song 'disarmed the senses', but this Keatsian melody is definitely 'Not to the sensual ear'.

369 *'beyond poetry . . .'.* Unpublished lecture on 'English

Letter Writers', delivered at Yale in 1933, quoted by F. O. Matthiessen, *The Achievement of T. S. Eliot*, 3rd ed. (1935; repr. NY: OUP, 1959), p. 90.

369 *'unimaginable'*. LG: I.

369 *'Thou canst not see my face'*. Exodus 33: 20.

369 *the poetry of the Bible*. Unpublished address on the Bible at King's Chapel, Boston (Dec. 1932), Houghton. I am grateful to Mrs Valerie Eliot for permission (in 1975) to see this.

370 *Eliot on* Le Spectre de la rose. LG: III and letter to JH: 'I was thinking of the Ballet', CFQ, p. 202.

371 *high points of his past*. First draft of LG: II.

371 *'Now and in England'*. LG: I.

371 *'Where prayer has been valid'*. LG: I.

372 *'rough road'*. LG: I.

372 *'breaks'*. LG: I.

373 *'the passage . . .'*. BN: I.

373 *maytime-playtime*. Drafts of LG: I.

373 *from well below the surface*. TSE told JH that what might be wrong with the first draft of LG was the lack of acute personal reminiscence working well below the surface. CFQ, p. 24.

374 *'the dark dove . . .'*. LG: II.

374 *Forster on* LG. Entry in his Commonplace Book (4 Jan. 1963), pp. 266–7. King's. Facsimile ed. by the Scolar Press, 1978. Forster was then eighty-five.

374 *'I would feel the need . . .'*. Quarterly Review of Literature, v (1967), quoted by Peter Ackroyd, *T. S. Eliot: A Life* (London: Hamish Hamilton; NY: Simon & Schuster, 1984), pp. 260–1.

375 *'falling down . . .'*. WL: V.

375 *the aftermath of air-raids*. TSE to W. T. Levy, CFQ, p. 166.

375 *London after an air-raid*. Precisely observed by Leonard Woolf, *The Journey Not the Arrival Matters* (London: Hogarth, 1969), p. 64.

375 *animated*. Letter to VW (Oct. [?] 1940). Berg. His tone is a

striking contrast to her harrowed descriptions of the ruined City squares in her diary.

376 *Eliot's climactic encounter with his other self.* A. Walton Litz, always alert to Eliot's ties with Henry James, has pointed out that it is as if the dramatic encounters of the *Inferno* and *Purgatorio* merge with the self-confrontation in 'The Jolly Corner' (review of *CFQ* 'From Burnt Norton to Little Gidding: The Making of T. S. Eliot's *Four Quartets*', *Review*, ii, 1980). Eliot refers us to Shelley's meeting with a disfigured Rousseau in 'The Triumph of Life' which, he said in 1950, 'made an indelible impression on me forty-five years ago'. ('What Dante Means to Me', CC, p. 130).

376 *first version of the ghost's prophecy.* CFQ gives the complete first draft of 7 July 1941 in App. A, pp. 225–33.

377 *'autumn'.* TSE to JH (5 Aug. 1941), CFQ, p. 29.

377 *JH on 'Zero summer'.* CFQ, p. 160.

377 *JH on 'silence'.* CFQ, p. 223: 'He put a cross against "silence".'

377 *'cost me . . .'.* 'What Dante Means to Me', CC, p. 129.

377 *'old rooted sin . . .'.* CFQ, p. 188.

377 *'Vacillation'.* , *Collected Poems* (London: Macmillan, 1958), p. 284. The lines are quoted by Helen Gardner and Ronald Bush.

378 *lust and rage.* Yeats, 'The Spur', *Collected Poems* p. 359. TSE quoted the poem in 'Yeats', *OPP*, p. 302.

378 *Yeats's fire.* 'Byzantium'. *Collected Poems*, pp. 280–1.

378 *'there is only the one remedy . . .'.* From a second prose outline of the ghost's revised speech. CFQ, p. 189.

378 *both versions are personal.* A. Walton Litz has noted that the personal urgency was already there in the last twenty-four lines of the first version. (Review of *CFQ*, op. cit.)

379 *'They vanish . . .'.* CFQ, p. 157.

379 *detachment.* LG: III. It is hard to see here the distinction that TSE makes between 'detachment' and 'indifference'. It is possible that 'indifference' should be preferred, but its connotations are colder than 'detachment'.

379 *'uncompromising'.* JH to TSE (1 Aug. 1941). This letter is quoted in full in App. A of CFQ.

380 The Cloud of Unknowing. Op. cit., p. 52.

380 Imitation of Christ. Thomas à Kempis, Book 2, ch. 8: 'Some Advice on the Inner Life'.

380 *'the purification of the motive'*. LG: III. The first type-script reads 'The perfection of the motive'. *CFQ*, p. 230.

380 *'love of a country'*. LG: III.

380 *'Love'*. 'Love is the unfamiliar Name . . .'. LG: IV.

380 *broke down*. JH's frank words to TSE. *CFQ*, p. 234.

380 *the descent of Christ*. This is a prayer based on 'Anima Christi sancifica me'. The quoted words are Eliot's additions. *CFQ*, p. 207.

380 *in tongues'*. *CFQ*, p. 213. The original (MS A) version of Part IV, Magdalene College, Cambridge.

381 *'sign that brands'*. *CFQ*, p. 213. The phrase comes from the original (MS A) version of part IV. Magdalene College, Cambridge.

381 'Unprofitable Sin', *etc*. First typescript, *CFQ*, p. 214.

381 *'already a kind of presence of the supernatural . . .'*. 'Baudelaire', *SE*, pp. 374–5.

381 *St Bernard's sermon*. Quoted by Thomas Merton, *The Silent Life* (NY: Farrar, Straus, 1957; repr. London: Sheldon Press, 1975), p. 112.

382 *'to spend much more time . . .'*. *CFQ*, p. 196.

382 *'Solidad'*. TSE wrote 'Solidos', corrected in *CFQ*, p. 213.

382 *'broken king'*. LG: I.

382 *'not wholly commendable'*. LG: III.

383 *TSE to Allen Tate*. (26 Mar. 1943). Tate Papers, Princeton.

383 *the rescue at the Shambles*. TSE to JH (19 Sept. 1942). King's.

383 *'. . . re-reading the poem . . .'*. TSE to JH (5 Aug. 1941). King's.

383 *Eliot's Kipling*. A. Walton Litz picked out the telling phrases from Eliot's introduction (repr. *OPP*, pp. 265–94), in his immensely suggestive review of *CFQ*, op. cit. How curiously TSE's Kipling and *EC* merge. TSE was thinking in particular of *Puck of Pook's Hill*, *Rewards and Fairies*, 'The Wish House', and 'The Friendly Brook'.

384 *a white rose.* Recalled by Hope Mirrlees in BBC TV programme 'The Mysterious Mr Eliot' (1974).

384 *history as 'timeless moments'.* LG: V.

384 *Hegel's* Philosophy of History. Eliot's copy is in the Houghton Library.

385 *talk on Shakespeare in Bristol.* Eliot used the two lectures on the development of Shakespeare's verse, composed in 1937 (see ch. 9), which he revised in July 1941. King's.

385 *Eliot to Martin Browne.* (20 Oct. 1942), *EMB*, p. 158.

385 *Eliot's visit to Sweden with Bishop Bell.* These details come verbatim from Roger Kojecky, *T. S. Eliot's Social Criticism* (NY: Farrar, Straus & Giroux, 1972), p. 150.

385 *hoped to revise* LG *in the winter.* TSE to McKnight Kauffer in New York (29 Aug. 1941), saying that he was putting *LG* aside until winter. Pierpont Morgan Library, NY.

385 *'smoke-screen'.* JH's word describing the first typescript of part IV. *CFQ*, p. 235.

385 *'Who heaped the brittle roseleaves?'* See *CFQ*, p. 216, which made the link with *BN*. Eliot did the revised versions on a pad called MS C. Magdalene.

385 *voices of two mystics.* Eliot made the additions to part III by 17 Aug. 1942. He added the line from *The Cloud of Unknowing* to part V by 27 Aug. 1942.

386 *'the two mystical extremes'.* TSE to JH (2 Sept. 1942). *CFQ*, p. 70.

386 LG *resonates into a future beyond the poem.* In his review of *CFQ*, 'The Making of *Four Quartets*', A. Walton Litz argues for the closure of *FQ* in contrast with *WL*, which is open-ended. I agree in the sense that Eliot does subdue the private search to the given formula for spiritual autobiography, which is final.

387 *'ease'.* LG: II.

387 *Eliot to Mrs Perkins.* (10 July 1936). He motored from Cambridge. *CFQ*, p. 35.

387 *A classic language.* Eliot posits a role for the poet as saviour and extender of the language in a brilliant radio

interview on 22 Nov. 1940, published as 'The Writer as Artist', *Listener* (28 Nov. 1940).

388 *beyond character*. 'The Development of Shakespeare's Verse'. King's.

388 *shedding his life like a husk*. Helen Gardner said rightly that *FQ* was autobiographical but not in the same way as Eliot's earlier poetry.

389 *cumulative effect*. These are Eliot's words from the above talk on Shakespeare's verse.

389 *behind it, the dead*. When JH asked about the yew tree (in *DS*: V), TSE described a dream.

389 *'We are born with the dead . . .'. LG*: V.

389 *Edith Sitwell to Eliot. Selected Letters 1919–64*, ed. John Lehmann and Derek Parker (NY: Vanguard Press, 1970), p. 203.

389 *eighteen months later. FQ* was published in England on 31 Oct. 1944.

389 *'the fourth is the best . . .'. Paris Review* interview with Donald Hall, repr. *Writers at Work*, ed. Van Wyck Brooks, 2nd series, (NY: Viking, 1963).

389 *told Helen Gardner*. Interview, *Sunday Times* (21 Sept. 1958).

390 *'I rest on those'. Paris Review* interview.

390 *'I stand or fall on them'*. TSE to W.T. Levy, in William Turner Levy and Victor Scherle, *Affectionately, T. S. Eliot*, (NY: Lippincott 1968), p. 41.

390 *'I have the A minor Quartet . . .'*. Spender, 'Remembering Eliot', Allen Tate's collection, op. cit., p. 54.

390 *'your heart . . .'. WL*: V.

390 *The true artist . . .'*. TSE quotes from Kipling's story 'The Bull that Thought' in his Introduction to *A Choice of Kipling's Verse*, repr. *OPP*, p. 273.

390 *the function of art*. 'Poetry and Drama' (1951) in *OPP*, p. 94.

391 *Mary Lee Settle. New York Times Book Review* (16 Dec. 1984), 10.

391 *'which we can only detect . . .'*. 'Poetry and Drama', op. cit., p. 93.

391 *wise woman*. Eliot called her this in a letter to JH (2 Sept. 1942).

Chapter 11 Lady of Silences

392 *'O God!'* Peter Ackroyd, *T. S. Eliot: A Life* (London: Hamish Hamilton; NY: Simon & Schuster, 1984), p. 256.

392 *'reality'*. 'human kind / Cannot bear very much reality.' *BN*: I.

392 *'Lady of silences'*. *AW*: II.

392 *TSE's letters to EH*. Princeton University.

393 *Bodleian Library*. EH to TSE (12 Sept. 1963). Copy in Willard Thorp Papers, Princeton. Printed in full below.

393 *'to protect me'*. EH to Willard Thorp (27 Nov. 1965). EH's correspondence with Willard Thorp is in the Thorp Papers, Princeton.

393 *Peter du Sautoy*. 'T. S. Eliot: Personal Reminiscences', *Southern Review* (Autumn 1985), pp. 947–56. Repr. *Essays from the Southern Review*. Details confirmed in letter to me (17 Mar. 1986).

393 *cheeseboard*. Hugh Kenner, *The Pound Era* (1972).

394 *false teeth*. TSE to Polly Tandy (3 Nov. 1941). Tandy Papers, British Library.

394 *psychological change of life*. Letter to MT included in PRS.

394 *shocked*. TSE to Violet Schiff (28 Jan. 1947). British Library.

394 *'I have met myself . . .'*. *CPy*, I. ii. *Plays*, p. 153.

395 *scenes*. MT's diary (28 Oct. 1954). PRS.

395 *feelings of guilt*. 'T. S. Eliot: a friendship', *Listener*, xcvii (28 Apr. 1977), 541–3.

396 *Lavinia's return*. *CPy*, I. iii.

396 *original acted version*. Author's TS copy of acting edition with MS corrections, Act II, p. 90. King's. (*Plays*, p. 176).

396 *'What is hell?'* *CPy*, I. iii. *Plays*, p. 169.

396 *'projections'*. See 'Cyril Tourneur', *SE*, p. 166: 'characters which seem merely to be spectres projected from the

poet's inner world of nightmare, some horror beyond words.'

396 *The whole oppression . . .'. CPy*, I. iii. *Plays*, p. 175.

396 *Roderick Usher*. 'The Fall of the House of Usher'.

397 *macabre fantasies*. 'The Love Song of Saint Sebastian'; *Sweeney Agonistes; The Family Reunion*.

397 *'face that sweats . . .'*. 'The wind sprang up at four o'clock'. *CP*, p. 134.

397 *Christopher Sykes*. 'Some Memories', *Book Collector* (Winter 1965).

397 *'disintegrated'*. TSE to MT (30 Jan. 1947), PRS.

397 *'tensely withdrawn'*. Hans Meyerhoff, *Partisan Review* (Jan. 1948).

397 *two operations*. Ackroyd, p. 258.

397 *Lambert Strether*. Henry James, *The Ambassadors*. A New Englander in Europe (1901, published 1903).

398 *Sir Herbert Read*. Allen Tate's collection, 31.

398 *Eliot did believe*. TSE to MT (2 June 1950). PRS.

398 *'emotionless'. DS*: II.

398 *catastrophe*. TSE to MT (27 Apr. 1949), PRS.

399 *family feeling*. Letter to Mrs Perkins (30 Sept. 1935), quoted in *CFQ*, p. 35.

399 *light verse*. Lines from 'Morgan Tries Again' are quoted in *Great Tom*, p. 142.

399 *'detachment'. LG*: III.

399 *'so perfect a solution'*. EH to Willard Thorp (17 Jan. 1965). Princeton.

400 *'many a passage . . .'*. EH to Willard Thorp (5 Jan. 1964). Princeton.

400 *'my eyes failed'. WL*: I.

401 *'I remember . . .'*. This comes from the draft of *WL*: II: *facs. WL*, pp. 12–13.

401 Notebook. *The Complete Notebooks of Henry James* ed. Leon Edel and Lyall H. Powers (OUP, 1987), pp. 112–13.

402 *Willard Thorp on 'Geronion'*. An excellent lecture (March 1947) at the Univ. of Virginia. Copy in the Eliot Collection, Houghton Library.

402 *'Cape Ann'. CP*, p. 142. Helen Gardner remarked to me

that this was 'Emily Hale's poem' (conversation, March 1985).

402 *over the heads.* See Henry James, 'The Jolly Corner', *Complete Stories*, v (NY: The Library of America, 1996). Eliot alludes to this tale in *FR*, I, i. (*Plays*, p. 60) and, too, with the ghost in *LG*: II. The latter, I think accurate suggestion was made by A. Walton Litz in a review of *CFQ*, 'The Making of Eliot's *Four Quartets*', *Review*, ii (1980), 14.

403 *'Hidden under the heron's wing'.* The poem is written in the post-Paris hand, i.e. after Nov. 1911 and before June 1914. See above, ch. 3.

403 *the lotus.* I am grateful to Andrew Topsfield, Curator of Indian Art at the Ashmolean Museum, Oxford, for his very interesting information.

405 *August and September.* Dates given in a letter from Valerie Eliot to Mrs Catherine Devas, owner of Stamford House.

405 *EH's long dress.* Janet Adam Smith, who was too pregnant to attend this occasion, heard this anecdote from her mother, who was present.

405 *'Miss Hale has brought her garden . . .'. Great Tom*, p. 143.

405 *EH includes Eliot's words in the service.* 'Order of the Service'. Smith College.

405 *July 1938.* TSE sent a letter to Hugh Gordon Porteus on 15 July 1938 from Chipping Campden. Beinecke.

405 *the woman who accompanied Eliot.* PRS.

405 *Cat Morgan.* TSE wrote EH a comic verse in this character in 1937 or 1938.

405 *uncomfortable castle.* Janet Adam Smith, in conversation, Sept. 1985.

405 *JH reported to Morley.* Letter. King's.

405 *A Campden friend. Great Tom*, p. 149.

406 *'The Jolly Corner' in* FR. See above, ch. 9.

406 *graduate essay.* Copy in EH Papers, Smith College. (She got an A.)

406 *Bennett Junior College.* EH put the address on a pamphlet

by TSE, 'Reunion by destruction' (1943), which he sent her. Denison Library.

406 *headmistress*. Trustees minutes (28 Sept. 1944). I am indebted to Philip McFarland for finding this and other facts about EH.

406 *Sarah F. Tomaino's memories of EH*. Letter to me (13 Nov. 1988), after the publication of *Eliot's New Life*. I am very grateful to her for writing and so delightfully.

407 *'my wretched way of living . . .'.* EH to President Hard of Scripps College (1 Oct. 1945). The letter offers a bequest of her Eliot collection.

408 *a good sort*. Janet Adam Smith in conversation.

408 *'now and in England'*. LG: V.

408 *'destiny'*. OPP, pp. 64–5. The copy of the essay that TSE sent to EH is in the Denison Library.

408 *Aeneas abandons Dido. Aeneid*, IV, ll. 542–5.

408 *Aeneas justifies himself. Aeneid*, IV, ll. 458–9, trans. Allen Mandelbaum (NY: Bantam, 1972), p. 92.

408 *'projection'*. OPP, p. 63.

408 *felt 'a worm'*. 'Virgil and the Christian World', BBC broadcast, 9 Sept. 1951, OPP, pp. 135–48.

408 *dreamlike scene of parting*. Cf. the imagined scene of parting in 'La Figlia che Piange'.

408 *'burning' etc. Aeneid*, VI. ll. 597–626.

409 *A. Walton Litz*. In conversation with the present author.

409 *'used to follow Emily . . .'.* Dorothy Elsmith, letter (1977).

410 *Janet Adam Smith*. See her delightful reminiscences of TSE in 'Tom Possum and the Roberts Family', *Southern Review* (Autumn 1985), repr. *Essays from the Southern Review*. TSE's correspondence with Michael Roberts is in the Berg Collection.

411 *Theresa Eliot*. I am grateful to Professor Eloise Hay for passing on this anecdote, which was told her by Theresa Eliot just before her death.

411 *at EH's instigation*. Miss Tucker told the trustees: 'It is to her, as you know, that we are wholly indebted for Mr Eliot's coming.' (With thanks, again, to Mr McFarland.)

411 *aged eagle*. *AW*: I. Richard Chase, 'T. S. Eliot in Concord', *The American Scholar*, xvi (Autumn 1947), 441.

411 *looking up with effort*. Ackroyd, p. 256.

411 *Emily to Lorraine Havens*. I am immensely grateful to Mrs Havens for photocopies of the two valuable letters from Emily Hale, in Aug. 1947 and in Sept. 1948, that she has preserved; also for her sympathetic picture of a woman she knew well for a great number of years.

412 *nursed plans*. See below her offer (8 Jan. 1948) to President Hard to give a public reading of TSE's poems.

413 *another letter to Lorraine Havens*. Written after EH's return from a summer vacation at Grand Nassau.

413 *drafting* The Cocktail Party. According to Browne, TSE was drafting the play between May and August 1948.

413 *'hidden meaning'*. Letter to Thorp (5 Jan. 1964). Princeton. TSE sent EH an (undated) typescript.

413 *less personal than a poem*. 'The Three Voices of Poetry' (1953), *OPP*, pp. 96–112.

414 *well below the surface*. See TSE's comment to JH, about the problem of *LG* being the lack of personal reminiscence working well below the surface, ch. 10 above.

414 *focus for sympathy*. Browne in *T. S. Eliot: A Symposium for his Seventieth Birthday*, ed. Neville Braybrooke (NY: Farrar, Straus, 1958).

415 *'moments . . .'*. *CPy*, I. i, *Plays*, p. 142.

415 *'There was a door'*. *CPy*, I. iii, *Plays*, p. 169.

416 *'the* daimon *. . .'*. King's. Quoted *EMB*, p. 184.

416 *shut up*. 'Of Individualism in Democracies', in *Democracy in America*, ii, part II, ch. 2, ed. J. P. Mayer (NY: Anchor, 1969), p. 508.

416 *as did less gifted men*. EH to Lorraine Havens, (Aug. 1947).

416 *still in love*. Letter (2 June 1950). PRS.

417 *'my way of thinking'*. PRS.

417 *a wireless talk*. 'Towards a Christian Britain', *Listener* (10 Apr. 1941), 525. 'I think it is through such men as Foucauld that the reborn Christian consciousness comes.'

417 *Celia's murder in the Edinburgh script*: Houghton bMS Am 1691.7 (69).

418 *EMB's critique of the ending.* TS notes on the final scene (26 Feb. 1950). Houghton bMS Am 1691.7 (81).

418 *'The ending is . . . repugnant.* Susannah Clapp, *Observer* (31 Aug. 1997).

419 *Geoffrey Faber.* Letter quoted in programme notes to John Dexter's 1986 production in London.

419 *against the bent. CFQ*, p. 15.

420 *'For what happened . . .'. CPy*, Act II. *Plays*, 189.

420 *'may remember . . .'.* Ibid.

421 *went with Eliot.* Dorothy Elsmith told me this in 1977.

421 *EH at opening night and Theodora's comment.* MT's diary (25 and 28 Aug. 1953). PRS.

421 *'a man's sense . . .'.* TSE to MT (2 June 1950). PRS.

421 Notebooks. 5 Feb. 1895.

422 *Ann Kennedy Irish.* Letter, *Abbot Academy Bulletin* (Oct. 1957). I am grateful to Margaret F. Crouch at Phillips Academy, Andover, for sending a copy.

422 *devastated.* I am very grateful to Barbara Burwell for a most perceptive description of EH. Her words were so well chosen that I have constantly used them.

423 *Caroline Willington.* Statement in the Scripps College Archives.

423 *TSE 'liked to think . . .' and 'It seemed to him . . .'.* Valerie Eliot, Introduction, *L*, i, xvi.

423 *shocked and angry'.* Letter from Mrs Eliot to *TLS* (24 Feb. 1984), 191.

423 *letter to Willard Thorp.* This, and all subsequent letters, in the Thorp Papers, Princeton.

424 *hoped to pick up a post.* EH to Thorp (summer 1957).

424 *appeared disturbed.* Matthews, *Great Tom*, pp. 149–50.

424 *'I miss the real exchange . . .'.* 22 Nov. 1961.

424 *a little house . . .'.* EH to Ricardo Quinones (23 Jan. 1965).

425 *Willard Thorp explained.* Conversation in Aug. 1985.

425 *EH's letter to 'Tom'.* A copy survives, sent to Willard Thorp. Princeton.

427 *By November*. EH, letter to Willard Thorp (29 Nov. 1963).

427 *'personal'*. See letter to President Hard at Scripps (20 Sept. 1945). Denison Library, which has all subsequent letters to Hard and his replies.

428 *'nothing to say'*. EH to Hard (8 Mar. 1948).

429 *offered* Sweeney Agonistes. This offer, I think, was conditional. In the end she kept it until her death.

429 *address at University College, Dublin*. First printed in Autumn 1985 in *Southern Review*, ed. A. Walton Litz, and entitled 'Tradition and the Practice of Poetry'. Professor Litz adds a most useful afterword on Eliot and Yeats. Repr. *Essays from the Southern Review*.

429 *reports from Eleanor Hinkley*. EH to Willard Thorp (17 Jan. 1965). Princeton.

430 *Mr Dix's compromise*. EH to Willard Thorp (8 Feb. 1965). Princeton.

431 *left her some money, etc.* I am indebted for these facts to a brief biography written for EH's friends at the time of her death in 1969, and given to me by Mrs Elsmith.

431 *'I did have . . .'*. EH to Margaret Thorp (4 July 1968). Smith College.

432 *a future mystery*. EH to Margaret Thorp (11 Jan. 1965). Thorp Papers. Princeton.

433 *'watchers and waiters'*. *FR*, I, ii, *Plays*, p. 77.

433 *perfect gentlemen in James*. See *The Ambassadors*; 'The Jolly Corner'; 'The Beast in the Jungle'.

433 *Winterbourne*. In *Daisy Miller* (1878). See ch. 8 above.

433 *Robert Acton*. In *The Europeans* (1878).

434 *'I think of it . . .'*. 'The Beast in the Jungle' (1903), Henry James, *Complete Stories*, v, op. cit.

434 *the notion of some infinite 'thing'*. 'Preludes': IV. *CP*, p. 15.

434 *'Something or other . . .'*. 'The Beast in the Jungle'.

434 *'Christ the tiger'*. 'Gerontion'. Note also the three white leopards, *AW*: II.

434 *'He hadn't disturbed people . . .'*. 'The Beast in the Jungle'.

434 *privilege*. Ibid.

434 *'the real truth'*. Ibid.

434 *'a man of extremes'*. Lecture on TSE at Scripps in Dec. 1932. See ch. 7 above.

435 *'burst upon the world'*. EH to Willard Thorp (27 Nov. 1965). Princeton.

Chapter 12 Fame and Friends

436 *the drink to The Guardians*. MT's diary (5 June 1950), PRS.

436 *'TS . . . TS . . . TS'*. Eileen Simpson, *Poets in their Youth* (1982; repr. London: Picador, 1984), p. 171.

437 *godlike authority*. Ibid. Eileen Simpson gives the best description of TSE's godlike aura, and I have used some of her phrases verbatim.

437 *'the most desperately lonely business'*. PRS. He said this in Dec. 1950, on his return from Chicago.

437 *TSE performing Sherlock Holmes*. Matthews, *Great Tom*, pp. 158–9.

437 *'No-one thinks of me as a poet . . .'*. Levy, p. 19.

437 *'utterly depleted'*. Allen Tate's coll., p. 32.

438 *Desmond MacCarthy*. Correspondence in King's.

438 *'Coriolan'*. See ch. 7 above.

439 *tapped their beaks in vain*. The phrase comes from Virginia Woolf's *The Waves* (London: Hogarth; NY: Harcourt, 1931), p. 181.

439 *'the private door . . .'*. Act I, *Plays*, p. 236.

440 *descriptions of MT*. I am grateful to Janet Adam Smith, Peter du Sautoy, and Ann Stokes for providing clear images.

440 *'SCUM List'*. Ann Stokes to me (28 Nov. 1991).

440 *MT's diary*. Extracts from the diary are part of her unpublished memoir of her friendship with Eliot (PRS), which is privately owned.

442 *godfather*. See Janet Adam Smith, 'Tom Possum and the Roberts Family', *Essays from the Southern Review*.

442 *'always suspect everybody'*. TSE to MT (19 Dec. 1944), PRS. Dickens, *The Old Curiosity Shop*, chs 36 and 66.

444 *'now and in England'*. LG: I: 'Now and in England'. LG: V: 'History is now and England'.

444 *'prayer, observance . . .'*. DS: V.

446 *had been in love with one woman*. TSE to MT (2 June 1950). PRS.

446 *psychological change of life*. TSE to MT (27 Apr. 1949), PRS. See above, ch. 11.

447 *native Calvinism*. MT to TSE (21 Feb. 1942), PRS.

448 *early London years*. See ch. 4 above.

448 *Archbishop Temple*. He died in autumn 1944.

448 I'll Walk Beside You. (Longman's, 1945). In 1943 MT had considered doing a book of letters, which TSE had brushed off on behalf of Faber. With Longman's, the book was successful.

449 *'I found . . .'*. Ibid., p. 21.

449 *None had had leave since the Normandy landing*. Ibid., p. 36.

449 *'Moaning Minnies'*. Ibid., p. 95.

450 *'for 48 hours is so short'*. Ibid., p. 54.

450 *'For the last four years . . .'*. Ibid., p. 59.

450 *'mental rehabilitation'*. Ibid., p. 54.

450 *'termites'*. TSE used this word in a 1917 letter to Lytton Strachey where he complains that he was ground down amongst the termites (see ch. 4 above); and he used the word again to MT in the fifties (in PRS).

450 *MT at an air-evacuation centre. I'll Walk Beside You*, pp. 40–1.

451 *Mrs Millington*. TSE to MT (30 Oct. 1944), PRS.

451 *'the most tragic and pitiable body of men'. I'll Walk Beside You*, p. 95.

451 *'I wish you could see . . .'*. Ibid., pp. 96–7.

451 *state of mind of the ex-prisoners*. Ibid., p. 98.

452 *'I wish . . .'*. Ibid., p. 99.

452 *'The horror'*. See Ronald Schuchard's definitive essay, 'Eliot and the Horrific Moment', *Southern Review* (Oct. 1985), 1045–56, repr. *Essays from the Southern Review*.

453 *'Oh it's YOU again, Julia'*. PRS (24 Nov. 1949).

453 *Julia 'is me'*. PRS (18 Aug. 1949).

453 *Eliot pictured her sailing* . . . . TSE to MT (23 Feb. 1948), PRS.

453 *the future of the East* . . . . Ibid.

453 *Eliot asked for tips* . . . . TSE to MT (3 Mar. 1949), PRS.

454 *fading. DS*: III: 'The future is a faded song . . . / Of wistful regret . . .'. For EH singing in 1913 see above, ch. 3.

455 *February–March 1946*. TSE moved into the flat in February, JH a month later. *CFQ*, p. 12.

455 *1935*. Ibid.

455 très-loyal serviteur. This is how JH signed a letter to TSE (5 Mar. 1941). King's.

455 *bored with all living*. TSE remarked on this in an address to Friends of Rochester Cathedral, 'Religious Drama: Medieval and Modern' (*Univ. of Edinburgh Journal*, ix (Autumn 1937), 8–17, repr. NY: House of Books, 1954): 'There is a very profound kind of boredom which is an essential moment in the religious life, the boredom with all living in so far as it has no religious meaning.'

455 *'at home'*. See references to TSE's 1935 letter to Mrs Perkins, above, ch. 7.

455 *even to his confessors*. PRS (in conversation on 27 Nov. 1951).

455 *an old man* . . . . Note to MT (6 Oct. 1953), PRS.

456 *in a cage*. PRS (20 June 1951). The phrase in a cage recalls the original title of *WL*: II: 'In the Cage'.

456 *eleven years with JH*. They lived together from March 1946 to January 1957. The chief sources for TSE's life during these years are PRS; *CFQ*; and *The Book Collector* (Winter 1965), which contains 'Some Memories', a series of obituaries for JH.

456 *stings*. Nicholas Barker (in *The Book Collector*, Winter 1965) is particularly good on the atmosphere in JH's company.

457 *strain*. PRS.

457 *'escape into living . . .'. The Confidential Clerk*, Act I, *Plays*, pp. 236–7.

457 *Winter and summer* .... Daily habits in Peter Ackroyd, *T. S. Eliot: A Life* (London: Hamish Hamilton, NY: Simon & Schuster, 1984), p. 249.

458 *commiserate.* MT describes a visit to JH when TSE was away in Nice in Mar. 1952. PRS.

458 *'He can't help hurting us'.* Easter Day, Apr. 1955. PRS.

458 *'man of letters'.* Kathleen Raine, *The Book Collector* (Winter 1965).

458 *'Metoikos'.* Signature on a paper for the Moot. *Great Tom*, p. 126. Confirmed in PRS.

458 *told Helen Gardner* .... CFQ, p. 13.

458 *wrote from Cambridge* .... JH to TSE (27 June 1940). King's.

459 *illustrated catalogue.* CFQ, p. 12.

459 *ran brilliantly as a dictator.* John Carter, *Sunday Times* obituary.

459 *took the Distillers Company to task.* Catherine Porteus, *The Book Collector* (Winter 1965).

459 *'a poem . . .'.* Kathleen Raine, ibid.

459 *'carpentry'.* Obituary, King's College *Annual Report*, (Nov. 1965), pp. 30–3.

459 *'Besides a strong personal affection . . .'.* PRS.

459 *He feared nobody.* Obituary, King's College *Annual Report*.

460 *'Be witty'.* Recalled by Gwen Watkins in conversation, Sept. 1986.

460 *Graham Green. The Book Collector* (Winter 1965).

460 *Janet Adam Smith.* Ibid.

461 *'the chill ascends . . .'. EC*: II.

461 *Hayward's desire.* Described sympathetically by Graham Greene, *The Book Collector* (Winter 1965).

461 *weird, ghostly, Strindbergian.* Frances Partridge, *Julia: A Portrait of Julia Strachey* (London: Gollancz, 1983), pp. 207–8.

462 *Their first housekeeper.* Recalled by Christopher Sykes in *The Book Collector* (Winter 1965).

462 *'confidential clerk' as divine agent.* Carol Smith, *T. S.*

Eliot's Dramatic Theory and Practice (Princeton Univ. Press, 1963), p. 210.

462 *would like to change his name.* TSE to MT (Oct. 1955), PRS.

462 *'Bonsir Nehemiah'.* MT's diary (Oct. 1955).

463 *adoptive nephew.* Signature to a note of Dec. 1955. On another occasion Bonsir was MT's son-in-law.

464 *'I set myself . . .'.* Preface to PRS.

465 *'he seemed to take fright . . .'.* PRS.

465 *on 27 April 1949.* Letter to MT, PRS.

465 *on 29 May 1950.* MT proposed by letter, PRS.

465 *'Will you be looking in . . .'.* MT's diary, PRS.

466 *'I never see . . .'.* MT's diary (3 Apr. 1950), PRS.

466 *reply of 2 June.* Letter, PRS.

466 *a pain that gnawed at his liver.* See *EC*: IV and Helen Gardner's commentary (*CFQ*, pp. 44–6) showing the allusion to Gide's handling of Prometheus's liver.

466 *on 5 June they had a talk . . . .* PRS.

467 *he no longer enjoyed his love's company.* TSE to MT (2 June 1950), PRS.

467 *'THE lady'.* PRS (23 July 1950).

467 *'mediocre' contemporaries.* MT's diary (2 Jan. 1955). PRS.

467 *Shaw.* Ibid. (2 Apr. 1951).

467 *F. R. Leavis.* Ibid. (Mar. 1955).

467 *Pound.* Ibid. (Mar. 1955).

468 *Muir, Auden, Day Lewis, Sitwell, Marianne Moore.* Ibid. (1 Nov. 1956).

468 *confessions.* MT's diary (27 Nov. 1951, 26 May 1953, and 7 Oct. 1954). PRS.

468 *'I believe in hell . . .'.* Diary, PRS.

468 *'the whole of me . . .'.* MT's diary (26 May 1953). PRS.

469 *over Tower Bridge.* This was in Sept. 1955. PRS.

469 *the cage.* See *facs. WL*, pp. 16–17: 'In the Cage' (the cancelled title of *WL*: II).

469 *the home of Mungojerrie and Rumpelteazer.* TSE explained to MT (Sept. 1956). Diary. PRS. He is referring to characters in *Old Possum's Book of Practical Cats*.

469 *football games*. Recalled by Christopher Sykes in 'Some Memories', *The Book Collector* (Winter 1965).

470 *Eliot would work the lift* . . . . PRS (30 Nov. 1954).

470 *'I love the* economy *of Mozart'*. MT's diary (15 May 1947), PRS.

470 *'After all* . . .'. MT's diary (30 Nov. 1952), PRS.

Chapter 13 A Prophet's Mission

473 *'on stilts'*. *Emerson in his Journals* (14 Nov. 1839), ed. Joel Porte (Cambridge, Mass: Belknap, 1982), p. 230.

473 *disseminates principles*. 'The American Scholar', *Selected Prose and Poetry*, p. 67.

473 *'He judges* . . .'. 1855 Preface to *Leaves of Grass*.

473 *The greatest poet* . . . . 'Goethe as the Sage', OPP, p. 253.

473 *the war had brought* . . . . Preface to *The Dark Side of the Moon* (London, 1946). Cited by Ackroyd, p. 246.

473 *'centuries of barbarism'*. Interview in *Horizon* (Aug. 1945). Cited by Ackroyd, p. 246.

473 *'prophetic gloom'*. NDC p. 185.

474 *speech at Aix-en-Provence*. Made on receiving the degree of Hon. D. ès L. Hayward Bequest: 'Miscellaneous Essays & Addresses'. King's.

474 *'. . . our own ability* . . .'. OPP, p. 10.

474 *The* Notes *warn* . . . . p. 91.

474 *letter to Desmond MacCarthy*. 14 Nov. 1947. King's.

474 *'We live in an* impossible *age'*. MT's diary (5 Dec. 1954). PRS.

474 *Gomorrah*. Letter to MT (St Wenceslas 1948) while on board the SS *America*. PRS.

474 *Nineveh*. In Apr. 1956 TSE wrote to MT that he had no hopes of a Christian Conference arranged by J. O. Oldham and Kathleen Bliss, whose vague aspirations seemed futile in the face of Nineveh.

474 *prayed in the Underground*. MT's diary (25 June 1952). PRS.

474 *explained this to MT*. PRS (24 June 1944).

474 *TSE on intolerance and Jews in Virginia: ASG.* pp. 18–20.

475 *Litvinoff incident.* Anthony Julius, *T. S. Eliot, Anti-Semitism, and Literary Form* (CUP, 1995), 37, 217–18.

475 *'spiritual organisation'.* Quoted by Ackroyd, p. 273.

476 *'What is man . . .'.* Psalm 8. He did not carry out this plan.

476 *Eden had not understood.* TSE to Pound (12 Oct. 1956). Beinecke. The talk had been delivered on 19 Apr. 1955, and is repr. as 'The Literature of Politics', *CC*, pp. 136–44.

476 *'Half of the harm . . .'. CPy,* II, *Plays,* p. 175.

476 *'I don't hear any voices . . .'.* Ibid., p. 185.

476 *'deranged society'.* 'The Frontiers of Criticism', *OPP*, p. 116.

476 *'chaos'. What is a Classic? OPP,* p. 74.

476 *'Whig? Tory?'* Auden's review, *New Yorker* (23 Apr. 1949), 85–6.

477 *'a voice in Ramah . . .'.* Ibid.

477 *the prophet has no being.* I am grateful to Dr Rachel Salmon of Bar-llan University, Israel, for her persuasive understanding of the prophets.

477 *'In the year that King Uzziah died . . .'.* TSE quoted the opening of Isaiah 6: 1 in a letter to MT (28 Nov. 1944), PRS.

477 *'And he laid it upon my mouth . . .'.* Isaiah 6: 7–9.

478 *went against the grain.* Helen Gardner said (*CFQ*, p. 15) that 'in writing plays Eliot was writing, to some extent, against the bent of his natural genius. Essentially he was an explorer, not an expounder . . .'.

478 *Mr McKnight.* TSE told this to MT. MT's diary (2 Apr. 1951), PRS.

478 *Mr Silvero.* 'Gerontion' (1919).

478 *Mme Sosostris. WL:* I.

479 *exclusion of a Jew from the Eliot collection:* TSE to Theodore Spencer (19 July 1948). Spencer Papers, Harvard Archives.

480 *looked beyond its time.* In *What is a Classic?* (*OPP*, p. 73) TSE admired 'the dedication of Aeneas . . . to a future far beyond his living achievement'.

480 *'Nihilism itself becomes boredom'*. Leslie Paul, 'A Conversation with T. S. Eliot', *Kenyon Review*, xxvii (1965), 11–21. Recorded in 1958.

480 *into the red Eye of the morning*. Sylvia Plath, 'Ariel' (1962), *Collected Poems* (London: Faber, 1981), p. 240.

480 *'indomitable spirit of mediocrity'*. CPy, I, ii, Plays, p. 153.

480 *make the best of a bad job*. CPy, II, *Plays*, p. 182.

481 'transparent' *words*. 'Poetry and Drama' (1951). This idea originated in his unpublished Shakespeare lecture of 1937, King's.

481 *'You will forget this phrase . . .'*. CPy, II, *Plays*, p. 182.

481 *'You've missed the point . . .'*. CPy, I, i, Plays, p. 125.

481 *'There's altogether too much mystery . . .'*. CPy, I, *Plays*, p. 137.

482 *the dog in the night*. 'Silver Blaze' (with thanks to Julie Akhurst Hall).

482 *the immortal hand*. Blake's 'Tyger', *Complete Writings*, ed. Geoffrey Keynes (OUP, 1966, repr. 1984), p. 214.

482 *provincialism of time. What is a Classic?* OPP, p. 72.

482 *'The Three Provincialities'*. Tyro, repr. *Essays in Criticism* (1951). See also Pound on provincialism (a shared concern) in *Selected Prose 1909–65*, ed. William Cookson (London: Faber, 1973), pp. 159–73.

482 *as it was for Henry James*. See Henry James, *Nathaniel Hawthorne* (1879). In 'From Poe to Valéry (1948) TSE said that Poe had 'the provinciality of the person who is not at home where he belongs, but cannot get to anywhere else.' CC, p. 29.

482 *'Provinciality . . . a vice'*. 'Professional, or . . .', *Egoist* (Apr. 1918), 61.

482 *'a positive literary vice'*. 'Tradition and the Practice of Poetry', Dublin talk (1936), ed. A. Walton Litz, *Essays from the Southern Review*, pp. 7–26.

482 *'emancipated'*. Essay on P. E. More (1937), Princeton. TSE criticised provincials of their time in a letter to P. E. More (20 July 1934), Princeton.

482 *Dante the 'least provincial'*. 'What Dante Means to Me', CC, pp. 134–5.

482 *'insupportable to posterity'. Tyro.*

483 *essay on James.* 'In Memory of Henry James', *Egoist,* v (Jan. 1918), 1. See above, ch. 4. Quoted by Ronald Bush in 'Nathaniel Hawthorne and T. S. Eliot's American Connection', *Essays from the Southern Review,* 65–74.

483 *'history had meaning'.* 'Virgil and the Christian World', *OPP,* p. 148. In a wireless talk on Aeneas in 1951 TSE said that 'for no one before his time except the Hebrew prophets, history had meaning'.

483 *Aeneas as prototype of Christian pilgrim.* Ibid., pp. 143–4.

483 *a by-product of his private poetry workshop.* 'The Frontiers of Criticism' (1956), *OPP,* p. 117, and 'To Criticize the Critic' (1961), *CC,* p. 13.

483 *'impersonality'.* 'Tradition and the Individual Talent' (1919), *SW,* pp. 53, 56–9.

483 *'objective correlative'.* 'Hamlet and His Problems' (1919), *SW,* p. 100.

483 *'unified' or 'dissociated sensibility'.* 'The Metaphysical Poets' (1921), *SE,* p. 247.

483 *A hundred years on . . . .* 'To Criticize the Critic', *CC,* p. 19.

484 *'I'm surprised we were allowed Milton . . .'.* John Pearson, *Façades* (London: Macmillan, 1978), p. 385.

484 *'bluff'.* 10 Aug. 1929, King's, cited by P. N. Furbank in 'Forster, Eliot, and the Literary Life', *Twentieth Century Literature,* xxxi (Summer/Fall 1985).

484 *'icy inviolability'.* 'Shorter Notices' *Egoist* article (June –July 1918), 87.

484 *'that parlour game . . .'.* 'Professional, or . . .', *Egoist* (Apr. 1918), 61.

484 *'called to the seat of judgement'.* 'To Criticize the Critic', *CC,* p. 12.

484 *'canonised and excommunicated.'* Harry Levin used the phrase in a letter to Matthiessen in 1934, printed as an appendix to *Memories of the Moderns* (London: Faber, 1981), p. 243.

485 *tone more English than the English.* Chris Baldick, *The*

Social Mission of English Criticism 1848–1932 (OUP, 1983), p. 110.

485 *introduced Eliot to Bruce Richmond.* TSE, 'Bruce Lyttleton Richmond', *TLS* (13 Jan. 1961). Richmond was ninety when TSE wrote this piece.

485 *'understanding'.* 'The Frontiers of Criticism', *OPP*, p. 121.

485 *the only criticism that he could recommend.* See TSE's letters to Helen Gardner, Bodleian Library. In Oct. 1949, Helen Gardner had a letter from the Cresset Press quoting TSE'S opinion that 'it seems to me the best book of its kind that has been done'. TSE confirmed this view in a letter to W. T. Levy, *Affectionately, T. S. Eliot*, p. 105.

485 *TSE's reservations about source-hunting.* His more private remarks were recalled by Helen Gardner in conversation with the present author.

485 *'transmutes'.* 'Yeats', *OPP*, p. 299.

485 *'The fact that . . .'.* TSE to Philip Mairet (30 Oct. 1956). Texas. Quoted by Jeffrey M. Perl and Andrew Tuck, 'The Hidden Advantage of Tradition: On the Significance of T. S. Eliot's Indic Studies', *Philosophy East and West*, xxxv (Apr. 1985), 122.

486 *'the greater expression of personality'.*'Yeats', *OPP*, p. 299.

486 *'A Note on War Poetry'.* CP, p. 215.

486 *'A poet may believe . . .'.* 'Virgil', *OPP*, p. 137.

487 *'the adjective of some transcendental self'.* KE, p. 21. Quoted by Calvin Bedient, *He Do The Police in Different Voices* (Univ. of Chicago Press, 1987), p. 16.

487 *'there is something integral'.* UPUC, p. 88.

487 *an 'inner compulsion'.* 'Kipling', *OPP*, p. 274.

487 *'a consistent view of life'.* 'From Poe to Valéry', *CC*, p. 35.

487 *the whole pattern.* This uses, almost verbatim, TSE's strictures on understanding Shakespeare in 'John Ford' (1932), *SE*, p. 170.

487 *his poetry came from America. Paris Review* interview with Donald Hall, repr. *Writers at Work*, ed. Van Wyck Brooks, 2nd series (NY: Viking, 1963).

487 'real significance...'. 'Stravinsky and Others', *New Republic* (10 Mar. 1926), repr. *T. S. Eliot: The Critical Heritage*, i, ed. Michael Grant, (London: Routledge, 1982), pp. 239–40.

487 *a distinctive sense of the past.* 'In Memory of Henry James', op. cit.

488 *'American Literature'.* CC, p. 56.

488 *'depravity's despair'.* 'What Dante Means to Me', CC, p. 134.

488 *Jansenism indistinguishable from Puritanism.* SE, p. 357.

488 *fragments of a greater Reality,* Jewel Spears Brooker gives an admirably concise and clear summary of what in Bradley's thought appealed to TSE in 'The Structure of Eliot's "Gerontion": An Interpretation Based on Bradley's Doctrine of the Systematic Nature of Truth', *ELH*, lxvi (1979), 314–40.

488 *'fractions are worth more to me...'.* (Nov.–Dec. 1833), *Emerson in His Journals*, 119.

488 *Auden.* Introduction to *The Faber Book of Modern American Verse* (1956), p. 18.

488 *tradition is not inherited ....* 'Tradition and the Individual Talent', *SW*, p. 49.

488 *'strong traits ....'.* 'The Custom House', introductory to *The Scarlet Letter*.

489 'To *the high mountain peaks ...'.* *The Scarlet Letter*, ch. 11: 'The Interior of a Heart'.

489 *the difference between a madman and an effective writer.* 'The Social Function of Poetry', *OPP*, p. 9.

489 *'To Carthage ...'.* WL: III.

490 *Dante's refining fire.* WL: V.

490 *the peace that passeth understanding.* TSE's note to 'Shantih', WL: V (needless to say, not one of the bogus or distracting notes).

490 *The rebel may appear as social conformist.* TSE was referring to Tennyson, 'In Memoriam' (1936), SE, p. 295.

490 *'When a man ...'.* (9 Dec. 1932), UPUC, p. 73.

490 *Wordsworth.* (17 Feb. 1933), UPUC, p. 87.

490 'a profound spiritual revival'. (9 Dec. 1932), UPUC, p. 80.

491 'see and hear more'. 'What Dante Means to Me', CC, p. 134.

491 'the obligation to explore'. Ibid.

491 'thing'. 'Preludes': IV.

491 'a fringe of indefinite extent . . .'. 'Poetry and Drama', OPP, p. 93.

491 'unattended' moments. DS: V.

491 the still point . . . . BN: II.

491 'The Word in the desert'. BN: V.

491 Denied the ultimate vision . . . . I draw here on what TSE says of Virgil (OPP, p. 74) because it seems equally true of himself.

492 'All genius . . .'. Ann Stokes in a letter to me (3 June 1991).

492 pills, and potions. The streak of hypochondria is confirmed by Sir Herbert Read in Allen Tate's coll., p. 32.

492 lesion. Medical details given by TSE's doctor to MT in June 1956. PRS.

493 chrysalis. The image derived from TSE's '2nd Debate between the Body and Soul' (1911). IMH, p. 68.

493 feared that he was coming to his end. His doctor told MT that the racing heart would have given a panic-stricken sense of approaching death.

493 'As for poetry . . .'. MT's diary (30 Nov. 1954), PRS.

493 'abnormal'. Diary (June 1956), PRS.

493 reading Paul Tillich. TSE took a copy of Systematic Theology to South Africa in 1950. He remarked to W. T. Levy in 1954 that vol. i was one of the profoundest theological books of recent times (Levy, p. 50).

493 Tillich on self-punishment. He proposed a 'proper human self-love' instead of the 'false' self-love that is connected with self-contempt. Systematic Theology, i (London: Nisbet, 1953; Univ. of Chicago, 1951), p. 313.

493 Tillich on forgiveness. The New Being (London: SCM Press, 1956), p. 48.

494 *torn between duty to God and duty to man.* Letter to MT
(28 Oct. 1955), PRS.

494 *neurotic depressive.* The query is in a letter to MT (Sept.
1956), PRS.

494 *'I, even I . . .'.* Isaiah 43: 25.

494 *'a peach of a girl'.* MT's diary, PRS.

494 *left to dine alone with Jean Kennerley.* TSE to JH (5 Aug.
1941). King's.

495 *'unattached devotion . . .'.* DS: II.

Chapter 14 Love: the Unfamiliar Name

496 *Laforgue married.* David Arkell discovered this neat
coincidence in his fine biography, *Looking for Laforgue*
(Manchester: Carcanet, 1979).

496 *'made for marriage'.* Blake Morrison, 'The Two Mrs
Eliots' (interview with Valerie Eliot), *Independent on
Sunday* (24 Apr. 1994).

497 *'thoughts without need of speech'.* Poem, 'To My Wife',
printed as a dedication to *The Elder Statesman* (1958). In a
revised form it appeared as 'A Dedication to My Wife' in
CP, p. 221.

497 *began in Oct.–Nov. 1955.* Dating of the composition of
the play comes from TSE's conversations with MT, PRS.

497 *'I was bowled over . . .'.* Valerie Eliot, interview, 'The
Poet's Wife and Letters', *The Times* (17 Sept. 1988).

498 *'had to get to Tom . . .'.* Interview, *Observer* (20 Feb.
1972).

498 *'It was very disappointing . . .'.* and collection box. 'The
Poet's Wife and Letters', op. cit.

498 *Queen Anne's School.* I am grateful to Dr Rosemary
Pountney of Jesus College, Oxford, for details about the
school, which she attended.

499 *'He was just . . .'.* 'The Poet's Wife and Letters', op. cit.

499 *'I can't get to know her . . .'.* MT's diary (27 Mar. 1955).
PRS.

499 *sudden impulse.* TSE to MT (28 Oct. 1950), PRS.

499 *a better collection.* Remarked by Peter du Sautoy in conversation (1986).

499 *would dodge into the lavatory.* TSE to MT. Postscript, PRS.

499 *work late.* Ibid.

499 *Vernon Watkins.* Recalled by Gwen Watkins in conversation (Sept. 1986).

500 *conceals a deep failure.* From a page of manuscript (n.d.) in Mrs Eliot's possession. *EMB*, p. 318.

500 *first draft.* The first drafts of Acts I and II, as well as the Green and White synopses, are at King's. The manuscript and typescripts of Act III are owned by Mrs Eliot.

500 *'sticky'.* MT's diary (Mar. 1956). PRS.

500 *'stricken' and Tomlin.* Tomlin, 'T. S. Eliot: a Friendship', op. cit.

500 *'cadaverous'.* Donald Hall, *Remembering Poets* (NY, 1978).

500 *looked after his affairs.* *EMB*, p. 316.

501 *'the ELD ST. begins to unburden his heart . . .'.* The second White synopsis for the play. King's. Quoted *EMB*, p. 310.

501 *introduces a love scene.* *EMB*, pp. 317–18.

501 *'changing'.* The word was retained in the final version, *Plays*, p. 298.

501 *'Love'.* III. *The Temple* (1633). *The Works of George Herbert*, ed. F. E. Hutchinson (OUP, 1941), pp. 188–9.

502 *things ill done.* LG: II.

502 *'morbid conscience'.* Act III, *Plays*, p. 345.

502 *'emotional situation'.* 'The Three Voices of Poetry', *OPP*, p. 111.

502 *biopic. Tom and Viv.* Reviewed by Lyndall Gordon, 'Truth about the Waste Land lives', *Evening Standard* (7 Apr. 1994).

503 *'in unison'.* 'The Three Voices of Poetry', *OPP*, p. 109. TSE distinguished speaking in unison from using a character as mouthpiece.

503 *call out latent potentialities.* *OPP*, p. 102. See discussion of Becket in *MC* in ch 7 above.

503 *'a pit . . .'.* The line comes from a rough first draft of lines

for *DS*: III. Manuscript at Magdalene College, Cambridge. Quoted *CFQ*, p. 137. The date would have been late 1940, for JH received a complete draft of *DS* on New Year's Day 1941.

503 *as an old man explores.* See *EC*: V: 'Old men ought to be explorers'.

503 *Mock humility.* 'The Rest Cure', Act II.

503 *'I can only say . . .'*. Letter to William Turner Levy, quoted in *Affectionately, T. S. Eliot*, p. 101.

504 *the blankness of the walls.* Quoted *EMB*, p. 319.

504 *'But have I still time?'* *Plays*, p. 338.

504 *'the heinousness . . .'*. Act III, *Plays*, p. 345.

504 *'spectral existence . . .'*. Ibid., p. 341.

504 *It is enough . . .'*. Ibid., p. 340.

505 *once again.* In *FR*. See ch. 9, above.

505 *In late Nov.* On 25 Nov. TSE told MT that he got out his typewriter and did several pages of Act II.

505 *'And more frightening . . .'*. Kept in Act II, *Plays*, p. 325.

505 *daring to strip the mask.* I have drawn on EMB's words about the Elder Statesman, *EMB*, p. 311.

506 *'One day . . .'*. Levy, p. 43.

506 *knit together.* Recalled by Gwen Watkins in conversation (Sept. 1986).

506 *pangs.* First draft, King's. Quoted *EMB*, pp. 315–16.

506 *'2nd Debate between the Body and Soul'.* *IMH*, p. 68. Discussed above, ch. 3.

507 *the way* from . . . . (Jan. 1861), *Emerson in his Journals*, ed. Joel Porte (Cambridge, Mass.: Belknap, 1982), p. 491.

507 *Monica.* I am guessing here about the associations of this name for Eliot. He might well have chosen it quite arbitrarily.

507 *March 1938 TSE told EMB* . . . . Letter (19 Mar. 1938) quoted *in toto* in *EMB*, pp. 106–8.

507 *'I am only a beginner . . .'*. *ES*, III. *Plays*, p. 354.

507 *Act I completed 9 Feb. 1958. EMB*, p. xiv.

508 *'like the asthmatic . . .'*. *ES*, III, *Plays*, p. 355.

508 *More rewriting* . . . . *EMB*, p. 317.

508 *first production of* ES. See *EMB*, p. 338.

508 *Act III at Edinburgh. EMB*, pp. 330–2.

509 *'a new person'*. Act III, *Plays*, p. 355.

509 *felt by his friends* . . . . Two who held such a view were Helen Gardner and Gwen Watkins.

509 *thought of calling the police*. JH told this to Gwen Watkins. It is not clear what time exactly he found Eliot's letter announcing his departure. JH possibly said different things to different people.

509 *Peter du Sautoy*. 'T. S. Eliot: Personal Reminiscences', *Southern Review* (Oct. 1985), 954. Repr. *Essays from the Southern Review*, 75–84.

509 *'My dear lady . . .'*. MT's diary (Trinity XVIII, 1956). PRS.

511 *'My dear chap . . .'*. Helen Gardner, recalling JH's account to her. In conversation.

511 *'I thought . . .'*. Recalled by Gwen Watkins, who said that several people were there at the time.

511 *felt his helplessness anew*. Christopher Sykes, 'Some Memories', *The Book Collector* (Winter 1965).

511 *morale never recovered*. Gwen Watkins. In conversation.

511 *Graham Greene*. Obituary for JH, *The Book Collector* (Winter 1965). See ch. 12 above.

511 *a union* . . . . Peter du Sautoy described the marriage in this way, *Essays from the Southern Review*. See also the relationship of Charles and Monica in *ES*.

512 *'a streak of sadism'*. TSE remarked on this comment in *Ushant* in a letter to Aiken (7 Nov. 1952). Huntington. Cited by Ackroyd, p. 213.

512 *would not be pinned*. See 'Prufrock', who is pinned.

512 *He paid his contribution*. Hilary Spurling, *Secrets of a Woman's Heart: The Later Life of I. Compton-Burnett 1920–1969* (London: Hodder & Stoughton, 1984), p. 241.

512 *removed acknowledgement to JH*. Noted in *Great Tom*, p. 124.

513 *'sacrifice others'*. Second draft of Act I, *EMB*, p. 318: 'In sacrificing himself he's had to sacrifice others.'

513 *Dimmesdale*. Nathaniel Hawthorne, *The Scarlet Letter*.

513 *'Explore your own higher latitudes'.* Conclusion (ch. 18) to *Walden.*

513 *spat out the butt-ends.* 'Prufrock': 'Then how should I begin / To spit out all the butt-ends of my days and ways?' *CP*, p. 5.

514 *'Love reciprocated . . .'.* Interview with Henry Hewes, *Saturday Review* (13 Sept. 1958), p. 32. Copy in Houghton.

514 *'None of my books . . .'.* Recorded by VW (25 July 1926) in *Diary*, iii, p. 99.

514 *'old man's frenzy'.* 'An Acre of Grass', *Collected Poems*, p. 347.

514 *'throbbings of noontide'.* 'I Look into My Glass', *Wessex Poems and Other Verses* (1898).

514 *affair.* See 'Portrait of a Lady' and 'adulterated' in 'Gerontion'. ('Adulterated' is, I think, a serious pun: see ch. 4 above.)

514 *like 'crawling bugs'. facs. WL*, pp. 44–5.

515 *dancing lessons. Photonews.*

515 *John Finlay's dinner.* An account of the evening is given by Harry Levin in 'Old Possum at Possum House', *Southern Review* (Oct. 1985), repr. *Essays from the Southern Review*, pp. 153–6.

515 *unbent to VW.* See above, ch. 4.

515 *unbent to Iowa students. Great Tom*, p. 154.

516 *correspondence with Groucho Marx. The Groucho Letters: Letters from and to Groucho Marx* (NY: Simon & Schuster; London: Michael Joseph, 1967), pp. 154–62.

516 *Groucho to Gummo Marx.* Ibid., pp. 162–3.

517 *child with nurse.* Photograph, Houghton.

517 *entertained Janet Adam Smith's children.* 'Tom Possum and the Roberts Family'.

518 *with Ivy Compton-Burnett.* Hilary Spurling, *Secrets of a Woman's Heart*, p. 241.

518 *very good mind.* Levy, pp. 98–9.

518 *madly happy.* Letter on return from honeymoon. Schiff Papers, British Library.

518 *'It is a wonderful thing . . .'.* Levy, pp. 98–9.

518 *fiftieth anniversary report on the class of 1910.* Copy in Houghton.

518 '. . . *art and love* . . .'. *Ushant* (Boston: Little, Brown, 1952), pp. 185–6.

519 *told Henry Hewes. Saturday Review* (13 Sept. 1958).

519 '*No peevish winter* . . .'. CP, p. 221. This is the last poem in CP.

520 '*You were the first sympathetic reader* . . .'. Letter to Cyril Connolly, quoted in obituary for TSE (10 Jan. 1965) in the *Sunday Times.*

520 '*This last part* . . .'. To Levy, p. 110.

520 The New Being. (London: SCM Press, 1956), p. 13.

520 *October chill.* Letter to Allen Tate (23 Oct. 1957). Princeton.

520 *November fogs.* Letter to Tate (26 Nov. 1958). Princeton.

520 *told Pound.* Letter (29 Jan. 1960). Beinecke.

521 *cruise to Jamaica.* The Eliots travelled on the *Santa Rosa* (Grace Line). They stayed at the Jamaica Inn, Ocho Rios, Jamaica, from 14 Jan. to 5 Mar. 1961.

521 *told Vernon Watkins.* Letter (26 Apr. 1962). Berg.

521 *bent over.* Levy, p. 126.

521 *said of More in 1937.* TSE to Willard Thorp (17 Feb. 1937). More Papers, Princeton.

521 *afraid of death.* MT's diary (8 Aug. 1949). PRS.

521 '*Death is not oblivion*'. Interview with Henry Hewes, *Saturday Review* (13 Sept. 1958).

521 *envied Joyce.* Letter to Pound (28 Dec. 1959). Beinecke.

522 *still spoke of things he wanted to do.* Letter to Pound (Nov. 1961). Beinecke.

522 '*foresees*'. CC, p. 19.

522 '*feeling*'. CC, p. 20.

522 '*emotional preferences*'. CC, p. 19.

522 *fed his emotions.* CC, p. 18.

522 *a paradox of the New England mind.* TSE analyses this in a review of Henry Adams, 'A Sceptical Patrician', *Athenaeum* (23 May 1919). See above, ch. 5.

522 *Emerson on his aunt. Emerson in his Journals* (6 May 1841), p. 253.

523 *'the comfort . . . .'.* CC, p. 23.

523 *'sequence which culminates in faith'.* SE, p. 360.

523 *'the pride of birth . . .'. George Herbert*, no. 152 in the series *Writers and their Work* (London: Longmans, 1962), pp. 12–13.

523 *unsparing self-examination.* Ibid., p. 13.

523 *temptation to the religious poet.* Ibid., p. 24.

524 *'the fluctuations of emotion . . .'.* Ibid, p. 23.

524 *'And now in age I bud again'.* From 'The Flower', quoted *ibid.*, p. 25. *Works*, p. 166.

524 *'Love'. George Herbert*, p. 34.

525 *'convalescence of the spirit'.* Ibid., p. 26.

525 *'The last time I saw him . . .'. Introduction to a Reading of Poems by TSE.* (Univ. of Minnesota, 15 Feb. 1965). Copy in Tate Papers, Princeton.

525 *tenderly.* Sykes, obituary for JH, *The Book Collector* (Winter 1965).

525 *'He was – my dear – friend'.* Helen Gardner recalled this in conversation, 1985.

525 *telephoned Kathleen Raine.* Obituary for JH, *The Book Collector* (Winter 1965).

525 *chose Beethoven's Seventh.* Said this to MT (23 Dec. 1949), PRS.

525 *Stravinsky's setting.* Dedicated to TSE in 1962.

526 *Emily Hale's letters.* Thorp Papers, Princeton.

527 *service for TSE at Harvard.* Emily Hale's letter to Willard Thorp.

527 *'little brown people'.* Nanu Mitchell, in conversation.

527 *Humphrey Carpenter.* In conversation.

527 *Vivienne as Daisy. Daisy Miller* (1878). See ch. 8 above.

527 *Emily as May.* 'The Beast in the Jungle' (1903). See ch. 11 above.

527 *Valerie Eliot like Alice Staverton.* 'The Jolly Corner' (1908).

528 *playing a part in his obituary.* ES, Act II, *Plays*, p. 324.

528 *C. Day Lewis.* Obituary for *The Times*, written in 1946 with JH's help. Revised by JH in 1959. Drafts in King's.

528 *TSE's photo of Poet's Corner.* A picture postcard. Houghton.

528 *next to Tennyson* . . . . Described thus in a letter from Valerie Eliot to Allen Tate (17 Jan. 1967). Tate Papers, Princeton.

528 '*And what the dead had no speech for* . . .'. *LG*: I.

528 '*Though our outward man perish* . . .'. The Lesson came from 2 Corinthians 4:16.

528 '*for the things which are seen* . . .'. Ibid., 4:18.

529 '*Can a lifetime represent a single motive?*' Prose summary for *LG*: III on scribbling pad (Magdalene MS A), quoted in *CFQ*, p. 197.

529 the '*life of a man of genius* . . .'. 'The Classics and the Man of Letters' (1942), *CC*, p. 147.

530 *TSE in Sweden.* TSE to Marian Eliot (18 Dec. 1948). Bodleian Library. The Swedish girls who burst into his room were celebrating St Lucy's Day.

530 '*the awful daring* . . .'. *WL*: V.

530 '*the deeper, unnamed feelings* . . .'. *UPUC*, p. 155.

531 '*art* makes *life*'. In a letter to H. G. Wells (10 July 1915), James wrote: 'It is art that *makes* life, makes interest, makes importance . . .'. *Letters*, ed. Leon Edel, iv (Cambridge, Mass.: Belknap, 1984), p. 770).

531 *wills etc.* See *WL*: V where existence

    . . . is not to be found in our obituaries
    Or in memories draped by the beneficent spider
    Or under seals broken by the lean solicitor
    In our empty rooms . . .

531 '*thing*'. 'Preludes': IV.

532 '*a Catholic cast of mind* . . .'. 'Goethe', *OPP*, p. 243.

532 '*in the sty*'. *Marina*.

532 '*a good deal* . . .'. The Rock, *CP*, p. 157, and *ICS*, pp. 48, 49.

533 '*prophesy*'. *AW*: II.

533 '*destiny*'. I am using phrases from *What is a Classic?*

because it seems to me that TSE has a special sense of affinity with Aeneas.

533 *peculiar detachment.* I have drawn on 'Kipling' (1941) where, again, there seems a particular affinity.

533 *the extremist.* Emily Hale's word for TSE, see ch. 7 above.

533 *'The loneliness of home ...'.* 'The Rest Cure', p. 18. King's. Quoted *EMB*.

533 *His youth was interred ....* Draws on *What is a Classic?*

533 *Hope Mirrlees.* BBC TV programme, 'The Mysterious Mr Eliot', *Listener*, lxxxv (14 Jan. 1971), p. 50.

533 *stressed his origins. Paris Review* interview. TSE was interviewed in the NY apartment of Mrs Cohn (of the House of Books) by Donald Hall. Repr. *Writers at Work*, ed. Van Wyck Brooks (NY: Viking, 1965).

533 *unique demand.* A set formula for salvation was laid down in seventeenth-century New England. Edmund S. Morgan, *Visible Saints: The History of a Puritan Idea* (Cornell Univ. Press, 1965), p. 91: 'The pattern is so plain as to give the experiences the appearance of a stereotype'.

533 *Increase Mather.* Quoted ibid., p. 147.

534 *the man 'who's been successful ...'.* Draft of *ES* owned by Valerie Eliot. Quoted *EMB*, p. 318.

534 *outpost.* Morgan, *Visible Saints*, p. 112.

534 *'For Thine is the Kingdom'.* 'The Hollow Men'.

534 *the devil of the stairs. AW*: III.

534 *'trying'.* 'Who are only undefeated / Because we have gone on trying'. *DS*: V.

535 *too clever to be a saint.* I am indebted to Dr Alison Shell for this remark in a first-year tutorial on Eliot at St Hilda's College, Oxford (1985).

535 *epitome.* Wording derived from review by Fiona MacCarthy, *Observer* (19 Apr. 1998).

535 *the prophetic role and introspection.* The Puritans adopted the modes, of course, from the Old Testament.

535 *is and was from the beginning. DS*: I.

535 *'the source of the longest river'. LG*: V.

535 *Some 'obstruction' and habitual barriers. UPUC*, p. 145.

536 *experienced. SE*, p. 325.

536 *'in a world of time beyond me'. Marina.*
536 *'the posterity of the desert'. AW: II.*
536 *re-enact. Song for Simeon.*

ACKNOWLEDGEMENTS

THIS BOOK IS dedicated to my mother, Rhoda Press, who has always spoken of the religious life with unusual clarity and who, throughout her life, wrote mystical poems which she stashed in a basket at the back of a dark cupboard (in her modesty as 'a housewife at the bottom of Africa'). My favourite of her poems, 'Klaver', linking the veld of her childhood with a vision of purity, is pinned at eye level as I revise this book.

It is dedicated, too, to Jon Stallworthy, its first editor before he left publishing to take up a post at Cornell. Jon Stallworthy is known as a poet and biographer, but for me he has continued to be, in a sense, the editor who divines what a writer has in mind, and promotes the longed-for risks. He certainly took a risk with me, a foreigner flouting the settled view of Eliot at that time.

I owe, also, special thanks to Sacvan Bercovitch, Professor of American Studies at Harvard, who supervised this work at an early stage, and to A. Walton Litz and Helen Gardner for generous help later on. After working alone at the Berg Collection, it was heady to meet in Professor Litz a scholar who understood as no one else the challenges of dating the *Waste Land* fragments. I have valued his continued encouragement to pursue Eliot's American background, in particular the ties with Henry James. He is a marvellous teacher, combining the excitement of new research with informal ease. We discussed this revision over lunch at the Century Club in New York in November 1995.

In the mid-seventies Walt Litz introduced me to two young Americans, Ronald Schuchard and Ronald Bush, who were soon to be foremost Eliot scholars. I must thank Ron Bush for stimulating discussions since he took up his post nearby, and for recent articles on Eliot which he passed on with his usual alacrity. Michael Holroyd, too, spared the time to consider the problems of revising a biography.

Earlier versions of the first six chapters were read in the mid-seventies by Jacques Barzun, Valerie Eliot, Ronald Schuchard, and Anne Elliott, and their corrections and suggestions are incorporated in the text. The notes do not acknowledge the influence of *The Art of T. S. Eliot* by Helen Gardner, whose chapter on *The Waste Land* must remain the classic account of the continuity of Eliot's career.

I am grateful to Maurice Haigh-Wood, brother and co-executor of Vivienne Eliot, for permission, given in 1976, to quote from his sister's papers.

Dorothy Elsmith of Woods Hole in Massachusetts, a close friend of Emily Hale, contacted me in the summer of 1977 after reading *Eliot's Early Years*. In a spirit of the utmost loyalty and discretion, she offered details about Emily Hale's relationship with Eliot. I met Mrs Elsmith twice, in 1977–8, once in London, once in Oxford, and then, after her death, her daughter, Barbara Gates Burwell, provided another memorable description of Emily Hale. I also benefited from Professor Willard Thorp of Princeton whose wife, Margaret, had been a lifelong friend of Emily Hale. I am grateful for the permission to quote from the Thorp papers.

A large batch of Emily Hale material, full of useful dates, was provided by Judy Harvey Sahak, Librarian and Assistant Director of the Ella Strong Denison Library in Claremont, California. In 1992 she sent copies of a batch of Eliot's letters to another friend of Emily Hale, Jeanette McPherrin, which give a closer idea of the critical years of the Eliot-Hale relationship, 1934–6. Judy Sahak has been nothing less than a co-researcher, with her ingenuity for sources beyond the official papers, like a Scripps College magazine of the early thirties, and she identified photographs of Emily Hale by the reappearance of a certain elegant pair of shoes. During the eighties, she also put me in touch with friends of Emily Hale who had striking memories, above all Lorraine Havens who gave me copies of two valuable letters in which Emily Hale describes her changing relationship with Eliot in 1947 and 1948. Other Scripps friends who shared wonderfully clear memories going back fifty years were Marie McSpadden Sands, Laurabel Neville Hume, and Margaret Ann Ingram. A few further details came from a relative, C. E. Dexter Morse, who was also a fellow-teacher at Concord Academy, and from a family intimate, Alice Whiting Ellis, of Boston. In 1989, John Mayer, the Boston author of *T. S. Eliot's Silent Voices*, took me with him on his hunt for Emily Hale's house in Concord. We knocked on the door, and the owners kindly showed us round. There is an image of Emily Hale coming on stage for her one-woman show, her arms full of flowers; the image was repeated for me in 1996 when her pupil, Nona Hanes Porter, 'the last protégée of Emily Hale', arrived at our meeting in London bearing an armful of flowers.

Eliot's friend and Faber colleague, Peter du Sautoy gave me lunch in April 1986 at one of Eliot's haunts, the Russell Hotel and, with grave, discreet judgement, described Eliot in later years. Lesley Roberts brought the Tandy letters on 20 December 1990, and Basil Saunders recalled the work of the Lunacy Law reformers in a substantial letter in 1993. (He died in May 1998, and I'd like to thank his son, Bill Saunders, for permission to print this letter.) Ann Rendall dug up an introduction Eliot wrote for an exhibition by her father, McKnight Kauffer, and Eloise B. Bender kindly gave permission to see and quote from Theodore Spencer's papers at Harvard.

The biographer and radio presenter, Humphrey Carpenter, allowed me to read his aunt, Mary Trevelyan's unpublished memoir of her twenty-year friendship with Eliot. I read it four times with increasing fascination.

Helen Gardner had an unsurpassed understanding of Eliot's work and character, and many of her comments have lingered in my mind. She pointed out Eliot's compassion for degraded women in *The Waste Land*, also his honesty in never claiming anything in religious terms which he did not experience. 'Do you think he ever attained his spiritual goal?' I asked, and shan't forget the way she looked me straight in the eye and after a significant pause said just one word: 'No'. I attended her class on the manuscripts of *Four Quartets* at the time when she was starting to edit them. 'Don't imagine an American seminar,' she warned in advance. 'I don't want to hear anyone's opinions.' She took us all to Burnt Norton on a glorious June day in 1974, followed by tea in Chipping Campden.

I have worked repeatedly at the Houghton Library which provided a timely visiting fellowship in 1997, and Susan Halpert her swift and expert skills as a research librarian. Others who helped are Ann Van Arsdale of Princeton's Special Collections; Robert L. Beare of the McKeldin Library, University of Maryland; Mary Clapinson, Keeper of Western Manuscripts at the Bodleian Library, Oxford; A. O. J. Cockshut with his deep understanding of conversion; Karen Eberhart, Archives Specialist at Smith College, who sent a large package of Emily Hale papers; Dr Michael Halls who was Modern Archivist at King's College, Cambridge; Sara S. Hodson, Curator of Literary Manuscripts at the Huntington Library; Dr J. R. L. Maddicott, a medieval historian who supplied useful facts about Thomas à Becket; the Revd Peter Mayhew of the Cowley Fathers, who corrected some misconceptions about Anglo-Catholicism; Mr Osborn, owner of the Osborn Collection at the Beinecke Library, who gave courteous assistance in the spring of 1975; Thomas Staley, director of the Humanities Research Center at Austin, Texas who offered airfare; and last but not least Dr Lola Szladits, who was curator of the Berg Collection in the New York Public Library.

I am grateful for permission to quote from the following copyright material: *The Making of T. S. Eliot's Plays* by E. Martin Browne, reprinted by permission of Cambridge University Press; T. S. Eliot's *Collected Poems 1909–1962*,

copyright 1936 by Harcourt Brace Jovanovich, copyright ©
1963, 1964 by T. S. Eliot; *Selected Essays*, copyright 1950 by
Harcourt Brace Jovanovich, Inc, renewed 1978 by Esme
Valerie Eliot; from *Complete Poems and Plays 1909–1950*
(HBJ, 1952; Faber, 1969), all reprinted by permission of
Faber & Faber Ltd., and Harcourt Brace Jovanovich, Inc.
Excerpts from *The Waste Land: A Facsimile and Transcript
of the Original Drafts, Including the Annotations of Ezra
Pound*, edited and copyright © 1971 by Valerie Eliot, are
reprinted by permission of Faber & Faber Ltd., and Harcourt
Brace Jovanovich, Inc. Excerpts from *On Poetry and Poets*
and *To Criticize the Critic*, are reprinted by permission of
Faber & Faber Ltd, and Farrar, Straus & Giroux, Inc.
Excerpts from Helen Gardner, *The Composition of the Four
Quartets*, copyright © 1978 by Helen Gardner, are reprinted
by permission of Faber & Faber Ltd., and Oxford University
Press Inc. Excerpts from *The Groucho Letters: Letters from
and to Groucho Marx*, copyright © 1967 by Groucho Marx,
are reprinted by permission of Simon & Schuster, Inc. Three
quotations from William Force Stead, in the Osborn Collec-
tion, are reprinted by permission of The Beinecke Rare Book
Library, Yale. Excerpts from *The Diary of Virginia Woolf*,
Vol. 3: 1925–1930, Vol. 4: 1931–1935, edited by Anne
Olivier Bell, copyright © 1980 and 1982 respectively by
Quentin Bell and Angelica Garnett and *The Letters of
Virginia Wolf*, Vol. III: 1923–1928, Vol. V: 1932–1935,
edited by Nigel Nicholson and Joanne Trautmann, copyright
© 1977 and 1979 respectively by Quentin Bell and Angelica
Garnett, are reprinted by permission of The Hogarth Press on
behalf of the estate of Virginia Woolf and the Editors, and
Harcourt Brace Jovanovich, Inc.

Several people were willing to comment on drafts of the
later chapters: Willard Thorp and Lorraine Havens confirmed
the accuracy of the portrait of Emily Hale in chapter 11;
Humphrey Carpenter checked and corrected details about
Mary Trevelyan in chapters 12–14; A. Walton Litz went
through the whole book; Andrew Topsfield, Curator of

Indian Art at the Ashmolean Museum, corrected misconceptions about Indian scriptures; my cousins Roger Press and Tamara Follini commented on style, as did Kate Lea, who gave meticulous attention to detail, and helped to sort out matters of theology after welcoming teas in her cottage in Beckley.

I am also grateful to Catherine Devas for showing me Stamford House in Chipping Campden, and to Viscount Sandon for allowing visits to Burnt Norton and providing historical details.

Siamon Gordon performed the essential 'caesarian operation', and found the anecdote about Eliot's attachment to *The House of the Seven Gables*. I enjoyed many talks with my daughter Anna who did a dissertation on Eliot and language in her final year at Cambridge. Finally, I am grateful to past editors, Judith Luna and Jonathan Galassi, and to the present editors, Caroline Michel, Jenny Uglow, Arzu Tahsin, and Alane Mason, for this opportunity to redo the biography.

BIOGRAPHICAL SOURCES

SINCE THERE IS an excellent bibliography of Eliot's works, as well as numerous bibliographies of secondary criticism, the aim here is to offer a selective guide to biographical sources, stressing rare items and the masses of buried, unpublished, or uncollected material.

Manuscript Sources

The unpublished sources are so abundant and widely-scattered that it is unlikely that anyone could cover them completely. A longheld myth is that research is made impossible by current restrictions. No one should be deterred, for though some manuscripts and typescripts may not be seen – mainly at the Houghton Library at Harvard University – the vast majority, by far, are available.

There are three major repositories apart from Mrs Eliot's private collection. The Houghton Library has a vast Eliot collection with the advantage of comprehensiveness. First in importance are the writings of Eliot's mother, Charlotte Champe Eliot, her immense Scrapbook and her published volumes: *Easter Songs* (Boston: James H. West, n.d.), *Savonarola* (London: Faber, 1926), as well as her biography of Eliot's impressive grandfather, *William Greenleaf Eliot* (Boston: Houghton Mifflin, 1904). A vital source of information is the Library's nine boxes of Eliot family documents, photographs, letters, and out-of-the-way newspaper clippings, most of which were collected by Eliot's elder brother, Henry Eliot. Here, Eliot appears in the context of the Eliot family. See one hundred and twelve letters from Henry Eliot to his mother – bMS Am 1691.6 (4–5) – a number of which concern themselves with Eliot's troubles. Other items of interest are the programme of a 'stunt show' in which Eliot performed with Emily Hale in 1913, and a substantial collection of material relating to his career as a dramatist, including drafts of his most confessional play, *The Family Reunion* (bMS Am 1691.14 (38), see Appendix V). Thoroughly absorbing are E. Martin Browne's scrapbooks on different productions of Eliot's plays, together with photographs of performances. Eliot's letters are restricted, including, alas, his correspondence with Emily Hale about the drafts of *The Family Reunion* in which she played a dual role as the source for one of the characters as well as consultant on the drafts.

Second, there is the choice Berg Collection in the New York Public Library. Here are the gems of Eliot's early years: *The Waste Land*, the 'Inventions of the March Hare' (a Notebook of Eliot's youth), and a folder of miscellaneous poems. In the holograph Notebook, Eliot made fair copies of numerous poems, most of which he never published. Luckily he dated them, so that, despite his frugal impulse from time to time to fill up unused blank spaces, a sequence may be reconstructed. The Notebook contains a draft of 'Prufrock' with a 1912 addition which was excised before publication. The Berg's acquisition (which came from the estate of John Quinn, a New York lawyer who was Eliot's benefactor) also includes a folder of early poems, some holographs but most of them in typescript. Here, too, are a few poems that were unpublished in his lifetime as well as drafts of published poems – in the case of 'Whispers of Immortality' about seven drafts. It is essential to see the changes in Eliot's handwriting in 1910–11 and the watermarks of the original paper in order to determine the chronology of Eliot's writings (see chapters 3 and 5 and Appendix II). The Berg Collection has an important exchange with Leonard Woolf on the management of Vivienne Eliot's ill-health in the mid-1920s.

Third: the Hayward Bequest at King's College, Cambridge University: here are the main manuscripts of Eliot's later years, including the drafts of *Four Quartets* and the crucial correspondence with John Hayward who advised Eliot on the three wartime *Quartets*. A few items to do with these poems were given to Magdalene College, Cambridge, where Eliot was made an honorary fellow.

The two most important Eliot manuscripts became widely available in the 1970s with a facsimile edition of the original drafts of *The Waste Land*, including the annotations of Ezra Pound, ed. with an introduction by Valerie Eliot (London: Faber; NY: Harcourt Brace, 1971) and Helen Gardner's study of *The Composition of Four Quartets* (London: Faber, 1978). Both are lasting works of scholarship, all the better for not overloading the reader with the kind of superfluous information that Eliot's obscurities make all too tempting to lesser scholars. In Mrs Eliot's introduction and Helen Gardner's chapters on the growth and sources of the *Quartets*, facts are selective and direct the reader towards the work. It is to be hoped that scholars of the twenty-first century will follow their lead in discerning the simplicity at the heart of Eliot's apparent difficulty.

Eliot's philosophy papers between 1911 and 1914 at the Houghton Library have been examined by a growing number of academics with Mrs Eliot's permission: the collection of index cards on which Eliot, as a young man, made notes from books that had interested him (see Appendix I); holograph notes on the Paris lectures of Henri Bergson (1910–11), also a draft of a paper on Bergson (c. 1912), catalogued as bMS Am 1691 (130, 132); Eliot's essay on the relationship between politics and metaphysics (c. 1914), catalogued as bMS Am 1691 (25); and eighty pages of notes from the extensive lectures (philosophy course: 24a) on Buddhism, given from 3 October 1913 till 15 May 1914 by a visiting scholar from Japan, Masaharu Anesaki, catalogued amongst the R. B. Perry Papers as bMS Am 1691.14 (12). One of his handouts which Eliot kept was Anesaki's entry on 'Buddhist Ethics and Morality' in the *Encyclopaedia of Religion and Ethics*, v, ed. James Hastings (NY: Scribner's, 1910) 447–55.

The largest unpublished source is Eliot's letters, the majority of which, though dispersed across Great Britain and the United States, are open to scholars. Eliot's more confidential batches were to Virginia Woolf (in the Berg); to Bertrand Russell (copies in the Russell Archive at McMaster University, Hamilton, Ontario, largely to do with Eliot's difficulties in his first marriage – the best parts are quoted in Russell's *Autobiography*); and to his Harvard friend, Conrad Aiken (at the Huntington Library, California). The letters to Aiken after 1916 are uninteresting with the exception of a letter of 1952, acknowledging the autobiographical *Ushant* (in which a young Eliot appears as 'the tsetse'). Faber's rejection of Aiken's poetry in the early thirties was obviously a source of grievance, and also Eliot's much greater fame. Eliot's letters sound like attempts to cheer on the friendship, for the most part, it appears, unsuccessfully. Aiken was also scornful of Eliot's becoming a Christian, but some warmth seems to have returned with the arrival of Valerie Eliot.

The letters that are vital to an understanding of Eliot's creative and religious development – the two go together – often come in small, isolated groups. Eliot's letters to William Force Stead form a background to his growing attachment to Anglicanism during the twenties, his conversion, his first confession, and his acceptance of celibacy. These letters are in the Osborn Collection at the Beinecke Library, Yale. There, too, are Stead's reminiscences, dated 29 April 1940, holograph notes on Eliot's character in response to a questionnaire by Dr Osborn. Though there are minor inaccuracies, two reported exchanges with Eliot on the subject of love (with Emily Hale in mind) do sound true. Another small batch of both religious and literary importance are twenty-two letters to Paul Elmer More, the Princeton theologian, from 1928 until More's death in 1937. The best of these letters (in the More Papers, Special Collections, Princeton University Library) debate the nature of hell.

There is a large collection of correspondence at the Humanities Research Center, Austin, Texas, including the letters of Lady Ottoline Morrell on the Eliots, notably Russell's affair with Vivienne, and her growing disturbance. Another large collection of letters from Eliot to various less intimate friends may be found at Princeton University. Eliot's letters to a friend Bonamy Dobrée are part of the Brotherton Collection at Leeds University, and his letters to another friend Sir Herbert Read are part of the Read Archive (lot 48, item 32) of McPherson Library at the University of Victoria, British Columbia in Canada. Eliot's letters to Professor Theodore Spencer are in the Spencer Papers, in the Harvard Archives: HUG 4806.5 Box 2, in Pusey Library. See also Professor Spencer's journal (HUG 4806.35). Theodore Spencer's copy of Eliot's *Poems 1909–1925* have annotations deriving from discussions with Eliot while he was a visiting professor at Harvard, 1932–3. The copy is in the Matthiessen Room in Eliot House, Harvard.

Donald Gallup owns letters to Emily Hale's aunt, Mrs Perkins – Helen Gardner quotes from them in *The Composition of Four Quartets*. The seven letters (1936–48) to Emily's close friend, Dorothy Elsmith are restricted at the Houghton (bMS Am 1691.3). Fortunately, researchers may examine an unusually confidential batch of thirteen letters from Eliot to Emily Hale's younger friend Jeanette McPherrin (1934–54, see ch. 9) which were acquired in 1992 for the fascinating Hale collection at the Ella Strong Denison Library, Claremont, California. This collection, another substantial one at Smith College, Northampton, Mass., and the Thorp collection at Princeton are the three main repositories of Emily Hale papers. Other sources are Simmons College in Boston; the archives of Milwaukee-Downer College, now part of the University of Wisconsin; and two Massachusetts schools, Concord Academy and Phillips Academy.

Eliot's letters reflect, as good letters do, a different relationship with each correspondent. His letters to Virginia Woolf reflect her enjoyment of this form, and her style of playful vivacity. His letters to Pound reflect Pound's bristle and contempt. His letters to P.E. More reflect the latter's theological seriousness and a common interest in spiritual autobiography. Another group of fifty-five letters to Sydney Schiff (who wrote under the name, Stephen Hudson), from 1919–43 (in the British Library: Add 52918) have, from the start, a rare note: open and affectionate. In their relative unguardedness, these letters might be classed with those to More and Virginia Woolf, but of the three, the letters to Schiff and his wife, Violet, are by far the most natural. There seems less wish to make an impression (with Virginia Woolf, he wished to be amusing, and with More, to be the most serious of converts). The naturalness with Schiff came partly from the fact that both had wives who suffered from chronic illness. Vivienne's letters show that she enjoyed her own relation to the Schiffs who treated the young Eliots with a sympathy that was not reserved for Eliot alone. It was a couple relationship, and perhaps the only genuine one that Eliot and Vivienne shared. Another reason for the special tone of these letters is that Schiff seems to have replaced Pound as Eliot's mentor when Pound left England towards the end of the Great War. At that point Eliot's letters confide work plans, and reveal that he was showing Schiff work in progress.

Though Eliot was adept at taking on the colouring of his correspondents, Pound's Brer Rabbit language was wearing to keep up, and Eliot imitated, with more success, the Southern drawl of Allen Tate (in the Tate Papers, Princeton). Eliot's later letters to Pound (in the Beinecke Library) blend American humour with weary exasperation and efforts to defuse Pound's epistolary outbursts and invective. Eliot could not treat Pound as he did young Faber authors – with kindly consideration – for Pound was his senior by a few years, with a prior claim to fame. He was a bit like a supervisor whose pupil overtakes him. For Eliot, it was that sort of difficult relationship. He could never forget what he owed to Pound, and Pound never relinquished the right (and chance) to prick Eliot's ambition to take cover as an English gentleman. Pound took the line that other Faber poets – Auden, Spender,

Wallace Stevens – were his inferiors, and that he only allowed Faber to publish him as a personal favour to Eliot and his American colleague, Frank Morley. On 25 Jan. 1934 Eliot tried to divert the tide of Pound's letters with the humorous complaint that his main occupation at Faber was now to superintend a department devoted to correspondence with Mr Ezra Pound. He complained too (21 Feb. 1938), and with justice, that Pound's letters were cryptograms which, like all Pound's explanations, assumed that the reader knew all about it already.

The letters to Pound have an atmosphere of boxing in the Underworld (as Virginia Woolf called the literary market-place). Most are about the minutiae of the literary life – rivals, money, reviewers – and reflect moods of aggression, particularly in the earlier letters with their masculine bravado, misogyny, and anti-Semitism. At some point in the late thirties Eliot began to detach himself from the blatant anti-Semitism that was to lead Pound into the arms of the enemy and a trial for treason, and on 13 Aug. 1954 let fly one rebuff to the effect that though Pound was at liberty to continue with personal insults, he would tolerate no further insult either to his nationality or to his religion which included the Jewish religion. This letter was signed T.S.E. instead of the usual Tp [Tom possum]. Pound, delighted to have provoked this steam, reaffirmed his attachment to the long friendship.

Two central batches of letters have been restricted but, in each case, it is not impossible to gain some insight into the ties they represent. The largest and most secret batch of letters, approximately a thousand to Emily Hale from about 1930 to 1957, is sealed at Princeton until 12 October 2019, the longest embargo Eliot enjoined. Emily Hale's letters to Eliot were probably destroyed (see ch. 11), but, fortunately, a letter of 1947 to Lorraine Havens, describing a crisis in their relationship, has survived and also a good number of her letters to Willard Thorp which give an idea of this relationship from her point of view. These are the letters in the Thorp Papers at Princeton, which include, too, a copy of Emily

Hale's final letter, sadly restrained in the face of Eliot's rejection, which she wrote to him in September 1963.

His letters to Mary Trevelyan (from about 1942 to 1957) are restricted at the Houghton Library, but she included a great number of Eliot's letters to her, or extracts, in her unpublished memoir of their friendship. This memoir, 'The Pope of Russell Square, 1938–1958', intersperses these letters with narrative and reports of conversations (from Mary's diary), providing a unique close-up of Eliot during his most inscrutable years of fame in the late forties and early fifties. Well-written, highly readable, and splendidly detailed, it must come out sooner or later, but cannot appear in its entirety until Faber completes an edition of Eliot's letters. The valuable typescript is privately owned by Mary Trevelyan's nephew, Humphrey Carpenter, and niece, Kate Trevelyan. There are entertaining details about Mary Trevelyan's work with foreign students, especially on the Goats' Club which she founded in 1956 with Eliot as its first president, in *Goats: A History of International Students House, London* by A. Adu Boahen (London: International Students Trust, 1983).

There are twelve unsigned editorials in *Lloyd's Bank Monthly* which Eliot may have written. They are not listed in the bibliography of Eliot's works. Henry Eliot mentions to his mother (29 September 1923) that his brother wrote an article for Lloyd's at that time.

Because Eliot drew so constantly on his life, especially his inward life, as a source for his writing, the earlier drafts and evolution of his works have a special interest. The scenarios and drafts of Eliot's plays, *Sweeney Agonistes*, *The Family Reunion*, *The Cocktail Party*, *The Confidential Clerk*, and *The Elder Statesman* (of the last, the scenarios and first two Acts), are part of the Hayward Bequest at King's. (Material relating to the final act of *The Elder Statesman*, written after Eliot's second marriage, is owned by Valerie Eliot.) In Eliot's early years, many of his drafts were handwritten; in later years, he tended to work directly from a few rough notes on to the typewriter. Some of these rough notes have survived. There are those for the *Quartets* in King's and

Magdalene College, Cambridge, and another, longer set for *Murder in the Cathedral*, available in the Houghton Library (see Appendix IV). The most intriguing page provides a source for the four Tempters in four of Eliot's contemporaries. Equally intriguing are two pages of a pencil draft that followed the *Murder* notes and that are filed with them: this is the 'Bellegarde' sketch (also described in Appendix IV).

The scenarios and drafts of *The Family Reunion* are divided between King's and the Houghton: they reveal ten stages of composition (see Appendix V). Eliot consulted Emily Hale at one stage, and her marginal comments may be seen at the Houghton.

Of the unpublished essays, Eliot's talk on the Bible, in the historic King's Chapel in Boston on 1 Dec. 1932, is the most profound, with its distinctions between scripture and litera-ture, and its suggestiveness for Eliot's poetic search for the Word. He mentions, for instance, the problem of patience for the religious poet who awaits an illumination he cannot command. This typescript was donated to the Houghton Library by Emily Hale's uncle, the Revd John Carroll Perkins who, at the time of Eliot's talk, was minister of King's Chapel. It has become modish to make much of Eliot's early philosophical essays (at the Houghton), but these obligatory academic exercises are of limited interest beside Eliot's mature thoughts on the Bible.

In *The Achievement of T. S. Eliot* (NY: OUP, 1935), F. O. Matthiessen printed a wonderful note he took down from an unpublished lecture (on English Letter Writers) which Eliot gave at Yale in 1933: it quotes Eliot's wish to go 'beyond poetry' in the way Beethoven went 'beyond music' in his late quartets (see ch. 10). Donald Gallup made notes on Eliot's unpublished lecture 'Walt Whitman and Modern Poetry' which he includes in 'Mr Eliot at the Churchill Club' in *T. S. Eliot: Essays from the Southern Review*, ed. James Olney (OUP, 1988).

Hayward collected several of Eliot's other unpublished addresses at King's. By far the most interesting are two lectures on 'The Development of Shakespeare's Verse', delivered at Edinburgh University in 1937 (the remarks on *Hamlet* being pertinent to the composition of the intensely introspective *Family Reunion*). He repeated the (revised) lectures at Bristol in 1941, and gave the carbons to Emily Hale who later gave them to Harvard. Necessary to our understanding of Eliot's dramatic aims are his theory, here, of the ultra-dramatic and his comments on the challenge of poetic language. Some points from these lectures went into 'Poetry and Drama' (1951).

Hayward also collected and bound the drafts of *Four Quartets*. These are well-documented by Helen Gardner in *The Composition of Four Quartets*, but she overlooked one draft of *Burnt Norton* which Eliot sent to Frank Morley in New York and which is now available at Harvard. This draft has an additional few lines at the end which attempt to express a visionary experience in spaced words (see ch. 10). It was cut on Morley's advice. The extant drafts of Eliot's other mature poems are fairly polished, with only the odd notable variant or epigraph. I suspect that, in some cases, he destroyed earlier drafts, as is likely in the case of *The Confidential Clerk* which Hayward labelled a first draft but appears close to a final one.

Serious students of Eliot's life will want to see the rather dull typescript Autobiography of his father, Henry Ware Eliot, in the Olin Library, Washington University, St. Louis.

When she died in 1947, Eliot's first wife, Vivienne, left her diaries to the Bodleian Library, Oxford. Those for 1914, 1919, 1934, and 1935 are catalogued as MSS Eng. misc. e. 876–8, f. 532. Her diary for 1935–6 is catalogued MSS. Eng. lett. c. 382. The diaries are less significant for the early years, for all but one were written before and after she lived with Eliot, but the diaries of the thirties do contain many memories (perhaps distorted, and to be read with caution), copies of letters, and contemporary records of the Eliots' separation – wholly, of course, from Vivienne's point of view. All the diaries, taken together, are a gripping document of moods, character, and behaviour. The Bodleian Library also has drafts and fragments of her attempts at fiction and a few poems in the early twenties, some of which Eliot edited or took down at her dictation, and some of which he published in the *Criterion* (MSS. Eng. misc. d. 936/1–4, and MSS. Eng. misc. c. 624). Twelve unbound copies of poems were in existence in 1934 when an inventory was made of the Eliots' belongings. There are two or three isolated poems, but no collection of them amongst her papers in the Bodleian Library. One notebook disappeared from the library in 1990. Perhaps for this reason Vivienne Eliot's papers are now on microfilm, and this is what the reader is given. Unfortunately, she writes her first drafts in pencil, and this is faint on microfilm. Show the librarian the problem, and request the originals.

Eliot's letters to the New York magazine, the *Dial*, as well as unpublished letters from Vivienne to its editor, Scofield Thayer, are in the Beinecke Library.

A hundred and forty-three letters to Doris (Polly) Tandy from 1934 to 1963, now in the British Library, were discovered in extraordinary circumstances in 1990 in the hands of an English pig-farmer, Edward Kidner. He had been about to throw them out when they were rescued by a neighbour Lesley Roberts of the BBC. Mr Kidner was the widower of Anthea (Poppet) Tandy, Eliot's goddaughter, the youngest of the three children of Geoffrey and Doris Tandy (see ch. 7). These comic letters cover Eliot's attributes as a house guest, advise on how to cope with children suffering from chickenpox and how to treat an ailing cat, discuss cat types and list suitable names for them; they also enclose working drafts of Eliot's collection of *Practical Cats*. (Other unpublished cat poems are in the Houghton – 'Cat's Prologue' bMS Am 1691.7 (66) – and at Princeton.) Eliot came to know the Tandy children through their father who worked at the Natural History Museum in the early 1930s and later became a broadcaster: he read a selection of Eliot's cat poems on the wireless at Christmas 1937. When they were published in 1939, the elder Tandy daughter, Alison (known as Pooney), was one of the four children to whom they were dedicated.

There was yet another find in 1996: the trail has vanished, but is bound to reappear. A past pupil who works with the homeless in Oxford told me that a man who came to the shelter had found some Eliot and related letters in a chest of drawers. He offered them to the Bodleian Library. The Department of Western Manuscripts confirmed this in March 1997 and said that in the end the owner did not sell them the letters because a manuscript dealer thought they were worth more than the Library had offered.

Printed Sources

After the drafts of the two great poems became available in the 1970s, the next major publication was *The Letters of T. S. Eliot: Volume 1 1898–1922*, ed. Valerie Eliot (London: Faber; NY: Harcourt Brace, 1988). This book changed my impression of Eliot as letter writer: he's absorbing, discreetly candid to certain correspondents, playful and stern by turns, offering the excitement of verbal precision but in a somewhat less studied way than in poetry or essays, drawing us closer perhaps than we've yet been to his milieu. The unexpected proximity is enhanced by the inclusion of letters from Eliot's correspondents, and not least, various letters from Vivienne which show more than her diaries do what she was like to live with in the early years of Eliot's first marriage: her combination of alertness and blinkeredness; her mercurial switch from eager spontaneity to demanding pathos. The notes provide abundant and accurate information without swamping the text – a difficult balance, well-judged here.

The two major publications of the 1990s were Eliot's Notebook and miscellaneous poems (from the Berg Collection) as *Inventions of the March Hare: Poems 1909–1917*, ed. Christopher Ricks (London: Faber; NY: Harcourt Brace, 1996), and two sets of Eliot lectures, the Clark Lectures at

Trinity College, Cambridge, 1926, and the Turnbull Lectures at The Johns Hopkins University, 1933, as *The Varieties of Metaphysical Poetry*, ed. and introduced by Ronald Schuchard (London: Faber; NY: Harcourt Brace, 1992).

Eliot's essays in spiritual biography, 'The *Pensées* of Pascal', 'Baudelaire', 'Paul Elmer More' (in the *Princeton Alumni Weekly*, 5 Feb. 1937), the account of Charles de Foucauld (in 'Towards a Christian Britain', *Listener*, 10 Apr. 1941, 524–5), and *George Herbert*, together with the collected editions of poems and plays, and in particular *The Family Reunion*, are more revealing of his inward life than any existing memoir or biography. For a curious self-characterisation, see his 'Eeldrop and Appleplex: I', *Little Review*, 4 (May 1917), 7–11, repr. *The Little Review Anthology*, ed. D. V. Baker (London, 1949), and also the strange 'Ode', published once only, in *Ara Vos Prec* (London: Ovid, 1920).

Donald Gallup's *T. S. Eliot: A Bibliography* (NY: Harcourt Brace, 1969) is the indispensable guide to printed works, particularly useful for its accurate year-by-year listing of uncollected critical articles, of introductions to books by other authors, and of books containing letters from Eliot. Short as they are, some of his pieces in the *Athenaeum* – 'A Sceptical Patrician' (23 May 1919) and 'The Preacher as Artist' (28 Nov. 1919) – and some of his London Letters to the *Dial* (lxx, Apr. 1921, 448–53, and June 1921, 686–91; lxxi, Aug. 1921, 213–17, and Oct. 1921, 452–5; lxxii, Apr. 1922, 510–13; lxxiii, Sept. 1922, 329–31) are of more enduring interest than his theory of impersonality which, as Ronald Schuchard's articles suggest, obscured the personal nature of Eliot's poetry.

The bibliography shows what a prolific reviewer he was in early years, what a frequent commentator and speaker in later years. There is a vast body of criticism that has now remained for half a century unread by new generations of readers, and many distinguished thoughts lie buried in obscure and, for many, unobtainable journals. We have only to leave the well-trodden paths of the volumes of selected criticism to find fresh approaches to Eliot through his own words. Two outstanding but almost unknown pieces of the mature years are 'A Commentary: That Poetry is Made with Words', *New English Weekly*, xxvii (Apr. 1939), which provides a gloss on *Four Quartets*, and a marvellously stimulating exchange on language with a radio interviewer, Desmond Hawkins, on 22 Nov. 1940, printed as 'The Writer as Artist' in the *Listener* (28 Nov. 1940), 773–4. These views on the writer's duty to his language lie behind *Little Gidding*: V.

Eliot often talked more freely to children. Two obscure school addresses are interesting for their reminiscences: one at Milton Academy, Milton, Mass., on 17 June 1933, which is printed in the *Milton Graduates Bulletin*, iii (Nov. 1933), 5–9; the other at the centennial of the Mary Institute, St Louis, on 11 Nov. 1959, which is printed in *From Mary to You* (St Louis, 1959), 133–6. See also an informal interview with Eliot in the *Granite Review*, xxiv, No. 3 (1962), 16–20. There were two full-scale interviews in Eliot's later years, the first with Helen Gardner, 'The "Aged Eagle" Spreads His Wings: a 70th-Birthday Talk with T. S. Eliot', *Sunday Times* (21 Sept. 1958). This gives an intelligent survey of the whole career, dominated by Eliot's conviction that the difference between his pre- and post-conversion poetry has been exaggerated by critics. A year later, Donald Hall did the fine *Paris Review* interview, containing Eliot's other telling assertion – also ignored for two decades – that his poetry came from America. This interview is repr. in *Writers at Work*, ed. Van Wyck Brooks, 2nd series (NY: Viking, 1963; re-edited by Dick Kay, London: Penguin, 1972). Eliot also reminisced, this time about his family in St Louis, in a 1953 address, repr. in *CC*, 'American Literature and the American Language'. Occasional recollections may be found in his various introductions to books by other writers. For memories of America, see his Preface to E. A. Mowrer, *This American World* (London: Faber, 1928) and his Introduction to the Cresset edition of *Huckleberry Finn* (1950); for memories of Harvard's Philosophy Department in the early years of this century see his Introduction to Josef Pieper, *Leisure: the Basis of Culture* (repr. NY: Mentor-Omega, 1963).

There have been numerous memoirs by people who knew Eliot in one way or another. The best have been cameos which do not venture beyond immediate knowledge. One of the liveliest came from Hope Mirrlees in an interview for the BBC TV programme, 'The Mysterious Mr Eliot', printed in the *Listener* (14 Jan. 1971), 50. W. G. Tinckom-Fernandez did a memoir of Eliot as a student, 'T. S. Eliot, '10, An Advocate Friendship' in the special Eliot issue of the *Harvard Advocate*, cxxv:3 (Dec. 1938), repr. *Harvard Advocate: Centennial Anthology*, ed. Jonathan D. Culler (Cambridge, Mass: Schenkman, 1966), pp. 63–81. An amusing collection was edited in honour of Eliot's sixtieth birthday by Tambimuttu and Richard March (London, 1948, repr. Frank & Cass, 1965), containing lively memoirs by Conrad Aiken ('King Bolo and Others'), Clive Bell ('How Pleasant to Know Mr. Eliot') and Wyndham Lewis ('Early London Environment'). Another good collection was edited by Allen Tate after Eliot's death, *T. S. Eliot: The Man and his Work* (NY: Dell, 1966; London: Chatto, 1967), with interesting memoirs by Frank Morley, Sir Herbert Read, Bonamy Dobrée, and Robert Giroux. Amongst the many fine articles in the *Southern Review*'s Eliot issue, ed. James Olney (Oct. 1985) and repr. by OUP in 1988 as *Essays from the Southern Review*, Janet Adam Smith has a delightful reminiscence of Eliot, showing his domestic aspect, in 'Tom Possum and the Roberts Family' and, in the same book, Harry Levin recalls Eliot at Harvard and Peter du Sautoy recalls Eliot as fellow-publisher. Mr du Sautoy gives a sympathetic image of Eliot's happiness in his second marriage, when their friendship was at its height.

Valerie Eliot has drawn a confident portrait of her husband as a good, sensitive, and loving man in three interviews: in the *Observer* (20 February 1972); 'A Poet's Wife and Letters' in the *Times* (17 September 1988); and 'Two Mrs Eliots' by Blake Morrison in the *Independent on Sunday* (24 April 1994).

There are numerous books and articles which are not primarily about Eliot but contain glimpses of him. *The Diary of Virginia Woolf* ed. Anne Olivier Bell, assisted by Andrew McNeillie (London: Hogarth; NY: Harcourt, Brace, 1977–84) provides the most perceptive, even clairvoyant portraits of Eliot in his first years in London, and shows the development of his friendship with a highly original novelist who was also Eliot's publisher and, at the same time, high priestess of Modernism. Other glimpses of Eliot may be found in Bertrand Russell's *Autobiography*, i–ii (Boston: Little, Brown; London: Allen & Unwin, 1967–9). Ray Monk corrects its fudging of the relation to Vivienne Eliot with a new mass of authenticated detail in *Bertrand Russell: The Spirit of Solitude* (London: Cape, 1996). Witty anecdotes of Eliot as an undergraduate may be found in Donald J. Adams, *Copey of Harvard* (Boston: Houghton Mifflin, 1960), and Conrad Aiken, *Ushant* (Boston: Little, Brown, 1952). Eliot's Oxford experience in wartime may be gauged from Robin Harrison, 'In the Shadow of War: Letters of an Oxford Freshman 1914–15', *Oxford Magazine* (Fourth Week, Michaelmas Term, 1996), 4–13. A vivid image of Eliot as a newcomer to London's literary scene may be found in Iris Barry, 'The Ezra Pound Period', *The Bookman* (Oct. 1931). See also Ezra Pound, *Selected Letters 1907–1941*, ed. D. D. Paige (repr. NY: New Directions, 1971); Leonard Woolf, *Downhill All the Way* (NY: Harcourt, 1967; London: Hogarth, repr. OUP); and *Letters of Leonard Woolf*, ed. Frederic Spotts (London: Weidenfeld, 1989), containing his initial overture as publisher to Eliot in 1918, and one reply to Eliot's appeal for help with Vivienne in the twenties. There is a rather snide picture of angelic coldness in Richard Aldington's *Life for Life's Sake* (NY: Viking, 1941). Finally, some rare close-ups of Eliot may be discerned in Vivienne Eliot's sketches: 'Letters of the Moment – I and II', *Criterion*, ii (Feb. and Apr. 1924), 220–2, 360–4; 'Thé Dansant', *Criterion*, iii (Oct. 1924), 72–8; 'A Diary of the Rive Gauche' and 'Necesse est Perstare?', *Criterion*, iii (Apr. 1925), 425–9, 364; and 'Fête Galante', *Criterion*, iii (July 1925), 557–63.

Eliot appears in interesting lights in several later biographies. The most useful is David Arkell's *Looking for*

Laforgue (Manchester: Carcanet, 1979) – overtly, there's not a lot on Eliot, but quotations from Laforgue's letters are full of suggestive parallels, like Laforgue's account of his youthful obsession with saintly stunts. Eliot is a marginal figure in Claire Tomalin, *Katherine Mansfield: A Secret Life* (London: Viking, 1987), but the image is strong. He's of course a central figure in Humphrey Carpenter, *A Serious Character: The Life of Ezra Pound* (London: Faber; Boston: Houghton Mifflin, 1988). Miranda Seymour, *Ottoline Morrell: Life on the Grand Scale* (London: Hodder, 1992) has fresh material on Vivienne as well as Eliot, while his friendship with the Sitwells and frictions in the marketplace are ably discussed in Philip Ziegler, *Osbert Sitwell* (London: Chatto, 1998). Mary Hutchinson's relationship with Eliot is filled out by David Bradshaw in 'Those Extraordinary Parakeets: Clive Bell and Mary Hutchinson', *The Charleston Magazine*, issue 16 (Autumn/Winter 1997), 5–12. Anthony Powell reflects on the different sides to Eliot – the publicity he commanded (no one has so much publicity without seeking it) and the other Eliot who 'liked pottering about . . . making the smallest of small talk' – in *Journals*, i (London: Heinemann, 1995–8), p. 230.

There are several full-length memoirs, all written with an uneasy blend of effusion and condescension. They are based on no more than a slight acquaintance with the man and show little feeling for his work. They are *Affectionately, T. S. Eliot* by William Turner Levy and Victor Scherle (NY: J. B. Lippincott, 1968); Robert Sencourt, *T. S. Eliot: A Memoir* (NY: Dodd; London: Garnstone Press, 1971); and T. S. Matthews' *Great Tom* (NY: Harper; London: Weidenfeld & Nicolson, 1974). The latter is full of inaccuracies, but it does uncover the important relationship with Emily Hale and has collected some genuine facts about her.

E. Martin Browne's *The Making of T. S. Eliot's Plays* (Cambridge: Cambridge University Press, 1969, repr. with supplement, 1970) is a special kind of memoir which recalls Eliot's work in the theatre. It has immensely valuable information about the evolution of his plays, backed by reports of conversations and abundant quotation from Eliot's drafts and letters, though, for all this, the book is less perceptive than Carol H. Smith's unsurpassed *T. S. Eliot's Dramatic Theory and Practice* (Princeton University Press, 1963).

For the American aspect of Eliot's genius, see his brilliant essays on Henry James for the *Little Review* (discussed in ch. 4). The best critical approach is by Ronald Bush, 'Nathaniel Hawthorne and T. S. Eliot's American Connection' in *T. S. Eliot: Essays from the Southern Review*, ed. James Olney (NY: OUP, 1988). Eliot's distinction of American from English poetry as a different rhythm in the blood is central to an unpublished talk, 'Tradition and the Practice of Poetry', which A. Walton Litz edited for *Essays from the Southern Review*. Eric Sigg has studied what Eliot called 'the extensive consanguinity in New England where everybody, if not nearly related, is at least a cousin of everybody else' (referring to his poem 'Cousin Nancy' and quoted in *T. S. Eliot, An Exhibition of Manuscripts and First Editions*, Humanities Research Center, Texas, June 1961). Extremely useful to the biographer are Sigg's article, 'Eliot as a product of America' in *A Cambridge Companion to T. S. Eliot*, ed. A. David Moody (CUP, 1994), and another article which has circulated in typescript, 'T. S. Eliot and the New England Literary Family', with fascinating detail on Andrew Eliott's involvement in the witch-trials of the 1690s, and amazing family trees showing Eliot's connections to many of the foremost American writers (1992). American scholars have cast their eye on Eliot's return to America in 1932–33: apart from Ronald Schuchard's helpful background to the Turnbull Lectures of 1933 in his edition of *The Varieties of Metaphysical Poetry*, James F. Louks has compiled 'The Exile's Return: Fragment of a T. S. Eliot Chronology', *ANQ*, ix: 2 (spring 1996), 16–39, and Ronald Bush is due to publish ' "As If You Were Hearing it from Mr. Fletcher or Mr. Tourneur in 1633": T. S. Eliot's 1933 Harvard lecture Notes for "English 26" ("Introduction to Contemporary Literature")'.

Ronald Schuchard's 'T. S. Eliot and the Horrific Moment' in *Essays from the Southern Review* is profoundly right. He explores the unnameable: the poet's strange capacity for horror. A. V. C. Schmidt, 'Eliot's Intolerable Wrestle: Speech, Silence, Words and Voices', *UNISA English Studies* (Pretoria, 1983), 17–22, is another outstanding essay which examines Eliot's struggles with language in his search for the ineffable Word. John Mayer, *T. S. Eliot's Silent Voices* (NY: OUP, 1989) follows the play of inner voices in Eliot's early poetry, including what was then the unpublished material in the Berg Collection.

Thirty years after Eliot's death, his reputation reached a low point in the 1990s as readers began to question his élitism and intolerance with increasing outspokenness. A more questioning approach was voiced in America by Cynthia Ozick in a long *New Yorker* article in 1989, and in England it came from within the citadel, as it were, at the Eliot lectures for the University of Canterbury, published afterwards by Eliot's own press: Christopher Ricks, *T. S. Eliot and Prejudice* (London: Faber, 1988) and John Carey, *The Intellectuals and the Masses: Pride and Prejudice among the Literary Intelligentsia 1880–1939* (London: Faber, 1992). The most widely-discussed book was a case against Eliot, built up with polemical relentlessness by a lawyer, Anthony Julius, in *T. S. Eliot, Anti-Semitism, and Literary Form* (Cambridge and NY: CUP, 1995). Julius declares a respect for Eliot in his final paragraph, but it seems more like respect for a worthy adversary than an understanding of 'literary form', of compassion for abused women in *The Waste Land*, of moments of tenderness and vision, the psychic daring on 'the frontiers of consciousness', and the height of Eliot's genius in *Four Quartets* – so much is left out to sharpen the tooth of an attack. It seems naïve not to assume that to be a genius does not preclude common faults. It's obvious, though, why Eliot in particular invited attack, with his moral loftiness (so antipathetic to this later age).

Where the above are factual books, an inaccurate play, *Tom and Viv*, by Michael Hastings, redone as a 'biopic' in 1994, has undermined Eliot's reputation with the wider public. A movie, unlike a biography, has to tell a story in two hours. How does it compare with biographical truth? Brian Gilbert, the director, would have it that the movie is 'imaginative truth'. No one will deny that in any art form, imaginative truth has its place. But what line should be drawn between artistic form and the licence to skew the truth in the case of people who were once alive? Biography is committed to factual truth, and in the movie two factual truths were plain wrong. First, Hastings (who co-scripted the movie) and Brian Gilbert were too stuck on the dotty charms of 'Viv' to admit any serious scene of a woman writing. 'Viv's' creative flair was confined, in the script, to supplying one title. (It had her coming up with 'The Waste Land' because that is Eliot's most famous poem.) Second, 'Tom' is presented as a man who mates once for life. But in real life, Eliot was, of course, in love with someone else. *Tom and Viv*'s claim to Art would seem to absolve it of the inconvenient complication of another woman, but Hastings was aware of another damaging omission. For his script lacked Eliot's own words, except for one reading. In short, it was hollow at the core – despite the glorious English landscape and Miranda Richardson acting up a storm as winsome, misunderstood 'Viv'. No one apparently told her the distinctly uncharming fact that the real Vivienne joined the Black Shirts and liked to parade her Fascist uniform. Is this excusable on the grounds of pre-menstrual tension and over-medication? For that provides Hastings with a simple source for all 'Viv's' troubles. His reductive scenarios do not draw on the mental torment of Harry – the furies of conscience in a man who believes he may have murdered his wife in the play Eliot was writing at the very time of Vivienne's committal. Eliot's own play is the closest we shall ever come to his private critique of his conduct. But the Eliot estate did not permit Hastings to quote the actual words. For years Hastings ranted against the estate. He would have it that the estate was against everyone, but in truth there has always been a vast industry of Eliot scholars endlessly quoting his words. Hastings was alone in a handicap to which his bluster repeatedly drew attention: the absence of a poet in his script.

Another phenomenon of the late 1980s and early 1990s was a spate of academic books on Eliot's work in the formal discipline of philosophy: William Skaff, *The Philosophy of T. S. Eliot: From Skepticism to a Surrealist Poetic, 1909–1927* (Philadelphia: Univ. of Philadelphia Press, 1986); Cleo McNelly Kearns, *T.S. Eliot and Indic Tradition: A Study in Poetry and Belief* (NY: CUP, 1987); Richard Shusterman, *T. S. Eliot and the Philosophy of Criticism* (London: Duckworth, 1988); Jeffrey M. Perl, *Skepticism and Modern Enmity: Before and After Eliot* (Baltimore: Johns Hopkins Univ. Press, 1989) which has material unpublished elsewhere; and Manju Jain, *T. S. Eliot and American Philosophy: The Harvard Years* (Cambridge: CUP, 1992).

H. W. H. Powel, Jr did pioneering biographic work in his Brown University master's essay, 'Notes on the Life of T. S. Eliot, 1888–1910' (1954), followed by John Soldo with his Harvard dissertation (1972) on Eliot's development from 1888 to 1915, published as *The Tempering of T. S. Eliot* (Ann Arbor, Mich: UMI Research Press, 1983). The first full-length biography was Peter Ackroyd's deft and readable *T. S. Eliot: A Life* (London: Hamish Hamilton; NY: Simon & Schuster, 1984). James Olney contributed 'Where is the real T. S. Eliot? or, The Life of the Poet' to *The Cambridge Companion to T. S. Eliot* (1994). 'The Bodily Biography of T. S. Eliot', parts I and II in the *Yeats Eliot Review*, xv: 1 (fall 1997), 2–9, 36–44, and xv: 2 (spring 1998), 27–44, by Chris Buttram Trombold, has gone to primary sources for a survey of Eliot's life as a drawn-out obsession with the body and its ills. I began my research in 1970 with Herbert Howarth's *Notes on Some Figures Behind T. S. Eliot* (Boston: Houghton Mifflin, 1964; London: Chatto, 1965) which remains a wonderfully intelligent source.

A short biography, combining readability, accuracy, critical insight, and a substantial bibliography, provides an ideal introduction for schools, colleges, and general readers of Eliot. It is by Ronald Bush who published the admirable *T. S. Eliot: A Study in Character and Style* (NY: OUP, 1984) and edited *T. S. Eliot: The Modernist in History* (Cambridge: CUP, 1991): 'T. S. Eliot 1888–1965' is in *Retrospective*

Supplement I of *American Writers: A Collection of Literary Biographies*. ed. A. Walton Litz and Molly Weigel (NY: Scribners, 1998).

For those whose definition of biography would include the inward and imaginative life, it is appropriate to add, finally, Paul Elmer More's 'Marginalia: I', *The American Review* (Nov. 1936), including a spiritual biography which, Eliot told him in a letter of 11 Jan. 1937, was more like his own than that of anyone he had known, particularly More's sentence: 'I have often wondered what line my experience might have taken had I been brought up in a form of belief and a practice of worship from which the office of the imagination and of the aesthetic emotions had not been so ruthlessly evicted.' P. E. More explores the Calvinistic inheritance, the attractions of 'pure spirituality' in the religious philosophy of India, scepticism in relation to conflicting impulses in some obscure region of the soul, the call, and a final state on 'the border' of the unknown.

INDEX

EH is Emily Hale; TSE is T. S. Eliot; all works are by TSE unless otherwise indicated.

'Brahma' and TSE's 'I am the Resurrection' 150–1; journals 153; and Communion 166; and 'angel-whispering' 184; on the 'sublime vision' 236; repetition in essays 340, 341; on tradition 384; self-reliance 416; and Henry James Senior 507; Transcendentalism 488; 'The American Scholar' 473; 'Nature' 15, 24
'Entretien dans un parc' 61
Evening Standard 333
Everett, Barbara 631
Everett, William 220
Every, George 352, 384n
'Exequy' (fragment) 163n, 173n, 175, 177n, 186, 543

Faber, Enid 259, 293, 367, 368
Faber, Geoffrey 219, 220, 258, 259, 293, 297, 305, 355, 419, 448, 496
Faber, Dr Thomas 525
Faber and Faber (formerly Faber & Gwyer) 219, 239, 259, 296, 299, 302, 353, 405, 440, 494, 498
Family Reunion, The 2, 92. 160 *and n*, 206, 240, 242, 267, 269, 282, 284, 286, 287, 289, 290, 301–2, 310, 321–36, 398, 405, 406, 415, 418, 420, 429, 433, 479, 481, 502, 503, 507; drafts 551–3
Fenton, James 475
Ferrand, Margaret *see* Thorp, Margaret
Ferrar, John 371, 372
Ferrar, Nicholas 371, 372, 524
Ferrar, Susanna 371, 372
Fiedler, Leslie A.: *Love and Death in the American Novel* 36
'Figlia che Piange, La' 81, 85, 203, 236, 266, 376, 433, 515, 531

Finlay, John 515
'Fire Sermon, The' *see Waste Land, The*
'First Debate between the Body and Soul, The' 34, 61, 236
Fisher, Archbishop 468 *and n*
Fiske, John 29
Fitzgerald, F. Scott 254
Fitzgerald, Robert 527
Flanagan, Hallie 619; TSE to 321, 551
Fonteyn, Margot 280
Ford, Ford Madox 99
Forster, E. M. 104, 374, 484; *Howards End* 142
Foucauld, Charles de 417 *and n*, 646
Four Quartets 4, 74n, 242, 302, 313, 323, 336, 338–91, 397, 409, 436, 458, 478, 479, 495, 507, 519, 522, 679; *see also Burnt Norton*; *Dry Salvages*; *East Coker*; *Little Gidding*
'Fourth Caprice in Montparnasse' 56
Fox, Edward 302
Frazer, Sir James 39, 86; *The Golden Bough* 110, 176
Freud, Sigmund 39, 364
'Frontiers of Criticism, The' 483, 500
Frost, Father Bede: *St John of the Cross* 351
Frost, Robert 512; *North of Boston* 117
Fry, Roger 102, 139, 145, 474
Flaubert, Gustave 480

Gallup, Donald 111n, 685, 689
Galsworthy, John: *The Pigeon* 234
Gardner, Helen 148n, 184n, 312, 324, 353, 384n, 419, 480, 485, 543, 546, 602, 603, 613, 634, 641, 655, 658, 672,

INDEX